EVOLUTION OF MS – DOS/PC – DOS

1981	**MS – DOS 1.0**	First operating system for the IBM PC.
	PC – DOS 1.0	Support for 160K single-sided floppy disks.
	MS – DOS 1.25	First operating system for the IBM PC.
	PC – DOS 1.1	Support for 160K single-sided floppy disks.
1983	**MS – DOS 2.0**	Support for background processing, batch files, device-drivers, file handles, subdirectories, 360K double-sided floppy disks.
	PC – DOS 2.0	
	MS – DOS 2.01	Support for foreign language characters and the IBM PCjr.
	MS – DOS 2.1	
	MS – DOS 2.11	DOS 2.X bug fix upgrade.
1984	**MS – DOS 3.0**	Support for 1.2MB high-density floppy disks. Let users set file attributes to read-only.
	PC – DOS 3.0	
	MS–DOS 3.1	Support for networks and disk drive aliases.
	PC – DOS 3.1	
1986	**MS – DOS 3.2**	Support for 3.5-inch floppy disks.
	PC – DOS 3.2	
1987	**MS – DOS 3.3**	Updated foreign language character support, nested batch files, ability to use 4 serial ports (earlier versions of DOS only supported 2 serial ports) at speeds up to 19,200 baud (earlier versions of DOS only supported up to 9600 baud).
	PC – DOS 3.3	
1988	**MS – DOS 4.01**	Support for disk partitions greater than 32MB. Provided a visual shell.
	PC – DOS 4.0	

EVOLUTION OF WINDOWS

1985	**Windows 1.0**	One of the first graphical user interfaces (GUIs) for MS – DOS.
1987	**Windows 2.0**	Compatability with OS/2 Presentation Manager.
	Windows/286	
	Windows/386	
1990	**Windows 3.0**	Support for memory beyond 640K, improved multi-tasking, updated graphics and color.

EVOLUTION OF THE INTEL FAMILY OF PROCESSORS

1972	**4004**	First microprocessor created. This device was designed to work in the confines of a desk calculator. Its shortcomings as a general-purpose chip were soon recognized. One of its greatest shortcomings was the 4-bit design, which severely hampered memory access. However, the 4004 did offer the first truly programmable processing environment on a single chip.
1974	**8008**	A second generation 8-bit microprocessor designed for use as a general-purpose device. This chip offered a multiplexed bi-directional data bus and full interrupt capability.

| 1975 | 8080 | This chip developed the concept of an external stack. Earlier chips had a limited stack size because the processor stored the stack internally. This chip also offered direct memory access, allowing a device to access memory without interference from the processor. |

| 1978 | 8086 8087 | This is the first third generation microprocessor. The 8086 provides a 16-bit data path. It provides 20-bit addressing which allows access of up to 1 MB of memory. The 8086 is limited to a 64 KByte segment size due to the segment:offset addressing scheme required to create a 20-bit address on a 16-bit bus. In addition to expanded memory support, the 8086 provided access to floating point math using the 8087 math co-processor. IBM chose to make the co-processor an optional part of the original PC. The 8086 also provides an expanded register set over the 8080. |

| 1980 | 8088 8089 80186 | Intel produced the 8088 as a less expensive alternative to the 8086. It uses a 16-bit internal structure, but an 8-bit external structure. This allows a manufacturer to produce a computer with all the benefits of the 8086, while using cost saving 8-bit support circuitry. The harm of this technology is slower execution speed. |

The 8089 Input/Output Processor provides an interface between the 8086/8088 and external peripheral devices or memory. Each 8089 contains two DMA (direct memory access) channels. The 8086/8088 builds a description of the I/O it wants performed. The 8089 responds when it completes the I/O task. This allows the 8086/8088 to concentrate on tasks other than system I/O. Intel designed the 8089 for I/O-intensive environments or multiprocessor applications.

The 80186 is a 16-bit microprocessor that uses a 16-bit bus. It uses the same instruction set as the 8086. In addition to these standard instructions, the 80186 provides several advanced instructions. These instructions reduce the amount of code required to perform a task. For example, instead of issuing the standard eleven instructions to save the register contents on the stack, the 80186 adds a new instruction that performs the task in one. In addition to these time saving instruction additions, the 80186 performs some 8086 commands in fewer execution cycles. This further enhances the chip's ability to perform high-speed calculations.

| 1982 | 80188 | The 80188 uses the same instruction set and provides the same features as the 80186. The main difference between the two chips is that the 80188 uses an 8-bit bus. This allows a manufacturer to produce a computer with all the benefits of the 80186, while using cost saving 8-bit support circuitry. The harm of this technology is slower execution speed. |

| 1983 | 80286 80287 | The 80286 is a full 16-bit microprocessor that uses a 16-bit bus. There are several differences between this chip and its predecessors. First, this chip provides an enhanced instruction set. The bulk of these commands affect the microprocessor's data transfer and processor control abilities. The second difference is the number of available address lines. The 80286 provides 24 address lines for a maximum memory access of 16 MBytes. To provide backward compatibility with the 8086/8088, the processor has two operating modes. *Real* mode makes the processor act like an 8086/8088. This includes the 1 MB address limitation. *Protected* mode provides full access to the 16 MB address capability. Protected mode |

also allows access to some multitasking capabilities. The 80287 provides a floating point capability for the 80286. Like its predecessors, the 80286 performs integer math only.

1985 80386
80387
The 80386 uses a 32-bit architecture. This includes the address, bus, and internal structures. The 32-bit address capability allows the chip to directly access 4 gigabytes of data. Using a virtual address mode the chip could access as much as 16 terabytes of data. In addition to the advanced memory capability, the 80386 has three modes of operation. The first mode *Real* emulates a single 8086/8088 processor. The second mode *Protected* allows the chip to provide a limited multitasking capability and access the full memory address range. The third mode *Virtual 86* provides full multitasking capability. Each task runs on its own fully functional 8086/8088. Although each task can only access 1 MB of memory, you can run as many tasks as will fit in the full address range available to the processor. Finally, the 80386 provides advanced 32-bit data transfer, bit manipulation, and string manipulation commands. As with the 80287, the 80387 provides the 80386 with a floating point math capability.

1988 80486
The 80486 provides a 32-bit computing environment similar to the 80386. Major differences between the two chips involve peripheral management rather than enhanced capability. For example, the 80486 provides the capabilities of the 80387 internally. Therefore, the chip does not require an external math co-processor. The 80486 also provides an internal cache controller and instruction cache memory. The 80386 required external chips to provide these capabilities. In addition to these standard enhancements, the 80486 provides a burst mode for data transfer between internal components. This burst mode effectively provides a 128-bit path between the processor and its attached devices (for example the cache controller/memory). Finally, the 80486 provides commands to manage these enhanced capabilities. Some 80386 instructions execute in fewer clock cycles on the 80486 as well. In other words, the 80486 provides a tightly integrated improved version of the 80386/80387 combination.

1991 80586
The 80586 is the next step in chip evolution. The exact capabilities provided by this chip are unknown as of this writing. However, industry authorities predict that the chip will have a virtual 80386 mode (multiple 80386 machines running in a multitasked environment). In addition to this capability, the chip will probably provide a better selection of high-speed data manipulation commands and enhanced floating point math capability.

The Ultimate DOS Programmer's Manual

John Mueller and Wallace Wang

 WINDCREST®

FIRST EDITION
FIRST PRINTING

© 1991 by **Windcrest Books**, an imprint of TAB BOOKS.
TAB BOOKS is a division of McGraw-Hill, Inc.
The name ''Windcrest'' is a registered trademark of TAB BOOKS.

Library of Congress Cataloging-in-Publication Data

Mueller, John (John P.)
    The ultimate DOS programmer's manual / by John Mueller, Wallace Wang.
      p.   cm.
    Includes index.
    ISBN 0-8306-7534-5   ISBN 0-8306-3534-3 (pbk.)
    1. PC DOS (Computer operating system) 2. MS-DOS (Computer operating system) I. Wang, Wally. II. Title.
QA76.76.063M84   1990
005.4'46—dc20
                                   90-41436
                                      CIP

TAB BOOKS offers software for sale. For information and a catalog, please contact TAB Software Department, Blue Ridge Summit, PA 17294-0850.

Questions regarding the content of this book should be addressed to:

Reader Inquiry Branch
Windcrest Books
Blue Ridge Summit, PA 17294-0850

Technical Editor: David M. Harter
Production: Katherine G. Brown
Book Design: Jaclyn J. Boone

This book is dedicated to those poor lost
souls who delved into DOS only to find its intri-
cacies elude them. May this book be the light you need
to find your way in the snarled world of DOS programming.

Contents

1   *Using DOS*   *1*

This chapter introduces DOS 4.0 and its unique
capabilities. This includes modifying the shell. It also
compares DOS 4.0 to previous DOS versions.

2   *Using CodeView*   *25*

This chapter gives a complete and concise overview of
CodeView options, command line semantics, and general
commands. It includes a tutorial complete with screen
displays to help you learn CodeView quickly and easily.

3 *Using the Microsoft Editor*   **53**

This chapter provides instructions for using the Microsoft editor. It includes discussions on some of the esoteric editor features.

4 *Processor Commands and Interfaces*   **94**

This chapter discusses various processor-specific commands. It provides programming examples of how to use some of the unique processor commands.

5 *Processor Ports*   **208**

This chapter provides detailed information on various processor ports. It includes programming examples showing how to use some of the ports.

6 *Video Controllers*   **234**

This chapter provides detailed programming information for the MDA, Hercules, CGA, EGA, VGA, Super VGA, 8514/A, and 34010-based display adapters. Each discussion includes a block diagram and concludes with a programming example.

7 ROM Interrupts   410

*This chapter describes all the ROM interrupts available
with a standard PC. It also includes some non-standard
interrupt descriptions. For example, it describes the
standard ROM interrupts for Super VGA display adapters.*

8 DOS Program Control Interrupts   535

*This chapter explains the DOS program control interrupts
in detail.*

9 DOS Video Service Interrupts 555

This chapter shows you how to use DOS to control the video adapter. It includes a programming example.

10 DOS Hard Disk/Floppy Diskette Service Interrupts 563

This chapter provides detailed information on the services available from DOS for controlling a hard disk/floppy diskette drive. The discussion includes a programming example.

11   DOS Keyboard Interrupts

This chapter describes how to get input from the user using DOS.

15 *DOS Expanded Memory Support Interrupts*   690

*This chapter describes the extensions provided by an
expanded memory driver to the basic set of DOS services.
It includes a programming example showing how to use
the services. In addition, it describes the equipment you
need to use these extensions.*

16   *DOS Input/Output Control Interrupts*   740

*This chapter describes the input/output services provided
by advanced versions of DOS. It includes a program
showing the advanced features the input/output services
provide for controlling a hard disk/floppy diskette drive.*

17   *DOS Miscellaneous Interrupts*

*This chapter describes the DOS Services that do not fall
into a major programming or device control category. It
includes an example of how to use some of these services.*

18 Memory-Resident Programming 811

This chapter describes some of the steps required to create a TSR program. It provides a programming example showing how to create a TSR program. Instead of placing the TSR functions in the main program, this chapter places them in a separate module. This allows you to see the interaction between the TSR functions and the program more clearly.

Appendices

List of Tables

Acknowledgments

There are three parties to which Wallace and I want to express our gratitude. Without their support in both time and product, we could not have produced the quality and quantity of information present in this book.

First, we want to thank Control Systems for the use of a 34010-based display adapter. Using this card greatly enhanced our appreciation of the complications of programming using the TIGA interface. Both of us especially want to thank Scott Fitzsimmons for his level of interest and unfailing assistance. We would also like to thank Les Peterson for his enthusiasm and technical support.

Second, we want to thank Texas Instruments for the use of the 34010 Software Development Kit. Using this kit helped us develop the information about the TIGA interface in general. We want to thank Joan Robertson and Scott Huckaby for their help in obtaining these products and other types of technical assistance.

Finally, we want to thank Microsoft Corporation for its support of the languages used throughout this book. In particular, we want to thank Tanya Van Dam for her assistance in getting the required products.

Introduction

The Ultimate DOS Programmer's Manual explains how to program in the DOS environment. This includes: memory resident programming; ROM BIOS and DOS BIOS function calls; EGA, VGA, and Super VGA displays; and the DOS 4.0 shell.

By explaining how particular DOS functions work, this book provides a solid foundation for programming in any language. This book provides example programs using assembly language, BASIC, C, and Quick Pascal that you can study and change for your own use. In addition to providing source code examples, this book will also show you how to create programs using a variety of languages. For example, you could write an assembly language program where speed is crucial, and use a C or Pascal program for creating the user interface. For best performance from your programs, use assembly language modules in time critical sections. Mixed language programming lets you choose the best language for a particular task.

WHO SHOULD USE THIS BOOK

Both beginners and experienced programmers can benefit from using this book. For beginners, this book explains how DOS works, how to use interrupts, how to access ROM and DOS functions, and what each function does. For experienced programmers, this book provides a handy reference to the many DOS and ROM functions available from any language.

You should be familiar with a programming language to benefit the most from this book. We tested all program examples in this book using Microsoft Macro Assembler 5.1, Microsoft BASIC 7.0, Microsoft C 5.1, Microsoft Quick Pascal 1.0, and Borland Turbo Pascal 5.5. We used Microsoft CodeView 2.2 as the debugger in most cases. If you use any of the

Quick language compilers—Quick Assembler, Quick BASIC, or Quick C— you may have to change the program examples in this book slightly to make them work properly. In addition, standard Pascal does not support many of the functions we included in the Pascal programming examples.

WHAT THIS BOOK WILL DO

This book provides three types of information necessary for programming an IBM compatible computer. First, this book will explain how to make maximum use of the DOS environment when writing programs. Second, it shows equivalent programs written in four of the most popular programming languages. Third, it shows how to mix the different languages to create a single program. For example, you could write part of a program to access the ROM BIOS using assembly language, design a user interface with Pascal, create data structures and file access routines in C, and draw graphics using BASIC. Not only does this book show you how programs in different languages work, but it also shows you how to integrate different languages together within the DOS environment.

WHY TO USE MICROSOFT COMPILERS

Although competing language compilers might offer more features or convenience than the Microsoft compilers, we chose to use Microsoft compilers for compatibility reasons. Only Microsoft offers a complete range of compatible language compilers that can work together. Thus you can write part of your program in assembly language for speed and direct access to hardware interrupts and functions, and mix your assembly language routines with the more structured C or Pascal languages.

In addition, both the Microsoft C and Pascal compilers closely adhere to their respective language standards. This means you can write code using the Microsoft C and Pascal compilers, and port them over to completely different machines. Using compilers that follow language standards ensures that this book will always provide relevant, accurate information no matter what new changes appear in future compiler versions.

Finally, no other compiler vendor now offers versions for both MS–DOS and OS/2. By using Microsoft compilers, you make sure that you can port any programs developed in MS–DOS directly to OS/2 without extensive rewriting of your code.

EQUIPMENT USED

We tested all programs in this book on three different machines. The first machine included a Hauppauge 386 motherboard, 80387 math co-processor, ATI VGA Wonder card, Logitech C7 serial mouse, and a Multi-

Sync 3D monitor. The second machine included a Northgate 386 with a Princeton VGA monitor and a Logitech Hi-Res serial mouse. The third machine was a Cordata PPC-400, 8088 running at 4.77 MHz. For our software we used the Microsoft compilers along with MS–DOS 4.01 and PC/MOS-386 version 3.0. We made every effort to ensure that the program examples work on any computer configuration. However, given the ever-changing state of computer equipment and software, this is not possible to verify.

If you experience any problems, try running the same program on a different computer. If the problem disappears, then you know that your computer equipment is at fault. If the problem persists, write and let us know so we can verify the problem and find a way around it for the next edition of this book.

WHAT THIS BOOK CONTAINS

Each chapter of *The Ultimate DOS Programmer's Manual* discusses a particular aspect of DOS programming in more detail. Where possible, program examples include assembly language, BASIC, C, and Pascal. Many of the low-level programming examples use assembly language only.

CHAPTER 1 discusses the differences between DOS 4.0 and earlier versions of DOS. In addition, this chapter explains the new features of DOS 4.0, how to use the DOS 4.0 shell program, and how to customize the shell for your own applications.

CHAPTER 2 explains how to use Microsoft CodeView for debugging assembly language, BASIC, C, and Pascal programs. You will learn how to use CodeView for tracing bugs and eliminating them, even if your program consists of different languages such as C and assembly language.

CHAPTER 3 explains how to use the Microsoft Editor. It shows how to customize the editor commands using Microsoft C.

CHAPTER 4 provides detailed explanations for the different microprocessors used in the IBM computer family. The chapter covers the 8088/8086, 80286, and 80386 along with their respective math co-processors 8087, 80287, and 80387.

CHAPTER 5 describes the 8253/8254 programmable timers, 8255A programmable peripheral interface, and 8259 interrupt controller. The programming examples show how you can program them. Chapter 5 also provides an input/output system map.

CHAPTER 6 explains the different video controllers available for the IBM. This includes monochrome, Hercules graphics, CGA, EGA VGA, Super VGA, 8514A, BGA, and the TIGA interface.

CHAPTER 7 lists the different ROM interrupts, their functions, and how you can access them in your own programs. Some of the interrupts available include printer services, keyboard interrupts, and disk drive functions.

CHAPTERS 8 through 13 provide detailed explanations and program examples on the DOS program control, video service, disk drive, keyboard, printer, and serial port services and interrupts.

CHAPTER 14 explains how DOS works with a mouse, the differences between two-button and three-button mice, the differences between serial and bus mice, and how to access a mouse in your own programs.

CHAPTER 15 explains how expanded memory works and how to access it. It focuses on the driver supplied with DOS 4.0. However, you can use this chapter with most LIM 4.0 compatible drivers.

CHAPTERS 16 and 17 discuss different DOS services such as input/output. Both chapters show how to use both old and new DOS services.

CHAPTER 18 discusses memory resident programs: how they work; what they can do; how to create them using assembly language, C, and Pascal. It also discusses the differences between creating .COM and .EXE memory resident programs.

APPENDIX A provides two types of ASCII charts: a standard one, and one that organizes related characters in groups for quick reference.

APPENDIX B lists the DOS commands available up to DOS 4.0.

APPENDIX C lists the DOS 4.0 shell commands.

APPENDIX D contains a one-megabyte memory map. This shows you how DOS allocates memory in the real mode environment.

1
Using DOS

DOS 4.0 represents a major enhancement of the IBM operating system. In addition to retaining compatibility with older versions of DOS, DOS 4.0 includes several new commands and support for hard disks greater than 32 megabytes. It also includes foreign language support for Japanese, Korean, and Chinese. In addition, DOS 4.0 includes support for expanded memory, enhanced keyboard support, and the introduction of a shell program to simplify choosing program commands. If you want to take more complete control over your IBM or compatible computer, you need DOS 4.0.

Unlike previous versions of DOS, DOS 4.0 requires at least 256K of memory. If you plan to use the DOS 4.0 shell, you need at least 360K of memory. Although you can use DOS 4.0 on a floppy-disk system, you should install DOS 4.0 on a hard disk to take maximum advantage of its features.

NEW FEATURES

The most immediate difference between DOS 4.0 and older versions of DOS is the DOS 4.0 installation procedure. Just like previous versions of DOS, you can copy the files from your DOS 4.0 disks to your hard disk. But if you want the option to run more than one operating system, such as running DOS 4.0 with an older version of DOS or with OS/2, you must use the installation procedure.

INSTALLATION PROCEDURE

The installation procedure lets you customize DOS 4.0 for your computer. During installation, you can choose the following options:

- DOS memory requirements
- Keyboard configuration

DOS Memory Requirements

You can install DOS 4.0 in three configurations:

- Minimum DOS function; maximum program work space
- Balance DOS function with program work space
- Maximum DOS function; minimum program work space

Minimum DOS function uses the least amount of memory for DOS. It also reduces the capabilities of the DOS shell program. In rare cases, programs with particularly ravenous appetites for memory will not run under DOS 4.0. For these programs, you must install DOS 4.0 using this option. If your computer only has 256K of memory, you must choose this option.

Balance DOS function divides memory equally between DOS 4.0 and any programs you want to run. If your computer has 512K of memory or less, then you must choose this option. This is the default option.

The Maximum DOS function allocates enough memory to use all the features of DOS 4.0 including the DOS shell. This still leaves enough memory for running other programs. If you have a hard disk and a computer with more than 512K of memory, this option provides the optimum configuration.

Keyboard Configuration

DOS 4.0 supports characters for a variety of countries including monetary symbols, decimal separator, and time and date format. The default country is the United States. DOS 4.0 provides support for the following countries:

Arabic Speaking	Italy	Spain
Austrailia	Japan	Sweeden
Canada (French speaking)	Korea	Switzerland
	Latin America	Taiwan
Denmark	Netherlands	United Kingdom
France	Norway	United States
Germany	People's Republic of	
Hebrew Speaking	China	

If you choose Denmark, Portugal, Norway, or French-speaking Canada, you must set the Code-Page Switching option to Y(es) during the Installation Option Review. Once you choose a country configuration for

DOS 4.0, you must choose one of the following keyboard configurations. The default configuration is None.

Belgian	Italian	Swedish
Canadian French	Latin American	Swiss (French)
Danish	Speaking	Swiss (German)
Dutch	None	UK English
Finnish	Norwegian	US English
French	Portuguese	
German	Spanish	

THE *MEM* COMMAND

Any time you want to determine you computer's total memory and the total available memory for running other programs, use the MEM command. The command line parameters for the MEM command appear below.

MEM [/PROGRAM] [/DEBUG]

The MEM command displays:

- Total memory
- Total available memory
- Largest block of available memory at the current time
- Total extended memory
- Total available extended memory

The /PROGRAM parameter displays the address, name, size, and type of each program loaded into memory in addition to the standard information. The /DEBUG parameter displays the same information as the /PROGRAM parameter. It also displays the address, name, size, and type of any internal device drivers.

DIFFERENCES

Previous versions of DOS could only access up to 32 megabytes of disk space. DOS 4.0 can access up to 2 gigabytes of disk space. In addition, DOS 4.0 adds enhancement to the commands listed below.

ANSI.SYS	FASTOPEN	PRINTER.SYS
APPEND	FDISK	REPLACE
BACKUP	FORMAT	SELECT
CHKDSK	GRAFTABL	SYS
COUNTRY	GRAPHICS	TIME
DEL	KEYB	TREE
DISPLAY.SYS	MODE	VDISK.SYS

ANSI.SYS

The ANSI.SYS device driver provides extended screen and keyboard functions to an IBM computer. DOS 4.0 adds three additional parameters /X, /K, and L.

The ANSI.SYS /X parameter The /X parameter causes ANSI.SYS to treat the cursor and numeric keys on an extended keyboard as separate keys. Thus, ANSI.SYS considers pressing the right-arrow key on the cursor pad and the right-arrow on the numeric pad as different keys.

The ANSI.SYS /K parameter The /K parameter causes ANSI.SYS to treat the cursor and numeric keys on the extended keyboard as identical keys. Thus, ANSI.SYS considers pressing the right-arrow key on the cursor pad and the right-arrow on the numeric pad as the same.

The ANSI.SYS /L parameter The /L parameter works with the Mode command and an EGA or VGA video card to fix the number of rows of text that appear on the screen. EGA monitors can display 43 lines, and VGA monitors can display 50 lines. The default is 25 lines. Because some programs attempt to change the display setting, the /L parameter ensures that these programs cannot change the number of lines.

Append

The Append command works like the Path command: While the Path command defines a search path for executable files (.EXE, .COM, and .BAT), the Append command defines a search path for nonexecutable files. This includes overlay files, device drivers, configuration files, and data files. DOS 4.0 adds two additional parameter switches to the APPEND command /X:<SETTING> and /PATH:<SETTING>.

The /X:<setting> The Append /X parameter defines a search path for both executable and nonexecutable files. This eliminates the need for using the PATH command. The setting can be ON or OFF.

The /PATH:<setting> The Append /PATH parameter searches for executable files in all files specified in the Append list. If you type the command C:\word\wp to run WP.EXE, and WP.EXE appears in a different directory, then the Append /PATH parameter ensures that DOS 4.0 will find and run the program anyway.

Backup

The Backup command backs up hard and floppy disk data. With older versions of DOS, you had to format floppy disks before running the Backup command. With DOS 4.0, you can use unformatted floppy disks. The Backup command formats the disks as it performs the backup. For this to work, the Format program must appear in the same directory as the Backup program, or on the search path specified by the Path or Append commands.

ChkDsk

The ChkDsk program examines disks for errors, filenames, and storage capacity. If you format a disk with DOS 4.0 and use the ChkDsk program, you will see a volume serial number report. This serial number is an eight-digit hexadecimal number that the DOS 4.0 Format command automatically assigns each formatted disk.

The DOS 4.0 ChkDsk command also displays an allocation unit report that tells the size of the disk clusters, how many clusters appear on the disk, and how many available clusters remain for storing data. Because DOS allocates storage by clusters and not by byte, the allocation unit report gives a more accurate estimation of the total capacity of the disk.

Del

The DOS 4.0 Del command includes an additional warning message, "All files in directory will be deleted!" when you attempt to erase all files in a directory. In addition, the DOS 4.0 DEL command includes a /P permission switch. Using the /P switch causes DOS to display the prompt, "Delete (Y/N)?" before deleting each file. Using the /P switch provides an extra measure of security to prevent you from deleting a file by mistake.

FastOpen

The FastOpen command creates a buffer for holding file and path names. This reduces the time needed for DOS to find files on disk. The default setting for the DOS 4.0 FastOpen command stores 50 path and file names, and 25 continuous space buffers on a hard disk. Older versions of DOS did not store buffers continually, resulting in slower performance.

FDisk

The DOS 4.0 FDisk command can create hard disk partitions up to four gigabytes in size. Generally you should partition a hard disk into smaller sections because many programs cannot read sectors or clusters larger than 32 megabytes.

Format

The DOS 4.0 FORMAT command automatically adds an eight-digit hexadecimal number on each disk it formats. DOS bases this hexadecimal number on the date and time of the formatting. In addition, the DOS 4.0 FORMAT command displays an allocation unit report listing how many bytes are in each allocation unit and how many allocation units appear on the disk.

GrafTabl

The GrafTabl command loads character graphics into memory for a CGA or Hercules graphics monitor. EGA and VGA monitors do not need it. In older versions of DOS, you could display a message telling which character set you loaded by typing GrafTabl /STATUS. In DOS 4.0, you can get the same message by typing GrafTabl /?.

Graphics

The Graphics command lets you print graphic screen displays to IBM printers, Epson printers with the GrafTrax option, or printers claiming Epson compatibility. The DOS 4.0 Graphics command can print EGA or VGA graphics. It stores information on how to print graphics for different printers in a file called GRAPHICS.PRO.

KeyB

The DOS 4.0 KeyB command offers two alternate keyboard layouts for France, Italy, and the United Kingdom by using the /<ID> switch and the appropriate number for the keyboard layout. TABLE 1-1 lists the num-

Table 1-1   DOS 4.0 Keyboard Nationality Codes

Country	Code	Identifier
Australia	US	103
Belgium	BE	120
Canada (English)	US	103
Canada (French)	CF	058
Denmark	DK	159
Finland	SU	153
France	FR	120 or 189
Germany	GR	129
Italy	IT	141 or 142
Latin America	LA	171
Netherlands	NL	143
Norway	NO	155
Portugal	PO	163
Spain	SP	172
Sweden	SV	153
Switzerland (France)	SF	150
Switzerland (German)	SG	000
United Kingdom	UK	168 or 166
United States	US	103

bers for various nations. To load a keyboard configuration type: KeyB
<CODE>, <IDENTIFIER>.

Once you load a keyboard configuration other than the default United
States layout, you can switch between layouts. Pressing Ctrl–Alt–F1
switches back to the United States layout. Pressing Ctrl–Alt–F2 switches
to the alternative layout.

Mode

The MODE command can configure the serial port, redirect printer
output, and configure the number of lines displayed on the screen.

Configuring the serial port   You must supply three parameters when configuring the serial port: data bits, stop bits, and parity type. TABLE 1-2
shows some typical serial port settings. DOS 4.0 provides support for two
seldom used parity types: mark and space.

Table 1-2   Typical Serial Port Settings

Data Bits	Stop Bits	Parity
7	1	Odd or Even
7	2	None
7 or 8	1 or 2	Mark
8	1	None
7	1 or 2	Space

Redirecting printer output   The MODE command can direct printer output
through a second parallel port or to a serial port. When configuring a serial
port for a printer, use the P parameter at the end of the command with
older versions of DOS, or the B parameter with DOS 4.0. The P or B parameter detects printer errors and tells DOS. Without the P or B parameter, the
print driver continues sending characters to the port until a time-out error
occurs.

DOS 4.0 provides three ways to handle errors: the E parameter, the B
parameter, and the R parameter. The E parameter displays an error message on the screen if the port is busy. The B parameter returns the actual
status of the port. The R parameter always reports that the port is ready to
receive data, even when it is not. Use the E, B, and R parameters as shown
below.

MODE 1ptn:[cols=chars],,[lines=lines] [,retry=c]

Configuring the screen   The MODE command can also set the number of
lines that appear on the screen. The default is 25 lines, but EGA monitors
can display 43 lines and VGA monitors can display 50. If you use the /L
parameter with ANSI.SYS, you can fix the number of lines that appear on

the screen. You must add ANSI.SYS to your CONFIG.SYS file to use the 43 and 50 line options.

Printer.SYS

The DOS 3.3 version of PRINTER.SYS provides foreign language support for the IBM Proprinter II, Model 4201 or an IBM Quietwriter III, Model 5202. The DOS 4.0 version of this file adds support for the IBM Proprinter XL, Model 4202, IBM Proprinter X24, Model 4207, and the IBM Proprinter XL24, Model 4208.

Replace

The REPLACE command selectively copies files by certain criteria, such as by date, archive status, or only those files that don't exist on the source disk. TABLE 1-3 lists the REPLACE command switches and describes what they do.

Table 1-3   Replace Command Switches

Switch	Effect
/A	Only copies files that do not already exist on the target directory.
/D	Replaces those files that exist on the target directory that have a date earlier than the same filenames on the source disk. (DOS 3.2 and above only.)
/U	Replaces those files that exist on the target directory that have a date earlier than the same filenames on the source disk. (DOS 4.0 only.)
/S	Replaces all files of the same name as those that appear on the source disk.
/R	Replaces read-only files.
/P	Displays each file name before copying. DOS then displays a prompt so you can choose whether or not to copy the file.
/W	Displays the message "Press any key to begin replacing file(s)." This lets you change disks if you want before copying files.

Select

The SELECT command lets you choose a default country code and keyboard layout. In addition you can format a disk and create AUTOEXEC .BAT/CONFIG.SYS files. Choosing this command in DOS 4.0 displays a menu for installing DOS 4.0 onto a hard or floppy disk.

The second menu displays options Minimum DOS function, Balance DOS function, and Maximum DOS function. This affects the installation of the AUTOEXEC.BAT, CONFIG.SYS, and DOSSHELL.BAT files. The default is Balance DOS function. The default CONFIG.SYS file appears below.

```
break=on
buffers=20
files=8
lastdrive=e
shell=c\dos400\command.com/p/e:256
device=c:\dos400\ansi.sys
install=c:\dos400\fastopen.exe c:=(50,25)
```

The number of buffers vary, depending on the size of your hard disk. The default AUTOEXEC.BAT file appears below.

```
@echo off
set compsec=c:\dos400\command.com
verify off
path c:\dos400
append/e
append c:\dos400
prompt $p$g
ver
graphics
print/d:lpt1
dosshell
```

Sys

The SYS command copies the operating system files to a formatted disk, making the formatted disk bootable. If you have formatted a disk using an older version of DOS, the DOS 4.0 SYS command cannot transfer the operating system files to the disk.

Time

Older versions of DOS kept track of time using the 24-hour clock. DOS 4.0 lets you display time using the 12-hour clock. Rather than displaying 13:00, DOS 4.0 can display the time as 1:00 pm.

Tree

The TREE command displays a list of files in each directory. DOS 4.0 draws the directory structure. Using the TREE command by itself displays a listing of the directories. Figure 1-1 shows a typical TREE display.

The /F parameter Using the /F parameter displays a list of directories plus the files that each one contains. This greatly increases the amount of space required to display the tree.

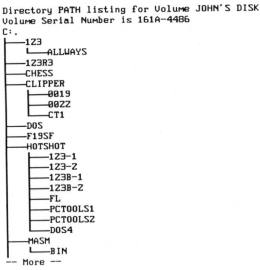

```
Directory PATH listing for Volume JOHN'S DISK
Volume Serial Number is 161A-4486
C:.
    ├──123
    │   └──ALLWAYS
    ├──123R3
    ├──CHESS
    ├──CLIPPER
    │   ├──0019
    │   ├──0022
    │   └──CT1
    ├──DOS
    ├──F19SF
    ├──HOTSHOT
    │   ├──123-1
    │   ├──123-2
    │   ├──123B-1
    │   ├──123B-2
    │   ├──FL
    │   ├──PCTOOLS1
    │   ├──PCTOOLS2
    │   └──DOS4
    ├──MASM
    │   └──BIN
-- More --
```

1-1 Directory path listing.

The /A parameter Some monitors cannot display the extended graphics characters that the TREE command uses. The /A parameter tells Tree to use dashes (-) and plus signs (+) to draw the directory structure.

VDisk.SYS

Include VDISK.SYS as part of the CONFIG.SYS file to create a RAM disk. With older versions of DOS, you could create a RAM disk in expanded memory using the /E parameter. With DOS 4.0, you can use the /E parameter or the /X parameter. Use the /X parameter only if you have a 386 PC. You must use the XMA2EMS.SYS device driver with the /X parameter. The maximum size for a RAM disk is 32,768K. The minimum size is 1K. The default is 64K.

USING THE *DOS* SHELL

DOS 4.0 gives you the option to use the traditional DOS prompt or the DOS shell. The shell displays menu options consisting of two parts: Start Programs and File System.

Start Programs

The Start Programs part of the DOS shell lets you run programs, such as Lotus 1-2-3 or WordPerfect, from within the DOS shell. You can organize programs into Groups, which appear in the DOS shell with three trailing dots. Groups can contain up to 16 programs. The DOS shell contains four initial groups:

- Command Prompt
- File System
- Change Colors
- DOS Utilities

Command prompt   The Command Prompt temporarily exits the DOS shell and displays the traditional DOS prompt. You can also choose this command by pressing Shift – F9. After choosing Command Prompt, you can return to the DOS shell by typing EXIT and pressing Enter.

Change colors   The Change Colors lets you use the left- and right-arrow keys to change the colors of the DOS shell. DOS 4.0 gives you four different color configurations from which to choose.

DOS utilities   The DOS Utilities contain menu commands for formatting and copying disks as well as setting the date and time of your computer. You can add your own programs in the DOS Utilities group if you wish.

File System

The File System consists of two windows displayed side by side. The left window, called the Directory Tree, displays the directory structure of the current drive. The right window, called the File List Area, displays the files within each directory. From the File System, you can perform standard DOS commands—such as copying, deleting, and renaming files.

MODIFYING THE *DOS* SHELL DISPLAY

To modify the DOS shell, you need to edit the DOSSHELL.BAT file using EDLIN, a programming editor. You can also use any word processor that can save and retrieve ASCII files. The DOSSHELL.BAT file can contain the options listed in TABLE 1-4. A typical DOSSHELL.BAT file appears below.

```
@C:
@CD C: \ DOS
@SHELLB DOSSHELL
@ I F ERRORLEVEL 255 GOTO END
: COMMON
@BREAK = OFF
SHELLC /TRAN/COLOR/DOS/MENU/MUL/SND/MEU : SHELL . MEU
CLR : SHELL . CLR/PROMPT/MA I NT/EX I T/SWAP/DATE
: END
@BREAK = ON
```

Modifying the DOS Shell Menus

Although the DOS 4.0 shell comes preconfigured, you can easily customize the shell by adding your own menus, programs, passwords, and help files. The DOS 4.0 shell provides the three main menus shown below.

Table 1-4   DOSSHELL.BAT Options

Option	Description
/CLR SHELL.CLR	Tells the DOS shell that the SHELL.CLR file contains information on displaying colors.
/COLOR	Allows you to change colors using the Color Change command from the DOS shell.
/CO1	Displays the DOS shell in 16-color, EGA 640x350 graphics.
/CO2	Displays the DOS shell in 16-color, Hercules or VGA graphics.
/CO3	Displays the DOS shell in 16-color, VGA graphics.
/DATE	Displays the date and time in the DOS shell menu bar.
/DOS	Includes the File System command in the DOS shell.
/EXIT	Lets you permanently exit the DOS shell by pressing F3 or choosing Exit shell program from the Exit menu.
/LF	Switches the mouse button functions for left-handed mouse users.
/MAINT	Lets you edit programs and groups displayed in the DOS shell.
/MENU	Lets you create new groups in the DOS shell.
/MEU:SHELL.MEU	Tells the DOS shell to look in the SHELL.MEU file for the list of programs that make up the Main Group on the Start Programs screen.
/MOS:PCIBMDRV.MOS	Lets the DOS shell use an IBM mouse.
/MUL	Keeps directory information in memory for faster performance.
/PROMPT	Lets you temporarily return to the DOS prompt.
/SND	Provides sound for warning messages when using the DOS shell.
/SWAP	Lets DOS 4.0 swap directories to a floppy disk drive.
/TEXT	Displays the DOS shell in text mode.
/TRAN	Clears the DOS shell from memory when you exit the DOS shell by pressing F3 or choosing Exit shell program from the Exit menu.

- Program
    - Start
    - Add...
    - Change...
    - Delete...
    - Copy...
- Group
    - Add...
    - Change...

Delete...
Reorder...
- Exit
    Exit Shell
    Resume Start Programs

Displaying Menus

To display a menu from the DOS 4.0 shell, you can use the keyboard or a mouse. Figures 1-2 through 1-5 show the four menus (including Help)

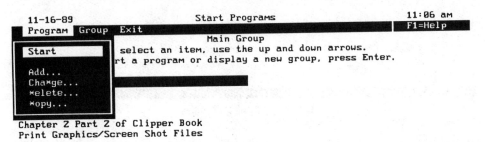

```
11-16-89                        Start Programs                      11:06 am
Program  Group  Exit                                                F1=Help
                                    Main Group
   Start                  select an item, use the up and down arrows.
                       rt a program or display a new group, press Enter.
   Add...
   Cha*ge...
   *elete...
   *opy...

Chapter 2 Part 2 of Clipper Book
Print Graphics/Screen Shot Files
```

```
F10=Actions              Shift+F9=Command Prompt
```

1-2 DOS Shell Program menu.

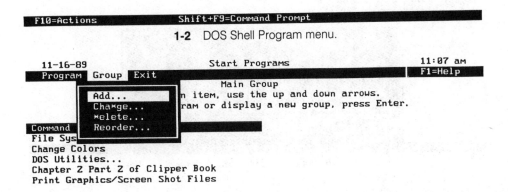

```
11-16-89                        Start Programs                      11:07 am
Program  Group  Exit                                                F1=Help
                                    Main Group
                 Add...       n item, use the up and down arrows.
                 Cha*ge...    ram or display a new group, press Enter.
                 *elete...
   Command       Reorder...
File Sys
Change Colors
DOS Utilities...
Chapter 2 Part 2 of Clipper Book
Print Graphics/Screen Shot Files
```

```
F10=Actions              Shift+F9=Command Prompt
```

1-3 DOS Shell Group menu.

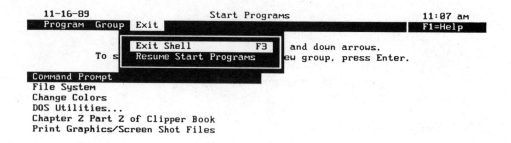

Exit Shell   F3   and down arrows.
      To s   Resume Start Programs   eu group, press Enter.

Command Prompt
File System
Change Colors
DOS Utilities...
Chapter 2 Part 2 of Clipper Book
Print Graphics/Screen Shot Files

F10=Actions   Shift+F9=Command Prompt

1-4   DOS Shell Exit menu.

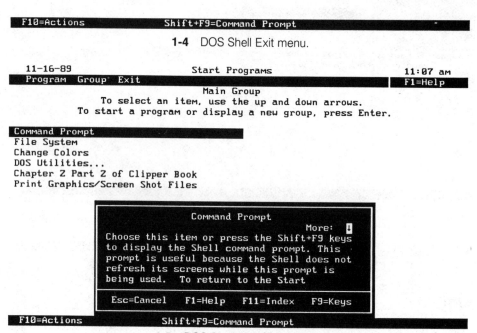

Main Group
To select an item, use the up and down arrows.
To start a program or display a new group, press Enter.

Command Prompt
File System
Change Colors
DOS Utilities...
Chapter 2 Part 2 of Clipper Book
Print Graphics/Screen Shot Files

Command Prompt
                                    More: ⬇
Choose this item or press the Shift+F9 keys
to display the Shell command prompt. This
prompt is useful because the Shell does not
refresh its screens while this prompt is
being used.   To return to the Start

Esc=Cancel   F1=Help   F11=Index   F9=Keys

F10=Actions   Shift+F9=Command Prompt

1-5   DOS Shell Help dialog box.

supplied with DOS 4.0. The following procedures show you how to use the
menus.

Keyboard method 1

1. Press F10 to highlight the menu bar.
2. Use the left- and right-arrow keys to highlight the menu you want
   to display.
3. Press Enter or the down-arrow to display the menu.

Keyboard method 2

1. Press F10 to highlight the menu bar.
2. Type the letter of the menu you want, such as P for Program, G for Group, or X for Exit.

Mouse method   Click the mouse pointer on the menu you want to display. If you use the standard mouse setup, press the left button. Otherwise, press the right button.

Removing Menus

After you display a menu, you can remove it without choosing a command. There are two methods of performing this task. First, you can press Esc. This removes the menu but highlights the menu name. Press Esc a second time to return to the DOS Shell. Second, click the mouse anywhere outside the menu.

THE PROGRAM MENU

The Program menu (FIG. 1-2) lets you add, edit, delete, or copy programs within a group. You can add a maximum of 16 programs within a single group.

Start

The Start command runs the program highlighted in the DOS shell. You can choose four different ways to use the Start command.

Keyboard method 1   Use the up/down arrow keys to highlight the program you want to run, then press Enter.

Keyboard method 2

1. Use the up/down arrow keys to highlight the program you want to run.
2. Press F10 to highlight the menu bar.
3. Use the left/right arrow keys to highlight the Program menu.
4. Press Enter to pull down the Program menu.
5. Type S to choose the Start command.

Keyboard method 3

1. Use the up/down arrow keys to highlight the program you want to run.
2. Press F10 to highlight the menu bar.
3. Use the left/right arrow keys to highlight the Program menu.

4. Press Enter to pull down the Program menu.
5. Use the up/down arrow keys to highlight the Start command.
6. Press Enter.

Mouse method 1 Click twice with the mouse on the program you want to run. If you use the standard mouse setup, press the left button. Otherwise, press the right button.

Add...

The Add command on the Program menu lets you add a new program within a group. (The Group menu Add command only lets you add a new group from within the Main Group.) When you choose the Add command, the Add Program dialog box shown in FIG. 1-6 appears. When adding a program within a group, you must supply the parameters listed in TABLE 1-5.

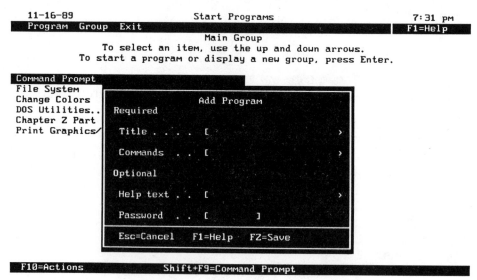

1-6 DOS Shell Add Program dialog box.

Table 1-5   Add Command Parameters

Parameter	Description
Title	The title field appears in the DOS shell. A title can contain up to 40 characters, including blank spaces. Ideally, the title should contain the actual program name, such as Microsoft Word or Lotus 1-2-3.
Commands	The commands field lists the drive, directory, and name of the file you want to run. The file

Table 1-5 Continued.

can be a .COM or .EXE file. The commands field can contain up to 500 characters, including blank spaces. The format for commands is D:||CD PATH||COMMAND. If you want to run a batch file, the format is D:||CD PATH||CALL BATCH FILENAME. The commands field offers the following startup options.

[ ]	Square brackets request a prompt for parameters. For example, if you typed WP [ ] into the command line and tried running the program, the DOS shell would display a Program Parameter dialog box.
/T<TITLE>	The /T parameter works with the square brackets [ ] to let you customize the title in the Program Parameters dialog box. Rather than display Program Parameters in the dialog box, the dialog box will display a specific title. The title can contain up to 40 characters, including spaces. The default title is "Program Parameters."
/L<N>	The /L parameter defines the maximum number of characters a user can enter into a parameter dialog box, where n is a number between 1 and 127.
/I<INSTRUCTIONS>	The /I parameter lets you customize the instructions provided in the parameter dialog box. The default instructions are "Type the parameters, then press Enter."
/P<PROMPT>	The /P parameter lets you customize the prompt in the parameter dialog box. A prompt can contain up to 20 characters. The default prompt is "Parameters . .:"
/D<DEFAULT>	The /D parameter lets you specify a default value for the parameter dialog box. The default value can contain up to 40 characters.

Table 1-5   Continued.

/R	The /R parameter works with the /D parameter. Including the /R parameter means that pressing a letter, number, or punctuation key will erase the default value specified by the /D parameter.
/M<FILENAME>	The /M parameter forces the DOS shell to verify the existence of the filename specified.
/F<PROGRAM>	The /F parameter is used when running programs stored on floppy disks. This checks the existence of a program on the specified floppy disk to ensure the program exists on that disk.
Help text	Help text can contain up to 478 characters, including blank spaces. DOS 4.0 automatically formats your help text to fit within the help panel. If you want to begin a new line, just type the ampersand (&) character.
Password	A password can contain up to 8 characters, including blank spaces. Passwords limit access to programs. If you forget your password, even you won't be able to access, delete, or change the program from within the DOS shell.

Change...

The Change command lets you edit the title, commands, help text, and password of a program that appears in the DOS shell. The following procedure shows you how to use the Change command.

1. Use the up/down arrows to highlight the program you want to edit. *Note*: If you highlight a group name, the Change command appears dimmed on the Program menu.
2. Press F10 and then type P to select the Program menu. Select the Change command. The Change Program dialog box shown in FIG. 1-7 appears. If you password-protected your program, the Password dialog box shown in FIG. 1-8 appears first. Type the correct password and press Enter.
3. Type any changes to the title, commands, help text, and password. When you finish making changes, press F2 to save your changes.

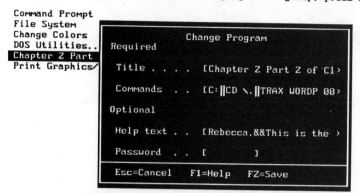

1-7   DOS Shell Change Password dialog box.

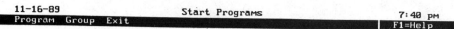

1-8   DOS Shell Request Password dialog box.

Delete...

The Delete command deletes a program from a group in the DOS shell. The following procedure shows you how to delete a program.

1. Use the up/down arrow keys to highlight the program you want to delete.
2. Press F10 and then type P to select the Program menu. Choose the

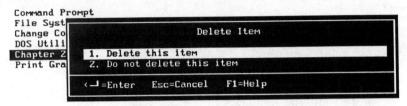

Program Group Exit   F1=Help

Main Group
To select an item, use the up and down arrows.
To start a program or display a new group, press Enter.

Command Prompt
File Syst
Change Co
DOS Utili
Chapter Z
Print Gra

Delete Item

1. Delete this item
2. Do not delete this item

←↵=Enter   Esc=Cancel   F1=Help

F10=Actions   Shift+F9=Command Prompt

1-9 DOS Shell Delete Program dialog box.

Delete command. The Delete Item dialog box shown in FIG. 1-9
appears.

3. Use the up/down arrow keys to highlight the "Delete this item"
option and press Enter.

Copy...

The Copy command lets you copy program names from one group to
another. To copy a program name, follow these steps:

1. Use the up/down arrow keys to highlight the program you want to
copy to another group.
2. Press F10 and then type P to select the Program menu. Choose
Copy from the Program menu. The DOS shell displays a prompt:
"To complete the copy, display the destination group, then press
F2. Press F3 to cancel copy."
3. Switch to another group by first pressing Esc to exit the current
group, then using the up/down arrow keys to highlight another
group.
4. Press F2 when the new group appears on the screen.

THE GROUP MENU

The group menu lets you add, change, delete, and reorder groups. The
reorder command will also let you reorder programs within a group. The
Main Group can contain up to 16 programs or subgroups. Subgroups can

contain up to 16 programs, but cannot contain any subgroups of their own. This means that the DOS shell can hold a maximum of 256 groups.

Add...

The Add command in the Group menu lets you add a new group within the DOS shell Main group. The Add command appears dimmed if you choose it within a subgroup. Choosing the Add command from the Group menu displays the Add Group dialog box shown in FIG. 1-10. It contains a title, filename, help text, and password. TABLE 1-6 describes these fields.

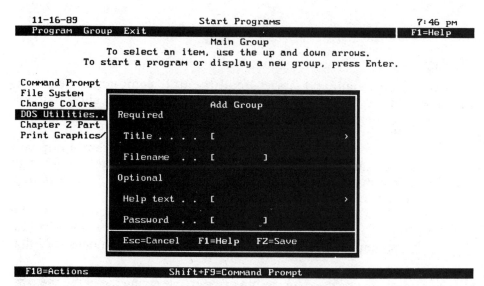

```
11-16-89                    Start Programs               7:46 PM
 Program  Group  Exit                                   F1=Help
                        Main Group
        To select an item, use the up and down arrows.
        To start a program or display a new group, press Enter.

Command Prompt
File System
Change Colors              Add Group
DOS Utilities..  Required
Chapter 2 Part
Print Graphics    Title . . . . [                        >

                  Filename . . [            ]

                 Optional

                  Help text . . [                        >

                  Password . . [            ]

                  Esc=Cancel   F1=Help   F2=Save

 F10=Actions              Shift+F9=Command Prompt
```

1-10 DOS Shell Add Group dialog box.

Table 1-6   Group Add Command Fields

Field	Description
Title	The title describes the group, such as Word Processors or Spreadsheets. A title can contain up to 38 characters.
Filename	The filename is the name of the file to store the DOS shell title, help text, and password about a group. The filename can contain up to 8 characters. File names must be unique between groups, and should be easy to remember. For example, WORDS for a group containing word processor programs.

Table 1-6   Continued.

Help text	Help text can contain up to 478 characters, including blank spaces. DOS 4.0 automatically formats your help text to fit within the help panel. If you want to begin a new line, just type the ampersand (&) character.
Password	A password can contain up to eight characters, including blank spaces. Passwords limit access to program groups. If you forget your password, even you won't be able to access, delete, or change the group from within the DOS shell.

Change...

The Change command lets you edit the title, commands, help text, and password of a program group that appears in the DOS shell. The following procedure shows you how to use the Change command.

1. Use the up/down arrow keys to highlight the program group you want to edit. *Note*: If you highlight a program name, the Change command appears dimmed on the Group menu. Group names appear with the ellipsis (...) following the name.
2. Press F10 and then type G to select the Group menu. Choose the Change command. The Change Group dialog box shown in FIG. 1-11 appears. If you password-protected the group, a password dia-

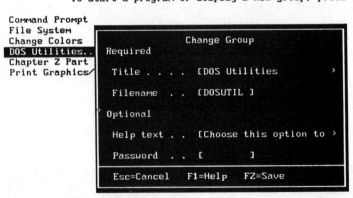

1-11   DOS Shell Change Group dialog box.

log box will appear first. You must type the correct password before you can change a group.

3. Enter any changes to the title, commands, help text, and password. When you finish making changes, press F2 to save your changes.

Delete...

The Delete command deletes a group in the DOS shell but does NOT delete the file that contains the group information. If you delete a group and want to restore it, add a new group and use the same filename as the previously deleted group. To delete a group permanently, you must erase the group filename with the .MEU extension. The following procedure shows you how to delete a group.

1. Use the up/down arrow keys to highlight the program you want to delete.
2. Press F10 and then type G to select the Group menu. Choose the Delete command. The Delete Item dialog box shown in FIG. 1-12 appears.
3. Use the up/down arrow keys to highlight the "Delete this item" option and press Enter.

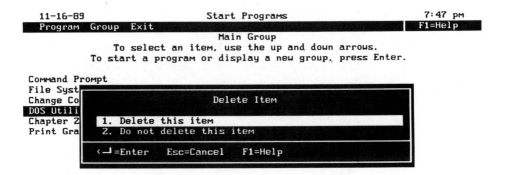

1-12 DOS Shell Delete Group dialog box.

Reorder...

The reorder command lets you rearrange the appearance of programs or groups in the DOS shell. The DOS shell always places the last program or group you added at the bottom of the program or group list. The following procedure shows you how to move a program or group name.

1. Use the up/down arrow keys to highlight the program or group you want to reorganize.
2. Press F10 and then type G to select the Group menu. Choose Reorder. The DOS shell displays the prompt: "To complete the reorder, highlight the new position, then press Enter. Press Esc to cancel."
3. Use the up/down arrow keys and highlight the program or group name where you want to move the program or group name.
4. Press Enter. The program or group name appears above the program or group name you highlighted in step 3.

THE EXIT MENU

The Exit menu lets you quit the DOS shell. To exit the DOS shell temporarily press Shift – F9 or choose Command Prompt from within the Main Group in the DOS shell. To exit the DOS shell permanently, press F3 or choose Exit from the Exit menu.

2
Using CodeView

This chapter does not present a complete explanation of all CodeView functions and operations. It does provide a complete and concise overview of CodeView options, command line semantics, and general commands. It explains some, but not all the differences between real and protected modes of operation. (You can use CodeView with OS/2.) Several features added to this chapter, which the Microsoft manuals do not include, are examples of functioning code and suggestions for optimizing code for easy maintenance using CodeView. Figure 2-1 shows a typical CodeView display. TABLE 2-1 describes each item labeled on FIG. 2-1.

OPERATION

Access the real mode version of the CodeView debugger using CV .EXE. The protected mode version produces an error message in the DOS environment. There are four main differences between the protected mode and real mode versions. First, the real mode version cannot use the /L option. Second, the real mode version does not support multiple threads of operation or the associated commands. Third, the display (\ ) function works differently in protected mode. In real mode the output screen display remains until the programmer presses a key. In protected mode the display changes after 3 seconds unless told to remain longer. Finally, the real mode version allows you to use only 640 Kbytes. Use the command line format below for real mode CodeView.

CV [*options*] *executable filename* [*arguments*]

The CodeView option descriptions appear below. The executable file

Table 2-1   CodeView Display Elements

Element	Description
1	*Menu Bar* - Contains a list of Main menu items and two commands. When you select one of the menu items, CodeView displays a submenu with lists of commands you can perform. Selecting Trace displays the results of the next command in line. Selecting Go continues program execution without stopping.
2	*Watch Window (Optional)* - Contains a list of selected variables and expressions, and their current status. CodeView displays this window whenever you define a variable or expression to monitor.
3	*Code Lines* - Codeview numbers each line of code within a file sequentially. Each external file called within a program uses its own numbering starting at one. Codeview highlights the numbers of lines selected as breakpoints.
4	*Current Location Line* - Shows the line of code that CodeView will execute next. This line is not always visible since you can scroll throughout the current file.
5	*Display/Dialog Window Separator* - This line separates the Display Window from the Dialog Window. Moving the line up or down changes the size of both windows.
6	*Dialog Window* - Use this window to enter commands you want CodeView to perform. You can scroll through this window to review the results of previous commands.
7	*Cursor* - Shows the location within the Dialog or Display Windows that Codeview allows you to enter commands. Entry always begins at the location directly under the cursor.
8	*Scroll Bars* - Allows you to scroll through the contents of the Dialog or Display Windows using a mouse. The highlighted area shows the current location of the cursor within the window. The arrows determine the direction of scrolling.
9	*Mouse Pointer* - Shows the current location of the mouse. CodeView displays the mouse pointer only if you have a mouse installed.
10	*Display Window* - Shows the program code loaded into CodeView for debugging. You can display the

Table 2-1   Continued.

code in one of three modes. Source mode shows the program code as you wrote it. Assembly-language mode displays the code as the compiler converted it for the processor. Mixed mode shows both the source code and assembly language equivalent.

11   *Register Window (Optional)* - The register window shows the current status of the 80x86 or 8088 processor registers. You can toggle this window open or closed by pressing F2. A special 80386 mode allows you to view all the registers associated with the 80386 processor. The operand address at the bottom of the display shows the physical location of an operand (variable) in memory.

12   *Menu Highlight* - Highlights the current menu selection. You change the highlight by pressing the Up or Down Arrows.

13   *Menu* - Contains selections relating to the category displayed on the Menu Bar. You can select a menu by pressing Alt then the highlighted letter of the Menu on the Menu Bar.

14   *Program Name* - Displays the name of the file loaded into memory. If you used the CodeView switches while compiling and linking your code, the Program Name changes as you go between library and other source code modules.

15 (Not Shown)   *Dialog Box* - Appears in the center of the display when you select a menu item requiring a response. The Dialog Box disappears when you type an answer and press Enter.

16 (Not Shown)   *Message Box* - Appears in the center of the display when an error occurs or CodeView needs to warn you about some condition. The Message Box disappears when you correct the error condition and press Enter.

---

name is any legitimate real mode or OS/2 family API program. The arguments are command line parameters to the executable file.

OPTIONS

The options listed below affect the way CodeView reacts to the system hardware and programs. All of these options are appropriate when using the real mode version. CodeView supports additional options when you use the protected mode version of the program.

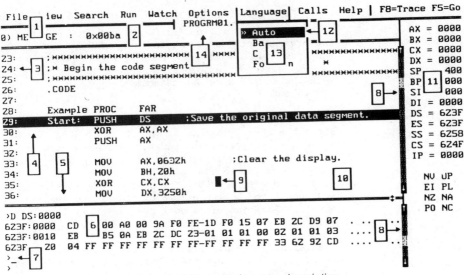

2-1 CodeView display area description.

The /2 Option

The /2 option permits using two monitors. The default monitor displays the program, while the other monitor displays CodeView information.

The /43 Option

The /43 option enables the 43 line display mode of EGA equipped computers.

The /50 Option

The /50 option enables the 50 line display mode of VGA equipped computers.

The /B Option

This option disables color presentation when using a two-color monitor with a CGA card.

The /C *commands* Option

Use this option to execute the command in the *commands* field automatically upon CodeView start-up.

The /D Option

The /D option disables Nonmaskable Interrupt (NMI) and 8259 interrupt trapping. This allows use of CodeView with computers that are less than 100% IBM compatible.

The /E Option

This option enables use of expanded (not extended) memory following the LIM 3.0 or higher specification.

The /F Option

Use this option to enable screen flipping. CodeView flips between two display pages in the graphic memory to display both CodeView and program screens. This option is faster than the screen swapping mode required for monochrome displays. CodeView disables this option when using two displays.

The /I Option

This option forces CodeView to handle both NMI and 8259 interrupt trapping. Use this option on computers that are not 100% IBM compatible.

The /M Option

This option disables mouse support.

The /P Option

Use this option to disable EGA palette register saving and restoration on non-IBM EGAs. Some EGAs cannot use this feature. Use this feature if the window mode appears to crash.

The /S Option

The /S option enables screen swapping. Use this option with a monochrome adapter, a non-IBM CGA/EGA adapter, or a program that uses multiple video pages. This option works slower than the standard screen flipping mode explained above. Do not use this option when using two displays.

The /T Option

The /T option enables the sequential mode of debugging. CodeView presents each display screen sequentially during the debugging session.

Use this option with non-IBM compatible computers and when using device redirection.

The /W Option

This option enables the window mode. The window mode displays up to four screens simultaneously so the programmer can monitor all aspects of the debugging session. This option might cause some non-IBM compatible displays/computers to crash.

COMMANDS AND CONTROLS

The commands and control keys listed below include all the keyboard commands used to control various aspects of the debugger display and program control. It also includes all commands entered at the prompt that affect program execution and control.

The 8087 (7) Command

This command tells CodeView to display the contents of the 8087/80287 chip registers in the dialog window as shown in FIG. 2-2. It also works with 8087 emulator libraries.

```
                                                    ═:┐   EI PL
                                                      │   NZ NA
>7                                                    │   PO NC
cControl 037F   (Projective closure, Round nearest, 64-bit precision)
                    iem=0 pm=1 um=1 om=1 zm=1 dm=1 im=1
cStatus   0000  cond=0000 top=0 pe=0 ue=0 oe=0 ze=0 de=0 ie=0
cTag      FFFF  instruction=00000  operand=00000  opcode=D800
Stack           Exp  Mantissa          Value
  >
```

2-2   CodeView 80X87 status display.

The Alt–C Key Combination

This key combination invokes the Calls menu shown in FIG. 2-3. The Calls menu displays a hierarchy of routines called during program execution. Selecting a call from the menu, displays that routine on screen. It does not affect program execution.

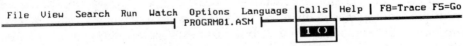

```
 File  View  Search  Run  Watch  Options  Language │Calls│ Help │ F8=Trace F5=Go
                                    ┤ PROGRM01.ASM ├
                                                      1 ()
```

2-3   CodeView Call Listing dialog box.

The Alt–F Key Combination

The Alt–F key combination brings up the File menu shown in FIG. 2-4. The File menu contains options for opening a new file, creating a DOS shell, and exiting from CodeView.

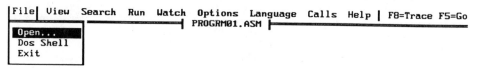

2-4   CodeView File menu.

The Alt–H Key Combination

Use this key combination to bring up the Help menu shown in FIG. 2-5. The Help menu presents the topics contained in the help system. Pressing the F1 key also invokes this option.

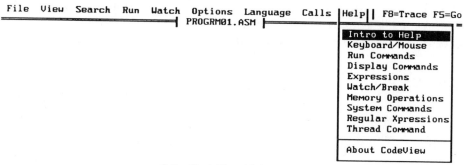

2-5   CodeView Help menu.

The Alt–L Key Combination

The Alt – L key combination brings up a menu that allows selection of programming languages as shown in FIG. 2-6. Using the auto mode allows

2-6   CodeView Language Selection menu.

CodeView to select the appropriate language based on the file extension of the source code file viewed. Source code files with an ASM extension automatically select the C language. Use this option to override the automatic C selection when using assembly language with other high-level languages. Type USE LANGUAGE NAME to select another language from the command line.

The Alt–O Key Combination

Use this option to change the default condition of CodeView as shown in FIG. 2-7. There are four options controlled by this menu. Flip/swap con-

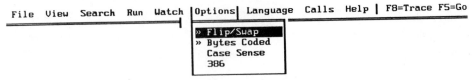

2-7 CodeView Options menu.

trols whether CodeView swaps the contents of the debugging with program output, or flips between two video pages during program execution. The "Bytes Coded" option affects only assembly language programs. When enabled, this option causes CodeView to display all instructions, instruction addresses, and bytes for each instruction. The case sense option enables/disables case sensitivity. The 386 option enables/disables the 386 register display. When disabled, CodeView discards all 32-bit register output and displays only 16-bit output.

The Alt–R Key Combination

The Alt–R key combination invokes the Run menu shown in FIG. 2-8. Use this menu to start, restart, or execute the program. This option also clears all current breakpoints.

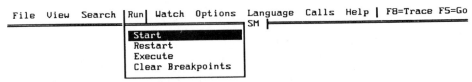

File View Search |Run| Watch Options Language Calls Help | F8=Trace F5=Go

2-8 CodeView Run Program menu.

The Alt–S Key Combination

This key combination invokes the Search menu shown in FIG. 2-9. Using the Ctrl–F key combination invokes the first option, Find, as well. The Find option looks through the current source code file for any regular expression and places the cursor at that point. The Next option finds the next occurrence of the expression; Previous finds the previous occurrence. The Label option searches executable code for an assembly language label.

File View |Search| Run Watch Options Language Calls Help | F8=Trace F5=Go

2-9 CodeView Search for Item menu.

The Alt–V Key Combination

This key combination invokes the View menu (FIG. 2-10) which contains three sets of options for changing the default display. The Source/Mixed/Assembly options change the way CodeView displays the file. The Registers option (also toggled using the F2 key) enables/disables display of the CPU registers. The Output option toggles the display between debugger and program output. Use the F4 key to toggle this option without invoking the menu.

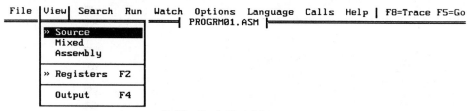

2-10 CodeView View menu.

The Alt–W Key Combination

The Alt–W key combination invokes the Watch menu shown in FIG. 2-11. The Watch menu contains five options for viewing variables and expressions during program execution. It also provides an option for setting conditional breakpoints.

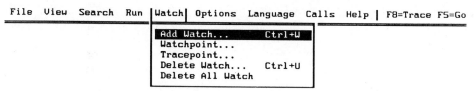

2-11 CodeView Watch menu.

The Add Watch option provides a means for viewing variables or expressions during program execution. CodeView provides three methods for entering a watch-expression statement. The first method uses the menu to invoke the option. Pressing Ctrl – W on the keyboard is the second method. The third method involves typing W? *expression* [*,format*] or W [*type*]*range* at the command line.

The Watchpoint option sets breakpoints on a conditional basis. When the watchpoint *expression* evaluates true, program execution discontinues. CodeView provides two methods of entering a watchpoint. Using the menu provides one method of entering the watchpoint. The second method involves typing WP? *expression* [*,format*] at the command line. CodeView accepts any valid *expression* and combination of Boolean operators as input.

Tracepoints monitor a range of memory for change. CodeView stops program execution when a tracepoint detects change. The two ways to set a tracepoint are: Using the menu, and typing a command. The command line formats for a tracepoint are TP? *expression* [,*format*] and TP [*type*] *range*.

The final two menu options are Delete Watchpoint and Delete All Watchpoint. Watchpoints include tracepoints. The first method of deleting a watchpoint uses the menu to select one or all. The second method involves pressing Ctrl–U and allows deletion of only one watchpoint. The third method uses the command line. Type Y [*watch number*] to delete a single watchpoint or Y* to delete them all.

The Assemble (A [*address*]) Command

The Assemble command converts 8088, 8086, 80286, and 80386 mnemonics to executable code. The optional *address* field specifies where to place the code; otherwise, assembly begins at the current address.

The Breakpoint Clear (BC [*list* ¦ *]) Command

The Breakpoint Clear command removes a single breakpoint (specified by *list*) or all breakpoints (specified by an asterisk).

The Breakpoint Disable (BD [*list* ¦ *]) Command

Use this command to disable one or all breakpoints. The *list* field specifies which breakpoints to disable. An asterisk disables all breakpoints.

The Breakpoint Enable (BE [*list* ¦ *]) Command

This command selectively enables the breakpoints specified by *list*. Using an asterisk with this command enables all breakpoints.

The Breakpoint List (BL) Command

This command displays a listing of both enabled and disabled breakpoints.

The Breakpoint Set
(BP [*address* [*passcount*] ["*commands*"]]) Command

The Breakpoint Set command places a breakpoint at the specified *address*. If the programmer does not specify an address, the breakpoint appears at the current program execution line. The *passcount* field provides a means of ignoring the breakpoint for the number of times specified. CodeView executes the commands entered in the "*commands*" field every time it encounters the breakpoint.

The Compare Memory (*C range address*) Command

CodeView compares the contents of memory specified by *range* with the contents of memory starting at *address*.

The Ctrl–C Key Combination

Pressing Ctrl – C halts program execution. The Ctrl – Break key combination performs the same function.

The Ctrl–F Key Combination

The Ctrl – F key combination invokes the Find option of the Search menu. Pressing Alt – S, then F, performs the same function.

The Ctrl–G Key Combination

Causes the dialog box or window currently occupied by the cursor to grow.

The Ctrl–S Key Combination

Use the Ctrl – S key combination to halt screen scrolling during display commands. Pressing any key restores scrolling.

The Ctrl–T Key Combination

Decreases the size of the dialog box or window currently occupied by the cursor.

The Ctrl–U Key Combination

The Ctrl – U key combination performs the same function as pressing Alt – W and then D. CodeView displays a listing of the current watchpoints as shown in FIG. 2-12. Selecting one of the watchpoints and pressing Enter deletes it.

The Ctrl–W Key Combination

Use the Ctrl – W key combination to invoke the Add Watch option of the Watch menu (FIG. 2-13). It performs the same function as pressing Alt – W and A. This option causes CodeView to display the contents of the selected variable or expression during program execution.

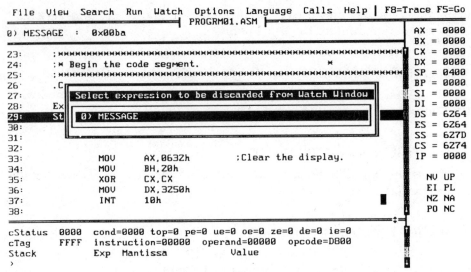

2-12 CodeView Delete Watch Expression dialog box.

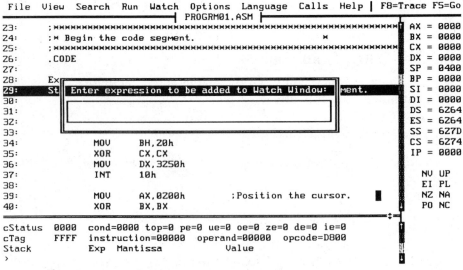

2-13 CodeView Add Watch Expression dialog box.

The Display Mode (S−, S+, or S&) Selection Command

These three commands select the CodeView display mode. S− selects assembly only mode, S+ selects source only mode, and S& selects mixed assembly and source mode.

The Display Expression (? *expression* [,*format*]) Command

Use this command to display any valid CodeView expression. The *expression* field contains the expression to evaluate. The optional *format* field specifies the display format.

The Down-Arrow Key

Moves the cursor down one line in the display or dialog box.

The Dump (D [*type*] [*address* ¦ *range*]) Command

The Dump command displays data contained in the area specified by *address* in both hexadecimal and ASCII formats. Using D by itself produces a display of the data pointed to by DS:0000 or the data after the previous display. The *range* field specifies a starting and ending address to display. Using a segment override allows display of data not pointed to by the DS register. Adding a dump *type* specifier changes the default dump display. The examples below show all the different forms of dump.

```
D  CS:0 50   ;Dumps the data pointed to by the CS
             ;register from offset 0 to 50.
DB CS:0 50   ;Dumps the same data in byte format.
DA CS:0 50   ;Dumps the same data in ASCII format.
DI CS:0 50   ;Dumps the same data in integer format.
DU CS:0 50   ;Dumps the same data in unsigned integer format.
DW CS:0 50   ;Dumps the same data in word format.
DD CS:0 50   ;Dumps the same data in double word format.
DS CS:0 50   ;Dumps the same data in short real format.
DL CS:0 50   ;Dumps the same data in long real format.
DT CS:0 50   ;Dumps the same data in 10-byte real format.
```

The End Key

Moves the cursor to the end of the command buffer in the dialog window or source file/program instructions in the display window.

The Enter (E [*type*] *address* [*list*]) Command

Use this command to change the contents of memory. There is one non-optional field associated with this command. CodeView will treat the E as execute unless the *address* field contains a valid address. As with other commands, this command assumes the segment address of the DS register unless the *address* field contains a segment override. The *list* field contains the data CodeView enters at that address. If the *list* field is empty, CodeView presents an area for entering the data. The *type* field determines the size of data entered into memory. The examples below show how to use this command.

```
E  0001 "D"        ;Enter data in the default type.
EB 0001 44         ;Enter a byte.
EA 0001 "HI"       ;Enter ASCII.
EI 0001 -12        ;Enter an integer.
EU 0001 12         ;Enter an unsigned integer.
EW 0001 ADOC       ;Enter a word.
ED 0001            ;Enter a double word.
ES 0001            ;Enter a short real.
EL 0001            ;Enter a long real.
ET 0001            ;Enter a 10-byte real.
```

The Examine Symbols
(X? [*module!*] [*symbol*] [*]) Command

The Examine Symbols command displays symbolic information about a program as shown in FIG. 2-14. When used by itself (X with no question mark), it displays all symbolic information for all modules. Specifying a module name with an asterisk, displays information for that module. Stipulating a specific symbol name without a module, displays information for each module in which the symbol appears. Using both options displays information for a specific symbol in a specific module.

2-14 CodeView Display Expression command.

The Execute (E) Command

The Execute command performs the same function as the Go command in slow motion. This allows the observer to see the changing of the contents of the CPU registers, and any watched variables or expressions.

The F1 Key

Performs the same function as Alt–H. Displays the on-line Help menu.

The F2 Key

Switches the display between showing/not showing the CPU register contents. Pressing Alt–V and R performs the same function.

The F3 Key

Use this key to change the output display between source code, mixed source code and assembly, and assembly only. Pressing Alt–V and the associated display mode performs the same function.

The F4 Key

This key toggles the display between the debugger and program outputs. Pressing Alt–V and O performs the same function.

The F5 Key

Performs the same function as the Go command. The program executes until CodeView encounters a breakpoint or the file ends.

The F6 Key

Toggles the cursor between the dialog and display windows.

The F7 Key

This option is active when the cursor is in the display window. If the line pointed to by the cursor represents code, and CodeView does not encounter another breakpoint or the end of the executable file, then the program executes to the cursor line.

The F8 Key

Use this key to execute a Trace command.

The F9 Key

This key tells CodeView to add a breakpoint to the line pointed to by the cursor.

The F10 Key

Pressing this key executes a program step command. CodeView steps over any calls or interrupts to the next displayed instruction.

The Fill Memory (F *range list*) Command

Use this command to fill a range of memory with the values specified by *list*.

The Go (G *break address*) Command

The Go command continuously executes program instructions until it encounters the address specified by the *break address*, a pre-set breakpoint, a Ctrl – C/Break, or the end of the executable file.

The Graphic Display (?? *variable* [,C]) Command

This command provides an enhanced view of structured variables. The *variable* field states which variable to observe. The optional C entry allows an ASCII display of single byte entries. The graphic display is similar in nature to the Watch command.

The Help (H) Command

Use this command to obtain help on various topics. It performs the same function as the F1 key.

The Home Key

Moves the cursor to the beginning of the command buffer in the dialog window or source file/program instructions in the display window.

The Input and Output Redirection (= *device name*) Command

This command changes both the default input and output to the device specified by *device name*. The example below shows commands specifically used during input/output redirection.

```
T>REDIR.TXT          ;Redirect the output.
*This is a Comment.   ;Add a comment to the file.

<INFILE.TXT          ;Redirect the input.
:                    ;Short command processing delay.
:::::                ;Longer command processing delay.
"                    ;Pause until the programmer
                     ;presses a key.
```

The Input Redirection (< *device name*) Command

The input redirection command changes default input from the console to the specified *device name*.

The Move Memory (M *range address*) Command

Use this command to move a *range* of memory to the *address* specified.

The Option (O [*option* [+ ¦ –]]) Command

The Option command changes the default condition of items appearing on the options menu. Valid options for the *option* field include F for flip/swap screens, B for bytes coded, C for case-sensitive, and 3 for 386 mode. Adding a + to the end of the option turns it on, – turns it off; otherwise, CodeView displays the current state of the option. Entering O with no arguments displays the current state of all options.

The Output Redirection ([T] > [>] *device name*) Command

The output redirection command changes the default output to the device specified by *device name*. The option T prefix allows simultaneous output to both display and device. Using the second greater-than symbol allows CodeView to append the new output to the end of an old file.

The Page Down Key

Moves the cursor one page down the command buffer in the dialog window or source file/program instructions in the display window.

The Page Up Key

Moves the cursor one page up the command buffer in the dialog window or source file/program instructions in the display window.

The Port Import (I *port*) Command

This command tells CodeView to import data from the specified *port*. It displays the data in the current default radix.

The Port Output (O *port byte*) Command

Use this command to output the value specified in the *byte* field to the specified *port*.

The Program Step (P *count*) Command

The program step command executes a program step. If it encounters a procedure, routine, or interrupt, it executes all the code to the next executable step in the displayed procedure. The program step command normally executes once; specifying a value in *count* executes it that number of times.

The Quit (Q) Command

The Quit command closes all program files and returns the programmer to the DOS prompt.

The Radix (N [*radix number*]) Command

Use this command to change the default base used to display numeric data. Entering N with no argument displays the current radix. Valid radix arguments are 8 for octal, 10 for decimal, and 16 for hexadecimal.

The Register (R [*register name*] [= [*expression*]]) Command

Use this command without any parameters to display the contents of all registers. When using an 80386 equipped machine, CodeView displays all 32-bit registers.

CodeView displays the current value of the register and asks for a new value, when the *register name* field contains a valid register name but the *expression* field is blank. It automatically replaces the designated register with an expression, when supplied.

The Redraw (@) Command

This command redraws the CodeView display.

The Restart (L *arguments*) Command

The restart command returns the CPU registers and program variables to the conditions encountered on program entry. CodeView passes any parameters placed in the *arguments* field to the program as command line variables.

The Screen Exchange (╲ [*time*]) Command

This command performs the same function as pressing the F4 key. Use it to see executing program output. The *time* field operates only with the protected mode version. The protected mode version screen returns to the debugging display automatically. The optional *time* field sets the amount of time that elapses before the screen returns to the debugging display.

The Search Memory (S *range list*) Command

CodeView searches memory specified by *range* for bytes or delimited strings specified by *list*. It returns a list of addresses holding the search value.

The Search Source File (/ [*regular expression*]) Command

This command is similar in nature to the Search Memory command. Instead of searching memory, CodeView searches a source file for the specified *regular expression*. CodeView then places the cursor where it found the expression.

The Shell Escape (! [*commands*]) Command

Use this command to suspend debugging temporarily to execute a DOS command. When no command appears in the *commands* field, CodeView executes a copy of the command processor; otherwise, it executes the command.

The Stack Trace (K) Command

The Stack Trace command displays a list of calls made by a program during program execution.

The Tab Set (# *number*) Command

Use this command to change the spacing between tabs.

The Trace (T *count*) Command

This command causes CodeView to execute one line of code. If the code calls another procedure/routine or interrupt, CodeView shows that code as the next executable instruction. The Trace command executes once or the number of times specified by the optional *count* field.

The Unassemble (U [*address¦range*]) Command

Use this command to produce an unassembled listing of an executable file. Unless the command includes an address, CodeView displays one screen of unassembled data starting at the address pointed to by CS:IP. When the command includes a range of addresses, CodeView unassembles code from the starting to ending address.

The Up-Arrow Key

Moves the cursor up one line in the display or dialog box.

The View (V [*expression*] or [.[*filename:*] *line number*]) Command

View provides the means to browse through a source code file. The two methods of determining the view start location include using a module/label name or the desired source code *line number*. CodeView allows the addition of a *filename* when specifying a source code line number.

EXPRESSIONS, SYMBOLS, CONSTANTS, STRINGS, DISPLAY FORMATS

Expressions The expressions used in MASM coincide with the same expressions used in C. However, MASM does not use some of the symbols used in C. TABLE 2-2 presents only the symbols used in MASM and their order of precedence.

Table 2-2   CodeView Assembly Language Expressions

Precedence	Operators
1	() [] -> .
2	! - (type) ++ -- * & sizeof
3	* / % :
4	+ -
5	< > <= >=
6	== !=
7	&&
8	|
9	= += -= *= /= %=
10	BY (byte) WO (word) DW (double word)

Notes:

1) The minus sign for the precedence 2 operators is the unary (number value) operator. The precedence 4 minus sign is the binary (subtraction) operator.

2) The asterisk sign for the precedence 2 operators represents the pointer operator. The precedence 3 asterisk is the multiplication operator.

3) The ampersand at precedence 2 is the address-of operator. CodeView does not support the ampersand as a bitwise AND

Symbols Symbols represent variables, registers, segment addresses, offset addresses, or full 32-bit addresses. CodeView accepts requests for information about any valid register, address, global variable, or variable in the current procedure.

Constants A constant is any integer number CodeView uses as part of a command. The default radix CodeView uses with assembly language programs is hexadecimal. To change the radix, use either the radix command described above to change the radix, or a radix override in front of the number permanently. The form of a number with a radix override is: override + number as shown below.

```
16      ;This represents 16 in the default radix.
016     ;This represents 16 octal.
0n16    ;This represents 16 decimal
0x16    ;This represents 16 hexadecimal
```

Strings   A string consists of characters delimited by double quotes. Code-View uses strings as part of some commands (for instance searches). The example below shows the difference between a string and non-string.

```
"This is a string."
This is not a string.
```

Display formats   CodeView provides a set of nine display format extensions to various commands. TABLE 2-3 provides a list of these extensions and their meanings.

Table 2-3   CodeView Display Format Specifiers

Character	Output Format
d	Signed Decimal Integer
i	Signed Decimal Integer
u	Unsigned Decimal Integer
o	Unsigned Octal Integer
f	Signed Floating Point Decimal Value (6 Places)
e or E	Signed Floating Point Decimal Value Using Scientific Notation (6 Places)
g or G	Either F or E Format (Whichever is More Compact)
c	Single Character
s	Characters Printed to the First Null Character

Note: Using the capitalized version of a format specifier results in upper case letters in the output.

RESTRICTIONS

The use of the CodeView debugger requires you to observe the following six restrictions on program type:

- CodeView can debug programs with include files. You cannot see the contents of the include file.
- You cannot use the standard EXEPAC utility or any LINK pack options on files used with CodeView. You can use the CVPACK utility to reduce executable file size.

- You can use CodeView on .COM extension files; however, none of the facilities associated with the symbolic information contained in executable files are present.
- You may never debug memory resident programs using CodeView.
- The programs may not alter the environment. CodeView discards any changes to the environment when it exits.
- Some programs might experience problems if they directly access the Program Segment Prefix (PSP). CodeView preprocesses the PSP the same way C programs do.

In addition to the restrictions above, the protected mode version of CodeView has the two restrictions listed below.

- Only one copy of CodeView can run at a time.
- If you don't use the /2 option when debugging and the program calls dynamic link library functions outside the API, then CodeView cannot access the program's environment, drive, or directory.

SAMPLE SESSION USING CODEVIEW

This sample session shows you the basics of using CodeView with a simple program. It does not show you how to troubleshoot a program. You can rely on this procedure as a basic method of starting the troubleshooting process.

Note: The following screen shots use the assembly language version of the program. You can still use the procedure with the other language versions listed. As stated in the Overview, source code listings ending with A represent assembly code, B represent BASIC code, C represent C code, and D represent Pascal code.

Due to differences between displays, display adapters, and other machine configurations, your display might not look exactly like the screens shown below. However, your screen should contain the same elements.

1. Type the program listing shown in FIG. 2-15. Compile and link your program.
2. Type CV PROGRM01 and press Enter. If you want, you can specify any command line parameters necessary to make CodeView work with your display or other hardware. CodeView displays the program and highlights the first line of the program code as shown in FIG. 2-16.
3. Press F3. Notice the display mode changes to show both source and assembly code (FIG. 2-17).
4. Press F3 twice. The display shows source code only.
5. Press F6. The cursor changes windows (appears in the Display Window).

2-15A Assembly language CodeView demonstration.

```
;**********************************************************************************************
;* Sample Program 1, CodeView Demonstration                    *
;* This program shows you how to use CodeView within a program.  It demonstrates various display aspects like *
;* loops.  You will also learn about various display modes.          *
;* Copyright 1989 John Mueller & Wallace Wang - Tab Books       *
;**********************************************************************************************

;**********************************************************************************************
;* Perform the program setup.                   *
;**********************************************************************************************

.MODEL MEDIUM   ; Use a medium model size.

.STACK ; Use the defalt stack of 1024 bytes.

;**********************************************************************************************
;* Begin the data area.  Declare all variables.          *
;**********************************************************************************************

.DATA

Message DB      '| This is a Message |$'

;**********************************************************************************************
;* Begin the code segment.                 *
;**********************************************************************************************

.CODE

Example PROC    FAR
Start:  PUSH    DS      ;Save the original data segment.
        XOR     AX,AX
        PUSH    AX
```

```
        MOV     AX,0619h        ;Clear the display.
        MOV     BH,7
        XOR     CX,CX
        MOV     DX,1950h
        INT     10h

        MOV     AX,0200h        ;Position the cursor.
        XOR     BX,BX
        MOV     DX,0C1Eh
        INT     10h

        MOV     AX,@Data        ;Display a message.
        MOV     DS,AX
        MOV     AX,0900h
        MOV     DX,OFFSET Message
        INT     21h

; Place a box around the message.

        MOV     AX,0200h        ;Position the cursor.
        XOR     BX,BX
        MOV     DX,0B1Eh
        INT     10h

        MOV     AX,0200h        ;Draw the first character.
        MOV     DL,201
        INT     21h
        MOV     CX,19   ;Draw a line.
Loop1:  MOV     AX,0200h        ;Draw a character.
        MOV     DL,205
        INT     21h
        LOOP    Loop1
```

```
          MOV     AX,0200h    ;Draw the last character.
          MOV     DL,187
          INT     21h

          MOV     AX,0200h    ;Position the cursor.
          XOR     BX,BX
          MOV     DX,0D1Eh
          INT     10h

          MOV     AX,0200h    ;Draw the first character.
          MOV     DL,200
          INT     21h

          MOV     CX,19       ;Draw a line.
Loop2:    MOV     AX,0200h    ;Draw a character.
          MOV     DL,205
          INT     21h
          LOOP    Loop2

          MOV     AX,0200h    ;Draw the last character.
          MOV     DL,188
          INT     21h

          RET

Example   ENDP
END       Start
```

2-15B BASIC CodeView demonstration.

```
' Sample Program 1, CodeView Demonstration
' This program shows you how to use CodeView within a program.
' It demonstrates various display aspects like loops
' You will also learn about various display modes.
' Copyright 1989 John Mueller & Wallace Wang - Tab Books

Message$ = "°  This is a Message  °"

CLS
LOCATE 12, 30
PRINT Message$;

LOCATE 11, 30
PRINT "ſ";

FOR C = 0 TO 20
  PRINT "ë";
NEXT C
PRINT "¡";

LOCATE 13, 30
PRINT "å";
FOR C = 0 TO 20
  PRINT "ë";
NEXT C
PRINT "ſ";
```

2-15C C language CodeView demonstration.

```
/* Sample Program 1, CodeView Demonstration
   This program shows you how to use CodeView within a program.
   It demonstrates various display aspects like loops.  You will
   also learn about various display modes.
   Copyright 1989 John Mueller & Wallace Wang - Tab Books */

#include <stdio.h>
#include <graph.h>

char *MESSAGE = "¤ This is a Message ¤";
int COUNT = 0;

main()
{
        _clearscreen(_GCLEARSCREEN);     /* Print the message. */
        _settextposition(12, 30);
        printf("%s", MESSAGE);

        _settextposition(11, 30);                /* Display the top line. */
        printf("%s", "è");
        for(COUNT=0; COUNT<19; COUNT++) /* Use a loop to display the line. */
                printf("%s", "ë");
        printf("%s", "£");
```

```
    _settextposition(13, 30);                    /* Display the bottom line. */
    printf("%s", "à");
    for(COUNT=0; COUNT<19; COUNT++) /* Use a loop to display the line. */
            printf("%s", "ë");
    printf("%s", "¥");
}
```

```
 File   View   Search   Run   Watch   Options   Language   Calls   Help | F8=Trace F5=Go
├══════════════════════════════════╡ PROGRM01.ASM ╞══════════════════════════
23:   ;××××××××××××××××××××××××××××××××××××××××××××××××××××××××××××××××  AX = 0000
24:   ;× Begin the code segment.                                     ×    BX = 0000
25:   ;××××××××××××××××××××××××××××××××××××××××××××××××××××××××××××××××  CX = 0000
26:   .CODE                                                               DX = 0000
27:                                                                       SP = 0400
28:   Example PROC     FAR                                                BP = 0000
29:       Start:  PUSH     DS          :Save the original data segment.   SI = 0000
30:               XOR      AX,AX                                          DI = 0000
31:               PUSH     AX                                             DS = 6264
32:                                                                       ES = 6264
33:               MOV      AX,0632h       :Clear the display.             SS = 627D
34:               MOV      BH,20h                                         CS = 6274
35:               XOR      CX,CX                                          IP = 0000
36:               MOV      DX,3250h
37:               INT      10h                                            NV UP
38:                                                                       EI PL
39:               MOV      AX,0200h      ;Position the cursor.            NZ NA
40:               XOR      BX,BX                                          PO NC
Microsoft (R) CodeView (R)  Version 2.2
(C) Copyright Microsoft Corp. 1986-1988.  All rights reserved.
>
```

2-16 Sample program 1 source code view.

```
 File   View   Search   Run   Watch   Options   Language   Calls   Help | F8=Trace F5=Go
├══════════════════════════════════╡ PROGRM01.ASM ╞══════════════════════════
START:                                                                    AX = 0000
29:        Start:  PUSH     DS          :Save the original data segment.   BX = 0000
6274:0000 1E              PUSH     DS                                      CX = 0000
30:                XOR      AX,AX                                          DX = 0000
6274:0001 33C0            XOR      AX,AX                                   SP = 0400
31:                PUSH     AX                                             BP = 0000
6274:0003 50              PUSH     AX                                      SI = 0000
33:                MOV      AX,0632h       :Clear the display.             DI = 0000
6274:0004 B83206          MOV      AX,0632                                 DS = 6264
34:                MOV      BH,20h                                         ES = 6264
6274:0007 B720            MOV      BH,20                                   SS = 627D
35:                XOR      CX,CX                                          CS = 6274
6274:0009 33C9            XOR      CX,CX                                   IP = 0000
36:                MOV      DX,3250h
6274:000B BA5032          MOV      DX,3250                                 NV UP
37:                INT      10h                                            EI PL
6274:000E CD10            INT      10                                      NZ NA
39:                MOV      AX,0200h      ;Position the cursor.            PO NC
Microsoft (R) CodeView (R)  Version 2.2
(C) Copyright Microsoft Corp. 1986-1988.  All rights reserved.
>
```

2-17 Sample program 1 mixed view.

6. Point to line 62 using down-arrow. Press Enter. Press F9. Code-View sets a breakpoint at line 62 (indicated by highlight or change of color).
7. Press F5. CodeView stops program execution at line 62.
8. Press F4. CodeView displays the output screen (FIG. 2-18). Press Enter. CodeView returns to the debug screen.

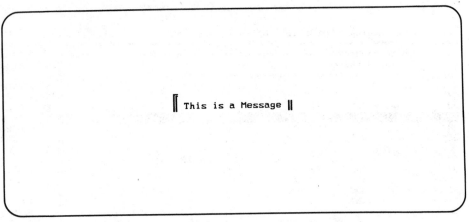

2-18 Sample program 1 breakpoint one screen.

9. Press F5. CodeView stops program execution at line 62. This shows the effects of a loop.
10. Press F9. CodeView removes the breakpoint from line 62.
11. Press F5. CodeView displays a termination message.
12. Press F4. Notice that the program completed the message box (FIG. 2-19).
13. Press Enter to return to the debug screen. Type Q and press Enter. The DOS prompt appears.

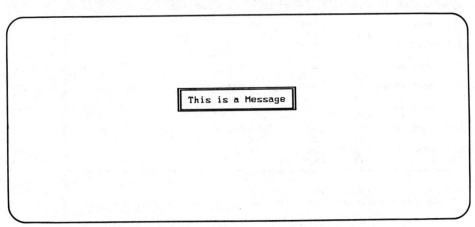

2-19 Sample program 1 breakpoint two screen.

3

Using the Microsoft Editor

The Microsoft Editor allows you to write programs using a word processor specifically designed for that task. In addition, it allows you to perform some programming tasks without leaving the editor. The following paragraphs describe the features and how to use the Microsoft Editor to its best advantage. Figure 3-1 shows a typical Microsoft Editor display with its various parts labeled.

USING COMMANDS

Giving commands to the Microsoft Editor involves three parts: Arg, Argument, and Function. Arg introduces the command. Argument defines what to use. Function defines what to do.

Throughout this chapter, we will show commands using the generic syntax (Arg Argument Function) and the equivalent Microsoft Editor default keystrokes (Alt – A). If you customize the editor, then the default keystrokes in this chapter might not work.

All examples in this chapter use the PROGRM01.C file included on the disk in this book. If you use any other language, use the PROGRM01 sample file included as an example.

Arg

Arg is the means used to issue commands to the editor. You provide the editor with an argument each time you wish to issue a command. There are three forms for Arg:

Arg	(Alt – A)
Arg Arg	(Alt – A Alt – A)
Meta	(F9)

```
/* Sample Program 1, CodeView Demonstration
    This program shows you how to use CodeView within a program.  It demonstrates
    loops.  You will also learn about various display modes.
    Copyright 1989 John Mueller & Wallace Wang - Tab Books, Inc. */

#include <stdio.h>
#include <graph.h>

char *MESSAGE = "‖ This is a Message ‖";
int COUNT = 0;

main()                              ┌─────────────┐
{                                   │ EDITING AREA │
                                    └─────────────┘
        _clearscreen(_GCLEARSCREEN);      /* Print the message. */
        _settextposition(12, 30);
        printf("%s", MESSAGE);

        _settextposition(11, 30);                /* Display the top line. */
        printf("%s", "┌");
        for(COUNT=0; COUNT<19; COUNT++) /* Use a loop to display the line. */
                printf("%s", "─");
        printf("%s", "┐");     ┌─────────────┐
                               │ COMMAND LINE │                           ┌─────────────┐
Copyright (C) Microsoft Co└─────────────┘    All rights reserve─┐│ STATUS LINE │
c:\c\0018\progrm01.c (C) Length=29  Window=(1,1)  ◄──────────────┘└─────────────┘
```

3-1 Microsoft Editor display area description.

Every command you give the Microsoft Editor begins with one of these three forms.

Text Arguments

Choosing one of three Arg forms (Arg, Arg Arg, Meta) tells the Microsoft Editor to begin a command. Next, the Microsoft Editor looks for the argument to use.

There are two types of argument: text and cursor movement. You can type in an argument (a text argument) or highlight existing text on the screen with the cursor (a cursor movement argument).

Three types of text arguments include textarg, numarg, and markarg. Three types of cursor movement arguments include streamarg, linearg, and boxarg. The following paragraphs describe the text argument types.

Textarg Textarg is text that you type from the keyboard. If you type the name of text marked using the Mark function (Ctrl–M), the Microsoft Editor interprets the text as the marked name and not as text. For example:

; Insert a file into the current file.
; Arg Arg Textarg Paste
Alt–A Alt–A <FILENAME> Shift–Ins

Numarg Numarg are integers you type from the keyboard.

; Move the cursor to a specific line on the display.
; Arg Numarg Mark
Alt–A <NUMBER> Ctrl–M

Markarg Markarg accepts any text defined with the Mark function (Ctrl – M). Once you define and name marked text with the Mark function, you can type the name as an argument.

```
; Copies the text between the specified marker and
; the cursor to the clipboard.
; Arg Markarg Copy
Alt – A <MARKER NAME> + ;Numeric Keypad +
```

Cursor Movement Arguments

You can type arguments directly from the keyboard, or highlight arguments on the screen instead. To highlight text on the screen, choose Arg (Alt – A) and then move the cursor anywhere on the screen.

Streamarg Streamarg consists of text on a single line. To highlight text, press the left- and right-arrow keys.

```
; Delete the text appearing between two cursor positions.
; Arg Streamarg Sdelete
Alt – A <MOVE CURSOR> Del
```

Linearg Linearg consists of a text block that you highlight by using only the down-arrow key.

```
; Perform a search and replace of the highlighted lines.
; Arg Linearg Replace
Alt – A <MOVE CURSOR DOWN> Ctrl – L
```

Boxarg Boxarg consists of a text block that you highlight by moving the right- and down-arrow keys.

```
; Insert a block of spaces into the highlighted area.
; Arg Boxarg Linsert
Alt – A <MOVE CURSOR DOWN AND RIGHT> Ctrl – N
```

EDITING COMMANDS

You can change the cursor movement commands by changing the hscroll and vscroll in the TOOLS.INI file. The hscroll switch determines the number of columns to shift left or right when you move the cursor off the left or right screen edge. The default is 10 columns.

The vscroll switch determines the number of rows to scroll up or down when you move the cursor off the top or bottom screen edge. The default is 7 rows.

Moving the Cursor

You can move the cursor up, down, left, and right by character, line, paragraph, or page. The Microsoft Editor defines a paragraph as the first blank line preceding or following lines of text. There are other cursor movement commands provided by the Microsoft Editor. TABLE 3-1 provides a complete listing of these commands.

Table 3-1   Moving the Cursor

Movement	Command (Key)
Moving the Cursor Up	
One line up	Up arrow key
Top of the screen	Meta Up (F9 Up)
Scrolls up by lines	Mlines (Ctrl+W)
Scroll up by paragraph	Mpara (Ctrl+PgUp)
Page up	Mpage (PgUp)
Page up a specific number of pages	Arg numarg Mpage (Alt+A numarg PgUp)
Page up the number of pages highlighted on the screen	Arg streamarg Mpage (Alt+A streamarg PgUp)
Upper-left corner of the current screen	Home (Ctrl+Home)
Beginning of the file	Arg Mpage (Alt+A PgUp) Mark (Ctrl+M)
Moving the Cursor Down	
One line down	Down arrow key
Bottom of the screen	Meta Down (F9 Down)
Scroll down by lines	Plines (Ctrl+Z)
Scroll down by paragraph	Ppara (Ctrl+PgDn)
Page down	Ppage (PgDn)
Page down a specific number of pages	Arg numarg Ppage (Alt+A numarg PgDn)
Page down the number of pages highlighted on the screen	Arg streamarg Ppage (Alt+A streamarg PgDn)
End of the file	Arg Ppage (Alt+A PgDn)
Moving the Cursor Right	
Right to next tab stop	Tab (Tab)
Right one character	Right arrow key
Right one word	Pword (Ctrl+Right)
End of line	Meta Right (F9 Right or End)
Moving the Cursor Left	
Left to previous tab stop	Backtab (Shift+Tab)
Left one character	Left arrow key
Left one word	Mword (Ctrl+Left)
Beginning of line	Meta Left (F9 Left or Home)

Inserting

You can insert characters, lines, dates, times, and complete text blocks. The following paragraphs describe how to perform this task.

Inserting characters   Choose Insert mode (Ins or Ctrl – V). The Microsoft Editor displays the "insert" command in the bottom of the screen. To turn off the Insert mode, choose this command again. To insert a single blank space at the cursor position, choose Sinsert (Ctrl – J).

Inserting lines   Choose Linsert (Ctrl – N) to insert one blank line above the current line. The cursor remains positioned at the new line position, allowing you to type on the new line without moving the cursor.

Inserting the current date   Curdate inserts the current date in the form of 2-May-1989. Because the Microsoft Editor does not provide default keystrokes for Curdate, you must assign your own keystrokes to Curdate in the form:

Arg Curdate:keystroke Assign

Using the Microsoft Editor default keystrokes, you could assign the keys Ctrl – D to Curdate using the following procedure.

1. Press Alt – A for the Arg function
2. Type Curdate:Ctrl – D
3. Press Alt – = for the Assign function

Now whenever you press Ctrl – D, the Microsoft Editor will recognize it as the Curdate command and enter the current date at the cursor's position.

Inserting the current day   Curday inserts the current day in the form of Sun, Mon, Tue, etc. Because the Microsoft Editor does not provide default keystrokes for Curday, you must assign your own keystrokes to Curday in the form:

Arg Curday:keystroke Assign

Using the Microsoft Editor default keystrokes, you could assign the keys Ctrl – D to Curday using the following procedure.

1. Press Alt – A for the Arg function
2. Type Curday:Ctrl – D
3. Press Alt – = for the Assign function

Now whenever you press Ctrl – D, the Microsoft Editor recognizes it as the Curday command and enters the current day at the cursor's position.

Inserting the current path name   Curfile inserts the current path name. Because the Microsoft Editor does not provide default keystrokes for Curfile, you must assign your own keystrokes to Curfile in the form:

Arg Curfile:keystroke Assign

Using the Microsoft Editor default keystrokes, you could assign the keys Ctrl – F to Curfile using the following procedure.

1. Press Alt – A for the Arg function
2. Type Curfile:Ctrl – F
3. Press Alt – = for the Assign function

Now whenever you press Ctrl – F, the Microsoft Editor will recognize it as the Curfile command and enter the current path name at the cursor's position.

Inserting the current file extension Curfileext inserts the current file-name's extension. Because the Microsoft Editor does not provide default keystrokes for Curfileext, you must assign your own keystrokes to Curfileext in the form:

Arg Curfileext:keystroke Assign

Using the Microsoft Editor default keystrokes, you could assign the keys Ctrl – F to Curfileext using the following procedure.

1. Press Alt – A for the Arg function
2. Type Curfileext:Ctrl – E
3. Press Alt – = for the Assign function

Now whenever you press Ctrl – E, the Microsoft Editor will recognize it as the Curfileext command. It enters the current filename's extension at the cursor position. If your current file was PROGRM01.C, this would print .C.

Inserting the current file base name Curfilenam inserts the current file-name's base name. Because the Microsoft Editor does not provide default keystrokes for Curfilenam, you must assign your own keystrokes to Curfilenam in the form:

Arg Curfilenam:keystroke Assign

Using the Microsoft Editor default keystrokes, you could assign the keys Ctrl – B to Curfilenam using the following procedure.

1. Press Alt – A for the Arg function
2. Type Curfilenam:Ctrl – B
3. Press Alt – = for the Assign function

Now whenever you press Ctrl – B, the Microsoft Editor would recognize it as the Curfilenam command and enter the current filename's base name at the cursor's position. If your current file was PROGRM01.C, this would print PROGRM01.

Inserting the current time   Curtime inserts the current time. Because the Microsoft Editor does not provide default keystrokes for Curtime, you must assign your own keystrokes to Curtime in the form:

Arg Curtime:keystroke Assign

Using the Microsoft Editor default keystrokes, you could assign the keys Ctrl – T to Curtime using the following procedure.

1. Press Alt – A for the Arg function
2. Type Curtime:Ctrl – T
3. Press Alt – = for the Assign function

Now whenever you press Ctrl – T, the Microsoft Editor will recognize it as the Curtime command and enter the current time at the cursor's position.

Inserting the current user name   Curuser inserts the current user name. Because the Microsoft Editor does not provide default keystrokes for Curuser, you must assign your own keystrokes to Curuser in the form:

Arg Curuser:keystroke Assign

Using the Microsoft Editor default keystrokes, you could assign the keys Ctrl – U to Curuser using the following procedure.

1. Press Alt – A for the Arg function.
2. Type Curuser:Ctrl – U
3. Press Alt – = for the Assign function

Now whenever you press Ctrl – U, the Microsoft Editor will recognize it as the Curuser command and enter the current user name at the cursor's position.

Inserting a file   To insert a file at the current cursor position, use the following command:

Arg Arg textarg Paste
(Alt – A Alt – A <FILENAME> Shift – Ins)

In place of textarg, type the name of the file you wish to insert, including any file extensions.

Inserting the output of a system-level command into a file   You can include the output of a system-level command into a file using the following command:

Arg Arg !textarg Paste
(Alt – A Alt – A !<FILENAME> Shift – Ins)

In place of textarg, type the name of the program you wish to run. The Microsoft Editor will run the program and insert the program's output directly into the file at the current cursor position.

Copy and Paste

You can copy single or multiple lines of text. When you copy text, the Microsoft Editor stores the copied text to a buffer called the *clipboard*. Once the Clipboard contains text, you can copy the text back to your file using the Paste command (Shift – Ins). The copy command works with both text and cursor-movement arguments. TABLE 3-2 provides a complete listing of the Copy commands.

Table 3-2   Copy Commands

Command	Description
Arg textarg Copy (Alt+A textarg +)	Copies text that you type to the Clipboard.
Arg numarg Copy (Alt+A numarg +)	Copies the specified number of lines from the current cursor position down.
Arg markarg Copy (Alt+A markarg +)	Copies previously marked text (Ctrl+M) to the Clipboard.
Arg streamarg Copy (Alt+A streamarg +)	Copies highlighted text on a single line to the Clipboard.
Arg linearg Copy (Alt+A linearg +)	Copies the highlighted text on multiple lines to the Clipboard.
Arg boxarg Copy (Alt+A boxarg +)	Copies the highlighted text block to the Clipboard.

Deleting

You can delete single characters, line breaks, and entire text blocks using Cdelete, Emacsdel, Ldelete, and Sdelete. Both Ldelete and Sdelete put lines into the Clipboard. You can cut and paste text from different parts of a document using Ldelete (Ctrl – Y) or Sdelete (Ctrl – Del) with Paste (Ins). TABLE 3-3 provides a complete listing of the Delete commands.

Search and Replace

The Microsoft Editor offers forward (Psearch) and backward (Msearch) searches. Psearch searches for text from the current cursor position to the end of the file. Msearch searches for text from the current cursor position

Table 3-3   Delete Commands

Command	Description
Cdelete (Ctrl+G)	Deletes the character immediately to the left of the cursor. Cdelete works only on single lines of text. If the cursor appears on line 1, then Cdelete will not begin deleting the text on the next line above. In other words, Cdelete cannot delete line breaks.
Emacsdel (BackSpace)	Deletes the character immediately to the left of the cursor. Works just like Cdelete except Emacsdel will delete line breaks.
Ldelete (Ctrl+Y)	Deletes a line of text.
Arg Ldelete (Alt+A Ctrl+Y)	Deletes from the current cursor position to the end of a line.
Arg boxarg Ldelete (Alt+A boxarg Ctrl+Y)	Deletes a highlighted text block.
Arg Sdelete (Alt+A Del)	Deletes text from the current cursor position to the line break at the end of the line. Using this command will join the bottom line with the top line.
Arg streamarg Sdelete(Alt+A streamarg Del)	Deletes text between the two cursor positions.

to the beginning of the file. TABLE 3-4 provides a complete listing of the Search and Replace commands.

To search an entire file, move the cursor to the top of the file using Arg Mpage (Alt–A PgUp), choose the text to search, and choose Psearch (F3). Or move the cursor to the bottom of the file using Arg Ppage (Alt–A PgDn) and choose Msearch (F4).

Table 3-4   Search and Replace Commands

Command	Description
Arg textarg Psearch (Alt+A textarg F3)	Searches forward for the string defined in textarg. When it finds a string, the search stops.
Psearch (F3)	Repeats the previous search. Searches forward.

Table 3-4   Continued.

Command	Description
Arg Psearch (Alt+A F3)	Searches forward for the string defined from the current cursor position to the first blank.
Arg streamarg Psearch (Alt+A streamarg F3)	Searches forward for the string highlighted on the screen.
Arg textarg Msearch (Alt+A textarg F4)	Searches backwards for the string defined in textarg. When it finds a string, the search stops.
Msearch (F4)	Repeats the previous search. Searches backwards.
Arg Msearch (Alt+A F4)	Searches backwards for the string backwards from the current cursor position to the first blank.
Arg streamarg Msearch (Alt+A streamarg F4)	Searches backwards for the string highlighted on the screen.

To search and replace text, choose the Replace (Ctrl–L) or Qreplace (Ctrl–\) function. The Replace function replaces text without asking for confirmation. The Qreplace function asks for confirmation before each replacement. Both Replace and Qreplace search and replace from the current cursor position to the end of the file. Use the following commands.

Arg Replace   or Arg Qreplace
(Alt–A Ctrl–L) or (Alt–A Ctrl–\)

Searches can look for exact string matches, or inexact matches. To look for inexact string matches, use special strings called *regular expressions*.

Regular Expressions

Regular expressions let you search for strings using inexact matching. For example, to search for all strings that begin with the letter 'a' and end with 'z,' you could search for the string [a-z]. TABLE 3-5 contains a complete listing of all the regular expressions.

The Microsoft Editor has predefined some regular expressions. To search for one of these predefined expressions, type a colon followed by the letter such as :a. To use a regular expression, you must use Arg Arg (Alt–A

Table 3-5   Regular Expressions

Command	Description
:a	This expression, which means [a-zA-Z0-9], searches for strings containing numbers and upper- and lowercase letters.
:b	This expression, which means ([\t]#), searches for blank spaces.
:c	This expression, which means [a-zA-Z], searches only for upper and lower case letters.
:d	This expression, which means [0-9], searches only for numbers.
:f	This expression, which means (['\[\]\:<|>+=;,.]#), searches for portions of a file name.
:h	This expression, which means ([0-9a-fA-F]#), searches for hexadecimal numbers.
:i	This expression, which means ([a-zA-Z_$][a-zA-Z0-9_$]@), searches for a C-language identifier.
:n	This expression, which means ([0-9]#[0-9]@![0-9]@.[0-9]#![0-9]#), searches for a single number.
:p	This expression, which means (([a-z]\:!)(\\!)(:f(:f!)\\)@:f(.:f!)), searches for a path.
:q	This expression, which means ("["]@"!'[']@'), searches for a string surrounded by quotes.
:w	This expression, which means ([a-zA-Z]#), searches for a single word.
:z	This expression, which means ([0-9]#), searches for a single integer.

Alt–A). Otherwise the Editor interprets the regular expression as a literal string like ':a.'

To search for these predefined expressions, use the following command:

Arg Arg :letter Psearch or Arg Arg :letter Msearch
(Alt–A Alt–A :letter F3) or (Alt–A Alt–A :letter F4)

To make your own expressions, the Microsoft Editor provides special characters. If you do not use a special character, or Arg Arg (Alt – A Alt – A) then the editor interprets the string literally.

Backslash (\ ) Causes the editor to ignore the special meaning of the next character. The editor would interpret two backslashes (\ \ ) as a command to search for a single backslash (\ ).

Question mark (?) Matches any single character. The expression a?c would match abc and a4c but not abbc or a323c.

Caret (^) Searches for strings at the beginning of a line. For example, ^mov would search for all 'mov' strings that begin a line.

Dollar sign ($) Opposite of caret, searches for strings at the end of a line. For example, ah$ would search for all 'ah' strings that end a line.

In character class [class] Matches any one character in the class. The expression a[123] would find the strings a1, a2, and a3. Use a dash (-) to specify a range such as a[1-3] which is equivalent to a[123].

Not in character class [~class] Opposite of character class, searches for characters not specified in the character class. For example, the expression a[4-9] would find the strings a1, a2, and a3 but not a4 or a9.

In addition to literal searches and inexact searches, the Microsoft Editor can also search for specific numbers of matches. For example, to search for all lines that do not begin with 'if' or 'while,' you would use the Not function as shown below.

~X Where X is any string or regular expression.

Minimal matching (X*) and Maximal matching (X@) Matches zero or more occurrences of X. For example, ab*c matches abc, ab3c, and aberdc.

Minimal matching plus (X +) and Maximal matching plus (X#) Matches one or more occurrences of X. For example, ab+c matches ab3c and aberdc but not abc.

Both minimal and maximal matching only work during search-and-replace operations. The difference between minimal and maximal matching lies in the number of characters that each finds. Minimal matching finds as few characters as possible while maximal matching finds as many characters as possible. The differences only appear when doing a search and replace.

Searching the string a+ (minimal matching plus) and replacing it with the string A would have the following effect.

Original string: aaa

1. Arg Arg (Alt – A Alt – A)
2. Ctrl – L or Ctrl – \

3. a+ (Search string)
4. A (Replacement string)

New string: AAA

Searching the string a# (maximal matching plus) and replacing it with the string A would have a different effect.

Original string: aaa

1. Arg Arg (Alt – A Alt – A)
2. Ctrl – L or Ctrl – \
3. a# (Search string)
4. A (Replacement string)

New string: A

In the above example, minimal matching plus immediately replaces a string with the new string when it finds a match. Maximal matching plus examines the entire string of letters that match, and then does the replacement.

Besides minimal and maximal matching, the Microsoft Editor lets you perform other selective matches.

Alternation (X1!X2!...!Xn)   Matches either X1 or X2 in that order. First the editor would search for the string X1Xn. If that fails, it would next search for X2Xn and so on.

1. Arg Arg (Alt – A Alt – A)
2. (X1!X2!)
3. F3 (Forward search)
    F4 (Backward search)
    Ctrl – L (Replace without asking)
    Ctrl – \ (Query replace)

Not function (˜X)   Matches all strings that do not appear in X. For example, ˜a˜b˜c would find all strings but abc.

Power function (X^n)   Matches exactly n copies of X. For example, a^3 matches aaa and aaaa but not a or aa.

Tagged expressions {...}   Tagged expressions only work during search-and-replace operations. A tagged expression appears within curly brackets. The editor tags the first string as $1. The editor tags the next string, separated by commas, as $2 and so on. The tag $0 refers to the entire string.

A tagged expression lets you manipulate text within a string. For example, to reverse a string you could search for the following string: {:w}{:z} and specify this replacement string: $2$1. This would accept a string beginning with letters, ending with numbers, and reverse them.

Original string: abc123

1. Arg Arg (Alt – A Alt – A)
2. Ctrl – L or Ctrl – \
3. {:w}{:z} (Search string)
4. $2$1 (Replacement string)

New string: 123abc

File Markers

File markers act like bookmarks, letting you quickly move to specific lines in a file. To save a single file marker, use the Savecur and Restcur functions. To save multiple file markers, use the Mark function. TABLE 3-6 contains a complete listing of the File Marker commands.

Table 3-6   File Markers

Command	Description
Mark (Ctrl+M)	Moves to the top of a file.
Arg numarg Mark (Alt+A numarg Ctrl+M)	Moves to a specific line in a file. The Microsoft Editor numbers the first line of a file as line 0.
Arg textarg Mark (Alt+A textarg Ctrl+M)	Moves to the file marker named by textarg.

Savecur and Restcur   Savecur saves the current cursor position. To return to this position, use Restcur. Note that you can only save one cursor position at a time using Savecur. If you use Savecur again, you will lose the previous cursor position. Because the Microsoft Editor does not provide default keystrokes for Savecur or Restcur, you must assign your own keystrokes to Savecur and Restcur using the following format.

Arg Savecur:keystroke Assign
Arg Restcur:keystroke Assign

Using the Microsoft Editor default keystrokes, you could assign the keys Ctrl – S to Savecur using the following procedure.

1. Press Alt – A for the Arg function
2. Type Savecur:Ctrl – S
3. Press Alt – = for the Assign function

Now whenever you press Ctrl – S, the Microsoft Editor would recognize it as the Savecur command and save the current cursor position. Likewise, you could assign the keys Ctrl – R to Restcur using the following procedure.

1. Press Alt – A for the Arg function
2. Type Restcur:Ctrl – R
3. Press Alt – = for the Assign function

Now whenever you press Ctrl – R, the Microsoft Editor would recognize it as the Restcur command and return the cursor to the previously saved cursor position. If you did not save the cursor position with Savecur before choosing Restcur, nothing happens.

The Restcur command only works once. If you saved a position with Savecur and then use Restcur, the editor displays the cursor at the Savecur position. If you move the cursor and then use Restcur again, nothing happens.

To save more than one cursor position in a file, or to make permanent file markers, use the Mark function (Ctrl – M).

Creating a file marker Move the cursor to the location to place the file marker and choose the following command:

Arg Arg textarg Mark
(Alt – A Alt – A textarg Ctrl – M)
Type in a word or phrase to name the file marker.

Moving to a file marker Using the file marker command (Ctrl – M), you can move to the top of a file, to specific lines in a file, or to file markers.

COMPILING AND LINKING WITHIN THE EDITOR

The Microsoft Editor lets you compile programs without exiting the editor. To tell the editor which files to compile every compilation, you can set the extmake switch in the TOOLS.INI file. Use the compile command as shown below.

Arg Compile
(Alt – A Shift – F3)

If you do not set the extmake switch, then you must name the file you wish to compile.

Arg Arg textarg Compile
(Alt – A Alt – A textarg Shift – F3)

or

Arg Arg streamarg Compile
(Alt – A Alt – A streamarg Shift – F3)

Reading Compiler Errors

When a program fails to compile, the compiler displays an error message. This error message lists the row and column where the compilation failed. The editor moves the cursor to the first error. To see the next error, use the Compile (Shift–F3) command. To see the previous error, use the Arg Meta Compile (Alt–A F9 Shift–F3) command.

Compatible Compilers

Only certain compilers can display compiler errors from within the Microsoft Editor. Those compilers include:

- Microsoft C Optimizing Compiler
- Microsoft Macro Assembler
- Microsoft Pascal Compiler
- Microsoft BASIC Compiler

If you do not have one of these compilers, you cannot read error messages from within the Microsoft Editor.

MACROS

Macros are keystrokes and functions that execute with the touch of a single keystroke. Functions can be any valid editor function. Keystrokes may be as simple as moving the cursor, or as complicated as asking for input and performing a command based on that input.

Macro Specifications

The maximum number of macros you can define is 1024. Macros disappear when you exit the editor unless you save them to the TOOLS.INI file.

Creating a Macro

You can create macros using the following command syntax:

Arg textarg Assign
(Alt – A textarg A + =)

where textarg takes the form:

macroname := {function | "text"}

You must use a unique name for each macroname. The Microsoft Editor allows you to use previously defined functions only. Separate multiple functions with a space. Macros must fit on a single line. The following macro scrolls the window by 11 lines and places the cursor in column 1:

Halfscreen : = Meta Up Arg "11" Plines Begline
      (F9 Up Alt – A 11 Ctrl – Z Home)

Because macros must fit on a single line, you must break large macros into several smaller ones like:

Head1 : = Arg...
Head2 : = Newline...
Head3 : = Newline...
Header : = Head1 Head2 Head3

Once you create a macro, you must assign it to a keystroke. You may not assign multiple macros to the same macroname.

Assigning Macros to Keystrokes

After creating a macro, assign it to a keystroke as follows.

Arg textarg Assign
(Alt – A textarg Alt – =)

where textarg is the macro name and keystroke such as:

Header: Alt – H

Note: Take care not to assign macros to existing keystrokes, such as Alt – A or Home, unless you wish to redefine these keys.

Viewing Macros

To see which macros you defined, use the Help function (F1). The Microsoft Editor displays a list of macros in alphabetical order. Figure 3-2

```
         Current function-to-key assignments and variable values
                          Press f2 to return

     Your current keyboard assignments are:

                          arg        alt+a
                       assign        alt+=
                      backtab        shift+tab
                      begline        home
                       cancel        esc
                      cdelete        ctrl+G
                      compile        shift+f3
                         copy        ctrl+ins and num+
                         down        ctrl+X and down
                     emacscdel       bksp
                     emacsnewl       numenter and enter
                      endline        end
                      execute        f7
                         exit        f8
                         home        ctrl+home
                  information        shift+f1
                   initialize        shift+f8
                   insertmode        ctrl+V and ins
     Copyright (C) Microsoft Corp 1987, 1988.  All rights reserved
     <assign> (pseudo NL) Length=122  Window=(1,1)
```

3-2   Microsoft Editor macro listing display.

shows a typical macro listing. When you finish looking at this list, use the
Setfile function (F2) to return to the editor.

Assigning ASCII Characters to Macros

If you need to display the ASCII characters in a file, assign them to a
macro. To assign a carriage return to the Ctrl–R key, use the following:

Arg Graphic:Ctrl–R Assign
(Alt–A Graphic:Ctrl–R Alt–=)

Removing Macros

You may erase macros from memory. If you define the Alt–H keystroke as a macro, you can erase it with the following command:

Arg textarg Assign
(Alt–A textarg Alt–=)

To erase the Alt–H macro, you would do the following:

Arg Unassigned:Alt–H Assign
(Alt–A Unassigned:Alt–H Alt–=)

Macro Conditionals

Macro conditionals alter the order that the macro invokes functions.
Using a macro conditional lets the macro test for certain conditions to
exist. If they exist, the macro performs a command. If the conditions do
not exist, the macro can perform a different command. TABLE 3-7 provides
a complete listing of macro conditionals.

Table 3-7   Macro Conditionals

Default Function	Keystroke	Returns TRUE	Returns FALSE
Arg	Alt+A	Always	Never
Argcompile	F5	Compile successful	Bad argument/ compiler not found
Assign	Alt+=	Assignment successful	Invalid assignment
Backtab	Shift+Tab	Cursor moved	Cursor at left margin
Begline	Home	Cursor moved	Cursor not moved
Cancel	Esc	Always	Never

Table 3-7   **Continued.**

Default Function	Keystroke	Returns TRUE	Returns FALSE
Cdelete	Ctrl+G	Cursor moved	Cursor not moved
Compile	Shift+F3	Compile successful	Bad argument/ compiler not found
Copy Down	Ctrl+Ins	Copy successful	Bad argument
Down arrow		Cursor moved	Cursor not moved
Emacscdel	BackSpace	Cursor moved	Cursor not moved
Emacsnewl	Enter	Cursor moved	Cursor not moved
Endline	End	Cursor moved	Cursor not moved
Execute	F7	Last command successful	Last command failed
Exit	F8	No return condition	No return condition
Help	F1	Always	Never
Home	Ctrl+Home	Cursor moved	Cursor not moved
Information	Shift+F1	Always	Never
Initialize	Shift+F8	Initialization successful	Bad argument
Insertmode	Ins	Insert mode now on	Insert mode now off
Lasttext	Ctrl+O	Function successful	Bad argument
Ldelete	Ctrl+Y	Line-delete successful	Bad argument
Left	Left arrow	Cursor moved	Cursor not moved
Linsert	Ctrl+N	Line insert successful	Bad argument

Table 3-7   Continued.

Default Function	Keystroke	Returns TRUE	Returns FALSE
Mark	Ctrl+M	Definition /move successful	Bad argument/ not found
Meta	F9	Meta now on	Meta now off
Mlines	Ctrl+W	Movement occurred	Bad argument
Mpage	PgUp	Movement occurred	Bad argument
Mpara	Ctrl+PgUp	Movement occurred	Bad argument
Msearch	F4	String found	Bad argument/ string not found
Mword	Ctrl+Left	Cursor moved	Cursor not moved
Newline	--	Always	Never
Paste	Shift+Ins	Always	Never
Pbal	Ctrl+[	Balance successful	Bad argument/ not balanced
Plines	Ctrl+Z	Movement occurred	Bad argument
Ppage	PgDn	Movement occurred	Bad argument
Ppara	Ctrl+PgDn	Movement occurred	Bad argument
Psearch	F3	String found	Bad argument/ string not found
Pword	Ctrl+Right	Cursor moved	Cursor not moved
Qreplace	Ctrl+\	At least one replacement	String not found/invalid pattern
Quote	Ctrl+P	Always	Never
Refresh	Shift+F7	File read in/ deleted	Canceled, bad argument

Table 3-7   Continued.

Default Function	Keystroke	Returns TRUE	Returns FALSE
Replace	Ctrl+L	At least one replacement	String not found/invalid pattern
Restcur	- -	Position previously saved with Savecur	Position not saved with Savecur
Right	Right arrow	Cursor over text of line	Cursor beyond end of line
Savecur	- -	Always	Never
Sdelete	Del	Delete successful	Bad argument
Setfile	F2	File-switch successful	Bad argument
Setwindow	Ctrl+]	Window-change successful	Bad argument
Shell	Shift+F9	Shell successful	Bad argument/ program not found
Sinsert	Ctrl+J	Insert successful	Bad argument
Tab	Tab	Cursor moved	Cursor not moved
Undo	Alt+BackSpace	Always	Never
Up	Up arrow	Cursor moved	Cursor not moved
Window	F6	Successful split, join, or move	Any error

Based on the Boolean values of these functions, the Microsoft Editor can invoke other functions. The editor offers four types of macro conditionals:

:> label - Defines a label
=> label - Transfers a label

—> label - Transfers to label if function returned FALSE
+ > label - Transfers to label if function returned TRUE

The format for a macro conditional looks like this:

Macroname := Function Label Function Label
Macroname : Keystroke

WINDOWS AND MULTIPLE FILES

The Microsoft Editor lets you open up to eight windows on the screen. The windows can display two or more files, or two or more parts of the same file. Each window must be a minimum of 5 lines and 10 columns in size. If you try to open a window with less than 5 lines or 10 columns, the Microsoft Editor ignores your command. Figure 3-3 shows a typical Microsoft Editor display with windows.

```
/* Sample Program 1, CodeView D/* Sample Program 1, CodeView Demonstration
   This program shows you how t   This program shows you how to use CodeView wi
   It demonstrates various disp   It demonstrates various display aspects like
   also learn about various dis   also learn about various display modes.
   Copyright 1989 John Mueller    Copyright 1989 John Mueller & Wallace Wang —

#include <stdio.h>                         ┌─────────────────┐
#include <graph.h>           ◄─────────────│VERTICAL WINDOW  │
                             #include <graph.└─────────────────┘

char *MESSAGE = "║ This is a Me  char *MESSAGE = "║ This is a Message ║":
═══════════════════════════════════════════════════════════════
/* Sample Program 1, CodeView Demonstration
   This program shows you how to use CodeView within a pr│gram.
   It demonstrates various display aspects like   ┌─────────────────┐
   also learn about various display modes.        │HORIZONTAL WINDOW│
   Copyright 1989 John Mueller & Wallace Wang —    └─────────────────┘

#include <stdio.h>
#include <graph.h>

char *MESSAGE = "║ This is a Message ║":
int COUNT = 0;

Copyright (C) Microsoft Corp 1987, 1988.  All rights reserved
c:\c\0018\progrm01.c (C) Length=30  Window=(1,1)
```

3-3 Microsoft Editor window display.

Opening a Window

You can create horizontal or vertical windows. The command for creating a horizontal window is:

Arg Window
(Alt – A F6)

The command for creating a vertical window is:

Arg Window
(Alt – A Alt – A F6)

Moving between Windows

To move between windows, press F6. This command moves the cursor to an adjacent window.

Closing a Window

When you close a window, the window merges to an adjacent window. The contents of the adjacent window will fill the new window. The command to close a window is:

Meta Window
(F9 F6)

Working with Multiple Files

To work with more than one file, first open a window, then load a file. Follow these steps:

1. Arg Window (Alt – A F6) or Arg Arg Window (Alt – A Alt – A F6) to create a horizontal or vertical window.
2. Arg Arg textarg Paste (Alt – A Alt – A textarg Shift – Ins) to load in the contents of a file where textarg is the name of the file you wish to load.

CUSTOMIZING THE EDITOR

You can customize the Microsoft Editor to make it work like several popular editors including WordStar, BRIEF, and Epsilon. The Microsoft Editor defaults to its own keystroke configuration if you do not choose one of your own. If you customize the editor, you should save your changes in the TOOLS.INI file. Otherwise you will lose your changes to the editor when you exit.

Using the TOOLS.INI File

The TOOLS.INI file stores the permanent changes you make to the Microsoft Editor. This file may contain comments, keystroke function assignments, macro definitions, switch settings, and tags.

Comments   The semicolon (;) marks a comment. The Microsoft Editor treats any text following a semicolon as a command and ignores it. Use comments to explain how your defined keystrokes and macros work.

; This is an example of a comment
Arg: = Alt – A ; Only this text is a comment

Keystroke function assignments   The syntax for assigning functions to keystrokes is:

functionname:keystroke
Functionname is the function like Setfile or Window.
Keystroke is the assigned key like Ctrl–F2 or Alt–3.

If you examine the TOOLS.INI file, you will see the default function key assignments like:

Arg:Alt–A
Argcompile:F5
Assign:Alt–=
Backtab:Shift–Tab

Macro definitions   The syntax for defining macros is:

macroname:={function ¦ "text"}
Macroname must be a unique name.
Function can be any function like Begline or Arg.

"Text" can be arguments for the function. You must separate functions and arguments by a space.

Switch settings   Three types of switch settings affect the Microsoft Editor. They include numeric, Boolean, and text switches.
You can change the switch settings temporarily using:

Arg textarg Assign
(Alt–A textarg Alt–=)

You can change switch settings permanently by typing them into the TOOLS.INI file.

Numeric switches   Numeric switches control the screen display such as colors, tab spacing, and the number of edit functions you can undo. To set a numeric switch, type the following:

switch : value

TABLE 3-8 contains a complete listing of the numeric switch settings.

Table 3-8   Numeric Switch Settings

Numeric Switch	Description and default value
entab	Controls the number of blank spaces the editor converts into tabs.
	0 means that the editor never replaces blank spaces with tabs
	1 means that the editor only replaces spaces outside quote marks with tabs
	2 means that the editor replaces all spaces with tabs

Table 3-8   Continued.

Numeric Switch	Description and default value
errcolor	Controls the background and foreground colors for displaying error message, (XY) where X is the background and Y is the foreground. The default to 04, red text on a black background.
fgcolor	Controls the color used by the editor, (XY) where X is the background and Y is the foreground. The default to 07, light gray text on a black background.
height	Controls the number of lines the editor displays. Default value is 23 lines. For EGA monitors, use 41. For VGA monitors, use 48.
hgcolor	Controls color for highlighted text, (XY) where X is the background and Y is the foreground. The default to 70, black text on a light gray background.
hike	Specifies the endling line position of the cursor when moved. Default is 4.
hscroll	Controls the number of columns shifted left or right when the cursor moves out of the editor window. The default is 10.
infcolor	Controls the color for informative text, (XY) where X is the background and Y is the foreground. The default to 06, brown text on a black background.
maxmsg	Controls the maximum number of messages saved in the message buffer (for OS/2 protected mode only). The default value is 10, set in the TOOLS.INI file as the tab [M-10.0].
noise	Controls the number of lines counted at a time when searching or loading a file, displayed in the lower-right corner of the editor. The default value is 50. To turn off the display, use 0.
rmargin	Controls the right column margin when using wordwrap mode. The default value is 72.
stacolor	Controls the color used for displaying the status line, (XY) where X is the background and Y is the foreground. The default to 03, cyan text on a black background.
tabdisp	Defines the ASCII character used to display tabs. The default value is 32, which displays tabs as spaces.

Table 3-8   Continued.

Numeric Switch	Description and default value
tmpsav	Controls the number of files the editor saves editing information for. The default value is 20, which means you can edit 20 different files and the editor will remember the last cursor position for all of them.
traildisp	Defines the ASCII character used to display trailing spaces. The default value is 0, and only takes effect if you have turned on the trailspace boolean switch.
undocount	Defines the number of levels you can undo commands in the editor.
vmbuf	Defines the number of 2K pages allocated to buffer the virtual-memory file. The default value is 128, and works in OS/2 protected mode only.
vscroll	Defines the number of lines shifted up or down when you move the cursor out of the editing window. The default value is 7 lines.
width	Defines the width of the display. The default value is 80 columns.

Colors	Hexadecimal value
Black	0
Blue	1
Green	2
Cyan	3
Red	4
Magenta	5
Brown	6
Light Gray	7
Dark Gray	8
Light Blue	9
Light Green	A
Light Cyan	B
Light Red	C
Light Magenta	D
Light Yellow	E
White	F

Boolean switches   Boolean switches turn editing functions on or off. The syntax to turn on a Boolean switch is:

switchname:

The syntax to turn off a Boolean switch is:

noswitchname:

TABLE 3-9 contains a complete listing of the Boolean switch settings.

Table 3-9   Boolean Switch Settings

Boolean Switch	Description and default value
askexit	Prompts for confirmation when you exit the editor. The default is Off.
askrtn	Prompts for you to press Enter when returning from the Shell command. The default is On.
autosave	Saves the current file whenever you exit the editor or switch to another file. The default value is On.
case	Sets case significant for search-and-replace commands. The default value is Off.
displaycursor	Shows the row and column position of the cursor in the upper-left corner. The default is Off.
enterinsmode	Starts the editor in insert mode. The default value is Off.
savescreen	Saves and restores the DOS screen for the Push and Exit functions. The default is On.
shortnames	Lets you name a file without its three letter file extension. The default is On.
Boolean Switch	Description and default value
softer	Indents text based on the format of surrounding text when you use the Newline or Emacsnewl functions. The default is On.
trailspace	Remembers trailing spaces in text. The default Off.
wordwrap	Breaks lines of text when they move beyond the right margin, specified by rmargin. The default is Off.

Text switches   Text switches alter how the editor works with files. There are five text switches available: backup, extmake, load, markfile, and readonly.

To set a text switch, use the following syntax:

textswitch:value

Backup. The backup text switch tells the Microsoft Editor what to do with files when you exit. This text switch can have three values: none, undel, or bak such as:

backup:none
backup:undel
backup:bak

"None" tells the editor not to make a backup copy of files that you change. If the filename already exists, the editor will overwrite it.

"Undel" tells the editor to move the old copy of a file to the hidden subdirectory called DELETED. To recover this backup copy of the file, you must use the UNDEL.EXE program. The Microsoft Editor sets the default text switch setting to undel.

"Bak" tells the editor to save the old copy of a file with the .BAK file extension.

Extmake. Works with the Compile function (Shift – F3) to specify the filename to use.

Load. Load specifies the name of the C-extension executable file to load. If you created your own extensions to the Microsoft Editor using C, and if you stored the file as C-EXT.EXE, then the load command would be:

load:c-ext.exe

Markfile. Markfile defines the filename the editor uses when looking for a marker.

Readonly. Specifies the DOS command to use when the editor tries to overwrite a read-only file. If you do not specify a DOS command, the editor will ask you for a new filename to store the current file.

Tags. Tags divide the TOOLS.INI file into sections. Sections let you create separate configurations for the Microsoft Editor.

For example, one section of the TOOLS.INI file might contain macrodefinitions and keystroke definitions for editing assembly language programs. Another section might contain definitions for editing Pascal or C programs.

Tags can also specify different operating systems and graphics displays. The syntax for making tags is:

[M-text]

Text is any name such as [M-Pascal], [M-C], or [M-Assembly]. The Microsoft Editor recognizes several built-in tags:

[M-3.20]   MS-DOS version 3.2
[M-3.30]   MS-DOS version 3.3
[M-10.0]   OS/2 protected mode
[M-10.0R]   OS/2 real mode

[M-mono]	Monochrome Display Adapter
[M-cga]	Color Graphics Adapter
[M-ega]	Enhanced Graphics Adapter
[M-vga]	Virtual Graphics Array
[M-viking]	Viking monitor display

To load a specific tagged part of the TOOLS.INI file, use:

Arg textarg Initialize
(Alt – A textarg Shift – F8)

Textarg is equal to "text" in [M-text]. In the above examples, to load the tagged section [M-3.30], you would choose:

Arg textarg Initialize
(Alt – A 3.30 Shift – F8)

WRITING NEW FUNCTIONS IN MICROSOFT C

Although you can customize the Microsoft Editor using macros and switch settings in the TOOLS.INI file, you can create your own functions with the Microsoft C Optimizing Compiler, version 4.0 or higher. When writing C extensions with the Microsoft C Optimizing Compiler, your programs may only use a certain number of functions.

Writing C Extensions

Any C extensions you write must follow the format defined by the SKEL.C program template provided with the Microsoft Macro Assembler disks.

```
#include "ext.h"

#define TRUE            -1
#define FALSE   0
#define        NULL            ((char *) 0)

flagType Pascal EXTERNAL Skel (argData, pArg, fMeta)
unsigned int argData;
ARG far *pArg;
flagType fMeta;
{
        return TRUE;
}

struct swiDesc swiTable[ ] = {
        { NULL, NULL, NULL }
};
```

```
struct cmdDesc cmdTable 0[ ] = 0{
        { "skel", Skel, 0, NOARG } ,
        { NULL, NULL, NULL, NULL }
};

WhenLoaded ( )
{
        return TRUE;
}
```

The EXT.H File

```
#include "ext.h"
```

The first line of a C extension includes the EXT.H file. This file declares structures and types that link your C extension program to the Microsoft Editor. This must be the first line of your C extension program. TABLE 3-10 provides a complete listing of functions that you may call from a C extension program.

Table 3-10   Functions Callable from C Extensions

Function Category	Callable Functions
Buffer Manipulation	All
Character Classification and Conversion	All
Data Conversion	All except strtod().
Directory Control	All except getcwd().
File Handling	All
Low-Level I/O Routines	All except write() in binary mode.
Console and Port I/O	All except: cgets() cprintf() cscanf()
Searching and Sorting	All except qsort().
String Manipulation	All except strdup().
BIOS Interface	All
MS-DOS Interface	All except: int86() int86x()

Table 3-10   Continued.

Function Category	Callable Functions
Time	All except: ctime() gmtime() localtime() utime()
Miscellaneous	All except: assert() getenv() perror() putenv() _searchenv()

The Switch Table

```
struct swiDesc swiTable[ ] =
{
        { NULL, NULL, NULL }
};
```

The switch table defines the switch settings your C extension will use. The preceding switch setting does nothing. You must keep this NULL row { NULL, NULL, NULL } as the last line in the switch table.

There are three fields in each entry. The first field defines the name of the switch setting. The second field defines a pointer to the switch. The third field defines the type of switch used. The three choices are SWI _BOOLEAN, SWI_NUMERIC, or SWI_SPECIAL. The following example defines a numeric switch with a default value of 20.

```
int n = 20;

struct swiDesc swiTable[ ] =
{
        { "newswitch", &n, SWI_NUMERIC },
        { NULL, NULL, NULL }
}
```

The Command Table

```
struct cmdDesc cmdTable[ ] =
{
        { NULL, NULL, NULL, NULL }
}
```

The command table defines a new editing function for the Microsoft Editor. The preceding switch setting does nothing. You must keep this NULL row { NULL, NULL, NULL } as the last line in the switch table. TABLE 3-11 provides a complete listing of command table functions.

Table 3-11   Command Table Functions

Value	Description
KEEPMETA	Reserves Meta (F9) prefix for next function.
CURSORFUNC	Executes cursor movement only. Does not take arguments.
WINDOWFUNC	Window-movement function.
NOARG	Does not need the Arg (Alt+A) prefix.
TEXTARG	Accepts a text argument.
BOXSTR	Accepts a streamarg argument.
NULLARG	Accepts Arg (Alt+A) without an argument.
NULLEOL	Accepts Arg (Alt+A) without an argument. The function is passed a pointer to textarg consisting of an ASCIIZ string from the cursor to the end of the line.
NULLEOW	Accepts Arg (Alt+A) without an argument. The function is passed a pointer to textarg cnsisting of an ASCIIZ string from the cursor to the end of the word.
LINEARG	Accepts a linearg.
STREAMARG	Accepts any kind of cursor movement: streamarg, linearg, or boxarg.
BOXARG	Accepts a boxarg.
NUMARG	Accepts a numarg.
MARKARG	Accepts a markarg.

There are four fields in each command table entry. The first field defines the name of the new editing function in quotes. This is the pointer to the function name. The second field defines the name of the new editing function without quotes. This is the address of the function. The third field is always NULL. The fourth field uses one or more of the values listed in TABLE 3-11. You may use two or more of these values on the same line by using the "¦" symbol such as KEEPMETA ¦ CURSORFUNC.

The WhenLoaded Function

```
WhenLoaded ( )
{
```

```
                        return;
        }
```

The preceding WhenLoaded function does nothing. Instead of the return statement, you could use one of three functions: SetKey, DoMessage, or BadArg.

SetKey SetKey assigns a function name to a keystroke. To set the Ctrl – Y keystroke to the name "Delete," use the following syntax.

```
WhenLoaded ( )
{
        SetKey ("Delete", "Ctrl-Y");
}
```

DoMessage DoMessage displays a message on the dialog line of the Microsoft Editor. To remind yourself what your newly defined keystrokes will do, display a message as shown below.

```
WhenLoaded ( )
{
DoMessage ("The function Delete is Ctrl-Y");
}
```

BadArg BadArg gives an error message if the user gives your function an incorrect argument. For example, a letter when the function needs an integer. Use BadArg to display a message as shown below.

```
WhenLoaded ( )
{
        BadArg ("Incorrect argument type");
}
```

Writing Your Function

```
#define TRUE    -1
#define FALSE    0
flagType Pascal EXTERNAL Skel (argData, pArg, fMeta)
unsigned int argData;
ARG far *pArg;
flagType fMeta;
{
return TRUE;
}
```

The first two lines of this function define the integer value for Boolean operations. The remaining lines define your actual function. The function definition appears between the curly brackets under flagType fMeta. Your functions can use three types of editing functions: Reading, Writing, and Initialization.

Reading files Three commands let you read files: FileNameToHandle, GetLine, and FileLength.

FileNameToHandle. To read or write to a file, you must use the File-NameToHandle command, which appears as:

```
PFILE filename;
filename = FileNameToHandle (pname, pShortName)
```

where pname is the actual filename and pShortName is a pointer to that name. To return the handle for the current file, use the following format.

```
PFILE curfile;
curfile = FileNameToHandle ("", NULL);
```

GetLine. Getline reads text from a file. Use the following format.

```
int Pascal GetLine (line, buf, pfile)
LINE line;
char far *buf
PFILE pfile;
```

The line parameter defines the line number. The buf parameter points to the buffer where the editor stores the text line. The pfile parameter points to the file defined by the FileNameToHandle command.

FileLength. FileLength finds the number of lines in a file using the following syntax.

```
variable = FileLength (filename);
```

Before using the FileLength command, you must identify the file to use with the FileNameToHandle command.

File writing Three commands let your functions modify a file: Replace, PutLine, CopyLine, and DelStream.

Replace. Replace inserts or replaces characters into text. The Replace declaration appears as shown below:

```
flagType Pascal Replace (c, x, y, pFile, fInsert)
char c;
COL x;
LINE y;
PFILE pFile;
flagType fInsert;
```

The c variable contains the replacement character or string. The x and y define the column (x) and line (y) to replace the existing text. The pFile parameter points to the file declared with the FileNameToHandle. The fInsert returns – 1 if the replacement is successful, and a 0 if unsuccessful.

```
char *p;
PFILE cfile;
cfile = FileNameToHandle ("",NULL); /* Current file */
for (p = "Hello"; *p; p++, y++)
Replace (*p, 12, 20, cfile, TRUE);
```

The preceding example replaces text at column 12 and line 20 with the string "Hello".

PutLine. PutLine replaces a line of text. Its declaration appears as shown below.

```
void Pascal PutLine (line, buf, pfile)
LINE line;
char far *buf;
PFILE pfile;
```

The line parameter contains a number which defines which line to replace. The buf parameter points to the string containing the replacement text. The pfile parameter points to the file defined by FileNameTo-Handle.

CopyLine. CopyLine copies lines of text from one location to another. The CopyLine declaration appears as shown below.

```
void Pascal CopyLine (pFileSrc, pFileDst, yStart, yEnd,
yDst)
PFILE pFileSrc, pFileDst;
LINE yStart, yEnd, yDst;
```

If pFileSrc is NULL, then the CopyLine function inserts a blank line. To do this, type CopyLines (NULL, cfile, NULL, NULL, 0).

DelStream. DelStream deletes text beginning with a starting coordinate and ending, but not including, with the ending coordinate. The Del-Stream declaration appears below.

```
void Pascal DelStream (pfile, xStart, yStart, xEnd, yEnd)
PFILE pfile;
COL xStart, xEnd
LINE yStart, yEnd;
```

The xStart and yStart parameters define the beginning coordinates and the xEnd and yEnd define the ending coordinates. The following example deletes text beginning at line 2 column 3 up to but not including line 5 column 4.

```
DelStream (cfile, 3, 2, 4, 5);
```

Initialization The three initialization functions include SetKey, DoMessage, and BadArg, SetKey assigns keystrokes to a function as shown below.

```
SetKey ("New", "Ctrl-N");
```

DoMessage displays a message on the Microsoft Editor dialog line as shown below.

```
DoMessage ("Enter an integer value");
```

BadArg displays an error message if the user gives an invalid or incorrect number of arguments.

Compiling C Extensions

You must compile your C program extension differently to use with the Microsoft Editor. To compile in Real Mode, use the following procedure:

1. Compile with the command-line options /Gs and /Asfu to use the proper memory model and calling convention as shown below.

   ```
   CL /c /Gs /Asfu myext.c
   ```

2. Link with the command-line options /NOD and /NOI followed by the EXTHDR.OBJ file. The /NOD and /NOI options link your program to the EXTHRD.OBJ file and not to the standard C libraries as shown below.

   ```
   LINK /NOI /NOD exthdr.obj myext.obj, myest.exe
   ```

3. Edit the TOOLS.INI file and add the line

   ```
   load:myext.exe.
   ```

Although your file compiles to a normal .EXE file, you cannot run it directly from DOS. You can only run it by defining it through the TOOLS.INI file for the Microsoft Editor. To compile in Protected Mode, use the following procedure.

1. Compile with the command-line options /G2, /Asfu, and /Lp to use the proper memory model and calling convention. You only need to use the /Lp option if you are compiling a protected-mode program from within the real mode of RAM.

   ```
   CL /c /Gs /Asfu /G2 /Lp myext.c
   ```

2. Link to produce a .DLL file instead of an .EXE file. Define SKEL.DEF as the module-definition file. Then place the resulting .DLL file in a directory listed in the LIBPATH directive from the CONFIG.SYS file.

EDITOR UTILITY PROGRAMS

Microsoft Macro Assembler comes with five utility programs. The MEGREP.EXE and CALLTREE.EXE files work with .ASM files you create with the Microsoft Editor.

The UNDEL.EXE, EXP.EXE, and RM.EXE files work with backup files created when you include the text switch "backup.undel" in the TOOLS.INI file. Backup files appear in a hidden subdirectory called DELETED. Each time you save a file, the Microsoft Editor saves the previous version to the DELETED subdirectory with the .BAK file extension.

MEGREP.EXE Utility

This program searches through program (ASCII) files for strings and regular expressions. You can run MEGREP from the DOS prompt, or you can run it within the Microsoft Editor. MEGREP.EXE has three options: /C, /c, and /f. Figure 3-4 shows typical output from the MEGREP program.

```
C:\C\SOURCE>MEGREP /C /c printf *.C
CFLOW.C: 17
DEMO.C: 2
SIEVE.C: 2
SORTDEMO.C: 2

C:\C\SOURCE>
```

3-4   MEGREP output example.

MEGREP.EXE [/C] [pattern] [files]

This command-line format searches files for a specific pattern. The /C option means that MEGREP searches for a pattern regardless of upper- or lowercase letters. Without the /C option, MEGREP.EXE will do a literal search, meaning that MEGREP.EXE will examine all letters in the pattern for specific case.

MEGREP.EXE [/c] [pattern] [files]

This command-line format searches files for specific patterns and records the number of matches made. Without the /c option, MEGREP does not count the number of matches found within a specific file.

MEGREP.EXE [/f] [patternfile ¦ pattern] [files]

This command-line format searches for patterns stored in a file, called a patternfile. Using this command, you can direct MEGREP.EXE to search for more patterns than you can type on the command line.

To use MEGREP.EXE from within the Microsoft Assembler, type:

Alt – A Alt – A textarg Shift – F3
where textarg represents:
/C pattern files
/c pattern files
/f patternfile ¦ pattern files
or any combination of these three options.

CALLTREE.EXE Utility

The CALLTREE.EXE program locates function calls within files. It prints the results in four files: a calltree listing file, a called-by listing file, a warning listing file, and a marker file. Figures 3-5 and 3-6 show the calltree

```
Screen
  VioGetMode?
  malloc?
  VioReadCellStr?
  VioGetCurPos?
  VioSetMode?
  VioWrtCellStr?
  VioSetCurPos?
VioGetMode?
VioSetMode?
Initialize
  srand?
  time?
  RandInt
    rand?
  Cls
    VioScrollDn?
  Reinitialize
    DosGetDateTime?
    PrintOneBar
      VioWrtNCell?
  BoxInit
    DrawFrame
      memset?
      VioWrtCharStrAtt?
    VioWrtCharStrAtt?
    strlen?
    sprintf?
SortMenu
  VioSetCurPos?
  KbdCharIn?
  toupper?
  Reinitialize...
  InsertionSort
    PrintOneBar...
    ElapsedTime
      DosGetDateTime?
      sprintf?
      VioWrtChrStrAtt?
      strlen?
      DosBeep?
      DosSleep?
  ElapsedTime...
  BubbleSort
    Swaps
    SwapBars
```

3-5 Calltree listing for SortDemo. C.

```
|   |   |   | PrintOneBar...
|   |   |   | ElapsedTime...
|   |   | HeapSort
|   |   |   | PercolateUp
|   |   |   | Swaps...
|   |   |   | SwapBars...
|   |   | Swaps...
|   |   | SwapBars...
|   |   | PercolateDown
|   |   |   | SwapBars...
|   | ExchangeSort
|   |   | ElapsedTime...
|   |   | Swaps...
|   |   | SwapBars...
|   | ShellSort
|   |   | Swaps...
|   |   | SwapBars...
|   | QuickSort
|   |   | Swaps...
|   |   | SwapsBars...
|   |   | QuickSort*
|   | BoxInit...
| Cls...
```

3-5 Continued.

BoxInit:	Initialize	SortMenu	
BubbleSort:	SortMenu		
Cls:	Initialize	main	
DrawFrame:	BoxInit		
ElapsedTime:	ExchangeSort	InsertionSort	SortMenu
	SwapBars		
ExchangeSort:	SortMenu		
HeapSort:	SortMenu		
Initialize:	main		
InsertionSort:	SortMenu		
PercolateDown:	HeapSort		
PercolateUp:	HeapSort		
PrintOneBar:	InsertionSort	Reinitialize	SwapBars
QuickSort:	QuickSort	SortMenu	
RandInt:	Initialize		
Reinitialize:	Initialize	SortMenu	
Screen:	main		
ShellSort:	SortMenu		
SortMenu:	main		
SwapBars:	BubbleSort	ExchangeSort	HeapSort
	PercolateDown	PercolateUp	QuickSort
	ShellSort		
Swaps:	BubbleSort	ExchangeSort	HeapSort
	PercolateDown	PercolateUp	QuickSort
	ShellSort		
main:			

3-6 Called by listing for SortDemo. C.

listing and called-by listing files for the SORTDEMO.C program provided on your Microsoft C disks. Other programming language output appears about the same.

The calltree listing file lists procedure names, indenting them four spaces per level. Procedure calls appearing for the second time appear as an ellipsis (...). Recursive calls appear as an asterisk (*). Any undefined procedures appear as a question mark (?). The command-line syntax for CALLTREE.EXE is:

CALLTREE [options]filename source-filename

The source-filename contains the files to use. You may use DOS wildcards:

CALLTREE [/a]filename

The /a option shows argument lists for function calls:

CALLTREE [/v]filename

The /v option displays a complete listing in the calltree listing file. Without this option, CALLTREE.EXE displays a function call once. The second time it encounters the same function call, it only displays an ellipsis (...).

CALLTREE [/i]filename

The /i option treats upper- and lowercase letters the same way.

CALLTREE [/q]filename

The /q option (quiet mode) prevents the output from appearing on the screen and just stores it in a file instead.

CALLTREE [/s]symbol filename

The /s option searches the filename for a specific symbol.

CALLTREE [/m]filename filename

The /m filename option uses the symbols listed in filename for calltree information.

CALLTREE [/c]filename

The /c option specifies the name of the calltree listing file. Otherwise CALLTREE.EXE defaults to its own listing file.

CALLTREE [/b]filename

The /b filename option specifies the name of the called-by listing file.

CALLTREE [/w]filename

The /w filename option specifies the name of the warning listing file.

CALLTREE [/z]filename

The /z filename option specifies the name of the marker file created for the Microsoft Editor.

UNDEL.EXE Utility

The Undel utility restores previous versions of files. This program moves files from the DELETED subdirectory to its parent directory. Use the following command-line syntax with Undel.

UNDEL [filename]

If you do not specify a filename, Undel displays the contents of the DELETED subdirectory. If more than one version of a file exists, Undel lets you choose which version you want to restore. If the filename already exists in the parent directory, Undel swaps the two files.

EXP.EXE Utility

The Exp program erases all files in the DELETED subdirectory. Use the command-line syntax shown below.

EXP [/r] [/q] [directory]

If you do not specify a directory, Exp deletes files in the DELETED subdirectory for the current directory. If you use the [/r] option, Exp deletes files in all DELETED subdirectories it finds. If you do not want to see a listing of the deleted files on screen, choose [/q] which specifies quiet mode.

RM.EXE Utility

This program works just like the Exp program, except that it selectively erases files from the DELETED subdirectory. Use the following command-line syntax.

RM [/i] [/r] [/f] filename

The [/i] option asks for confirmation to delete each file. The [/r] option searches all DELETED subdirectories for files to delete. The [/f] option only deletes read-only files.

4
Processor Commands and Interfaces

This chapter discusses processor-specific commands. The chapter arranges the processor commands in mnemonic alphabetical order. There are sections for the 8086/8088, 8087, 80286, 80287, 80386, and 80387 processors. Each general-purpose processor builds upon the commands available to its predecessor; therefore, each command appears once. The math co-processor commands appear once for each command. The applicable processor appears in parentheses beside the command. TABLE 4-1

Table 4-1   8086/8088 Processor Instructions

Command	Meaning	Page
Data Transfer		
IN	Input Data from Port	120
LAHF	Load the AH Register with Flags	129
LDS	Load the DS Register	129
LEA	Load the Effective Address	129
LES	Load the ES Register	129
MOV	Move	131
OUT	Output Data to Port	134
POP	Remove Data from the Stack	134
POPF	Remove Flags from the Stack	134
PUSH	Place Data on the Stack	134
PUSHF	Place Flags on the Stack	134
SAHF	Store AH into the Flag Register	138
XCHG	Exchange	142
XLAT	Translate	142

Table 4-1   Continued.

Command	Meaning	Page
Arithmetic		
AAA	ASCII Adjust for Addition	112
AAD	ASCII Adjust for Division	112
AAM	ASCII Adjust for Multiplication	112
AAS	ASCII Adjust for Subtraction	113
ADC	Add with Carry	113
ADD	Add without Carry	114
CBW	Convert Byte to Word	115
CMP	Compare	116
DAA	Decimal Adjust for Addition	117
DAS	Decimal Adjust for Subtraction	117
DEC	Decrement	118
DIV	Divide	118
IDIV	Integer Divide	119
IMUL	Integer Multiply	120
INC	Increment	121
MUL	Multiply	132
NEG	Negate	133
SBB	Subtract with Borrow	139
SUB	Subtract	142
Bit Manipulation		
AND	Logical AND on Bits	114
NOT	Logical NOT on Bits	133
OR	Logical OR on Bits	133
RCL	Rotate Left through Carry	135
RCR	Rotate Right through Carry	135
ROL	Rotate Left	137
ROR	Rotate Right	137
SAL	Arithmetic Shift Left	138
SAR	Arithmetic Shift Right	138
SHL	Shift Left	140
SHR	Shift Right	140
TEST	Test Bits	142
XOR	Logical Exclusive-OR on Bits	143
String Manipulation		
CMPSB	Compare Strings, Byte-by-Byte	116
CMPSW	Compare Strings, Word-by-Word	116
LODSB	Load Byte from String into AL	130
LODSW	Load Word from String into AX	130
MOVSB	Move String Byte-by-Byte	132
MOVSW	Move String Word-by-Word	132
REP	Repeat	136
REPE	Repeat if Equal	136
REPNE	Repeat if Not Equal	136
REPNZ	Repeat if Not Zero	136
REPZ	Repeat if Zero	136
SCASB	Scan String for Byte	139
SCASW	Scan String for Word	139
STOSB	Store Byte in AL at String	141
STOSW	Store Word in AX at String	141

Table 4-1   Continued.

Command	Meaning	Page
Control Transfer		
CALL	Execute a Subprogram	114
INT	Software Interrupt	121
INTO	Interrupt on Overflow	122
IRET	Return from Interrupt	122
JA	Jump if Above	122
JAE	Jump if Above or Equal	122
JB	Jump if Below	123
JBE	Jump if Below or Equal	123
JC	Jump on Carry	123
JCXZ	Jump if CX Equals Zero	123
JE	Jump if Equal	123
JG	Jump if Greater Than	124
JGE	Jump if Greater Than or Equal	124
JL	Jump if Less Than	124
JLE	Jump if Less Than or Equal	124
JMP	Jump Unconditionally	124
JNA	Jump if Not Above	125
JNAE	Jump if Not Above or Equal	125
JNB	Jump if Not Below	125
JNBE	Jump if Not Below or Equal	125
JNC	Jump on No Carry	126
JNE	Jump if Not Equal	126
JNG	Jump if Not Greater Than	126
JNGE	Jump if Not Greater Than or Equal	126
JNL	Jump if Not Less Than	126
JNLE	Jump if Not Less Than or Equal	127
JNO	Jump on No Overflow	127
JNP	Jump on No Parity	127
JNS	Jump on Not Sign	127
JNZ	Jump on Not Zero	127
JO	Jump on Overflow	128
JP	Jump on Parity	128
JPE	Jump on Parity Even	128
JPO	Jump on Parity Odd	128
JS	Jump on Sign	128
JZ	Jump on Zero	128
LOOP	Loop	130
LOOPE	Loop While Equal	130
LOOPNE	Loop While Not Equal	131
LOOPNZ	Loop While Not Zero	131
LOOPZ	Loop While Zero	131
RET	Return from a Subprogram	136
Flag and Processor Control		
CLC	Clear the Carry Flag	115
CLD	Clear the Direction Flag	115
CLI	Clear the Interrupt Flag	115
CMC	Complement the Carry Flag	116
ESC	Escape	119
HLT	Halt	119
LOCK	Lock the Bus	130

Table 4-1   Continued.

Command		Meaning	Page
	NOP	No Operation	133
	STC	Set the Carry Flag	141
	STD	Set the Direction Flag	141
	STI	Set the Interrupt Flag	141
	WAIT	Wait	142

lists the 8086/8088 processor instructions by functional area. TABLE 4-2 lists the 8087/80287/80387 co-processor commands by functional area. TABLE 4-3 lists the 80286 processor additions and TABLE 4-4 lists the 80386 processor additions by functional area.

Table 4-2   8087/80287/80387 Co-processor Instructions

Command		Meaning	Page
Data Transfer			
	FBLD	BCD Load	164
	FBSTP	BCD Store and Pop	164
	FILD	Integer Load	167
	FIST	Integer Store	168
	FISTP	Integer Store and Pop	168
	FLD	Load Real	168
	FST	Store Real	173
	FSTP	Store Real and Pop	173
	FXCH	Exchange Registers	175
Arithmetic			
	FABS	Absolute Value	163
	FADD	Add Real	164
	FADDP	Add Real and Pop	164
	FCHS	Change Sign	164
	FDIV	Divide Real	165
	FDIVP	Divide Real and Pop	165
	FDIVR	Divide Real Reversed	166
	FDIVRP	Divide Real Reversed and Pop	166
	FIADD	Integer Add	166
	FIDIV	Integer Divide	167
	FIDIVR	Integer Divide Reversed	167
	FIMUL	Integer Multiply	167
	FISUB	Integer Subtraction	168
	FISUBR	Integer Subtraction Reversed	168
	FMUL	Multiply Real	170
	FMULP	Multiply Real and Pop	170
	FPREM	Partial Remainder	171
	FPREM1	IEEE Partial Remainder	206
	FRNDINT	Round to an Integer	172
	FSCALE	Scale	172

Table 4-2   Continued.

Command	Meaning	Page
FSQRT	Square Root	172
FSUB	Subtract Real	173
FSUBP	Subtract Real and Pop	174
FSUBR	Subtract Real Reversed	174
FSUBRP	Subtract Real Reversed and Pop	174
FXTRACT	Extract Exponent and Significand	175

Comparisons

Command	Meaning	Page
FCOM	Compare Real	164
FCOMP	Compare Real and Pop	165
FCOMPP	Compare Real and Pop Twice	165
FICOM	Integer Compare	166
FICOMP	Integer Compare and Pop	167
FTST	Test	174
FUCOM	Unordered Compare	206
FUCOMP	Unordered Compare and Pop	206
FUCOMPP	Unordered Compare and Pop Twice	207
FXAM	Examine	174

Transcendental

Command	Meaning	Page
F2XM1	Value of 2X - 1	162
FCOS	Cosine	206
FPATAN	Partial Arctangent	171
FPTAN	Partial Tangent	172
FSIN	Sine	206
FSINCOS	Sine and Cosine	206
FYL2X	Value of Y * log2 X	175
FYL2XP1	Value of Y * log2 (X+1)	175

Constant

Command	Meaning	Page
FLD1	Load Value of 1.0	168
FLDL2E	Load Value of log2e	169
FLDL2T	Load Value of log210	169
FLDLG2	Load Value of log102	169
FLDLN2	Load Value of loge2	169
FLDPI	Load Value of Pi	169
FLDZ	Load Value of 0.0	169

Processor Control

Command	Meaning	Page
FCLEX	Clear Exceptions with Wait	164
FDECSTP	Decrement the Stack Pointer	165
FDISI	Disable Interrupts with Wait	165
FENI	Enable Interrupts with Wait	166
FFREE	Free Register	166
FINCSTP	Increment the Stack Pointer	167
FINIT	Initialize the Processor with Wait	168
FLDCW	Load a Control Word	169
FLDENV	Load the Environment	169
FNCLEX	Clear Exceptions	170
FNDISI	Disable Interrupts	165
FNENI	Enable Interrupts	170

Table 4-2 Continued.

Command	Meaning	Page
FNINIT	Initialize Processor	170
FNOP	No Operation	170
FNSAVE	Save State	171
FNSTCW	Store Control Word	171
FNSTENV	Store Environment	171
FNSTSW	Store Status Word	171
FRSTOR	Restore State	172
FSAVE	Save State with Wait	172
FSETPM	Set Protected Mode	186
FSTCW	Store Control Word with Wait	173
FSTENV	Store Environment with Wait	173
FSTSW	Store Status Word with Wait	173
FWAIT	CPU Wait	174

Table 4-3   80286 Processor Instruction Additions

Command	Meaning	Page
Data Transfer		
INS	Input String from Port	179
INSB	Input String Byte from Port	179
INSW	Input String Word from Port	179
LAR	Load Access-Rights Byte	180
LGDT	Load Global Descriptor Table Register	180
LIDT	Load Interrupt Descriptor Table Register	180
LLDT	Load Local Descriptor Table Register	181
LMSW	Load Machine Status Word	181
LSL	Load Segment Limit	181
LTR	Load Task Register	181
OUTS	Output String to Port	181
OUTSB	Output String Byte to Port	182
OUTSW	Output String Word to Port	182
POPA	Pop All General Registers	182
PUSHA	Push All General Registers	183
SGDT	Store Global Descriptor Table Register	183
SIDT	Store Interrupt Descriptor Table Register	184
SLDT	Store Local Descriptor Table Register	184
SMSW	Store Machine Status Word	184
STR	Store Task Register	184
Bit Manipulation		
ARPL	Adjust RPL Field of Selector	177
Flag and Processor Control		
BOUND	Check Array Index Against Bounds	177
CLTS	Clear the Task Switched Flag	178
ENTER	Make Stack Frame for Procedure	178

Table 4-4 Continued.

Command	Meaning	Page
Data Transfer		
SETPE	Set Byte on Parity Even	202
SETPO	Set Byte on Parity Odd	203
SETS	Set Byte on Sign	203
SETZ	Set Byte on Zero	203
Arithmetic		
CDQ	Convert Doubleword to Quadword	193
CWDE	Convert Word to Doubleword Extended	194
Bit Manipulation		
BSF	Bit Scan Forward	192
BSR	Bit Scan Reverse	193
BT	Bit Test	193
BTC	Bit Test and Complement	193
BTR	Bit Test and Reset	193
BTS	Bit Test and Set	193
SHLD	Shift Left, Double Precision	203
SHRD	Shift Right, Double Precision	204
String Manipulation		
CMPSD	Compare Strings, Doubleword-by-	194
Doubleword		
LODSD	Load a Doubleword from String into EAX	195
MOVSD	Move String, Doubleword-by-Doubleword	196
SCASD	Scan String for Doubleword	198
STOSD	Store Doubleword in EAX at String	204
Control Transfer		
JECXZ	Jump if ECX Equals Zero	195

Note: The % symbol shows the modulo of a number and the & symbol shows a logical AND when used below.

8086/8088 COMMANDS

The paragraphs below describe each 8086/8088 processor-specific command. The 80286 and 80386 processors use these commands as well. TABLE 4-1 lists all the processor commands by functional area. The table includes the page number of the instruction description. Figure 4-1 shows a mixture of 8086/8088 specific commands used in an assembly language program. There are no listings for BASIC, C and Pascal because it is impossible to see the processor commands using these languages.

```
;* Sample Program 2, 8088/8086 Instruction Demonstration              *
;* This program demonstrates some of the 8088/8086 processor commands.  You do not require any special  *
;* equipment to use this program.  While it does not show you every processor command available, this    *
;* program does provide insights into some of the more esoteric commands.  While the program performs a task,  *
;* it does not perform that task efficiently.              *
;* Copyright 1989 John Mueller & Wallace Wang - Tab Books*
;***********************************************************************************************************


;***********************************************************************************************************
;* Perform the program setup.              *
;***********************************************************************************************************


.MODEL MEDIUM   ; Use a medum model size.

.STACK  ; Use the defalt stack of 1024 bytes.

;***********************************************************************************************************
;* Begin the data area.  Declare all variables.              *
;***********************************************************************************************************
.DATA

BSpc      EQU     8
LF        EQU     10
CR        EQU     13
StrEnd    EQU     36
CalcScrn     DB        ' ┌──────────────────┐ ',CR,LF
             DB        '|  ┌────────────────┐  |',CR,LF
             DB        '|  |                |  |',CR,LF
             DB        '|  └────────────────┘  |',CR,LF
             DB        '|                      |',CR,LF
             DB        '|  ┌──┐ ┌──┐ ┌──┐ ┌──┐ |',CR,LF
             DB        '|  | 7 | | 8 | | 9 | |+| |',CR,LF
             DB        '|  └──┘ └──┘ └──┘ └──┘ |',CR,LF
             DB        '|  ┌──┐ ┌──┐ ┌──┐ ┌──┐ |',CR,LF
             DB        '|  | 4 | | 5 | | 6 | |-| |',CR,LF
             DB        '|  └──┘ └──┘ └──┘ └──┘ |',CR,LF
             DB        '|  ┌──┐ ┌──┐ ┌──┐ ┌──┐ |',CR,LF
             DB        '|  | 1 | | 2 | | 3 | |=| |',CR,LF
             DB        '|  └──┘ └──┘ └──┘ └──┘ |',CR,LF
             DB        '|  ┌──┐                |',CR,LF
             DB        '|  | 0 |                |',CR,LF
             DB        '|  └──┘                |',CR,LF
             DB        ' └──────────────────┘ ',CR,LF,StrEnd
DispPg   DB      0
DecNum   DB      19 DUP (' '),'0',StrEnd
DecNum2  DB      20 DUP (' '),StrEnd
ClrStr   DB      19 DUP (' '),'0',StrEnd
Posit    DW      0
Posit2   DW      0
Posit3   DW      0
```

4-1 Continued.

```
MathStat      DB     0
Carry   DB    0
Borrow  DB    0
LastNum DB    0


;***********************************************************************************************************
;* Begin the code segment.                        *
;***********************************************************************************************************
.CODE

Example PROC   FAR
Start:  PUSH   DS       ;Save the original data segment.
        XOR    AX,AX
        PUSH   AX

        MOV    AX,@DATA        ;Point DS & ES to our data segment.
        MOV    DS,AX
        MOV    ES,AX


;***********************************************************************************************************
;* Demonstate the Math/String commands using a two function calculator.  This example begins by checking  *
;* the last character input into the calculator.  The calculator performs integer math only.  It also only *
;* shows subtraction and addition.  One unique characteristic of the calculator is its ability to add or   *
;* subtract numbers of any size by using character math.              *
;***********************************************************************************************************

        MOV    AX,0F00h        ;Get the display status.
        INT    10h
        MOV    DispPg,BH       ;Save the display page.
        INC    BH       ;Use next page for display.
        MOV    AH,05h
        MOV    AL,BH
        INT    10h

        MOV    AX,0200h        ;Change the cursor position.
        MOV    DH,0     ;Row 0
        MOV    DL,0     ;Column 0
        INT    10h

        LEA    DX,CalcScrn     ;Display the calculator.
        MOV    AX,0900h
        INT    21h
        CALL   DispNum ;Display the number.

NextKey:       XOR     AX,AX   ;Get keyboard input.
        INT    16h

        CALL   ChckKey ;Check Decimal input.
        CMP    AL,1Bh   ;Compare key input to escape.
        JE     Exit     ;If equal, leave calculator.
        JMP    NextKey ;Get another character.
```

4-1 Continued.

```
Exit:   MOV    AH,05h  ;Restore the display page.
        MOV    AL,DispPg
        INT    10h

        RET

Example ENDP


;********************************************************************************************
;* This procedure validates the keystroke input by the user.    *
;********************************************************************************************


ChckKey PROC    NEAR

ChckNum:        CMP    AL,'0'  ;Is input a number?
        JL     BckSpc  ;If less, check backspace.
        CMP    AL,'9'
        JG     MathKey2
        CMP    Posit,19        ;If it is, is buffer full?
        JG     NoKey   ;If so, skip.
        LEA    DX,DecNum       ;Otherwise, place in buffer,
        ADD    DX,Posit        ; then display.
        MOV    SI,DX
        MOV    [SI],AL
        MOV    [DecNum+19],' ' ;Remove 0 from end of buffer.
        INC    Posit   ;Advance to next buffer position.
        CALL   DispNum ;Display character buffer.
        JMP    NoKey

BckSpc: CMP    AL,BSpc ;Check for a backspace.
        JNE    MathKey1        ;If not, check math symbols.
        CMP    Posit,0 ;See if buffer contains characters.
        JE     NoKey   ;If not, exit.
        DEC    Posit   ;Go to the previous position.
        LEA    DX,DecNum       ;Erase the buffer character.
        ADD    DX,Posit
        MOV    SI,DX
        MOV    AL,' '
        MOV    [SI],AL
        CALL   DispNum ;Display character buffer.
        JMP    NoKey

MathKey1:       CMP    AL,'+'  ;Check addition.
        JNE    MathKey2        ;If not, check subtraction.
        CALL   DoAdd
        JMP    MathKey1
MathKey2:       CMP    AL,'-'  ;Check subtraction.
        JNE    MathKey3        ;If not, check equals.
        CALL   DoSub
        JMP    MathKey1
MathKey3:       CMP    AL,'='  ;Check equals.
```

```
        JNE     NoKey   ;If not, not a key.
        CALL    DoEqual
        JMP     ChckNum


NoKey:  RET


ChckKey ENDP

;*******************************************************************************************************
;* This procedure displays the current product or entry number in the appropriate area of the calculator.  *
;*******************************************************************************************************


DispNum PROC    NEAR

        MOV     AX,0200h        ;Change the cursor position.
        MOV     DH,2    ;Row 2
        MOV     DL,3    ;Column 3
        MOV     BH,DispPg       ;Use the correct page number.
        INC     BH
        INT     10h
        LEA     DX,DecNum       ;Display the number.
        MOV     AX,0900h
        INT     21h


        RET
DispNum ENDP


;*******************************************************************************************************
;* This procedure adds two numbers.  It begins by placing the contents of DecNum into DecNum2 and clearing  *
;* DecNum. After clearing DecNum, it waits for a new entry.  After the user enters the number, DoAdd   *
;* converts and adds the two numbers one digit at a time.  It places the result in DecNum for display.  *
;*******************************************************************************************************

DoAdd   PROC    NEAR

        LEA     SI,DecNum       ;Locate the beginning of the
        LEA     DI,ClrStr       ; current number.
        MOV     CX,20
        REPE    CMPSB
        DEC     SI      ;Place pointers on exact
        INC     CX      ; position.
        PUSH    CX      ;Save the starting position.
        LEA     DI,DecNum2      ;Move the current number to
        REP     MOVSB   ; the storage string.
        POP     AX      ;Compute the number of spaces
        MOV     CX,20   ; to add to the end of the
        SUB     CX,AX   ; storage string.
        CMP     CX,0    ;If none, skip.
        JLE     DoAddB
        MOV     Posit,AX        ;Update posit to the correct string length.
DoAddA: MOV     BYTE PTR [DI],' '       ;Pad the end of the storage
```

```
          INC      DI        ; string with spaces.
          LOOP     DoAddA
DoAddB:   LEA      SI,ClrStr       ;Clear the current number
          LEA      DI,DecNum       ; storage string.
          MOV      CX,10
          REP      MOVSW
          MOV      AX,Posit        ;Place the length of the current
          MOV      Posit2,AX       ; number in the temporary storage area.
          MOV      Posit,0 ;Clear the length variable.
          CALL     DispNum


DoAdd1: XOR      AX,AX    ;Get keyboard input.
          INT      16h
          CMP      AL,1Bh   ;Compare key input to escape.
          JNE      DoAdd1A
          JMP      DoAddEnd        ;If equal, leave calculator.


DoAdd1A:      CMP      AL,'0'  ;Is input a number?
          JL       DoAdd2  ;If less, check backspace.
          CMP      AL,'9'
          JG       DoAdd7
          CMP      Posit,19        ;If it is, is buffer full?
          JG       DoAdd1  ;If so, skip.
          LEA      DX,DecNum       ;Otherwise, place in buffer,
          ADD      DX,Posit        ; then display.
          MOV      SI,DX
          MOV      [SI],AL
          MOV      [DecNum+19],' ' ;Remove 0 from end of buffer.
          INC      Posit   ;Advance to next buffer position.
          CALL     DispNum ;Display character buffer.
          JMP      DoAdd1


DoAdd2: CMP      AL,BSpc ;Check for a backspace.
          JNE      DoAdd3  ;If not, check math symbols.
          CMP      Posit,0 ;See if buffer contains characters.
          JE       DoAdd1  ;If not, exit.
          DEC      Posit   ;Go to the previous position.
          LEA      DX,DecNum       ;Erase the buffer character.
          ADD      DX,Posit
          MOV      SI,DX
          MOV      AL,' '
          MOV      [SI],AL
          CALL     DispNum ;Display character buffer.
          JMP      DoAdd1


DoAdd3: CMP      AL,'+'  ;Check for a math symbol.
          JNE      DoAdd4  ;If it exists, store the
          JMP      DoAdd8  ; symbol for later.
DoAdd4: CMP      AL,'-'
          JNE      DoAdd7
          JMP      DoAdd8
```

```
DoAdd7: CMP    AL,'='
        JNE    DoAdd1
DoAdd8: MOV    MathStat,AL
        LEA    AX,DecNum       ;Load the addresses of the numbers.
        ADD    AX,Posit        ;Use Posit and Posit2 to
        DEC    AX       ; compensate for string
        MOV    DI,AX    ; length.
        LEA    AX,DecNum2
        ADD    AX,Posit2
        DEC    AX
        MOV    SI,AX
        MOV    AX,20
        SUB    AX,Posit
        MOV    Posit3,AX
DoAdd9: XOR    AX,AX    ;Zero the registers used
        XOR    DX,DX    ; for addition.
        MOV    DL,[SI] ;Load the add values.
        MOV    AL,[DI]
        SUB    DL,30h   ;Change DL to a number.
        CMP    DL,0     ;If DL doesn't contain a
        JGE    DoAdd9A ; number between 0 and 9 skip.
        MOV    LastNum,1        ;Indicate that this is the
        JMP    DoAdd9B ; last temporary number.
DoAdd9A:    ADD    AL,DL        ;Perform the addition.
DoAdd9B:    CMP    Carry,1 ;Add 1 for carry if required.
        JNE    DoAdd9C
        INC    AL
        DEC    Carry
DoAdd9C:    CMP    AL,'9'  ;Change AL back to number
        JLE    DoAdd10 ; character, if required.
        SUB    AL,10
        INC    Carry   ;Set carry, if required.
DoAdd10:    MOV    BX,Posit3
        MOV    BYTE PTR [DI+BX],AL      ;Place the new number in
        DEC    Posit    ; storage and decrement the
        DEC    Posit2 ; two string pointers.
        CMP    Posit,0 ;See if this is the last number.
        JE     DoAdd11 ;If so, exit.
        CMP    LastNum,1        ;If this is not the last
        JE     DoAdd10B ; temporary number.
        DEC    SI       ;Decrement to next position
DoAdd10B:   DEC    DI       ; for addition of numbers.
        JMP    DoAdd9
DoAdd11:    CMP    Posit2,0         ;See if we added all the
        JLE    DoAdd11C ; numbers in the temporary
        MOV    CX,Posit2        ; string (DecNum2).
DoAdd11A:   DEC    SI      ;If not, move them to the
        DEC    DI      ; current number (DecNum).
        MOV    AL,[SI]
        CMP    Carry,1 ;Make sure we add any
        JNE    DoAdd11B         ; required carries.
```

4-1 Continued.

```
            INC     AL
            DEC     Carry
            CMP     AL,'9'
            JLE     DoAdd11B
            SUB     AL,10
            INC     Carry
DoAdd11B:   MOV     BYTE PTR [DI+BX],AL
            LOOP    DoAdd11A
DoAdd11C:   CMP     Carry,1
            JNE     DoAdd12
            DEC     Carry
            DEC     DI
            MOV     BYTE PTR [DI+BX],'1'
DoAdd12:    MOV     CX,BX
            DEC     BX
DoAdd13:    MOV     BYTE PTR [DI+BX],' '
            DEC     BX
            LOOP    DoAdd13
            MOV     AL,MathStat     ;Place the last math key in AL.

DoAddEnd:   RET

DoAdd   ENDP

;***********************************************************************************************************
;* This procedure subtracts two numbers.  It begins by placing the contents of DecNum into DecNum2 and  *
;* clearing DecNum. After clearing DecNum, it waits for a new entry. After the user enters the number, DoAdd  *
;* converts and subtracts the two numbers one digit at a time.  It places the result in DecNum for display.   *
;***********************************************************************************************************

DoSub   PROC    NEAR

            LEA     SI,DecNum       ;Locate the beginning of the
            LEA     DI,ClrStr       ; current number.
            MOV     CX,20
            REPE    CMPSB
            DEC     SI      ;Place pointers on exact
            INC     CX      ; position.
            PUSH    CX      ;Save the starting position.
            LEA     DI,DecNum2      ;Move the current number to
            REP     MOVSB   ; the storage string.
            POP     AX      ;Compute the number of spaces
            MOV     CX,20   ; to add to the end of the
            SUB     CX,AX   ; storage string.
            CMP     CX,0    ;If none, skip.
            JLE     DoSubB
            MOV     Posit,AX        ;Update posit to the correct string length.
DoSubA: MOV     BYTE PTR [DI],' '       ;Pad the end of the storage
            INC     DI      ; string with spaces.
            LOOP    DoSubA
DoSubB: LEA     SI,ClrStr       ;Clear the current number
```

108   CHAPTER 4

```
        LEA     DI,DecNum         ; storage string.
        MOV     CX,10
        REP     MOVSW
        MOV     AX,Posit          ;Place the length of the current
        MOV     Posit2,AX         ; number in the temporary storage area.
        MOV     Posit,0 ;Clear the length variable.
        CALL    DispNum

DoSub1: XOR     AX,AX    ;Get keyboard input.
        INT     16h
        CMP     AL,1Bh   ;Compare key input to escape.
        JNE     DoSub1A
        JMP     DoSubEnd          ;If equal, leave calculator.

DoSub1A:        CMP     AL,'0'  ;Is input a number?
        JL      DoSub2   ;If less, check backspace.
        CMP     AL,'9'
        JG      DoSub7
        CMP     Posit,19          ;If it is, is buffer full?
        JG      DoSub1   ;If so, skip.
        LEA     DX,DecNum         ;Otherwise, place in buffer,
        ADD     DX,Posit          ; then display.
        MOV     SI,DX
        MOV     [SI],AL
        MOV     [DecNum+19],' ' ;Remove 0 from end of buffer.
        INC     Posit    ;Advance to next buffer position.
        CALL    DispNum ;Display character buffer.
        JMP     DoSub1

DoSub2: CMP     AL,BSpc ;Check for a backspace.
        JNE     DoSub3   ;If not, check math symbols.
        CMP     Posit,0 ;See if buffer contains characters.
        JE      DoSub1   ;If not, exit.
        DEC     Posit    ;Go to the previous position.
        LEA     DX,DecNum         ;Erase the buffer character.
        ADD     DX,Posit
        MOV     SI,DX
        MOV     AL,' '
        MOV     [SI],AL
        CALL    DispNum ;Display character buffer.
        JMP     DoSub1

DoSub3: CMP     AL,'+'   ;Check for a math symbol.
        JNE     DoSub4   ;If it exists, store the
        JMP     DoSub8   ; symbol for later.
DoSub4: CMP     AL,'-'
        JNE     DoSub7
        JMP     DoSub8
DoSub7: CMP     AL,'='
        JNE     DoSub1
DoSub8: MOV     MathStat,AL
```

```
          LEA     AX,DecNum       ;Load the addresses of the numbers.
          ADD     AX,Posit        ;Use Posit and Posit2 to
          DEC     AX        ; compensate for string
          MOV     DI,AX     ; length.
          LEA     AX,DecNum2
          ADD     AX,Posit2
          DEC     AX
          MOV     SI,AX
          MOV     AX,20
          SUB     AX,Posit
          MOV     Posit3,AX
DoSub9:   XOR     AX,AX     ;Zero the registers used
          XOR     DX,DX     ; for addition.
          MOV     AL,[SI]   ;Load the add values.
          MOV     DL,[DI]
          SUB     DL,30h    ;Change DL to a number.
          CMP     DL,0      ;If DL doesn't contain a
          JL      DoSub9A   ; number between 0 and 9 skip.
          SUB     AL,DL     ;Perform the addition.
DoSub9A:          CMP     Borrow,1        ;Sub 1 for Borrow if required.
          JNE     DoSub9B
          DEC     AL
          DEC     Borrow
DoSub9B:          CMP     AL,'0'  ;Change AL back to number
          JGE     DoSub10 ; character, if required.
          ADD     AL,10
          INC     Borrow    ;Set Borrow, if required.
DoSub10:          MOV     BX,Posit3
          MOV     BYTE PTR [DI+BX],AL     ;Place the new number in
          DEC     Posit   ; storage and decrement the
          DEC     Posit2  ; two string pointers.
          CMP     Posit,0 ;See if this is the last number.
          JE      DoSub11 ;If so, exit.
          DEC     SI        ;Decrement to next position
          DEC     DI        ; for addition of numbers.
          JMP     DoSub9
DoSub11:          CMP     Posit2,0        ;See if we added all the
          JLE     DoSub12 ; numbers in the temporary
          MOV     CX,Posit2       ; string (DecNum2).
DoSub11A:         DEC     SI        ;If not, move them to the
          DEC     DI        ; current number (DecNum).
          MOV     AL,[SI]
          CMP     Borrow,1        ;Make sure we add any
          JNE     DoSub11B        ; required carries.
          DEC     AL
          DEC     Borrow
          CMP     AL,'0'
          JGE     DoSub11B
          ADD     AL,10
          INC     Borrow
```

```
DoSub11B:        MOV      BYTE PTR [DI+BX],AL
        LOOP     DoSub11A
DoSub12:         MOV      CX,BX
        DEC      BX
DoSub13:         MOV      BYTE PTR [DI+BX],' '
        DEC      BX
        LOOP     DoSub13
        LEA      SI,DecNum        ;Locate the beginning of the
        LEA      DI,ClrStr        ; current number.
        MOV      CX,20
        REPE     CMPSB
        DEC      SI       ;Place pointers on exact
        INC      CX       ; position.
DoSub14:         CMP      BYTE PTR [SI],'0'
        JNE      DoSub15
        MOV      BYTE PTR [SI],' '
        INC      SI
        LOOP     DoSub14
DoSub15:         MOV      AL,MathStat      ;Place the last math key in AL.
DoSubEnd:        RET


DoSub   ENDP


;********************************************************************************************************************
;* This procedure displays the results of all the math operations as stored in the current number variable      *
;* (DecNum).  It uses the get keyboard interrupt (16h) to hold the display.  The procedure passes this new       *
;* key back to the calling procedure in AL.            *
;********************************************************************************************************************


DoEqual PROC     NEAR

        MOV      AX,0200h         ;Change the cursor position.
        MOV      DH,2     ;Row 2
        MOV      DL,3     ;Column 3
        MOV      BH,DispPg        ;Use the correct page number.
        INC      BH
        INT      10h
        LEA      DX,DecNum        ;Display the number.
        MOV      AX,0900h
        INT      21h

        XOR      AX,AX    ;Get keyboard input.
        INT      16h

        RET

DoEqual ENDP

END     Start
```

The flags used for various instructions below include the following.

- Overflow (OF)
- Direction (DF)
- Interrupt (IF)
- Trap (TF)
- Sign (SF)
- Zero (ZF)
- Auxiliary Carry (AF)
- Parity (PF)
- Carry (CF)

ASCII Adjust for Addition (AAA)

Category: Arithmetic Instructions

The ASCII adjust for addition instruction changes the AL register contents from packed to unpacked decimal format. Zero the auxiliary carry flag (AF) before using this command. The command logic appears below.

If (AL & 0Fh) > 9 or AF = 1 then
AL = AL + 6 (high order nibble zeroed)
AH = AH + 1
AF = 1
CF = AF

The ASCII adjust for addition instruction affects the flags shown below.

AF, CF   1
OF, PF, XF, ZF   Undefined

ASCII Adjust for Division (AAD)

Category: Arithmetic Instructions

The ASCII adjust for division instruction changes the AX register contents from unpacked to packed decimal format. The command logic appears below.

AL = AH * 0Ah + AL
AH = 0

The ASCII adjust for division instruction affects the flags shown below.

PF, SF, ZF   Updated to Reflect Conditions
AF, CF, OF   Undefined

ASCII Adjust for Multiplication (AAM)

Category: Arithmetic Instructions

The ASCII adjust for multiplication instruction corrects the result of multiplying two unpacked decimal format numbers. The command logic appears below.

AH = AL / 0Ah
AL = AL MOD 0Ah

The ASCII adjust for multiplication instruction affects the flags shown below.

PF, SF, ZF   Updated to Reflect Conditions
AF, CF, OF   Undefined

ASCII Adjust for Subtraction (AAS)

Category: Arithmetic Instructions
The ASCII adjust for subtraction instruction corrects the results of subtracting two unpacked decimal format numbers. Zero the auxiliary carry flag (AF) before using this command. The command logic appears below.

If (AL & 0Fh) > 9 or AF = 1 then
AL = AL – 6 (high order nibble zeroed)
AH = AH – 1
AF = 1
CF = AF

The ASCII adjust for subtraction instruction affects the flags shown below.

AF, CF   1
OF, PF, XF, ZF   Undefined

Add with Carry (ADC)

Category: Arithmetic Instructions
Use the add with carry instruction to add two numbers and account for carries generated from previous additions. The add with carry instruction logic appears below.

If CF = 1 then
Destination = Destination + Source + 1
else
Destination = Destination + Source

The add with carry instruction updates the AF, CF, OF, PF, SF, and ZF flags.

Add without Carry (ADD)

Category: Arithmetic Instructions
This instruction adds two operands without regard for CF status. The

add without carry instruction logic appears below.

> Destination = Destination + Source

The add without carry instruction updates the AF, CF, OF, PF, SF, and ZF flags as required.

Logical AND on Bits (AND)

Category: Bit-Manipulation Instructions

Use this instruction to logically AND two values together at the bit level. The logical AND instruction logic appears below.

> Destination = Destination & Source
> CF = 0
> OF = 0

Example:

```
MOV   BL,10101010
AND   BL,01010110
;BL equals 00000010b
```

The logical AND instruction affects the flags as shown below.

> CF, OF   0
> PF, SF, ZF   Updated to Reflect Conditions
> AF   Undefined

Execute a Subprogram (CALL)

Category: Control-Transfer Instructions

The CALL instruction executes an out-of-line subprogram. Two types of call instruction exist. The first type is a near call to subprograms ±32 Kbytes or less distant from the current instruction. For this type, the processor updates IP to the next instruction position and pushes this value on the stack. It then places the new instruction value in IP and continues execution until a return instruction appears. The second type is a far call to subprograms greater than ±32 Kbytes distant from the current instruction. The processor pushes CS and replaces it with the segment of the call instruction. Then the processor updates IP to the next instruction position and pushes this value on the stack. It then places the new instruction value in IP and continues execution until a RETURN instruction appears. The CALL instruction logic appears below.

> If Inter-Segment Call then
> SP = SP - 2
> SP + 1:SP = CS

```
CS = New_Segment
SP = SP - 2
SP + 1:SP = IP
IP = Destination
```

Convert Byte to Word (CBW)

Category: Arithmetic Instructions

This instruction converts a byte value stored in AL to a word value by extending the sign-bit in AL through AH. The convert byte to word logic appears below.

```
If AL < 80h then
AH = 0
else
AH = FFh
```

Clear the Carry Flag (CLC)

Category: Flag- and Processor-Control Instructions

The clear the carry flag instruction sets CF to zero. Its logic appears below.

```
CF = 0
```

Clear the Direction Flag (CLD)

Category: Flag- and Processor-Control Instructions

The clear the direction flag instruction sets DF to zero. Its logic appears below.

```
DF = 0
```

Clear the Interrupt Flag (CLI)

Category: Flag- and Processor-Control Instructions

The clear the interrupt flag instruction sets IF to zero. Its logic appears below.

```
IF = 0
```

Complement the Carry Flag (CMC)

Category: Flag- and Processor-Control Instructions

This instruction toggles the value of CF. The complement the carry flag logic appears below.

```
If CF = 0 then
```

```
CF = 1
else
CF = 0
```

Compare (CMP)

Category: Arithmetic Instructions

This instruction compares by subtracting the value of the destination from the value of the source. It updates the AF, CF, OF, PF, SF, and ZF registers to reflect the subtraction results, but does not place the results in the destination. The compare instruction logic appears below.

```
Flag_Values = Destination – Source
```

Compare Strings, Byte-by-Byte (CMPSB)

Category: String-Manipulation Instructions

This instruction changes the value of the AF, CF, OF, PF, SF, and ZF flags to show the relationship between two bytes in a string. The results of the comparison do not affect the contents of either operand. After comparing the two string bytes, the instruction updates both SI and DI to point to the next string element. DF controls the direction of comparison. The compare strings, byte-by-byte logic appears below.

```
Flag_Values = Destination_String – Source_String
If DF = 0 then
SI = SI + 1
DI = DI + 1
else
SI = SI – 1
DI = DI – 1
```

Compare Strings, Word-by-Word (CMPSW)

Category: String-Manipulation Instructions

This instruction changes the value of the AF, CF, OF, PF, SF, and ZF flags to show the relationship between two words in a string. The results of the comparison do not affect the contents of either operand. After comparing the two string words, the instruction updates both SI and DI to point to the next string element. DF controls the direction of comparison. The compare strings, word-by-word logic appears below.

```
Flag_Values = Destination_String – Source_String
If DF = 0 then
```

```
SI = SI + 2
DI = DI + 2
else
SI = SI - 2
DI = DI - 2
```

Convert Word to Doubleword (CWD)

Category: Arithmetic Instructions

Use this instruction to convert a word value to a doubleword value. It extends the sign-bit in AX through DX. The convert word to doubleword logic appears below.

```
If AX < 8000h then
DX = 0
else
DX = FFFFh
```

Decimal Adjust for Addition (DAA)

Category: Arithmetic Instructions

The decimal adjust for addition instruction corrects the result of adding two packed decimal operands. The logic below shows the instruction's operation.

```
If AL & 0Fh > 9 or AF = 1 then
AL = AL + 6
AF = 1
If AL > 9Fh or CF = 1 then
AL = AL + 60h
CF = 1
```

The decimal adjust for addition instruction affects the registers as shown below.

```
CF or AF    1
PF, SF, ZF  Updated to Reflect Current Conditions
OF  Undefined
```

Decimal Adjust for Subtraction (DAS)

Category: Arithmetic Instructions

The decimal adjust for subtraction instruction corrects the result of subtracting two packed decimal operands. The logic below shows the instruction's operation.

If AL & 0Fh > 9 or AF = 1 then
AL = AL – 6
AF = 1

If AL > 9Fh or CF = 1 then
AL = AL – 60h
CF = 1

The decimal adjust for subtraction instruction affects the registers as shown below.

CF or AF   1
PF, SF, ZF   Updated to Reflect Current Conditions
OF   Undefined

Decrement (DEC)

Category: Arithmetic Instructions

This instruction reduces the contents of a register or memory variable by one. The decrement instruction logic appears below.

Destination = Destination – 1

The decrement instruction updates AF, OF, PF, SF, and ZF as required.

Divide (DIV)

Category: Arithmetic Instructions

The divide instruction performs unsigned division. It divides the quantity in the accumulator by the divisor. When using byte values, the quotient appears in AL and the remainder appears in AH. The value divided appears in AX. When using word values, the quotient appears in AX and the remainder appears in DX. The value divided appears in the AX:DX register pair. Using doubleword values places the quotient in EAX and the remainder in EDX. The processor divides the numerator in the EAX:EDX register pair by the divisor. The divide instruction logic appears below.

Temp = Numerator
If Temp / Divisor > Maximum_Value then
Quotient, Remainder = Undefined
SP = SP – 2
SP + 1:SP = Flags
IF = 0
TF = 0
SP = SP – 2
SP + 1:SP = CS
CS = 2 (The contents of memory locations 2 & 3.)
SP = SP – 2

SP + 1:SP = IP
IP = 0 (The contents of memory locations 0 & 1.)
else
Quotient = Temp / Divisor (/ = Unsigned Divisor)
Remainder = Temp % Divisor (% = Unsigned Modulo)

The processor leaves the AF, CF, OF, PF, SF, and ZF undefined upon exit from the divide instruction.

Escape (ESC)

Category: Flag- and Processor-Control Instructions

The escape instruction provides a means for co-processing chips to access data using the 8086/8088/80286/80386 processing stream. It causes the processor to place the operand on the bus while internally performing a no operation (NOP) instruction. This instruction does not affect any flags.

Halt (HLT)

Category: Flag- and Processor-Control Instructions

This instruction stops the processor temporarily while waiting for an interrupt. It provides a means of creating a wait state without resorting to endless software loops. The halt instruction does not affect any flags.

Integer Divide (IDIV)

Category: Arithmetic Instructions

The integer divide instruction performs signed division on the value contained in the accumulator. When using byte values, the quotient appears in AL and the remainder appears in AH. The value divided appears in AX. When using word values, the quotient appears in AX and the remainder appears in DX. The value divided appears in the AX:DX register pair. Using doubleword values places the quotient in EAX and the remainder in EDX. The processor divides the numerator in the EAX:EDX register pair by the divisor.

Using byte values, the minimum and maximum values allowed equal ±127. When using word values, the minimum and maximum values allowed equal ±32,767. Doubleword values allow a range of ±2,147,483,647. Flags affected by the instruction include AF, CF, OF, PF, SF, and ZF. The processor leaves all flags undefined. The integer divide instruction logic appears below.

Temp = Numerator
If Temp / Divisor > 0 and Temp / Divisor > MAX
    or Temp / Divisor < 0 and Temp / Divisor < MIN
then

Quotient, Remainder = Undefined
SP = SP − 2
SP + 1:SP = Flags
IF = 0
TF = 0
SP = SP − 2
SP + 1:SP = CS
CS = 2
SP = SP − 2
SP + 1:SP = IP
IP = 0
else
Quotient = Temp / Divisor (/ = Signed Division)
Remainder = Temp % Divisor (% = Signed Modulo)

Integer Multiply (IMUL)

Category: Arithmetic Instructions

This instruction performs signed multiplication on the value in the accumulator by the multiplicand. When using byte values, the AX register contains the double length result. Using word values returns the result in the AX:DX register pair. Doubleword values return a result in the EAX:EDX register pair.

The minimum/maximum values returned by each multiplication type are ±127 for byte values, ±32,767 for word values, and ±2,147,483,647 for doubleword values. The integer multiplication instruction logic appears below.

Destination = Destination * Multiplicand
(* = Signed Multiply)
If Extension = Sign − Extension of Low then
CF = 0
else
CF = 1
OF = CF

The flags integer multiplication effects appear below.

CF   0 for Normal, 1 for Overflow Condition
OF = CF
AF, PF, SF, ZF   Undefined

Input Data from Port (IN)

Category: Data-Transfer Instructions

This instruction allows data input from a port to the AX register. Use either the DX register or a constant to specify a port number less than 256. For port numbers greater than 255, use the DX register only. This instruction does not affect the flags. The input instruction logic appears below.

Destination = Source

Increment (INC)

Category: Arithmetic Instructions

This instruction increases the contents of a register or memory variable by one. The increment instruction logic appears below.

Destination = Destination + 1

The increment instruction updates AF, OF, PF, SF, and ZF as required.

Software Interrupt (INT)

Category: Control-Transfer Instructions

This instruction activates the interrupt processing procedure outlined below.

1. Decrement SP by 2. Push the flags on the stack using the same format as PUSHF.
2. Clear TF and IF to prevent other single-step or maskable interrupts from occurring.
3. Decrement SP. Push CS.
4. Calculate the interrupt pointer address by multiplying the interrupt type by four. Place the second word of the interrupt pointer in CS.
5. Decrement SP and push IP. Place the first word of the interrupt pointer in IP.

The assembler generates a one-byte form of the instruction for interrupt 3 (known as the *breakpoint interrupt*). Only device drivers or operating systems normally create their own interrupt code. The only flags affected are IF and TF, which the interrupt processor sets to 1. The interrupt instruction logic appears below.

SP = SP – 2
SP + 1:SP = Flags
IF = 0
TF = 0
SP = SP – 2
SP + 1:SP = CS
CS = Interrupt_Type * 4 + 2
SP = SP – 2
SP + 1:SP = IP
IP = Interrupt_Type * 4

Interrupt on Overflow (INTO)

Category: Control-Transfer Instructions

Use this instruction to generate an interrupt 4 when the overflow flag (OF) equals 1. It operates in all respects like the interrupt instruction when executed. If OF equals 0, the processor ignores this instruction. The interrupt on overflow logic appears below.

```
If OF = 1 then
SP = SP - 2
SP + 1:SP = Flags
IF = 0
TF = 0
SP = SP - 2
SP + 1:SP = CS
CS = 12h
SP = SP - 2
SP + 1:SP = IP
IP = 10h
```

Return from Interrupt (IRET)

Category: Control-Transfer Instructions

This instruction returns control to a procedure calling an interrupt after the interrupt completes. It pops CS, IP, and all flags. The return from interrupt logic appears below.

```
IP = SP + 1:SP
SP = SP + 2
CS = SP + 1:SP
SP = SP + 2
Flags = SP + 1:SP
SP = SP + 2
```

Jump if Above (JA)

Category: Control-Transfer Instructions

This instruction transfers control to the instruction pointed to by IP + Displacement when CF and ZF equal 0. The instruction logic appears below.

```
If CF & ZF = 0 then
IP = IP + Displacement (Sign Extended to 16 bits)
```

Jump if Above or Equal (JAE)

Category: Control-Transfer Instructions

This instruction transfers control to the instruction pointed to by IP + Displacement when CF equals 0. The instruction logic appears below.

If CF = 0 then
IP = IP + Displacement (Sign Extended to 16 bits)

Jump if Below (JB)

Category: Control-Transfer Instructions

This instruction transfers control to the instruction pointed to by IP +
Displacement when CF equals 1. The instruction logic appears below.

If CF = 1 then
IP = IP + Displacement (Sign Extended to 16 bits)

Jump if Below or Equal (JBE)

Category: Control-Transfer Instructions

This instruction transfers control to the instruction pointed to by IP +
Displacement when CF or ZF equals 1. The instruction logic appears
below.

If CF or ZF = 1 then
IP = IP + Displacement (Sign Extended to 16 bits)

Jump on Carry (JC)

Category: Control-Transfer Instructions

This instruction transfers control to the instruction pointed to by IP +
Displacement when CF equals 1. The instruction logic appears below.

If CF = 1 then
IP = IP + Displacement (Sign Extended to 16 bits)

Jump if CX Equals Zero (JCXZ)

Category: Control-Transfer Instructions

This instruction transfers control to the instruction pointed to by IP +
Displacement when CX equals 0. The instruction logic appears below.

If CX = 0 then
IP = IP + Displacement (Sign Extended to 16 bits)

Jump if Equal (JE)

Category: Control-Transfer Instructions

This instruction transfers control to the instruction pointed to by IP +
Displacement when ZF equals 1. The instruction logic appears below.

If ZF = 1 then
IP = IP + Displacement (Sign Extended to 16 bits)

Jump if Greater Than (JG)

Category: Control-Transfer Instructions

This instruction transfers control to the instruction pointed to by IP + Displacement when SF equals OF or ZF equals 0. The instruction logic appears below.

If (SF = OF) or (ZF = 0) then
IP = IP + Displacement (Sign Extended to 16 bits)

Jump if Greater Than or Equal (JGE)

Category: Control-Transfer Instructions

This instruction transfers control to the instruction pointed to by IP + Displacement when SF equals OF. The instruction logic appears below.

If SF = OF then
IP = IP + Displacement (Sign Extended to 16 bits)

Jump if Less Than (JL)

Category: Control-Transfer Instructions

This instruction transfers control to the instruction pointed to by IP + Displacement when SF does not equal OF. The instruction logic appears below.

If SF < > OF then
IP = IP + Displacement (Sign Extended to 16 bits)

Jump if Less Than or Equal (JLE)

Category: Control-Transfer Instructions

This instruction transfers control to the instruction pointed to by IP + Displacement when SF does not equal OF or ZF equals 1. The instruction logic appears below.

If (SF < > OF) or (ZF = 1) then
IP = IP + Displacement (Sign Extended to 16 bits)

Jump Unconditionally (JMP)

Category: Control-Transfer Instructions

This instruction unconditionally transfers control to the instruction referenced by an operand. There are three types of unconditional jump. The first type, short, allows jumps of only ± 127 bytes, but produces only 2 bytes of code. The second type, near, allows jumps of ± 32 Kbytes. It produces 3 bytes of code. The third type uses both CS and IP for far jumps. It uses 5 bytes of code. The unconditional jump logic appears below.

> If Far Jump then
> CS = Segment
> IP = Offset
> else If Near Jump then
> IP = IP + Displacement (Sign Extended to 16 bits)
> else
> IP = IP + Displacement (Not Sign Extended)

Jump if Not Above (JNA)

Category: Control-Transfer Instructions

This instruction transfers control to the instruction pointed to by IP + Displacement when CF or ZF equal 1. The instruction logic appears below.

> If CF or ZF = 1 then
> IP = IP + Displacement (Sign Extended to 16 bits)

Jump if Not Above or Equal (JNAE)

Category: Control-Transfer Instructions

This instruction transfers control to the instruction pointed to by IP + Displacement when CF equals 1. The instruction logic appears below.

> If CF = 1 then
> IP = IP + Displacement (Sign Extended to 16 bits)

Jump if Not Below (JNB)

Category: Control-Transfer Instructions

This instruction transfers control to the instruction pointed to by IP + Displacement when CF equals 0. The instruction logic appears below.

> If CF = 0 then
> IP = IP + Displacement (Sign Extended to 16 bits)

Jump if Not Below or Equal (JNBE)

Category: Control-Transfer Instructions

This instruction transfers control to the instruction pointed to by IP + Displacement when CF and ZF equal 0. The instruction logic appears below.

> If CF & ZF = 0 then
> IP = IP + Displacement (Sign Extended to 16 bits)

Jump on No Carry (JNC)

Category: Control-Transfer Instructions

This instruction transfers control to the instruction pointed to by IP + Displacement when CF equals 0. The instruction logic appears below.

If CF = 0 then
IP = IP + Displacement (Sign Extended to 16 bits)

Jump if Not Equal (JNE)

Category: Control-Transfer Instructions

This instruction transfers control to the instruction pointed to by IP + Displacement when ZF equals 0. The instruction logic appears below.

If ZF = 0 then
IP = IP + Displacement (Sign Extended to 16 bits)

Jump if Not Greater Than (JNG)

Category: Control-Transfer Instructions

This instruction transfers control to the instruction pointed to by IP + Displacement when SF does not equal OF or ZF equals 1. The instruction logic appears below.

If (SF < > OF) or (ZF = 1) then
IP = IP + Displacement (Sign Extended to 16 bits)

Jump if Not Greater Than or Equal (JNGE)

Category: Control-Transfer Instructions

This instruction transfers control to the instruction pointed to by IP + Displacement when SF does not equal OF. The instruction logic appears below.

If SF < > OF then
IP = IP + Displacement (Sign Extended to 16 bits)

Jump if Not Less Than (JNL)

Category: Control-Transfer Instructions

This instruction transfers control to the instruction pointed to by IP + Displacement when SF equals OF. The instruction logic appears below.

If SF = OF then
IP = IP + Displacement (Sign Extended to 16 bits)

Jump if Not Less Than or Equal (JNLE)

Category: Control-Transfer Instructions

This instruction transfers control to the instruction pointed to by IP + Displacement when SF equals OF or ZF equals 0. The instruction logic appears below.

If (SF = OF) or (ZF = 0) then
IP = IP + Displacement (Sign Extended to 16 bits)

Jump on No Overflow (JNO)

Category: Control-Transfer Instructions

This instruction transfers control to the instruction pointed to by IP + Displacement when OF equals 0. The instruction logic appears below.

If OF = 0 then
IP = IP + Displacement (Sign Extended to 16 bits)

Jump on No Parity (JNP)

Category: Control-Transfer Instructions

This instruction transfers control to the instruction pointed to by IP + Displacement when PF equals 0. The instruction logic appears below.

If PF = 0 then
IP = IP + Displacement (Sign Extended to 16 bits)

Jump on Not Sign (JNS)

Category: Control-Transfer Instructions

This instruction transfers control to the instruction pointed to by IP + Displacement when SF equals 0. The instruction logic appears below.

If SF = 0 then
IP = IP + Displacement (Sign Extended to 16 bits)

Jump on Not Zero (JNZ)

Category: Control-Transfer Instructions

This instruction transfers control to the instruction pointed to by IP + Displacement when ZF equals 0. The instruction logic appears below.

If ZF = 0 then
IP = IP + Displacement (Sign Extended to 16 bits)

Jump on Overflow (JO)

Category: Control-Transfer Instructions

This instruction transfers control to the instruction pointed to by IP + Displacement when OF equals 1. The instruction logic appears below.

If OF = 1 then
IP = IP + Displacement (Sign Extended to 16 bits)

Jump on Parity (JP)

Category: Control-Transfer Instructions

This instruction transfers control to the instruction pointed to by IP + Displacement when PF equals 1. The instruction logic appears below.

If PF = 1 then
IP = IP + Displacement (Sign Extended to 16 bits)

Jump on Parity Even (JPE)

Category: Control-Transfer Instructions

This instruction transfers control to the instruction pointed to by IP + Displacement when PF equals 1. The instruction logic appears below.

If PF = 1 then
IP = IP + Displacement (Sign Extended to 16 bits)

Jump on Parity Odd (JPO)

Category: Control-Transfer Instructions

This instruction transfers control to the instruction pointed to by IP + Displacement when PF equals 0. The instruction logic appears below.

If PF = 0 then
IP = IP + Displacement (Sign Extended to 16 bits)

Jump on Sign (JS)

Category: Control-Transfer Instructions

This instruction transfers control to the instruction pointed to by IP + Displacement when SF equals 1. The instruction logic appears below.

If SF = 1 then
IP = IP + Displacement (Sign Extended to 16 bits)

Jump on Zero (JZ)

Category: Control-Transfer Instructions

This instruction transfers control to the instruction pointed to by IP + Displacement when ZF equals 1. The instruction logic appears below.

If ZF = 1 then
IP = IP + Displacement (Sign Extended to 16 bits)

Load the AH Register with Flags (LAHF)

Category: Data-Transfer Instructions

Use this instruction during assembly language conversions from 8080/8085 processor to 8086/8088 processor format. It transfers the low order byte of the flags register to AH. The flags transferred include SF, ZF, AF, PF, and CF. The load AH register with flags instruction logic appears below.

AH = SF:ZF:X:AF:X:PF:X:CF

Load the DS Register (LDS)

Category: Data-Transfer Instructions

This instruction transfers a 32-bit pointer from the source operand (memory only) to the destination operand (offset) and the DS register (segment). The destination operand is any 16-bit general purpose register. The instruction logic appears below.

Register = Effective_Address
DS = Effective_Address + 2

Load the Effective Address (LEA)

Category: Data-Transfer Instructions

The load effective address instruction transfers the offset of the source operand (rather than its value) to the destination operand. The source operand is always a memory variable. The destination is always a general-purpose 16-bit register. The load effective address instruction logic appears below.

Register = Effective_Address

Load the ES Register (LES)

Category: Data-Transfer Instructions

This instruction transfers a 32-bit pointer from the source operand (memory only) to the destination operand (offset) and the ES register (segment). The destination operand is any 16-bit general purpose register. The instruction logic appears below.

Register = Effective_Address
ES = Effective_Address + 2

Lock the Bus (LOCK)

Category: Flag- and Processor-Control Instructions

The lock instruction prevents interference by any co-processors during the next instruction. Always use lock with other instructions.

Load a Byte from String into AL (LODSB)

Category: String-Manipulation Instructions

Use this instruction to transfer a byte from the string pointed to by SI to AL. The SI register automatically advances to the next string element in the direction pointed to by the direction flag. The instruction logic appears below.

```
AL = String_Element
If DF = 0 then
SI = SI + 1
else
SI = SI - 1
```

Load a Word from String into AX (LODSW)

Category: String-Manipulation Instructions

Use this instruction to transfer a word from the string pointed to by SI to AX. The SI register automatically advances to the next string element in the direction pointed to by the direction flag. The instruction logic appears below.

```
AX = String_Element
If DF = 0 then
SI = SI + 2
else
SI = SI - 2
```

Loop (LOOP)

Category: Control-Transfer Instructions

The loop instruction decrements CX by 1 and then tests to see if CX equals 0. If CX is greater than 0, loop transfers control to the target instruction. Otherwise, it passes control to the next in-line instruction. The instruction logic appears below.

```
CX = CX - 1
If CX < > 0 then
IP = IP + Displacement (Sign Extended to 16 bits)
```

Loop while Equal (LOOPE)

Category: Control-Transfer Instructions

The loop instruction decrements CX by 1 and then tests to see if CX equals 0. If CX is greater than 0 and ZF equals 1, loop transfers control to the target instruction. Otherwise, it passes control to the next in-line instruction. The instruction logic appears below.

```
CX = CX – 1
If (CX < > 0) and (ZF = 1) then
IP = IP + Displacement (Sign Extended to 16 bits)
```

Loop while Not Equal (LOOPNE)

Category: Control-Transfer Instructions

The loop instruction decrements CX by 1 and then tests to see if CX equals 0. If CX is greater than 0 and ZF equals 0, loop transfers control to the target instruction. Otherwise, it passes control to the next in-line instruction. The instruction logic appears below.

```
CX = CX – 1
If (CX < > 0) and (ZF = 0) then
IP = IP + Displacement (Sign Extended to 16 bits)
```

Loop while Not Zero (LOOPNZ)

Category: Control-Transfer Instructions

The loop instruction decrements CX by 1 and then tests to see if CX equals 0. If CX is greater than 0 and ZF equals 0, loop transfers control to the target instruction. Otherwise, it passes control to the next in-line instruction. The instruction logic appears below.

```
CX = CX – 1
If (CX < > 0) and (ZF = 0) then
IP = IP + Displacement (Sign Extended to 16 bits)
```

Loop While Zero (LOOPZ)

Category: Control-Transfer Instructions

The loop instruction decrements CX by 1 and then tests to see if CX equals 0. If CX is greater than 0 and ZF equals 1, loop transfers control to the target instruction. Otherwise, it passes control to the next in-line instruction. The instruction logic appears below.

```
CX = CX – 1
If (CX < > 0) and (ZF = 1) then
IP = IP + Displacement (Sign Extended to 16 bits)
```

Move (MOV)

Category: Data-Transfer Instructions

This instruction transfers data from the source operand to a destination operand of the same length. The instruction logic appears below.

    Destination = Source

Move String Byte-by-Byte (MOVSB)

Category: String-Manipulation Instructions

This instruction moves the byte pointed to by SI to the destination pointed to by DI. Using the REP instruction with this instruction repeats the move the number of times shown in CX. After each move, the instruction advances both SI and DI to the next position in the direction indicated by DF. The instruction logic appears below.

    Destination = Source
    DI = DI + 1
    SI = SI + 1

Move String Word-by-Word (MOVSW)

Category: String-Manipulation Instructions

This instruction moves the word pointed to by SI to the destination pointed to by DI. Using the REP instruction with this instruction repeats the move the number of times shown in CX. After each move, the instruction advances both SI and DI to the next position in the direction indicated by DF. The instruction logic appears below.

    Destination = Source
    DI = DI + 2
    SI = SI + 2

Multiply (MUL)

Category: Arithmetic Instructions

This instruction performs unsigned multiplication on the value in the accumulator by the multiplicand. When using byte values, the AX register contains the double length result. Using word values returns the result in the AX:DX register pair. Doubleword values return a result in the EAX :EDX register pair. The multiplication instruction logic appears below.

    Destination = Destination * Multiplicand
    (* = Unsigned Multiply)
    If Extension = 0 then
    CF = 0
    else
    CF = 1
    OF = CF

The flags integer multiplication effects appear below.

CF   0 for Normal, 1 for Overflow Condition
OF = CF
AF, PF, SF, ZF   Undefined

Negate (NEG)

Category: Arithmetic Instructions
This instruction calculates the two's complement of the destination operand. This is effectively the same as subtracting the destination operand from 0. The instruction logic appears below.

Destination = 0 − Destination

This instruction updates AF, CF, OF, PF, SF, and ZF as required.

No Operation (NOP)

Category: Flag- and Processor-Control Instructions
This instruction tells the CPU to do nothing.

Logical NOT on Bits (NOT)

Category: Bit-Manipulation Instructions
The NOT instruction produces the one's complement of the destination operand by inverting its bits. This instruction does not affect any flags. The logic for this instruction appears below.

Destination = FFFFh − Destination

Logical OR on Bits (OR)

Category: Bit-Manipulation Instructions
This instruction performs an inclusive OR of the source and destination operands. It places the results in the destination operand. A bit equals 1 in the destination operand when either or both operands contain a 1 in that bit position. The logic for this instruction appears below.

Destination = Source OR Destination
CF = 0
OF = 0

The decimal adjust for subtraction instruction affects the registers as shown below.

CF OF   0
PF, SF, ZF   Updated to Reflect Current Conditions
AF   Undefined

Output Data to Port (OUT)

Category: Data-Transfer Instructions

This instruction allows data output to a port from the AX register. Use either the DX register or a constant to specify port numbers less than 256. For port numbers greater than 255 use the DX register only. This instruction does not affect the flags. The input instruction logic appears below.

Destination = Source

Remove Data from the Stack (POP)

Category: Data-Transfer Instructions

POP removes the word pointed to by the stack pointer (SP) and places it in a memory operand or register. It then increments SP by 2. The logic for the POP instruction appears below.

Destination = SP + 1:SP
SP = SP + 2

Remove Flags from the Stack (POPF)

Category: Data-Transfer Instructions

POPF removes the word pointed to by the stack pointer (SP) and places it in the flag register. It then increments SP by 2. The logic for the POPF instruction appears below.

Flags = SP + 1:SP
SP = SP + 2

Place Data on the Stack (PUSH)

Category: Data-Transfer Instructions

PUSH decrements SP by 2. It then adds the word contained in a register or memory operand to the location pointed to by the stack pointer (SP). The logic for the PUSH instruction appears below.

SP = SP – 2
SP + 1:SP = Source

Place Flags on the Stack (PUSHF)

Category: Data-Transfer Instructions

PUSHF decrements SP by 2. It then adds the flag register contents to the location pointed to by the stack pointer (SP). The logic for the PUSHF instruction appears below.

SP = SP – 2
SP + 1:SP = Flags

Rotate Left through Carry (RCL)

Category: Bit-Manipulation Instructions

This instruction rotates the bits in the destination to the left the number of places specified in the count operand. The carry flag receives the value dropped from the high-order bit. The low-order bit receives the value contained in the carry flag. In this way, no bits disappear during the rotation. The logic for this instruction appears below.

```
Temp = Count
Do While Temp < > 0
Temp_CF = CF
CF = Destination_High_Order_Bit
Destination = Destination * 2 + Temp_CF
Temp = Temp - 1

If Count = 1 then
If Destination_High_Order_Bit < > CF then
OF = 1
else
OF = 0
else
OF = Undefined
```

Rotate Right through Carry (RCR)

Category: Bit-Manipulation Instructions

This instruction rotates the bits in the destination to the right the number of places specified in the count operand. The carry flag receives the value dropped from the low-order bit. The high-order bit receives the value contained in the carry flag. In this way, no bits disappear during the rotation. The logic for this instruction appears below.

```
Temp = Count
Do While Temp < > 0
Temp_CF = CF
CF = Destination_Low_Order_Bit
Destination = Destination / 2
Destination_High_Order_Bit = Temp_CF
Temp = Temp - 1

If Count = 1 then
If Destination_High_Order_Bit < >
   Destination_Next_To_High_Order_Bit then
OF = 1
else
OF = 0
else
OF = Undefined
```

Repeat (REP)

Category: String-Manipulation Instructions
   Use this instruction with string manipulation instructions to repeat the instruction the number of times specified in CX.

Repeat if Equal (REPE)

Category: String-Manipulation Instructions
   Use this instruction with string manipulation instructions to repeat the instruction the number of times specified in CX. It repeats only while ZF = 1 when used with the CMPSB, CMPSW, SCASB, or SCASW instructions.

Repeat if Not Equal (REPNE)

Category: String-Manipulation Instructions
   Use this instruction with string manipulation instructions to repeat the instruction the number of times specified in CX. It repeats only while ZF = 0 when used with the CMPSB, CMPSW, SCASB, or SCASW instructions.

Repeat if Not Zero (REPNZ)

Category: String-Manipulation Instructions
   Use this instruction with string manipulation instructions to repeat the instruction the number of times specified in CX. It repeats only while ZF = 0 when used with the CMPSB, CMPSW, SCASB, or SCASW instructions.

Repeat if Zero (REPZ)

Category: String-Manipulation Instructions
   Use this instruction with string manipulation instructions to repeat the instruction the number of times specified in CX. It repeats only while ZF = 1 when used with the CMPSB, CMPSW, SCASB, or SCASW instructions.

Return from a Subprogram (RET)

Category: Control-Transfer Instructions
   Use this instruction at the end of a subprogram to return control to the calling program. The assembler generates two types of return: far and near. The near return pops only IP from the stack. A far return pops both IP and CS from the stack.
   The return instruction also provides a means of discarding parame-

ters by specifying a pop value. It adds the pop value to SP before returning to the calling procedure. The return instruction logic appears below.

```
IP = SP + 1:SP
SP = SP + 2
If Far Return then
CS = SP + 1:SP
SP = SP + 2
If ADD Immediate to Stack Pointer then
SP = SP + Pop_Value
```

Rotate Left (ROL)

Category: Bit-Manipulation Instructions

This instruction rotates the bits in the destination to the left the number of places specified in the count operand. It affects both OF and CF. The logic for this instruction appears below.

```
Temp = Count
Do While Temp < > 0
CF = Destination_High_Order_Bit
Destination = Destination * 2 + CF
Temp = Temp – 1

If Count = 1 then
If Destination_High_Order_Bit < > CF then
OF = 1
else
OF = 0
else
OF = Undefined
```

Rotate Right (ROR)

Category: Bit-Manipulation Instructions

This instruction rotates the bits in the destination to the right the number of places specified in the count operand. It affects both OF and CF. The logic for this instruction appears below.

```
Temp = Count
Do While Temp < > 0
CF = Destination_Low_Order_Bit
Destination = Destination /2
Destination_High_Order_Bit = CF
Temp = Temp – 1

If Count = 1 then
If Destination_High_Order_Bit < > CF then
```

OF = 1
else
OF = 0
else
OF = Undefined

Store AH into the Flag Register (SAHF)

Category: Data-Transfer Instructions

Use this instruction during assembly language conversions from 8080/8085 processor to 8086/8088 processor format. It transfers the contents of AH to low-order byte of the flags register. The flags transferred include SF, ZF, AF, PF, and CF. The store AH into the flags instruction logic appears below.

AH = SF:ZF:X:AF:X:PF:X:CF

Arithmetic Shift Left (SAL)

Category: Bit-Manipulation Instructions

The arithmetic shift left instruction shifts all bits in the destination operand left the number of bits specified by the source operand. It affects CF, OF, PF, SF, ZF, and AF (undefined). The instruction logic appears below.

Temp = Count
Do While Temp < > 0
CF = Destination_High_Order_Bit
Destination = Destination * 2
Temp = Temp − 1
If Count = 1 then
If Destination_High_Order_Bit < > CE then
OF = 1
else
OF = 0
else
OF = Undefined

Arithmetic Shift Right (SAR)

Category: Bit-Manipulation Instructions

The arithmetic shift right instruction shifts all bits in the destination operand right the number of bits specified by the source operand. It affects CF, OF, PF, SF, ZF, and AF (undefined). The instruction logic appears below.

Temp = Count
Do While Temp < > 0

```
CF = Destination_Low_Order_Bit
Destination = Destination / 2
(/ = Signed Division Rounding Down)
Temp = Temp − 1
If Count = 1 then
If Destination_High_Order_Bit < >
    Destination_Next_To_High_Order_Bit then
OF = 1
else
OF = 0
else
OF = Undefined
```

Subtract with Borrow (SBB)

Category: Arithmetic Instructions

This instruction subtracts the source value from the destination value and stores the result in the destination. It decrements the result by one if CF = 1. The subtract with borrow instruction affects AF, CF, OF, PF, SF, and ZF. The instruction logic appears below.

```
If CF = 1 then
Destination = Destination − Source − 1
else
Destination = Destination − Source
```

Scan String for Byte (SCASB)

Category: String-Manipulation Instructions

Use this instruction with any of the repeat instructions to scan strings for the value contained in AL. After each scan, DI advances to point to the next string element. This instruction affects AF, CF, OF, PF, SF, and ZF. The instruction logic appears below.

```
AL − Destination
If DF = 0 then
DI = DI + 1
else
DI = DI − 1
```

Scan String for Word (SCASW)

Category: String-Manipulation Instructions

Use this instruction with any of the repeat instructions to scan strings for the value contained in AX. After each scan, DI advances to point to the next string element. This instruction affects AF, CF, OF, PF, SF, and ZF. The instruction logic appears below.

```
AX − Destination
```

```
If DF = 0 then
DI = DI + 2
else
DI = DI - 2
```

Shift Left (SHL)

Category: Bit-Manipulation Instructions

The shift left instruction shifts all bits in the destination operand left the number of bits specified by the source operand. It affects CF, OF, PF, SF, ZF, and AF (undefined). The instruction logic appears below.

```
Temp = Count
Do While Temp < > 0
CF = Destination_High_Order_Bit
Destination = Destination * 2
Temp = Temp - 1
If Count = 1 then
If Destination_High_Order_Bit < > CE then
OF = 1
else
OF = 0
else
OF = Undefined
```

Shift Right (SHR)

Category: Bit-Manipulation Instructions

The shift right instruction shifts all bits in the destination operand right the number of bits specified by the source operand. It affects CF, OF, PF, SF, ZF, and AF (undefined). The instruction logic appears below.

```
Temp = Count
Do While Temp < > 0
CF = Destination_Low_Order_Bit
Destination = Destination / 2
(/ = Unsigned Division)
Temp = Temp - 1
If Count = 1 then
If Destination_High_Order_Bit < >
   Destination_Next_To_High_Order_Bit then
OF = 1
else
OF = 0
else
OF = Undefined
```

Set the Carry Flag (STC)

Category: Flag- and Processor-Control Instructions

This instruction sets CF regardless of its present condition. The instruction logic appears below.

CF = 1

Set the Direction Flag (STD)

Category: Flag- and Processor-Control Instructions

This instruction sets DF regardless of its present condition. The instruction logic appears below.

DF = 1

Set the Interrupt Flag (STI)

Category: Flag- and Processor-Control Instructions

This instruction sets IF regardless of its present condition. The instruction logic appears below.

IF = 1

Store Byte in AL at String (STOSB)

Category: String-Manipulation Instructions

Use this instruction alone or with any repeat instruction to send the value in AL to the string pointed at by DI. DI automatically advances to the next string location after each store operation. This instruction does not affect any flags. The instruction logic appears below.

Destination = AL
If DF = 0 then
DI = DI + 1
else
DI = DI – 1

Store Word in AX at String (STOSW)

Category: String-Manipulation Instructions

Use this instruction alone or with any repeat instruction to send the value in AX to the string pointed at by DI. DI automatically advances to the next string location after each store operation. This instruction does not affect any flags. The instruction logic appears below.

Destination = AX
If DF = 0 then
DI = DI + 2

```
else
DI = DI - 2
```

Subtract (SUB)

Category: Arithmetic Instructions

The subtract instruction subtracts the value in the source from the destination. It affects AF, CF, OF, PF, SF, and ZF. The instruction logic appears below.

Destination = Destination - Source

Test Bits (TEST)

Category: Bit-Manipulation Instructions

This instruction performs a logical AND of two operands then updates the flags. The flags reflect how the two operands compared. Test does nothing with the results. The flags it affects include CF, OF, PF, SF, and ZF. The processor leaves AF undefined after this instruction. The instruction logic appears below.

```
Operand_1 & Operand_2
CF = 0
OF = 0
```

Wait (WAIT)

Category: Flag- and Processor-Control Instructions

This instruction causes the CPU to enter its wait state until it receives an external interrupt on the test line. Wait does not affect any flags.

Exchange (XCHG)

Category: Data-Transfer Instructions

This instruction swaps the contents of the source and destination operands. It does not affect any flags. The logic for this instruction appears below.

```
Temp = Destination
Destination = Source
Source = Temp
```

Translate (XLAT)

Category: Data-Transfer Instructions

The translate instruction places the value in a table pointed to by BX in AL. The AL register initially contains an offset into the table. The translate instruction does not affect any flags. The instruction logic appears below.

AL = Value Pointed to by BX + AL

Logical Exclusive-OR on Bits (XOR)

Category: Bit-Manipulation Instructions

This instruction performs an exclusive-OR on two operands. It returns a value in the destination operand. XOR sets a bit in the destination operand if the corresponding bits in the comparison operands are different. The exclusive-OR instruction affects CF, OF, PF, SF, ZF, and AF (undefined). The instruction logic appears below.

Destination = Destination XOR Source
CF = 0
OF = 0

8087 COMMANDS

The paragraphs below describe each 8087 math co-processor specific command. The 80287 and 80387 math co-processors use some of these commands as well. Each command identifies which processor uses it. TABLE 4-2 lists all the processor commands by functional area. The table includes the page number of the instruction description. Figure 4-2 shows an example of an 8087 co-processor specific program. Figure 4-3 shows an example of an 80287 co-processor specific program. Figure 4-4 shows an example of an 80387 co-processor specific program. All three programs appear in assembly language for maximum clarity of the co-processor specific commands. There are no listings for BASIC, C and Pascal because it is impossible to see the co-processor commands using these languages. These languages invoke the math co-processor automatically when detected.

The 8087/80287/80387 math co-processors do not use flags. Instead, they contain a status and control word. The status word indicates the current math co-processor condition. The control word affects math co-processor operation. The breakdown for both the control word and status word appears below.

Status Word (bit)

0	Invalid Operation Exception (IE)
1	Denormalized Operation Exception (DE)
2	Zero Divide Exception (ZE)
3	Overflow Exception (OE)
4	Underflow Exception (UE)
5	Precision Exception (PE)
7	Interrupt Request (IR)

8	Condition Code 0 (C0)
9	Condition Code 1 (C1)
10	Condition Code 2 (C2)
11 – 13	Stack Top Pointer (ST)
14	Condition Code 3 (C3)
15	Busy Signal (B)

Control Word (Bit)

0	Invalid Operation Exception Mask (IM)
1	Denormalized Operation Exception Mask (DM)
2	Zero Divide Exception Mask (ZM)
3	Overflow Exception Mask (OM)
4	Underflow Exception Mask (UM)
5	Precision Exception Mask (PM)
7	Interrupt Enable Mask (IEM); 0 = Enabled, 1 = Disabled
8 – 9	Precision Control (PC); 00 = 24 bits, 01 = (Reserved), 10 = 53 bits, 11 = 64 bits
10 – 11	Rounding Control (RC); 00 = Round to Nearest or Even, 01 = Round Down, 10 = Round Up, 11 = Truncate
12	Infinity Control (IC); 0 = Projective, 1 = Affine
13 – 15	Reserved

4-2 Sample program 3 source code listing.

```
;***************************************************************************************
;* Sample Program 3, 8087 Instruction Demonstration            *
;* This program shows you how to diffentiate between different types of math co-processors.  While this is   *
;* not the only method available, it is the most reliable.  To perform this task the program performs three  *
;* tasks.  First, it checks for the existance of any type of co-processor by loading the co-processor control *
;* word.  If memory contains a control word, then a co-processor exists.  Next, it performs an 8087 only     *
;* instruction.  If the co-processor returns the correct results, then it is an 8087.  Finally, the 8087 and  *
;* 80287 return equality if you compare positive and negative infinity, an 80387 does not.  The third test    *
;* uses this feature to look for an 80287.  To use this program you need the following special equipment:     *
;*      8087, 80287, or 80387 equipped computer.                 *
;* Copyright 1989 John Mueller & Wallace Wang - Tab Books *
;***************************************************************************************


;***************************************************************************************
;* Perform the program setup.                 *
;***************************************************************************************

.MODEL MEDIUM    ; Use a medum model size.

.STACK  ; Use the defalt stack of 1024 bytes.

;***************************************************************************************
;* Begin the data area.  Declare all variables.        *
;***************************************************************************************
.DATA
```

```
LF       EQU      10
CR       EQU      13
StrEnd   EQU      36
CtrlWord          DW       0
StatWord          DW       0
CPresent          DB       'Co-Processor is present.  Type: ',StrEnd
NPresent          DB       'No co-processor installed.',LF,CR,StrEnd
Type1    DB       '8087',LF,CR,StrEnd
Type2    DB       '80287',LF,CR,StrEnd
Type3    DB       '80387',LF,CR,StrEnd


;********************************************************************************************************
;* Begin the code segment.                                   *
;********************************************************************************************************
.CODE


Example PROC     FAR
Start:  PUSH     DS       ;Save the original data segment.
        XOR      AX,AX
        PUSH     AX

        MOV      AX,@DATA          ;Point DS & ES to our data segment.
        MOV      DS,AX
        MOV      ES,AX

        FNINIT            ;Initialize the co-processor.
        FNSTCW   CtrlWord          ;Store the control word in AX.
        MOV      AX,CtrlWord
        CMP      AH,03h   ;See if co-processor installed.
        JE       Present
        LEA      DX,NPresent       ;If not, display message.
        MOV      AX,0900h
        INT      21h
        JMP      Exit


;********************************************************************************************************
;* This section of the program determines the co-processor type and displays an appropriate message.    *
;********************************************************************************************************

Present:         LEA      DX,CPresent      ;If installed, display
        MOV      AX,0900h          ; first part of message.
        INT      21h
        AND      CtrlWord,0FF7Fh ;Turn on co-processor interrupts
        FLDCW    CtrlWord          ; by loading new control word.
        FDISI             ;Disable interrupts (works on 8087 only)
        FSTCW    CtrlWord          ;Store the control word in AX.
        MOV      AX,CtrlWord
        TEST     AX,0080h          ;See if instruction worked.
        JE       Test2    ;If it didn't, not 8087.
        LEA      DX,Type1          ;Load type message.
        JMP      DispType
```

4-2 Continued.

```
Test2:   FNINIT          ;Re-initialize the co-processor.
         FLD1            ;Load 1, then 0, then divide
         FLDZ            ; to generage infinity
         FDIV
         FLD     ST      ;Generate negative inifity by pushing the current
         FCHS            ; stack contents and changing the sign.
         FCOMPP          ;Compare the two infinities. Equal
         FSTSW   StatWord        ; for 8087/80287 co-processors.
         FWAIT           ;Wait for FSTSW to finish.
         MOV     AX,StatWord
         SAHF            ;Move AH to the flag register.
         JNZ     Test3   ;If not zero, then must be 80387.
                         ;The zero flag corresponds to condition code
                         ; 3 on the co-processor.
         LEA     DX,Type2        ;Load type message.
         JMP     DispType
Test3:   LEA     DX,Type3        ;Load type message.
DispType:        MOV     AX,0900h        ;Display the second part
         INT     21h     ; of the message.

Exit:    RET

Example ENDP

END     Start
```

4-3 Sample program 4 source code listing.

```
;****************************************************************************************
;* Sample Program 4, 80287 Instruction Demonstration         *
;* This program allows you to enter two integers for the lengths of two sides of a triangle.  It then  *
;* calculates the third side using the Pythagorean theorem.  The program outputs the result to four decimal  *
;* places.  To use this program you need the following special equipment:      *
;*      80287 or 80387 equipped computer.            *
;* Copyright 1989 John Mueller & Wallace Wang - Tab Books *
;****************************************************************************************


;****************************************************************************************
;* Perform the program setup.                 *
;****************************************************************************************


.MODEL MEDIUM   ; Use a medum model size.

.286P   ; Use the correct processor instruction set.
.287

.STACK  ; Use the defalt stack of 1024 bytes.

;****************************************************************************************
;* Begin the data area.  Declare all variables.       *
;****************************************************************************************
```

4-3 Continued.

```
.DATA

Beep      EQU     07
LF        EQU     10
CR        EQU     13
StrEnd    EQU     36
Ten       DW      10
TenTh     DW      10000
CtrlWord          DW      0
AddLine DB        LF,LF,CR,StrEnd
NPresent          DB      Beep,'You need a math co-processor to use '
          DB      'this program.',LF,CR,StrEnd
WPresent          DB      Beep,'You need an 80287 or 80387 installed '
          DB      'to use this program.',LF,CR,StrEnd
InData1 DB        'Type a number for the first side of the '
          DB      'triangle. ',StrEnd
InData2 DB        'Type a number for the second side of the '
          DB      'triangle. ',StrEnd
OutData DB        'The third side of the triangle equals. '
ConvNum DB        10 DUP(0),StrEnd
Input     LABEL   BYTE
PartAdd DW        0
SideA     DQ      0
SideB     DQ      0
SideCI  DW        0
SideCD  DW        0


;***************************************************************************************************************
;* Begin the code segment.                            *
;***************************************************************************************************************
.CODE

Example PROC    FAR
Start:  PUSH    DS      ;Save the original data segment.
        XOR     AX,AX
        PUSH    AX
        MOV     AX,@DATA        ;Point DS & ES to our data segment.
        MOV     DS,AX
        MOV     ES,AX


;***************************************************************************************************************
;* Check for the presence of a math co-processor, then an 80287 or 80387 math co-processor.  If one isn't    *
;* installed or if the machine contains an 8087, exit the program.        *
;***************************************************************************************************************

        FNINIT          ;Initialize the co-processor.
        FNSTCW  CtrlWord        ;Store the control word in AX.
        MOV     AX,CtrlWord
        CMP     AH,03h  ;See if co-processor installed.
        JE      Present
        LEA     DX,NPresent     ;If not, display error message.
```

```
              MOV      AX,0900h
              INT      21h
              JMP      Exit

Present:      AND      CtrlWord,0FF7Fh ;Turn on co-processor interrupts
              FLDCW    CtrlWord         ; by loading new control word.
              FDISI             ;Disable interrupts (works on 8087 only)
              FSTCW    CtrlWord         ;Store the control word in AX.
              MOV      AX,CtrlWord
              TEST     AX,0080h         ;See if instruction worked.
              JE       Correct ;If it didn't, not 8087.
              LEA      DX,WPresent      ;If it did, display error message.
              MOV      AX,0900h
              INT      21h
              JMP      Exit
```

```
;*********************************************************************************************************
;* This section calculates the third side of the triangle using the equation sqrt(SideA^2 * SideB^2).   *
;*********************************************************************************************************
```

```
Correct:      FLDZ               ;Load co-processor with zero.
              LEA      DX,InData1       ;Request length of first side.
              MOV      AX,0900h
              INT      21h
GetNum1:      XOR      AX,AX   ;Get the number.
              INT      16h
              CMP      AL,CR   ;If enter pressed, get next
              JE       NextNum ; number.
              CMP      AL,'0'  ;Is actually a number?
              JL       GetNum1 ;If not, ignore.
              MOV      AH,2    ;Display the number.
              MOV      DL,AL
              INT      21h
              SUB      AL,30h  ;Convert character to number.
              MOV      Input,AL         ;Store number in variable.
              FIMUL    Ten     ;Multiply prev number by 10.
              FIADD    PartAdd ;Add current number
              JMP      GetNum1

NextNum:      FSTP     SideA   ;Store the first number.
              LEA      DX,AddLine       ;Add space between answers.
              MOV      AX,0900h
              INT      21h
              FLDZ               ;Load co-processor with zero.
              LEA      DX,InData2       ;Request length of first side.
              MOV      AX,0900h
              INT      21h
GetNum2:      XOR      AX,AX   ;Get the number.
              INT      16h
              CMP      AL,CR   ;If enter pressed, calculate
              JE       CalcSide         ; the third side.
```

4-3 Continued.

```
        CMP     AL,'0'  ;Is actually a number?
        JL      GetNum2 ;If not, ignore.
        MOV     AH,2    ;Display the number.
        MOV     DL,AL
        INT     21h
        SUB     AL,30h  ;Convert character to number.
        MOV     Input,AL        ;Store number in variable.
        FIMUL   Ten     ;Multiply prev number by 10.
        FIADD   PartAdd ;Add current number
        JMP     GetNum2

CalcSide:       FLD     ST      ;Push the stack contents.
        FMUL            ;Square the second number.
        FSTP    SideB   ;Store the second number.
        FLD     SideA   ;Get the first number.
        FLD     ST      ;Push the stack contents.
        FMUL            ;Square the first number.
        FADD    SideB   ;Add the second side.
        FSQRT           ;Obtain the square root.
```

;**
;* This part of the program takes the answer contained in the math co-processor, splits it into an integer   *
;* and decimal section, and converts the two sections to character representations.   *
;**

```
        OR      CtrlWord,0C00h  ;Change rounding to truncate
        FLDCW   CtrlWord        ; by loading new control word.
        FIST    SideCI  ;Store integer part of third side.
        FLD     ST      ;Push the stack contents.
        FRNDINT         ;Compute decimal part of third
        FSUB            ; side by subtracting the
        FIMUL   TenTh   ; integer part.
        FIST    SideCD  ;Store to decimal part of the third side.

        LEA     AX,ConvNum      ;Load the storage address.
        ADD     AX,9    ;Find the end.
        MOV     DI,AX   ;Place results in DI.
        MOV     AX,SideCD       ;Get the decimal part.
        CALL    HexConv

        DEC     DI      ;Place decimal point.
        MOV     BYTE PTR [DI],'.'
        DEC     DI

        MOV     AX,SideCI       ;Convert integer part.
        CALL    HexConv

        LEA     DX,AddLine      ;Add space between answers.
        MOV     AX,0900h
        INT     21h
        LEA     DX,OutData      ;Display third side length.
```

```
        MOV     AX,0900h
        INT     21h
Exit:   RET


Example ENDP


;**************************************************************************************************
;* This procedure converts an integer to a character representation.        *
;**************************************************************************************************


HexConv PROC    NEAR

        MOV     CX,10    ;Load the divisor.
NextChar:       XOR     DX,DX    ;Clear DX.
        DIV     CX       ;Place first number in DX.
        ADD     DL,30h   ;Convert to a character.
        MOV     [DI],DL  ;Move to string location.
        DEC     DI       ;Update string pointer.
        CMP     AX,10    ;See if we need to divide.
        JGE     NextChar
        ADD     AL,30h   ;If not, AX less than 10.
        MOV     [DI],AL  ;Convert to character and store.

        RET


HexConv ENDP


END     Start
```

4-4 Sample program 5 source code listing.

```
;**************************************************************************************************
;* Sample Program 5, 80387 Instruction Demonstration              *
;* This program demonstrates the trignometric functions added to the 80387 math co-processor.  It also *
;* shows the tangent function provided with the original 8087 math co-processor.  To use this program you        *
;* need the following special equipment:              *
;*      80387 equipped computer                *
;*      EGA or VGA display.                    *
;* Copyright 1989 John Mueller & Wallace Wang - Tab Books*
;**************************************************************************************************


;**************************************************************************************************
;* Perform the program setup.                 *
;**************************************************************************************************


.MODEL MEDIUM   ; Use a medum model size.

.386P   ; Use the correct processor instruction set.
.387


.STACK  ; Use the defalt stack of 1024 bytes.
```

4-4 Continued.

```
;**************************************************************************************************
;* Begin the data area.  Declare all variables.             *
;**************************************************************************************************
.DATA

Beep    EQU     07
LF      EQU     10
CR      EQU     13
StrEnd  EQU     36
CtrlWord        DW      0
StatWord        DW      0
NPresent        DB      Beep,'You need a math co-processor to use '
        DB      'this program.',LF,CR,StrEnd
WPresent        DB      Beep,'You need an 80387 installed '
        DB      'to use this program.',LF,CR,StrEnd
TypeScr DB      ' ┌───────────────┐ ',CR,LF
        DB      '| Display the  |',CR,LF
        DB      '|   Value  of  |',CR,LF
        DB      '├───────────────┤',CR,LF
        DB      '| Sine         |',CR,LF
        DB      '| Cosine       |',CR,LF
        DB      '| Sine/Cosine  |',CR,LF
        DB      '| Tangent      |',CR,LF
        DB      '| Quit         |',CR,LF
        DB      ' └───────────────┘ ',StrEnd
Type1   DB      'Sine        ',StrEnd
Type2   DB      'Cosine      ',StrEnd
Type3   DB      'Sine/Cosine',StrEnd
Type4   DB      'Tangent     ',StrEnd
Type5   DB      'Quit        ',StrEnd
TypeSel DB      1
XPosit  DW      26
YPosit  DW      0
XLen    DW      270
YLen    DW      300
XDot    DW      1
YDot    DW      1
Two     DW      2
Seventy DW      70
PtFive  LABEL   QWORD
        DW      3 DUP(0),3FE0h
SineStr DB      'Value of Sine',CR,LF,StrEnd
CosineStr       DB      'Value of Cosine',CR,LF,StrEnd
CSineStr        DB      'Value of Sine/Cosine',CR,LF,StrEnd
TangStr DB      'Value of Tangent',CR,LF,StrEnd
GridStr DB      '|',CR,LF
        DB      '|',CR,LF
        DB      '|',CR,LF
        DB      '|',CR,LF
        DB      '|',CR,LF
        DB      '|',CR,LF
```

4-4 Continued.

```
         DB      '|',CR,LF
         DB      '|',CR,LF
         DB      '|',CR,LF
         DB      '|',CR,LF
         DB      '|',CR,LF
         DB      '├──────────────────────────────'
         DB      '──────────────────────',CR,LF
         DB      '|',CR,LF
         DB      '|',CR,LF
         DB      '|',CR,LF
         DB      '|',CR,LF
         DB      '|',CR,LF
         DB      '|',CR,LF
         DB      '|',CR,LF
         DB      '|',CR,LF
         DB      '|',CR,LF
         DB      '└──────────────────────────────'
         DB      '──────────────────────',CR,LF
         DB      'Press Any Key When Ready...',StrEnd
```

```
;**************************************************************************************************
;* Begin the code segment.                          *
;**************************************************************************************************
.CODE


Example PROC    FAR
Start:  PUSH    DS      ;Save the original data segment.
        XOR     AX,AX
        PUSH    AX

        MOV     AX,@DATA        ;Point DS & ES to our data segment.
        MOV     DS,AX
        MOV     ES,AX


;**************************************************************************************************
;* Check for the presence of a math co-processor, then an 80287 or 80387 math co-processor.  If an 80387    *
;* isn't installed exit the program.              *
;**************************************************************************************************

        FNINIT          ;Initialize the co-processor.
        FNSTCW  CtrlWord        ;Store the control word in AX.
        MOV     AX,CtrlWord
        CMP     AH,03h  ;See if co-processor installed.
        JE      Present
        LEA     DX,NPresent     ;If not, display error message.
        JMP     DispMsg


;**************************************************************************************************
;* This section of the program determines the co-processor type and displays an appropriate message.    *
;**************************************************************************************************
```

```
Present:        AND     CtrlWord,0FF7Fh ;Turn on co-processor interrupts
        FLDCW   CtrlWord        ; by loading new control word.
        FDISI                   ;Disable interrupts (works on 8087 only)
        FSTCW   CtrlWord        ;Store the control word in AX.
        MOV     AX,CtrlWord
        TEST    AX,0080h        ;See if instruction worked.
        JE      Test2   ;If it didn't, not 8087.
        LEA     DX,WPresent     ;If 8087, display error message.
        JMP     DispMsg
Test2:  FNINIT                  ;Re-initialize the co-processor.
        FLD1                    ;Load 1, then 0, then divide
        FLDZ                    ; to generate infinity
        FDIV
        FLD     ST      ;Generate negative inifity by pushing the current
        FCHS                    ; stack contents and changing the sign.
        FCOMPP                  ;Compare the two infinities. Equal
        FSTSW   AX              ; for 8087/80287 co-processors.
        SAHF                    ;Move AH to the flag register.
        JNZ     Correct ;If not zero, then must be 80387.
                                ;The zero flag corresponds to condition code
                                ; 3 on the co-processor.
        LEA     DX,WPresent     ;If 80287, display error message.
DispMsg:        MOV     AX,0900h
        INT     21h
        JMP     Exit
```

```
;****************************************************************************************************
;* This section of the program displays the menu, determines which display procedure the user selected, and    *
;* calls the appropriate display procedure.             *
;****************************************************************************************************
```

```
Correct:        CALL    BarSel  ;Display the menu until user presses enter.

        CMP     AL,1    ;User select Sine?
        JNE     D2
        MOV     AX,16   ;Set video adapter to graphics
        INT     10h     ; mode (640 X 350).
        MOV     AX,0200h        ;Set the cursor position.
        XOR     BX,BX
        MOV     DX,0022h
        INT     10h
        MOV     AX,0900h        ;Display the heading.
        LEA     DX,SineStr
        INT     21h
        LEA     DX,GridStr      ;Display the grid.
        INT     21h
D1A:    CALL    SDisp   ;Compute display point.
        INC     XDot    ;Advance the X Posit pointer.
        CMP     XDot,541        ;See if we computed the last
        JNE     D1A     ; display point.
        XOR     AX,AX   ;Get keyboard input.
```

```
          INT     16h
          MOV     XDot,1  ;Reset X Position pointer.
          MOV     AX,0003h        ;Reset the video mode to text.
          INT     10h
          JMP     Correct ;Get next menu selection.
D2:       CMP     AL,2    ;User select Cosine?
          JNE     D3
          MOV     AX,16   ;Set video adapter to graphics
          INT     10h     ; mode (640 X 350).
          MOV     AX,0200h        ;Set the cursor position.
          XOR     BX,BX
          MOV     DX,0021h
          INT     10h
          MOV     AX,0900h        ;Display the heading.
          LEA     DX,CosineStr
          INT     21h
          LEA     DX,GridStr      ;Display the grid.
          INT     21h
D2A:      CALL    CDisp   ;Compute display point.
          INC     XDot    ;Advance the X Posit pointer.
          CMP     XDot,541        ;See if we computed the last
          JNE     D2A     ; display point.
          XOR     AX,AX   ;Get keyboard input.
          INT     16h
          MOV     XDot,1  ;Reset X Position pointer.
          MOV     AX,0003h        ;Reset the video mode to text.
          INT     10h
          JMP     Correct ;Get next menu selection.
D3:       CMP     AL,3    ;User select Sine/Cosine?
          JNE     D4
          MOV     AX,16   ;Set video adapter to graphics
          INT     10h     ; mode (640 X 350).
          MOV     AX,0200h        ;Set the cursor position.
          XOR     BX,BX
          MOV     DX,001Dh
          INT     10h
          MOV     AX,0900h        ;Display the heading.
          LEA     DX,CSineStr
          INT     21h
          LEA     DX,GridStr      ;Display the grid.
          INT     21h
D3A:      CALL    CSDisp  ;Compute display point.
          INC     XDot    ;Advance the X Posit pointer.
          CMP     XDot,541        ;See if we computed the last
          JNE     D3A     ; display point.
          XOR     AX,AX   ;Get keyboard input.
          INT     16h
          MOV     XDot,1  ;Reset X Position pointer.
          MOV     AX,0003h        ;Reset the video mode to text.
          INT     10h
          JMP     Correct ;Get next menu selection.
```

4-4 Continued.

```
D4:        CMP      AL,4      ;User select Tangent?
           JNE      Exit      ;User selected Quit.
           MOV      AX,16     ;Set video adapter to graphics
           INT      10h       ; mode (640 X 350).
           MOV      AX,0200h          ;Set the cursor position.
           XOR      BX,BX
           MOV      DX,0020h
           INT      10h
           MOV      AX,0900h          ;Display the heading.
           LEA      DX,TangStr
           INT      21h
           LEA      DX,GridStr        ;Display the grid.
           INT      21h
D4A:       CALL     TDisp     ;Compute display point.
           INC      XDot      ;Advance the X Posit pointer.
           CMP      XDot,541          ;See if we computed the last
           JNE      D4A       ; display point.
           XOR      AX,AX     ;Get keyboard input.
           INT      16h
           MOV      XDot,1    ;Reset X Position pointer.
           MOV      AX,0003h          ;Reset the video mode to text.
           INT      10h
           JMP      Correct

Exit:      RET                ;User selected Quit.


Example ENDP

;****************************************************************************************************
;* This procedure presents a scrolling bar menu for the user to select a display type.  It passes the  *
;* selected value back to the calling procedure in AX.          *
;****************************************************************************************************

BarSel PROC       NEAR

           MOV      AH,6      ;Clear the screen.
           MOV      AL,25     ;Scroll 25 lines.
           XOR      BH,BH     ;Use black.
           XOR      CX,CX     ;Start in upper left corner.
           MOV      DH,25     ;End in line 25 and
           MOV      DL,80     ; column 80.
           INT      10h

           MOV      AX,0200h          ;Position the cursor.
           XOR      BX,BX     ;Use display page 0.
           MOV      DH,08     ;Row 8.
           MOV      DL,00     ;Column 0.
           INT      10h

           LEA      DX,TypeScr        ;Display the menu.
           MOV      AX,0900h
           INT      21h
```

4-4 Continued.

```
        CALL    Highlight

NextKey:        XOR     AX,AX   ;Get keyboard input.
        INT     16h

        CMP     AL,CR   ;Compare to return.
        JE      Selected        ;If return, user selected type.
        CMP     AH,50h  ;Compare to down arrow.
        JNE     UpCheck ;If not, check up arrow.
        CMP     TypeSel,5       ;See if already at bottom.
        JNE     AddOne  ;If not, add to level.
        JMP     SetOne  ;Otherwise set level to one.
UpCheck:        CMP     AH,48h  ;Compare to up arrow.
        JNE     NextKey ;If not, invalid keystroke.
        CMP     TypeSel,1       ;See if already at top.
        JNE     SubOne  ;If so, subtract level.
        JMP     SetFive ;Otherwise, set level to four.

AddOne: CALL    Dim     ;Dim the old selection.
        INC     TypeSel ;Increment the level.
        CALL    Highlight       ;Highlight the new selection.
        JMP     NextKey ;Get the next keystroke.

SubOne: CALL    Dim     ;Dim the old selection.
        DEC     TypeSel ;Decrement the level.
        CALL    Highlight       ;Highlight the new selection.
        JMP     NextKey ;Get the next keystroke.

SetOne: CALL    Dim     ;Dim the old selection.
        MOV     TypeSel,1       ;Set level to 1.
        CALL    Highlight       ;Highlight the new selection.
        JMP     NextKey ;Get the next keystroke.

SetFive:        CALL    Dim     ;Dim the old selection.
        MOV     TypeSel,5       ;Set level to 4.
        CALL    Highlight       ;Highlight the new selection.
        JMP     NextKey ;Get the next keystroke.

Selected:       MOV     AL,TypeSel
        RET

BarSel  ENDP

;*****************************************************************************************************************
;* This procedure highlights one of the bar menu selections.  It bases the highlight on the current value of    *
;* TypeSel, which determines which display procedure the program executes.      *
;*****************************************************************************************************************

Highlight       PROC    NEAR

        CMP     TypeSel,2
```

```
        JE      Line2
        CMP     TypeSel,3
        JE      Line3
        CMP     TypeSel,4
        JE      Line4
        CMP     TypeSel,5
        JE      Line5


Line1:  MOV     AH,13h  ;Write a string to screen.
        MOV     AL,1    ;BL contains attribute.
        XOR     BH,BH   ;Use page 0.
        MOV     BL,70h  ;Use white background.
        MOV     CX,11   ;String length.
        MOV     DH,12   ;Starting row.
        MOV     DL,2    ;Starting column.
        LEA     BP,Type1        ;String address.
        INT     10h
        JMP     Exit2


Line2:  MOV     AH,13h  ;Write a string to screen.
        MOV     AL,1    ;BL contains attribute.
        XOR     BH,BH   ;Use page 0.
        MOV     BL,70h  ;Use white background.
        MOV     CX,11   ;String length.
        MOV     DH,13   ;Starting row.
        MOV     DL,2    ;Starting column.
        LEA     BP,Type2        ;String address.
        INT     10h
        JMP     Exit2


Line3:  MOV     AH,13h  ;Write a string to screen.
        MOV     AL,1    ;BL contains attribute.
        XOR     BH,BH   ;Use page 0.
        MOV     BL,70h  ;Use white background.
        MOV     CX,11   ;String length.
        MOV     DH,14   ;Starting row.
        MOV     DL,2    ;Starting column.
        LEA     BP,Type3        ;String address.
        INT     10h
        JMP     Exit2


Line4:  MOV     AH,13h  ;Write a string to screen.
        MOV     AL,1    ;BL contains attribute.
        XOR     BH,BH   ;Use page 0.
        MOV     BL,70h  ;Use white background.
        MOV     CX,11   ;String length.
        MOV     DH,15   ;Starting row.
        MOV     DL,2    ;Starting column.
        LEA     BP,Type4        ;String address.
        INT     10h
        JMP     Exit2
```

4-4 Continued.

```
Line5:  MOV     AH,13h   ;Write a string to screen.
        MOV     AL,1     ;BL contains attribute.
        XOR     BH,BH    ;Use page 0.
        MOV     BL,70h   ;Use white background.
        MOV     CX,11    ;String length.
        MOV     DH,16    ;Starting row.
        MOV     DL,2     ;Starting column.
        LEA     BP,Type5          ;String address.
        INT     10h


Exit2:  RET


Highlight       ENDP
```

```
;*********************************************************************************************************
;
;* This procedure dims one of the bar menu selections.  It bases the dim on the current value of         *
;* TypeSel, which determines which display procedure the program executes.         *
;*********************************************************************************************************
;
```

```
Dim     PROC    NEAR

        CMP     TypeSel,2
        JE      Dim2
        CMP     TypeSel,3
        JE      Dim3
        CMP     TypeSel,4
        JE      Dim4
        CMP     TypeSel,5
        JE      Dim5

Dim1:   MOV     AH,13h   ;Write a string to screen.
        MOV     AL,1     ;BL contains attribute.
        XOR     BH,BH    ;Use page 0.
        MOV     BL,07h   ;Use white background.
        MOV     CX,11    ;String length.
        MOV     DH,12    ;Starting row.
        MOV     DL,2     ;Starting column.
        LEA     BP,Type1          ;String address.
        INT     10h
        JMP     Exit3

Dim2:   MOV     AH,13h   ;Write a string to screen.
        MOV     AL,1     ;BL contains attribute.
        XOR     BH,BH    ;Use page 0.
        MOV     BL,07h   ;Use white background.
        MOV     CX,11    ;String length.
        MOV     DH,13    ;Starting row.
        MOV     DL,2     ;Starting column.
        LEA     BP,Type2          ;String address.
        INT     10h
        JMP     Exit3
```

```
Dim3:   MOV     AH,13h  ;Write a string to screen.
        MOV     AL,1    ;BL contains attribute.
        XOR     BH,BH   ;Use page 0.
        MOV     BL,07h  ;Use white background.
        MOV     CX,11   ;String length.
        MOV     DH,14   ;Starting row.
        MOV     DL,2    ;Starting column.
        LEA     BP,Type3        ;String address.
        INT     10h
        JMP     Exit3

Dim4:   MOV     AH,13h  ;Write a string to screen.
        MOV     AL,1    ;BL contains attribute.
        XOR     BH,BH   ;Use page 0.
        MOV     BL,07h  ;Use white background.
        MOV     CX,11   ;String length.
        MOV     DH,15   ;Starting row.
        MOV     DL,2    ;Starting column.
        LEA     BP,Type4        ;String address.
        INT     10h
        JMP     Exit3

Dim5:   MOV     AH,13h  ;Write a string to screen.
        MOV     AL,1    ;BL contains attribute.
        XOR     BH,BH   ;Use page 0.
        MOV     BL,07h  ;Use white background.
        MOV     CX,11   ;String length.
        MOV     DH,16   ;Starting row.
        MOV     DL,2    ;Starting column.
        LEA     BP,Type5        ;String address.
        INT     10h

Exit3:  RET

Dim     ENDP
```

```
;************************************************************************************************************
;* This procedure displays a graphic representation of all the values of sine from 0 to 360 degrees.  Since  *
;* the 80387 requires radians instead of degrees for input, the procedure uses a two step process for        *
;* determining the current display position.  The display value (fractional part of 360 degrees) is a        *
;* function of the number of dots in the entire display area of 540 dots.  To find this fractional part we    *
;* divide the current X position by the total number of dots in the display, then multiply by pi.  This      *
;* value provides the current radian position within the circle.  The program then finds the value of sine   *
;* for that radian value and determines the Y offset from the Y axis.    *
;************************************************************************************************************
```

```
SDisp   PROC    NEAR

        FILD    XDot    ;Load current X Posit.
        FILD    XLen    ;Divide by total length.
        FDIV
```

```
        FLDPI           ;Load Pi to determine the
        FMUL            ; number of radians/2.
        FSIN            ;Find the sine of angle.
        FIDIV   Two     ; values in upper half o
        FADD    PtFive  ; display. Add required
        FIMUL   YLen    ; corrections.
        FILD    YLen
        FSUBR
        FIADD   XPosit  ;Add display offset.
        FISTP   YPosit  ;Save value.

        MOV     AX,0C39h        ;Display the pixel
        XOR     BX,BX   ;Use display page 0.
        MOV     CX,XDot ;Load the column.
        ADD     CX,5    ;Add the display offset.
        MOV     DX,YPosit       ;Load the row.
        INT     10h

        RET

SDisp   ENDP


;*******************************************************************************************************************
;* This procedure displays a graphic representation of all the values of cosine from 0 to 360 degrees.  *
;* It uses the same basic procedure as SDisp.                *
;*******************************************************************************************************************
;

CDisp   PROC    NEAR

        FILD    XDot    ;Load current X Posit.
        FILD    XLen    ;Divide by total length.
        FDIV
        FLDPI           ;Load Pi to determine the
        FMUL            ; number of radians/2.
        FCOS            ;Find the cosine of angle
        FIDIV   Two     ; values in upper half of
        FADD    PtFive  ; display. Add required
        FIMUL   YLen    ; corrections.
        FILD    YLen
        FSUBR
        FIADD   XPosit  ;Add display offset.
        FISTP   YPosit  ;Save value.

        MOV     AX,0C3Ah        ;Display the pixel
        XOR     BX,BX   ;Use display page 0.
        MOV     CX,XDot ;Load the column.
        ADD     CX,5    ;Add the display offset.
        MOV     DX,YPosit       ;Load the row.
        INT     10h
```

4-4 Continued.

```
            RET

CDisp   ENDP

;*****************************************************************************************************
;* This procedure displays a graphic representation of all the values of sine/cosine from 0 to 360 degrees.   *
;* It uses the same basic procedure as SDisp. Notice the procedure only performs one transcendental function  *
;* using the dual sine/cosine function.          *
;*****************************************************************************************************

CSDisp  PROC    NEAR

        FILD    XDot     ;Load current X Posit.
        FILD    XLen     ;Divide by total length.
        FDIV
        FLDPI            ;Load Pi to determine the
        FMUL             ; number of radians/2.
        FSINCOS          ;Find cosine/sine of angle.
        FIDIV   Two      ; values in upper half of
        FADD    PtFive   ; display. Add required
        FIMUL   YLen     ; corrections.
        FILD    YLen
        FSUBR
        FIADD   XPosit   ;Add display offset.
        FISTP   YPosit   ;Save value.

        MOV     AX,0C3Ah         ;Display the pixel
        XOR     BX,BX    ;Use display page 0.
        MOV     CX,XDot  ;Load the column.
        ADD     CX,5     ;Add the display offset.
        MOV     DX,YPosit        ;Load the row.
        INT     10h

        FIDIV   Two      ; values in upper half of
        FADD    PtFive   ; display. Add required
        FIMUL   YLen     ; corrections.
        FILD    YLen
        FSUBR
        FIADD   XPosit   ;Add display offset.
        FISTP   YPosit   ;Save value.

        MOV     AX,0C39h         ;Display the pixel
        XOR     BX,BX    ;Use display page 0.
        MOV     CX,XDot  ;Load the column.
        ADD     CX,5     ;Add the display offset.
        MOV     DX,YPosit        ;Load the row.
        INT     10h

        RET

CSDisp  ENDP
```

4-4 Continued.

```
;**************************************************************************************************
;* This procedure displays a graphic representation of all the values of tangent from 0 to 360 degrees. *
;* It uses the same basic procedure as SDisp.              *
;**************************************************************************************************
;

TDisp    PROC    NEAR

         FILD    XDot     ;Load current X Posit.
         FILD    XLen     ;Divide by total length.
         FDIV
         FLDPI            ;Load Pi to determine the
         FMUL             ; number of radians/2.
         FPTAN            ;Find the tangent of angle
         FDIV             ; values in upper half of
         FIDIV   Seventy  ; display. Add required
         FADD    PtFive   ; corrections.
         FIMUL   YLen
         FILD    YLen
         FSUBR
         FIADD   XPosit   ;Add display offset.
         FISTP   YPosit   ;Save value.

         MOV     AX,0C3Ch         ;Display the pixel
         XOR     BX,BX    ;Use display page 0.
         MOV     CX,XDot  ;Load the column.
         ADD     CX,5     ;Add the display offset.
         MOV     DX,YPosit        ;Load the row.
         INT     10h

         RET

TDisp    ENDP

END      Start
```

Each math co-processor contains 8 stack elements 80 bits long. Bits 11 through 13 of the co-processor status word tells you which element appears at the top of the stack. For example, if element 8 was at the top of the stack, then element 1 would appear second. Each element uses a floating point format consisting of 64 significand bits, 15 exponent bits, and 1 sign bit. The co-processors use these stack elements for most math operations. Figure 4-5 depicts the relationship between the stack elements. It also shows how the math co-processor stores real numbers.

Value of $2^X - 1$ (F2XM1) (8087/80287/80387)

Category: Transcendental Instructions

This instruction calculates the value of $Y = 2^X - 1$. X is the top stack

Stack Element 1, ST(0)
Stack Element 2, ST(1)
Stack Element 3, ST(2)
Stack Element 4, ST(3)
Stack Element 5, ST(4)
Stack Element 6, ST(5)
Stack Element 7, ST(6)
Stack Element 8, ST(7)

**8087/80287/80387
Stack Structure
(Each Element 80 Bits Wide)**

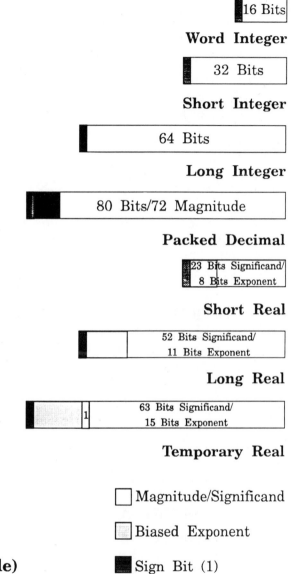

16 Bits

Word Integer

32 Bits

Short Integer

64 Bits

Long Integer

80 Bits/72 Magnitude

Packed Decimal

23 Bits Significand/
8 Bits Exponent

Short Real

52 Bits Significand/
11 Bits Exponent

Long Real

63 Bits Significand/
15 Bits Exponent

Temporary Real

☐ Magnitude/Significand

▨ Biased Exponent

■ Sign Bit (1)

■ Not Used/Ignored

4-5 Math co-processor internal logical structure.

element. Y replaces X as the top stack element. This instruction affects the PE and UE status bits.

Absolute Value (FABS) (8087/80287/80387)

Category: Arithmetic Instructions

Use this instruction to replace the top stack element with its absolute value. It affects the IE status bit.

Add Real (FADD) (8087/80287/80387)

Category: Arithmetic Instructions

The add real instruction adds two numbers together and places the result in the destination operand. The instruction uses the stack as the default destination. This instruction affects the PE, UE, OE, DE, and IE status bits.

Add Real and Pop (FADDP) (8087/80287/80387)

Category: Arithmetic Instructions

This instruction adds two operands, places the result at the destination, and pops a value from the stack. The instruction uses the stack as the default destination. This instruction affects the PE, UE, OE, DE, and IE status bits.

BCD Load (FBLD)(8087/80287/80387)

Category: Data-Transfer Instructions

Use this instruction to convert a BCD number (at the specified operand address) to a temporary real format and push it on the stack. This instruction affects the IE status bit.

BCD Store and Pop (FBSTP) (8087/80287/80387)

Category: Data-Transfer Instructions

This instruction pops a value from the stack, converts it to a BCD integer, and places it at the operand address. It affects the IE status bit.

Change Sign (FCHS) (8087/80287/80387)

Category: Arithmetic Instructions

Use this instruction to change the sign of the top stack element. It affects the IE status bit.

Clear Exceptions with Wait (FCLEX) (8087/80287/80387)

Category: Processor-Control Instructions

Precede this instruction with a CPU wait prefix. It clears the B, PE, UE, OE, ZE, DE, IE, and IR status bits.

Compare Real (FCOM) (8087/80287/80387)

Category: Comparison Instructions

This instruction compares the top stack element with the second stack element or other specified operand. It affects the C0, C1, C3, DE, and IE status bits.

Compare Real and Pop (FCOMP) (8087/80287/80387)

Category: Comparison Instructions

This instruction compares the top stack element with the second stack element or other specified operand. It then pops the stack. The compare real and pop instruction affects the C0, C1, C3, DE, and IE status bits.

Compare Real and Pop Twice (FCOMPP) (8087/80287/80387)

Category: Comparison Instructions

This instruction compares the top stack element with the second stack element or other specified operand. It then pops the stack twice. The compare real and pop instruction affects the C0, C1, C3, DE, and IE status bits.

Decrement the Stack Pointer (FDECSTP) (8087/80287/80387)

Category: Processor-Control Instructions

This instruction decrements the 8087 status word stack pointer. It affects only the ST status bits.

Disable Interrupts with Wait (FDISI) (8087 Only)

Category: Processor-Control Instructions

Precede this instruction with a CPU wait prefix. It sets the IEM control word bit preventing the 8087 from generating interrupts. This instruction does not affect the status word.

Divide Real (FDIV) (8087/80287/80387)

Category: Arithmetic Instructions

This instruction divides the destination by the source operand. It places the result in the destination. The instruction uses the stack as the default destination. The divide real instruction affects the PE, UE, OE, ZE, DE, and IE status bits.

Divide Real and Pop (FDIVP)(8087/80287/80387)

Category: Arithmetic Instructions

This instruction divides the destination by the source operand. It places the result in the destination and pops the stack. The instruction uses the stack as the default destination. The divide real and pop instruction affects the PE, UE, OE, ZE, DE, and IE status bits.

Divide Real Reversed (FDIVR) (8087/80287/80387)

Category: Arithmetic Instructions

This instruction divides the source by the destination operand. It places the result in the destination. The instruction uses the stack as the default destination. The divide real reversed instruction affects the PE, UE, OE, ZE, DE, and IE status bits.

Divide Real Reversed and Pop (FDIVRP) (8087/80287/80387)

Category: Arithmetic Instructions

This instruction divides the source by the destination operand. It places the result in the destination and pops the stack. The instruction uses the stack as the default destination. The divide real reversed and pop instruction affects the PE, UE, OE, ZE, DE, and IE status bits.

Enable Interrupts with Wait (FENI) (8087 Only)

Category: Processor-Control Instructions

Precede this instruction with a CPU wait prefix. It clears the IEM control word bit allowing the 8087 to generate interrupts. This instruction does not affect the status word.

Free Register (FFREE) (8087/80287/80387)

Category: Processor-Control Instructions

This instruction changes the specified stack register tag to indicate an empty element. It does not affect the status word.

Integer Add (FIADD) (8087/80287/80387)

Category: Arithmetic Instructions

This instruction adds two operands as integers and stores the result at the destination. It assumes a default stack destination. The integer add instruction affects the PE, OE, DE, and IE status bits.

Integer Compare (FICOM) (8087/80287/80387)

Category: Comparison Instructions

This instruction converts the operand to an integer (if required) and compares it to the top stack element. It then changes the condition of the status word bits to match the comparison result. The status word bits affected include C0, C2, C3, DE, and IE.

Integer Compare and Pop (FICOMP) (8087/80287/80387)

Category: Comparison Instructions

This instruction converts the operand to an integer (if required) and compares it to the top stack element. It then changes the condition of the status word bits to match the comparison result and pops the stack. The status word bits affected include C0, C2, C3, DE, and IE.

Integer Divide (FIDIV) (8087/80287/80387)

Category: Arithmetic Instructions

The integer divide instruction divides the destination by the source operand as integers. It stores the result in the destination operand. The instruction uses the stack as the default destination. It affects the PE, UE, OE, ZE, DE, and IE status bits.

Integer Divide Reversed (FIDIVR) (8087/80287/80387)

Category: Arithmetic Instructions

The integer divide reversed instruction divides the source by the destination operand as integers. It stores the result in the destination operand. The instruction uses the stack as the default destination. It affects the PE, UE, OE, ZE, DE, and IE status bits.

Integer Load (FILD) (8087/80287/80387)

Category: Data-Transfer Instructions

This instruction converts the binary integer pointed to by the operand address to a temporary real format and pushes it on the stack. It affects only the IE status bit.

Integer Multiply (FIMUL) (8087/80287/80387)

Category: Arithmetic Instructions

The integer multiply instruction multiplies the destination by the source operand as integers. It stores the result in the destination operand. The instruction uses the stack as the default destination. It affects the PE, OE, DE, and IE status bits.

Increment the Stack Pointer (FINCSTP) (8087/80287/80387)

Category: Processor-Control Instructions

This instruction increments the stack status word bits.

Initialize the Processor with Wait (FINIT) (8087/80287/80387)

Category: Processor-Control Instructions

This instruction equals a hardware reset instruction for the math co-processor chip. Precede this instruction with a CPU wait prefix.

Integer Store (FIST) (8087/80287/80387)

Category: Data-Transfer Instructions

Use this instruction to round the top stack element to a binary integer and store it at the operand address. This instruction affects the PE and IE status bits.

Integer Store and Pop (FISTP) (8087/80287/80387)

Category: Data-Transfer Instructions

Use this instruction to round the top stack element to a binary integer and store it at the operand address. It pops the stack after storing the integer. This instruction affects the PE and IE status bits.

Integer Subtract (FISUB) (8087/80287/80387)

Category: Arithmetic Instructions

This instruction subtracts the source from the destination operand and places the result in the destination. The instruction assumes a stack default destination. The arithmetic instruction affects the PE, OE, DE, and IE status bits.

Integer Subtract Reversed (FISUBR) (8087/80287/80387)

Category: Arithmetic Instructions

This instruction subtracts the destination from the source operand and places the result in the destination. The instruction assumes a stack default destination. The arithmetic instruction affects the PE, OE, DE, and IE status bits.

Load Real (FLD) (8087/80287/80387)

Category: Data-Transfer Instructions

Use this instruction to push the source operand on the stack. It affects the DE and IE status bits.

Load Value of 1.0 (FLD1) (8087/80287/80387)

Category: Constant Instructions

This instruction pushes the constant 1.0 on the stack. It affects the IE status bit.

Load a Control Word (FLDCW) (8087/80287/80387)

Category: Processor-Control Instructions

Use this instruction to load the control word with the value pointed to by the source operand. This instruction does not affect any status bits.

Load the Environment (FLDENV) (8087/80287/80387)

Category: Processor-Control Instructions

The load the environment instruction restores all the environment variables from the 14-word memory location pointed to by the source operand. It affects all the status bits.

Load Value of $\log_2 e$ (FLDL2E) (8087/80287/80387)

Category: Constant Instructions

This instruction pushes the value of $\log_2 e$ onto the stack. It affects the IE status bit.

Load Value of $\log_2 10$ (FLDL2T) (8087/80287/80387)

Category: Constant Instructions

This instruction pushes the value of $\log_2 10$ onto the stack. It affects the IE status bit.

Load Value of $\log_{10} 2$ (FLDLG2) (8087/80287/80387)

Category: Constant Instructions

This instruction pushes the value of $\log_{10} 2$ onto the stack. It affects the IE status bit.

Load Value of $\log_e 2$ (FLDLN2) (8087/80287/80387)

Category: Constant Instructions

This instruction pushes the value of $\log_e 2$ onto the stack. It affects the IE status bit.

Load Value of Pi (FLDPI) (8087/80287/80387)

Category: Constant Instructions

This instruction pushes the value of Pi onto the stack. It affects the IE status bit.

Load Value of 0.0 (FLDZ) (8087/80287/80387)

Category: Constant Instructions

This instruction pushes 0 onto the stack. It affects the IE status bit.

Multiply Real (FMUL) (8087/80287/80387)

Category: Arithmetic Instructions

This instruction multiplies the source by the destination operand. It stores the result in the destination operand. The instruction assumes a default stack destination. The multiply real instruction affects the PE, UE, OE, DE, and IE status bits.

Multiply Real and Pop (FMULP) (8087/80287/80387)

Category: Arithmetic Instructions

This instruction multiplies the source by the destination operand. It stores the result in the destination operand, then pops the stack. The instruction assumes a default stack destination. The multiply real instruction affects the PE, UE, OE, DE, and IE status bits.

Clear Exceptions (FNCLEX) (8087/80287/80387)

Category: Processor-Control Instructions

Use this instruction to clear the exception flags, interrupt request, and busy flags of the status word without using a CPU wait prefix. It affects the B, IR, PE, UE, OE, ZE, DE, and IE status bits.

Disable Interrupts (FNDISI) (8087 Only)

Category: Processor-Control Instructions

This instruction sets the interrupt enable mask of the control word without using a CPU wait prefix. It prevents the co-processor from issuing interrupts. The disable interrupts instruction does not affect any status bits.

Enable Interrupts (FNENI) (8087 Only)

Category: Processor-Control Instructions

This instruction clears the interrupt enable mask of the control word without using a CPU wait prefix. It enables the co-processor to issue interrupts. The disable interrupts instruction does not affect any status bits.

Initialize Processor (FNINIT) (8087/80287/80387)

Category: Processor-Control Instructions

This instruction initializes the math co-processor without issuing a CPU wait prefix. It is functionally equivalent to a hardware reset.

No Operation (FNOP) (8087/80287/80387)

Category: Processor-Control Instructions

This instruction tells the CPU to do nothing. This instruction does not affect the status bits.

Save State (FNSAVE) (8087/80287/80387)

Category: Processor-Control Instructions

This instruction saves the contents of all math co-processor registers and environment variables, without issuing a CPU wait, to the place pointed to by the destination operand. It requires 94 words of memory per save for an 8087 math co-processor. The instruction then issues the equivalent of an FNINIT instruction.

Store Control Word (FNSTCW) (8087/80287/80387)

Category: Processor-Control Instructions

This instruction copies the control word to the place pointed to by the destination operand without using a CPU wait prefix. It does not affect any status bits.

Store Environment (FNSTENV) (8087/80287/80387)

Category: Processor-Control Instructions

This instruction copies the environment variable to the place pointed to by the destination operand without using a CPU wait prefix. The store requires 14 words when using an 8087 math co-processor. It does not affect any status bits.

Store Status Word (FNSTSW) (8087/80287/80387)

Category: Processor-Control Instructions

This instruction copies the status word to the place pointed to by the destination operand without using a CPU wait prefix. It does not affect any status bits.

Partial Arctangent (FPATAN) (8087/80287/80387)

Category: Transcendental Instructions

This instruction computes $\Theta = $ ARCTAN (Y/X) when X is the top stack element and Y is the second stack element. It pops both stack elements and places the result on the stack. This instruction performs no input number validation. It affects the PE and UE status bits.

Partial Remainder (FPREM) (8087/80287/80387)

Category: Arithmetic Instructions

The partial arctangent instruction calculates the modulo of the top two stack elements. It performs this by successively subtracting the second element from the first. The calculated remainder remains in the first element. The instruction affects the C0, C1, C3, UE, DE, and IE status bits.

Partial Tangent (FPTAN) (8087/80287/80387)

Category: Transcendental Instructions

This instruction computes $Y/X = TAN (\Theta)$ where Θ is the top stack element. The instruction replaces the top stack element with Y, then pushes the computed X. This instruction performs no input value checking. It affects the PE and IE status bits.

Round to an Integer (FRNDINT) (8087/80287/80387)

Category: Arithmetic Instructions

This instruction rounds the number located on the top stack element to an integer. It affects the PE and IE status bits.

Restore State (FRSTOR) (8087/80287/80387)

Category: Processor-Control Instructions

This instruction restores the state of all registers and environment variables from the location pointed to by the destination operand. It affects all the status bits.

Save State with Wait (FSAVE) (8087/80287/80387)

Category: Processor-Control Instructions

This instruction saves the contents of all math co-processor registers and environment variables to the place pointed to by the destination operand. It uses the CPU wait prefix and requires 94 words of memory per save for an 8087 math co-processor. The instruction then issues the equivalent of an FINIT instruction.

Scale (FSCALE) (8087/80287/80387)

Category: Arithmetic Instructions

Use this instruction to calculate the value of $X = X * 2^Y$, where X is the value of the top stack element, and Y is the second stack element. This instruction affects the UE, OE, and IE status bits.

Square Root (FSQRT) (8087/80287/80387)

Category: Arithmetic Instructions

Use this instruction to calculate the square root of the top stack element. The square root value replaces the old stack value. This instruction affects the PE, DE, and IE status bits.

Store Real (FST) (8087/80287/80387)

Category: Data-Transfer Instructions

The store real instruction copies the top stack element value to the position pointed to by the destination operand. This instruction affects the PE, UE, OE, and IE status bits.

Store Control Word with Wait (FSTCW) (8087/80287/80387)

Category: Processor-Control Instructions

This instruction copies the control word to the place pointed to by the destination operand using a CPU wait prefix. It does not affect any status bits.

Store Environment with Wait (FSTENV) (8087/80287/80387)

Category: Processor-Control Instructions

This instruction copies the environment variable to the place pointed to by the destination operand using a CPU wait prefix. The store requires 14 words when using an 8087 math co-processor. It does not affect any status bits.

Store Real and Pop (FSTP) (8087/80287/80387)

Category: Data-Transfer Instructions

The store real instruction copies the top stack element value to the position pointed to by the destination operand. It pops the stack after transferring the value. This instruction affects the PE, UE, OE, and IE status bits.

Store Status Word with Wait (FSTSW) (8087/80287/80387)

Category: Processor-Control Instructions

This instruction copies the status word to the place pointed to by the destination operand using a CPU wait prefix. It does not affect any status bits.

Subtract Real (FSUB) (8087/80287/80387)

Category: Arithmetic Instructions

This instruction subtracts the source from the destination operand and places the result in the destination. The instruction assumes a default destination of stack. It affects the PE, UE, OE, DE, and IE status bits.

Subtract Real and Pop (FSUBP) (8087/80287/80387)

Category: Arithmetic Instructions

This instruction subtracts the source from the destination operand and places the result in the destination. Upon instruction completion, it pops the stack. The instruction assumes a default destination of stack. It affects the PE, UE, OE, DE, and IE status bits.

Subtract Real Reversed (FSUBR) (8087/80287/80387)

Category: Arithmetic Instructions

This instruction subtracts the destination from the source operand and places the result in the destination. The instruction assumes a default destination of stack. It affects the PE, UE, OE, DE, and IE status bits.

Subtract Real Reversed and Pop (FSUBRP) (8087/80287/80387)

Category: Arithmetic Instructions

This instruction subtracts the destination from the source operand and places the result in the destination. It pops the stack upon instruction completion. The instruction assumes a default destination of stack. It affects the PE, UE, OE, DE, and IE status bits.

Test (FTST) (8087/80287/80387)

Category: Comparison Instructions

This instruction compares the top stack element with zero and sets the status bits accordingly. It affects the C0, C2, C3, DE, and IE status bits.

CPU Wait (FWAIT) (8087/80287/80387)

Category: Processor-Control Instructions

The CPU wait instruction performs essentially the same function for the math co-processor as it does for the main processor. This permits synchronization of both processors. The main processor suspends operations until the co-processor completes its activities.

Examine (FXAM) (8087/80287/80387)

Category: Comparison Instructions

This instruction examines the top stack element and updates the status bits to reflect its condition. The examine instruction affects the C0, C1, C2, and C3 status bits.

Exchange Registers (FXCH) (8087/80287/80387)

Category: Data-Transfer Instructions

This instruction switches the value contained in the top stack element with the destination operand. It only affects the IE status bit.

Extract Exponent and Significand (FXTRACT) (8087/80287/80387)

Category: Arithmetic Instructions

This instruction pops the top stack element, separates the exponent from the significand, and pushes both values on the stack. It affects only the IE status bit.

Value of Y * log$_2$ X (FYL2X) (8087/80287/80387)

Category: Transcendental Instructions

This instruction calculates the value of $Z = Y * \log_2 X$, where X is the top stack element and Y is the second stack element. The instruction pops both stack elements and pushes the new value, Z, onto the stack. This instruction does not validate the input values. It affects the PE status bit.

Value of Y * log$_2$ (X + 1) (FYL2XP1) (8087/80287/80387)

Category: Transcendental Instructions

This instruction calculates the value of $Z = Y * \log_2 (X + 1)$, where X is the top stack element and Y is the second stack element. The instruction pops both stack elements and pushes the new value, Z, onto the stack. This instruction does not validate the input values. It affects the PE status bit.

80286 COMMAND ADDITIONS

The paragraphs below describe the commands available to the 80286 processor in addition to the standard 8086/8088 instruction set. See TABLE 4-1 for a listing of 8086/8088 processor instruction by functional area. TABLE 4-3 lists all the additional 80286 processor commands by functional area. The table includes the page number of the instruction description. Figure 4-6 shows a mixture of 80286-specific commands used in an assembly language program. There are no listings for BASIC, C and Pascal because it is impossible to see the processor commands using these languages.

The flags used for various instructions below include the following.

- Nested Task (NT)
- Input/Output Privilege Level (IOPL)

- Overflow (OF)
- Direction (DF)
- Interrupt (IF)
- Trap (TF)
- Sign (SF)
- Zero (ZF)
- Auxiliary Carry (AF)
- Parity (PF)
- Carry (CF)

4-6 Sample program 6 source code listing.

```
;***********************************************************************************************
;* Sample Program 6, 80286 Instruction Demonstration            *
;* This is the second half of a two part program showing you how to create a stack frame using the Enter and    *
;* Leave instructions. With an 8088/8086 processor, you must perform a two step process to create a stack    *
;* frame and a single step process to destroy it. With an 80286 you can use these two single step     *
;* instructions to quickly create a stack frame. Both instructions use fewer clock cycles than their    *
;* 8088/8086 counterparts. To use this program you need the following special equipment:         *
;*      80286 equipped computer            *
;* Copyright 1989 John Mueller & Wallace Wang - Tab Books *
;***********************************************************************************************


;***********************************************************************************************
;* Perform the program setup.                   *
;***********************************************************************************************

.MODEL SMALL    ; Use a medum model size.

.286P   ; Use the correct processor instruction set.


;***********************************************************************************************
;* Begin the data area.  Declare all variables.        *
;***********************************************************************************************
.DATA

LF      EQU     10
CR      EQU     13
StrEnd  EQU     36
Message1        DB      24 DUP(' '),"┌───────────────────────────┐",LF,CR
        DB      24 DUP(' '),"│ This is the Assembly Message │",LF,CR
        DB      24 DUP(' '),"└───────────────────────────┘",LF,CR,StrEnd
Message2        DB      28 DUP(' '),"┌──────────────────────┐",LF,CR
        DB      28 DUP(' '),"│ This is the C Message │",LF,CR
        DB      28 DUP(' '),"└──────────────────────┘",LF,CR,StrEnd


;***********************************************************************************************
;* Begin the code segment.               *
;***********************************************************************************************
.CODE
```

4-6 Continued.

```
PUBLIC  _Example

_Example      PROC    NEAR

      ENTER   512,0   ;Allocate 512 stack, level 0.
      PUSHA           ;Save all the registers.
      MOV     AX,[BP+4]       ;Retrieve the passed value and
      CMP     AX,1    ; display appropriate string.
      JNE     Do2     ;Progrm selected string 2.
      LEA     DX,Message1     ;Load the address of string 1
      JMP     Display ; and jump to interrupt.
Do2:  LEA     DX,Message2     ;Load the address of string 2.
Display:      MOV     AX,0900h        ;Display the message.
      INT     21h
      POPA            ;Restore all the registers.
      LEAVE           ;Deallocate stack frame.

      RET             ;Return to calling program.

_Example      ENDP
END
```

Adjust RPL Field of Selector (ARPL)

Category: Bit-Manipulation Instructions

Use this instruction to compare the two RPL bits (bits 0 and 1) of the first operand with those in the second. If the RPL bits of the first operand are less than those of the second, the instruction sets the first operand's RPL bits equal to those of the second. The adjust RPL field of selector instruction affects ZF only. It then sets ZF. Otherwise, this instruction clears ZF. The instruction logic appears below.

First_Operand_RPL & Second_Operand_RPL
If First_Operand_RPL < Second_Operand_RPL then
First_Operand_RPL = Second_Operand_RPL
ZF = 1
else
ZF = 0

Check Array Index Against Bounds (BOUND)

Category: Flag- and Processor-Control Instructions

This instruction compares the signed value of the first operand against the values pointed to by the second operand. The word at the second word is the lower boundary. The word after the second word is the upper boundary. This instruction generates an interrupt 5 whenever the first operand falls outside of either boundary. The bound instruction affects none of the flags. Its logic appears below.

```
If First_Operand < Second_Operand then
SP = SP – 2
SP + 1:SP = Flags
IF = 0
TF = 0
SP = SP – 2
SP + 1:SP = CS
CS = 22
SP = SP – 2
SP + 1:SP = IP
IP = 20
If First_Operand > Word_After_Second_Operand then
SP = SP – 2
SP + 1:SP = Flags
IF = 0
TF = 0
SP = SP – 2
SP + 1:SP = CS
CS = 22
SP = SP – 2
SP + 1:SP = IP
IP = 20
```

Clear the Task Switched Flag (CLTS)

Category: Flag- and Processor-Control Instructions

This instruction (normally used in operating systems) clears the task switched flag of the machine register.

Make Stack Frame for Procedure Parameters (ENTER)

Category: Flag- and Processor-Control Instructions

Use this instruction to modify the stack for entry into a high-level language. The first operand specifies the number of stack storage bytes to allocate. The second operand indicates the routine nesting level. This instruction does not modify any of the flags. The instruction logic appears below.

```
SP = SP – 2
SP + 1:SP = BP
FP = SP
If Level > 0 then
    Repeat (Level – 1) Times
        BP = BP – 2
        SP = SP – 2
        SP + 1:SP = BP
```

```
        End Repeat
        SP = SP – 2
        SP + 1:SP = FP
     End If
     BP = FP
     SP = SP – Storage_Allocation
```

Input String from Port (INS)

Category: Data-Transfer Instructions

This instruction allows string input from a port to the destination operand. Use the DX register to specify the port number and the DI register to specify destination. The instruction automatically switches between word or byte to accommodate the size of the destination operand. This instruction does not affect the flags. The input string from port instruction logic appears below.

```
     Destination = Source
```

Input String Byte from Port (INSB)

Category: Data-Transfer Instructions

This instruction allows byte input from a port to the destination operand. Use the DX register to specify the port number and the DI register to specify destination. This instruction does not affect the flags. The input instruction logic appears below.

```
     Destination = Source
     If DF = 0 then
     DI = DI + 1
     else
     DI = DI – 1
```

Input String Word from Port (INSW)

Category: Data-Transfer Instructions

This instruction allows word input from a port to the destination operand. Use the DX register to specify the port number and the DI register to specify destination. This instruction does not affect the flags. The input instruction logic appears below.

```
     Destination = Source
     If DF = 0 then
     DI = DI + 2
     else
     DI = DI – 2
```

Load Access-Rights Byte (LAR)

Category: Data-Transfer Instructions

This instruction overwrites the high byte of the destination with the access-rights byte and zeroes the low byte. The instruction operates only when the descriptor appears at the current privilege level and at the selector RPL. The instruction sets ZF when successful.

High-Level Procedure Exit (LEAVE)

Category: Flag- and Processor-Control Instructions

Use this instruction when leaving a high-level language procedure to reverse the effects of the ENTER instruction. It deallocates all variables, then restores SP and BP to their original state. This instruction does not affect any flags. The instruction logic appears below.

```
SP  = BP
BP  = SP + 1:SP
SP  = SP + 2
```

Load Global Descriptor Table Register (LGDT)

Category: Data-Transfer Instructions

Use this instruction to load the global descriptor table from the memory address operand specified. The global descriptor table is six bytes long. Normally this instruction appears in protected mode operating system software only. It does not affect any registers. The instruction logic appears below.

```
Global_Desc_Table [1] = Memory_Address_Operand [1]
Global_Desc_Table [2] = Memory_Address_Operand [2]
Global_Desc_Table [3] = Memory_Address_Operand [3]
Global_Desc_Table [4] = Memory_Address_Operand [4]
Global_Desc_Table [5] = Memory_Address_Operand [5]
Global_Desc_Table [6] = Memory_Address_Operand [6]
```

Load Interrupt Descriptor Table Register (LIDT)

Category: Data-Transfer Instructions

Use this instruction to load the interrupt descriptor table from the memory address operand specified. The interrupt descriptor table is six bytes long. Normally this instruction appears in protected mode operating system software only. It does not affect any registers. The instruction logic appears below.

```
Int_Desc_Table [1] = Memory_Address_Operand [1]
Int_Desc_Table [2] = Memory_Address_Operand [2]
Int_Desc_Table [3] = Memory_Address_Operand [3]
```

Int_Desc_Table [4] = Memory_Address_Operand [4]
Int_Desc_Table [5] = Memory_Address_Operand [5]
Int_Desc_Table [6] = Memory_Address_Operand [6]

Load Local Descriptor Table Register (LLDT)

Category: Data-Transfer Instructions

Use this instruction to transfer the global descriptor table to the local descriptor table based on the current selector. Normally this instruction appears in protected mode operating system software only. It does not affect any registers. The instruction logic appears below.

Global_Desc_Table [1] = Local_Desc_Table [1]
Global_Desc_Table [2] = Local_Desc_Table [2]
Global_Desc_Table [3] = Local_Desc_Table [3]
Global_Desc_Table [4] = Local_Desc_Table [4]
Global_Desc_Table [5] = Local_Desc_Table [5]
Global_Desc_Table [6] = Local_Desc_Table [6]

Load Machine Status Word (LMSW)

Category: Data-Transfer Instructions

The load machine status word instruction transfers the value of the operand to the machine status word. Normally this instruction appears in operating system software only. It does not affect any registers.

Load Segment Limit (LSL)

Category: Data-Transfer Instructions

This instruction loads the descriptor's limit field (if present) into the destination operand based on the selector specified in the source operand. When successful, the instruction sets ZF; otherwise, it clears ZF.

Load Task Register (LTR)

Category: Data-Transfer Instructions

Use this instruction to load the task register with the value contained in the source operand. Normally this instruction appears in operating system software only. It does not affect any registers.

Output String to Port (OUTS)

Category: Data-Transfer Instructions

This instruction allows string output to a port from the source operand. Use the DX register to specify the port number and the SI register to specify source. The instruction automatically switches between word or byte to accommodate the size of the destination operand. This instruction does not affect the flags. The output string to port instruction logic appears below.

Destination = Source

Output String Byte to Port (OUTSB)

Category: Data-Transfer Instructions
This instruction allows byte output to a port from the source operand. Use the DX register to specify the port number and the SI register to specify source. This instruction does not affect the flags. The output string to port instruction logic appears below.

Destination = Source
If DF = 0 then
SI = SI + 1
else
SI = SI - 1

Output String Word to Port (OUTSW)

Category: Data-Transfer Instructions
This instruction allows byte output to a port from the source operand. Use the DX register to specify the port number and the SI register to specify source. This instruction does not affect the flags. The output string to port instruction logic appears below.

Destination = Source
If DF = 0 then
SI = SI + 2
else
SI = SI - 2

Pop All General Registers (POPA)

Category: Data-Transfer Instructions
POPA removes the general-purpose registers from the stack and discards the SP value. It then increments SP by 16. The logic for the POPA instruction appears below.

DI = SP + 1:SP
SP = SP + 2
SI = SP + 1:SP
SP = SP + 2
BP = SP + 1:SP
SP = SP + 2
SP = SP + 1:SP

```
SP  = SP + 2
BX  = SP + 1:SP
SP  = SP + 2
DX  = SP + 1:SP
SP  = SP + 2
CX  = SP + 1:SP
SP  = SP + 2
AX  = SP + 1:SP
SP  = SP + 2
```

Push All General Registers (PUSHA)

Category: Data-Transfer Instructions

PUSHA decrements SP by 2 for each value pushed. It then adds the register contents to the location pointed to by the stack pointer (SP). The SP value pushed equals SP before instruction execution begins. The logic for the PUSHA instruction appears below.

```
SP = SP − 2
SP + 1:SP = AX
SP = SP − 2
SP + 1:SP = CX
SP = SP − 2
SP + 1:SP = DX
SP = SP − 2
SP + 1:SP = BX
SP = SP − 2
SP + 1:SP = SP
SP = SP − 2
SP + 1:SP = BP
SP = SP − 2
SP + 1:SP = SI
SP = SP − 2
SP + 1:SP = DI
```

Store Global Descriptor Table Register (SGDT)

Category: Data-Transfer Instructions

Use this instruction to transfer the six bytes of the global descriptor table to the memory address operand. Normally this instruction appears in protected mode operating system software only. It does not affect any registers. The instruction logic appears below.

```
Memory_Address_Operand [1] = Global_Desc_Table [1]
Memory_Address_Operand [2] = Global_Desc_Table [2]
Memory_Address_Operand [3] = Global_Desc_Table [3]
Memory_Address_Operand [4] = Global_Desc_Table [4]
```

Memory_Address_Operand [5] = Global_Desc_Table [5]
Memory_Address_Operand [6] = Global_Desc_Table [6]

Store Interrupt Descriptor Table Register (SIDT)

Category: Data-Transfer Instructions

Use this instruction to transfer the six bytes of the interrupt descriptor table to the memory address operand. Normally this instruction appears in protected mode operating system software only. It does not affect any registers. The instruction logic appears below.

Memory_Address_Operand [1] = Int_Desc_Table [1]
Memory_Address_Operand [2] = Int_Desc_Table [2]
Memory_Address_Operand [3] = Int_Desc_Table [3]
Memory_Address_Operand [4] = Int_Desc_Table [4]
Memory_Address_Operand [5] = Int_Desc_Table [5]
Memory_Address_Operand [6] = Int_Desc_Table [6]

Store Local Descriptor Table Register (SLDT)

Category: Data-Transfer Instructions

Use this instruction to transfer the two bytes of the local descriptor table to the memory address operand. Normally this instruction appears in protected mode operating system software only. It does not affect any registers. The instruction logic appears below.

Memory_Address_Operand [1] = Local_Desc_Table [1]
Memory_Address_Operand [2] = Local_Desc_Table [2]

Store Machine Status Word (SMSW)

Category: Data-Transfer Instructions

Use this instruction to transfer the machine status word to the operand. Normally this instruction appears in operating system software only. It does not affect any registers.

Store Task Register (STR)

Category: Data-Transfer Instructions

Use this instruction to transfer the task register contents to the operand. Normally this instruction appears in operating system software only. It does not affect any registers.

Verify a Segment for Reading (VERR)

Category: Flag- and Processor-Control Instructions

Use this instruction to determine if the selector specified by the operand appears at the current privilege level and is readable. The instruction sets ZF for accessible selectors.

Verify a Segment for Writing (VERW)

Category: Flag- and Processor-Control Instructions

Use this instruction to determine if the selector specified by the operand appears at the current privilege level and is writeable. The instruction sets ZF for accessible selectors.

80287 COMMAND ADDITIONS

The paragraph below explains the only 80287 math co-processor specific command. In addition to the command below, the 80287 math co-processor uses many of the 8087 commands. TABLE 4-2 lists all the co-processor commands by functional area. The table includes the page number of the instruction description. Figure 4-3 contains an assembly language program showing the 80287 command addition. There are no listings for BASIC, C and Pascal because it is impossible to see the co-processor commands using these languages. The language implements the co-processor automatically (when detected).

The 8087/80287/80387 math co-processors do not use flags. Instead, they contain a status and control word. The status word indicates the current math co-processor condition. The control word affects math co-processor operation. The breakdown for both the control word and status word appears below.

Status Word (bit)

0	Invalid Operation Exception (IE)
1	Denormalized Operation Exception (DE)
2	Zero Divide Exception (ZE)
3	Overflow Exception (OE)
4	Underflow Exception (UE)
5	Precision Exception (PE)
7	Error Summary Status (ES)
8	Condition Code 0 (C0)
9	Condition Code 1 (C1)
10	Condition Code 2 (C2)
11–13	Stack Top Pointer (ST)
14	Condition Code 3 (C3)
15	Busy Signal (B)

Control Word (bit)

0	Invalid Operation Exception Mask (IM)
1	Denormalized Operation Exception Mask (DM)
2	Zero Divide Exception Mask (ZM)
3	Overflow Exception Mask (OM)

4	Underflow Exception Mask (UM)
5	Precision Exception Mask (PM)
8–9	Precision Control (PC); 00 = 24 bits, 01 = (Reserved), 10 = 53 bits, 11 = 64 bits
10–11	Rounding Control (RC); 00 = Round to Nearest or Even, 01 = Round Down, 10 = Round Up, 11 = Truncate
12	Infinity Control (IC); 0 = Projective, 1 = Affine
13–15	Reserved

Each math co-processor contains 8 stack elements 80 bits long. Each element uses a floating point format consisting of 64 significand bits, 15 exponent bits, and 1 sign bit. The co-processors use these stack elements for most math operations.

Set Protected Mode (FSETPM) (80287 Only)

Category: Processor-Control Instructions

This instruction sets the 80287 to protected mode operation.

80386 COMMAND ADDITIONS

The paragraphs below describe the commands available to the 80386 processor in addition to the standard 8086/8088/80286 instruction set. See TABLE 4-1 for a listing of 8086/8088 processor instructions and TABLE 4-3 for a listing of 80286 processor instructions listed by functional area. TABLE 4-4 lists all the additional 80386 processor commands by functional area. The table includes the page number of the instruction description. Figure 4-7 shows a mixture of 80386-specific commands used in an assembly language program. There are no listings for BASIC, C and Pascal because it is impossible to see the processor commands using these languages.

The 80386 flag register is 32-bits wide. The 80386 chip reserves the upper 14 bits. The flags used for various instructions below include the following.

- Virtual Mode (VM)
- Resume (R)
- Nested Task (NT)
- Input/Output Privilege Level (IOPL)
- Overflow (OF)
- Direction (DF)
- Interrupt (IF)
- Trap (TF)
- Sign (SF)
- Zero (ZF)
- Auxiliary Carry (AF)
- Parity (PF)
- Carry (CF)

4-7 Sample program 7 source code listing.

```
;**********************************************************************************************
;* Sample Program 7, 80386 Instruction Demonstration              *
;* This program allows you to scan an ASCII file for a particular string.  If it finds the string, the  *
;* program displays the position.  Otherwise, it exits with a "String Not Found" message.  You must provide    *
;* a search string of at least 6 characters to use this program.  To use this program you need the following   *
;* special equipment:                          *
;*       80386 equipped computer              *
;* Copyright 1989 John Mueller & Wallace Wang - Tab Books *
;**********************************************************************************************


;**********************************************************************************************
;* Perform the program setup.                 *
;**********************************************************************************************

.MODEL MEDIUM   ; Use a medum model size.

.386P   ; Use the correct processor instruction set.

.STACK  ; Use the defalt stack of 1024 bytes.

;**********************************************************************************************
;* Begin the data area.  Declare all variables.           *
;**********************************************************************************************
.DATA

Beep     EQU    07
BS       EQU    08
LF       EQU    10
CR       EQU    13
Space    EQU    32
StrEnd   EQU    36
Buffer   DD     1024 DUP ('    ')
FileName        DB     12 DUP (' '),0
Handle   DW     0
InString        LABEL  BYTE
SearchStr       DD     20 DUP ('    ')
ErrMsg1 DB      Beep,'String Not Found',LF,CR,StrEnd
ErrMsg2 DB      Beep,'File Not In Current Directory',LF,CR,StrEnd
ErrMsg3 DB      Beep,'Could not open file:       ',LF,CR,StrEnd
ErrMsg4 DB      Beep,'File empty:          ',LF,CR,StrEnd
ErrMsg5 DB      Beep,'Search string not found in:  ',LF,CR,StrEnd
ErrMsg6 DB      Beep,'Search string not found.',LF,CR,StrEnd
Msg1     DB     'Type a filename and extension: ',StrEnd
Msg2     DB     LF,CR,'Type up to an 80 character search'
         DB     ' string:',LF,CR,StrEnd
Msg3     DB     'Press any key when ready...',StrEnd
StrLen  DW      0


;**********************************************************************************************
;* Begin the code segment.                    *
;**********************************************************************************************
```

```
.CODE

Example PROC    FAR
Start:  PUSH    DS      ;Save the original data segment.
        XOR     AX,AX
        PUSH    AX

        MOV     AX,@DATA        ;Point DS & ES to our data segment.
        MOV     DS,AX
        MOV     ES,AX


;*********************************************************************************************
;* This section of the program performs the individual checks required to open the file, search for the *
;* string, and display the file on screen.  If the program fails to perform any of these steps, it displays    *
;* an error message and exits to the DOS prompt.                         *
;*********************************************************************************************

        MOV     AX,0619h        ;Clear the screen.
        MOV     BH,7
        XOR     CX,CX
        MOV     DX,1950h
        INT     10h

        MOV     AX,0200h        ;Position the cursor
        XOR     BX,BX   ; at row 0, column 0.
        XOR     DX,DX
        INT     10h

        CALL    OpenFile        ;Open the file.
        CMP     AX,0    ;Look for error code.
        JE      GoodFile        ;If no error, go to next step.
        JMP     Exit    ;Otherwise, exit program.

GoodFile:       CALL    ReadFile        ;Read 4000 bytes.
        CMP     AX,0    ;See if file contained any
        JNE     ChkBuf  ; data.  If so, scan it.
        MOV     AX,0900h        ;Otherwise, display an error
        LEA     DX,ErrMsg4      ; message.
        INT     21h
        JMP     Exit

ChkBuf: CALL    ScanData        ;Search for user string.
        CMP     AX,0    ;If no error, display the file
        JE      DispBuf ; on screen.
        JMP     Exit    ;Otherwise, exit program.

DispBuf:        CALL    DispFile        ;Display the file.

Exit:   RET

Example ENDP
```

4-7 Continued.

```
;*********************************************************************************************************
;* This procedure obtains the filename, determines if the file exists, and either exits with an error message   *
;* or opens the file for use.                              *
;*********************************************************************************************************

OpenFile      PROC    NEAR

        MOV     AX,0900h        ;Display the input message.
        LEA     DX,Msg1
        INT     21h

        LEA     SI,FileName     ;Load file variable address.
        MOV     CX,12   ;Maximum number of input chars.
Input1: MOV     AX,0100h        ;Get user input.
        INT     21h
        CMP     AL,CR   ;See if user pressed enter.
        JE      EInput1 ;If so, exit loop.
        CMP     AL,BS   ;See if user pressed backspace.
        JNE     Input1A ;If not, add character
        INC     CX      ;Restore CX.
        DEC     SI      ;Restore SI.
        MOV     BYTE PTR [SI],Space     ;Place space in string.
        MOV     AX,0A20h        ;Write space to screen.
        XOR     BX,BX
        PUSH    CX      ;Save CX then input number
        MOV     CX,1    ; of characters to display.
        INT     10h
        POP     CX
        JMP     Input1  ;Get the next character.
Input1A:        MOV     [SI],AL ;Store the character.
        INC     SI      ;Point to the next position.
        LOOP    Input1  ;Get the next character.

EInput1:        MOV     AX,4E00h        ;See if the file exists.
        MOV     CX,0007h
        LEA     DX,FileName
        INT     21h
        JNC     Open1   ;If it exists, open file.
        LEA     DX,ErrMsg2      ;If not, display an error
        MOV     AX,0900h        ; message.
        INT     21h
        MOV     AX,1    ;Place error code in AX.
        RET

Open1:  MOV     AX,3D00h        ;Open file for reading.
        LEA     DX,FileName
        INT     21h
        JNC     FileOpen        ;If DOS opened it, exit.
        LEA     DX,ErrMsg3      ;If not, display an error
        MOV     AX,0900h        ; message.
        INT     21h
```

```
        MOV     AX,1        ;Place error code in AX.
        JMP     Exit2

FileOpen:   MOV     Handle,AX       ;Save file handle.
        XOR     AX,AX   ;No Error.

Exit2:  RET

OpenFile        ENDP
```

```
;********************************************************************************************
;* This procedure reads the file 4096 bytes at a time (or any part of 4000 bytes).  If the file pointer is at   *
;* the end of file or the file does not contain any information, then the procedure returns an error code.      *
;********************************************************************************************

ReadFile        PROC    NEAR

        MOV     AX,3F00h
        MOV     BX,Handle
        MOV     CX,4096
        LEA     DX,Buffer
        INT     21h

        RET

ReadFile        ENDP
```

```
;********************************************************************************************
;* This procedure prompts the user for a search string and stores it in a variable.  The procedure then scans   *
;* the file buffer for the first character of the search string.  If it finds the first character,      *
;* the procedure completes the comparison four characters at a time until the search string contains less   *
;* than four characters.  If the program runs out of buffer to check, it loads more of the disk file into   *
;* the buffer.  The program displays an error message when it reaches end of file and the end of the buffer.    *
;********************************************************************************************

ScanData        PROC    NEAR

        MOV     AX,0900h        ;Prompt the user for a search
        LEA     DX,Msg2 ; string.
        INT     21h

        LEA     SI,InString     ;Load search string address.
        MOV     CX,80   ;Maximum number of input chars.
Input2: MOV     AX,0100h        ;Get user input.
        INT     21h
        CMP     AL,CR   ;See if user pressed enter.
        JE      EInput2 ;If so, exit loop.
        CMP     AL,BS   ;See if user pressed backspace.
        JNE     Input2A ;If not, add character
        INC     CX      ;Restore CX.
```

4-7 Continued.

```
        DEC     SI      ;Restore SI.
        MOV     BYTE PTR [SI],Space     ;Place space in string.
        MOV     AX,0A20h        ;Write space to screen.
        XOR     BX,BX
        PUSH    CX      ;Save CX then input number
        MOV     CX,1    ; of characters to display.
        INT     10h
        POP     CX
        JMP     Input2  ;Get the next character.
Input2A:        MOV     [SI],AL ;Store the character.
        INC     SI      ;Point to the next position.
        INC     StrLen  ;Increment the length counter.
        LOOP    Input2  ;Get the next character.

EInput2:        LEA     EDI,Buffer      ;Load the buffer address.
        MOV     ECX,4096        ;Load buffer size.
EInput3:        LEA     ESI,SearchStr   ;Load search string address.
        LODSB           ;Place first character in AL.
        REPNE   SCASB   ;Search for character.
        CMP     ECX,0   ;If found, finish comparison.
        JE      EInput4 ;Otherwise, exit.

        MOV     CX,StrLen       ;Load the string length.
        DEC     CX      ;Subtract 1 then divide by 4
        SHR     CX,2    ; to find number of DWORDS.
        REPE    CMPSD   ;Compare four characters at a time.

        XOR     AX,AX   ;Assume no error exists.
        CMP     CX,0    ;See if entire string matched.
        JE      Exit3   ;If so, exit.
        LEA     ECX,Buffer      ;Otherwise, see we are at the
        ADD     ECX,4096        ; end of the buffer.
        SUB     ECX,EDI
        CMP     ECX,0   ;If not, scan again.
        JNE     EInput3
EInput4:        CALL    ReadFile        ;See if we are at end of file.
        CMP     AX,0
        JNE     EInput2 ;If not, scan again.
        MOV     AX,0900h        ;Otherwise, display an error
        LEA     DX,ErrMsg6      ; message and exit program.
        INT     21h
        MOV     AX,1

Exit3:  RET

ScanData        ENDP
```

```
;******************************************************************************************************
;* This procedure clears the screen and displays the file starting at the position the program found the   *
;* search string.  It stops displaying the file when it reaches the end of the buffer or the bottom of the  *
;* screen.                              *
;******************************************************************************************************
```

```
DispFile          PROC    NEAR

        PUSHA             ;Save the registers.

        MOV     AX,0619h        ;Clear the screen.
        MOV     BH,7
        XOR     CX,CX
        MOV     DX,1950h
        INT     10h

        SUB     DI,StrLen       ;Move the file pointer to the
        DEC     DI      ; begining of search string.

        MOV     AX,0200h        ;Set the cursor position.
        XOR     BX,BX
        XOR     DX,DX
        INT     10h

Print1: MOV     AH,2    ;Print a character
        MOV     DL,[DI]
        INT     21h
        INC     DI      ;Move to next character.

        MOV     AH,3    ;Read cursor position.
        INT     10h
        CMP     DH,24   ;Last Row?
        JE      Exit4   ;If so, exit.
        JMP     Print1  ;Otherwise, print next char.

Exit4:  MOV     AH,9    ;Print exit message.
        LEA     DX,Msg3
        INT     21h
        XOR     AX,AX   ;Wait for keypress.
        INT     16h

        POPA              ;Restore the registers.

        RET

DispFile          ENDP

END     Start
```

Bit Scan Forward (BSF)

Category: Bit-Manipulation Instructions

    Use this instruction to scan the bits of the second operand (beginning at the low-order bit) for any set bits. If the instruction finds a set bit, it places the bit number in the first operand and clears ZF. If it does not find any set bits, it sets ZF and does nothing to the first operand.

Bit Scan Reverse (BSR)

Category: Bit-Manipulation Instructions

Use this instruction to scan the bits of the second operand (beginning at the high-order bit) for any set bits. If the instruction finds a set bit, it places the bit number in the first operand and clears ZF. If it does not find any set bits, it sets ZF and does nothing to the first operand.

Bit Test (BT)

Category: Bit-Manipulation Instructions

This instruction uses the value of the second operand as a bit index to the first operand. It copies the bit at the indexed position to the carry flag.

Bit Test and Complement (BTC)

Category: Bit-Manipulation Instructions

This instruction uses the value of the second operand as a bit index to the first operand. It copies the complement of the bit at the indexed position to the carry flag.

Bit Test and Reset (BTR)

Category: Bit-Manipulation Instructions

This instruction uses the value of the second operand as a bit index to the first operand. It copies the bit at the indexed position to the carry flag and clears the original bit.

Bit Test and Set (BTS)

Category: Bit-Manipulation Instructions

This instruction uses the value of the second operand as a bit index to the first operand. It copies the bit at the indexed position to the carry flag and sets the original bit.

Convert Doubleword to Quadword (CDQ)

Category: Arithmetic Instructions

Use this instruction to convert a doubleword value to a quadword value. It extends the sign-bit in EAX through EDX. The convert doubleword to quadword logic appears below.

If EAX < 8000000h then

```
EDX = 0
else
EDX = FFFFFFFFh
```

Compare Strings, Doubleword-by-Doubleword (CMPSD)

Category: String-Manipulation Instructions

This instruction changes the value of the AF, CF, OF, PF, SF, and ZF flags to show the relationship between two doublewords in a string. The results of the comparison do not affect the contents of either operand. After comparing the two string words, the instruction updates both ESI and EDI to point to the next string element. DF controls the direction of comparison. The compare strings, doubleword-by-doubleword logic appears below.

```
Flag_Values = Destination_String - Source_String
If DF = 0 then
ESI = ESI + 4
EDI = EDI + 4
else
ESI = ESI - 4
EDI = EDI - 4
```

Convert Word to Doubleword Extended (CWDE)

Category: Arithmetic Instructions

Use this instruction to convert a word value to a doubleword value. It extends the sign-bit in AX through EAX. The convert word to doubleword logic appears below.

```
If AX < 8000h then
EAX = 0000 + AX
else
EAX = FFFFh + AX
```

Input String Doubleword from Port (INSD)

Category: Data-Transfer Instructions

This instruction allows doubleword input from a port to the destination operand. Use the DX register to specify the port number and the EDI register to specify destination. This instruction does not affect the flags. The input instruction logic appears below.

```
Destination = Source
If DF = 0 then
```

```
EDI = EDI + 4
else
EDI = EDI - 4
```

Jump if ECX Equals Zero (JECXZ)

Category: Control-Transfer Instructions

This instruction transfers control to the instruction pointed to by IP + Displacement when ECX equals 0. The instruction logic appears below.

```
If ECX = 0 then
IP = IP + Displacement (Sign Extended to 16 bits)
```

Load the FS Register (LFS)

Category: Data-Transfer Instructions

This instruction transfers a 32-bit pointer from the source operand (memory only) to the destination operand (offset) and the FS register (segment). The destination operand is any 16-bit general-purpose register. The instruction logic appears below.

```
Register = Effective_Address
FS = Effective_Address + 2
```

Load the GS Register (LGS)

Category: Data-Transfer Instructions

This instruction transfers a 32-bit pointer from the source operand (memory only) to the destination operand (offset) and the GS register (segment). The destination operand is any 16-bit, general-purpose register. The instruction logic appears below.

```
Register = Effective_Address
GS = Effective_Address + 2
```

Load a Doubleword from String into EAX (LODSD)

Category: String-Manipulation Instructions

Use this instruction to transfer a doubleword from the string pointed to by ESI to EAX. The ESI register automatically advances to the next string element in the direction pointed to by the direction flag. The instruction logic appears below.

```
EAX = String_Element
If DF = 0 then
ESI = ESI + 4
else
ESI = ESI - 4
```

Load the SS Register (LSS)

Category: Data-Transfer Instructions

This instruction transfers a 32-bit pointer from the source operand (memory only) to the destination operand (offset) and the SS register (segment). The destination operand is any 16-bit, general-purpose register. The instruction logic appears below.

Register = Effective_Address
SS = Effective_Address + 2

Move String, Doubleword-by-Doubleword (MOVSD)

Category: String-Manipulation Instructions

This instruction moves the doubleword pointed to by ESI to the destination pointed to by EDI. Using the REP instruction with this instruction repeats the move the number of times shown in ECX. After each move, the instruction advances both ESI and EDI to the next position in the direction indicated by DF. The instruction logic appears below.

Destination = Source
EDI = EDI + 4
ESI = ESI + 4

Move with Sign Extended (MOVSX)

Category: Data-Transfer Instructions

Use this instruction to move data from a smaller to a larger operand. It extends the sign-bit of the second operand to fill the first operand.

Move with Zero Extended (MOVZX)

Category: Data-Transfer Instructions

Use this instruction to move data from a smaller to larger operand. It clears the bits in the first operand not filled by the second operand.

Output String Doubleword to Port (OUTSD)

Category: Data-Transfer Instructions

This instruction allows doubleword output to a port from the source operand. Use the EDX register to specify the port number and the ESI register to specify source. This instruction does not affect the flags. The output string to port instruction logic appears below.

Destination = Source
If DF = 0 then
ESI = ESI + 4

```
else
ESI = ESI – 4
```

Pop All General Doubleword Registers (POPAD)

Category: Data-Transfer Instructions

POPAD removes the extended general-purpose registers from the stack and discards the ESP value. It then increments ESP by 32. The logic for the POPAD instruction appears below.

```
EDI = ESP + 3:ESP + 2:ESP + 1:ESP
ESP = ESP + 4
ESI = ESP + 3:ESP + 2:ESP + 1:ESP
ESP = ESP + 4
EBP = ESP + ESP + 3:ESP + 2:1:ESP
ESP = ESP + 4
ESP = ESP + ESP + 3:ESP + 2:1:ESP
ESP = ESP + 4
EBX= ESP + 3:ESP + 2:ESP + 1:ESP
ESP = ESP + 4
EDX= ESP + 3:ESP + 2:ESP + 1:ESP
ESP = ESP + 4
ECX= ESP + 3:ESP + 2:ESP + 1:ESP
ESP = ESP + 4
EAX= ESP + 3:ESP + 2:ESP + 1:ESP
ESP = ESP + 4
```

Remove Extended Flags from Stack (POPFD)

Category: Data-Transfer Instructions

POPFD removes the two words pointed to by the stack pointer (ESP) and places it in the extended flag register. It then increments ESP by 4. The logic for the POPFD instruction appears below.

```
Flags = ESP + 3:ESP + 2:ESP + 1:ESP
ESP = ESP + 4
```

Push All General Doubleword Registers (PUSHAD)

Category: Data-Transfer Instructions

PUSHAD decrements ESP by 4 for each value pushed. It then adds the register contents to the location pointed to by the stack pointer (ESP). The ESP value pushed equals ESP before instruction execution begins. The logic for the PUSHAD instruction appears below.

```
ESP = ESP – 4
ESP + 3:ESP + 2:ESP + 1:ESP = EAX
```

ESP = ESP – 4
ESP + 3:ESP + 2:ESP + 1:ESP = ECX
ESP = ESP – 4
ESP + 3:ESP + 2:ESP + 1:ESP = EDX
ESP = ESP – 4
ESP + 3:ESP + 2:ESP + 1:ESP = EBX
ESP = ESP – 4
ESP + 3:ESP + 2:ESP + 1:ESP = ESP
ESP = ESP – 4
ESP + 3:ESP + 2:ESP + 1:ESP = EBP
ESP = ESP – 4
ESP + 3:ESP + 2:ESP + 1:ESP = ESI
ESP = ESP – 4
ESP + 3:ESP + 2:ESP + 1:ESP = EDI

Place Extended Flags on Stack (PUSHFD)

Category: Data-Transfer Instructions

PUSHF decrements ESP by 4. It then adds the extended flag register contents to the location pointed to by the stack pointer (ESP). The logic for the PUSHF instruction appears below.

ESP = ESP – 4
ESP + 3:ESP + 2:ESP + 1:ESP = Flags

Scan String for Doubleword (SCASD)

Category: String-Manipulation Instructions

Use this instruction with any of the repeat instructions to scan strings for the value contained in EAX. After each scan, EDI advances to point to the next string element. This instruction affects AF, CF, OF, PF, SF, and ZF. The instruction logic appears below.

EAX – Destination
If DF = 0 then
EDI = EDI + 4
else
EDI = EDI – 4

Set Byte if Above (SETA)

Category: Data-Transfer Instructions

This instruction checks the status of both CF and ZF. If both flags equal 0, then the instruction stores a 1 in the operand; otherwise, it stores a 0 in the operand.

Set Byte if Above or Equal (SETAE)

Category: Data-Transfer Instructions

This instruction checks the status of CF. If CF equals 0, then the instruction stores a 1 in the operand; otherwise, it stores a 0 in the operand.

Set Byte if Below (SETB)

Category: Data-Transfer Instructions

This instruction checks the status of CF. If CF equals 1, then the instruction stores a 1 in the operand; otherwise, it stores a 0 in the operand.

Set Byte if Below or Equal (SETBE)

Category: Data-Transfer Instructions

This instruction checks the status of CF and ZF. If CF or ZF equals 1, then the instruction stores a 1 in the operand; otherwise, it stores a 0 in the operand.

Set Byte on Carry (SETC)

Category: Data-Transfer Instructions

This instruction checks the status of CF. If CF equals 1, then the instruction stores a 1 in the operand; otherwise, it stores a 0 in the operand.

Set Byte if Equal (SETE)

Category: Data-Transfer Instructions

This instruction checks the status of ZF. If ZF equals 1, then the instruction stores a 1 in the operand; otherwise, it stores a 0 in the operand.

Set Byte if Greater Than (SETG)

Category: Data-Transfer Instructions

This instruction checks the status of ZF, SF and OF. If ZF equals 0 or SF equals OF, then the instruction stores a 1 in the operand; otherwise, it stores a 0 in the operand.

Set Byte if Greater Than or Equal (SETGE)

Category: Data-Transfer Instructions

This instruction checks the status of SF and OF. If SF equals OF, then the instruction stores a 1 in the operand; otherwise, it stores a 0 in the operand.

Set Byte if Less Than (SETL)

Category: Data-Transfer Instructions
This instruction checks the status of SF and OF. If SF does not equal OF, then the instruction stores a 1 in the operand; otherwise, it stores a 0 in the operand.

Set Byte if Less Than or Equal (SETLE)

Category: Data-Transfer Instructions
This instruction checks the status of ZF, SF and OF. If SF does not equal OF or ZF equals 1, then the instruction stores a 1 in the operand; otherwise, it stores a 0 in the operand.

Set Byte if Not Above (SETNA)

Category: Data-Transfer Instructions
This instruction checks the status of CF and ZF. If CF or ZF equals 1, then the instruction stores a 1 in the operand; otherwise, it stores a 0 in the operand.

Set Byte if Not Above or Equal (SETNAE)

Category: Data-Transfer Instructions
This instruction checks the status of CF. If CF equals 1, then the instruction stores a 1 in the operand; otherwise, it stores a 0 in the operand.

Set Byte if Not Below (SETNB)

Category: Data-Transfer Instructions
This instruction checks the status of CF. If CF equals 0, then the instruction stores a 1 in the operand; otherwise, it stores a 0 in the operand.

Set Byte if Not Below or Equal (SETNBE)

Category: Data-Transfer Instructions
This instruction checks the status of both CF and ZF. If both flags equal 0, then the instruction stores a 1 in the operand; otherwise, it stores a 0 in the operand.

Set Byte on No Carry (SETNC)

Category: Data-Transfer Instructions

This instruction checks the status of CF. If CF equals 0, then the instruction stores a 1 in the operand; otherwise, it stores a 0 in the operand.

Set Byte if Not Equal (SETNE)

Category: Data-Transfer Instructions

This instruction checks the status of ZF. If ZF equals 0, then the instruction stores a 1 in the operand; otherwise, it stores a 0 in the operand.

Set Byte if Not Greater Than (SETNG)

Category: Data-Transfer Instructions

This instruction checks the status of ZF, SF and OF. If SF does not equal OF or ZF equals 1, then the instruction stores a 1 in the operand; otherwise, it stores a 0 in the operand.

Set Byte if Not Greater Than or Equal (SETNGE)

Category: Data-Transfer Instructions

This instruction checks the status of SF and OF. If SF does not equal OF, then the instruction stores a 1 in the operand; otherwise, it stores a 0 in the operand.

Set Byte if Not Less Than (SETNL)

Category: Data-Transfer Instructions

This instruction checks the status of SF and OF. If SF equals OF, then the instruction stores a 1 in the operand; otherwise, it stores a 0 in the operand.

Set Byte if Not Less Than or Equal (SETNLE)

Category: Data-Transfer Instructions

This instruction checks the status of ZF, SF and OF. If ZF equals 0 or SF equals OF, then the instruction stores a 1 in the operand; otherwise, it stores a 0 in the operand.

Set Byte on No Overflow (SETNO)

Category: Data-Transfer Instructions

This instruction checks the status of OF. If OF equals 0, then the instruction stores a 1 in the operand; otherwise, it stores a 0 in the operand.

Set Byte on No Parity (SETNP)

Category: Data-Transfer Instructions
This instruction checks the status of PF. If PF equals 0, then the instruction stores a 1 in the operand; otherwise, it stores a 0 in the operand.

Set Byte on Not Sign (SETNS)

Category: Data-Transfer Instructions
This instruction checks the status of SF. If SF equals 0, then the instruction stores a 1 in the operand; otherwise, it stores a 0 in the operand.

Set Byte on Not Zero (SETNZ)

Category: Data-Transfer Instructions
This instruction checks the status of ZF. If ZF equals 0, then the instruction stores a 1 in the operand; otherwise, it stores a 0 in the operand.

Set Byte on Overflow (SETO)

Category: Data-Transfer Instructions
This instruction checks the status of OF. If OF equals 1, then the instruction stores a 1 in the operand; otherwise, it stores a 0 in the operand.

Set Byte on Parity (SETP)

Category: Data-Transfer Instructions
This instruction checks the status of PF. If PF equals 1, then the instruction stores a 1 in the operand; otherwise, it stores a 0 in the operand.

Set Byte on Parity Even (SETPE)

Category: Data-Transfer Instructions
This instruction checks the status of PF. If PF equals 1, then the instruction stores a 1 in the operand; otherwise, it stores a 0 in the operand.

Set Byte on Parity Odd (SETPO)

Category: Data-Transfer Instructions

This instruction checks the status of PF. If PF equals 0, then the instruction stores a 1 in the operand; otherwise, it stores a 0 in the operand.

Set Byte on Sign (SETS)

Category: Data-Transfer Instructions

This instruction checks the status of SF. If SF equals 1, then the instruction stores a 1 in the operand; otherwise, it stores a 0 in the operand.

Set Byte on Zero (SETZ)

Category: Data-Transfer Instructions

This instruction checks the status of ZF. If ZF equals 1, then the instruction stores a 1 in the operand; otherwise, it stores a 0 in the operand.

Shift Left, Double Precision (SHLD)

Category: Bit-Manipulation Instructions

The shift left double precision instruction shifts all bits in the first operand left the number of bits specified by the third operand. It loses high-order bits and copies low-order bits from the second operand starting at the second operand's low-order bit. This instruction affects CF, OF, PF, SF, ZF, and AF (undefined). The instruction logic appears below.

```
Temp = Count
Do While Temp < > 0
CF = First_High_Order_Bit
First = First * 2 + Second_Low_Order_Bit
Second = Second /2
(/ = Unsigned Division)
Temp = Temp – 1
If Count = 1 then
If First_High_Order_Bit < > CE then
OF = 1
else
OF = 0
else
OF = Undefined
```

Shift Right, Double Precision (SHRD)

Category: Bit-Manipulation Instructions

The shift right double precision instruction shifts all bits in the first operand right the number of bits specified by the third operand. It loses the low-order bits and copies the high-order bits from the second operand start and the second operand's high-order bit. This instruction affects CF, OF, PF, SF, ZF, and AF (undefined). The instruction logic appears below.

```
Temp = Count
Do While Temp < > 0
CF = First_Low_Order_Bit
First = First / 2 + Second_High_Order_Bit
(/ = Unsigned Division)
Second = Second * 2
Temp = Temp - 1
If Count = 1 then
If First_High_Order_Bit < > First_Next_To_High_Order_Bit then
OF = 1
else
OF = 0
else
OF = Undefined
```

Store Doubleword in EAX at String (STOSD)

Category: String-Manipulation Instructions

Use this instruction alone or with any repeat instruction to send a value in EAX to the string pointed at by EDI. EDI automatically advances to the next string location after each store operation. This instruction does not affect any flags. The instruction logic appears below.

```
Destination = EAX
If DF = 0 then
EDI = EDI + 4
else
EDI = EDI - 4
```

80387 COMMAND ADDITIONS

The paragraphs below explain the 80387 math co-processor specific commands. In addition to the commands below, the 80387 math co-processor uses many of the 8087 commands. It does not use any 80287 specific commands. TABLE 4-2 lists all the co-processor commands by functional area. The table includes the page number of the instruction description. Figure 4-4 contains assembly language examples of the 80387 command additions. There are no listings for BASIC, C and Pascal because it is impossible to see the co-processor commands using these languages. These languages provide library routines to use a co-processor automatically (when detected).

The 8087/80287/80387 math co-processors do not use flags. Instead, they contain a status and control word. The status word indicates the current math co-processor condition. The control word affects math co-processor operation. The breakdown for both the control word and status word appears below.

Status Word (bit)

0	Invalid Operation Exception (IE)
1	Denormalized Operation Exception (DE)
2	Zero Divide Exception (ZE)
3	Overflow Exception (OE)
4	Underflow Exception (UE)
5	Precision Exception (PE)
6	Stack Flag (SF); When SF = 1 and C0 = 0 then stack underflow. When SF = 1 and C0 = 1 then stack overflow.
7	Error Summary Status (ES)
8	Condition Code 0 (C0)
9	Condition Code 1 (C1)
10	Condition Code 2 (C2)
11 – 13	Stack Top Pointer (ST)
14	Condition Code 3 (C3)
15	Busy Signal (B)

Control Word (bit)

0	Invalid Operation Exception Mask (IM)
1	Denormalized Operation Exception Mask (DM)
2	Zero Divide Exception Mask (ZM)
3	Overflow Exception Mask (OM)
4	Underflow Exception Mask (UM)
5	Precision Exception Mask (PM)
8 – 9	Precision Control (PC); 00 = 24 bits, 01 = (Reserved), 10 = 53 bits, 11 = 64 bits
10 – 11	Rounding Control (RC); 00 = Round to Nearest or Even, 01 = Round Down, 10 = Round Up, 11 = Truncate
12	Infinity Control (IC); 0 = Projective, 1 = Affine
13 – 15	Reserved

Each math co-processor contains 8 stack elements 80 bits long. Each element uses a floating point format consisting of 64 significand bits, 15 exponent bits, and 1 sign bit. The co-processors use these stack elements for most math operations.

Cosine (FCOS) (80387 Only)

Category: Transcendental Instructions

This instruction computes $Y = COS(\Theta)$ where Θ is the top stack element. The instruction replaces the top stack element with Y. If Θ exceeds 26^3 then the instruction sets C2; otherwise, it clears C2. It affects the C2, PE and IE status bits.

IEEE Partial Remainder (FPREM1) (80387 Only)

Category: Arithmetic Instructions

The partial arctangent instruction calculates the modulo of the top two stack elements. It performs this by successively subtracting the second element from the first. The calculated remainder remains in the first element. The instruction affects the C0, C1, C3, UE, DE, and IE status bits.

Sine (FSIN) (80387 Only)

Category: Transcendental Instructions

This instruction computes $Y = SIN(\Theta)$ where Θ is the top stack element. The instruction replaces the top stack element with Y. If Θ exceeds 26^3 then the instruction sets C2; otherwise, it clears C2. It affects the C2, PE and IE status bits.

Sine and Cosine (FSINCOS) (80387 Only)

Category: Transcendental Instructions

This instruction computes $Y = SIN(\Theta)$ and $X = COS(\Theta)$ where Θ is the top stack element. The instruction replaces the top stack element with Y, then pushes X. If Θ exceeds 26^3 then the instruction sets C2; otherwise, it clears C2. It affects the C2, PE and IE status bits.

Unordered Compare (FUCOM) (80387 Only)

Category: Comparison Instructions

This instruction converts the operand to an integer (if required) and compares it to the top stack element. It then changes the condition of the status word bits to match the comparison result. The difference between this instruction and the standard compare is that non-comparable results do not raise the invalid operation exception. The status word bits affected include C0, C2, C3, DE, and IE.

Unordered Compare and Pop (FUCOMP) (80387 Only)

Category: Comparison Instructions

This instruction converts the operand to an integer (if required) and compares it to the top stack element. It then changes the condition of the status word bits to match the comparison result and pops the stack. The difference between this instruction and the standard compare and pop is that non-comparable results do not raise the invalid operation exception. The status word bits affected include C0, C2, C3, DE, and IE.

Unordered Compare and Pop Twice (FUCOMPP) (80387 Only)

Category: Comparison Instructions

This instruction converts the operand to an integer (if required) and compares it to the top stack element. It then changes the condition of the status word bits to match the comparison result and pops the stack twice. The difference between this instruction and the standard compare and pop twice is that non-comparable results do not raise the invalid operation exception. The status word bits affected include C0, C2, C3, DE, and IE.

5
Processor Ports

A processor port provides the means for communication with devices outside the CPU. Figure 5-1 shows typical port relationships to the CPU. As you can see from the diagram, direct hardware manipulation using ports requires that you know three pieces of information: the port address, the device reaction, and the port read/write privileges. Of these three pieces of information, the port address is the most important. By knowing the port address, you can usually experiment to find the other two pieces of essential information. Writing a program and viewing the port reaction with a debugger usually helps you determine the characteristics of the port. However, you can always achieve better results with less wasted time by knowing all three pieces from the outset.

Each port number addresses a specific device input/output, register, or index. The CPU uses the IN instruction to retrieve information from the port. Likewise, it uses the OUT instruction to send information to the port. The DX register of the CPU or a memory location always contains the port address. The CPU uses the AL, AX, or EAX register as a buffer for port input or output. Most ROM and DOS interrupts use IN and OUT instructions to perform the tedious work of sending and receiving information to or from the port for you. However, some programs need to access the ports directly to reduce the time required to perform an interrupt. When using the IN and OUT instructions to control the devices at the specified address directly, you assume responsibility for knowing how it reacts. You must also know if the port allows you to read, write, or both. The paragraphs below discuss the major processor ports and how to program them. TABLE 5-1 provides a listing of most processor ports and their functions.

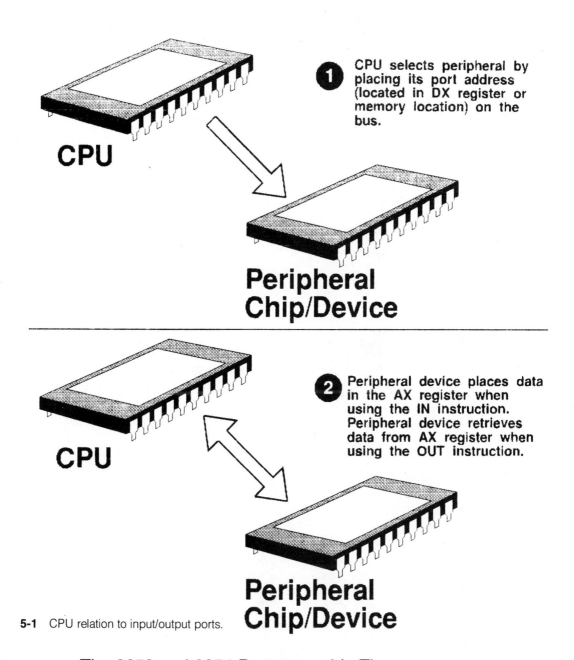

① CPU selects peripheral by placing its port address (located in DX register or memory location) on the bus.

CPU

Peripheral Chip/Device

② Peripheral device places data in the AX register when using the IN instruction. Peripheral device retrieves data from AX register when using the OUT instruction.

CPU

5-1   CPU relation to input/output ports.

Peripheral Chip/Device

The 8253 and 8254 Programmable Timers

Both the 8253 and 8254 timers output pulses at regular intervals. The PC uses these pulses to control the sequence of events within the computer. In this way, both timers act like a clock circuit. However, they differ from a clock in two important aspects. First, a clock circuit uses a crystal to generate a specific, unchangeable frequency. The 4.77 MHz base frequency of the original PC is an example of a clock circuit output. Chang-

Table 5-1   Input/Output Port Addresses

Address   Function

PC and PC/XT System Board Ports

000 - 00F   8273A DMA Controller
010   Manufacturer Test Point
020 - 021   8259A Interrupt Controller
040 - 043   8253 Timer
060 - 063   8255A Programmable Peripheral Interface
080 - 083   DMA Page Registers
0A0 - 0AF   NMI Mask Registers
0C8 - 0CF   Reserved
0E0 - 0EF   Reserved

PC/AT System Board Ports

000 - 01F   8237A-5 DMA Controller Number 1
020 - 03F   8259A Interrupt Controller Number 1
040 - 05F   8254.2 Timer
060 - 06F   8042 Keyboard
070 - 07F   Realtime Clock and NMI Mask Register
080 - 09F   DMA Page Register
0A0 - 0BF   8259A Interrupt Controller Number 2
0C0 - 0DF   8237A-5 DMA Controller Number 2
0E0 - 0EF   Reserved
0F0   Clear Math Co-Processor Busy
0F1   Reset Math Co-Processor
0F8 - 0FF   Math Co-Processor

PS/2 Model 30 System Board Ports

000 - 01F   8237A-5 DMA Controller
020 - 03F   I/O Support Gate Array: Interrupt Controller
040 - 05F   8253 Timer
060   I/O Support Gate Array: Keyboard Input Port
061 - 062   I/O Support Gate Array: Speaker
                       and Configuration Control
063 - 06A   System Support Gate Array: (Undocumented)
06B   System Support Gate Array: RAM Enable/Remap
06C - 06F   System Support Gate Array: (Undocumented)
080 - 08F   System Support Gate Array: DMA Page Registers
0A0 - 0AF   I/O Support Gate Array: NMI Enable
0B0 - 0BF   Realtime Clock/Calender (Undocumented)
0E0 - 0EF   Realtime Clock/Calender (Undocumented)

PS/2 Models 50, 60, and 80

000 - 01F   8237A-5 DMA Controller
020 - 021   8259A Interrupt Controller Number 1
040   System Timer
042   System Timer
043   System Timer
044   System Timer
047   System Timer

Table 5-1 Continued.

Address   Function

PS/2 Models 50, 60, and 80

Address	Function
060	Keyboard Auxiliary Device
061	System Control Port B
064	Keyboard Auxiliary Device
070 - 071	Realtime Clock and NMI Mask Register
074 - 076	Reserved
081 - 083	DMA Page Registers
087	DMA Page Registers
089 - 08B	DMA Page Registers
08F	DMA Page Registers
090	Central Arbitration Control Port
091	Card Selected Feedback
092	System Control Port A
093	Reserved
094	System Board Setup
096 - 097	Programmable Option Select, Channel Connector Select
0A0 - 0A1	8259A Interrupt Controller Number 2
0C0 - 0DF	8237A-5 DMA Controller Number 2
0F0 - 0FF	Math Co-Processor
100 - 107	Programmable Option Select

I/O Channel Ports

Address	Function
1F0 - 1F8	PC/AT Hard-Disk Controller
200 - 20F	Game Control
210 - 217	Expansion Unit
21F	Voice Communications Adapter
220 - 24F	Reserved
278 - 27F	Parallel Printer LPT3:
2C0 - 2CF	3270-PC
2E8 - 2EF	Serial Port COM4:
2F0 - 2F7	Reserved
2F8 - 2FF	Serial Port COM2:
300 - 31F	Prototype Card
320 - 32F	Hard-Disk Controller (Except PC/AT)
330 - 337	XT-370
360 - 36F	PC Network Adapter
378 - 37F	Parallel Printer LPT2:
380 - 38F	Secondary Bisynchronous Interface
3A0 - 3AF	Primary Bisynchronous Interface
3B0 - 3BB	Monochrome Display
3BC - 3BF	Parallel Printer LPT1:
3C0 - 3CF	Enhanced Graphics Adapter
3D0 - 3DF	Color Graphics Adapter
3E0 - 3E7	Reserved
3E8 - 3EF	Serial Port COM3:
3F0 - 3F7	Floppy Disk Controller
3F8 - 3FF	Serial Port COM1:

ing the clock circuit crystal provides the only way to change the circuit output. These timers accept clock input and output—a changeable frequency based, in part, on that input. Second, a clock circuit does not provide a programming interface. You cannot change the clock's purpose. A timer can perform several different functions simultaneously. The specific function depends on the status of its registers.

The 8253 programmable timer (used in PCs) operates at a base frequency of 1.19318 MHz. The 8254 timer (used in ATs) can operate at frequencies up to 10 MHz. For all practical purposes, both chips operate the same. They control certain system functions with three channels that can operate in one of six modes each. The listing below shows the I/O ports used for each function.

- Channel 0—Port 40h
- Channel 1—Port 41h
- Channel 2—Port 42h
- Mode Control—Port 43h

The mode control port affects the appearance and method used to derive the timer output. This port is common to all three channels. Bits 6 and 7 affect which output channel you select. The mode control functions appear in TABLE 5-2.

Table 5-2   8253/8254 Mode Control Bits

Bit	Function
0	Counter Operation (1 = BCD, 0 = Binary)
1 - 3	Operating Mode
4 - 5	00b - Latch Present Counter Value 01b - Read/Write Only MSB 10b - Read/Write Only LSB 11b - Read/Write LSB Followed by MSB
6 - 7	Channel Selection

In theory you could change system operation by changing the output of each channel. However, in practice you usually change only the output of Channel 3. Some programs do derive special effects by changing the other two channels. Changing these channels could adversely affect computer operation. Each channel provides services for a different system function as listed below.

- Channel 0—System Timer
- Channel 1—DMA Memory-Refresh Operations
- Channel 2—General Purpose, Normally Associated with the Speaker Port

The three channels provide interrupts at given periods. To calculate the time, divide the timer base frequency (1,193,180 Hz) by the channel divisor. The divisor ranges in value from 0 to 65,536. A value of zero results in a divisor of 65,536. The standard divisor for Channel 0 is 65,536, and for Channel 1 is 18. Channel 2 does not use a standard divisor. Figure 5-2 at the end of this chapter shows a typical method of changing the output of one of the timer channels.

5-2 Sample program 8 source code listing.

```
;**********************************************************************************************
;* Sample Program 8, 8253/8254 Programmable Timer Demonstration *
;* This program shows you how to program the 8253/8254 timer.  It also shows you how to create interrupt      *
;* driven programs that depend not on timing loops, but the timer tick to monitor the timing of a program.    *
;* To use this program you need the following special equipment:        *
;*      80286 equipped computer                      *
;* Copyright 1989 John Mueller & Wallace Wang - Tab Books, *
;**********************************************************************************************


;**********************************************************************************************
;* Perform the program setup.                      *
;**********************************************************************************************

.MODEL MEDIUM    ; Use a medum model size.

.286

.STACK  ; Use the defalt stack of 1024 bytes.

;**********************************************************************************************
;* Begin the data area.  Declare all variables.           *
;**********************************************************************************************
.DATA

Beep      EQU     07
BS        EQU     08
LF        EQU     10
CR        EQU     13
Space     EQU     32
StrEnd    EQU     36
Ch2       DW      42h
Mode      DW      43h
PPI       DW      61h
SpOn      DB      00001011b
SpOff     DB      00001001b
SetMode   DB      10110110b
Timer     DB      0
EightN    DB      8
FourN     DB      16
TwoN      DB      32
NumNotes        DB      72
```

5-2 Continued.

```
;*********************************************************************************************
;* To derive the value for each note used to create Greensleeves, divide 1,193,180 (the base frequency of the   *
;* timer) by the frequecny value of the note.  For example, to get the value for C octive 3 you use the *
;* following equation: Value = 1,193,180/130.81.  Value equals 9121.      *
;*********************************************************************************************

Notes   DW      5424,4561,4063,3620,3417,3620,4063,4832,6088
        DW      5424,4832,4561,5424,5424,5736,5424,4832,5736
        DW      7240,5424,4561,4063,3620,3417,3620,4063,4832
        DW      6088,5424,4832,4561,4832,5424,5736,6439,5736
        DW      5424,5424,3044,3044,3220,3620,4063,4832,6088
        DW      5424,4832,4561,5424,5424,5736,5424,4832,5736
        DW      7240,3044,3044,3220,3620,4063,4832,6088,5424
        DW      4832,4561,4832,5424,5736,6439,5736,5424,5424


;*********************************************************************************************
;* To determine the time duration, multiply the time value by 1/18 (the interval between occurrences of *
;* interrupt 08h).  For example, the value 6 equals 6/18ths of a second or 1/3rd of a second.    *
;*********************************************************************************************

Times   DB      6,24,12,18,6,12,24,12,18,6,12,24,12,18,6,12
        DB      24,12,24,12,24,12,18,6,12,24,12,18,6,12,18,6
        DB      12,18,6,12,36,36,36,18,6,12,24,12,18,6,12,24
        DB      12,18,6,12,24,12,36,36,18,6,12,24,12,18,6,12
        DB      18,6,12,18,6,12,36,36

DoOld8  LABEL   DWORD
Old8    DW      2 DUP (0)
Msg     DB      '█████████████████████',LF,CR
        DB      '█ Playing Greensleeves █',LF,CR
        DB      '█████████████████████',LF,CR,StrEnd


;*********************************************************************************************
;* Begin the code segment.                        *
;*********************************************************************************************
.CODE


Example PROC    FAR
Start:  PUSH    DS      ;Save the original data segment.
        XOR     AX,AX
        PUSH    AX

        MOV     AX,@DATA        ;Point DS & ES to our data segment.
        MOV     DS,AX
        MOV     ES,AX


;*********************************************************************************************
;* This section of the program displays a message that tells the user what the program is doing.       *
;*********************************************************************************************
```

```
        LEA     DX,Msg   ;Display starting message.
        MOV     AX,0900h
        INT     21h


;********************************************************************************************
;* This section of the program initializes the interrupt, plays the song, then restores the interrupt vector    *
;* to its original value.  Every interrupt driven program follows a procedure similar to this one.  If you       *
;* fail to restore the interrupt, your machine will hang-up upon exit to DOS.  *
;********************************************************************************************


        MOV     AX,3508h        ;Get interrupt 8 vector.
        INT     21h
        MOV     WORD PTR Old8,BX        ;Save the vector.
        MOV     WORD PTR [Old8+2],ES

        MOV     AX,2508h        ;Point interrupt 8 to our
        PUSH    DS      ; procedure
        PUSH    CS
        POP     DS
        LEA     DX,DoSounds
        INT     21h
        POP     DS      ;Restore DS.

        CLI             ;Disable interrupts.
        MOV     AL,SetMode      ;Set the output mode of timer
        MOV     DX,Mode ; channel 2.
        OUT     DX,AL
        LEA     SI,Notes        ;Place first note in timer
        MOV     DX,Ch2  ; channel 2 register.
        OUTSB
        OUTSB
        DEC     NumNotes        ;Decrement the number of notes
        LEA     DI,Times        ; left to play.  Load amount
        MOV     BL,[DI] ; of time to play note.
        MOV     Timer,BL

TimeWait:       CLI             ;Disable interrupts.
        MOV     DX,PPI  ;Turn the speaker on.
        MOV     AL,SpOn
        OUT     DX,AL

        STI
        HLT             ;Wait for an interrupt.
        CMP     Timer,0 ;See if timer set to zero.
        JNE     TimeWait        ;If not, wait until it is.

        CLI             ;Disable interrupts.
        MOV     DX,PPI  ;Turn the speaker off.
        MOV     AL,SpOff
```

```
        OUT     DX,AL
        STI              ;Enable interrupts.
        HLT              ;Wait 1/18th of a second.


        CMP     NumNotes,0     ;See if we played last note.
        JE      Exit    ;If so, leave program.
        MOV     DX,Ch2  ;Otherwise, output next note
        OUTSB            ; to the timer.
        OUTSB
        DEC     NumNotes        ;Decrement the number of notes
        MOV     BL,[DI] ; left to play.  Load amount
        MOV     Timer,BL        ; of time to play note.
        JMP     TimeWait

Exit:   MOV     AX,2508h        ;Point interrupt 8 to its
        PUSH    DS      ; original vector.
        MOV     DX,Old8
        MOV     DS,[Old8+2]
        INT     21h
        POP     DS

        RET

Example ENDP


;*******************************************************************************************************
;* This procedure provides an interface to the interrupt.  We replace the original interrupt vector with the   *
;* address for this procedure.  The procedure decrements the timer every 1/18th of a second then calls the     *
;* original interrupt.  In essence this removes variances usually found in programs relying on timing loops.    *
;* Since the timer interrupt gets called every 1/18th of a second reguardless of clock speed, you do not need   *
;* to worry about timing differences between machines.  You can easily change the timing by changing the       *
;* timer tick.  Small variances in the timer tick frequency produce large changes in program execution speed.   *
;* Notice that since we call the original interrupt vector, the program is not responsible for the normal       *
;* interrupt housekeeping.                          *
;*******************************************************************************************************

DoSounds        PROC    FAR

        DEC     Timer
        JMP     CS:DoOld8       ;Call interrupt 8.
        RET

DoSounds        ENDP

END     Start
```

The 8255A Programmable Peripheral Interface (PPI)

The 8255A programmable peripheral interface controls the keyboard, speaker, and system configuration switches. Some computers control other devices using this chip. Of all the peripheral chips, this one is the most flexible. There are five ports commonly associated with this chip. Port 60h allows you to read input from the keyboard when bit 7 of Port 61h is clear. On some PCs, setting bit 7 on Port 61h allows you to read the configuration switches using Port 60h. In all other cases, setting bit 7 returns an acknowledge to (clears) the keyboard. These are the common uses for Port 60h. Changing Port 63h bits 4, 5 and 6 allows you to use Port 60h for other purposes. As you can see, you must consider the interactions between ports carefully when programming this chip.

The listings in TABLES 5-3 through 5-6 provide standard 8255A port

Table 5-3   Port 61h Status Bits

Bit	Function
0	Speaker Control 0b = Direct 1b = Through 8253/8254 Timer
1	Speaker Condition 0b = Off 1b = On
2	Configuration Switch Selection 0b = Read Spare Switches Port 62h (PC) 1b = Read RAM Size Switches Port 62h (PC) AT and XT - Not Used
3	Cassette Motor Condition/Configuration Switch Selection 0b = Cassette Motor On (PC), Read Configuration Switch Port 62h High Nibble (XT) 1b - Cassette Motor Off (PC), Read Configuration Switch Port 62h Low Nibble (XT)
4	RAM Parity Error Checking 0b = Enabled 1b = Disabled
5	Expansion Port RAM Parity Error Checking 0b = Enabled 1b = Disabled
6	Keyboard Click 0b = Off 1b = On
7	0b = Keyboard Enabled 1b = Read Configuration Switches (PC), Keyboard Acknowledge (XT)

Table 5-4   Port 62h Status Bits

Bit	Function
0 - 3	Configuration Switch Status (Selected by Port 61h Bit 2 for PC and Bit 3 for XT)
4	Cassette Data Input
5	8253/8254 Timer Output
6	Expansion Slot RAM Parity Error When Set
7	RAM Parity Error When Set

Table 5-5   Port 63h Status Bits

Bit	Function
0	Port 62h Bits 0 through 3 status 0b = Output 1b = Input
1	Port 61h Usage 0b = Output 1b = Input
2	Port 61h Mode
3	Port 62h Bits 4 through 7 status 0b = Output 1b = Input
4	Port 60h Usage 0b = Output 1b = Input
5 - 6	Port 60h Mode
7	Port Status 0b = Active 1b = Inactive

uses and bit definition. Only an AT computer normally uses port 64h which reports the status of the 8042 controller connected to the 8255A. Most computers use ports 61h through 63h as shown in the tables. Because each computer varies in its usage of the 8255A PPI (there is no

Table 5-6   Port 64h Status Bits

Bit Position	When Set	When Clear
During Output		
0	Ouput Buffer Full	Output Buffer Empty
1	Input Buffer Full	Input Buffer Empty
2	Return From Shutdown	Normal POST
3	Last Input was Command	Last Input was Data
4	Keyboard Locked	Keyboard Unlocked
5	8042-6805 XMIT Timeout	No Timeout
6	6805-8042 XMIT Timeout	No Timeout
7	Parity Error (6805)	No Parity Error
During Input		
0	Enable Keyboard Int.	Disable Keyboard Int.
2	Return From Shutdown	Normal POST
3	Disable Keylock	Enable Keylock
4	Disable Keyboard	Enable Keyboard
5	PC Keyboard Mode	AT Keyboard Mode
6	Translate Scan Codes	Does Not Translate

standard configuration for this chip), consult the technical reference for your computer before using the ports. Figure 5-3 at the end of this chapter shows an example of how to use the 8255A PPI.

5-3 Sample program 9 source code listing.

```
;******************************************************************************
;* Sample Program 9, Programmable Peripheral Interface (PPI) Demonstration    *
;* This program shows you how to control the keyboard through the use of ports and interrupts.  The program  *
;* begins by storing a password.  It then diverts the standard interrupt 9 vector to a special routine.  The *
;* program waits for each interrupt 9 to determine if the user entered the correct password a second time.   *
;* When the user does enter the correct password, the program reinstalls the original interrupt 9 vector.    *
;* This routine does not allow the user to reboot the computer or perform any other escape maneuvers    *
;* (including Ctrl-C and Ctrl-Alt-Del) while the password section (starting with FREEZE) is enabled.  You do  *
;* not require any special equipment to use this program.           *
;*                            *
;* Copyright 1989 John Mueller & Wallace Wang - Tab Books *
;******************************************************************************


;******************************************************************************
;* Perform the program setup.                 *
;******************************************************************************

.MODEL SMALL    ; Use a medum model size.

.STACK  ; Use the defalt stack of 1024 bytes.
```

5-3 Continued.

```
;****************************************************************************************************
;* Begin the data area.  Declare all variables.            *
;****************************************************************************************************
.DATA

FullBuff      EQU     02
Beep    EQU     07
BS      EQU     08
LF      EQU     10
CR      EQU     13
Space   EQU     32
StrEnd  EQU     36
CharPort      EQU     60h
Control EQU     64h
KeyOff  EQU     10101101b
KeyOn   EQU     10101110b
Msg1    DB      ' ┌────────────────────────┐ ',CR,LF
        DB      '| Type a password: _____ |',CR,LF
        DB      '|      Then press Enter.    |',CR,LF
        DB      ' └────────────────────────┘ ',CR,LF,StrEnd
TypeChar      DB      '*'
Password      DB      10 DUP (' ')
Openword      DB      10 DUP (' ')
Empty   DB      10 DUP (' ')
DoOld9  LABEL   DWORD
Old9    DW      2 DUP (0)
Compare DB      0
NumChar DW      0


;****************************************************************************************************
;* This list of values provides part of the conversion required to change keyboard scan codes into ASCII
;* characters.  The keyboard always returns a scan code instead of ASCII characters.       *
;****************************************************************************************************

ScanConv      DB      0,0,'1234567890-=',0,0,'QWERTYUIOP[]',CR,0
        DB      'ASDFGHJKL;',39,'`',0,'\ZXCVBNM,./',0,'*'
        DB      0,' ',0,0,0,0,0,0,0,0,0,0,0,0,0,'789-456+'
        DB      '1230.',0,0,0,0,0


;****************************************************************************************************
;* Begin the code segment.                              *
;****************************************************************************************************
.CODE

Example PROC    FAR
Start:  PUSH    DS      ;Save the original data segment.
        XOR     AX,AX
        PUSH    AX

        MOV     AX,@DATA        ;Point DS & ES to our data segment.
```

5-3 Continued.

```
        MOV     DS,AX
        MOV     ES,AX


;*****************************************************************************************************
;* Display an intialization message, get a password from the user, and lock the keyboard.         *
;*****************************************************************************************************

        MOV     AX,0632h        ;Clear the screen.
        XOR     BX,BX
        XOR     CX,CX
        MOV     DX,3250
        INT     10h

        MOV     AX,0200h        ;Position the cursor.
        XOR     BX,BX
        XOR     DX,DX
        INT     10h

        MOV     AX,0900h        ;Display the initial
        LEA     DX,Msg1 ; password entry message.
        INT     21h

        LEA     SI,Password     ;Load storage variable address.
        MOV     AX,0200h        ;Position the cursor.
        XOR     BX,BX
        MOV     DX,0113h
        INT     10h
        MOV     CX,10   ;Load maximum password size.

GetChar1:       XOR     AX,AX   ;Get a character.
        INT     16h
        CMP     AL,CR   ;See if user pressed enter.
        JE      Freeze  ;If so, password entered.
        CMP     AL,'a'  ;Convert character to upper
        JL      GetChar1A       ; case if necessary.
        CMP     AL,'z'
        JG      GetChar1A
        SUB     AL,32   ;Perform conversion.
GetChar1A:      MOV     [SI],AL ;Store the character and move
        INC     SI      ; to the next position.
        MOV     AX,0200h        ;Display an asterisk to show
        MOV     DL,TypeChar     ; character entry.
        INT     21h
        LOOP    GetChar1        ;Get next character.


;*****************************************************************************************************
;* This section of the program saves the old interrupt 9 vector, then points interrupt 9 to our procedure.  *
;* This, in effect, freezes the keyboard. Notice this code section also clears the display. This removes   *
;* any clues left on the screen. Preventing anyone from guessing the password. Notice you can no longer    *
;* use Ctrl-Alt-Del.                                *
;*****************************************************************************************************
```

5-3 Continued.

```
Freeze: MOV     AX,0632h        ;Clear the screen.
        XOR     BX,BX
        XOR     CX,CX
        MOV     DX,3250
        INT     10h

        MOV     AX,0200h        ;Position the cursor.
        XOR     BX,BX
        XOR     DX,DX
        INT     10h

        PUSH    ES      ;Save ES.
        MOV     AX,3509h        ;Get interrupt 9 vector.
        INT     21h
        MOV     WORD PTR Old9,BX        ;Save the vector.
        MOV     WORD PTR [Old9+2],ES
        POP     ES      ;Restore ES.

        MOV     AX,2509h        ;Point interrupt 9 to our
        PUSH    DS      ; procedure
        PUSH    CS
        POP     DS
        LEA     DX,GetKey
        INT     21h
        POP     DS      ;Restore DS.

Frozen: HLT             ;Check the keyboard.
        CMP     Compare,1       ;See if user entered password.
        JE      Equal   ;If so, enable interrupt 9.
        JMP     Frozen  ;Else, get next character.

Equal:  MOV     AX,2509h        ;Point interrupt 9 to its
        PUSH    DS      ; original vector.
        MOV     DX,Old9
        MOV     DS,[Old9+2]
        INT     21h
        POP     DS

        RET
```

```
;****************************************************************************************************
;
;* This section of the program replaces the standard interrupt 9 routine.  Notice that it turns the keyboard   *
;* off before interpreting the character by sending a control sequence to port 64h.  This procedure works      *
;* with the translation table SCANCONV to interpret the scan codes returned from port 60h.  After it         *
;* interprets the scan code, the procedure place the character into the password variable OPENWORD.  If the     *
;* user pressed enter (CR), the procedure checks the contents of OPENWORD against the original password *
;* (PASSWORD).  If the two match, the procedure sets a flag true; otherwise, it resets all the input         *
;* parameters.  The procedure reenables the keyboard before returning to the main procedure.       *
;****************************************************************************************************
;
```

```
GetKey: PUSHF               ;Save flags and registers.
        PUSH    AX
        PUSH    BX
        PUSH    CX
        PUSH    DX
        PUSH    DI
        PUSH    SI

        CLI                 ;Turn off the keyboard.
KeyWait:        IN      AL,Control
        TEST    AL,FullBuff
        LOOPNZ  KeyWait
        MOV     AL,KeyOff
        OUT     Control,AL
        STI

        CLI                 ;Get a character.
KeyGet: IN      AL,Control
        TEST    AL,FullBuff
        LOOPNZ  KeyGet
        IN      AL,CharPort
        STI

        TEST    AL,80h  ;Ignore Acknoledgements.
        JNZ     NoProc

        LEA     BX,ScanConv     ;Convert it from a scan code
        XLAT            ; to an ASCII character.
        CMP     AL,0    ;If not character, exit.
        JE      NoProc
        PUSH    AX      ;Otherwise, save character.

        MOV     BH,0    ;Display an asterisk for any
        CMP     AL,CR   ; character than the carriage
        JE      NoAst   ; return.
        MOV     AL,TypeChar
NoAst:  MOV     AH,0Eh
        INT     10h

        LEA     SI,OpenWord     ;Load compare variable address.
        ADD     SI,NumChar      ;Point to end of string.

GetChar2:       POP     AX      ;Restore the character.
        CMP     AL,CR   ;See if user pressed enter.
        JE      PCompare        ;If so, password entered.
        MOV     [SI],AL ;Save character and update
        INC     NumChar ; pointer.
        JMP     NoProc

PCompare:       MOV     CX,10   ;Load number of characters.
        LEA     SI,Password     ;Point to original and opening
```

```
            LEA      DI,Openword      ; passwords.
            REP      CMPSB    ;Compare the two entries.
            CMP      CX,0     ;See if they compared.
            JE       PassEqual
            LEA      SI,Empty         ;Clear the open password.
            LEA      DI,Openword
            MOV      CX,10
            REP      MOVSB
            MOV      NumChar,0        ;Reset the character pointer.
            JMP      NoProc   ;Get a new password.

PassEqual:  MOV      Compare,1        ;Set Compare flag true.

NoProc: MOV  AL,20h   ;Reset the interrupt
        OUT  20h,AL   ; controller.
        CLI           ;Reenable the keyboard.
KeyEnd: IN   AL,Control
        TEST AL,FullBuff
        LOOPNZ KeyEnd
        MOV  AL,KeyOn
        OUT  Control,AL
        STI

        POP      SI       ;Restore flags and registers.
        POP      DI
        POP      DX
        POP      CX
        POP      BX
        POP      AX
        POPF

        IRET              ;Return to the main procedure.

Example ENDP

END     Start
```

The 8259 Programmable Interrupt Controller (PIC)

Every maskable hardware interrupt generated within a PC goes through a central control chip called the programmable interrupt controller. The 8259 PIC handles up to eight interrupts using a priority sequence. Every time the PIC detects a hardware interrupt, it checks to see if the CPU is servicing another interrupt. If not, the PIC passes control of the interrupt to the interrupt handler. For example, both the timer tick (Channel 0 of the 8253/8254 Timer) and keyboard generate hardware interrupts. When the PIC receives a timer tick interrupt, it calls interrupt 08h to service it. Likewise, it calls interrupt 09h to service a keyboard interrupt. When the interrupt completes its service of the hardware interrupt, it clears the 8259 PIC. Figure 5-4 at the end of this chapter shows a typical example of how to use the 8259 PIC.

The CPU follows the same basic procedure for every interrupt it processes. First it pushes all the flags. This allows the CPU to return to an

5-4 Sample program 10 source code listing.

```
;***********************************************************************************************
;* Sample Program 10, Programmable Interrupt Controller (PIC) Demonstration      *
;* This program shows you how to disable the keyboard to prevent user interference during a critical   *
;* operation, then reenable the keyboard.  Unlike the keyboard shutoff method used in program 9, this   *
;* method allows you to retrieve the user keystrokes stored in the keyboard buffer.  You do not need any   *
;* special equipment to use this program.                        *
;*                        *
;* Copyright 1989 John Mueller & Wallace Wang - Tab Books *
;***********************************************************************************************


;***********************************************************************************************
;* Perform the program setup.                  *
;***********************************************************************************************

.MODEL MEDIUM    ; Use a medum model size.

.STACK   ; Use the defalt stack of 1024 bytes.


;***********************************************************************************************
;* Begin the data area.  Declare all variables.          *
;***********************************************************************************************
.DATA

Beep     EQU     07
BS       EQU     08
LF       EQU     10
CR       EQU     13
Space    EQU     32
StrEnd   EQU     36
PICPort  EQU     21h
KeyOff   EQU     00000010b
KeyOn    EQU     11111101b

Msg1     DB      'Keyboard interrupt disabled. Press Ctrl-Alt-Del.',CR,LF
         DB      'Notice machine does not reboot.',CR,LF,LF,StrEnd
Msg2     DB      'Keyboard interrupt enabled.',CR,LF
         DB      'Machine reboots automatically',CR,LF,LF,LF,StrEnd
WaitVar  DB      126
DoOld8   LABEL   DWORD
Old8     DW      2 DUP (0)


;***********************************************************************************************
;* Begin the code segment.                  *
;***********************************************************************************************
.CODE
```

5-4 Continued.

```
Example PROC    FAR
Start:  PUSH    DS          ;Save the original data segment.
        XOR     AX,AX
        PUSH    AX

        MOV     AX,@DATA         ;Point DS & ES to our data segment.
        MOV     DS,AX
        MOV     ES,AX


;***********************************************************************************************************
;* This part of the program stores the original interrupt 8 vector (used for timing) and points it our  *
;* procedure.  The program then uses interrupt 8 to provide timing by decrementing a variable.  The first    *
;* time period allows the user to press Ctrl-Alt-Del and notice that the machine does nothing.  The second   *
;* time period allows the user to view the reboot message before the machine reboots.   *
;***********************************************************************************************************


        MOV     AX,3508h         ;Get interrupt 8 vector.
        INT     21h
        MOV     WORD PTR Old8,BX        ;Save the vector.
        MOV     WORD PTR [Old8+2],ES

        MOV     AX,2508h         ;Point interrupt 8 to our
        PUSH    DS      ; procedure
        PUSH    CS
        POP     DS
        LEA     DX,DoWait
        INT     21h
        POP     DS          ;Restore DS.

        CLI             ;Disable interrupts.
        IN      AL,PICPort      ;Import the current PIC status.
        OR      AL,KeyOff       ;Modify to turn keyboard off.
        OUT     PICPort,AL      ;Output to PIC.
        STI             ;Enable interrupts.

        MOV     AX,0900h         ;Tell user to press
        LEA     DX,Msg1 ; Ctrl-Alt-Del.
        INT     21h

LoopIt: HLT             ;Wait for some amount of time.
        CMP     WaitVar,0
        JNE     LoopIt

        CLI             ;Disable interrupts.
        IN      AL,PICPort      ;Import the current PIC status.
        AND     AL,KeyOn        ;Modify to turn keyboard on.
        OUT     PICPort,AL      ;Output to PIC
        STI             ;Enable interrupts.

        MOV     AX,0900h         ;Display a reboot message.
```

```
        LEA     DX,Msg2
        INT     21h

        MOV     WaitVar,36      ;Reset WaitVar.
Loop2:  HLT                     ;Wait for some amount of time.
        CMP     WaitVar,0
        JNE     Loop2

        XOR     AX,AX   ;Get Ctrl-Alt-Del.
        INT     16h

        MOV     AX,2508h        ;Point interrupt 8 to its
        PUSH    DS      ; original vector.
        MOV     DX,Old8
        MOV     DS,[Old8+2]
        INT     21h
        POP     DS

        RET

Example ENDP

;**************************************************************************************************
;* This procedure updates the timing variable then calls the original interrupt 8 vector to process any *
;* timing critical functions.  Notice we do not need to perform any house keeping tasks by using the vector     *
;* in this manner.                              *
;**************************************************************************************************

DoWait  PROC    FAR

        DEC     WaitVar ;Update the timing variable.
        JMP     CS:DoOld8       ;Call interrupt 8.
        RET

DoWait  ENDP

END     Start
```

exact state after processing the interrupt. Next it disables the interrupt flag. This prevents any other interrupts while the CPU processes the current interrupt. Next it pushes the code segment (CS) and instruction pointer (IP). This allows the CPU to return to a specific point in program execution. Finally, the CPU acknowledges the interrupt by signaling the 8259 PIC. The PIC places the interrupt number on the bus. The CPU retrieves the interrupt number and multiplies it by 4 (the number of bytes for each interrupt in the interrupt vector table). For example, interrupt 4 uses address 0000:0016 in low memory. The CPU then passes control to the address pointed to by the interrupt vector table in low memory. Once the CPU performs this task it can process the interrupt. The interrupt handler must preserve the CPU registers before it services the hardware. Otherwise, the CPU will return from the interrupt in an unknown condition. After the CPU processes the interrupt, it outputs 20h to port 20h of the PIC. This allows the PIC to process other interrupts. Before the CPU returns control to the program it interrupted to service the hardware, it places the old values in CS and IP. It also pops the flags off the stack.

Each device connected to the PIC uses its own interrupt request line (IRQ). Because the AT has more devices to handle than a PC, the AT uses two cascaded 8259 PICs. The INT (output) line of the slave PIC connects to IRQ2 of the master PIC. This effectively gives the AT 15 IRQ lines. Every line is a different priority. Therefore, if two interrupts arrive at the same time, the 8259 PIC services the higher priority interrupt first, then the lower priority interrupt.

The 8259 PIC uses four ports to accomplish the goal of servicing hardware interrupts. Two of the ports (22h and 23h) remain undocumented. Port 20h controls the interrupt controller command center. The interrupt control assembly commands control the contents of port 20h. Port 21h controls the interrupt controller interrupt mask register. TABLE 5-7 shows the use of the port at 21h.

Table 5-7   8259 Interrupt Controller Port 21h Status Bits

Bit Position	When Set	When Clear
0	System Timer Disabled	System Timer Enabled
1	Keyboard Interrupt Disabled	Keyboard Interrupt Enabled
2	Reserved	Reserved
3	COM2: Interrupt Disabled	COM2: Interrupt Enabled
4	COM1: Interrupt Disabled	COM1: Interrupt Enabled
5	Fixed Disk Int. Disabled	Fixed Disk Int. Enabled
6	Floppy Disk Int. Disabled	Floppy Disk Int. Enabled
7	Parallel Port Int. Disabled	Parallel Port Int. Enabled

Serial Ports

There are four standard serial port address ranges. Many add-in devices allow you to use more serial ports by subdividing these address ranges. The discussion below uses the values for COM1. The addresses used by the other three ports perform similar functions. Each table below shows the addresses for the other three ports in order. For example, the first port appearing between the parentheses is COM2.

Addresses 3F8h and 3F9h change the baud rate setting for COM1 (beside their normal function) when a program sets bit 7 of port 3FBh. TABLE 5-8 shows the baud rate resulting from various inputs to the two

Table 5-8   Standard Baud Rate Divisor Settings (1.8432 MHz Clock)

MSB 3F9h	LSB 3F8h	Resulting Baud Rate
4	17h	110 bps
1	80h	300 bps
0	60h	1,200 bps
0	30h	2,400 bps
0	18h	4,800 bps
0	0Ch	9,600 bps
0	07h	19,200 bps

ports. Port 3F8h normally sends and receives data between the computer and attached device. Port 3F9h provides access to the interrupt enable/disable register. Port 3FAh provides access to the interrupt identification register and port 3FBh provides access to the line control register. TABLES 5-9 through 5-11 show the standard uses for the ports described above.

Table 5-9   Interrupt Enable Register (Ports 3F9h, 2F9h, 3E9h, and 2E9h)

Bit	Function
0	Enable Interrupt on Data Available
1	Enable Interrupt on Transmit Holding Register Empty
2	Enable Interrupt on Receive Line Status Change
3	Enable Interrupt on Modem Status Change
4 - 7	Not Used

**Table 5-10   Interrupt Identification Register
(Ports 3FAh, 2FAh, 3EAh, and 2EAh)**

Bit	Function
0	Interrupt Pending When Clear
1 - 2	00b = Modem Status Change 01b = Transmitter Holding Register Empty 10b = Received Data Available 11b = Receiver Line Status Interrupt
3 - 7	Not Used

Table 5-11   Line Control Register

Bit	Function
0 - 1	Data Length 00b = 5 Bits 01b = 6 Bits 10b = 7 Bits 11b = 8 Bits
2	Number of Stop Bits 0b = 1 Stop Bit 1b = 2 Stop Bits/1.5 When Bits 0 and 1 Are Clear
3	Parity Enabled When Set
4	Even Parity When Set
5	0 = Parity Held at Value in Bit 4 1 = Parity Operates Normally
6	Transmit Break Condition When Set
7	0 = Normal Access to Ports 3F8h/3F9h 1 = Use Ports 3F8h/3F9h to Specify Baud Rate

Parallel Ports

There are three parallel port address ranges. The discussion of parallel port addresses refers to LPT1. The other two parallel port address sets perform similar functions. The tables described below contain the appropriate addresses for the other two ports in order. For example, the first address within the parentheses is LPT2.

The first port (3BCh) outputs data to the printer. Most parallel ports are uni-directional. The parallel port on the IBM PS/2 models, and on some other AT class machines, is bi-directional—allowing both input and output. Port 3BDh accesses the printer-status register. TABLE 5-12 shows the printer-status register functions. Port 3BEh accesses the printer-con-

Table 5-12   Parallel Printer Adapter Status Register (Ports 3BDh, 379h, and 279h)

Bit	Function
0	Time Out When Set
1 - 2	Not Used
3	Printer Error When Set
4	Printer On-Line When Set
5	Out of Paper When Set
6	Acknowledged When Clear
7	Printer Busy When Clear

trol register. TABLE 5-13 shows the printer-control register functions. The remaining ports (3BFh, 37Bh, 37Fh, and 27Bh through 27Fh) do not serve any documented function.

Table 5-13   Parallel Printer Adapter Control Register (Ports 3BEh, 37Ah, and 27Ah)

Bit	Function
0	Output Data to Printer When Set (Strobe)
1	Enable Auto Linefeed When Set
2	Initialize Paper When Set
3	Printer Reads Output When Set
4	Enable IRQ7 For Printer Acknowledge
5 - 7	Not Used

Input/Output System Map

The different processors discussed above communicate with the outside world using ROM, RAM, and input/output ports. These processors have two access modes: memory or I/O port. All the processors described above use 10 input/output address lines (1024 ports) even though they can potentially access many more. A standard 8086/8088 uses 20 memory address lines (1 MB memory). The 80286 provides 24 memory address lines (16 MB memory). The 80386 uses 32 memory address lines (4 GB memory). The memory map in TABLE 5-14 shows memory allocation for basic DOS access using an 8086/8088 processor. The 80286 and 80386 processors access memory above 1 MB using operating system-specific methods.

Table 5-14   One-Megabyte Memory Map (Most Operating Systems)

Address	Function
00000 - 0003F	Hardware/Software* Interrupt Vectors
00000 - 00003	Divide-by-Zero
00004 - 00007	Single Step
00008 - 0000B	Non-Maskable Interrupt (NMI)
0000C - 0000F	Breakpoint
00010 - 00013	Overflow
00014 - 00017	BOUND Exceeded, Print Screen* (Int 5)
00018 - 0001B	Invalid Opcode, Reserved* (Int 6)
0001C - 0001F	Processor Extension Not Available, Reserved* (Int 7)
00020 - 00023	Double Fault, IRQ0 Timer Tick* (Int 8)
00024 - 00027	Segment Overrun, IRQ1 Keyboard* (Int 9)
00028 - 0002B	Invalid Task-State Segment, IRQ2 Cascade from Slave 8259A PIC* (Int Ah)
0002C - 0002F	Segment Not Present, IRQ3 Serial Communications COM2* (Int Bh)
00030 - 00033	Stack Segment Overrun, IRQ4 Serial Communications COM1* (Int Ch)
00034 - 00037	General Protection Fault, IRQ5 Fixed Disk - PC or Parallel Printer LPT2 - AT* (Int Dh)
00038 - 0003B	Page Fault, IRQ6 Floppy Disk* (Int Eh)
0003C - 0003F	Reserved, IRQ7 Parallel Printer LPT1 (Int Fh)
00040 - 0007F	BIOS Interrupt Vectors
00040 - 00043	Numeric Co-Processor Error, Video Services* (Int 10h)
00044 - 00047	Equipment Check* (Int 11h)
00044 - 0007F	Reserved
00048 - 0004B	Conventional Memory Size* (Int 12h)
0004C - 0004F	Disk Driver* (Int 13h)
00050 - 00053	Communications Driver* (Int 14h)
00054 - 00057	Cassette Driver - PC, I/O System Extensions - AT* (Int 15h)
00058 - 0005B	Keyboard Driver* (Int 16h)
0005C - 0005F	Printer Driver* (Int 17h)
00060 - 00063	BASIC* (Int 18h)
00064 - 00067	ROM BIOS Bootstrap* (Int 19h)
00068 - 0006B	Time of Day* (Int 1Ah)
0006C - 0006F	Ctrl-Break* (Int 1Bh)
00070 - 00073	ROM BIOS Timer Tick* (Int 1Ch)
00074 - 00077	Video Parameter Table* (Int 1Dh)
00078 - 0007B	Floppy Disk Parameters* (Int 1Eh)
0007C - 0007F	ROM BIOS Font - Characters 80h to FFh* (Int 1Fh)

Table 5-14   Continued.

Address	Function
00080 - 000FF	DOS Interrupt Vectors
00080 - 00083	Terminate Process* (Int 20h)
00084 - 00087	Function Dispatcher* (Int 21h)
00088 - 0008B	Terminate Address* (Int 22h)
0008C - 0008F	Ctrl-C Handler Address* (Int 23h)
00090 - 00093	Critical Error Handler Address* (Int 24h)
00094 - 00097	Absolute Disk Read* (Int 25h)
00098 - 0009B	Absolute Disk Write* (Int 26h)
0009C - 0009F	Terminate and Stay Resident* (Int 27h)
00100 - 003FF	Assignable Interrupt Vectors
00100 - 00103	Idle Interrupt* (Int 28h)
00104 - 00107	Reserved (Int 29h)
00108 - 0010B	Network Redirector* (Int 2Ah)
0010C - 0011B	Reserved (Int 2Bh - 2Eh)
0011C - 0011F	Multiplex Interrupt* (Int 2Fh)
00120 - 0015F	Reserved (Int 30h - 3Fh)
00400 - 004FF	ROM BIOS Data Area
00400 - 00416	Hardware Parameters
00417 - 0043D	Keyboard Buffer/Status Bytes
0043E - 00448	Disk Status Bytes
00449 - 00466	Video Display Data
00467 - 00470	Option ROM and Timer Data
00471 - 00487	Additional Status Bytes
00488 - 004FF	Reserved
00500 - 005FF	DOS Data Area
A0000 - BFFFF	Video Display Area
A0000 - AFFFF	EGA 64KB
A0000 - BFFFF	EGA 128KB
B0000 - B0FFF	Monochrome 4KB
B0000 - B7FFF	EGA Monochrome Emulation 32KB
B8000 - BBFFF	CGA 16KB
B8000 - BFFFF	EGA CGA Emulation 32KB
C0000 - F3FFF	BIOS Extensions
F4000 - FDFFF	System ROM/Stand-Alone BASIC
FE000 - FFFFF	ROM BIOS

* These addresses are assigned by software only. Because they are not hardwired into the machine, these addresses could change at any time.

6
Video Controllers

The paragraphs below discuss seven different types of display adapters. Even though more display adapters exist, these seven kinds encompass the most common types used. The 34010 series (including Business Graphics Array) accounts for a single type of adapter, even though there are many implementations of that type. For the most precise information about your display adapter, refer to the manufacturer specification manual.

In addition to descriptions of the display adapters, the following paragraphs reference tables containing detailed information about the registers used by each adapter. These registers allow you to control the activities of each adapter directly. The tables appear at the end of the chapter for your convenience in referencing them. Some of the display adapter descriptions use block diagrams to help you visualize the relationship between various elements of the display adapter. Finally, some descriptions reference a typical programming example. This example shows you how to use the information appearing in the tables. All programming examples use assembly language to provide you with maximum information. Other programming languages tend to hide the details of register manipulation within the language.

MONOCHROME DISPLAY ADAPTER (MDA)

The monochrome display adapter discussed here differs from the Hercules graphics card discussed below in memory access and graphics display abilities. The standard monochrome display adapter uses only 4 Kbytes of video memory. Because of this memory limitation, the MDA does not display graphics. It uses four of the ports assigned to it for

234

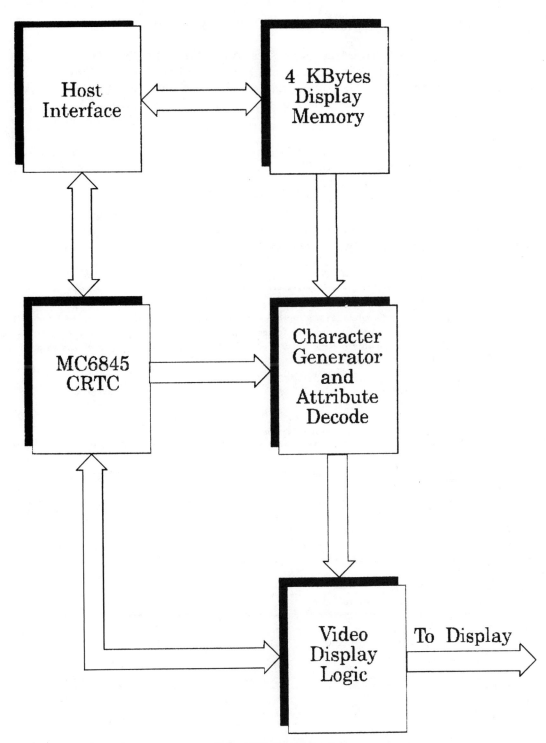

6-1 MDA block diagram.

control/informational purposes. Figure 6-1 shows a typical MDA block diagram.

Each port assigned to the MDA addresses some part of the 6845 CRTC (cathode ray-tube controller) chip shown in FIG. 6-1. Notice that the MDA buffers the port input through a host interface. Port 3B4h, the index register, tells the adapter which register to access through Port 3B5h. The CRTC allows reading from or writing to only one of the 18 registers at a time.

TABLE 6-1 shows the internal monochrome display adapter registers accessed from port 3B5h. Port 3B8h accesses the CRT control register. TABLE 6-2 shows the CRT control register bit meanings. The final port, 3BAh (CRT status register), contains read-only information. Most programs need to look at only two bits of this register. Bit 2 indicates video enabled when clear and bit 3 indicates a vertical retrace when set. Figure 6-2 shows an example of how to program the MDA registers directly.

6-2 Sample program 11 source code listing.

```
;*********************************************************************************************
;* Sample Program 11, MDA Programming Techniques Demonstration  *
;* This program shows you how to detect an MDA capable display by directly manipulating the registers.  It    *
;* also shows you how to send characters directly to the display.  Always set EGA and VGA color monitors to   *
;* display monochrome when using this program.  You need the following special equipment to use this program. *
;*      MDA Display Adapter & Appropriate Monitor or    *
;*      Hercules Display Adapter & Appropriate Monitor or        *
;*      EGA Display Adapter & Appropriate Monitor or    *
;*      VGA Display Adapter & Appropriate Monitor       *
;*                              *
;* Copyright 1989 John Mueller & Wallace Wang - Tab Books*
;*********************************************************************************************


;*********************************************************************************************
;* Perform the program setup.                   *
;*********************************************************************************************

.MODEL MEDIUM   ; Use a medum model size.

.STACK ; Use the defalt stack of 1024 bytes.


;*********************************************************************************************
;* Begin the data area.  Declare all variables.         *
;*********************************************************************************************
.DATA

;Standard equates.

True    EQU     01
Beep    EQU     07
LF      EQU     10
CR      EQU     13
StrEnd  EQU     36
```

```
MDA      EQU      81h
HGC      EQU      82h
HGCPlus EQU       83h
InColor EQU       84h
CGA      EQU      85h
EGA      EQU      86h
MCGA     EQU      87h
VGA      EQU      88h


;Strings for display adapter type.
TypeStr DB        'Display adapter type: ',StrEnd
MDAStr  DB        'MDA',CR,LF,StrEnd
HGCStr  DB        'HGC',CR,LF,StrEnd
HGCPlusStr        DB      'HGC Plus',CR,LF,StrEnd
InColorStr        DB        'InColor',CR,LF,StrEnd
CGAStr  DB        'CGA',CR,LF,StrEnd
EGAStr  DB        'EGA',CR,LF,StrEnd
MCGAStr DB        'MCGA',CR,LF,StrEnd
VGAStr  DB        'VGA',CR,LF,StrEnd
OtherStr          DB      'Other/Unknown',CR,LF,StrEnd
ErrMsg1 DB        'Must use a monochrome card!!',Beep,CR,LF,StrEnd


;Program variables.

TCode    DB      0
NotGood DB       0
CColumns         DB      0
DMode    DB      0
DPage    DB      0
Finished         DB      'Press any key when ready...',StrEnd
Heading DB       'MDA Display Attributes',StrEnd


;Attribute number grid.

AttrNum DB        ' ',7,'0',7,'1',7,'2',7,'3',7,'4',7,'5',7
        DB        '6',7,'7',7,'8',7,'9',7,'A',7,'B',7,'C',7
        DB        'D',7,'E',7,'F',7,'0',7
        DB        'XXXXXXXXXXXXXXXX'
        DB        '1XXXXXXXXXXXXXXX'
        DB        '2XXXXXXXXXXXXXXX'
        DB        '3XXXXXXXXXXXXXXX'
        DB        '4XXXXXXXXXXXXXXX'
        DB        '5XXXXXXXXXXXXXXX'
        DB        '6XXXXXXXXXXXXXXX'
        DB        '7XXXXXXXXXXXXXXX'
        DB        '8XXXXXXXXXXXXXXX'
        DB        '9XXXXXXXXXXXXXXX'
        DB        'AXXXXXXXXXXXXXXX'
        DB        'BXXXXXXXXXXXXXXX'
        DB        'CXXXXXXXXXXXXXXX'
        DB        'DXXXXXXXXXXXXXXX'
```

6-2 Continued.

```
        DB        'EXXXXXXXXXXXXXXXXX'
        DB        'FXXXXXXXXXXXXXXXXX'

;******************************************************************************************************
;* Begin the code segment.                              *
;******************************************************************************************************
.CODE

Example PROC     FAR
Start:  MOV      AX,@DATA          ;Point DS & ES to our data segment.
        MOV      DS,AX
        MOV      ES,AX


;******************************************************************************************************
;* This part of the program gets the display adapter type and displays it.  If the default adapter is not   *
;* monochrome compatible, then display an error message and exit.  Otherwise, proceed with the demonstration. *
;******************************************************************************************************

        LEA      DX,TypeStr        ;Display heading.
        MOV      AX,0900h
        INT      21h

        CALL     GetType ;Determine type then display it.
        MOV      AH,TCode          ;Load type number.
        CMP      AH,VGA  ;See if VGA.
        JNE      Disp1   ;If not, check next type.
        LEA      DX,VGAStr          ;If so, load display string.
        JMP      DispStr

Disp1:  CMP      AH,MCGA ;See if MCGA.
        JNE      Disp2   ;If not, check next type.
        LEA      DX,MCGAStr         ;If so, load display string.
        MOV      NotGood,True       ;Can't run this program.
        JMP      DispStr

Disp2:  CMP      AH,EGA  ;See if EGA.
        JNE      Disp3   ;If not, check next type.
        LEA      DX,EGAStr          ;If so, load display string.
        JMP      DispStr

Disp3:  CMP      AH,CGA  ;See if CGA.
        JNE      Disp4   ;If not, check next type.
        LEA      DX,CGAStr          ;If so, load display string.
        MOV      NotGood,True       ;Can't run this program.
        JMP      DispStr

Disp4:  CMP      AH,HGC  ;See if HGC.
        JNE      Disp5   ;If not, check next type.
        LEA      DX,HGCStr          ;If so, load display string.
        JMP      DispStr
```

```
Disp5:  CMP     AH,HGCPlus      ;See if HGC Plus.
        JNE     Disp6   ;If not, check next type.
        LEA     DX,HGCPlusStr   ;If so, load display string.
        JMP     DispStr

Disp6:  CMP     AH,InColor      ;See if InColor.
        JNE     Disp7   ;If not, check next type.
        LEA     DX,InColorStr   ;If so, load display string.
        MOV     NotGood,True    ;Can't run this program.
        JMP     DispStr

Disp7:  CMP     AH,MDA  ;See if MDA.
        JNE     Disp8   ;If not, check next type.
        LEA     DX,VGAStr       ;If so, load display string.
        JMP     DispStr

Disp8:  LEA     DX,OtherStr     ;Display doesn't match known types.
        MOV     NotGood,True    ;Can't run this program.
DispStr:        MOV     AX,0900h        ;Display the type string.
        INT     21h
        LEA     DX,Finished     ;Display keypress message.
        INT     21h
        XOR     AX,AX   ;Wait for a keypress.
        INT     16h

        CMP     NotGood,True    ;See if we can run program.
        JNE     GoodCard        ;If so, start demo.
        MOV     AX,0900h        ;If not, display error
        LEA     DX,ErrMsg1      ; message.
        INT     21h
        JMP     Exit

;***********************************************************************************************************
;* This part of the program displays the attributes available on an MDA or compatible display by going  *
;* through attributes 0 through FF.  It uses direct memory access to show these attributes.      *
;***********************************************************************************************************

GoodCard:       MOV     AX,0F00h        ;Get the current video mode.
        INT     10h
        MOV     CColumns,AH     ;Save parameters to variables.
        MOV     DMode,AL
        MOV     DPage,BH

        MOV     AX,0007h        ;Set the video mode.
        INT     10h
;Get ready to output attributes.

        MOV     AX,0200h        ;Position the cursor.
        XOR     BX,BX   ;Video page 0.
        MOV     DX,001Dh        ;Row 0, Column 29.
        INT     10h
```

```
        MOV     AX,0900h        ;Display the heading.
        LEA     DX,Heading
        INT     21h

        MOV     AX,0B000h       ;Set destination segment.
        PUSH    ES
        MOV     ES,AX
        MOV     AX,17Eh ;Set destination offset.
        MOV     DI,AX
        XOR     AX,AX   ;Zero the attribute counter.
        LEA     SI,AttrNum      ;Set the source address.

        MOV     CX,22h  ;Display top row of characters.
        REP     MOVSB
        ADD     DI,7Eh  ;Display first character of
        MOVSB           ; next row.
        MOVSB

        MOV     CX,10Fh ;Number of attributes.
        XOR     BX,BX   ;Zero character counter.
OutAttr:        MOVSB           ;Output character.
        MOV     ES:[DI],AL      ;Output attribute.
        INC     AX      ;Increment attribute.
        INC     DI      ;Increment destination.
        INC     BX      ;Increment character counter.
        CMP     BX,10h  ;See if we are at end of line.
        LOOPNE  OutAttr ;If not, display next char.
        CMP     CX,0    ;See if we displayed the last
        JE      LastDisp        ; character. Jump out of loop.
        ADD     DI,7Eh  ;Go to the next line.
        XOR     BX,BX   ;Zero character counter.
        MOVSB           ;Display first character of
        MOV     ES:[DI],AL      ; next row.
        INC     DI
        LOOP    OutAttr

LastDisp:       POP     ES      ;Restore ES.
        MOV     AX,0200h        ;Position the cursor.
        XOR     BX,BX   ;Video page 0.
        MOV     DX,1601h        ;Row 22, Column 1.
        INT     10h

        MOV     AX,0900h        ;Display finished string.
        LEA     DX,Finished
        INT     21h
        XOR     AX,AX   ;Wait for keypress.
        INT     16h

        XOR     AH,AH   ;Reset the video mode.
        MOV     AL,DMode
        INT     10h
```

```
Exit:   MOV     AX,4C00h        ;Exit to DOS.
        INT     21h
        RET

Example ENDP

;*************************************************************************************************
;* This procedure allows you to determine the current display adapter type.  Even if the target machine has   *
;* two display adapters, it only reports the type of the active display adapter.  This procedure works by      *
;* using BIOS routines or direct hardware manipulation methods that only work with the target adapter and all  *
;* upwardly compatible adapters.  It begins by checking VGA using a VGA only BIOS routine that enables/ *
;* disables the display.  The user doesn't notice a change because the routine uses the screen on parameter.   *
;* The procedure continues with similar approaches for the MCGA, EGA, CGA, InColor, HGC+, HGC, and finally     *
;* MDA.  This procedure places a number corresponding to the value of the display in a variable named TCode.   *
;* If the display adapter does not match any of these known types, the procedure does not change the value of  *
;* TCode.                           *
;*************************************************************************************************
;

GetType PROC    NEAR

        MOV     AX,1200h        ;Check for VGA by using a VGA
        MOV     BL,36h  ; only display enable.
        INT     10h
        CMP     AL,12h  ;Was interrupt successful?
        JNE     Type2   ;If not, different display.
        MOV     TCode,VGA       ;If so, save type and exit.
        JMP     Exit1

Type2:  MOV     AX,1200h        ;Check for MCGA by using the
        MOV     BL,32h  ; CPU access enable/disable
        INT     10h     ; interrupt (norm=enabled).
        CMP     AL,12h  ;Was interrupt successful?
        JNE     Type3   ;If not, different display.
        MOV     TCode,MCGA      ;If so, must be MCGA since we
        JMP     Exit1   ; already checked VGA.

Type3:  MOV     AX,1200h        ;Check for EGA by attempting
        MOV     BL,10h  ; to load memory allocation
        INT     10h     ; data.
        CMP     BH,10h  ;Was interrupt successful?
        JNE     Type4   ;If not, different display.
        MOV     TCode,EGA       ;If so, must be EGA since we
        JMP     Exit1   ; already checked VGA.

Type4:  MOV     DX,3D4h ;Check for CGA by getting then
        MOV     AL,0Ah  ; changing the cursor end scan
        OUT     DX,AL   ; line value.
        INC     DX
        IN      AL,DX
        XCHG    AH,AL   ;Save value.
        MOV     AL,6    ;Output new value.
```

```
                OUT     DX,AL
                MOV     CX,50h   ;Wait for CRTC to respond.
Type4A:  LOOP   Type4A
                IN      AL,DX    ;Get value in CRTC.
                XCHG    AH,AL    ;Place original value back in
                OUT     DX,AL    ; CRTC.
                CMP     AH,6     ;See if CRTC recieved our scan line
                JNE     Type5    ; value.  If not, different display.
                MOV     TCode,CGA        ;If so, must be CGA.
                JMP     Exit1


Type5:   MOV    DX,3B4h ;Check for monochrome by
                MOV     AL,0Ah   ; getting then changing the
                OUT     DX,AL    ; cursor end scan line value.
                INC     DX
                IN      AL,DX
                XCHG    AH,AL    ;Save value.
                MOV     AL,6     ;Output new value.
                OUT     DX,AL
                MOV     CX,50h   ;Wait for CRTC to respond.
Type5A:  LOOP   Type5A
                IN      AL,DX    ;Get value in CRTC.
                XCHG    AH,AL    ;Place original value back in
                OUT     DX,AL    ; CRTC.
                CMP     AH,6     ;See if CRTC recieved our scan line
                JNE     Exit1    ; value.  If not, different display.

                MOV     CX,50000        ;Perform this step 50,000 times.
                MOV     BX,0080h        ;Check status register for
                XOR     AX,AX    ; changing bit 7.  This bit
                MOV     DX,3BAh ; does not change on MDA.
Type5B:  IN     AL,DX
                TEST    AX,BX
                LOOPNZ  Type5B
                JZ      Type5C   ;Jump if Hercules display.
                MOV     TCode,MDA       ;If not, set for MDA display.
                JMP     Exit1

Type5C:  AND    AL,01110000b     ;Mask bits 4 through 6.
                CMP     AL,01010000b    ;See if this is an InColor.
                JNE     Type5D   ;If not, different display.
                MOV     TCode,InColor   ;If so, set for InColor.
                JMP     Exit1

Type5D:  CMP    AL,00010000b     ;See if this is an HGC Plus
                JNE     Type5E   ;If not, different display.
                MOV     TCode,HGCPlus   ;If so, set for HGC Plus.
                JMP     Exit1

Type5E:  MOV    TCode,HGC        ;Must be an HGC adapter.
```

```
Exit1:  RET

GetType ENDP

END     Start
```

HERCULES GRAPHICS CARD (HGC)

There are actually several versions of the Hercules Graphics Card (HGC). Not only has Hercules improved the HGC, but also clone copies of the HGC exist. The HGC combines the cost and resolution advantage of the MDA with the graphics capabilities of the CGA. Of course, the HGC does not provide color output. It also requires special programming to allow you to use graphics mode. There are, however, several shareware programs that allow you to simulate CGA graphics modes using the HGC. Most HGC registers and ports remain compatible with the MDA registers above. The CRT control register attributes (TABLE 6-3) differ from the definitions shown in TABLE 6-1 for the MDA. The HGC also adds three registers as shown in TABLE 6-4. Figure 6-3 shows an example of how to program the HGC registers directly.

6-3 Sample program 12 source code listing.

```
;*********************************************************************************************
;* Sample Program 12, Hercules Programming Techniques Demonstration    *
;* This program shows you how to create a graphics program using the Hecules graphics card (HGC).  This *
;* program will work on any Hercules compatible display adapter.  It will not work with an MDA or CGA   *
;* compatible display adapter.  You need the following special equipment to use this program.   *
;*      Hercules Display Adapter & Appropriate Monitor or        *
;*      EGA Display Adapter & Appropriate Monitor or       *
;*      VGA Display Adapter & Appropriate Monitor         *
;*                              *
;*      NOTE:                     *
;*      You may need to perform a special setup to use this program with an EGA or VGA adapter. *
;*      Some EGA and VGA adapters will not allow you to display Hercules graphics mode programs.      *
;*                              *
;* Copyright 1989 John Mueller & Wallace Wang - Tab Books. *
;*********************************************************************************************

;*********************************************************************************************
;* Perform the program setup.               *
;*********************************************************************************************

Video_Data    SEGMENT AT 40h   ;Video BIOS Data Area Address
         ORG   49h
Video_Offs    DB      ?
Video_Data    ENDS

Video_Buff    SEGMENT AT 0B000h     ;Start of Video Memory
```

6-3 Continued.

```
        ORG     0000h
Buff_Start     DB       ?
        ORG     2000h
Buff_Sect2     DB       ?
        ORG     4000h
Buff_Sect3     DB       ?
        ORG     6000h
Buff_Sect4     DB       ?
Video_Buff     ENDS


.MODEL MEDIUM   ; Use a medum model size.

.STACK  ; Use the defalt stack of 1024 bytes.

;************************************************************************************************************
;* Begin the data area.  Declare all variables.              *
;************************************************************************************************************
.DATA

;Standard equates.

Beep    EQU     07
BS      EQU     08
LF      EQU     10
CR      EQU     13
Space   EQU     32
StrEnd  EQU     36
HGC     EQU     82h
HGCPlus EQU     83h
InColor EQU     0h
EGA     EQU     86h
VGA     EQU     88h

;Program variables.
TCode   DB      0
NotGood DB      0
ErrMsg1 DB          'You Must use a Hercules compatible card!!',Beep,CR,LF,StrEnd

;The program uses this set of variables to print the phrase
; "Hello World" in the middle of the display.  Notice this
; display uses proportionally spaced type.

Prop1   DB      03Fh,0C3h,0FCh,000h,01Eh,03Ch,000h,000h
        DB      00Fh,0FFh,0F0h,0FFh,000h,000h,000h,01Eh
        DB      000h,03Ch
Prop2   DB      03Fh,0C3h,0FCh,000h,01Eh,03Ch,000h,000h
        DB      00Fh,0FFh,0F0h,0FFh,000h,000h,000h,01Eh
        DB      000h,03Ch
Prop3   DB      00Fh,000h,0F0h,000h,00Ch,018h,000h,000h
        DB      003h,0C3h,0C0h,03Ch,000h,000h,000h,00Ch
        DB      000h,018h
```

6-3 Continued.

```
Prop4    DB        006h,000h,060h,000h,00Ch,018h,000h,000h
         DB        001h,081h,080h,018h,000h,000h,000h,00Ch
         DB        000h,018h
Prop5    DB        006h,000h,060h,000h,00Ch,018h,000h,000h
         DB        001h,081h,080h,018h,000h,000h,000h,00Ch
         DB        000h,018h
Prop6    DB        006h,000h,060h,000h,00Ch,018h,000h,000h
         DB        000h,0C0h,0C0h,030h,000h,000h,000h,00Ch
         DB        000h,018h
Prop7    DB        007h,000h,0E0h,000h,00Ch,018h,000h,000h
         DB        000h,0C0h,0C0h,030h,000h,000h,000h,00Ch
         DB        000h,018h
Prop8    DB        007h,0FFh,0E0h,03Eh,00Ch,018h,01Fh,080h
         DB        000h,060h,060h,060h,03Fh,007h,08Fh,00Ch
         DB        00Fh,0D8h
Prop9    DB        007h,0FFh,0E0h,063h,00Ch,018h,030h,0C0h
         DB        000h,060h,060h,060h,061h,087h,09Fh,00Ch
         DB        018h,078h
Prop10   DB        007h,000h,0E0h,063h,00Ch,018h,030h,0C0h
         DB        000h,030h,0F0h,0C0h,061h,083h,030h,00Ch
         DB        018h,078h
Prop11   DB        006h,000h,060h,063h,00Ch,018h,060h,060h
         DB        000h,030h,0F0h,0C0h,0C0h,0C3h,060h,00Ch
         DB        030h,038h
Prop12   DB        006h,000h,060h,07Eh,00Ch,018h,060h,060h
         DB        000h,019h,099h,080h,0C0h,0C3h,0C0h,00Ch
         DB        030h,038h
Prop13   DB        006h,000h,060h,060h,00Ch,018h,060h,060h
         DB        000h,019h,099h,080h,0C0h,0C3h,080h,00Ch
         DB        030h,038h
Prop14   DB        00Fh,000h,0F0h,060h,00Ch,018h,030h,0C0h
         DB        000h,00Fh,00Fh,000h,061h,083h,000h,00Ch
         DB        030h,038h
Prop15   DB        03Fh,0C3h,0FCh,063h,01Eh,03Ch,030h,0C0h
         DB        000h,00Fh,00Fh,000h,061h,087h,080h,01Eh
         DB        018h,07Ch
Prop16   DB        03Fh,0C3h,0FCh,03Eh,01Eh,03Ch,01Fh,080h
         DB        000h,006h,006h,000h,03Fh,007h,080h,01Eh
         DB        00Fh,0FCh


PChar    DW        18
PSpace   DW        72
POffset  DW        3096      ;90 Bytes/Line X 34 Lines
```

```
;The program uses this set of variables to print the phrase
; "PRESS ANY KEY WHEN READY" at the bottom of the display.
; Notice this display uses mono-spaced type.
```

```
Block1   DB        3Eh,3Eh,3Fh,1Fh,1Fh,00h,0Ch,23h,33h,00h
         DB        33h,3Fh,33h,00h,63h,33h,3Fh,23h,00h,3Eh
         DB        3Fh,0Ch,3Eh,33h,00h,00h,00h
```

6-3 Continued.

```
Block2  DB      33h,33h,30h,30h,30h,00h,1Eh,33h,33h,00h
        DB      33h,30h,33h,00h,63h,33h,30h,33h,00h,33h
        DB      30h,1Eh,33h,33h,00h,00h,00h
Block3  DB      33h,33h,30h,30h,30h,00h,33h,3Bh,33h,00h
        DB      36h,30h,33h,00h,63h,33h,30h,3Bh,00h,33h
        DB      30h,33h,33h,33h,00h,00h,00h
Block4  DB      33h,33h,3Eh,1Ch,1Ch,00h,33h,37h,1Eh,00h
        DB      3Ch,3Eh,1Eh,00h,6Bh,33h,3Eh,37h,00h,33h
        DB      3Eh,33h,33h,1Eh,00h,00h,00h
Block5  DB      3Eh,3Eh,30h,0Eh,0Eh,00h,3Fh,33h,0Ch,00h
        DB      36h,30h,0Ch,00h,6Bh,3Fh,30h,33h,00h,3Eh
        DB      30h,3Fh,33h,0Ch,00h,00h,00h
Block6  DB      30h,36h,30h,03h,03h,00h,33h,33h,0Ch,00h
        DB      33h,30h,0Ch,00h,6Bh,33h,30h,33h,00h,36h
        DB      30h,33h,33h,0Ch,00h,00h,00h
Block7  DB      30h,33h,30h,03h,03h,00h,33h,33h,0Ch,00h
        DB      33h,30h,0Ch,00h,77h,33h,30h,33h,00h,33h
        DB      30h,33h,33h,0Ch,0Ch,0Ch,0Ch
Block8  DB      30h,33h,3Fh,3Eh,3Eh,00h,33h,33h,0Ch,00h
        DB      33h,3Fh,0Ch,00h,22h,33h,3Fh,33h,00h,33h
        DB      3Fh,33h,3Eh,0Ch,0Ch,0Ch,0Ch
NumChar DW      27
NumSpace        DW      63
B_Offset        DW      7200    ;90 Bytes/Line X 80 Lines
```

```
;Video BIOS Parameter Table Values.  These values fill the BIOS
; parameter table with the correct values for monochrome text
; mode.
```

```
Vid_Param       DB      7       ;CRT Mode
        DW      80      ;CRT Columns
        DW      8000H   ;CRT Length
        DW      0       ;CRT Start
        DW      8 DUP (0)       ;Cursor Position
        DW      0       ;Cursor Mode
        DB      0       ;Active Page
CRTC_Port       DW      3B4h    ;6845 Port Address
Mode_Set        DB      0Ah     ;Graphics Video Mode
        DB      0       ;Not Used, Must Be Zero
```

```
Vid_Len EQU     $-Vid_Param     ;Current Address - Initial Address
```

```
;Graphics mode parameters.  Each parameter is a single word
; consisting of a CRTC register number (loaded in AL) and data
; for that register (loaded in AH).  These are the parameters
; recommended by Hercules for a display of 16 pixels/character
; and 4 scan lines/character.
```

```
Graph_Parm      DW      3500h   ;Horizontal Total
        DW      2D01h   ;Horizontal Displayed
        DW      2E02h   ;Horizontal Sync Position
```

```
        DW      0703h   ;Horizontal Sync Width
        DW      5B04h   ;Vertical Total
        DW      0205h   ;Vertical Adjust
        DW      5706h   ;Vertical Displayed
        DW      5707h   ;Vertical Sync Displayed
        DW      0309h   ;Max Scan Line

Graph_Len    EQU    $-Graph_Parm    ;Current Address - Initial

;*********************************************************************************************
;* Begin the code segment.                              *
;*********************************************************************************************
.CODE

Example PROC    FAR
Start:  MOV     AX,@DATA        ;Point DS & ES to our data segment.
        MOV     DS,AX
        MOV     ES,AX


;*********************************************************************************************
;* This part of the program checks for the existence of an appropriate display adapter. It calls the GetType   *
;* procedure to determine the exact adapter type. If GetType finds an appropriate adapter, it changes the       *
;* value of TCode. Otherwise, the value of the TCode remains the same. Upon reentry to the main procedure,      *
;* the procedure checks for a zero in TCode. If TCode does equal zero, then the procedure exits to DOS.         *
;*********************************************************************************************

        CALL    GetType ;Check for acceptable adapter.
        CMP     TCode,0 ;If acceptable, proceed.
        JNE     GoodCard
        MOV     AX,0900h        ;Otherwise, display an error
        LEA     DX,ErrMsg1      ; message and exit to the DOS
        INT     21h     ; prompt.
        JMP     Exit


;*********************************************************************************************
;* This section of the program places the Hercules display adapter in graphics mode. You must directly *
;* manipulate the registers to accomplish the graphics mode transition since the video BIOS does not support  *
;* graphics mode. There are four steps to this process. First, the program updates the Video BIOS Parameter   *
;* table with the values required for monochrome text mode. Second, the program sets the 6845 CRTC      *
;* configuration switch at port 3BFh. Third, the program programs the CRTC after blanking the screen. You     *
;* must blank the screen to reduce interference. Finally, the program places the display adapter in graphics   *
;* mode.                                 *
;*********************************************************************************************

GoodCard:       PUSH    ES      ;Save the original segment.
        MOV     AX,Video_Data   ;Place the Video BIOS Address
        MOV     ES,AX   ; segment in ES and the data
        LEA     DI,ES:Video_Offs        ; offset in DI.
        LEA     SI,Vid_Param    ;Offset of BIOS Parameters.
        MOV     CX,Vid_Len      ;Length of BIOS Parameters.
```

6-3 Continued.

```
        REP     MOVSB       ;Transfer the parameters.
        POP     ES          ;Restore the original segment.

        MOV     DX,3BFh     ;Output the configuration bit.
        MOV     AL,1
        OUT     DX,AL

        MOV     DX,3B8h     ;Output blank bit to CRTC
        XOR     AL,AL       ; configuration port. (Blanks
        OUT     DX,AL       ; the display.)
        MOV     DX,3B4h     ;CRTC Address Register Port.
        LEA     SI,Graph_Parm ;Load parameter table address.
        MOV     CX,Graph_Len  ;Length of parameter table.
Next_Reg:   LODSW           ;Load first parameter.
        OUT     DX,AX       ;Output the parameter.  AH is
        LOOP    Next_Reg    ; parameter data, AL is
                            ; register number.  Get next
                            ; parameter.

        MOV     DX,3B8h     ;Enable graphics mode and
        MOV     AL,Mode_Set ; video refresh using the
        OUT     DX,AL       ; configuration port.

        PUSH    ES          ;Save the original segment.
        MOV     AX,Video_Buff ;Place video memory segment in
        MOV     ES,AX       ; ES and starting offset in
        LEA     DI,Buff_Start ; DI.

        MOV     CX,4000h    ;Clear the display by writing
        XOR     AX,AX       ; zeros to every video memory
ClearIt:    MOV     ES:[DI],AX      ; location.
        INC     DI
        INC     DI
        LOOP    ClearIt
```

```
;***************************************************************************************************
;* This section of the program displays the proportionally spaced message "Hello World" in the middle of the   *
;* display.                                        *
;***************************************************************************************************
```

```
        LEA     DI,Buff_Start   ;Display the 1st, 5th, 9th,
        ADD     DI,POffset      ; and 13th scan lines.
        LEA     SI,Prop1
        MOV     CX,PChar
        REP     MOVSB
        ADD     DI,PSpace
        LEA     SI,Prop5
        MOV     CX,PChar
        REP     MOVSB
        ADD     DI,PSpace
        LEA     SI,Prop9
```

```
        MOV     CX,PChar
        REP     MOVSB
        ADD     DI,PSpace
        LEA     SI,Prop13
        MOV     CX,PChar
        REP     MOVSB

        LEA     DI,Buff_Sect2    ;Display the 2nd, 6th, 10th,
        ADD     DI,POffset       ; and 14th scan lines.
        LEA     SI,Prop2
        MOV     CX,PChar
        REP     MOVSB
        ADD     DI,PSpace
        LEA     SI,Prop6
        MOV     CX,PChar
        REP     MOVSB
        ADD     DI,PSpace
        LEA     SI,Prop10
        MOV     CX,PChar
        REP     MOVSB
        ADD     DI,PSpace
        LEA     SI,Prop14
        MOV     CX,PChar
        REP     MOVSB

        LEA     DI,Buff_Sect3    ;Display the 3rd, 7th, 11th,
        ADD     DI,POffset       ; and 15th scan lines.
        LEA     SI,Prop3
        MOV     CX,PChar
        REP     MOVSB
        ADD     DI,PSpace
        LEA     SI,Prop7
        MOV     CX,PChar
        REP     MOVSB
        ADD     DI,PSpace
        LEA     SI,Prop11
        MOV     CX,PChar
        REP     MOVSB
        ADD     DI,PSpace
        LEA     SI,Prop15
        MOV     CX,PChar
        REP     MOVSB

        LEA     DI,Buff_Sect4    ;Display the 4th, 8th, 12th,
        ADD     DI,POffset       ; and 16th scan lines.
        LEA     SI,Prop4
        MOV     CX,PChar
        REP     MOVSB
        ADD     DI,PSpace
        LEA     SI,Prop8
        MOV     CX,PChar
```

```
        REP     MOVSB
        ADD     DI,PSpace
        LEA     SI,Prop12
        MOV     CX,PChar
        REP     MOVSB
        ADD     DI,PSpace
        LEA     SI,Prop16
        MOV     CX,PChar
        REP     MOVSB


;***********************************************************************************************************
;* This section of the program displays a finished message (PRESS ANY KEY WHEN READY...) at the bottom of the   *
;* display.  It waits for the user to press a key, resets the display mode, and exits to DOS.    *
;***********************************************************************************************************

        LEA     DI,Buff_Start   ;Display the 1st and 5th scan lines.
        ADD     DI,B_Offset
        LEA     SI,Block1
        MOV     CX,NumChar
        REP     MOVSB
        ADD     DI,NumSpace
        LEA     SI,Block5
        MOV     CX,NumChar
        REP     MOVSB

        LEA     DI,Buff_Sect2   ;Display the 2nd and 6th scan lines.
        ADD     DI,B_Offset
        LEA     SI,Block2
        MOV     CX,NumChar
        REP     MOVSB
        ADD     DI,NumSpace
        LEA     SI,Block6
        MOV     CX,NumChar
        REP     MOVSB

        LEA     DI,Buff_Sect3   ;Display the 3rd and 7th scan lines.
        ADD     DI,B_Offset
        LEA     SI,Block3
        MOV     CX,NumChar
        REP     MOVSB
        ADD     DI,NumSpace
        LEA     SI,Block7
        MOV     CX,NumChar
        REP     MOVSB

        LEA     DI,Buff_Sect4   ;Display the 4th and 8th scan lines.
        ADD     DI,B_Offset
        LEA     SI,Block4
        MOV     CX,NumChar
        REP     MOVSB
        ADD     DI,NumSpace
```

```
        LEA     SI,Block8
        MOV     CX,NumChar
        REP     MOVSB

        POP     ES      ;Restore the original segment.

        XOR     AX,AX   ;Wait for a keypress.
        INT     16h

        MOV     AX,0007h        ;Restore text mode
        INT     10h

Exit:   MOV     AX,4C00h        ;Return to DOS.
        INT     21h
        RET


Example ENDP


;****************************************************************************************************
;* This procedure allows you to determine the current display adapter type.  Even if the target machine has  *
;* two display adapters, it only reports the type of the active display adapter.  This procedure works by    *
;* using BIOS routines or direct hardware manipulation methods that only work with the target adapter and all *
;* upwardly compatible adapters.  It begins by checking VGA using a VGA only BIOS routine that enables/ *
;* disables the display.  The user doesn't notice a change because the routine uses the screen on parameter.  *
;* The procedure continues with similar approaches for the MCGA, EGA, CGA, InColor, HGC+, HGC, and finally    *
;* MDA.  This procedure places a number corresponding to the value of the display in a variable named TCode.  *
;* If the display adapter does not match any of these known types, the procedure does not change the value of *
;* TCode.                                *
;****************************************************************************************************


GetType PROC    NEAR

        MOV     AX,1200h        ;Check for VGA by using a VGA
        MOV     BL,36h  ; only display enable.
        INT     10h
        CMP     AL,12h  ;Was interrupt successful?
        JNE     Type2   ;If not, different display.
        MOV     TCode,VGA       ;If so, save type and exit.
        JMP     Exit1

Type2:  MOV     AX,1200h        ;Check for EGA by attempting
        MOV     BL,10h  ; to load memory allocation
        INT     10h     ; data.
        CMP     BH,10h  ;Was interrupt successful?
        JNE     Type3   ;If not, different display.
        MOV     TCode,EGA       ;If so, must be EGA since we
        JMP     Exit1   ; already checked VGA.

Type3:  MOV     DX,3B4h ;Check for monochrome by
        MOV     AL,0Ah  ; getting then changing the
        OUT     DX,AL   ; cursor end scan line value.
```

```
          INC     DX
          IN      AL,DX
          XCHG    AH,AL    ;Save value.
          MOV     AL,6     ;Output new value.
          OUT     DX,AL
          MOV     CX,50h   ;Wait for CRTC to respond.
Type3A: LOOP     Type3A
          IN      AL,DX    ;Get value in CRTC.
          XCHG    AH,AL    ;Place original value back in
          OUT     DX,AL    ; CRTC.
          CMP     AH,6     ;See if CRTC recieved our scan line
          JNE     Exit1    ; value. If not, different display.

          MOV     CX,50000         ;Perform this step 50,000 times.
          MOV     BX,0080h         ;Check status register for
          XOR     AX,AX    ; changing bit 7.  This bit
          MOV     DX,3BAh  ; does not change on MDA.
Type3B: IN      AL,DX
          TEST    AX,BX
          LOOPNZ  Type3B

Type3C: AND     AL,01110000b     ;Mask bits 4 through 6.
          CMP     AL,01010000b     ;See if this is an InColor.
          JNE     Type3D   ;If not, different display.
          MOV     TCode,InColor    ;If so, set for InColor.
          JMP     Exit1

Type3D: CMP     AL,00010000b     ;See if this is an HGC Plus
          JNE     Type3E   ;If not, different display.
          MOV     TCode,HGCPlus    ;If so, set for HGC Plus.
          JMP     Exit1

Type3E: MOV     TCode,HGC        ;Must be an HGC adapter.

Exit1:  RET

GetType ENDP

END     Start
```

COLOR GRAPHICS ADAPTER (CGA)

The color graphics adapter (CGA) uses 7 ports for control, information, and data transfer. Instead of the 4 KBytes of RAM provided by the MDA, the CGA uses 16 KBytes. This additional memory allows the CGA to provide low-resolution graphics in four colors and high-resolution graphics in two colors. Notice that the CGA allows you to connect to a composite monitor. Only the output to the green gun connects to the composite monitor output. Figure 6-4 shows a simplified block diagram of the structure of the CGA.

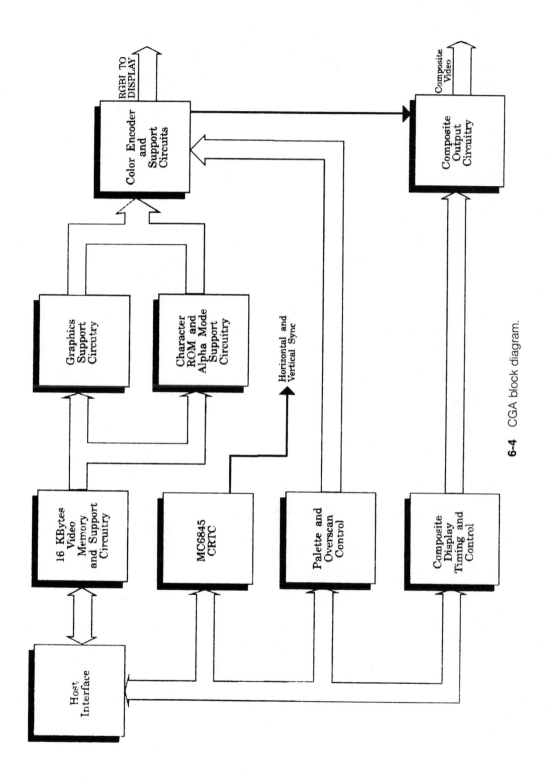

6-4 CGA block diagram.

As you can see from FIG. 6-4, the CGA is an enhanced version of the MDA. Port 3D4h specifies which CRTC register port 3D5h accesses. Because the MDA and CGA use the same CRTC, TABLE 6-1 lists the CGA control registers as well. Port 3D8h accesses the mode control register. TABLE 6-5 shows the meanings for the register bits. TABLE 6-6 shows the contents of the color-select register accessed using port 3D9h. Port 3DAh provides access to the CRT status register. TABLE 6-7 shows the contents of this register. Anything written to Port 3DBh clears the light-pen latch (bit 1 at port 3DAh). Likewise, port 3DCh presets the light-pen latch. TABLE 6-8 contains a listing of CGA display modes. Figure 6-5 shows an example of how to program the CGA registers directly.

6-5 Sample program 13 source code listing.

```
;*********************************************************************************************
;* Sample Program 13, CGA Programming Techniques Demonstration  *
;* This program shows you how to directly manipulate the colors displayed on screen.  It introduces procedures  *
;* for performing logical comparisons between an original and supplied color.  These comparisons include AND,  *
;* OR, XOR, and NOT.  In addition, it shows you how to provide 16 foreground and 16 background colors in text  *
;* mode.  Of course, you must disable blinking to perform this task.  You need the following special equipment  *
;* to use this program.          *
;*      CGA Display Adapter & Appropriate Monitor or    *
;*      EGA Display Adapter & Appropriate Monitor or    *
;*      VGA Display Adapter & Appropriate Monitor      *
;*              *
;*      NOTE:          *
;*      You may need to perform a special setup to use this program with an EGA or VGA adapter. *
;*              *
;* Copyright 1989 John Mueller & Wallace Wang - Tab Books *
;*********************************************************************************************


;*********************************************************************************************
;* Perform the program setup.        *
;*********************************************************************************************

.MODEL MEDIUM   ; Use a medum model size.

.STACK  ; Use the defalt stack of 1024 bytes.


;*********************************************************************************************
;* Begin the data area.  Declare all variables.    *
;*********************************************************************************************
.DATA

;Standard equates.

True    EQU    01
Beep    EQU    07
BS      EQU    08
LF      EQU    10
CR      EQU    13
```

```
Space     EQU    32
StrEnd    EQU    36
MDA       EQU    0
HGC       EQU    0
HGCPlus EQU      0
InColor EQU      0
CGA       EQU    85h
EGA       EQU    86h
MCGA      EQU    0
VGA       EQU    88h
BlinkOff         EQU    00001001b
BlinkOn EQU      00101001b


;Program variables.


TCode     DB     0
NotGood DB       0
ErrMsg1 DB       'You must use a CGA compatible card!!',Beep,CR,LF,StrEnd
SetBlink         DB       'Press any key to enable blinking...',StrEnd
Finished         DB       'Press any key when ready...         ',StrEnd
SStr      DB     'This is an example'
StrLen    EQU    $ - SStr
ORStr     DB     'Press any key to OR...'
ORLen     EQU    $ - ORStr
XORStr    DB     'Press any key to XOR...'
XORLen    EQU    $ - XORStr
ANDStr    DB     'Press any key to AND...'
ANDLen    EQU    $ - ANDStr
NOTStr    DB     'Press any key to NOT...'
NOTLen    EQU    $ - NOTStr
AreaLen DW       0
AreaRow DB       0
```

;The program uses these two variables to display the color
; attributes with blinking disabled and enabled.

```
Heading DB       'CGA Display Attributes',StrEnd

AttrNum DB       ' ',7,'0',7,'1',7,'2',7,'3',7,'4',7,'5',7
        DB       '6',7,'7',7,'8',7,'9',7,'A',7,'B',7,'C',7
        DB       'D',7,'E',7,'F',7,'0',7
        DB       'XXXXXXXXXXXXXXX'
        DB       '1XXXXXXXXXXXXXXX'
        DB       '2XXXXXXXXXXXXXXX'
        DB       '3XXXXXXXXXXXXXXX'
        DB       '4XXXXXXXXXXXXXXX'
        DB       '5XXXXXXXXXXXXXXX'
        DB       '6XXXXXXXXXXXXXXX'
        DB       '7XXXXXXXXXXXXXXX'
        DB       '8XXXXXXXXXXXXXXX'
        DB       '9XXXXXXXXXXXXXXX'
```

```
        DB      'AXXXXXXXXXXXXXXXX'
        DB      'BXXXXXXXXXXXXXXXX'
        DB      'CXXXXXXXXXXXXXXXX'
        DB      'DXXXXXXXXXXXXXXXX'
        DB      'EXXXXXXXXXXXXXXXX'
        DB      'FXXXXXXXXXXXXXXXX'


;*****************************************************************************************************
;* Begin the code segment.                           *
;*****************************************************************************************************
.CODE

Example PROC    FAR
Start:  MOV     AX,@DATA         ;Point DS & ES to our data segment.
        MOV     DS,AX
        MOV     ES,AX



;*****************************************************************************************************
;* This part of the program checks for the existence of an appropriate display adapter.  It calls the GetType    *
;* procedure to determine the exact adapter type.  If GetType finds an appropriate adapter, it changes the        *
;* value of TCode.  Otherwise, the value of the TCode remains the same.  Upon reentry to the main procedure,      *
;* the procedure checks for a zero in TCode.  If TCode does equal zero, then the procedure exits to DOS.          *
;*****************************************************************************************************

        CALL    GetType ;Check for acceptable adapter.
        CMP     TCode,0 ;If acceptable, proceed.
        JNE     GoodCard
        MOV     AX,0900h         ;Otherwise, display an error
        LEA     DX,ErrMsg1       ; message and exit to the DOS
        INT     21h     ; prompt.
        JMP     Exit


;*****************************************************************************************************
;* This section of the program displays all the attributes available when using a CGA display adapter with       *
;* blink set off.  It then enables the blink attribute to show the effect of this setting in the video control    *
;* register.  Notice that you effectively halve the number of available colors by enabling the blink bit.         *
;*****************************************************************************************************

GoodCard:       MOV     AL,BlinkOff      ;Send a blink off signal to
        MOV     DX,3D8h ; the CRTC control port.
        OUT     DX,AL

        ;Get ready to output attributes.

        CALL    ClearScr         ;Clear the display.

        MOV     AX,0200h         ;Position the cursor.
        XOR     BX,BX   ;Video page 0.
        MOV     DX,001Dh         ;Row 0, Column 29.
```

```
          INT      10h

          MOV      AX,0900h          ;Display the heading.
          LEA      DX,Heading
          INT      21h

          MOV      AX,0B800h         ;Set destination segment.
          PUSH     ES
          MOV      ES,AX
          MOV      AX,17Eh ;Set destination offset.
          MOV      DI,AX
          XOR      AX,AX    ;Zero the attribute counter.
          LEA      SI,AttrNum        ;Set the source address.

          MOV      CX,22h   ;Display top row of characters.
          REP      MOVSB
          ADD      DI,7Eh   ;Display first character of
          MOVSB             ; next row.
          MOVSB

          MOV      CX,10Fh ;Number of attributes.
          XOR      BX,BX    ;Zero character counter.
OutAttr:  MOVSB             ;Output character.
          MOV      ES:[DI],AL        ;Output attribute.
          INC      AX       ;Increment attribute.
          INC      DI       ;Increment destination.
          INC      BX       ;Increment character counter.
          CMP      BX,10h   ;See if we are at end of line.
          LOOPNE   OutAttr ;If not, display next char.
          CMP      CX,0     ;See if we displayed the last
          JE       LastDisp          ; character. Jump out of loop.
          ADD      DI,7Eh   ;Go to the next line.
          XOR      BX,BX    ;Zero character counter.
          MOVSB             ;Display first character of
          MOV      ES:[DI],AL        ; next row.
          INC      DI
          LOOP     OutAttr

LastDisp: POP      ES       ;Restore ES.
          MOV      AX,0200h          ;Position the cursor.
          XOR      BX,BX    ;Video page 0.
          MOV      DX,1601h          ;Row 22, Column 1.
          INT      10h

          MOV      AX,0900h          ;Display blink enable string.
          LEA      DX,SetBlink
          INT      21h
          XOR      AX,AX    ;Wait for keypress.
          INT      16h

          MOV      AL,BlinkOn        ;Send a blink on signal to
```

```
        MOV     DX,3D8h ; the CRTC control port.
        OUT     DX,AL

        MOV     AX,0200h        ;Position the cursor.
        XOR     BX,BX   ;Video page 0.
        MOV     DX,1601h        ;Row 22, Column 1.
        INT     10h

        MOV     AX,0900h        ;Display finished string.
        LEA     DX,Finished
        INT     21h
        XOR     AX,AX   ;Wait for keypress.
        INT     16h


;******************************************************************************************************
;* This section of the program shows you the differences between the results of the four logical operators:    *
;* OR, XOR, AND, and NOT.  The program passes the same value to each of the first three operators.  This        *
;* value interacts with the current screen attribute and produces a new screen color.  The NOT operator does    *
;* not require any extra input.                         *
;******************************************************************************************************


        CALL    ClearScr        ;Clear the display.

        MOV     AX,09DBh        ;Color the display with green.
        MOV     BX,0002h
        MOV     CX,2000 ;80 characters X 25 rows.
        INT     10h

        MOV     AX,1300h        ;Display a color string.
        MOV     BX,0017h        ;Blue back, white foreground.
        MOV     CX,StrLen
        MOV     DX,0C1Fh        ;Row 12, Column 31
        PUSH    BP      ;Save BP.
        LEA     BP,SStr ;Place string offset in BP.
        INT     10h
        POP     BP      ;Restore BP.

        MOV     AX,1300h        ;Display a color string.
        MOV     BX,002Fh        ;Green back, white foreground.
        MOV     CX,ORLen
        MOV     DX,1800h        ;Row 24, Column 00
        PUSH    BP      ;Save BP.
        LEA     BP,ORStr        ;Place string offset in BP.
        INT     10h
        POP     BP      ;Restore BP.
        XOR     AX,AX   ;Wait for keypress.
        INT     16h

        MOV     CX,0B1Eh        ;Starting row 11, column 30.
        MOV     DX,0D32h        ;Ending row 13, column 50.
```

```
MOV     BL,55h  ;OR color value.
CALL    ORArea  ;OR the desired screen area.

MOV     AX,1300h        ;Display a color string.
MOV     BX,002Fh        ;Green back, white foreground.
MOV     CX,XORLen
MOV     DX,1800h        ;Row 24, Column 00
PUSH    BP      ;Save BP.
LEA     BP,XORStr       ;Place string offset in BP.
INT     10h
POP     BP      ;Restore BP.
XOR     AX,AX   ;Wait for keypress.
INT     16h

MOV     CX,0A1Dh        ;Starting row 10, column 29.
MOV     DX,0E33h        ;Ending row 14, column 51.
MOV     BL,55h  ;XOR color value.
CALL    XORArea ;XOR the desired screen area.

MOV     AX,1300h        ;Display a color string.
MOV     BX,002Fh        ;Green back, white foreground.
MOV     CX,ANDLen
MOV     DX,1800h        ;Row 24, Column 00
PUSH    BP      ;Save BP.
LEA     BP,ANDStr       ;Place string offset in BP.
INT     10h
POP     BP      ;Restore BP.
XOR     AX,AX   ;Wait for keypress.
INT     16h

MOV     CX,091Ch        ;Starting row 9, column 28.
MOV     DX,0F34h        ;Ending row 15, column 52.
MOV     BL,55h  ;AND color value.
CALL    ANDArea ;AND the desired screen area.

MOV     AX,1300h        ;Display a color string.
MOV     BX,002Fh        ;Green back, white foreground.
MOV     CX,NOTLen
MOV     DX,1800h        ;Row 24, Column 00
PUSH    BP      ;Save BP.
LEA     BP,NOTStr       ;Place string offset in BP.
INT     10h
POP     BP      ;Restore BP.
XOR     AX,AX   ;Wait for keypress.
INT     16h

MOV     CX,081Bh        ;Starting row 8, column 27.
MOV     DX,1035h        ;Ending row 16, column 53.
CALL    NOTArea ;NOT the desired screen area.

MOV     AX,0200h        ;Position the cursor.
```

```
        XOR     BX,BX    ;Video page 0.
        MOV     DX,1800h        ;Row 22, Column 1.
        INT     10h

        MOV     AX,0900h        ;Display finished string.
        LEA     DX,Finished
        INT     21h
        XOR     AX,AX    ;Wait for keypress.
        INT     16h
        CALL    ClearScr        ;Clear the display.

Exit:   MOV     AX,4C00h        ;Exit to DOS.
        INT     21h
        RET

Example ENDP

;********************************************************************************************************
;* This procedure allows you to determine the current display adapter type.  Even if the target machine has    *
;* two display adapters, it only reports the type of the active display adapter.  This procedure works by       *
;* using BIOS routines or direct hardware manipulation methods that only work with the target adapter and all   *
;* upwardly compatible adapters.  It begins by checking VGA using a VGA only BIOS routine that enables/ *
;* disables the display.  The user doesn't notice a change because the routine uses the screen on parameter.    *
;* The procedure continues with similar approaches for the MCGA, EGA, CGA, InColor, HGC+, HGC, and finally      *
;* MDA.  This procedure places a number corresponding to the value of the display in a variable named TCode.    *
;* If the display adapter does not match any of these known types, the procedure does not change the value of   *
;* TCode.                                     *
;********************************************************************************************************

GetType PROC    NEAR

        MOV     AX,1200h        ;Check for VGA by using a VGA
        MOV     BL,36h   ; only display enable.
        INT     10h
        CMP     AL,12h   ;Was interrupt successful?
        JNE     Type2    ;If not, different display.
        MOV     TCode,VGA       ;If so, save type and exit.
        JMP     Exit1

Type2:  MOV     AX,1200h        ;Check for MCGA by using the
        MOV     BL,32h   ; CPU access enable/disable
        INT     10h      ; interrupt (norm=enabled).
        CMP     AL,12h   ;Was interrupt successful?
        JNE     Type3    ;If not, different display.
        MOV     TCode,MCGA      ;If so, must be MCGA since we
        JMP     Exit1    ; already checked VGA.

Type3:  MOV     AX,1200h        ;Check for EGA by attempting
        MOV     BL,10h   ; to load memory allocation
        INT     10h      ; data.
        CMP     BH,10h   ;Was interrupt successful?
```

```
        JNE     Type4    ;If not, different display.
        MOV     TCode,EGA        ;If so, must be EGA since we
        JMP     Exit1    ; already checked VGA.


Type4:  MOV     DX,3D4h ;Check for CGA by getting then
        MOV     AL,0Ah  ; changing the cursor end scan
        OUT     DX,AL   ; line value.
        INC     DX
        IN      AL,DX
        XCHG    AH,AL   ;Save value.
        MOV     AL,6    ;Output new value.
        OUT     DX,AL
        MOV     CX,50h  ;Wait for CRTC to respond.
Type4A: LOOP    Type4A
        IN      AL,DX   ;Get value in CRTC.
        XCHG    AH,AL   ;Place original value back in
        OUT     DX,AL   ; CRTC.
        CMP     AH,6    ;See if CRTC recieved our scan line
        JNE     Type5   ; value.  If not, different display.
        MOV     TCode,CGA        ;If so, must be CGA.
        JMP     Exit1


Type5:  MOV     DX,3B4h ;Check for monochrome by
        MOV     AL,0Ah  ; getting then changing the
        OUT     DX,AL   ; cursor end scan line value.
        INC     DX
        IN      AL,DX
        XCHG    AH,AL   ;Save value.
        MOV     AL,6    ;Output new value.
        OUT     DX,AL
        MOV     CX,50h  ;Wait for CRTC to respond.
Type5A: LOOP    Type5A
        IN      AL,DX   ;Get value in CRTC.
        XCHG    AH,AL   ;Place original value back in
        OUT     DX,AL   ; CRTC.
        CMP     AH,6    ;See if CRTC recieved our scan line
        JNE     Exit1   ; value.  If not, different display.


        MOV     CX,50000        ;Perform this step 50,000 times.
        MOV     BX,0080h        ;Check status register for
        XOR     AX,AX   ; changing bit 7.  This bit
        MOV     DX,3BAh ; does not change on MDA.
Type5B: IN      AL,DX
        TEST    AX,BX
        LOOPNZ  Type5B
        JZ      Type5C  ;Jump if Hercules display.
        MOV     TCode,MDA        ;If not, set for MDA display.
        JMP     Exit1


Type5C: AND     AL,01110000b    ;Mask bits 4 through 6.
        CMP     AL,01010000b    ;See if this is an InColor.
```

6-5 Continued.

```
        JNE     Type5D  ;If not, different display.
        MOV     TCode,InColor  ;If so, set for InColor.
        JMP     Exit1

Type5D: CMP     AL,00010000b    ;See if this is an HGC Plus
        JNE     Type5E  ;If not, different display.
        MOV     TCode,HGCPlus   ;If so, set for HGC Plus.
        JMP     Exit1

Type5E: MOV     TCode,HGC       ;Must be an HGC adapter.

Exit1:  RET

GetType ENDP
```

```
;*****************************************************************************************************************
;* This procedure clears the display and places the cursor at coordinates 0,0.  *
;*****************************************************************************************************************

ClearScr        PROC    NEAR

        MOV     AX,0619h        ;Scroll 25 lines.
        MOV     BH,7    ;Use gray.
        XOR     CX,CX   ;Start at coordinate 0,0.
        MOV     DX,1950h        ;End at coordinate 25,80.
        INT     10h
        MOV     AX,0200h        ;Set cursor position.
        XOR     BH,BH   ;Use page 0.
        XOR     DX,DX   ;Use coordinate 0,0.
        INT     10h

        RET

ClearScr        ENDP
```

```
;*****************************************************************************************************************
;* This procedure performs a logical OR of the selected screen attribute with the comparison color in BL.  It  *
;* performs this comparison over the square area defined by the values in CX and DX.   *
;*      BL - Comparison Color     *
;*      CH - Start Row     *
;*      CL - Start Column         *
;*      DH - End Row     *
;*      DL - End Column     *
;*****************************************************************************************************************

ORArea  PROC    NEAR

        MOV     AH,CL   ;Get the length of the area
        MOV     AL,DL   ; by subtracting the left
        SUB     AL,AH   ; column from the right.
        XOR     AH,AH
```

6-5 Continued.

```
        MOV     AreaLen,AX      ;Save the length.

        MOV     AH,DH    ;Get the total number of rows
        MOV     AL,CH    ; by subtracting upper row
        SUB     AH,AL    ; from lower row.
        MOV     AreaRow,AH      ;Save the number of rows.
        INC     AreaRow  ;Increment by 1 for looping.

        MOV     AL,CH    ;Determine the starting place
        XOR     AH,AH    ; in memory.
        MOV     DL,160   ;80 characters/line * 2 bytes
        MUL     DL
        XOR     CH,CH
        ADD     AX,CX    ;Add characters in from line
        ADD     AX,CX    ; starting point.
        MOV     DI,AX    ;Save offset.
        INC     DI       ;Increment to first attribute.

        PUSH    ES       ;Save ES.
        MOV     AX,0B800h       ;Store the video segment.
        MOV     ES,AX

NextRow1:       MOV     CX,AreaLen

NextAttr1:      MOV     AL,ES:[DI]
        OR      AL,BL
        MOV     ES:[DI],AL
        INC     DI
        INC     DI
        LOOP    NextAttr1

        ADD     DI,160   ;Add one row.
        SUB     DI,AreaLen      ;Subtract string length.
        SUB     DI,AreaLen
        DEC     AreaRow  ;Decrement row counter.
        CMP     AreaRow,0       ;See if this is the last row.
        JNE     NextRow1        ;If not, do another row.

        POP     ES

        RET

ORArea  ENDP

;**************************************************************************************************
;
;* This procedure performs a logical XOR of the selected screen attribute with the comparison color in BL.  It  *
;* performs this comparison over the square area defined by the values in CX and DX.      *
;*      BL - Comparison Color             *
;*      CH - Start Row                    *
;*      CL - Start Column                       *
;*      DH - End Row                    *
```

```
;*        DL - End Column                      *
;**********************************************************************************************************


XORArea PROC    NEAR

        MOV     AH,CL    ;Get the length of the area
        MOV     AL,DL    ; by subtracting the left
        SUB     AL,AH    ; column from the right.
        XOR     AH,AH
        MOV     AreaLen,AX       ;Save the length.

        MOV     AH,DH    ;Get the total number of rows
        MOV     AL,CH    ; by subtracting upper row
        SUB     AH,AL    ; from lower row.
        MOV     AreaRow,AH       ;Save the number of rows.
        INC     AreaRow ;Increment by 1 for looping.

        MOV     AL,CH    ;Determine the starting place
        XOR     AH,AH    ; in memory.
        MOV     DL,160   ;80 characters/line * 2 bytes
        MUL     DL
        XOR     CH,CH
        ADD     AX,CX    ;Add characters in from line
        ADD     AX,CX    ; starting point.
        MOV     DI,AX    ;Save offset.
        INC     DI       ;Increment to first attribute.

        PUSH    ES       ;Save ES.
        MOV     AX,0B800h        ;Store the video segment.
        MOV     ES,AX

NextRow2:       MOV     CX,AreaLen

NextAttr2:      MOV     AL,ES:[DI]
        XOR     AL,BL
        MOV     ES:[DI],AL
        INC     DI
        INC     DI
        LOOP    NextAttr2

        ADD     DI,160   ;Add one row.
        SUB     DI,AreaLen       ;Subtract string length.
        SUB     DI,AreaLen
        DEC     AreaRow ;Decrement row counter.
        CMP     AreaRow,0        ;See if this is the last row.
        JNE     NextRow2         ;If not, do another row.

        POP     ES

        RET
```

```
XORArea ENDP

;*****************************************************************************************************
;* This procedure performs a logical AND of the selected screen attribute with the comparison color in BL.  It  *
;* performs this comparison over the square area defined by the values in CX and DX.     *
;*                                                                    *
;*       BL - Comparison Color            *
;*       CH - Start Row                   *
;*       CL - Start Column                       *
;*       DH - End Row                 *
;*       DL - End Column              *
;*****************************************************************************************************
;

ANDArea PROC     NEAR

        MOV      AH,CL     ;Get the length of the area
        MOV      AL,DL     ; by subtracting the left
        SUB      AL,AH     ; column from the right.
        XOR      AH,AH
        MOV      AreaLen,AX      ;Save the length.

        MOV      AH,DH     ;Get the total number of rows
        MOV      AL,CH     ; by subtracting upper row
        SUB      AH,AL     ; from lower row.
        MOV      AreaRow,AH      ;Save the number of rows.
        INC      AreaRow ;Increment by 1 for looping.

        MOV      AL,CH     ;Determine the starting place
        XOR      AH,AH     ; in memory.
        MOV      DL,160    ;80 characters/line * 2 bytes
        MUL      DL
        XOR      CH,CH
        ADD      AX,CX     ;Add characters in from line
        ADD      AX,CX     ; starting point.
        MOV      DI,AX     ;Save offset.
        INC      DI        ;Increment to first attribute.

        PUSH     ES        ;Save ES.
        MOV      AX,0B800h          ;Store the video segment.
        MOV      ES,AX

NextRow3:       MOV      CX,AreaLen

NextAttr3:      MOV      AL,ES:[DI]
        AND      AL,BL
        MOV      ES:[DI],AL
        INC      DI
        INC      DI
        LOOP     NextAttr3

        ADD      DI,160    ;Add one row.
```

```
          SUB      DI,AreaLen       ;Subtract string length.
          SUB      DI,AreaLen


          DEC      AreaRow ;Decrement row counter.
          CMP      AreaRow,0        ;See if this is the last row.
          JNE      NextRow3         ;If not, do another row.


          POP      ES


          RET


ANDArea ENDP


;*****************************************************************************************************
;* This procedure performs a logical NOT of the selected screen attribute.  A logical NOT reverses the value   *
;* of each bit.  In other words, each 1 becomes a 0 and each 0 becomes a 1.  This procedure performs this       *
;* comparison over the square area defined by the values in CX and DX.  *
;*        CH - Start Row                      *
;*        CL - Start Column                         *
;*        DH - End Row                       *
;*        DL - End Column                    *
;*****************************************************************************************************


NOTArea PROC      NEAR


          MOV      AH,CL    ;Get the length of the area
          MOV      AL,DL    ; by subtracting the left
          SUB      AL,AH    ; column from the right.
          XOR      AH,AH
          MOV      AreaLen,AX       ;Save the length.


          MOV      AH,DH    ;Get the total number of rows
          MOV      AL,CH    ; by subtracting upper row
          SUB      AH,AL    ; from lower row.
          MOV      AreaRow,AH       ;Save the number of rows.
          INC      AreaRow ;Increment by 1 for looping.


          MOV      AL,CH    ;Determine the starting place
          XOR      AH,AH    ; in memory.
          MOV      DL,160   ;80 characters/line * 2 bytes
          MUL      DL
          XOR      CH,CH
          ADD      AX,CX    ;Add characters in from line
          ADD      AX,CX    ; starting point.
          MOV      DI,AX    ;Save offset.
          INC      DI       ;Increment to first attribute.


          PUSH     ES       ;Save ES.
          MOV      AX,0B800h         ;Store the video segment.
          MOV      ES,AX


NextRow4:       MOV      CX,AreaLen
```

```
NextAttr4:        MOV      AL,ES:[DI]
          NOT      AL
          MOV      ES:[DI],AL
          INC      DI
          INC      DI
          LOOP     NextAttr4

          ADD      DI,160   ;Add one row.
          SUB      DI,AreaLen      ;Subtract string length.
          SUB      DI,AreaLen
          DEC      AreaRow ;Decrement row counter.
          CMP      AreaRow,0       ;See if this is the last row.
          JNE      NextRow4        ;If not, do another row.

          POP      ES

          RET

NOTArea ENDP

END     Start
```

ENHANCED GRAPHICS ADAPTER (EGA)

The enhanced graphics adapter (EGA) is more complex and contains more registers than any of the display adapters discussed so far. In most cases the EGA supports HGC, CGA, and enhanced graphics modes. The EGA provides HGC and CGA support through a compatibility mode. Figure 6-6 provides a simplified block diagram of the structure of an EGA. Unlike the CGA and MDA standards, different manufacturers use different techniques to achieve EGA compatibility. Therefore, FIG. 6-6 represents a typical rather than absolute block diagram. As you can see, some EGAs use 64 KBytes and others 128 KBytes of RAM. The tables discussed throughout this section help you see the distinction between the two memory models. In most cases the additional memory equates to increased graphics capability, display pages, font storage, or resolution. TABLE 6-9 contains a listing of EGA display modes. Chapter 7 contains a discussion of the EGA video BIOS extensions.

There are five register groups: external, sequencer, cathode ray tube controller (CRTC), graphics, and attribute. The external registers provide miscellaneous external interfaces. The sequencer registers control memory access, timing, and data flow between other registers. The CRTC registers control display timing. The graphics controller registers manipulate parts of the display in graphics mode. Finally, the attribute registers control color palette selections.

Each register group (except the external register group) uses ports in groups of two. Each group contains an address register and a data register (two different ports). To access an individual register within a group, the

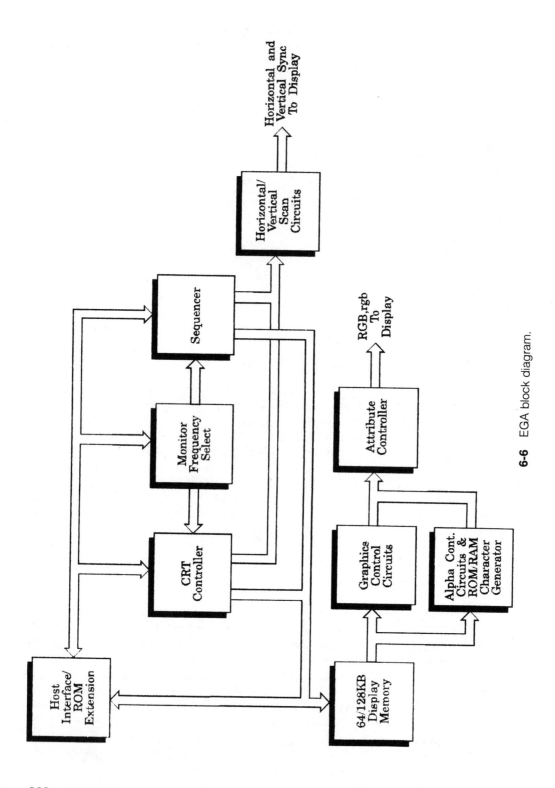

6-6 EGA block diagram.

programmer sends the address register an index to the specific data register. Then, the programmer uses the data port number to access the individual data register. The programmer has direct access to all external registers; each external register uses a unique port number.

Note: The values listed in the tables below represent example EGA register contents. Because the register contents vary from model to model, check the manufacturer's manual for defaults affecting your specific adapter.

There are three external group register ports. Each port performs a different function for input and output. Port 3C2h is the miscellaneous output register/input status register zero. TABLE 6-10 contains a listing of all miscellaneous output register bits. As you can see, this port affects video output interfaces. These interfaces include the CPU, clock, feature port, and display memory. The feature control register (output to ports 3BAh monochrome or 3DAh color) bit listing appears in TABLE 6-11. Several manufacturers plan to use the feature connector to add features to EGA and VGA displays. For example, one manufacturer plans to add enhanced display capabilities by connecting an EGA or VGA to another display adapter through the feature connector. Because each manufacturer plans to implement the feature connector differently, refer to the manufacturer's manual for a complete description of the purpose of this port. The EGA provides access to two input status registers. TABLE 6-12 contains a listing of all input status register zero bits. This register provides you access to the EGA and feature connector switch settings. The bit listing for input status register one (input from ports 3BAh monochrome or 3DAh color) appears in TABLE 6-13. This register provides information about display status, light-pen condition, and diagnostics.

The sequencer register group uses two ports. Port 3C4h is the sequencer address register. You must place the address of the data register you want to access in this register before attempting to access the data register. There are five index settings for this port which affect the data register selected by port 3C5h. Index 0 selects the reset register. TABLE 6-14 contains a bit listing for the reset register. As you can see, the reset register performs a reset of the entire display adapter. Although no standard defines the purpose for each type of reset absolutely, most applications use the synchronous clear for display resolution changes and asynchronous clear for diagnostics. TABLE 6-15 contains the bit listing for the clocking mode register (index 1). This register affects how the EGA presents information on screen. For example, it changes display output from 8-bit width to 9-bit width characters. It also affects display bandwidth (resolution capability), attribute register loading (number of colors), and dot clock frequency. Always perform a synchronous reset before changing the contents of the clocking mode register. TABLE 6-16 contains the bit listing for the map mask register (index 2). This register affects the read/write status of each bit plane of display memory. The EGA uses four bit planes to create 16 colors. The host can read any bit plane. It can only write to bit planes enabled for writing. Using this register can block inadvertent corruption of display memory. TABLE 6-17 contains the bit listing for the character map select register (index 3). When using alphanumeric display mode, bit plane 2 contains the character generators. Depending on the amount of memory installed, each EGA can use from 1 to 4 character generators. Character Map Select A contains the number (1 through 4) of the primary character map. Character Map Select B contains the number of the secondary character map. Each character map consumes exactly 8K of RAM (even if it requires less). Finally, index 4 selects the memory mode register. TABLE 6-18 lists its bit functions. This register affects how the EGA uses memory.

The CRTC register group uses four ports. One group of two ports (3B4h and 3B5h) supports monochrome modes, the other group of two (3D4h and 3D5h) supports color. The CRTC address register port 3?4h supports 24 indexes to other registers at port 3?5h. Use TABLE 6-19 as a guide for finding the individual index value, function, and related table except indexes Ch through Fh. TABLE 6-23 lists the default video mode values and bit functions for the end horizontal blanking register (index 3). This register uses a format different from the previous ones. All the other registers use all eight bits to represent the desired value. The end horizontal blanking register uses bits 0 – 4 for display value. This is the count used to stop horizontal blanking. It uses bits 5 – 7 to skew the start of the displayable area. The display adapter uses this skew time to access the character, attribute, character generator, and Pel Panning register. The adapter uses the information acquired to convert ASCII characters to a displayable bit stream. The display adapter assumes the display value of bits 5 – 7 equal the start horizontal blanking value for bits 5 – 7. Indexes Ch and Dh access the address of the first pixel or character in display memory. The CRTC looks at this address before it begins to display data. Some programs use the contents of these two indexes to implement smooth scrolling. Index Ch accesses the eight most significant bits. Index Dh accesses the eight least significant bits. When you use the four bit planes singularly, the two indexes point to a byte boundary. When using two bits planes chained together, index Ch and Dh always point to a word boundary. Indexes Eh and Fh access the current cursor address. The CRTC uses the address to place the cursor on the display. Index Eh accesses the eight most significant bits. Index Fh accesses the eight least significant bits.

The EGA graphics mode uses two graphics control chips to write and read graphics memory. The buffers used for these reads and writes include four latches—one for each bit plane. Each latch contains one byte of data for the most currently read memory address. The graphics control registers control the technique used to combine the CPU data with latch data. There are two graphics control registers named "Graphics 1" and "Graphics 2." Each register controls two latches. The port address for graphics 1 is 3CCh. This port usually contains 00h for all modes. The port address for graphics 2 is 3CAh. This port usually contains 01h for all modes. The graphics 1 and 2 address register (port 3CEh) contains an index to the registers accessed using port 3CFh. TABLE 6-41 shows the index, associated register name, and reference table.

The attribute register controls the color assignments derived from the four-bit input of the four-bit planes. Access these registers using port 3C0h (an undocumented access port for reading the registers exists at 3C1h). Change the registers only during a vertical retrace. TABLE 6-51 shows the index, associated register name and reference table for the attribute address register. Because the address register shares the same port as the other attribute registers, set the register to the address mode using an IN instruction to port 3BAh (monochrome) or 3DAh (color). Figure 6-7 shows an example of how to program the EGA registers directly.

6-7 Sample program 14 source code listing.

```
;********************************************************************************************
;* Sample Program 14, EGA Programming Techniques Demonstration  *
;* This program shows you how to turn off the EGA blink bit.  This procedure performs a task similar to *
;* program 15 for CGA.  Notice the differences between CGA and EGA/VGA programming requirements.  After the    *
;* program sets the blink bit off, it shows you the results of changing the palette register contents.  The    *
;* programs restores the original palette register values upon exit from the palette register demo.  You       *
;* need the following special equipment to use this program.    *
;*      EGA Display Adapter & Appropriate Monitor or    *
;*      VGA Display Adapter & Appropriate Monitor       *
;*      128 KBytes Display Memory (minimum)             *
;*                          *
;* Copyright 1989 John Mueller & Wallace Wang - Tab Books. *
;********************************************************************************************


;********************************************************************************************
;* Perform the program setup.                 *
;********************************************************************************************

.MODEL MEDIUM    ; Use a medum model size.

.STACK  ; Use the defalt stack of 1024 bytes.


;********************************************************************************************
;* Begin the data area.  Declare all variables.        *
;********************************************************************************************
.DATA

;Standard equates.

True    EQU    01
Beep    EQU    07
BS      EQU    08
LF      EQU    10
CR      EQU    13
Space   EQU    32
StrEnd  EQU    36
```

6-7 Continued.

```
EGA       EQU      86h
VGA       EQU      88h

;Program variables.

TCode   DB       0
NotGood DB       0
ErrMsg1 DB       'You must use a EGA compatible card!!',Beep,CR,LF,StrEnd
Finished        DB        'Press any key when ready...          ',StrEnd
```

;The program uses these two variables to display the color
; attributes with blinking disabled and enabled.

```
Heading DB       'EGA Display Attributes',StrEnd

AttrNum DB       ' ',7,'0',7,'1',7,'2',7,'3',7,'4',7,'5',7
        DB       '6',7,'7',7,'8',7,'9',7,'A',7,'B',7,'C',7
        DB       'D',7,'E',7,'F',7,'0',7
        DB       'XXXXXXXXXXXXXXX'
        DB       '1XXXXXXXXXXXXXXX'
        DB       '2XXXXXXXXXXXXXXX'
        DB       '3XXXXXXXXXXXXXXX'
        DB       '4XXXXXXXXXXXXXXX'
        DB       '5XXXXXXXXXXXXXXX'
        DB       '6XXXXXXXXXXXXXXX'
        DB       '7XXXXXXXXXXXXXXX'
        DB       '8XXXXXXXXXXXXXXX'
        DB       '9XXXXXXXXXXXXXXX'
        DB       'AXXXXXXXXXXXXXXX'
        DB       'BXXXXXXXXXXXXXXX'
        DB       'CXXXXXXXXXXXXXXX'
        DB       'DXXXXXXXXXXXXXXX'
        DB       'EXXXXXXXXXXXXXXX'
        DB       'FXXXXXXXXXXXXXXX'
```

;This variable contains the original color values for the palette
; registers. The program uses it to restore the original the
; registers to their original state.

```
OrgColor        DB       00h, 01h, 02h, 03h, 04h, 05h, 14h, 07h
        DB       38h, 39h, 3Ah, 3Bh, 3Ch, 3Dh, 3Eh, 3Fh
```

```
;************************************************************************************************************
;* Begin the code segment.                        *
;************************************************************************************************************
.CODE

Example PROC     FAR
Start:  MOV      AX,@DATA         ;Point DS & ES to our data segment.
        MOV      DS,AX
        MOV      ES,AX
```

6-7 Continued.

```
;**********************************************************************************************************
;* This part of the program checks for the existence of an appropriate display adapter.  It calls the GetType    *
;* procedure to determine the exact adapter type.  If GetType finds an appropriate adapter, it changes the        *
;* value of TCode.  Otherwise, the value of the TCode remains the same.  Upon reentry to the main procedure,      *
;* the procedure checks for a zero in TCode.  If TCode does equal zero, then the procedure exits to DOS.          *
;**********************************************************************************************************
;

          CALL    GetType ;Check for acceptable adapter.
          CMP     TCode,0 ;If acceptable, proceed.
          JNE     GoodCard
          MOV     AX,0900h        ;Otherwise, display an error
          LEA     DX,ErrMsg1      ; message and exit to the DOS
          INT     21h     ; prompt.
          JMP     Exit


;**********************************************************************************************************
;* This part of the program sets the blink attribute off.  Setting this attribute off effectively doubles the    *
;* available number of background display colors.                    *
;**********************************************************************************************************
;

GoodCard:    CALL    BlinkOff        ;Display high intensity
                             ; colors on background.

          ;Get ready to output attributes.

          CALL    ClearScr        ;Clear the display.

          MOV     AX,0200h        ;Position the cursor.
          XOR     BX,BX   ;Video page 0.
          MOV     DX,001Dh        ;Row 0, Column 29.
          INT     10h
          MOV     AX,0900h        ;Display the heading.
          LEA     DX,Heading
          INT     21h

          MOV     AX,0B800h       ;Set destination segment.
          PUSH    ES
          MOV     ES,AX
          MOV     AX,17Eh ;Set destination offset.
          MOV     DI,AX
          XOR     AX,AX   ;Zero the attribute counter.
          LEA     SI,AttrNum      ;Set the source address.

          MOV     CX,22h  ;Display top row of characters.
          REP     MOVSB
          ADD     DI,7Eh  ;Display first character of
          MOVSB           ; next row.
          MOVSB

          MOV     CX,10Fh ;Number of attributes.
          XOR     BX,BX   ;Zero character counter.
```

```
OutAttr:        MOVSB           ;Output character.
        MOV     ES:[DI],AL      ;Output attribute.
        INC     AX      ;Increment attribute.
        INC     DI      ;Increment destination.
        INC     BX      ;Increment character counter.
        CMP     BX,10h  ;See if we are at end of line.
        LOOPNE  OutAttr ;If not, display next char.
        CMP     CX,0    ;See if we displayed the last
        JE      LastDisp        ; character. Jump out of loop.
        ADD     DI,7Eh  ;Go to the next line.
        XOR     BX,BX   ;Zero character counter.
        MOVSB           ;Display first character of
        MOV     ES:[DI],AL      ; next row.
        INC     DI
        LOOP    OutAttr


LastDisp:       POP     ES      ;Restore ES.
        MOV     AX,0200h        ;Position the cursor.
        XOR     BX,BX   ;Video page 0.
        MOV     DX,1601h        ;Row 22, Column 1.
        INT     10h

        MOV     AX,0200h        ;Position the cursor.
        XOR     BX,BX   ;Video page 0.
        MOV     DX,1601h        ;Row 22, Column 1.
        INT     10h

        MOV     AX,0900h        ;Display finished string.
        LEA     DX,Finished
        INT     21h
        XOR     AX,AX   ;Wait for keypress.
        INT     16h


;****************************************************************************************************
;* This part of the program demonstrates the effects of changing the values within the 16 palette registers   *
;* (index 0 through 0Fh of port 03C0h).         *
;****************************************************************************************************

        CALL    CDemo   ;Display various palette
                        ; register display values.
        CALL    RestPal ;Restore the original
                        ; palette register values.

        MOV     AX,0200h        ;Position the cursor.
        XOR     BX,BX   ;Video page 0.
        MOV     DX,1601h        ;Row 22, Column 1.
        INT     10h

        MOV     AX,0900h        ;Display finished string.
        LEA     DX,Finished
        INT     21h
```

6-7 Continued.

```
        XOR     AX,AX    ;Wait for keypress.
        INT     16h

        CALL    ClearScr        ;Clear the display.

Exit:   MOV     AX,4C00h        ;Exit to DOS.
        INT     21h
        RET

Example ENDP
```

```
;****************************************************************************************************
;* This procedure allows you to determine the current display adapter type.  Even if the target machine has   *
;* two display adapters, it only reports the type of the active display adapter.  This procedure works by      *
;* using BIOS routines or direct hardware manipulation methods that only work with the target adapter and all  *
;* upwardly compatible adapters.  It begins by checking VGA using a VGA only BIOS routine that enables/ *
;* disables the display.  The user doesn't notice a change because the routine uses the screen on parameter.   *
;* The procedure continues with similar approaches for the MCGA, EGA, CGA, InColor, HGC+, HGC, and finally     *
;* MDA.  This procedure places a number corresponding to the value of the display in a variable named TCode.   *
;* If the display adapter does not match any of these known types, the procedure does not change the value of  *
;* TCode.                                    *
;****************************************************************************************************
```

```
GetType PROC    NEAR

        MOV     AX,1200h        ;Check for VGA by using a VGA
        MOV     BL,36h  ; only display enable.
        INT     10h
        CMP     AL,12h  ;Was interrupt successful?
        JNE     Type2   ;If not, different display.
        MOV     TCode,VGA       ;If so, save type and exit.
        JMP     Exit1

Type2:  MOV     AX,1200h        ;Check for EGA by attempting
        MOV     BL,10h  ; to load memory allocation
        INT     10h     ; data.
        CMP     BH,10h  ;Was interrupt successful?
        JNE     Exit1   ;If not, different display.
        MOV     TCode,EGA       ;If so, must be EGA since we
                        ; already checked VGA.

Exit1:  RET

GetType ENDP
```

```
;****************************************************************************************************
;* This procedure clears the display and places the cursor at coordinates 0,0.  *
;****************************************************************************************************
ClearScr        PROC    NEAR
```

```
        MOV     AX,0619h        ;Scroll 25 lines.
        MOV     BH,7    ;Use gray.
        XOR     CX,CX   ;Start at coordinate 0,0.
        MOV     DX,1950h        ;End at coordinate 25,80.
        INT     10h

        MOV     AX,0200h        ;Set cursor position.
        XOR     BH,BH   ;Use page 0.
        XOR     DX,DX   ;Use coordinate 0,0.
        INT     10h

        RET

ClearScr        ENDP
;**************************************************************************************************
;* This procedure sets the the blink bit to off.                *
;**************************************************************************************************
;

BlinkOff        PROC    NEAR

        CALL    SetFF   ;Set the Flip Flop to Address.
        CLI             ;Clear interrupts
        MOV     DX,3C0h ;Output the index number for
        MOV     AL,30h  ; the mode control register.
        OUT     DX,AL
        INC     DX      ;Get the current mode control
        IN      AL,DX   ; register contents.
        DEC     DX
        AND     AL,0F7h ;Turn off blink.
        OUT     DX,AL
        JMP     SHORT $+2       ;Add a short wait.
        STI             ;Set interrupts.
        CALL    SetFF   ;Set the Flip Flop to Address.

        RET

BlinkOff        ENDP

;**************************************************************************************************
;* This procedure sets the specified palette register to the requested color.  There are 16 palette registers  *
;* (index 0 through 0Fh of port 03C0h).  The palette registers share the port with the attribute control       *
;* register.  To access the palette registers, you send an index value to the attribute control register       *
;* first, then the palette register value.  You must set the attribute control register to address mode before *
;* attempting to change an palette register value.  You must supply the following values when using this        *
;* procedure.                    *
;*      BH - Palette Register Color           *
;*      BL - Palette Register Number          *
;**************************************************************************************************
;

SetPalette      PROC    NEAR
```

6-7 Continued.

```
        CALL    SetFF    ;Set the Flip Flop to Address.
Wait1:  IN      AL,DX    ;See if vertical retrace, if
        TEST    AL,08    ; not, wait.
        JZ      Wait1
        MOV     AL,BL    ;Set palette register number.
        MOV     DX,3C0h
        OUT     DX,AL
        JMP     $+2      ;Wait for mode control
        JMP     $+2      ; register reaction.
        MOV     AL,BH    ;Set the palette color.
        OUT     DX,AL
        MOV     AL,20h
        OUT     DX,AL
        CALL    SetFF    ;Set the Flip Flop to Address.

        RET

SetPalette      ENDP

;*****************************************************************************************************
;* This procedure sets the attribute control register to address mode by reading the Input Status Register.  *
;*****************************************************************************************************

SetFF   PROC    NEAR

        CLI
        PUSH    ES
        MOV     AX,40h   ;Get the Input Status Register
        MOV     ES,AX    ; port number (3BA or 3DA).
        MOV     DX,ES:[63h]
        ADD     DX,6
        POP     ES       ;Initialize the attribute
        IN      AL,DX
        STI

        RET

SetFF   ENDP


;*****************************************************************************************************
;* This procedure changes each one of the palette registers in turn to a different value.  After it changes  *
;* all the palette registers, the procedure uses a loop to provide a wait state.  This allow to the user to   *
;* view the results of the color palette change.         *
;*****************************************************************************************************

CDemo   PROC    NEAR

        MOV     BH,00h   ;Move the initial color in BH.
CLoop:  XOR     BL,BL    ;Move the initial reg in BL.
        CALL    SetPalette      ;Set the palette color.
```

```
        INC     BH      ;Change the contents of
        INC     BL      ; register 01h.
        CALL    SetPalette      ;Set the palette color.

        INC     BH      ;Change the contents of
        INC     BL      ; register 02h.
        CALL    SetPalette      ;Set the palette color.

        INC     BH      ;Change the contents of
        INC     BL      ; register 03h.
        CALL    SetPalette      ;Set the palette color.

        INC     BH      ;Change the contents of
        INC     BL      ; register 04h.
        CALL    SetPalette      ;Set the palette color.

        INC     BH      ;Change the contents of
        INC     BL      ; register 05h.
        CALL    SetPalette      ;Set the palette color.

        INC     BH      ;Change the contents of
        INC     BL      ; register 06h.
        CALL    SetPalette      ;Set the palette color.

        INC     BH      ;Change the contents of
        INC     BL      ; register 07h.
        CALL    SetPalette      ;Set the palette color.

        INC     BH      ;Change the contents of
        INC     BL      ; register 08h.
        CALL    SetPalette      ;Set the palette color.

        INC     BH      ;Change the contents of
        INC     BL      ; register 09h.
        CALL    SetPalette      ;Set the palette color.

        INC     BH      ;Change the contents of
        INC     BL      ; register 0Ah.
        CALL    SetPalette      ;Set the palette color.

        INC     BH      ;Change the contents of
        INC     BL      ; register 0Bh.
        CALL    SetPalette      ;Set the palette color.

        INC     BH      ;Change the contents of
        INC     BL      ; register 0Ch.
        CALL    SetPalette      ;Set the palette color.

        INC     BH      ;Change the contents of
        INC     BL      ; register 0Dh.
        CALL    SetPalette      ;Set the palette color.
```

```
        INC     BH      ;Change the contents of
        INC     BL      ; register OEh.
        CALL    SetPalette      ;Set the palette color.

        INC     BH      ;Change the contents of
        INC     BL      ; register OFh.
        CALL    SetPalette      ;Set the palette color.

        CMP     BH,3Fh  ;Check for last color.
        JE      EndColor        ;If so, exit.
        SUB     BH,14   ;Otherwise, setup for next color.

        MOV     CX,OFFFFh       ;Wait for user view time.
WaitChng:       NOP
        NOP
        LOOP    WaitChng
        JMP     CLoop   ;Begin next sequence.

EndColor:       RET

CDemo   ENDP

;****************************************************************************************************************
;* This procedure restores the original colors contained in the palette registers.  It works exactly the same  *
;* as procedure CDemo.                        *
;****************************************************************************************************************
;

RestPal PROC    NEAR

        LEA     DI,OrgColor     ;Load the address for the
                                ; original color table.
        MOV     BH,[DI] ;Store the color.
        MOV     BL,0    ;Change the contents of
        CALL    SetPalette      ; register OOh.

        INC     DI      ;Get next color and store.
        MOV     BH,[DI]
        INC     BL      ;Change the contents of
        CALL    SetPalette      ; register O1h.

        INC     DI      ;Get next color and store.
        MOV     BH,[DI]
        INC     BL      ;Change the contents of
        CALL    SetPalette      ; register O2h.

        INC     DI      ;Get next color and store.
        MOV     BH,[DI]
        INC     BL      ;Change the contents of
        CALL    SetPalette      ; register O3h.
```

```
        INC     DI      ;Get next color and store.
        MOV     BH,[DI]
        INC     BL      ;Change the contents of
        CALL    SetPalette      ; register 04h.


        INC     DI      ;Get next color and store.
        MOV     BH,[DI]
        INC     BL      ;Change the contents of
        CALL    SetPalette      ; register 05h.


        INC     DI      ;Get next color and store.
        MOV     BH,[DI]
        INC     BL      ;Change the contents of
        CALL    SetPalette      ; register 06h.


        INC     DI      ;Get next color and store.
        MOV     BH,[DI]
        INC     BL      ;Change the contents of
        CALL    SetPalette      ; register 07h.


        INC     DI      ;Get next color and store.
        MOV     BH,[DI]
        INC     BL      ;Change the contents of
        CALL    SetPalette      ; register 08h.


        INC     DI      ;Get next color and store.
        MOV     BH,[DI]
        INC     BL      ;Change the contents of
        CALL    SetPalette      ; register 09h.


        INC     DI      ;Get next color and store.
        MOV     BH,[DI]
        INC     BL      ;Change the contents of
        CALL    SetPalette      ; register 0Ah.


        INC     DI      ;Get next color and store.
        MOV     BH,[DI]
        INC     BL      ;Change the contents of
        CALL    SetPalette      ; register 0Bh.


        INC     DI      ;Get next color and store.
        MOV     BH,[DI]
        INC     BL      ;Change the contents of
        CALL    SetPalette      ; register 0Ch.


        INC     DI      ;Get next color and store.
        MOV     BH,[DI]
        INC     BL      ;Change the contents of
        CALL    SetPalette      ; register 0Dh.


        INC     DI      ;Get next color and store.
```

```
        MOV    BH,[DI]
        INC    BL       ;Change the contents of
        CALL   SetPalette     ; register 0Eh.

        INC    DI       ;Get next color and store.
        MOV    BH,[DI]
        INC    BL       ;Change the contents of
        CALL   SetPalette     ; register 0Fh.

        RET

RestPal ENDP

END     Start
```

VIRTUAL GRAPHICS ARRAY (VGA) AND SUPER VGA

The virtual graphics array (VGA) is very similar to the EGA. It contains all the same registers with a few added. These additional registers increase VGA flexibility. A standard VGA also provides 256K of display memory. Programs can use this extra memory for enhanced display resolutions/color combinations and font storage. Super VGA is a VGA enhancement. These enhancements include additional memory (usually 256K for a total of 512K for the adapter) and extended BIOS functions. At present, there is no standard for Super VGA. The Video Electronics Standards Association (VESA) is working with vendors to produce a standard Super VGA interface. To determine the capabilities and programming interface for Super VGA modes supported by your adapter, check the vendor manual.

Figure 6-8 is a simplified block diagram of a typical VGA/Super VGA. Unlike the CGA and MDA standards, different manufacturers use different techniques to achieve VGA compatibility. Therefore, FIG. 6-8 represents a typical rather than absolute block diagram. As you can see, standard VGAs use 256 KBytes and Super VGAs use 512 KBytes of RAM. Some vendors might allow you to use more RAM. However, due to memory constraints, every VGA has at least 256 KBytes of RAM. TABLE 6-57 contains a listing of VGA display modes. Notice that the table shows you the VESA specific Super VGA display modes. Some vendors implement these same modes as 7-bit mode numbers accessed through standard BIOS calls. Chapter 14 contains a discussion of the VGA video BIOS extensions. It also describes the programming interface currently promoted by VESA for Super VGA display modes.

The VGA uses registers similarly to, but not exactly the same as, the EGA. One exception is the addition of the digital-to-analog converter register group. There are six register groups: external, sequencer, cathode ray tube controller (CRTC), graphics, attribute, and digital-to-analog converter (DAC). The external registers provide miscellaneous external interfaces.

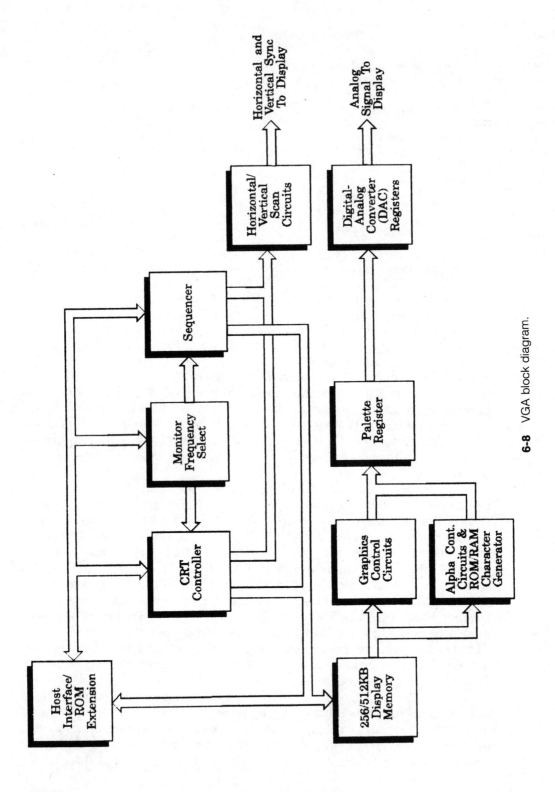

6-8 VGA block diagram.

The sequencer registers control memory access, timing, and data flow between other registers. The CRTC registers control display timing. The graphics controller registers manipulate parts of the display in graphics mode. The attribute registers control color palette selections. Finally, the DAC registers make final color selections and convert the colors to three analog signals.

Each register group (except the external register group) uses ports in groups of two. Each group contains an address register and a data register (two different ports). To access an individual register within a group, the programmer sends the address register and index to the specific data register. Then, the programmer uses the data port number to access the individual data register. The programmer has direct access to all external registers; each external register uses a unique port number.

Note: Most values contained in the VGA tables are defaults based on the EGA model. They show typical register contents. Because the BIOS defaults vary from model to model, check the manufacturer's manual for defaults affecting your specific model.

There are four external group register ports. Each port performs a different function for input and output. Port 3C2h is the miscellaneous output register/input status register zero (use port 3CCh to read the register contents). TABLE 6-58 contains a listing of all miscellaneous output register bits. As you can see, this port affects video output interfaces. These interfaces include the CPU, clock, feature port, and display memory. The feature control register (output to ports 3BAh monochrome or 3DAh color, input from port 3CAh) bit listing appears in TABLE 6-59. Several manufacturers plan to use the feature connector to add features to EGA and VGA displays. For example, one manufacturer plans to add enhanced display capabilities by connecting an EGA or VGA to another display adapter through the feature connector. Because each manufacturer plans to implement the feature connector differently, refer to the manufacturer's manual for a complete description of the purpose of this port. The VGA/Super VGA provides access to two input status registers. These registers provide enhanced features over their EGA counterpart. TABLE 6-60 contains a listing of all input status register zero bits. This register provides you access to the VGA switch settings and CRT interrupt (video retrace). The bit listing for input status register one (input from ports 3BAh monochrome or 3DAh color) appears in TABLE 6-61. This register provides information about display status, vertical retrace, and diagnostics. The video subsystem enable register (port 3C3h) controls VGA activity. Setting bit 0 allows the VGA to display a screen image even when in sleep mode. Most manufacturers reserve bits 1 through 7 for future expansion.

The sequencer register group uses two ports. Port 3C4h is the sequencer address register. You must place the address of the data register you want to access in this register before attempting to access the data register. There are five index settings for this port that affect the register selected by port 3C5h. Index 0 selects the reset register. TABLE 6-62 contains a bit listing for the reset register. As you can see, the reset register performs a reset of the entire display adapter. Although no standard defines the purpose for each type of reset absolutely, most applications use the synchronous clear for display resolution changes and asynchronous clear for diagnostics.

TABLE 6-63 contains the bit listing for the clocking mode register (index 1). This register affects how the VGA presents information on screen. For example, it changes display output from 8-bit width to 9-bit width characters. You must use an 8-bit character width for CGA and EGA modes. Use a 9-bit character width for MDA, HGC, and VGA display modes. The clocking mode register also affects attribute register loading (number of colors) and dot clock frequency. Unlike the EGA, you can use a divide by two (16-bit output) or divide by four (32-bit output) dot clock output. Always perform a synchronous reset before changing the contents of the clocking mode register.

TABLE 6-64 contains the bit listing for the map mask register (index 2). This register affects the read/write status of each bit plane of display memory. The VGA uses four bit planes to create 16 color references. The host can read any bit plane. It can only write to bit planes enabled for writing. Using this register can block inadvertent corruption of display memory.

TABLE 6-65 contains the bit listing for the character map select register (index 3). When using alphanumeric display mode, bit plane 2 contains the character generators. Depending on the amount of memory installed, each VGA can use from 1 to 8 character generators. Character Map Select A works with Character Map Select High Bit A to determine the number (1 through 8) of the primary character map. Character Map Select B works with Character Map Select High Bit B to determine the number of the secondary character map. Each character map consumes exactly 8K of RAM (even if it requires less). Finally index 4 selects the memory mode register.

TABLE 6-66 lists its bit functions. This register affects how the VGA uses memory. Notice that unlike the EGA, the VGA can chain its entire memory area into one contiguous division. The EGA and VGA can create two contiguous divisions to simulate CGA graphics mode.

The CRTC register group uses four ports. One group of two ports (3B4h and 3B5h) supports monochrome modes, the other group of two (3D4h and 3D5h) supports color. The CRTC address register port 3?4h supports 24 indexes to other registers at port 3?5h. Use TABLE 6-67 as a guide for finding the individual index value, function, and related table except indexes Ch through Fh. TABLE 6-23 lists the default video mode values and bit functions for the end horizontal blanking register (index 3). This register uses a format different from the previous ones. All the other registers use all eight bits to represent the desired value. The end horizontal blanking register uses bits 0 – 4 for display value. This is the count used to stop horizontal blanking. It uses bits 5 – 7 to skew the start of the displayable area. The display adapter uses this skew time to access the character, attribute, character generator, and Pel Panning register. The adapter uses the information acquired to convert ASCII characters to a displayable bit stream. The display adapter assumes the display value of bits 5 – 7 equals the start horizontal blanking value for bits 5 – 7. Indexes Ch and Dh access the address of the first pixel or character in display memory. The CRTC looks at this address before it begins to display data. Some programs use the contents of these two indexes to implement smooth scrolling. Index Ch accesses the eight most significant bits. Index Dh accesses the eight least significant bits. When you use the four bit planes singularly, the two indexes point to a byte boundary. When using two bits planes chained together, index Ch and Dh always point to a word boundary.

When using all four bit planes as a contiguous memory area, index Ch and Dh always point to a double word boundary. Indexes Eh and Fh access the current cursor address. The CRTC uses the address to place the cursor on the display. Index Eh accesses the eight most significant bits. Index Fh accesses the eight least significant bits.

The VGA graphics mode does not use two graphics control chips to write and read graphics memory like the EGA does. You can directly read graphics memory with the VGA. Like the EGA, the VGA still uses the graphics 1 and 2 address register (port 3CEh) to index a data port (3CFh). TABLE 6-41 shows the index, associated register name, and reference table.

The attribute register controls the color assignments derived from the four-bit input of the four bit planes. It sends these four bits to the serializers with four static bits (8 bits total) to the DAC. The DAC looks for this value in the color table and outputs the appropriate analog signals. Access these registers using port 3C0h. Use port 3C1h to read the register contents. Change the registers only during a vertical retrace. TABLE 6-89 shows the index, associated register name and reference table for the attribute address register. Because the address register shares the same port as the other attribute registers, set the register to the address mode using an IN instruction to port 3BAh (monochrome) or 3DAh (color).

The digital-to-analog converter (DAC) registers convert binary signals to analog signals used to drive an analog monitor. The DAC registers directly affect mode 13h output because this mode does not use the standard register set discussed above. The other modes can display 16 of the 256 selected colors at any given time; however, they still have access to all 256 colors through the color select register. The following paragraph describes the DAC registers.

Port 3C7h performs two functions. When read (bits 0 and 1), it outputs 11b if the DAC is in the write state, or 00b if the DAC is in the read state. When written to, it selects a PEL data register address for reading (0 – 255). Port 3C8h selects a PEL data register address for writing (0 – 255). Port 3C9h contains the PEL data register. To read or write to port 3C9h, the DAC state register must indicate the PEL data register is in the required state first. During reads or writes, the PEL data registers input/ output three 6-bit values. The first value contains red intensity, the second green intensity, and the third blue intensity. After a read or write, the address registers automatically select the next PEL data register address. Always disable interrupts during a PEL data register read. Never read the registers during active display time—blank the screen first.

The final DAC port is 3C6h. It contains the PEL mask register. Reading or writing this register could damage the DAC color table. Figure 6-9 shows an example of how to program the VGA registers directly. The lack of standards for Super VGA resolution prevents most software vendors from creating programs that use the increased capability. Refer to your vendor manual for a description of Super VGA modes available with your adapter.

6-9 Sample program 15 source code listing.

```
;***************************************************************************************************
;* Sample Program 15, VGA Programming Techniques Demonstration  *
;* This program shows you how to create a graphics display for a VGA.  Once you create the graphic (in this    *
;* case a diamond), the program waits until you press a key.  This allows you to wait for display settling.    *
;* The program then places the VGA in split screen mode.  It uses this mode to replicate the upper half of     *
;* the diamond in the lower half of the screen.  It then scrolls the diamond up the screen and recenters it.   *
;* Press a key to exit the program.  You need the following special equipment to use this program.        *
;*      VGA Display Adapter & Appropriate Monitor        *
;*                          *
;* Copyright 1989 John Mueller & Wallace Wang - Tab Books *
;***************************************************************************************************
;

;***************************************************************************************************
;* Perform the program setup.              *
;***************************************************************************************************
;

.MODEL MEDIUM   ; Use a medum model size.

.STACK  ; Use the defalt stack of 1024 bytes.

;***************************************************************************************************
;* Begin the data area.  Declare all variables.          *
;***************************************************************************************************
;
.DATA

;Standard equates.

DSplit8 EQU     00      ;Center of Display Bit 8
DSplit9 EQU     00      ;Center of Display Bit 9
True    EQU     01
BPLine  EQU     05      ;Displayed Bytes per Line
Beep    EQU     07
BS      EQU     08
LF      EQU     10
CR      EQU     13
Space   EQU     32
StrEnd  EQU     36
UBPRow  EQU     75      ;Unused Bytes per Row
```

6-9 Continued.

```
BPRow    EQU     80       ;Bytes per Row
DSplit0  EQU     240      ;Center of Display Bits 0 - 7
DOffset  EQU     17637    ;((480 Rows - 40 Display Rows)
                          ; * 80 Bytes per Row / 2) +
                          ; ((80 Bytes per Row - 5
                          ; Displayed Bytes per Line)
                          ; / 2)
VGA      EQU     88h
```

;Program variables.

```
TCode    DB      0
NotGood  DB      0
ErrMsg1  DB      'You must use a VGA compatible card!!',Beep,CR,LF,StrEnd
Finished DB      'Press any key when ready...        ',StrEnd
```

;The program uses these variables to draw a diamond on the screen.

```
Row01  DB      000h,000h,018h,000h,000h
Row02  DB      000h,000h,03Ch,000h,000h
Row03  DB      000h,000h,07Eh,000h,000h
Row04  DB      000h,000h,0FFh,000h,000h
Row05  DB      000h,001h,0FFh,080h,000h
Row06  DB      000h,003h,0FFh,0C0h,000h
Row07  DB      000h,007h,0FFh,0E0h,000h
Row08  DB      000h,00Fh,0FFh,0F0h,000h
Row09  DB      000h,01Fh,0FFh,0F8h,000h
Row10  DB      000h,03Fh,0FFh,0FCh,000h
Row11  DB      000h,07Fh,0FFh,0FEh,000h
Row12  DB      000h,0FFh,0FFh,0FFh,000h
Row13  DB      001h,0FFh,0FFh,0FFh,080h
Row14  DB      003h,0FFh,0FFh,0FFh,0C0h
Row15  DB      007h,0FFh,0FFh,0FFh,0E0h
Row16  DB      00Fh,0FFh,0FFh,0FFh,0F0h
Row17  DB      01Fh,0FFh,0FFh,0FFh,0F8h
Row18  DB      03Fh,0FFh,0FFh,0FFh,0FCh
Row19  DB      07Fh,0FFh,0FFh,0FFh,0FEh
Row20  DB      0FFh,0FFh,0FFh,0FFh,0FFh
Row21  DB      0FFh,0FFh,0FFh,0FFh,0FFh
Row22  DB      07Fh,0FFh,0FFh,0FFh,0FEh
Row23  DB      03Fh,0FFh,0FFh,0FFh,0FCh
Row24  DB      01Fh,0FFh,0FFh,0FFh,0F8h
Row25  DB      00Fh,0FFh,0FFh,0FFh,0F0h
Row26  DB      007h,0FFh,0FFh,0FFh,0E0h
Row27  DB      003h,0FFh,0FFh,0FFh,0C0h
Row28  DB      001h,0FFh,0FFh,0FFh,080h
Row29  DB      000h,0FFh,0FFh,0FFh,000h
Row30  DB      000h,07Fh,0FFh,0FEh,000h
Row31  DB      000h,03Fh,0FFh,0FCh,000h
Row32  DB      000h,01Fh,0FFh,0F8h,000h
Row33  DB      000h,00Fh,0FFh,0F0h,000h
```

```
Row34    DB        000h,007h,0FFh,0E0h,000h
Row35    DB        000h,003h,0FFh,0C0h,000h
Row36    DB        000h,001h,0FFh,080h,000h
Row37    DB        000h,000h,0FFh,000h,000h
Row38    DB        000h,000h,07Eh,000h,000h
Row39    DB        000h,000h,03Ch,000h,000h
Row40    DB        000h,000h,018h,000h,000h


Count    DB        40

;**********************************************************************************************************
;* Begin the code segment.                          *
;**********************************************************************************************************
.CODE

Example PROC     FAR
Start:  MOV      AX,@DATA          ;Point DS & ES to our data segment.
        MOV      DS,AX
        MOV      ES,AX


;**********************************************************************************************************
;* This part of the program checks for the existence of an appropriate display adapter.  It calls the GetType   *
;* procedure to determine the exact adapter type.  If GetType finds an appropriate adapter, it changes the      *
;* value of TCode.  Otherwise, the value of the TCode remains the same.  Upon reentry to the main procedure,    *
;* the procedure checks for a zero in TCode.  If TCode does equal zero, then the procedure exits to DOS.        *
;**********************************************************************************************************

        CALL     GetType ;Check for acceptable adapter.
        CMP      TCode,0 ;If acceptable, proceed.
        JNE      GoodCard
        MOV      AX,0900h          ;Otherwise, display an error
        LEA      DX,ErrMsg1        ; message and exit to the DOS
        INT      21h      ; prompt.
        JMP      Exit


;**********************************************************************************************************
;* This section of the program displays the diamond in the center of the screen.  Notice that unlike other     *
;* displays, the VGA and EGA use contiguous, not interleaved bytes for the display.  This allows the use of a   *
;* simple algorithm to place the image on the display.          *
;**********************************************************************************************************

GoodCard:        MOV      AX,0012h          ;Switch to graphics mode.
        INT      10h

        MOV      AX,0A000h         ;Store video segment in ES.
        MOV      ES,AX
        LEA      SI,Row01          ;Load location of first row.
        MOV      DI,DOffset        ;Load first video offset.
NextRow:         MOV      CX,BPLine        ;Load number of bytes.
        REP      MOVSB    ;Output the data.
        ADD      DI,UBPRow        ;Go to next line
```

6-9 Continued.

```
         DEC      Count   ;Number of rows.
         CMP      Count,0 ;See if last row.
         JE       DComplete      ;If so, exit.
         JMP      NextRow ;If not, draw next row.

DComplete:        XOR      AX,AX   ;Wait for user keypress.
         INT      16h


;*****************************************************************************************************
;* This section of the program places the VGA in split screen mode.  Before the program can send the correct   *
;* values to the overflow, max scan line, and line compare registers, it must determine the exact beginning     *
;* of vertical retrace.  It does this by waiting for the end of vertical retrace, then the beginning of *
;* vertical retrace (since the VGA does not specifically supply a beginning of vertical retrace indicator).      *
;*****************************************************************************************************

         CALL     CEndR   ;Wait until end of retrace.
         CALL     CStartR ;Wait until start of retrace.
         CALL     SetSplit        ;Split the screen.


;*****************************************************************************************************
;* This section of the program scrolls the graphic up the display.      *
;*****************************************************************************************************

         MOV      CX,240  ;Load the number of lines to scroll.
MoveIt:  PUSH     AX      ;Save the contents of AX
         PUSH     DX      ; and DX.
         CALL     CEndR   ;Wait until end of retrace.
         CALL     CStartR ;Wait until start of retrace.
         POP      DX      ;Restore the contents of DX
         POP      AX      ; and AX.
         DEC      AH      ;Decrement the line compare
         OUT      DX,AX   ; register value.
         LOOP     MoveIt

         XOR      AX,AX   ;Wait for user keypress.
         INT      16h

         MOV      AX,0003h        ;Switch to text mode.
         INT      10h
Exit:    MOV      AX,4C00h        ;Exit to DOS.
         INT      21h
         RET


Example ENDP


;*****************************************************************************************************
;* This procedure allows you to determine the current display adapter type.  Even if the target machine has     *
;* two display adapters, it only reports the type of the active display adapter.  This procedure works by        *
;* using BIOS routines or direct hardware manipulation methods that only work with the target adapter and all    *
;* upwardly compatible adapters.  It begins by checking VGA using a VGA only BIOS routine that enables/ *
;* disables the display.  The user doesn't notice a change because the routine uses the screen on parameter.     *
```

6-9 Continued.

```
;* The procedure continues with similar approaches for the MCGA, EGA, CGA, InColor, HGC+, HGC, and finally    *
;* MDA.  This procedure places a number corresponding to the value of the display in a variable named TCode.  *
;* If the display adapter does not match any of these known types, the procedure does not change the value of *
;* TCode.                                  *
;*************************************************************************************************************

GetType PROC    NEAR

        MOV     AX,1200h        ;Check for VGA by using a VGA
        MOV     BL,36h  ; only display enable.
        INT     10h
        CMP     AL,12h  ;Was interrupt successful?
        JNE     Exit1   ;If not, different display.
        MOV     TCode,VGA       ;If so, save type and exit.
        JMP     Exit1

Exit1:  RET

GetType ENDP

;*************************************************************************************************************
;* This procedure determines whether the display adapter is performing a vertical retrace.  This procedure   *
;* returns each time it is called during a vertical retrace.  You cannot use it to determine a specific *
;* point in the vertical retrace period.                *
;*************************************************************************************************************

CStartR PROC    NEAR

        CLI
        PUSH    ES
        MOV     AX,40h  ;Get the Input Status Register
        MOV     ES,AX   ; port number (3BA or 3DA).
        MOV     DX,ES:[63h]
        ADD     DX,6
        POP     ES      ;Restore ES.
ReCheck1:       IN      AL,DX   ;Wait until the start of
        TEST    AL,8    ; vertical retrace.
        JZ      ReCheck1        ;If start of retrace, exit.
        STI

        RET

CStartR ENDP

;*************************************************************************************************************
;* This procedure determines the exact end of the vertical retrace period.        *
;*************************************************************************************************************
CEndR   PROC    NEAR

        CLI
```

6-9 Continued.

```
        PUSH    ES
        MOV     AX,40h   ;Get the Input Status Register
        MOV     ES,AX    ; port number (3BA or 3DA).
        MOV     DX,ES:[63h]
        ADD     DX,6
        POP     ES       ;Restore ES.
ReCheck2:   IN      AL,DX    ;Wait until the end of
        TEST    AL,8     ; vertical retrace.
        JNZ     ReCheck2         ;If end of retrace, exit.
        STI

        RET

CEndR   ENDP

;**************************************************************************************************************
;* This procedure sets the attribute control register to address mode by reading the Input Status Register.    *
;**************************************************************************************************************

SetFF   PROC    NEAR

        CLI
        PUSH    ES
        MOV     AX,40h   ;Get the Input Status Register
        MOV     ES,AX    ; port number (3BA or 3DA).
        MOV     DX,ES:[63h]
        ADD     DX,6
        POP     ES       ;Initialize the attribute
        IN      AL,DX
        STI

        RET

SetFF   ENDP

;**************************************************************************************************************
;* This procedure places the display in split screen mode by changing the default value of the max scan line   *
;* (bit 6 is bit 9 of the screen line value), overflow (bit 4 is bit 8 of the screen line value), and line      *
;* compare registers (bits 0 - 7 of the screen line value).          *
;**************************************************************************************************************

SetSplit    PROC    NEAR

        CLI
        PUSH    ES
        MOV     AX,40h   ;Get the CRTC Control Register
        MOV     ES,AX    ; port number (3B4 or 3D4).
        MOV     DX,ES:[63h]
        POP     ES       ;Restore ES.

        MOV     AL,7     ;Select the overflow register.
```

```
        OUT    DX,AL
        INC    DX       ;Get the current contents.
        IN     AL,DX
        XCHG   AL,AH    ;Move current value to AH.
        AND    AH,11101111b   ;Zero bit 4.
        MOV    AL,DSplit8     ;Get the value of bit 8.
        OR  ·  AH,AL    ;Update bit 4 as required.
        DEC    DX       ;Output new value.
        MOV    AL,7
        OUT    DX,AX

        MOV    AL,9     ;Select the max scan line
        OUT    DX,AL    ; register.
        INC    DX       ;Get the current contents
        IN     AL,DX
        XCHG   AL,AH    ;Move current value to AH.
        AND    AH,10111111b   ;Zero bit 6.
        MOV    AL,DSplit9     ;Get the value of bit 9.
        OR     AH,AL    ;Update bit 6 as required.
        DEC    DX       ;Output new value.
        MOV    AL,9
        OUT    DX,AX

        MOV    AL,18h   ;Select and update the line
        MOV    AH,DSplit0     ; compare register.
        OUT    DX,AX

        STI

        RET

SetSplit       ENDP

END     Start
```

8514/A DISPLAY ADAPTER

The 8415/A display adapter differs from the adapters discussed above. Only the on-board CPU normally accesses the registers. The user access consists of calls to a terminate-and-stay-resident (TSR) program called an application interface (AI). Another difference is that this display adapter does not operate by itself. It requires the addition of a VGA to access lower resolution compatibility modes. TABLE 6-96 shows the display modes accessible with a system equipped with both a VGA and 8514/A display adapter.

As stated previously, the standard 8514/A AI consists of a TSR program. To access this program, use interrupt 7Fh after loading AX with the value 0105h. If successful, the CX:DX pair returns a segment and offset to the program entry table and the carry flag equals 0. The table contains 59 segment offset pairs for the calls listed in TABLE 6-97 in the order listed.

You can, however, directly access the ports on an 8514/A adapter. VESA has adopted a standard set of register names, mnemonics, and addresses (standard VS890804) as listed in TABLE 6-98. As indicated in the table, some registers use the read-only attribute, while others use the read-write attribute. Because each vendor could provide different functionality for each register, you should refer to the vendor manual for a detailed description of the register functions. A generalized listing of register functions as listed in Chips and Technologies 82C480 Programmer's Spec (Rev 2.1) follow.

Ports 100h, 101h, and 102h are Micro Channel Architecture (MCA) specific. You may read, but not write to ports 100h and 101h. They provide the POS ID for the installed card. The IBM 8514/A adapter returns a value of EF7Fh. Use this port to determine if the machine contains an 8514/A adapter. Port 102h enables or disables the 8514/A adapter. Placing a 1 in bit zero enables the card. You must set all other bits to zero.

Ports 2E8h, 6E8h, AE8h, EE8h, 12E8h, 16E8h, 1AE8h, and 1EE8h provide information about the vertical and horizontal sync parameters. Port 2E8h provides sync status when read. It sets the horizontal total register when written. The horizontal total equals the total length of the scan line including blanking. Horizontal total always begins with the first pixel of the scan line. TABLE 6-99 contains a complete bit listing for port 2E8h. Ports 6E8h, AE8h, and EE8h provide the means to read and write the remaining horizontal registers. These parameters include horizontal blank, horizontal sync, and horizontal sync pulse. TABLES 6-100 through 6-102 provide bit information about these ports. Ports 12E8h, 16E8h, 1AE8h, and 1EE8h provide read and write capability for all vertical registers. These registers include vertical total, vertical displayed, vertical sync start, and vertical sync width. TABLES 6-103 through 6-106 provide bit information about these ports. Figure 6-10 illustrates the relationship between the various display synchronization parameters.

The DAC register set includes ports 2EAh, 2EBh, 2ECh, and 2EDh. These registers include: DAC Mask, DAC Read Index, DAC Write Index, and DAC Data. All four registers contain eight bits of information. The 8514/A ANDs the bit stream with the contents DAC Mask register before sending them to the palette. This allows you to remove one or more bit planes from the data stream prior to display. The DAC Read Index addresses data at a specific address for the host. Use this register in combination with the DAC Data register (port 2EDh) to read a palette location. The DAC Write Index addresses a specific palette location for writing. The host uses the DAC Data register to place information at the specified palette location.

The control register set consists of ports 22E8h, 42E8h, 46E8h, 4AE8h, and 9AE8h. This includes the Display Control, Subsystem Status,

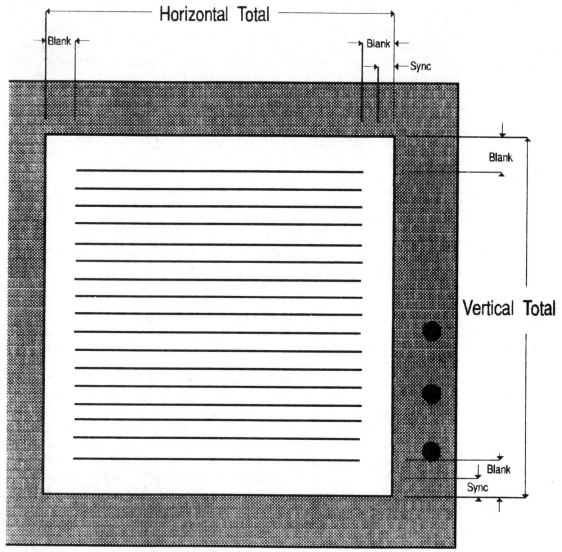

6-10 Horizontal/Vertical display register relationship.

Subsystem Control, ROM Page Select, Advanced Function Control, Graphics Processor Status, and Command registers. Each register controls a different area of 8514/A operation. TABLES 6-107 through 6-111 describe the display elements controlled by each register. Note that you may read the Subsystem Status and Graphics Processor Status registers. The Subsystem Control and Command registers are write-only.

The graphics register set includes position, status, and control registers. The position registers consist of Current X Position (port 82E8h), Current Y Position (port 86E8h), Destination X Position (port 8AE8h), and Destination Y Position (port 8EE8h). Each of these ports contain a number representing the start and finish of a graphics operation. The Y Position register contains a 10-bit number; all other registers contain 11-bit numbers.

The status registers consist of Error Term (port 92E8h) and Major Axis Pixel Count (port 96E8h). The Error Term register contains a 12-bit number used as a constant for the Bresenham algorithm. The host must place a number equal to $2*dy-dx$ in the register before starting the algorithm. The 8514/A automatically updates the register as it draws. The Major Axis Pixel Count register contains a 10-bit number. The 8514/A uses this number for CopyRect commands and as the constant dx term for the Bresenham algorithm. You must use a positive number for dx. The 8514/A automatically updates this register.

Finally, the control registers consist of Short Stroke Vector Transfer, Background Color, Foreground Color, Write Mask, Read Mask, Color Compare, Background Mix, Foreground Mix, Multi-Function Control, and Pixel Data Transfer. TABLE 6-112 contains a bit description of the Short Stroke Vector Transfer Register (port 9EE8h). Notice you can write two SSVs at once in 16-bit mode. The Background Color (port A2E8h) and Foreground Color (port A6E8h) registers contain 8-bit numbers. The 8514/A uses the contents of the Background Color register for writing pixels if you select Foreground Color Mix and FSS=00, or select the Background Color Mix and BSS=00. Likewise, it uses the contents of the Foreground Color register for writing pixels if you select the Foreground Color Mix and FSS=01, or select the Background Color Mix and BSS=01. The Write Mask register (port AAE8h) contains 8 bits, one for each plane. Placing a 1 in a bit allows writing to that plane's bit. Bit 0 corresponds to plane 0. The Read Mask register (port AEE8h) contains 8 bits, one for each plane. Placing a 0 in a bit allows reading of the selected plane's bit. Bit 0 corresponds to plane 0. The Color Compare register (port B2E8h) contains an 8-bit color number. The 8514/A compares the value of this color to the value of the destination during BITBLT operations. If the comparison is true, the CPU changes the destination. The comparison may use any type of equality including greater-than and less-than. The 8514/A uses the contents of bits 3, 4, and 5 of the Pixel Control register (port BEE8 index A) to control the comparison type. The 8514/A uses the contents of the Background Mix (port B6E8h) and Foreground Mix (port BAE8h) registers to control display color during drawing operations. This includes selection of both the mix color source and mix method. The Pixel Control register controls the selection of either the Foreground Mix or Background Mix register. TABLES 6-113 and 6-114 describe these two registers.

The Multi-Function Control register (port BEE8h) provides multiple services. You access each service by using an index number as part of the input. In all cases bits 12 through 15 contain the index number. Index 0 accesses the Minor Axis Pixel Count register. This register contains an 11-bit number which determines the rectangular height for BITBLTs. The next four indexes (1 through 4) control the scissors registers. The Top Scissors register (index 1) determines the upper limit of the boundary. The Left Scissors register (index 2) determines the minimum X limit of the boundary. The Bottom Scissors register (index 3) determines the lower limit of the boundary. Finally, the Right Scissors register (index 4) determines the maximum (right) X limit of the boundary. Each register contains a 12-bit number. Each time the 8514/A draws an object within the boundary described by these four registers, it outputs an interrupt (when enabled). The Memory Control register (index 5) determines the physical configuration of memory on the adapter. TABLE 6-115 describes the bit contents of this register. The Pattern X and Pattern Y registers (index 8 and 9) mix colors on a pixel-by-pixel basis. The Pattern X register contains the mix for even-numbered nuggets (four bits per plane) and the Pattern Y register contains the mix for odd numbered nuggets. Each register uses bits 1 through 4 to provide the mix pattern. Bit 4 controls pixel 0. The Pixel Control register (index A) determines the color mix modes and methods logic. TABLE 6-116 describes each bit in this register.

BUSINESS GRAPHICS ARRAY (BGA)

The Business Graphics Array (BGA) is one implementation of the 34010 Graphics System Processor (GSP). In most cases, the GSP requires discrete logic to perform its task. The addition of the 34092 BGA chip allows a simple implementation of a basic GSP design. As with all TMS340 family graphics processors, this board uses the Texas Instruments Graphics Architecture (an application interface) without modification. This means that the BGA should run most TIGA-compatible software, though at a lower resolution than some display adapters. Figure 6-11 shows a simplified block diagram of a typical BGA adapter.

Although the BGA produces resolutions similar to the 8514/A adapter, it has two advantages. First, you can program the 34010 like any computer. It does not rely on the host computer for program instructions or memory. This means that unlike a graphics co-processor, the BGA reduces the load on the host CPU. The second advantage is speed. Because the BGA performs most of its own processing, it should update the display more quickly than co-processor designs (depending on board design and application software). The paragraphs below describe the register set for the 34010 and the TIGA interface.

The TMS34092 BGA chip contains three internal 16-bit registers. You reference these registers as CR0, CR1, and CR2. Control Register 0 controls pixel size, monitor interface, pixel clock frequency, and VGA pass-through enable. Control Register 1 provides for programmable pixel size, memory bank enables, DRAM address multiplexing, external video interface control, programmable resets, and test support. Control Register 2 is a data register for pixel sizes of less than 8 bits.

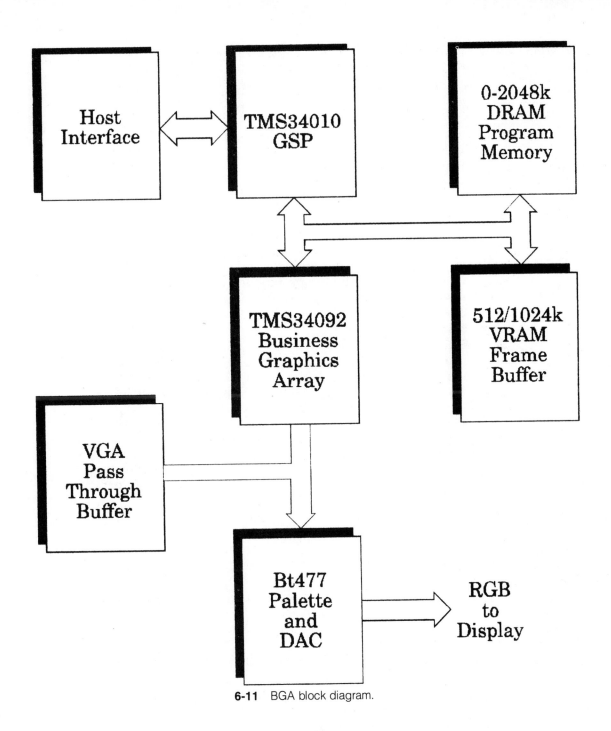

6-11 BGA block diagram.

34010 GRAPHICS SYSTEM PROCESSOR (GSP)

TMS34010 Graphics System Processor (GSP) programming requires three pieces of information. First, the programmer must know the memory mapping used by the interface software/ROM to provide access to the GSP. Second, the programmer must know how to use the registers provided by the GSP to manipulate data in program and display memory. Some vendor boards do not allow direct access to either memory area. To read or write host data, you must first program the register set, then use processor commands to initiate the transfer. Third, the programmer must know the GSP instruction set. Refer to the vendor manual for your GSP to obtain the addresses of various GSP components. You can eliminate this requirement by using the TIGA interface. The paragraphs below describe both the GSP registers and instruction set. Figure 6-12 shows a typical TMS34010 implementation. Notice that the block diagram looks similar to other display implementations. The programmability of the GSP adds the functionality provided by this system. The block diagram shows a generalized version of a typical GSP implementation. Most manufacturers deviate from this basic design.

The 34010 GSP contains four sets of registers: general-purpose, special-purpose, input/output, and memory-control. Each register set performs a specific task and contains more than one register. The general-purpose registers work with the execution unit to manipulate data. The special-purpose registers contain CPU execution flags and settings. The input/output registers provide an interface between the GSP, host, and external display related devices. The memory-control registers affect the internal memory operations of the GSP. The following paragraphs describe the registers in detail.

The general-purpose registers consist of two banks of 15 registers (30 total registers). You refer to the first bank as Register File A, and the second bank as Register File B. The GSP does not use Register File A for any special purpose. Therefore, you can use Register File A to store any semipermanent variables. The GSP does use Register File B for special purposes. This includes PIXBLT and line drawing operations. TABLE 6-117 describes the special uses for Register File B. Always load Register File B with the required information before executing a line drawing or PIXBLT operation. When not in use, Register File B reacts exactly like Register File A. In addition to standard registers, each register file contains a stack pointer (SP). The 34010 locks the two stack pointers together, meaning that the GSP provides one physical SP. The reason that each register file contains a reference to SP is to reduce the number of clock cycles required to perform a task. You may use SP like any other general register.

There are three special-purpose registers: status, program counter, and instruction cache. Each special-purpose register is 32 bits long. The status register (ST) contains information about CPU status. TABLE 6-118 describes the status information contained in this register. The program

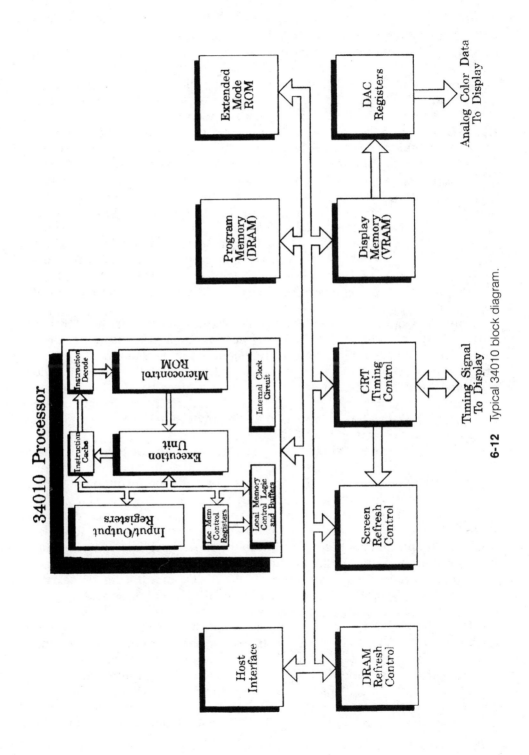

6-12 Typical 34010 block diagram.

counter (PC) points to the next instruction in the execution sequence. The GSP aligns all instructions on 16-bit boundaries. Therefore, the four LSB bits of this register always contain 0. An instruction may consist of more than one instruction word. As the GSP retrieves each instruction word, it automatically updates PC. There are occasions when the GSP replaces the contents of PC with another value. TABLE 6-119 describes each occurrence.

The instruction cache is 256 bytes long. It contains four segments. Each segment provides access to 64 bytes of cache memory. The segments are further broken down into 8 subsegments (also called data registers). Each subsegment contains 8 bytes (four 16-bit words) of code or data. The GSP aligns each segment on an even 32-bit word boundary. It addresses each word within the segment as shown in TABLE 6-120. The GSP provides access to the cache register pointed to by PC. A program may not read the contents of any of the other cache registers.

The instruction cache uses a least-recently used algorithm to replace the contents of the cache. Each time the GSP requests a segment not currently in memory, the cache controller fetches a new 64-byte segment from main memory. It replaces the least-recently used segment with the new segment contents.

The input/output register affects most display parameters used by the 34010. Both the host and 34010 may access the input/output register. There are 28 different input/output registers. As shown in TABLE 6-121, a program may access a register by name or address. The host accesses the registers through the host interface registers. It does this by loading the input/output register address in HSTADRL and HSTADRH registers. It then reads or writes the contents of the HSTDATA register. These registers occupy the address range from C0000000h to C00001FFh.

Each of the registers shown in TABLE 6-121 fall into one of four groups. Each group performs a specific task. The host interface registers provide host to 34010 communications. The host computer performs most communication with the display adapter through this interface. The local memory-control register controls how the 34010 manipulates data in VRAM. This includes the size of various display adapter constructs like pixel depth and window size. The interrupt-control register provides status information to the 34010 and host computer. The host computer can perform display-related tasks more efficiently by monitoring these two registers. The physical characteristics of the display adapter and display mode affect the video timing and screen refresh registers.

In addition to registers, the 34010 uses the instruction set summarized in TABLE 6-122. Notice that this instruction set contains instructions specifically designed for display data manipulation. Also, note that although Texas Instruments optimized the 34010 for graphic operations, it also uses generalized instructions like jump. This differentiates the 34010 from both a standard display adapter BIOS or co-processor and a general-purpose processor like the 8088. The 34010 can perform any task performed by a general-purpose processor. This gives it display data manipulation capabilities not found in standard display adapter BIOS or co-processor chips.

As you can see from TABLES 6-121 and 6-122, the 34010 provides a complex, but flexible programming interface. This book cannot provide the detailed information required by the novice programmer to create programs for the 34010. Refer to the Texas Instruments TMS34010 Software Development Kit for detailed programming information. However, you can use the tables in this book as a quick reference to the 34010. In addition to the information provided by the tables, you need to know the addresses used by the display adapter for the host interface. Obtain this information from the manufacturer's technical manuals.

34010 TEXAS INSTRUMENTS GRAPHICS ARCHITECTURE (TIGA)

The Texas Instruments Graphics Architecture (TIGA) application interface allows you to program the TMS34010 using the simplified procedures provided in multiple assembly and C libraries. TABLE 6-123 provides a summary of the TIGA instructions and their use. As with the processor instructions, this book does not provide the detailed instruction required by the novice programmer. Unlike the processor instructions, you must own a copy of the software development kit to use the TIGA interface. However, this book does provide a quick reference to the TIGA instruction set. In addition to the information provided by TABLE 6-123, you need to know the addresses used by the display adapter for the host interface. Obtain this information from the manufacturer's technical manuals.

As shown by TABLE 6-123, the TIGA instruction set falls into 14 main categories. In addition, each instruction also falls into one of two types. TIGA instruction types include core and extended. Core instructions are always available. They remain constant over the entire range of TIGA compatible boards. You must load an extended function into the TIGA environment before using it. This allows you to substitute one instruction for another. Always consult the manufacturer documentation before using an extended function.

There are 14 TIGA instruction categories. The graphics system initialization functions allow you to determine the presence of a TIGA compatible board and place the 340XX in a predefined state. There are different methods of performing this task. Each instruction performs the task of initialization in a different way. The clear functions allow you to clear all or part of display memory. The graphics attribute control functions allow you to change how the graphics processor executes various instructions. These attributes include foreground color, background color, plane mask, pixel processing, transparency, windowing, drawing origin, fill pattern, and drawing pen. The palette function allows you to change the final color used to paint the display on screen. These functions vary in scope from manufacturer to manufacturer. The graphics output function performs the actual drawing of objects in display memory. The poly drawing function provides extended graphics drawing functions. The workspace functions provide a method of temporarily allocating memory to manipulate a graphics object. The pixel array functions allow you to define pixel blocks and move them within display memory. The text functions provide the means to send text to the display. These functions depend on the availability of TIGA font files. You must install a font before using these functions. The cursor functions change the appearance and position of the cursor on-screen. The graphics utility functions consist of miscellaneous housekeeping instructions. The pointer-based memory management functions allow you to allocate and deallocate dynamic memory. In addition, these functions provide statistics on memory status. The communication functions determine how and when the display adapter communicates with the host. Finally, the extensibility functions allow you to add or delete functions from the TIGA environment.

As you can see, each category of TIGA instruction performs a specific task in relation to the graphics environment. Using this interface not only allows you to create portable code, but also to develop programs quickly and easily.

Table 6-1   Registers Accessed Using Port 3B5h or 3D5h

Register	Use
0	Total Horizontal Characters
01h	Total Displayed Horizontal Characters
02h	Horizontal Sync Position
03h	Horizontal Sync Width
04h	Total Vertical Rows
05h	Vertical Scan Line Adjust Value
06h	Total Displayed Vertical Rows
07h	Vertical Sync Position
08h	Interlace Mode
09h	Maximum Scan Line Address
0Ah	Scan Line At Which Cursor Starts
0Bh	Scan Line At Which Cursor Ends
0Ch	High-Byte Start Address
0Dh	Low-Byte Start Address
0Eh	High-Byte Cursor Address
0Fh	Low-Byte Cursor Address
10h	Light Pen (High Byte)
11h	Light Pen (Low Byte)

Table 6-2   Monochrome Adapter Mode Control Register (Port 3B8h)

Bit	Function
0	80 X 25 Display Mode When Set
1 - 2	Not Used
3	Video Enable When Set
4	Not Used
5	Enable Blink When Set
6 - 7	Not Used

Table 6-3   HGC Port 3B8h Status Bits

Bit Number	7	6	5	4	3	2	1	0
Normal Text Mode								
No Display	B	0	0	0	I	0	0	0
Underscore	B	0	0	0	I	0	0	1
Normal	B	0	0	0	I	1	1	1
Reverse	B	1	1	1	I	0	0	0
RAMFont 48KB Mode	H	R	O	U	F	F	F	F

Symbol Key

B	Bit Plane Masks
	Blinker Off - 1 = High Intensity, 0 = Normal Intensity
	Blinker On - 1 = Blink, 0 = No Blink
I	Normal Intensity = 0, High Intensity = 1
H	High Intensity or Boldface = 1
R	Reverse Video = 1 Blinker Off, Blink = 1 Blinker On
O	Overstrike = 1
U	Underscore = 1
F	Font Plane Masks

Table 6-4   HGC Registers Accessed Using Port 3B5h

Register	Use
0	Total Horizontal Characters
01h	Total Displayed Horizontal Characters
02h	Horizontal Sync Position

Table 6-4   Continued.

Register	Use
03h	Horizontal Sync Width
04h	Total Vertical Rows
05h	Vertical Scan Line Adjust Value
06h	Total Displayed Vertical Rows
07h	Vertical Sync Position
08h	Interlace Mode
09h	Maximum Scan Line Address
0Ah	Scan Line At Which Cursor Starts
0Bh	Scan Line At Which Cursor Ends
0Ch	High-Byte Start Address
0Dh	Low-Byte Start Address
0Eh	High-Byte Cursor Address
0Fh	Low-Byte Cursor Address
10h	Light Pen (High Byte)
11h	Light Pen (Low Byte)
14h	Fonts and Width of Fonts
15h	Scan Line for Underscore
16h	Scan Line for Overstrike

Table 6-5   Color Graphics Adapter Mode Control Register (Port 3D8h)

Bit	Function
0	Display Mode Setting 1 0 = 40 X 25 1 = 80 X 25
1	Display Mode Setting 2 0 = 320 X 200 Graphics Mode 1 = Alphanumeric Mode
2	Color Select 0 = Color Mode 1 = Black and White Mode
3	Video Enable When Set
4	Resolution Selection 0 = Normal Resolution 1 = 640 X 200 High Resolution
5	Enable Blink When Set
6 - 7	Not Used

Table 6-6   Color Graphics Adapter Color Select Register (Port 3D9h)

Bit	Function
0	Selects Blue Border in 40 X 25 Mode Selects Blue Background in 320 X 200 Graphics Mode Selects Blue Foreground in 640 X 200 Graphics Mode
1	Selects Green Border in 40 X 25 Mode Selects Green Background in 320 X 200 Graphics Mode Selects Green Foreground in 640 X 200 Graphics Mode
2	Selects Red Border in 40 X 25 Mode Selects Red Background in 320 X 200 Graphics Mode Selects Red Foreground in 640 X 200 Graphics Mode
3	Selects Intensified Border in 40 X 25 Mode Selects Intensified Background in 320 X 200 Graphics Mode Selects Red Foreground in 640 X 200 Graphics Mode
4	Selects Intensified Color Set in Graphics Mode Selects Background Colors in Alphanumeric Mode
5	0 = Green/Red/Brown Color Set 1 = Cyan/Magenta/White Color Set

Table 6-7   Color Graphics Adapter Status Register (Port 3DAh)

Bit	Function
0	Video Enabled When Set
1	Light Pen Trigger Set
2	Light Pen Triggered When Clear
3	Vertical Retrace in Progress When Set
4 - 7	Not Used

Table 6-8   Color Graphics Adapter Display Modes

Mode	Type	Colors	Resolution	Glyph Cell
0h	Text	16	200 by 320	8 by 8
1h	Text	16	200 by 320	8 by 8
2h	Text	16	200 by 640	8 by 8
3h	Text	16	200 by 640	8 by 8
4h	Graphics	4	200 by 320	8 by 8
5h	Graphics	4	200 by 320	8 by 8
6h	Graphics	2	200 by 640	8 by 8

Table 6-9   Enhanced Graphics Adapter Display Modes

Mode	Type	Colors	Resolution	Glyph Cell
Enhanced Color Display				
0h	Text	16/64	350 by 320	8 by 14
1h	Text	16/64	350 by 320	8 by 14
2h	Graphics	16/64	350 by 640	8 by 14
3h	Graphics	16/64	350 by 640	8 by 14
Standard Display				
0h	Text	16	200 by 320	8 by 8
1h	Text	16	200 by 320	8 by 8
2h	Graphics	16	200 by 640	8 by 8
3h	Graphics	16	200 by 640	8 by 8
Enhanced Color and Standard Displays				
4h	Graphics	4	200 by 320	8 by 8
5h	Graphics	4	200 by 320	8 by 8
6h	Graphics	2	200 by 640	8 by 14
7h	Text	4	350 by 720	9 by 14
Dh	Graphics	16	200 by 320	8 by 8
Eh	Graphics	16	200 by 640	8 by 8
64 KByte Boards				
Fh	Graphics	4	350 by 640	8 by 14
10h	Graphics	4/64	350 by 640	8 by 14
128 KByte Boards				
Fh	Graphics	4	350 by 640	8 by 14
10h	Graphics	16/64	350 by 640	8 by 14

Table 6-10   EGA Miscellaneous Output Register (Port 3C2h)

Bit	Function
0	3B/3D CRTC I/O Address (Selects monochrome or CGA addresses.)
1	Enable RAM (Disables CPU access to RAM when set.)
2 - 3	Clock Select 00b 14 MHz (From Bus) 01b 16 MHz (From EGA Board) 10b External Source (Feature Connector) 11b Not Used
4	Disable Internal Video Drivers (When set, uses the signal output pins of the feature connector to drive the monitor.)
5	Page Bit for Odd/Even (Selects one of two 64 KByte video pages when the EGA is in the odd/even mode. A one selects the high page.)
6	Horizontal Retrace Polarity (Selects a negative polarity when set.)
7	Vertical Retrace Polarity (Selects a negative polarity when set.)
6 & 7	The default condition of bits 6 & 7 appears below. 00b 200 lines 01b 350 lines 10b Not Used 11b Not Used

Table 6-11   EGA Feature Control Register (Ports 3BAh & 3DAh)

Bit	Function
0	Feature Control Bit 0 (Pin 21)
1	Feature Control Bit 1 (Pin 20)
2 - 3	Reserved
4 - 7	Not Used

Table 6-12   EGA Input Status Register Zero (Port 3C2h)

Bit	Function
0 - 3	Unused
4	Switch Sense (Reads the switch setting of the switch selected by bits 2 - 3 of the miscellaneous output register; where switch number = switch number - 2.)
5	Feature Code Bit 0 (Feature Connector Pin 19)
6	Feature Code Bit 1 (Feature Connector Pin 17)
7	CRT Interrupt (Indicates the occurrance of a video retrace interrupt when set.)

Table 6-13   EGA Input Status Register One (Port 3BAh & 3DAh)

Bit	Function
0	Display Enable (Set during active display, cleared during horizontal and vertical retrace.)
1	Light Pen Strobe (Set for light pen trigger.)
2	Light Pen Switch (Set when light pen switch is open.)
3	Vertical Retrace (Indicates vertical retrace when set.
4 - 5	Diagnostic Usage (Return value of attribute register diagnostic bits.)
6 - 7	Not Used

Table 6-14   EGA Reset Register (Index 0)

Bit	Function
0	Asynchronous Clear (0 causes a asynchronous clear and halts the sequencer register. Sets all outputs to a high impedance state)
1	Synchronous Clear (0 causes a synchronous clear and halts the sequencer register. Use this bit to reset the sequencer prior to changing clock frequencies.)
2- 7	Not Used

Table 6-15   EGA Clocking Mode Register (Index 1)

Bit	Function
0	8/9 Dot Clocks (Generates 8-bit wide characters when set.)
1	Bandwidth 0b - Gives CRT 2 of every 5 memory cycles. 1b - Gives CRT 4 of every 5 memory cycles.
2	Shift Load 0b - Fetches 8 bits from each memory plane. Provides four 8-bit serial bit streams to attribute register. 1b - Fetches 8 bits from each memory plane and combines the output into two 16-bit serial bit streams.
3	Dot Clock (Divide dot clock by 2 when set.)
4	Not used
5	Screen Off (Disables display without disrupting internal adapter functions when set.)
6 - 7	Not Used

Note:

The register default values follow, with the display mode number followed by the register value in parentheses. The 64 KByte adapter values are: 0 - 1 (0Bh), 2 - 3 (01h), 4 - 5 (0Bh), 6 (01h), 7 (00h), Dh (0Bh), Eh (01h), Fh - 10h (05h). The 128 KByte adapter values are: 0 - 1 (0Bh), 2 - 3 (01h), 4 - 5 (0Bh), 6 (01h), 7 (00h), Dh (0Bh), Eh - 10h (01h).

Table 6-16   EGA Map Mask Register (Index 2)

Bit	Function
0	Bit Plane 0 Enabled for Memory Write
1	Bit Plane 1 Enabled for Memory Write
2	Bit Plane 2 Enabled for Memory Write
3	Bit Plane 3 Enabled for Memory Write
4 - 7	Not Used

Note:

The register default values follow, with the display mode number followed by the register value in parentheses: 0 - 5 (03h), 6 (01h), 7 (03h), Dh - 10h (0Fh).

Table 6-17   EGA Character Map Select Register (Index 3)

Bit	Function
0 - 1	Character Map Select A
2 - 3	Character Map Select B
4 - 7	Not Used

Table 6-18   EGA Memory Mode Register (Index 4)

Bit	Function
0	Alpha (Selects alphanumeric modes when set.)
1	Extended Memory (Set when adapter contains more than 64 KBytes of memory.)
2	Odd/Even Mode (CGA Graphics Mode Emulation)
3 - 7	Not Used

Note:

The register default values follow, with the display mode number followed by the register value in parentheses. The values for 64 KByte boards are: 0 - 3 (03h), 4 - 5 (02h), 6 (06h), 7 (03h), Dh - Eh (06h), Fh - 10h (00h). The values for 128 KByte boards are: 0 - 3 (03h), 4 - 5 (02h), 6 (06h), 7 (03h), Dh - 10h (06h).

Table 6-19   CRTC Register Group Index Values

Index	Function	Table
0	Horizontal Total	6-20
1h	Horizontal Display End	6-21
2h	Start Horizontal Blanking	6-22
3h	End Horizontal Blanking	6-23
4h	Start Horizontal Retrace	6-24
5h	End Horizontal Retrace	6-25
6h	Vertical Total	6-26
7h	Overflow	6-27
8h	Preset Row Scan	6-28
9h	Max Scan Line	6-29
Ah	Cursor Start	6-30
Bh	Cursor End	6-31
10h	Vertical Retrace Start (Write)	6-32
10h	Light Pen High (Read)	6-33

Table 6-19   Continued.

Index	Function	Table
11h	Vertical Retrace End (Write)	6-34
11h	Light Pen Low (Read)	6-35
12h	Vertical Display End	6-36
13h	Offset	6-37
14h	Underline Location	6-38
15h	Start Vertical Blanking	6-39
16h	End Vertical Blanking	6-40
17h	Mode Control	6-41
18h	Line Compare	6-42

Table 6-20   EGA Horizontal Total Register Values (Index 0)

Mode	Scan (Dec)	Retrace (Dec)	Value (Dec)	Value (Hex)
Enhanced Color Display				
0h - 40 X 25 CGA Text (16)	40	6	45	2D
1h - 40 X 25 CGA Text (16)	40	6	45	2D
2h - 80 X 25 CGA Text (16)	80	12	91	5B
3h - 80 X 25 CGA Text (16)	80	12	91	5B
Standard Display				
0h - 40 X 25 CGA Text (16)	40	16	55	37
1h - 40 X 25 CGA Text (16)	40	16	55	37
2h - 80 X 25 CGA Text (16)	80	33	112	70
3h - 80 X 25 CGA Text (16)	80	33	112	70
Enhanced Color and Standard Displays				
4h - 320 X 200 CGA Graph (4)	40	16	55	37
5h - 320 X 200 CGA Graph (4)	40	16	55	37
6h - 640 X 200 CGA Graph (2)	80	33	112	70
7h - 80 X 25 Mono Text (4)	80	17	96	60
Dh - 320 X 200 EGA Graph (16)	40	16	55	37
Eh - 640 X 200 EGA Graph (16)	80	33	112	70
64 Kbyte Boards				
Fh - 640 X 350 Mono Graph (4)	80	17	96	60
10h - 640 X 350 EGA Graph (4)	80	12	91	5B
128 Kbyte Boards				
Fh - 640 X 350 Mono Graph (4)	80	17	96	60
10h - 640 X 350 EGA Graph (16)	80	12	91	5B

Notes:

1. Numbers appearing in parentheses show the number of colors available.

2. The horizontal total register value = scan value + retrace value - 1

3. The actual horizontal total is 2 greater than the amount shown. The scan count begins at 0, reducing the count by one. The EGA expends 1 extra count during retrace before starting the count over.

Table 6-21   EGA Horizontal Display Enable End Register Values (Index 1)

Mode	Scan (Dec)	Value (Dec)	Value (Hex)
0h - 40 X 25 CGA Text	40	39	27
1h - 40 X 25 CGA Text	40	39	27
2h - 80 X 25 CGA Text	80	79	4f
3h - 80 X 25 CGA Text	80	79	4f
4h - 320 X 200 CGA Graph	40	39	27
5h - 320 X 200 CGA Graph	40	39	27
6h - 640 X 200 CGA Graph	80	79	4f
7h - 80 X 25 Mono Text	80	79	4f
Dh - 320 X 200 EGA Graph	40	39	27
Eh - 640 X 200 EGA Graph	80	79	4f
Fh - 640 X 350 Mono Graph	80	79	4f
10h - 640 X 350 EGA Graph	80	79	4f

Note:

The horizontal display enable end register value = scan - 1 because the scan counter begins at 0.

Table 6-22   EGA Start Horizontal Blanking Register Values (Index 2)

Mode	Scan (Dec)	Overscan (Dec)	Value (Dec)	Value (Hex)
Enhanced Color Display				
0h - 40 X 25 CGA Text	40	4	43	2B
1h - 40 X 25 CGA Text	40	4	43	2B
2h - 80 X 25 CGA Text	80	4	83	53
3h - 80 X 25 CGA Text	80	4	83	53
Standard Display				
0h - 40 X 25 CGA Text	40	6	45	2D
1h - 40 X 25 CGA Text	40	6	45	2D
2h - 80 X 25 CGA Text	80	13	92	5C
3h - 80 X 25 CGA Text	80	13	92	5C

Table 6-22   Continued.

Mode	Scan (Dec)	Overscan (Dec)	Value (Dec)	Value (Hex)
Enhanced Color and Standard Displays				
4h - 320 X 200 CGA Graph	40	6	45	2D
5h - 320 X 200 CGA Graph	40	6	45	2D
6h - 640 X 200 CGA Graph	80	10	89	59
7h - 80 X 25 Mono Text	80	7	86	56
Dh - 320 X 200 EGA Graph	40	6	45	2D
Eh - 640 X 200 EGA Graph	80	10	89	59
Fh - 640 X 350 Mono Graph	80	7	86	56
10h - 640 X 350 EGA Graph	80	4	83	53

Table 6-23   EGA End Horizontal Blanking Register Values (Index 3)

Mode	Scan (Dec)	Actual (Hex)	Register (Hex)
Bits 0 - 4			
Enhanced Color Display			
0h - 40 X 25 CGA Text	40	2D	2D
1h - 40 X 25 CGA Text	40	2D	2D
2h - 80 X 25 CGA Text	80	57	37
3h - 80 X 25 CGA Text	80	57	37
Standard Display			
0h - 40 X 25 CGA Text	40	37	37
1h - 40 X 25 CGA Text	40	37	37
2h - 80 X 25 CGA Text	80	4F	2F
3h - 80 X 25 CGA Text	80	4F	2F
Enhanced Color and Standard Displays			
4h - 320 X 200 CGA Graph	40	37	37
5h - 320 X 200 CGA Graph	40	37	37
6h - 640 X 200 CGA Graph	80	4D	2D
7h - 80 X 25 Mono Text	80	3A	3A
Dh - 320 X 200 EGA Graph	40	37	37
Eh - 640 X 200 EGA Graph	80	4D	2D
64 KByte Boards			
Fh - 640 X 350 Mono Graph	80	5A	1A
10h - 640 X 350 EGA Graph	80	57	17
128 KByte Boards			
Fh - 640 X 350 Mono Graph	80	5A	3A
10h - 640 X 350 EGA Graph	80	57	37

Table 6-23   Continued.

Mode	Scan (Dec)	Actual (Hex)	Register (Hex)
Bits 5 - 6			
Enhanced Color Display			
0h - 40 X 25 CGA Text	01	2D	
1h - 40 X 25 CGA Text	01	2D	
2h - 80 X 25 CGA Text	01	37	
3h - 80 X 25 CGA Text	01	37	
Standard Display			
0h - 40 X 25 CGA Text	01	37	
1h - 40 X 25 CGA Text	01	37	
2h - 80 X 25 CGA Text	01	2F	
3h - 80 X 25 CGA Text	01	2F	
Enhanced Color and Standard			
4h - 320 X 200 CGA Graph	01	37	
5h - 320 X 200 CGA Graph	01	37	
6h - 640 X 200 CGA Graph	01	2D	
7h - 80 X 25 Mono Text	01	3A	
Dh - 320 X 200 EGA Graph	01	37	
Eh - 640 X 200 EGA Graph	01	2D	
64 KByte Boards			
Fh - 640 X 350 Mono Graph	00	1A	
10h - 640 X 350 EGA Graph	00	17	
128 KByte Boards			
Fh - 640 X 350 Mono Graph	01	3A	
10h - 640 X 350 EGA Graph	01	37	

Notes:

1. The register value equals the individual values from bit 7 (0), bits 5 - 6, and the five least significant end horizontal blanking value bits 0 - 4. The MSB for the end horizontal blanking value is the same as the start value.

2. Bit values for bits 5 and 6 show the character delay used before display of the next displayable area. These values are: 00 = no delay, 01 = 1 character, 10 = 2 characters, and 11 = 3 characters.

3. The EGA does not use bit 7.

Table 6-24   EGA Start Horizontal Retrace Register Values (Index 4)

Mode	Scan (Dec)	Value (Dec)	Value (Hex)
Enhanced Color Display			
0h - 40 X 25 CGA Text	40	43	28
1h - 40 X 25 CGA Text	40	43	28
2h - 80 X 25 CGA Text	80	83	51
3h - 80 X 25 CGA Text	80	83	51
Standard Display			
0h - 40 X 25 CGA Text	40	45	31
1h - 40 X 25 CGA Text	40	45	31
2h - 80 X 25 CGA Text	80	92	5F
3h - 80 X 25 CGA Text	80	92	5F
Enhanced Color and Standard Displays			
4h - 320 X 200 CGA Graph	40	45	30
5h - 320 X 200 CGA Graph	40	45	30
6h - 640 X 200 CGA Graph	80	89	5E
7h - 80 X 25 Mono Text	80	86	51
Dh - 320 X 200 EGA Graph	40	45	30
Eh - 640 X 200 EGA Graph	80	89	5E
64 KByte Boards			
Fh - 640 X 350 Mono Graph	80	86	50
10h - 640 X 350 EGA Graph	80	83	50
128 KByte Boards			
Fh - 640 X 350 Mono Graph	80	86	50
10h - 640 X 350 EGA Graph	80	83	52

Note:

The end horizontal retrace register may delay the horizontal retrace.

Table 6-25   EGA End Horizontal Retrace Register Values (Index 5)

Mode	Scan (Dec)	Actual (Hex)	Register (Hex)
Bits 0 - 4			
Enhanced Color Display			
0h - 40 X 25 CGA Text	40	2D	6D
1h - 40 X 25 CGA Text	40	2D	6D

Table 6-25   Continued.

Mode	Scan (Dec)	Actual (Hex)	Register (Hex)
2h - 80 X 25 CGA Text	80	4B	5B
3h - 80 X 25 CGA Text	80	4B	5B

Standard Display

0h - 40 X 25 CGA Text	40	35	15
1h - 40 X 25 CGA Text	40	35	15
2h - 80 X 25 CGA Text	80	47	07
3h - 80 X 25 CGA Text	80	47	07

Enhanced Color and Standard Displays

4h - 320 X 200 CGA Graph	40	34	14
5h - 320 X 200 CGA Graph	40	34	14
6h - 640 X 200 CGA Graph	80	46	06
7h - 80 X 25 Mono Text	80	50	60
Dh - 320 X 200 EGA Graph	40	34	14
Eh - 640 X 200 EGA Graph	80	46	06

64 KByte Boards

Fh - 640 X 350 Mono Graph	80	40	60
10h - 640 X 350 EGA Graph	80	5A	BA

128 KByte Boards

Fh - 640 X 350 Mono Graph	80	40	60
10h - 640 X 350 EGA Graph	80	40	00

Bits 5 - 6

Enhanced Color Display

0h - 40 X 25 CGA Text		11	6D
1h - 40 X 25 CGA Text		11	6D
2h - 80 X 25 CGA Text		10	5B
3h - 80 X 25 CGA Text		10	5B

Standard Display

0h - 40 X 25 CGA Text		00	15
1h - 40 X 25 CGA Text		00	15
2h - 80 X 25 CGA Text		00	07
3h - 80 X 25 CGA Text		00	07

Enhanced Color and Standard

4h - 320 X 200 CGA Graph		00	14
5h - 320 X 200 CGA Graph		00	14
6h - 640 X 200 CGA Graph		00	06
7h - 80 X 25 Mono Text		11	60

Table 6-25   Continued.

Mode	Scan (Dec)	Actual (Hex)	Register (Hex)
Dh - 320 X 200 EGA Graph		00	14
Eh - 640 X 200 EGA Graph		00	06
64 KByte Boards			
Fh - 640 X 350 Mono Graph		11	60
10h - 640 X 350 EGA Graph		01	BA
128 KByte Boards			
Fh - 640 X 350 Mono Graph		11	60
10h - 640 X 350 EGA Graph		00	00

Bit 7

The default for this bit for all modes is 0. This bit allows horizontal smooth scrolling when using EGAs with less than 64 KBytes. The sequence of scrolling involves setting the bit to 0, scrolling 8 bits, setting the bit to 1, and scrolling the next 8 bits.

Notes:

1. The register value equals the individual values from bit 7, bits 5 - 6, and the five least significant end horizontal retrace value bits 0 - 4. The MSB for the end horizontal retrace value is the same as the start value.

2. Bit values for bits 5 and 6 show the character delay used during retrace. These values are: 00 = no delay, 01 = 1 character, 10 = 2 characters, and 11 = 3 characters.

Table 6-26   EGA Vertical Total Register Values (Index 6)

Mode	Scan (Dec)	Retrace (Dec)	Actual Value	Reg. Value
Enhanced Color Display				
0h - 40 X 25 CGA Text (16)	350	14	16C	6C
1h - 40 X 25 CGA Text (16)	350	14	16C	6C
2h - 80 X 25 CGA Text (16)	350	14	16C	6C
3h - 80 X 25 CGA Text (16)	350	14	16C	6C
Standard Display				
0h - 40 X 25 CGA Text (16)	200	60	104	04
1h - 40 X 25 CGA Text (16)	200	60	104	04
2h - 80 X 25 CGA Text (16)	200	60	104	04
3h - 80 X 25 CGA Text (16)	200	60	104	04

Table 6-26   Continued.

Mode	Scan (Dec)	Retrace (Dec)	Actual Value	Reg. Value
Enhanced Color and Standard Displays				
4h - 320 X 200 CGA Graph (4)	200	60	104	04
5h - 320 X 200 CGA Graph (4)	200	60	104	04
6h - 640 X 200 CGA Graph (2)	200	60	104	04
7h - 80 X 25 Mono Text (4)	348	20	170	70
Dh - 320 X 200 EGA Graph (16)	200	20	104	04
Eh - 640 X 200 EGA Graph (16)	200	20	104	04
Fh - 640 X 350 Mono Graph (4)	348	20	170	70
10h - 640 X 350 EGA Graph (4)	350	14	16C	6C

Notes:

1. Numbers appearing in parentheses show the number of colors available.

2. Vertical total register value = scan value + retrace value.

Table 6-27   EGA CRT Controller Overflow Register (Index 7)

Bit	Function
0	Vertical Total Ninth Bit (see Index 6)
1	Vertical Display Enable End Ninth Bit (see Index 12h)
2	Vertical Retrace Start Ninth Bit (See Index 10h)
3	Start Vertical Blank Ninth Bit (see Index 9)
4	Line Compare Ninth Bit (see Index 9)
5 - 7	Not Used

Note:

The register default values follow with the mode number followed by the value in parentheses. The standard display values are: 0 - 6 (11h), 7 (1Fh), Dh - Eh (11h), Fh - 10h (1Fh). The enhanced color display values are: 0 - 3 (1Fh), 4 - 6 (11h), 7 (1Fh), Dh - Eh (11h), Fh - 10h (1Fh).

Table 6-28   EGA Preset Row Scan Register (Index 8)

Bit	Function
0 - 4	Preset Row Scan (Starting pixel row number after retrace).
5 - 7	Not Used

Table 6-28   Continued.

Note:

The register default values follow, with the display mode
number followed by the register value in parentheses: 0 - 7
(00h), dh - 10h (00h).

Table 6-29   EGA Maximum Scan Line Register (Index 9)

Bit	Function
0 - 4	Maximum Scan Line (Alphanumeric character height - 1)
5 - 7	Not Used

Note:

The register default values follow, with the display mode
number followed by the register value in parentheses. The
standard display values are: 0 - 3 (07h), 4 - 6 (01h), 7 (0Dh),
Dh - 10h (00h). The enhanced color display value are: 0 - 3
(0Dh), 4 - 6 (01h), 7 (0Dh), Dh - 10h (00h).

Table 6-30   EGA Cursor Start Register (Index Ah)

Bit	Function
0 - 4	Cursor Start Position (First cursor row position - 1)
5 - 7	Not Used

Note:

The register default values follow, with the display mode
number followed by the register value in parentheses: 0 - 3
(06h), 4 - 6 (00h), 7 (0Bh), Dh - 10h (00h).

Table 6-31   EGA Cursor End Register (Index Bh)

Bit	Function
0 - 4	Cursor End Position (Last cursor row position)
5 - 6	Cursor Skew (Cursor control signal delay) 00b - No Delay 01b - 1 Character Delay 10b - 2 Character Delay 11b - 3 Character Delay
7	Not Used

Table 6-31   Continued.

Note:

The register default values follow, with the display mode
number followed by the register value in parentheses: 0 - 3
(07h), 4 - 6 (00h), 7 (0Ch), Dh - 10h (00h).

Table 6-32   EGA Start Vertical Retrace Register Values (Index 10h)

Mode	Scan (Dec)	Actual Value (Dec)	Actual Value	Reg Value
Write Values				
Enhanced Color Display				
0h - 40 X 25 CGA Text	350	350	15E	5E
1h - 40 X 25 CGA Text	350	350	15E	5E
2h - 80 X 25 CGA Text	350	350	15E	5E
3h - 80 X 25 CGA Text	350	350	15E	5E
Standard Display				
0h - 40 X 25 CGA Text	200	225	E1	E1
1h - 40 X 25 CGA Text	200	225	E1	E1
2h - 80 X 25 CGA Text	200	225	E1	E1
3h - 80 X 25 CGA Text	200	225	E1	E1
Enhanced Color and Standard Displays				
4h - 320 X 200 CGA Graph	200	225	E1	E1
5h - 320 X 200 CGA Graph	200	225	E1	E1
6h - 640 X 200 CGA Graph	200	224	E0	E0
7h - 80 X 25 Mono Text	348	350	15E	5E
Dh - 320 X 200 EGA Graph	200	225	E1	E1
Eh - 640 X 200 EGA Graph	200	224	E0	E0
Fh - 640 X 350 Mono Graph	348	350	15E	5E
10h - 640 X 350 EGA Graph	350	350	15E	5E

Read Value

Index 10h accesses the eight most significant bits of the light
pen interface during reads.

Table 6-33   EGA End Vertical Retrace Register Values (Index 11h)

Mode	Scan (Dec)	Actual Value (Dec)	Actual Value	Reg Value
Write Values				
Enhanced Color Display				
0h - 40 X 25 CGA Text	350	299	12B	2B
1h - 40 X 25 CGA Text	350	299	12B	2B
2h - 80 X 25 CGA Text	350	299	12B	2B
3h - 80 X 25 CGA Text	350	299	12B	2B
Standard Display				
0h - 40 X 25 CGA Text	200	36	24	24
1h - 40 X 25 CGA Text	200	36	24	24
2h - 80 X 25 CGA Text	200	36	24	24
3h - 80 X 25 CGA Text	200	36	24	24
Enhanced Color and Standard Displays				
4h - 320 X 200 CGA Graph	200	36	24	24
5h - 320 X 200 CGA Graph	200	36	24	24
6h - 640 X 200 CGA Graph	200	35	23	23
7h - 80 X 25 Mono Text	348	302	12E	2E
Dh - 320 X 200 EGA Graph	200	36	24	24
Eh - 640 X 200 EGA Graph	200	35	23	23
Fh - 640 X 350 Mono Graph	348	302	12E	2E
10h - 640 X 350 EGA Graph	350	299	12B	2B

Read Value

Index 11h accesses the eight least significant bits of the light pen interface during reads.

Table 6-34   EGA Vertical Display Enable End Register Values (Index 12h)

Mode	Scan (Dec)	Actual Value (Dec)	Actual Value	Reg Value
0h - 40 X 25 CGA Text	200	199	C7	C7
1h - 40 X 25 CGA Text	200	199	C7	C7
2h - 80 X 25 CGA Text	200	199	C7	C7
3h - 80 X 25 CGA Text	200	199	C7	C7
4h - 320 X 200 CGA Graph	200	199	C7	C7
5h - 320 X 200 CGA Graph	200	199	C7	C7
6h - 640 X 200 CGA Graph	200	199	C7	C7
7h - 80 X 25 Mono Text	348	34D	15D	5D
Dh - 320 X 200 EGA Graph	200	199	C7	C7
Eh - 640 X 200 EGA Graph	200	199	C7	C7
Fh - 640 X 350 Mono Graph	348	349	15D	5D
10h - 640 X 350 EGA Graph	350	349	15D	5D

Table 6-35   EGA Offset Register Values (Index 13h)

Mode	Memory Row (Dec)	Memory Row(Hex)
0h - 40 X 25 CGA Text	20	14
1h - 40 X 25 CGA Text	20	14
2h - 80 X 25 CGA Text	40	28
3h - 80 X 25 CGA Text	40	28
4h - 320 X 200 CGA Graph	20	14
5h - 320 X 200 CGA Graph	20	14
6h - 640 X 200 CGA Graph	40	28
7h - 80 X 25 Mono Text	40	28
Dh - 320 X 200 EGA Graph	20	14
Eh - 640 X 200 EGA Graph	40	28
64 KByte Boards		
Fh - 640 X 350 Mono Graph	20	14
10h - 640 X 350 EGA Graph	20	14
128 KByte Boards		
Fh - 640 X 350 Mono Graph	40	28
10h - 640 X 350 EGA Graph	40	28

Table 6-36   EGA Underline Location Register (Index 14h)

Bit	Function
0 - 4	Underline Location (Position within character cell)
5 - 7	Not Used

Note:

The register default values follow, with the display mode
number followed by the register value in parentheses. Standard
display adapter values are: 0 - 3 (08h), 4 - 6 (00h), 7 (0Dh),
Dh - Eh (00h), Fh (0Dh), 10h (0Fh). Enhanced color display values
are: 0 - 3 (0Fh), 4 - 6 (00h), 7 (0Dh), Dh - Eh (00h), Fh (0Dh),
10h (0Fh).

Table 6-37   EGA Start Vertical Blanking Register Values (Index 15h)

Mode	Scan (Dec)	Overscan (Dec)	Actual Value	Reg. Value
Enhanced Color Display				
0h - 40 X 25 CGA Text	350	1	15E	5E
1h - 40 X 25 CGA Text	350	1	15E	5E
2h - 80 X 25 CGA Text	350	1	15E	5E
3h - 80 X 25 CGA Text	350	1	15E	5E
Standard Display				
0h - 40 X 25 CGA Text	200	25	E0	E0
1h - 40 X 25 CGA Text	200	25	E0	E0
2h - 80 X 25 CGA Text	200	25	E0	E0
3h - 80 X 25 CGA Text	200	25	E0	E0
Enhanced Color and Standard Displays				
4h - 320 X 200 CGA Graph	200	25	E0	E0
5h - 320 X 200 CGA Graph	200	25	E0	E0
6h - 640 X 200 CGA Graph	200	24	DF	DF
7h - 80 X 25 Mono Text	348	1	15E	5E
Dh - 320 X 200 EGA Graph	200	25	E0	E0
Eh - 640 X 200 EGA Graph	200	24	DF	DF
Fh - 640 X 350 Mono Graph	348	1	15E	5E
10h - 640 X 350 EGA Graph	350	1	15F	5F

Table 6-38   EGA End Vertical Blanking Register Values (Index 16h)

Mode	Scan (Dec)	Actual Value	Reg. Value
Enhanced Color Display			
0h - 40 X 25 CGA Text	350	14A	0A
1h - 40 X 25 CGA Text	350	14A	0A
2h - 80 X 25 CGA Text	350	14A	0A
3h - 80 X 25 CGA Text	350	14A	0A
Standard Display			
0h - 40 X 25 CGA Text	200	F0	F0
1h - 40 X 25 CGA Text	200	F0	F0
2h - 80 X 25 CGA Text	200	F0	F0
3h - 80 X 25 CGA Text	200	F0	F0
Enhanced Color and Standard Displays			
4h - 320 X 200 CGA Graph	200	F0	F0
5h - 320 X 200 CGA Graph	200	F0	F0

Table 6-38 Continued.

Mode	Scan (Dec)	Actual Value	Reg. Value
6h - 640 X 200 CGA Graph	200	CF	EF
7h - 80 X 25 Mono Text	348	14E	6E
Dh - 320 X 200 EGA Graph	200	F0	F0
Eh - 640 X 200 EGA Graph	200	CF	EF
Fh - 640 X 350 Mono Graph	348	14E	6E
10h - 640 X 350 EGA Graph	350	14A	0A

Note:

This register uses only bits 0 - 4. Bits 5 - 8 are the same as the start vertical blanking register. Bits 5 - 7 of this register are not used.

Table 6-39   EGA Mode Control Register (Index 17h)

Bit	Function
0	Compatability Mode Support (CGA Graphics Mode = 0)
1	Select Row Scan Counter (Setting this bit to 0 replaces bit 14 of the address register with bit 1 of the row counter.)
2	Horizontal Retrace Select (0 = Vertical Retrace Reset Every Horizontal Retrace, 1 = Vertical Retrace Reset Every Other Horizontal Retrace)
3	Count by Two (0 = Memory Address Updated Every Character Clock, 1 = Memory Address Updated Every Other Character Clock)
4	Output Control (0 = Normal, 1 = All Outputs High)
5	Address Wrap (Operates When Bit 6 = 1, 1 Places Memory Address Bit 15 in Address Bit 0, 0 Places Memory Address Bit 13 in Address Bit 0)
6	Word or Byte Mode (1 = Byte Mode, 0 = Word Mode)
7	Hardware Reset (1 = Enable Vertical/Horizontal Retraces, 0 = Clears Retraces)

Note:

The register default values follow, with the display mode number followed by the register value in parentheses. The standard display adapter values are: 0 - 3 (A3h), 4 - 5 (A2h),

Table 6-39   Continued.

6 (C2), 7 (A3h), Dh - Eh (E3h), Fh - 10h (8Bh). Enhanced color display values are: 0 - 3 (A3h), 4 - 5 (A2h), 6 (C2), 7 (A3h), Dh - 10h (E3h).

Table 6-40   EGA Line Compare Register Values (Index 18h)

Mode	Scan (Dec)	Actual Value	Reg. Value
Enhanced Color Display			
0h - 40 X 25 CGA Text	350	1FF	FF
1h - 40 X 25 CGA Text	350	1FF	FF
2h - 80 X 25 CGA Text	350	1FF	FF
3h - 80 X 25 CGA Text	350	1FF	FF
Standard Display			
0h - 40 X 25 CGA Text	200	1FF	FF
1h - 40 X 25 CGA Text	200	1FF	FF
2h - 80 X 25 CGA Text	200	1FF	FF
3h - 80 X 25 CGA Text	200	1FF	FF
Enhanced Color and Standard Displays			
4h - 320 X 200 CGA Graph	200	1FF	FF
5h - 320 X 200 CGA Graph	200	1FF	FF
6h - 640 X 200 CGA Graph	200	1FF	FF
7h - 80 X 25 Mono Text	348	1FF	FF
Dh - 320 X 200 EGA Graph	200	1FF	FF
Eh - 640 X 200 EGA Graph	200	1FF	FF
Fh - 640 X 350 Mono Graph	348	1FF	FF
10h - 640 X 350 EGA Graph	350	1FF	FF

Table 6-41   Graphics Registers 1 and 2 Group Index Values

Index	Function	Table
0	Set/Reset	13-59
1	Enable Set/Reset	13-60
2	Color Compare	13-61
3	Data Rotate	13-62
4	Read Map Select	13-63
5	Mode Register	13-64
6	Miscellaneous	13-65
7	Color Don't Care	13-66
8	Bit Mask	13-67

Table 6-42   EGA Set/Reset Register (Index 0)

Bit	Function
0	Set/Reset Bit Plane 0
1	Set/Reset Bit Plane 1
2	Set/Reset Bit Plane 2
3	Set/Reset Bit Plane 3

Note:

The register default values follow, with the display mode number followed by the register value in parentheses: 0 - 7 (00h), Dh - 10h (00h).

Table 6-43   EGA Enable Set/Reset Register (Index 1)

Bit	Function
0	Enable Set/Reset for Bit Plane 0
1	Enable Set/Reset for Bit Plane 1
2	Enable Set/Reset for Bit Plane 2
3	Enable Set/Reset for Bit Plane 3

Note:

The register default values follow, with the display mode number followed by the register value in parentheses: 0 - 7 (00h), Dh - 10h (00h).

Table 6-44   EGA Color Compare Register (Index 2)

Bit	Function
0 - 3	Comparison Color Number
4 - 8	Not Used

Note:

The register default values follow, with the display mode number followed by the register value in parentheses: 0 - 7 (00h), Dh - 10h (00h).

Table 6-45   EGA Data Rotate Register (Index 3)

Bit	Function
0 - 2	Rotate Count (Right Rotation)
3 - 4	Function Select 00b Write Data Without Modification 01b AND Data With Latch Contents 10b OR Data With Latch Contents 11b XOR Data With Latch Contents
5 - 7	Not Used

Note:

The register default values follow, with the display mode number followed by the register value in parentheses: 0 - 7 (00h), Dh - 10h (00h).

Table 6-46   EGA Read Map Select Register (Index 4)

Bit	Function
0 - 1	Bit Plane Number to Read
2 - 7	Not Used

Note:

The register default values follow, with the display mode number followed by the register value in parentheses: 0 - 7 (00h), Dh - 10h (00h).

Table 6-47   EGA Mode Register (Index 5)

Bit	Function
0 - 1	Write Mode 00b Use the map mask to enable/disable bit planes for writing and the bit mask to set/clear individual pixels. 01b Write the contents of the latch registers to memory. 10b Use the bit mask register to enable/disable the specific pixels within the one-byte CPU address.

Table 6-47   Continued.

Bit	Function
2	Test Condition (Sets all outputs high for diagnostics.)
3	Read Mode
	00b The CPU reads memory bit-for-bit from the bit plane selected by the read map select register.
	01b The CPU reads set bits when they match the color in the color in the color compare register. The color don't care register affects these results.
4	Odd/Even (When set, the CPU data at odd addresses affects odd bit planes and even addresses affect even bit planes.)
5	Shift Register (Emulates CGA four color graphics.)
6 - 7	Not Used

Note:

The register default values follow, with the display mode number followed by the register value in parentheses. Values for a 64 Kbyte board are: 0 - 3 (10h), 4 - 5 (30h), 6 (00h), 7 (10h), Dh - Eh (00h), Fh - 10h (10h). Values for a 128 Kbyte board are: 0 - 3 (10h), 4 - 5 (30h), 6 (00h), 7 (10h), Dh - 10h (00h).

Table 6-48   EGA Miscellaneous Register (Index 6)

Bit	Function
0	Graphics Mode (When Set)
1	Chain Odd Maps to Even Maps (Emulates CGA four color graphics.)
2 - 3	Memory Map
	00b A000h / 128K
	01b A000h / 64K
	10b B000h / 32K
	11b B800h / 32K
4 - 7	Not Used

Table 6-49   EGA Color Don't Care Register (Index 7)

Bit	Function
0	Contents of bit plane 0 match color compare register setting for bit plane 0 when cleared.
1	Contents of bit plane 1 match color compare register setting for bit plane 1 when cleared.
2	Contents of bit plane 2 match color compare register setting for bit plane 2 when cleared.
3	Contents of bit plane 3 match color compare register setting for bit plane 3 when cleared.
4 - 7	Not Used

Table 6-50   EGA Bit Mask Register (Index 8)

Bit	Function
0 - 7	Each set bit allows that CPU bit to change. Each cleared bit prevents that CPU bit from changing.

Table 6-51   Attribute Controller Register Group Index Values

Index	Function	Table
0 - Fh	Palette Registers	13-69
10	Enable Set/Reset	13-70
11	Color Compare	13-71
12	Data Rotate	13-72
13	Read Map Select	13-73

Table 6-52   EGA Palette Register Values (Index 0h - fh)

Color Bit	R' 5	G' 4	B' 3	R 2	G 1	B 0	Value
Black	0	0	0	0	0	0	0
Blue	0	0	0	0	0	1	1
Green	0	0	0	0	1	0	2
Cyan	0	0	0	0	1	1	3
Red	0	0	0	1	0	0	4
Magenta	0	0	0	1	0	1	5

Table 6-52   Continued.

Color	R'	G'	B'	R	G	B	Value
Bit	5	4	3	2	1	0	
Brown	0	1	0	1	0	0	14h
White	0	0	0	1	1	1	7
Dark Gray	1	1	1	0	0	0	38h
Light Blue	1	1	1	0	0	1	39h
Light Green	1	1	1	0	1	0	3Ah
Light Cyan	1	1	1	0	1	1	3Bh
Light Red	1	1	1	1	0	0	3Ch
Light Magenta	1	1	1	1	0	1	3Dh
Yellow	1	1	1	1	1	0	3Eh
Intensified White	1	1	1	1	1	1	3Fh

Note:

The color patterns shown above are the default 16 colors out of 64 available.

Table 6-53   EGA Mode Control Register (Index 10h)

Bit	Function
0	Graphics/Alphanumeric Mode (1 = Graphics Mode)
1	Monochrome/Color Display (1 = Monochrome)
2	Enable Line Graphics Character Codes (When set, the ninth bit equals the eight bits of the line graphics characters.)
3	Enable Blink/Set Background Intensity (1 = Blink Bit)
4 - 7	Not Used

Table 6-54   EGA Overscan Color Register (Index 11h)

Bit	Function
0	Primary Blue
1	Primary Green
2	Primary Red
3	Secondary Blue

Table 6-54   Continued.

Bit	Function
4	Secondary Green
5	Secondary Red
6 - 7	Not Used

Table 6-55   EGA Color Plane Enable Register (Index 12h)

Bit	Function
0	Enables Bit Plane 0 When Set
1	Enables Bit Plane 1 When Set
2	Enables Bit Plane 2 When Set
3	Enables Bit Plane 3 When Set
4 - 5	Video Status MUX (Used for diagnostics.) 00b Red/Blue 01b Blue'/Green 10b Red'/Green'
6 - 7	Not Used

Table 6-56   EGA Horizontal PEL Panning Register (Index 13h)

Bit	Function
0 - 3	Amount to Shift Display
4 - 7	Not Used

Table 6-57   VGA Display Modes

Mode	Type	Colors	Resolution	Glyph Cell
0h	Text	16	400 by 360	9 by 16
1h	Text	16	400 by 360	9 by 16
2h	Graphics	16	400 by 720	9 by 16
3h	Graphics	16	400 by 720	9 by 16
4h	Graphics	4	200 by 320	8 by 8
5h	Graphics	4	200 by 320	8 by 8
6h	Graphics	2	200 by 640	8 by 8
7h	Text	Mono	400 by 720	9 by 16

Table 6-57   Continued.

Mode	Type	Colors	Resolution	Glyph Cell
Dh	Graphics	16	200 by 320	8 by 8
Eh	Graphics	16	200 by 640	8 by 8
Fh	Graphics	Mono	350 by 640	8 by 16
10h	Graphics	16	350 by 640	8 by 16
11h	Graphics	2	480 by 640	8 by 16
12h	Graphics	16	480 by 640	8 by 16
13h	Graphics	256	200 by 320	8 by 8
6Ah*	Graphics	16	600 by 800	10 by 24
100h*	Graphics	256	400 by 640	8 by 16
101h*	Graphics	256	480 by 640	8 by 16
102h*	Graphics	16	600 by 800	10 by 24
103h*	Graphics	256	600 by 800	10 by 24
104h*	Graphics	16	768 by 1024	12 by 30
105h*	Graphics	256	768 by 1024	12 by 30
106h*	Graphics	16	1024 by 1280	16 by 40
107h*	Graphics	256	1024 by 1280	16 by 40

Note:

* 15-bit mode numbers are based on VESA (Video Electronics Standards Association) standard VS891001-7 for Super VGA resolution. Not all manufacturers use the 15-bit sequence. Some Super VGA display adapters use a 7-bit mode from 14h-7Fh. Mode 6Ah is the only 7-bit Super VGA mode currently supported by the VESA standard.

Table 6-58   VGA Miscellaneous Output Register (Port 3C2h)

Bit	Function
0	3B/3D CRTC I/O Address (Selects monochrome or CGA addresses.)
1	Enable RAM (Disables CPU access to RAM when set.)
2 - 3	Clock Select 00b 25 MHz VGA 01b 28 MHz VGA 10b External Source (Feature Connector) 11b Not Used
4	Not Used
5	Page Bit for Odd/Even (Selects one of two 64 KByte video pages when the VGA is in the odd/even mode. A one selects the high page.)
6	Horizontal Retrace Polarity (Selects a negative polarity when set.)

Table 6-58 Continued.

```
Bit        Function

7          Vertical Retrace Polarity (Selects a negative polarity
           when set.)

6 & 7      The default condition of bits 6 & 7 appears below.
           00b Not Used
           01b 350 lines
           10b 400 lines
           11b 480 lines
```

Table 6-59 VGA Feature Control Register (Ports 3BAh & 3DAh)

```
      Bit        Function

      0 - 7      Reserved (Bit 3 set to 0)
```

Table 6-60 VGA Input Status Register Zero (Port 3C2h)

```
Bit        Function

0 - 3      Unused

4          Switch Sense (Reads the switch setting of the switch
           selected by bits 2 - 3 of the miscellaneous output
           register; where switch number = switch number - 2.)

5 - 6      Reserved

7          CRT Interrupt (Indicates the occurrance of a video
           retrace interrupt when set.)
```

Table 6-61 VGA Input Status Register One (Port 3BAh & 3DAh)

```
Bit        Function

0          Display Enable (Set during active display, cleared
           during horizontal and vertical retrace.)

1 - 2      Reserved

3          Vertical Retrace (Indicates vertical retrace when set.)

4 - 5      Diagnostic Usage (Return value of attribute register
           diagnostic bits.)

6 - 7      Not Used
```

Table 6-62   VGA Reset Register (Index 0)

Bit	Function
0	Asynchronous Clear (0 causes a asynchronous clear and halts the sequencer register. Sets all outputs to a high impedance state)
1	Synchronous Clear (0 causes a synchronous clear and halts the sequencer register. Use this bit to reset the sequencer prior to changing clock frequencies.)
2- 7	Not Used

Table 6-63   VGA Clocking Mode Register (Index 1)

Bit	Function
0	8/9 Dot Clocks (Generates 8-bit wide characters when set.)
1	Not Used
2	Shift Load 0b - Fetches 8 bits from each memory plane. Provides four 8-bit serial bit streams to attribute register. 1b - Fetches 8 bits from each memory plane and combines the output into two 16-bit serial bit streams.
3	Dot Clock (Divide dot clock by 2 when set.)
4	Shift 4 (Same as 2 above, except it outputs one 32-bit serial bit stream.)
5	Screen Off (Disables display without disrupting internal adapter functions when set.)
6 - 7	Not Used

Note:

The register default values follow, with the display mode number followed by the register value in parentheses. The 64 KByte adapter values are: 0 - 1 (0Bh), 2 - 3 (01h), 4 - 5 (0Bh), 6 (01h), 7 (00h), Dh (0Bh), Eh (01h), Fh - 10h (05h). The 128 KByte adapter values are: 0 - 1 (0Bh), 2 - 3 (01h), 4 - 5 (0Bh), 6 (01h), 7 (00h), Dh (0Bh), Eh - 10h (01h).

Table 6-64   VGA Map Mask Register (Index 2)

Bit	Function
0	Bit Plane 0 Enabled for Memory Write
1	Bit Plane 1 Enabled for Memory Write
2	Bit Plane 2 Enabled for Memory Write
3	Bit Plane 3 Enabled for Memory Write
4 - 7	Not Used

Note:

The register default values follow, with the display mode number followed by the register value in parentheses: 0 - 5 (03h), 6 (01h), 7 (03h), Dh - 10h (0Fh).

Table 6-65   VGA Character Map Select Register (Index 3)

Bit	Function
0 - 1	Character Map Select A
2 - 3	Character Map Select B
4	Character Map Select High Bit A
5	Character Map Select High Bit B
6 - 7	Not Used

Table 6-66   VGA Memory Mode Register (Index 4)

Bit	Function
0	Not Used
1	Extended Memory (Set when adapter contains more than 64 KBytes of memory.)
2	Odd/Even Mode (CGA Graphics Mode Emulation)
3	Chain 4 (Allows CPU to see all four bit planes as contiguous memory.)
4 - 7	Not Used

Table 6-66   Continued.

Note:

The register default values follow, with the display mode number followed by the register value in parentheses. The values for 64 KByte boards are: 0 - 3 (03h), 4 - 5 (02h), 6 (06h), 7 (03h), Dh - Eh (06h), Fh - 10h (00h). The values for 128 KByte boards are: 0 - 3 (03h), 4 - 5 (02h), 6 (06h), 7 (03h), Dh - 10h (06h).

Table 6-67   VGA CRTC Register Group Index Values (Ports 3D4h & 3D5h)

Index	Function	Table
0	Horizontal Total	6-68
1h	Horizontal Display End	6-69
2h	Start Horizontal Blanking	6-70
3h	End Horizontal Blanking	6-71
4h	Start Horizontal Retrace	6-72
5h	End Horizontal Retrace	6-73
6h	Vertical Total	6-74
7h	Overflow	6-75
8h	Preset Row Scan	6-76
9h	Max Scan Line	6-77
Ah	Cursor Start	6-78
Bh	Cursor End	6-79
10h	Vertical Retrace Start (Read & Write)	6-80
11h	Vertical Retrace End (Read & Write)	6-81
12h	Vertical Display End	6-82
13h	Offset	6-83
14h	Underline Location	6-84
15h	Start Vertical Blanking	6-85
16h	End Vertical Blanking	6-86
17h	Mode Control	6-87
18h	Line Compare	6-88

Table 6-68   VGA Horizontal Total Register Values (Index 0)

Mode	Scan (Dec)	Retrace (Dec)	Value (Dec)	Value (Hex)
0h - 40 X 25 CGA Text (16)	40	9	45	2D
1h - 40 X 25 CGA Text (16)	40	9	45	2D
2h - 80 X 25 CGA Text (16)	80	15	91	5B
3h - 80 X 25 CGA Text (16)	80	15	91	5B
4h - 320 X 200 CGA Graph (4)	40	19	55	37
5h - 320 X 200 CGA Graph (4)	40	19	55	37
6h - 640 X 200 CGA Graph (2)	80	36	112	70
7h - 80 X 25 Mono Text (4)	80	20	96	60
Dh - 320 X 200 EGA Graph (16)	40	19	55	37

Table 6-68   Continued.

Mode	Scan (Dec)	Retrace (Dec)	Value (Dec)	Value (Hex)
Eh - 640 X 200 EGA Graph (16)	80	36	112	70
Fh - 640 X 350 Mono Graph (4)	80	20	96	60
10h - 640 X 350 EGA Graph (16)	80	15	91	5B
11h - 640 X 480 VGA Graph (2)	80	36	112	70
12h - 640 X 480 VGA Graph (16)	80	36	112	70
13h - 320 X 200 VGA Graph (256)	40	19	55	37

Notes:

1. Numbers appearing in parenthesis show the number of colors available.

2. The horizontal total register value = scan value + retrace value - 4

3. The actual horizontal total is 5 greater than the amount shown. The scan count begins at 0, reducing the count by one.

Table 6-69   VGA Horizontal Display Enable End Register Values (Index 1)

Mode	Scan (Dec)	Value (Dec)	Value (Hex)
0h - 40 X 25 CGA Text	40	39	27
1h - 40 X 25 CGA Text	40	39	27
2h - 80 X 25 CGA Text	80	79	4f
3h - 80 X 25 CGA Text	80	79	4f
4h - 320 X 200 CGA Graph	40	39	27
5h - 320 X 200 CGA Graph	40	39	27
6h - 640 X 200 CGA Graph	80	79	4f
7h - 80 X 25 Mono Text	80	79	4f
Dh - 320 X 200 EGA Graph	40	39	27
Eh - 640 X 200 EGA Graph	80	79	4f
Fh - 640 X 350 Mono Graph	80	79	4f
10h - 640 X 350 EGA Graph	80	79	4f
11h - 640 X 480 VGA Graph	80	79	4f
12h - 640 X 480 VGA Graph	80	79	4f
13h - 320 X 200 VGA Graph	40	39	27

Notes:

The horizontal display enable end register value = scan - 1 because the scan counter begins at 0.

Table 6-70   VGA Start Horizontal Blanking Register Values (Index 2)

Mode	Scan (Dec)	Overscan (Dec)	Value (Dec)	Value (Hex)
0h - 40 X 25 CGA Text	40	4	43	2B
1h - 40 X 25 CGA Text	40	4	43	2B
2h - 80 X 25 CGA Text	80	4	83	53
3h - 80 X 25 CGA Text	80	4	83	53
4h - 320 X 200 CGA Graph	40	6	45	2D
5h - 320 X 200 CGA Graph	40	6	45	2D
6h - 640 X 200 CGA Graph	80	10	89	59
7h - 80 X 25 Mono Text	80	7	86	56
Dh - 320 X 200 EGA Graph	40	6	45	2D
Eh - 640 X 200 EGA Graph	80	10	89	59
Fh - 640 X 350 Mono Graph	80	7	86	56
10h - 640 X 350 EGA Graph	80	4	83	53
11h - 640 X 480 VGA Graph	80	4	83	53
12h - 640 X 480 VGA Graph	80	4	83	53
13h - 320 X 200 VGA Graph	40	6	45	2D

Table 6-71   VGA End Horizontal Blanking Register Values (Index 3)

Mode	Scan (Dec)	Actual (Hex)	Register (Hex)
Bits 0 - 4			
0h - 40 X 25 CGA Text	40	2D	AD
1h - 40 X 25 CGA Text	40	2D	AD
2h - 80 X 25 CGA Text	80	57	B7
3h - 80 X 25 CGA Text	80	57	B7
4h - 320 X 200 CGA Graph	40	37	B7
5h - 320 X 200 CGA Graph	40	37	B7
6h - 640 X 200 CGA Graph	80	4D	AD
7h - 80 X 25 Mono Text	80	3A	BA
Dh - 320 X 200 EGA Graph	40	37	B7
Eh - 640 X 200 EGA Graph	80	4D	AD
Fh - 640 X 350 Mono Graph	80	5A	9A
10h - 640 X 350 EGA Graph	80	57	97
11h - 640 X 480 VGA Graph	80	4D	AD
12h - 640 X 480 VGA Graph	80	4D	AD
13h - 320 X 200 VGA Graph	40	37	B7
Bits 5 - 6			
0h - 40 X 25 CGA Text		01	AD
1h - 40 X 25 CGA Text		01	AD
2h - 80 X 25 CGA Text		01	B7
3h - 80 X 25 CGA Text		01	B7
4h - 320 X 200 CGA Graph		01	B7
5h - 320 X 200 CGA Graph		01	B7
6h - 640 X 200 CGA Graph		01	AD

Table 6-71   Continued.

Mode	Scan (Dec)	Actual (Hex)	Register (Hex)
7h - 80 X 25 Mono Text		01	BA
Dh - 320 X 200 EGA Graph		01	B7
Eh - 640 X 200 EGA Graph		01	AD
Fh - 640 X 350 Mono Graph		01	9A
10h - 640 X 350 EGA Graph		01	97
11h - 640 X 480 VGA Graph		01	AD
12h - 640 X 480 VGA Graph		01	AD
13h - 320 X 200 VGA Graph		01	B7

Bit 7

Set to 1 for all modes. (Used for chip testing only.)

Notes:

1. The register value equals the individual values from bit 7 (1), bits 5 - 6, and the five least significant end horizontal blanking value bits 0 - 4. The VGA uses an additional bit for the character count (bit 5) located in the end horizontal retrace register. The MSB (bits 6 and 7) for the end horizontal blanking value is the same as the start value.

2. Bit values for bits 5 and 6 show the character delay used before display of the next displayable area. These values are: 00 = no delay, 01 = 1 character, 10 = 2 characters, and 11 = 3 characters.

Table 6-72   VGA Start Horizontal Retrace Register Values (Index 4)

Mode	Scan (Dec)	Value (Dec)	Value (Hex)
0h - 40 X 25 CGA Text	40	43	28
1h - 40 X 25 CGA Text	40	43	28
2h - 80 X 25 CGA Text	80	83	51
3h - 80 X 25 CGA Text	80	83	51
4h - 320 X 200 CGA Graph	40	45	30
5h - 320 X 200 CGA Graph	40	45	30
6h - 640 X 200 CGA Graph	80	89	5E
7h - 80 X 25 Mono Text	80	86	51
Dh - 320 X 200 EGA Graph	40	45	30
Eh - 640 X 200 EGA Graph	80	89	5E
Fh - 640 X 350 Mono Graph	80	86	50
10h - 640 X 350 EGA Graph	80	83	52
11h - 640 X 480 VGA Graph	80	86	50
12h - 640 X 480 VGA Graph	80	86	50
13h - 320 X 200 VGA Graph	40	45	30

Table 6-72   Continued.

Note:

The end horizontal retrace register may delay the horizontal
retrace.

Table 6-73   VGA End Horizontal Retrace Register Values (Index 5)

Mode	Scan (Dec)	Actual (Hex)	Register (Hex)
Bits 0 - 4			
0h - 40 X 25 CGA Text	40	2D	6D
1h - 40 X 25 CGA Text	40	2D	6D
2h - 80 X 25 CGA Text	80	4B	5B
3h - 80 X 25 CGA Text	80	4B	5B
4h - 320 X 200 CGA Graph	40	34	14
5h - 320 X 200 CGA Graph	40	34	14
6h - 640 X 200 CGA Graph	80	46	06
7h - 80 X 25 Mono Text	80	50	60
Dh - 320 X 200 EGA Graph	40	34	14
Eh - 640 X 200 EGA Graph	80	46	06
Fh - 640 X 350 Mono Graph	80	40	60
10h - 640 X 350 EGA Graph	80	40	00
11h - 640 X 480 VGA Graph	80	40	00
12h - 640 X 480 VGA Graph	80	40	00
13h - 320 X 200 VGA Graph	40	34	14
Bits 5 - 6			
0h - 40 X 25 CGA Text		11	6D
1h - 40 X 25 CGA Text		11	6D
2h - 80 X 25 CGA Text		10	5B
3h - 80 X 25 CGA Text		10	5B
4h - 320 X 200 CGA Graph		00	14
5h - 320 X 200 CGA Graph		00	14
6h - 640 X 200 CGA Graph		00	06
7h - 80 X 25 Mono Text		11	60
Dh - 320 X 200 EGA Graph		00	14
Eh - 640 X 200 EGA Graph		00	06
Fh - 640 X 350 Mono Graph		11	60
10h - 640 X 350 EGA Graph		00	00
11h - 640 X 480 VGA Graph		00	00
12h - 640 X 480 VGA Graph		00	00
13h - 320 X 200 VGA Graph		00	14

Bit 7 End Horizontal Blanking Bit 5

This is the sixth bit of the VGA's end horizontal blanking
register.

Table 6-73   Continued.

Notes:

1. The register value equals the individual values from bit 7, bits 5 - 6, and the five least significant end horizontal retrace value bits 0 - 4. The MSB for the end horizontal retrace value is the same as the start value.

2. Bit values for bits 5 and 6 show the character delay used during retrace. These values are: 00 = no delay, 01 = 1 character, 10 = 2 characters, and 11 = 3 characters.

Table 6-74   VGA Vertical Total Register Values (Index 6)

Mode	Scan (Dec)	Retrace (Dec)	Actual Value	Reg. Value
0h - 40 X 25 CGA Text (16)	400	14	19E	9E
1h - 40 X 25 CGA Text (16)	400	14	19E	9E
2h - 80 X 25 CGA Text (16)	400	14	19E	9E
3h - 80 X 25 CGA Text (16)	400	14	19E	9E
4h - 320 X 200 CGA Graph (4)	200	60	104	04
5h - 320 X 200 CGA Graph (4)	200	60	104	04
6h - 640 X 200 CGA Graph (2)	200	60	104	04
7h - 80 X 25 Mono Text (4)	400	20	170	70
Dh - 320 X 200 EGA Graph (16)	200	60	104	04
Eh - 640 X 200 EGA Graph (16)	200	60	104	04
Fh - 640 X 350 Mono Graph (4)	350	20	170	70
10h - 640 X 350 EGA Graph (16)	350	14	16C	6C
11h - 640 X 480 VGA Graph (2)	480	14	1EE	EE
12h - 640 X 480 VGA Graph (16)	480	14	1EE	EE
13h - 320 X 200 VGA Graph (256)	200	60	104	04

Notes:

1. Numbers appearing in parentheses show the number of colors available.

2. Vertical total register value = scan value + retrace value.

3. This register uses values contained in the CRTC overflow register for bits 8 and 9. The actual value column above shows the results of these two additional bits.

Table 6-75   VGA CRT Controller Overflow Register (Index 7)

Bit	Function
0	Vertical Total Ninth Bit (see Index 6)
1	Vertical Display Enable End Ninth Bit (see Index 12h)
2	Vertical Retrace Start Ninth Bit (See Index 10h)

Table 6-75   Continued.

Bit	Function
3	Start Vertical Blank Ninth Bit (see Index 9)
4	Line Compare Ninth Bit (see Index 9)
5	Vertical Total Tenth Bit (see Index 6)
6	Vertical Display Enable End Tenth Bit (see Index 12h)
7	Vertical Retrace Start Tenth Bit (see Index 10h)

Note:

The register default values follow with the mode number followed by the value in parentheses. The standard display values are: 0 - 6 (11h), 7 (1Fh), Dh - Eh (11h), Fh - 10h (1Fh). The enhanced color display values are: 0 - 3 (1Fh), 4 - 6 (11h), 7 (1Fh), Dh - Eh (11h), Fh - 10h (1Fh).

Table 6-76   VGA Preset Row Scan Register (Index 8)

Bit	Function
0 - 4	Preset Row Scan (Starting pixel row number after retrace).
5 - 6	Byte Panning Control (Provides two extra horizontal pel panning register bits.)
7	Not Used

Note:

The register default values follow, with the display mode number followed by the register value in parentheses: 0 - 7 (00h), dh - 13h (00h).

Table 6-77   VGA Maximum Scan Line Register (Index 9)

Bit	Function
0 - 4	Maximum Scan Line (Alphanumeric character height - 1)
5	Start Vertical Blank Register Tenth Bit (see Index 15h)
6	Line Compare Register Tenth Bit (see Index 7)
7	200 to 400 Line Coversion (Scan Doubling Disabled = 0)

Table 6-78   VGA Cursor Start Register (Index Ah)

Bit	Function
0 - 4	Cursor Start Position (First cursor row position - 1)
5	Cursor Off (VGA Cursor Off = 1)
6 - 7	Not Used

Table 6-79   VGA Cursor End Register (Index Bh)

Bit	Function
0 - 4	Cursor End Position (Last cursor row position)
5 - 6	Cursor Skew (Cursor control signal delay) 00b - No Delay 01b - 1 Character Delay 10b - 2 Character Delay 11b - 3 Character Delay
7	Not Used

Table 6-80   VGA Start Vertical Retrace Register Values (Index 10h)

Mode	Scan (Dec)	Actual Value (Dec)	Actual Value	Reg Value
0h - 40 X 25 CGA Text	400	400	190	90
1h - 40 X 25 CGA Text	400	400	190	90
2h - 80 X 25 CGA Text	400	400	190	90
3h - 80 X 25 CGA Text	400	400	190	90
4h - 320 X 200 CGA Graph	200	225	E1	E1
5h - 320 X 200 CGA Graph	200	225	E1	E1
6h - 640 X 200 CGA Graph	200	224	E0	E0
7h - 80 X 25 Mono Text	400	400	190	90
Dh - 320 X 200 EGA Graph	200	225	E1	E1
Eh - 640 X 200 EGA Graph	200	224	E0	E0
Fh - 640 X 350 Mono Graph	348	350	15E	5E
10h - 640 X 350 EGA Graph	350	350	15E	5E
11h - 640 X 480 VGA Graph	480	480	1E0	E0
12h - 640 X 480 VGA Graph	480	480	1E0	E0
13h - 320 X 200 VGA Graph	200	224	E0	E0

Table 6-81   VGA End Vertical Retrace Register Values (Index 11h)

Bit	Function
0 - 3	Vertical Retrace End Count (Four Least Significant Bits, MSB equals Vertical Retrace Start Register MSB)
4	Clear Vertical Interrupt
5	Enable Vertical Interrupt
6	Select 5 Refresh Cycles (Sets the number of RAM refresh cycles per horizontal scan.)
7	Protect RO-7 (Write protects CRTC registers 0 through 7 when set.)

Table 6-82   VGA Vertical Display Enable End Register Values (Index 12h)

Mode	Scan (Dec)	Actual Value (Dec)	Actual Value	Reg Value
0h - 40 X 25 CGA Text	400	399	18F	8F
1h - 40 X 25 CGA Text	400	399	18F	8F
2h - 80 X 25 CGA Text	400	399	18F	8F
3h - 80 X 25 CGA Text	400	399	18F	8F
4h - 320 X 200 CGA Graph	200	199	C7	C7
5h - 320 X 200 CGA Graph	200	199	C7	C7
6h - 640 X 200 CGA Graph	200	199	C7	C7
7h - 80 X 25 Mono Text	400	399	18F	8F
Dh - 320 X 200 EGA Graph	200	199	C7	C7
Eh - 640 X 200 EGA Graph	200	199	C7	C7
Fh - 640 X 350 Mono Graph	350	349	15D	5D
10h - 640 X 350 EGA Graph	350	349	15D	5D
11h - 640 X 480 VGA Graph	480	479	1DF	DF
12h - 640 X 480 VGA Graph	480	479	1DF	DF
13h - 320 X 200 VGA Graph	200	199	C7	C7

Table 6-83   VGA Offset Register Values (Index 13h)

Mode	Memory Row (Dec)	Memory Row(Hex)
0h - 40 X 25 CGA Text	22	16
1h - 40 X 25 CGA Text	22	16
2h - 80 X 25 CGA Text	44	2C
3h - 80 X 25 CGA Text	44	2C
4h - 320 X 200 CGA Graph	20	14
5h - 320 X 200 CGA Graph	20	14
6h - 640 X 200 CGA Graph	40	28

Table 6-83   Continued.

Mode	Memory Row (Dec)	Memory Row (Hex)
7h - 80 X 25 Mono Text	44	2C
Dh - 320 X 200 EGA Graph	20	14
Eh - 640 X 200 EGA Graph	40	28
Fh - 640 X 350 Mono Graph	40	28
10h - 640 X 350 EGA Graph	40	28
11h - 640 X 480 VGA Graph	40	28
12h - 640 X 480 VGA Graph	40	28
13h - 320 X 200 VGA Graph	20	14

Table 6-84   VGA Underline Location Register (Index 14h)

Bit	Function
0 - 4	Underline Location (Position within character cell)
5	Count by 4 (Divides the character clock by 4.)
6	Double Word Mode (Double Word Memory Addressing = 1)
7	Not Used

Note:

The register default values follow, with the display mode number followed by the register value in parentheses: 0 - 3 (0Fh), 4 - 6 (00h), 7 (0Fh), Dh - Eh (00h), Fh - 12h (0Fh), 13h (00h).

Table 6-85   VGA Start Vertical Blanking Register Values (Index 15h)

Mode	Scan (Dec)	Overscan (Dec)	Actual Value	Reg. Value
0h - 40 X 25 CGA Text	400	1	19E	9E
1h - 40 X 25 CGA Text	400	1	19E	9E
2h - 80 X 25 CGA Text	400	1	19E	9E
3h - 80 X 25 CGA Text	400	1	19E	9E
4h - 320 X 200 CGA Graph	200	25	E0	E0
5h - 320 X 200 CGA Graph	200	25	E0	E0
6h - 640 X 200 CGA Graph	200	24	DF	DF
7h - 80 X 25 Mono Text	400	1	19E	9E
Dh - 320 X 200 EGA Graph	200	25	E0	E0
Eh - 640 X 200 EGA Graph	200	24	DF	DF
Fh - 640 X 350 Mono Graph	350	1	15E	5F
10h - 640 X 350 EGA Graph	350	1	15F	5F
11h - 640 X 480 VGA Graph	480	1	1E1	E1
12h - 640 X 480 VGA Graph	480	1	1E1	E1
13h - 320 X 200 VGA Graph	200	24	DF	DF

Table 6-86   VGA End Vertical Blanking Register Values (Index 16h)

Mode	Scan (Dec)	Actual Value	Reg. Value
0h - 40 X 25 CGA Text	400	14A	0A
1h - 40 X 25 CGA Text	400	14A	0A
2h - 80 X 25 CGA Text	400	14A	0A
3h - 80 X 25 CGA Text	400	14A	0A
4h - 320 X 200 CGA Graph	200	F0	F0
5h - 320 X 200 CGA Graph	200	F0	F0
6h - 640 X 200 CGA Graph	200	CF	EF
7h - 80 X 25 Mono Text	400	14E	6E
Dh - 320 X 200 EGA Graph	200	F0	F0
Eh - 640 X 200 EGA Graph	200	CF	EF
Fh - 640 X 350 Mono Graph	348	14E	6E
10h - 640 X 350 EGA Graph	350	14A	0A
11h - 640 X 480 VGA Graph	480	14A	0A
12h - 640 X 480 VGA Graph	480	14A	0A
13h - 320 X 200 VGA Graph	200	CF	EF

Table 6-87   VGA Mode Control Register (Index 17h)

Bit	Function
0	Compatibility Mode Support (CGA Graphics Mode = 0)
1	Select Row Scan Counter (Setting this bit to 0 replaces bit 14 of the address register with bit 1 of the row counter.)
2	Horizontal Retrace Select (0 = Vertical Retrace Reset Every Horizontal Retrace, 1 = Vertical Retrace Reset Every Other Horizontal Retrace)
3	Count by Two (0 = Memory Address Updated Every Character Clock, 1 = Memory Address Updated Every Other Character Clock)
4	Not Used
5	Address Wrap (Operates When Bit 6 = 1, 1 Places Memory Address Bit 15 in Address Bit 0, 0 Places Memory Address Bit 13 in Address Bit 0)
6	Word or Byte Mode (1 = Byte Mode, 0 = Word Mode)
7	Hardware Reset (1 = Enable Vertical/Horizontal Retraces, 0 = Clears Retraces)

Table 6-87   Continued.

Note:

The register default values follow, with the display mode
number followed by the register value in parentheses: 0 - 3
(A3h), 4 - 5 (A2h), 6 (C2), 7 (A3h), Dh - 13h (E3h).

Table 6-88   VGA Line Compare Register Values (Index 18h)

Mode	Scan (Dec)	Actual Value	Reg. Value
0h - 40 X 25 CGA Text	400	3FF	FF
1h - 40 X 25 CGA Text	400	3FF	FF
2h - 80 X 25 CGA Text	400	3FF	FF
3h - 80 X 25 CGA Text	400	3FF	FF
4h - 320 X 200 CGA Graph	200	3FF	FF
5h - 320 X 200 CGA Graph	200	3FF	FF
6h - 640 X 200 CGA Graph	200	3FF	FF
7h - 80 X 25 Mono Text	400	3FF	FF
Dh - 320 X 200 EGA Graph	200	3FF	FF
Eh - 640 X 200 EGA Graph	200	3FF	FF
Fh - 640 X 350 Mono Graph	348	3FF	FF
10h - 640 X 350 EGA Graph	350	3FF	FF
11h - 640 X 480 VGA Graph	480	3FF	FF
12h - 640 X 480 VGA Graph	480	3FF	FF
13h - 320 X 200 VGA Graph	200	3FF	FF

Table 6-89   VGA Attribute Controller Register Group Index Values

Index	Function	Table
0 - Fh	Palette Registers	13-107
10h	Enable Set/Reset	13-108
11h	Color Compare	13-109
12h	Data Rotate	13-110
13h	Read Map Select	13-111
14h	Color Select	13-112

Table 6-90   VGA Palette Register Values (Index 0h - Fh)

Bit	Function
0 - 5	Palette (Selects a color from one of the DAC registers.)
6 - 7	Not Used

Table 6-90   Continued.

Note:

These registers do not affect VGA mode 13h. The software directly manipulates the DAC during this mode.

Table 6-91   VGA Mode Control Register (Index 10h)

Bit	Function
0	Graphics/Alphanumeric Mode (1 = Graphics Mode)
1	Monochrome/Color Display (1 = Monochrome)
2	Enable Line Graphics Character Codes (When set, the ninth bit equals the eight bits of the line graphics characters.)
3	Enable Blink/Set Background Intensity (1 = Blink Bit)
4	Not Used
5	PEL Panning Compatibility (Allows panning of only the upper window in split screen mode when set.)
6	PEL Width (The pixels are eight bits wide when set. This allows use of up to 256 colors.)
7	P5, P4 Select (Replaces bits 4 and 5 of the palette register with bits 0 and 1 of the color select register when set.)

Table 6-92   VGA Overscan Color Register (Index 11h)

Bit	Function
0 - 7	Palette (Selects one of the DAC register colors.)

Table 6-93   VGA Color Plane Enable Register (Index 12h)

Bit	Function
0	Enables Bit Plane 0 When Set
1	Enables Bit Plane 1 When Set

Table 6-93   Continued.

2	Enables Bit Plane 2 When Set
3	Enables Bit Plane 3 When Set
4 - 5	Video Status MUX (Used for diagnostics.) 00b Red/Blue 01b Blue'/Green 10b Red'/Green'
6 - 7	Not Used

Table 6-94   VGA Horizontal PEL Panning Register (Index 13h)

Shift Value	7, 0-3	Modes 13h	All Others
Bits 0 - 3			
000b	1	0	0
001b	2	N/A	1
010b	3	1	2
011b	4	N/A	3
100b	5	2	4
101b	6	N/A	5
110b	7	3	6
111b	8	N/A	7
100b	0	N/A	N/A
Bits 4 - 7			
Not Used			

Table 6-95   VGA Color Select Register (Index 14h)

Bit	Function
0 - 1	S_Color 4 - 5 (The VGA replaces bits 4 and 5 of the palette registers with these bits when the attribute control mode register bit 7 equals 1.)
2 - 3	S_Color 6 - 7 (These bits are the MSB of the palette register.)

Table 6-96 8514/A Display Modes

Mode	Type	Colors	Resolution	Glyph Cell
VGA Mode				
0h	Text	16	400 by 360	9 by 16
1h	Text	16	400 by 360	9 by 16
2h	Graphics	16	400 by 720	9 by 16
3h	Graphics	16	400 by 720	9 by 16
4h	Graphics	4	200 by 320	8 by 8
5h	Graphics	4	200 by 320	8 by 8
6h	Graphics	2	200 by 640	8 by 8
7h	Text	Mono	400 by 720	9 by 16
Dh	Graphics	16	200 by 320	8 by 8
Eh	Graphics	16	200 by 640	8 by 8
Fh	Graphics	Mono	350 by 640	8 by 16
10h	Graphics	16	350 by 640	8 by 16
11h	Graphics	2	480 by 640	8 by 16
12h	Graphics	16	480 by 640	8 by 16
13h	Graphics	256	200 by 320	8 by 8
Advanced Function (AF) Mode2				
14h	Graphics	16/2561	480 by 640	8 by 16
15h	Graphics	16/2561	768 by 1024	12 by 20
16h	Graphics	16/2561	768 by 1024	8 by 14
17h	Graphics	16/2561	768 by 1024	7 by 15

Notes:

1. 16 colors from a palette of 262,144 colors available with the standard 512 KBytes of VRAM. 256 colors available with an additional 512 KBytes of VRAM (1 MByte total).

2. Application Interface (AI) specific modes. Some 8514/A adapters support additional modes through the use of direct register programming.

Table 6-97 8514/A Application Interface (AI) Commands

Command	Number	Function
ABLOCKCGA	53	Writes a CGA formatted alphanumeric character block.
ABLOCKMF1	52	Writes an alphanumeric character block.
ACURSOR	56	Sets the alphanumeric cursor position.
AERASE	54	Erases a character cell rectangle.

Table 6-97   Continued.

Command	Number	Function
ASCROLL	55	Scrolls the character cell rectangle.
ASCUR	57	Sets the alphanumeric cursor shape.
ASFONT	58	Selects the alphanumeric character font.
AXLATE	59	Selects the alphanumeric attribute color index table.
HBAR	5	Begins a filled area.
HBBC	14	Performs Bit-BLT exclusively in display memory.
HBBCHN	13	Performs Bit-BLT to or from system memory.
HBBR	12	Defines the Bit-BLT source at an absolute address.
HBBW	10	Defines the Bit-BLT destination at an absolute address.
HCBBW	11	Defines the Bit-BLT destination at the current cursor position.
HCCHST	50	Places a text string at the current cursor position.
HCHST	49	Places a text string at an absolute position.
HCLINE	2	Draws an absolute polyline starting at the current cursor position.
HCLOSE	16	Closes the display adapter interface.
HCMRK	9	Draws a marker symbol at the current cursor position.
HEAR	6	Ends a filled area.
HEGS	26	Clears the screen.
HESC	37	Terminate adapter processing.
HINIT	20	Initializes the task-dependent state buffer.
HINT	22	Waits for the vertical retrace signal.
HLDPAL	29	Load a palette.
HLINE	1	Draws an absolute polyline starting at an absolute cursor position.

Table 6-97   Continued.

Command	Number	Function
HMRK	8	Draws a marker symbol at an absolute position.
HOPEN	15	Opens the display adapter interface.
HQCOORD	35	Gets the coordinate types.
HQCP	18	Gets the current cursor position.
HQDFPAL	19	Get default palette information.
HQDPS	38	Gets drawing process buffer size.
HQMODE	24	Gets the display adapter mode.
HQMODES	25	Sees if a display adapter mode is available.
HRCLINE	4	Draws a relative polyline starting at the current cursor position.
HRECT	7	Draws a filled rectangle.
HRLINE	3	Draws a relative polyline starting at an absolute position.
HRLPC	33	Restores a saved line pattern position.
HRPAL	31	Restores a saved palette.
HSBCOL	45	Sets the background color.
HSBP	34	Sets the display and masking bitplane controls.
HSCMP	47	Sets the color comparison register.
HSCOL	44	Sets the foreground color.
HSCOORD	36	Sets the coordinate types.
HSCP	17	Moves the cursor to an absolute position.
HSCS	48	Selects a character set.
HSGQ	27	Sets the graphics quality/drawing styles.
HSHS	28	Clips a rectangle (scissors).
HSLPC	32	Saves the current line pattern position.
HSLT	42	Sets the current line type.
HSLW	43	Sets the current line width.

Table 6-97   Continued.

Command	Number	Function
HSMARK	39	Sets the current marker shape.
HSMODE	23	Sets the display adapter mode.
HSMX	46	Sets the drawing raster operation (mix).
HSPAL	30	Save the current palette.
HSPATT	40	Sets the current pattern shape.
HSPATTO	41	Sets the current pattern origin.
HSYNC	21	Sets the adapter to a task-dependent state.
HXLATE	51	Assigns a color index table for text.

Table 6-98   Standard 8514/A Registers

Port Address	Register Name	Mnemonic	Type
0100	Setup Mode Identification	SETUP_ID1	Read-Only
0101	Setup Mode Identification	SETUP_ID2	Read-Only
0102	Setup Mode Option	SETUP_OPT	Read-Write
02E8	Display Status	DISP_STAT	Read-Only
02E8	Horizontal Total	H_TOTAL	Write-Only
02EA	DAC Mask	DAC_MASK	Read-Write
02EB	DAC Read Index	DAC_R_INDEX	Read-Write
02EC	DAC Write Index	DAC_W_INDEX	Read-Write
02ED	DAC Data	DAC_DATA	Read-Write
06E8	Horizontal Displayed	H_DISP	Read-Write
0AE8	Horizontal Sync Start	H_SYNC_STRT	Read-Write
0EE8	Horizontal Sync Width	H_SYNC_WID	Read-Write
12E8	Vertical Total	V_TOTAL	Read-Write
16E8	Vertical Displayed	V_DISP	Read-Write
1AE8	Vertical Sync Start	V_SYNC_STRT	Read-Write
1EE8	Vertical Sync Width	V_SYNC_WID	Read-Write
22E8	Display Control	DISP_CNTL	Read-Write
42E8	Subsystem Status	SUBSYS_STAT	Read-Only
42E8	Subsystem Control	SUBSYS_CNTL	Write-Only
46E8	ROM Page Select	ROM_PAGE_SEL	Read-Write
4AE8	Advanced Function Control	ADVFUNC_CNTL	Read-Write

Table 6-98 Continued.

Port Address	Register Name	Mnemonic	Type
82E8	Current Y Position	CUR_Y	Read-Write
86E8	Current X Position	CUR_X	Read-Write
8AE8	Destination Y Position/Axial Step Constant	DESTY_AXSTP	Read-Write
8EE8	Destination X Position/Axial Step Constant	DESTX_AXSTP	Read-Write
92E8	Error Term	ERR_TERM	Read-Write
96E8	Major Axis Pixel Count	MAJ_AXIS_PCNT	Read-Write
9AE8	Graphics Processor Status	GP_STAT	Read-Only
9AE8	Command	CMD	Write-Only
9EE8	Short Stroke Vector Transfer	SHORT_STROKE	Read-Write
A2E8	Background Color	BKGD_COLOR	Read-Write
A6E8	Foreground Color	FRGD_COLOR	Read-Write
AAE8	Write Mask	WRT_MASK	Read-Write
AEE8	Read Mask	RD_MASK	Read-Write
B2E8	Color Compare	COLOR_CMP	Read-Write
B6E8	Background Mix	BKGD_MIX	Read-Write
BAE8	Foreground Mix	FRGD_MIX	Read-Write
BEE8	Multi-Function Control	MULTIFUNC_CNTL	N/A
BEE8 Index 0	Minor Axis Pixel Count	MIN_AXIS_PCNT	Read-Write
BEE8 Index 1	Top Scissors	SCISSORS_T	Read-Write
BEE8 Index 2	Left Scissors	SCISSORS_L	Read-Write
BEE8 Index 3	Bottom Scissors	SCISSORS_B	Read-Write
BEE8 Index 4	Right Scissors	SCISSORS_R	Read-Write
BEE8 Index 5	Memory Control	MEM_CNTL	Read-Write
BEE8 Index 8	Fixed Pattern Low	PATTERN_L	Read-Write
BEE8 Index 9	Fixed Pattern High	PATTERN_H	Read-Write
BEE8 Index A	Pixel Control	PIX_CNTL	Read-Write
E2E8	Pixel Data Transfer	PIX_TRANS	Read-Write

Table 6-99 Sync Status and Horizontal Total (Port 02E8h)

Bit	Function
Read - Sync Status	
0	Video Sense 0 - No Monitor Attached 1 - Monitor Attached

Table 6-99   Continued.

```
Bit        Function

1                        Horizontal Sync - End of Scan Line

2                        Vertical Sync - Start of Vertical Retrace

3 - 15                   Not Used

Write - Horizontal Total

0 - 7                    Horizontal Total - Total Scan Line Width

8 - 15                   Not Used
```

Table 6-100   Horizontal Displayed (Port 6E8h)

```
Bit             Function

0 - 7           Horizontal Blank - Start of Blank Pulse

8 - 15          Not Used
```

Table 6-101   Horizontal Sync Start (Port AE8h)

```
Bit             Function

0 - 7           Horizontal Sync Start

8 - 15          Not Used
```

Table 6-102   Horizontal Sync Width (Port EE8h)

```
Bit             Function

0 - 4           Horizontal Sync Width

5               Horizontal Sync Polarity
                1 - Negative
                0 - Positive

6 - 15          Not Used
```

Table 6-103   Vertical Total (Port 12E8h)

Bit	Function
1 - 11	Vertical Total - The total number of half scan lines in the frame.
12 - 15	Not Used

Table 6-104   Vertical Displayed (Port 16E8h)

Bit	Function
1 - 11	Vertical Blank - The starting position of the vertical blank pulse in half scan lines.
12 - 15	Not Used

Table 6-105   Vertical Sync Start (Port 1AE8h)

Bit	Function
1 - 11	Vertical Sync Pulse
12 - 15	Not Used

Table 6-106   Vertical Sync Width (Port 1EE8h)

Bit	Function
1 - 4	Vertical Sync Width
5	Vertical Sync Polarity 1 - Negative 0 - Positive
6 - 15	Not Used

Table 6-107   Display Control Register (Port 22E8h)

Bit	Function
0	Nugget Phase Enable (Not used on some 8514/A implementations.)
1 - 2	Pre-Scaler Bits 00 - Divide NCLK by 2 (Pseudo 8-Plane Mode) 01 - Divide NCLK by 4 (Standard 8514/A) 10 - Divide NCLK by 6 (Not Used) 11 - Divide NCLK by 8 (Not Used)
3	Double Scan Select 1 - Display each scan line once (normal). 0 - Display each scan line twice.
4	Interlaced Sync Select 1 - Interlaced Sync 0 - Non-Interlaced Sync
5 - 6	Display Enable 11 - Disable HSYNC, VSYNC, and BLANK* 10 - Disable HSYNC, VSYNC, and BLANK* 01 - Enable HSYNC, VSYNC, and BLANK* 00 - Not Used
7 - 15	Not Used

Note:

* Not Function (Setting bit disables input or output.)

Table 6-108   Subsystem Status/Control Register (Port 42E8h)

Bit	Function

Read - Subsytem Status

0 - 3

IRQ - Interrupt Request (Determines state of interupt request lines.)

1XXX - Idle. The 8514/A is idle and waiting for input. This bit provides the same information as the BSY bit of the Queue Status Register.

X1XX - Queue Overflow/Underflow. The host attempted to write to a full write queue or read from an empty read queue.

XX1X - Inside Scissor Rectangle. The 8514/A drew

Table 6-108   Continued.

Bit   Function

Read - Subsytem Status

0 - 3

current object within an area bounded by
a scissor rectangle. You can use this bit
to determine when two object coincide.

XXX1 - Vertical Blanking Active. Shows when it
is safe to send data to the 8514/A for
display.

4 - 6   Monitor Sense - Determines type monitor attached
to 8514/A.
000 - Reserved
001 - 8507 (1024 X 768 Interlaced Monochrome)
010 - 8514 (1024 X 768 Interlaced Color)
011 - Reserved
100 - Reserved
101 - 8503 (640 X 480 Non-Interlaced Monochrome)
110 - 8512/8513 (640 X 480 Non-Interlaced Color)
111 - Reserved

7   8 Bit Plane Select (8BP)
0 - 4 Bit Planes
1 - 8 Bit Planes

8 - 15   Not Used

Write - Subsytem Control

0 - 3

IRQ Clear - Interrupt Request (Write 1 to clear
flag.)

1XXX - Idle.

X1XX - Queue Overflow/Underflow.

XX1X - Inside Scissor Rectangle.

XXX1 - Vertical Blanking Active.

8 - 11

IRQ Enable - Interrupt Request (Write 1 to
enable flag.)

1XXX - Idle.

X1XX - Queue Overflow/Underflow.

XX1X - Inside Scissor Rectangle.

XXX1 - Vertical Blanking Active.

Table 6-108   Continued.

Bit   Function

Write - Subsytem Control

12 - 13

                     Memory Controller Disable

                     00 - No Effect

                     01 - Enable synchronization with memory
                             controller chip.

                     10 - Disable synchronization from memory
                             controller chip. (8514/A does not operate
                             correctly.)

                     11 - Disable synchronization from memory
                             controller chip. (8514/A does not operate
                             correctly.)

14 - 15   Graphics Processor Reset
                     00 - No Effect
                     01 - Enable Chip
                     10 - Reset Chip
                     11 - Reset Chip

Table 6-109   ROM Page Select Register (Port 46E8h)

Bit	Function
0 - 2	ROM Page Number - Remaps one of eight 4 KByte ROM pages into the address area from C0000h - C5FFFh.
3 - 15	Not Used

Table 6-110   Advanced Function Control Register (Port 4AE8h)

Bit	Function
0	Advanced Function Mode Select 0 - VGA drives video connector. 1 - 8514/A drives video connector.
1	Not Used
2 - 4	Clock Select - Not Used, Set To 0
5 - 7	Not Used

Table 6-111   Graphics Processor Status/Command Registers (Port 9AE8h)

Bit	Function

Read - Graphics Processor Status Register

0 - 7
Queue Full Status
00000000 - 8 Words Available (Queue Empty)
00000001 - 7 Words Available
00000011 - 6 Words Available
00000111 - 5 Words Available
00001111 - 4 Words Available
00011111 - 3 Words Available
00111111 - 2 Words Available
01111111 - 1 Word Available
11111111 - 0 Words Available (Queue Full)

8
Variable Data Ready
0 - Data Not Ready
1 - Data Ready to Read from Data Register

9
Busy
0 - 8514/A Not Busy
1 - 8514/A Executing a Drawing Command

10 - 15
Not Used

Write - Command Register

0
Pixel Write Operation
0 - Write disabled. Rectangle commands copy
rectangular blocks from bitmap to system memory.
1 - Write enabled. Rectangle commands copy
rectangular blocks from system memory to bitmap.

1
Across Planes
0 - Through Plane Mode
1 - Across Plane Mode

2
Last Pixel Null
0 - 8514/A draws last pixel for line and SVV
commands.
1 - 8514/A moves current position pointer
without drawing pixel. Use this with commands
that produce the wrong pixel color on the last
pixel of a row. For example, XOR.

3
Short Stroke Enable
0 - Short stroke vectors not enabled.
1 - Short stroke vectors enabled. 8514/A draws
contents of SSV register after each data write.

4
Marking Enable
0 - Marking disabled for line and BITBLTS (bit
block transfers). 8514/A moves current position
without changing pixels.
1 - Marking enabled.

Table 6-111   Continued.

Bit   Function

Write - Command Register

5   Increment X Positive
                           0 - 8514/A draws lines in X negative direction
                           (right).
                           1 - 8514/A draws lines in X positive direction
                           (left).

6   Y Major Axis
                           0 - X is major (independent) axis for Bresenham
                           algorithm.
                           1 - Y is major (independent) axis for Bresenham
                           algorithm.

7   Increment Y Positive
                           0 - 8514/A draws lines in Y negative direction
                           (up).
                           1 - 8514/A draws lines in Y positive direction
                           (down).

8   Variable Data Enable
                           0 - 8514/A draws normally.
                           1 - 8514/A waits for read/write of variable data
                           from host.

9   16-bit Operation (16B)
                           0 - SSV and VAR are accessed as 8-bit registers.
                           1 - SSV and VAR are accessed as 16-bit
                           registers.

10   Read Byte Swap (RBS) - 8514/A reads bytes in
                           opposite order written.
                           RBS & 16B = 0 - No Swap
                           RBS & 16B = 1 - Swap

11   Always set to zero.

12   Byte Order (Does not affect 16-bit registers.)
                           0 - Read high byte first.
                           1 - Read low byte first.

13 - 15   Draw Command
                           000 - No Operation
                           001 - Line
                           010 - Fill rectangle in X direction.
                           011 - Fill rectangle in Y direction.
                           100 - Fast filled rectangle.
                           101 - Outline
                           110 - Copy Rectangle
                           111 - Illegal (Generates error IRQ.)

Table 6-112   Short Stroke Vector (SSV) Transfer Register (Port 9EE8h)

Bit	Function
0 - 3	Length - The number of pixels that the 8514/A moves the Current Position pointer. If length contains 0, the 8514/A does not change Current Position.
4	Mark Pixels 0 - Move Current Position, but do not mark vector. 1 - Mark Pixels
5 - 7	Direction 000 - 0° 001 - 45° 010 - 90° 011 - 135° 100 - 180° 101 - 225° 110 - 270° 111 - 315°
8 - 11	Length - The number of pixels that the 8514/A moves the Current Position pointer. If length contains 0, the 8514/A does not change Current Position.
12	Mark Pixels 0 - Move Current Position, but do not mark vector. 1 - Mark Pixels
13 - 15	Direction 000 - 0° 001 - 45° 010 - 90° 011 - 135° 100 - 180° 101 - 225° 110 - 270° 111 - 315°

Table 6-113   Background Mix Register (Port B6E8h)

Bit	Function
0 - 5	Mix Method 00000 - DST 00001 - 0 (Destination always false.) 00010 - 1 (Destination always true.) 00011 - DST 00100 - SRC 00101 - SRC ^ DST

Table 6-113   Continued.

Bit   Function

                              00110 - (SRC ^ DST)
                              00111 - SRC
                              01000 - (SRC * DST)
                              01001 - (SRC * DST)
                              01010 - (SRC * DST)
                              01011 - (SRC * DST)
                              01100 - SRC * DST
                              01101 - SRC * DST
                              01110 - SRC * DST
                              01111 - SRC * DST
                              10000 - min(SRC,DST)
                              10001 - DST - SRC (With Underflow)
                              10010 - SRC - DST (With Underflow)
                              10011 - SRC + DST (With Overflow)
                              10100 - max(SRC,DST)
                              10101 - (DST - SRC)/2 (With Underflow)
                              10110 - (SRC - DST)/2 (With Underflow)
                              10111 - (SRC + DST)/2 (With Overflow)
                              11000 - DST - SRC (With Saturate)
                              11001 - DST - SRC (With Saturate)
                              11010 - SRC - DST (With Saturate)
                              11011 - SRC + DST (With Saturate)
                              11100 - (DST - SRC)/2 (With Saturate)
                              11101 - (DST - SRC)/2 (With Saturate)
                              11110 - (SRC - DST)/2 (With Saturate)
                              11111 - (SRC + DST)/2 (With Saturate)

5 - 7   Background Source Select
                              00 - Background Color Register Contents
                              01 - Foreground Color Register Contents
                              10 - Variable Data
                              11 - Bitmap Data

Legend:

DST - Destination
SRC - Source
 - Not
^ - XOR
* - And
+ - Numeric Addition
- - Numeric Subtraction
/ - Integer Division

Table 6-114   Foreground Mix Register (Port BAE8h)

Bit   Function

0 - 5   Mix Method
                              00000 - DST

Table 6-114   Continued.

```
Bit                    Function

0 - 5                  Mix Method
                       00001 - 0 (Destination always false.)
                       00010 - 1 (Destination always true.)
                       00011 - DST
                       00100 - SRC
                       00101 - SRC ^ DST
                       00110 - (SRC ^ DST)
                       00111 - SRC
                       01000 - (SRC * DST)
                       01001 - (SRC * DST)
                       01010 - (SRC * DST)
                       01011 - (SRC * DST)
                       01100 - SRC * DST
                       01101 - SRC * DST
                       01110 - SRC * DST
                       01111 - SRC * DST
                       10000 - min(SRC,DST)
                       10001 - DST - SRC (With Underflow)
                       10010 - SRC - DST (With Underflow)
                       10011 - SRC + DST (With Overflow)
                       10100 - max(SRC,DST)
                       10101 - (DST - SRC)/2 (With Underflow)
                       10110 - (SRC - DST)/2 (With Underflow)
                       10111 - (SRC + DST)/2 (With Overflow)
                       11000 - DST - SRC (With Saturate)
                       11001 - DST - SRC (With Saturate)
                       11010 - SRC - DST (With Saturate)
                       11011 - SRC + DST (With Saturate)
                       11100 - (DST - SRC)/2 (With Saturate)
                       11101 - (DST - SRC)/2 (With Saturate)
                       11110 - (SRC - DST)/2 (With Saturate)
                       11111 - (SRC + DST)/2 (With Saturate)

5 - 7                  Foreground Source Select
                       00 - Background Color Register Contents
                       01 - Foreground Color Register Contents
                       10 - Variable Data
                       11 - Bitmap Data
```

Legend:

```
DST - Destination
SRC - Source
 - Not
^ - XOR
* - And
+ - Numeric Addition
- - Numeric Subtraction
/ - Integer Division
```

Table 6-115   Memory Control Register (Port BEE8h Index 5)

Bit	Function
0	Not Used
1	X Coordinate Divisor - Determines the memory bank interleave factor in a horizontal direction. 0 - 1 Bank, No Interleave 1 - 2 Horizontally Interleaved Banks (Normal)
2 - 3	Y Coordinate Divisor - Determines the memory bank interleave factor in a vertical direction. 00 - 2 banks of 256 Kbyte VRAM. Extended modes, no pseudo 8-plane mode. 01 - 4 banks of 256 Kbyte or 1 bank of 1 Mbyte VRAM. 8514/A compatible modes. 10 - 2 banks of 1 Mbyte VRAM. Extended modes. 11 - 4 banks of 1 Mbyte VRAM. Extended modes.
4	SWP - Active in Pseudo 8 Plane Mode (Always Set to 0 When Not in Use.) 0 - Select buffer number zero, lower four planes. 1 - Select buffer number one, upper four planes.
5 - 11	Not Used
12 - 15	Index - Always Equals 5

Table 6-116   Pixel Control Register (Port BEE8h Index Ah)

Bit	Function
0	Not Used
1	MOD1 0 - Normal Operation 1 - Disables mixes. Opposite polarity of MOD2.
2	MOD2 0 - Normal Operation 1 - Disables mixes and prevents VRAM RMW cycles if bits 3 through 5 equal zero.
3 - 5	Color Comparison 000 - Always False 001 - Always True 010 - DST >= CCMP 011 - DST < CCMP 100 - DST = CCMP 101 - DST = CCMP

Table 6-116   Continued.

Bit	Function
	110 - DST <= CCMP
	111 - DST > CCMP
6 - 7	Foreground Select 00 - Foreground Mix register is always used. 01 - PATX and PATY select mix (1 equals Foreground Mix register). 10 - Variable data selects mix (1 equals Foreground Mix register). 11 - SRC selects mix (used to implement transparency).
8 - 11	Not Used
12 - 15	Index - Always Equals 10

Legend:

DST - Destination
SRC - Source
CCMP - Color Comparison

Table 6-117   34010 Register File B Functions

Register	Function
B0	Source Address (SADDR) - Contains a linear or XY address describing the upper left corner (lower address in array) of the source pixel array.
B1	Source Pitch (SPTCH) - The distance between adjacent rows of the source pixel array.
B2	Destination Address (DADDR) - Contains a linear or XY address describing the upper left corner (lower address in array) of the destination pixel array.
B3	Destination Pitch (DPTCH) - The distance between adjacent rows of the destination pixel array.
B4	Offset (OFFSET) - Linear address of the XY coordinate origin (X = 0, Y = 0). The GSP uses this address during XY to linear address conversions.
B5	Window Start Address (WSTART) - An address describing the upper left corner (lowest address) of the window area.

Table 6-117   Continued.

Register	Function
B6	Window End Address (WEND) - An address describing the lower right corner (highest address) of the window area.
B7	Delta X/Delta Y (DYDX) - Two 16-bit numbers describing the width (DX) and height (DY) of the destination array. The MSB holds DY, while the LSB holds DX.
B8	Color 0 (COLOR0) - The 16 MSB bits contain the background color used for fill, color expand, or draw and advance operations. The 16 LSB bits contain all ones or a pattern of ones and zeros for dithered output. The 34010 ignores the 16 MSB bits during color expand operations.
B9	Color 1 (COLOR1) - The 16 MSB bits contain the foreground color used for fill, color expand, or draw and advance operations. The 16 LSB bits contain all ones or a pattern of ones and zeros for dithered output. The 34010 ignores the 16 MSB bits during color expand operations.
B10 - B14 (PIXBLT)	Temporary Storage (TEMP) - Contain temporary information during PIXBLT operations.
B10 (Line Draw)	Count (COUNT) - Contains the number of pixels drawing during a line draw operation.
B11 (Line Draw)	Increment 1 (INC1) - Contains the X and Y values for a diagonal step.
B12 (Line Draw)	Increment 2 (INC2) - Contains the X and Y values for a non-diagonal step.
B13 (Line Draw)	Pattern (PATTRN) - Future Expansion. Always set this register to 0FFFFFFFFh (all ones) before performing a line draw operation. Failure to do so will result in software compatibility problems.
SP	Stack Pointer - Points to the top (lowest address) of the stack.

Table 6-118   34010 Status Register

Bit	Function
0 - 4	Field Size 0 (FS0) - Length of the first data field in bits. A field size of 00001b

Table 6-118   Continued.

Bit	Function
	corresponds to a 1-bit field length. A field size of 11111b corresponds to a 31-bit field length. A field size of 00000b corresponds to the maximum field length of 32 bits.
5	Field Extend 0 (FE0) - Determines method of extending field 0 when loaded into a 32-bit register. 0 - Zero extend field. 1 - Sign extend field.
6 - 10	Field Size 1 (FS1) - Length of the second data field in bits. A field size of 00001b corresponds to a 1-bit field length. A field size of 11111b corresponds to a 31-bit field length. A field size of 00000b corresponds to the maximum field length of 32 bits.
11	Field Extend 1 (FE1) - Determines method of extending field 1 when loaded into a 32-bit register. 0 - Zero extend field. 1 - Sign extend field.
12 - 20	Not Used
21	Interrupt Enable (IE) 0 - Disables all maskable interrupts. 1 - Enables all maskable interrupts.
22 - 24	Not Used
25	PIXBLT Executing (PBX) - Indicates if an interrupt occurred in the middle of a PIXBLT or FILL instruction. 0 - Interrupt occurred at PIXBLT or FILL instruction boundary. 1 - Interrupt occurred in the middle of a PIXBLT or FILL instruction.
26 - 27	Not Used
28	Overflow Flag (V) - Set according to instruction execution parameters.
29	Zero Flag (Z) - Set according to instruction execution parameters.
30	Carry Flag (C) - Set according to instruction execution parameters.
31	Negative Flag (N) - Set according to instruction execution parameters.

Table 6-119   34010 Program Counter Replace Values

Type	GSP Replace Value
Standard Instructions (Non-Branch)	GSP increments PC by 16 (10h) after each instruction word retrieval. Execution proceeds with the next instruction in sequence.
Absolute Branch To Instruction Address (TRAP, CALL, JAxx)	GSP loads specified address (instruction word contents after instruction). It automatically zeros four LSB bits. Execution proceeds with instruction pointed to by PC.
Relative Branch To Instruction Address (JRxx, DSJxx)	GSP shifts instruction offset by four bits to zero four LSB bits. It adds the offset to PC. Execution proceeds with instruction pointed to by PC.
Indirect Branch To Register Address (JUMP, EXGPC)	GSP loads PC with register contents. It automatically zeros four LSB bits. Execution proceeds with instruction pointed to by PC.

Table 6-120   34010 Instruction Cache Segment Start Address (SSA) Format

Bit	Contents/Value
0 - 3	Always set to zero.
4 - 5	Instruction word address within subsegment. 00 - First Word 01 - Second Word 10 - Third Word 11 - Fourth Word
6 - 8	Subsegment address within segment. 000 - Subsegment 1 001 - Subsegment 2 010 - Subsegment 3 011 - Subsegment 4 100 - Subsegment 5 101 - Subsegment 6 110 - Subsegment 7 111 - Subsegment 8
9 - 31	Segment Start Address (SSA). Corresponds to segment address in main memory.

Table 6-121 34010 Input/Output Registers

Address	Register	Function
C0000170h - C00001A0h	RESERVED	These register addresses reserved for future expansion.

Host Interface Registers

Address	Register	Function
C00000C0h	HSTDATA	Host Interface Data - A buffer used to transfer data between the host and the 34010 local memory.
C00000D0h	HSTADRL	Host Interface Address Low Word - This register contains the 16 LSB bits of the local memory address accessed by the host computer. Local memory addresses include register addresses.
C00000E0h	HSTADRH	Host Interface Address High Word - This register contains the 16 MSB bits of the local memory address accessed by the host computer. Local memory addresses include register addresses.
C00000F0h	HSTCTLL	Host Interface Control Low Byte - Controls host interface functions as shown below.

Bit	Function
0-2	Input Message Buffer (MSGIN)
3	Input Interrupt Bit (INTIN)
4-6	Output Message Buffer (MSGOUT)
7	Output Interrupt Bit (INTOUT)
8-15	Reserved

Address	Register	Function
C0000100h	HSTCTLH	Host Interface Control High Byte - Controls host interface functions as shown below.

Bit	Function
0-7	Reserved

Table 6-121 **Continued.**

Address	Register	Function

Host Interface Registers

		8	Nonmaskable Interrupt (NMI)
		9	NMI Mode Bit
		10	Reserved
		11	Increment Pointer Address on Write (INCW)
		12	Increment Pointer Address on Read (INCR)
		13	Lower Byte Last (LBL)
		14	Cache Flust (CF)
		15	Halt 34010 Execution (HLT)

Local Memory Interface Registers

C00000B0h   CONTROL   Memory Control - Controls local memory interface operations as shown below.

Bit	Function
0-1	Reserved
2	DRAM Refresh Mode (RM)
3-4	DRAM Refresh Rate (RR)
5	Transparency Enable (T)
6-7	Window Violation Detection Mode (W)
8	PIXBLT Horizontal Direction (PBH)
9	PIXBLT Vertical Direction (PBV)
10-14	Pixel Processing Operation Select (PPOP)
15	Cache Disable (CD)

C0000130h   CONVSP   Source Pitch Conversion Factor - Used by 34010 during XY to linear conversion of a source memory address.

C0000140h   CONVDP   Destination Pitch Conversion Factor - Used by 34010 during XY/linear conversion of a memory address.

C0000150h   PSIZE   Pixel Size Register - Specifies the pixel size in bits. Possible sizes include 1, 2, 4, 8, and 16 bits (2, 4, 16, 256, and 65,536 colors).

C0000160h   PMASK   Plane Mask Register - Enables/disables bits in the bit map plane. For example, setting bit 0 to 1 enables bit plane 0.

Table 6-121   Continued.

Address	Register	Function

Local Memory Interface Registers

C00001F0h   REFCNT

Refresh Count Register -
Generates the addresses output
during DRAM refresh cycles and
counts delay between next
refresh cycles.

Bit	Function
0-1	Reserved
2-7	Refresh Interval Counter (RINTVL)
8-15	Row Address (ROWADR)

Interrupt Control Registers

C0000110h   INTENB

Interrupt Enable - Selectively
enables or disables three
internal and two external
interrupts as shown below.

Bit	Function
0	Reserved
1	External Interrupt 1 Enable (X1E)
2	External Interrupt 2 Enable (X2E)
3-8	Reserved
9	Host Interrupt Pending (HIP)
10	Display Interrupt Pending (DIP)
11	Window Violation Interrupt Pending (WVP)
12-15	Reserved

C0000120h   INTPEND

Interrupt Pending - Shows
which interrupts are pending
using the same bit mask as
INTENB.

Video Timing and Refresh Registers

C0000000h   HESYNC

Horizontal End Sync - Contains
the ending value of the
horizontal sync interval.

C0000010h   HEBLNK

Horizontal End Blank -
Contains the ending value of
the horizontal blank interval.

Table 6-121   Continued.

Address	Register	Function

Video Timing and Refresh Registers

Address	Register	Function
C0000020h	HSBLNK	Horizontal Start Blank - Contains the starting value of the horizontal blank interval.
C0000030h	HTOTAL	Horizontal Total - Contains the total value of the horizontal scan line in VCLK periods.
C0000040h	VESYNC	Vertical End Sync - Contains the ending value of the vertical sync interval.
C0000050h	VEBLNK	Vertical End Blank - Contains the ending value of the vertical blank interval.
C0000060h	VSBLNK	Vertical Start Blank - Contains the starting value of the vertical blank interval.
C0000070h	VTOTAL	Vertical Total - Contains the total value of the vertical scan line in VCLK periods.
C0000080h	DPYCTL	Display Control - Controls several video timing signal values as shown below.

Bit	Function
0	Horizontal Sync Direction (HSD)
1	Reserved
2-9	Display Address Update (DUDATE)
10	Screen Origin Select (ORG)
11	VRAM Serial Register Transfer Enable (SRT)
12	Screen Refresh Enable (SRE)
13	Disable External Video (DXV)
14	Noninterlaced Video Enable (NIL)
15	Enable Video (ENV)

Address	Register	Function
C0000090h	DPYSTRT	Display Start Address - Controls the automatic memory-to-register cycles required to refresh a screen as shown below.

Table 6-121   Continued.

Address	Register	Function

Video Timing and Refresh Registers

		Bit	Function
		0-1	Specifies the number of scan lines displayed between refresh cycles. (LCSTRT)
		2-15	Starting Screen-Refresh Address. (SRSTRT)

Address	Register	Function
C00000A0h	DPYINT	Display Interrupt - Contains the number of the next scan line which causes a display interrupt request.
C00001B0h	DPYTAP	Display Tap Point Address - Used during shift register transfer cycles. Contains a VRAM tap point address.
C00001C0h	HCOUNT	Horizontal Count - Contains the number of VCLK cycles per horizontal scan line.
C00001D0h	VCOUNT	Vertical Count - Contains the number of horizontal scan lines in a display.
C00001E0h	DPYADR	Display Address - Counts the number of scan lines output between screen refresh cycles. Also contains the source of the row and column addresses output during a screen refresh cycle as shown below.

		Bit	Function
		0-1	Scan Line Counter (LNCNT)
		2-15	Screen Refresh Address (SRFADR)

Table 6-122   34010 Instruction Set

Instruction	Type	Function
ABS	Arithmetic	Stores the absolute value of a number in a destination register.

Table 6-122   Continued.

Instruction	Type	Function
ADD	Arithmetic	Adds the source register to the destination register.
ADDC	Arithmetic	Adds the source register to the destination register and sets the carry flag if necessary.
ADDI	Arithmetic	Adds an immediate value to the destination register. The immediate value may be 16 or 32-bits long.
ADDK	Arithmetic	Adds a 5-bit constant to the destination register.
ADDXY	Arithmetic	Adds the source register to the destination register in XY mode.
AND	Logical	Performs a logical and of the value in the destination register with the source register.
ANDI	Logical	Performs a logical and of the value in the destination register with a 32-bit immediate value.
ANDN	Logical	Performs a logical and of the value in the destination register with the source register, then complements the result.
ANDNI	Logical	Complements a 32-bit immediate value, then performs a logical and of the value in the destination register with the 32-bit immediate value.
BTST	Compare	Tests the bit specified by a constant or source register in the destination register.
CALL	Program Control and Context Switching	Calls the subroutine address placed in the source register.
CALLA	Program Control and Context Switching	Calls the absolute subroutine address specified by an immediate value.

Table 6-122   Continued.

Instruction	Type	Function
CALLR	Program Control and Context Switching	Calls the relative subroutine address specified by an immediate value.
CLR	Compare	Clears the specified register.
CLRC	Compare	Clears the carry flag.
CMP	Compare	Nondestructively compares the value in the source register to the destination register. Sets or clears the appropriate status bits.
CMPI	Compare	Nondestructively compares an immediate value to the destination register. Sets or clears the appropriate status bits. The immediate value may be 16 or 32-bits long.
CMPXY	Compare	Nondestructively compares the X and Y half of a register. Sets or clears the appropriate status bits.
CPW	Graphics	Compares a point specified by an X and Y coordinate in the source register to the window limits in the WEND or WSTART registers. X and Y are 16-bit signed values. WEND and WSTART must contain positive values. Used to reject objects drawn outside the confines of a window.
CVXYL	Graphics	Convert an XY address to a linear address.
DEC	Arithmetic	Reduces the contents of the specified register by one.
DINT	Program Control and Context Switching	Disable maskable interrupts.
DIVS	Arithmetic	Perform a signed division of the destination register by the source register. The 34010 performs the division on a 64-bit number if the destination register number is even (for example A14). Otherwise, it

Table 6-122   Continued.

Instruction	Type	Function
		performs the division on a 32-bit number. The source and destination registers must appear in the same register file.
DIVU	Arithmetic	Perform an unsigned division of the destination register by the source register. The 34010 performs the division on a 64-bit number if the destination register number is even (for example A14). Otherwise, it performs the division on a 32-bit number. The source and destination registers must appear in the same register file.
DRAV	Graphics	Draws a pixel at the address pointed to by the destination register using the color in COLOR1. The 34010 then adds the value in the source register to the destination register.
DSJ	Jump	If the destination register is greater than 0, the 34010 decrements it by one and advances to the specified address. Otherwise, it skips the jump and proceeds with the next sequential instruction.
DSJEQ	Jump	This instruction first checks to see if the zero flag (Z) is set. If Z = 1, then the 34010 skips the jump. Otherwise, if the destination register is greater than 0, the 34010 decrements it by one and advances to the specified address. Otherwise, it skips the jump and proceeds with the next sequential instruction.
DSJNE	Jump	This instruction first checks to see if the zero flag (Z) is clear. If Z = 0, then the 34010 skips the jump. Otherwise, if the destination register is greater than 0, the 34010 decrements it by one

Table 6-122   Continued.

Instruction	Type	Function
		and advances to the specified address. Otherwise, it skips the jump and proceeds with the next sequential instruction.
DSJS	Jump	If the destination register is greater than 0, the 34010 decrements it by one. If the direction bit (D) equals 0, the 34010 adds the specified value to the program counter. Otherwise, the 34010 subtracts the specified value from the program counter. If the destination register equals 0, the 34010 skips the jump and proceeds with the next sequential instruction.
EINT	Program Control and Context Switching	Enable maskable interrupts.
EMU	Program Control and Context Switching	The 34010 enters emulation mode. This instruction is intended for systems level programming only.
EXGF	Program Control and Context Switching	Exchanges the six LSB bits of the destination register with the specified field bits. The 34010 clears the upper 26-bits of the destination register.
EXGPC	Program Control and Context Switching	Exchanges the value contained in the destination register with the program counter. Program execution continues with the new program counter address.
FILL L	Graphics	Fills a two dimensional array with the value contained in COLOR1. DADDR contains the pixel array starting address (linear value). DPTCH contains the pixel array pitch (linear value). DYDX contains the pixel array dimensions.
FILL XY	Graphics	Fills a two dimensional array with the value contained in COLOR1. DADDR contains the pixel array starting address

Table 6-122   Continued.

Instruction	Type	Function
		(XY value). DPTCH contains the pixel array pitch (linear value). OFFSET contains the address of the screen origin (linear value). WSTART contains the window starting address(XY value). WEND contains the window ending address (XY value). DYDX contains the pixel array dimensions.
GETPC	Program Control and Context Switching	Increments the program counter value by 16 (to point past the current instruction) and places the value in the destination register.
GETST	Program Control and Context Switching	Copies the contents in the status register to the destination register.
INC	Arithmetic	Increases the contents of the specified register by one.
JAcc	Jump	Jump to the specified address (absolute) if the status flag(s) listed below contain the correct values.

cc	NCZV	NCZV	NCZV
B	X1XX		
C	X1XX		
EQ	XX1X		
GE	0XX0	1XX1	
GT	0X00	1X01	
HI	X00X		
HS	X00X	XX1X	
LE	0XX1	1XX0	XX1X
LO	X1XX		
LS	XX1X	X1XX	
LT	0XX1	1XX0	
N	1XXX		
NB	X0XX		
NC	X0XX		
NE	XX0X		
NN	0XXX		
NV	XXX0		
NZ	XX0X		
P	0X0X		
UC	XXXX		
V	XXX1		
Z	XX1X		

Table 6-122   Continued.

Instruction	Type	Function
JRcc	Jump	Add the specified value to the program counter (relative jump) if the status flag(s) listed below contain the correct values.

cc	NCZV	NCZV	NCZV
C	X1XX		
GE	0XX0	1XX1	
GT	0X00	1X01	
HI	X00X		
LE	0XX1	1XX0	XX1X
LS	XX1X	X1XX	
LT	0XX1	1XX0	
N	1XXX		
NC	X0XX		
NN	0XXX		
NV	XXX0		
NZ	XX0X		
P	0X0X		
UC	XXXX		
V	XXX1		
Z	XX1X		

Instruction	Type	Function
JUMP	Jump	Perform an absolute jump to the specified address.
LINE [0,1]	Graphics	Selects one of two available line drawing algorithms.
LMO	Compare	Locates the leftmost 1 in the source register and places the 1's complement of its location in the destination register (5 LSB bits). If the source register does not contain a 1, the 34010 loads the destination register with zeros and sets the zero flag.
MMFM	Move	Moves the contents of memory to the specified register list. All registers in the list must appear in the same register file.
MMTM	Move	Moves the contents of a specified register list to memory. All registers in the list must appear in the same register file.

Table 6-122   Continued.

Instruction	Type	Function
MODS	Arithmetic	Returns the signed remainder of the division of the destination register by the source register. Both registes always contain a 32-bit number. Both registers must appear in the same register file.
MODU	Arithmetic	Returns the unsigned remainder of the division of the destination register by the source register. Both registes always contain a 32-bit number. Both registers must appear in the same register file.
MOVB	Move	Moves a byte from the source register to the memory address pointed to by the destination register. Both registers must appear in the same register file.
MOVE	Move	Moves the contents of the source register, source register address, or explicitly specified memory address to the destination register, the memory address pointed to by the destination register, or an explicitly specified memory address.
MOVI	Move	Stores a 16-bit, sign extended or 32-bit immediate value in the destination register.
MOVK	Move	Stores a 5-bit constant in the destination register.
MOVX	Move	Moves the X half of the source register to the X half of the destination register. Does not affect the Y half of either register. Both registers must appear in the same register file.
MOVY	Move	Moves the Y half of the source register to the Y half of the destination register. Does not affect the X half of either register. Both registers must appear in the same register file.

Table 6-122   Continued.

Instruction	Type	Function
MPYS	Arithmetic	Performs a signed multiplication of the source register by the destination register. The 34010 stores a 32-bit result if the destination register is odd. Otherwise, it stores a 64-bit result. Both registers must appear in the same register file.
MPYU	Arithmetic	Performs an unsigned multiplication of the source register by the destination register. The 34010 stores a 32-bit result if the destination register is odd. Otherwise, it stores a 64-bit result. Both registers must appear in the same register file.
NEG	Arithmetic	Stores the 2s complement of the number in the destination register back into the destination register.
NEGB	Arithmetic	Stores the 2s complement of the number in the destination register back into the destination register. The 34010 decrements the result by one if the borrow bit is set.
NOP	Program Control and Context Switching	The processor does not perform any instruction. The program counter is set to the next instruction.
NOT	Logical	Stores the 1s complement of the number in the destination register back into the destination register.
OR	Logical	Performs a logical or of the source register with the destination register. Both registers must appear in the same register file.
ORI	Logical	Performs a logical or of an immediate value with the destination register.

Table 6-122   Continued.

Instruction	Type	Function
PIXBLT B, L	Graphics	Pixel Block Transfers the contents of a binary pixel array to a linear array.
PIXBLT B, XY	Graphics	Pixel Block Transfers the contents of a binary pixel array to an XY array.
PIXBLT L, L	Graphics	Pixel Block Transfers the contents of a linear pixel array to a linear array.
PIXBLT L, XY	Graphics	Pixel Block Transfers the contents of a linear pixel array to an XY array.
PIXBLT XY, L	Graphics	Pixel Block Transfers the contents of an XY pixel array to a linear array.
PIXBLT XY, XY	Graphics	Pixel Block Transfers the contents of an XY pixel array to an XY array.
PIXT	Graphics	Transfers the contents of the source register to the address pointed to by the destination register. It can also transfer the contents of the address pointed to by the source register to the destination register. PSIZE determines the size of the pixel. The address contained in the source or destination register is either XY or linear.
POPST	Program Control and Context Switching	Pops the status register from the stack and increments SP by 32.
PUSHST	Program Control and Context Switching	Pushes the status register onto the stack and decrements SP by 32.
PUTST	Program Control and Context Switching	Places the contents of the specified register into the status register.
RETI	Program Control and Context Switching	Returns to an interrupted routine from an interrupt service routine. ST and PC are popped from the stack and SP is incremented by 64.

Table 6-122   Continued.

Instruction	Type	Function
RETS *N*	Program Control and Context Switching	Returns to an interrupted routine from a subroutine. This return may contain an optional stack increment value (32 + 16N). If N is not specified, SP is incremented by 32.
REV	Program Control and Context Switching	Returns the revision number of the TMS34010 installed on the display adapter.
RL	Shift	Rotate the value in the destination register left by the amount specified in a constant or the source register.
SETC	Compare	Sets the carry bit of the status register to 1.
SETF	Program Control and Context Switching	Loads the field size and field extension values into the status register. This does not affect the value of the flags.
SEXT	Arithmetic	Sign extends the right justified field of the destination register using the MSB of the field.
SLA	Shift	Shifts the destination register field left by the value contained in a constant or the five LSB bits of the source register. The MSB of the destination register is always shifted to the carry bit of the status register. This instruction provides overflow detection and sets the overflow bit of the status register as required.
SLL	Shift	Shifts the destination register field left by the value contained in a constant. The MSB of the destination register is always shifted to the carry bit of the status register. This instruction does not provide overflow detection.

Table 6-122   Continued.

Instruction	Type	Function
SRA	Shift	Shifts the destination register field right by the value contained in a constant or the five LSB bits of the source register. The LSB of the destination register is always shifted to the carry bit of the status register. This instruction provides overflow detection and sets the overflow bit of the status register as required.
SRL	Shift	Shifts the destination register field left by the value contained in a constant. The LSB of the destination register is always shifted to the carry bit of the status register. This instruction does not provide overflow detection.
SUB	Arithmetic	Subtracts the value in the source register from the destination register and stores the result in the destination register.
SUBB	Arithmetic	Subtracts the value in the source register and carry bit of the status register from the destination register and stores the result in the destination register.
SUBI	Arithmetic	Subtracts a 16 or 32-bit immediate value from the destination register and stores the result in the destination register.
SUBK	Arithmetic	Subtracts a 5-bit constant value from the destination register and stores the result in the destination register.
SUBXY	Arithmetic	Individually subtract the X and Y halves of the source register from the X and Y halves of the destination register and stores the result in the destination register.

Table 6-122   Continued.

Instruction	Type	Function
TRAP *N*	Program Control and Context Switching	Executes the software interrupt specified by *N*. Trap pushes PC and ST on the stack, then places the address pointed to by the track number. N is a number from 0 to 31 as shown below.

N	*Trap Function*
0	Reset
1	External Interrupt 1
2	External Interrupt 2
3-7	Traps 3 through 7
8	Nonmaskable Interrupt
9	Host Interrupt
10	Display Interrupt
11	Window Violation
12-29	Traps 12 through 29
30	Illegal Opcode
31	Trap 31

Instruction	Type	Function
XOR	Logical	Performs a logical XOR of the contents of the destination register with the source register and stores the results in the destination register.
XORI	Logical	Performs a logical XOR of the contents of the destination register with an immediate value and stores the results in the destination register.
ZEXT	Arithmetic	Zero extends the right justified field in the destination register. If the field size is not specified, the 34010 uses the default field size as a reference.

Table 6-123   TIGA Instruction Set

Instruction	Type	Function
Void BITBLT (*Width*, *Height*, *SRCX*, *SRCY*, *DSTX*, *DSTY*)	Pixel Array (Extended)	Copies data from the source bitmap to the destination bitmap. Width and height describe the size of both

Table 6-123   Continued.

Instruction	Type	Function
		bitmaps. SRCX and SRCY describe the starting coordinates of the the source. DSTX and DSTY describe the starting coordinates of the destination.
Int CD_IS_ALIVE ()	Graphics System Initialization (Core)	Returns 0 if the communication driver is not installed. Otherwise, returns a non-zero result.
Void CLEAR_FRAME_BUF FER *(Color)*	Clear (Core)	Clears the entire display memory by setting it to the specified color. Use the CLEAR_SCREEN function to preserve offscreen data.
Void CLEAR_PAGE *(Color)*	Clear (Core)	Clears the current drawing page by setting it to the specified color. Use the CLEAR_SCREEN function to preserve offscreen data.
Void CLEAR_SCREEN *(Color)*	Clear (Core)	Clears only the visible portion of display memory by setting it to the specified color.
Void COP2GSP *(COPID, COPADDR, GSPADDR, Length)*	Communication (Core)	Copies data from the coprocessor address space to the TMS340 address space. Transfers occur in 32-bit length words.
Short CPW *(X, Y)*	Graphics Attribute Control (Core)	Outputs a 4-bit outcode based on a pixel's position within a window as shown below.

Code   Function

0000	Point lies within window.
01XX	Point lies above window.
10XX	Point lies below window.
XX01	Point lies left of window.
XX10	Point lies right of window.

Instruction	Type	Function
Int CREATE_ALM *(RLM_Name, ALM_Name)*	Extensibility (Core)	Converts a relocatable load module to an absolute load module. Exits with a value of 0 if successful.

Table 6-123   Continued.

Instruction	Type	Function
Int CREATE_ESYM *(GM_Name)*	Extensibility (Core)	Creates an external symbol table of global symbols. The linking loader uses this table to resolve references in a relocatable load module. Exits with a value of 0 if successful.
Int DELETE_FONT *(ID)*	Text (Extended)	Removes the font specified by ID (number) from the font table. Returns 0 if the font was not installed. Returns non-zero value if font removed successfully.
Void DRAW_LINE *(X1, Y1, X2, Y2)*	Graphics Output (Extended)	Draws a line on-screen. X1 and Y1 contain the starting coordinate. X2 and Y2 contain the ending coordinate.
Void DRAW_OVAL *(W, H, XLeft, YTop)*	Graphics Output (Extended)	Draws an oval on-screen. W contains the width. H contains the height. XLeft and YTop contain the coordinates of the upper left corner of the oval.
Void DRAW_OVALARC *(W, H, XLeft, YTop, Theta, Arc)*	Graphics Output (Extended)	Draws an eliptical arc on-screen. W contains the width. H contains the height. XLeft and YTop contain the coordinates of the upper left corner of the oval. Theta contains the start angle. Arc contains the number of degrees of arc.
Void DRAW_PIEARC *(W, H, XLeft, YTop, Theta, Arc)*	Graphics Output (Extended)	Draws an eliptical arc on-screen. Two lines emanate from the center of the arc to each end. W contains the width. H contains the height. XLeft and YTop contain the coordinates of the upper left corner of the oval. Theta contains the start angle. Arc contains the number of degrees of arc.
Void DRAW_POINT *(X, Y)*	Graphics Output (Extended)	Draws a single pixel on-screen. X and Y contain the coordinate of the pixel.
Void	Graphics Output	Draws a group of lines whose

Table 6-123   Continued.

Instruction	Type	Function
DRAW_POLYLINE (N, Points)	(Extended)	end points are suppied as a set of points. N indicates the number of lines to draw. Each point consists of an X and Y coordinate. To draw a closed polygon, use the same coordinates for the first and last set of points.
Void DRAW_POLYLINE (N, Points)	Poly Drawing (Extended)	See previous description.
Void DRAW_RECT (W, H, XLeft, YTop)	Graphics Output (Extended)	Draws a rectangle on-screen. W contains the width. H contains the height. XLeft and YTop contain the coordinates of the upper left corner.
Unsigned Long FIELD_EXTRACT (GPTR, FS)	Communication (Core)	Returns the 32-bit data in the TMS340 memory space pointed to by GPTR. FS contains the field size (number of significant bits).
Void FIELD_INSERT (GPTR, FS, Data)	Communication (Core)	Writes Data to the address in TMS340 memory pointed to by GPTR. FS contains the field size.
Void FILL_CONVEX (N, Points)	Graphics Output (Extended)	Draws a filled convex polygon. N indicates the number of vetices in the polygon. Each point consists of an X and Y coordinate. To draw a closed polygon, use the same coordinates for the first and last set of points.
Void FILL_CONVEX (N, Points)	Poly Drawing (Extended)	See previous description.
Void FILL_OVAL (W, H, XLeft, YTop)	Graphics Output (Extended)	Draws a filled oval on-screen. W contains the width. H contains the height. XLeft and YTop contain the coordinates of the upper left corner of the oval.
Void FILL_PIEARC (W, H, XLeft, YTop, Theta, Arc)	Graphics Output (Extended)	Draws a filled pie-shaped wedge on-screen. W contains the width. H contains the height. XLeft and YTop contain

Table 6-123   Continued.

Instruction	Type	Function
		the coordinates of the upper left corner of the oval. Theta contains the start angle. Arc contains the number of degrees of arc.
Void FILL_POLYGON *(N, Points)*	Graphics Output (Extended)	Draws a filled polygon. N indicates the number of vetices in the polygon. Each point consists of an X and Y coordinate. To draw a closed polygon, use the same coordinates for the first and last set of points.
Void FILL_POLYGON *(N, Points)*	Poly Drawing (Extended)	See previous description.
Void FILL_POLYGON *(N, Points)*	Workspace (Extended)	See previous description.
Void FILL_RECT *(W, H, XLeft, YTop)*	Graphics Output (Extended)	Draws a filled rectangle on-screen. W contains the width. H contains the height. XLeft and YTop contain the coordinates of the upper left corner.
Int FLUSH_ESYM *()*	Extensibility (Core)	Flushes an external symbol table of external symbols. The linking loader uses this table to resolve references in a relocatable load module. Exits with a value of 0 if successful.
Void FLUSH_EXTENDED *()*	Extensibility (Core)	Flushes the TIGA extended functions and installed user functions. Then, removes the symbol table stored on the host.
Void FRAME_OVAL *(W, H, XLeft, Ytop, DX, DY)*	Graphics Output (Extended)	Fills the area between two concentric ovals with the current foreground color. W contains the width. H contains the height. XLeft and YTop contain the coordinates of the upper left corner of the oval. DX specifies the horizontal distance between the outer and inner ovals. DY specifies the

Table 6-123   Continued.

Instruction	Type	Function
		vertical distance between the two ovals.
Void FRAME_RECT *(W, H, XLeft, Ytop, DX, DY)*	Graphics Output (Extended)	Fills the area between two concentric rectangles with the current foreground color. W contains the width. H contains the height. XLeft and YTop contain the coordinates of the upper left corner. DX specifies the horizontal distance between the outer and inner rectangles. DY specifies the vertical distance between the two rectangles.
Int FUNCTION_IMPLEM ENTED *(Function Code)*	Graphics System Initialization (Core)	Queries if a board supports a specific function. Some TIGA implementations do not support the following functions. COP2GSP GET_PALET GET_PALET_ENTRY GSP2COP INIT_PALET SET_PALET SET_PALET_ENTRY SET_TRANSP
Void GET_COLORS *(FColor, BColor)*	Graphics Attribute Control (Core)	Obtains the foreground and background color values.
Void GET_CONFIG *(Config)*	Graphics System Initialization (Core)	Obtains the current display adapter configuration and returns it in a structure.
Int GET_CURS_STATE ()	Cursor (Core)	Returns 0 if the cursor is not enabled.
Void GET_CURS_XY *(PX, PY)*	Cursor (Core)	Returns the coordinates of the cursor. Coordinates are relative to the upper left corner of the visible screen.
Void GET_ENV *(Env)*	Graphics Attribute Control (Core)	Returns the current graphics environment variable status in the structure pointed to by ENV.
Int GET_FONTINFO *(ID, PFontInfo)*	Text (Core)	Returns information about the current font in a structure pointed to by PFontInfo. ID determines which font the

Table 6-123   Continued.

Instruction	Type	Function
		function polls. 0 returns system font information. -1 returns current font information.
Void GET_ISR_PRIORIT IES *(NumISRs, PTR)*	Extensibility (Core)	Returns the priorities of interrupt service routines installed using the INSTALL_RLM and INSTALL_ALM functions. NumISRs contains the number of ISRs installed. PTR points to an array of short containing the priority data.
Int GET_MODEINFO *(Index, ModeInfo)*	Graphics System Initialization (Core)	Returns a structure containing the board configuration supported by the current board and monitor. Index contains the mode number.
Long GET_NEAREST_COL OR *(R, G, B, I)*	Palette (Core)	Obtains the color number that most closely matches the specified parameters. R is red, G is green, B is blue, and I is intensity.
Void GET_OFFSCREEN_M EMORY *(Num_Blocks, Offscreen)*	Pointer-Based Memory Management (Core)	Returns a description of the offscreen memory areas not in use. These blocks normally consist of display memory not used for the frame buffer or alternate frame buffer. You obtain the Num_Blocks parameter using the GET_CONFIG function. Offscreen is a pointer to memory allocated for offscreen entry storage.
Void GET_PALET *(Palet Size, Palet)*	Palette (Core)	Reads an entire palette register into the palette array. You obtain the Palet Size parameter using the GET_CONFIG function.
Int GET_PALET_ENTRY *(Index, R, G, B, I)*	Palette (Core)	Reads the color values contained in a single pallete. Index specifies which pallete to read. R is red, G is green, B is blue, and I is intensity. This function returns 0 if you specify an invalid index.
Long GET_PIXEL *(X, Y)*	Graphics Utility (Extended)	Returns the value of the pixel at the address specified by X

Table 6-123   Continued.

Instruction	Type	Function
		and Y. The coordinate is relative to the drawing origin.
Long GET_PMASK ()	Graphics Attribute Control (Core)	Returns the value of the plane mask (planes enabled/disabled for writing).
Int GET_PPOP ()	Graphics Attribute Control (Core)	Returns a 5-bit code for the current pixel processing operation.

Code   Function

0	Source
1	Source AND Destination
2	Source AND NOT Destination
3	All 0s
4	Source OR NOT Destination
5	Source EQU Destination
6	NOT Destination
7	Source NOR Destination
8	Source OR Destination
9	Destination
10	Source XOR Destination
11	NOT Source AND Destination
12	All 1s
13	NOT Source OR Destination
14	Source NAND Destination
15	NOT Source
16	Source + Destination
17	ADDS (Source, Destination)
18	Destination - Source
19	SUBS (Destination, Source)
20	MAX (Source, Destination)
21	MIN (Source, Destination)

Instruction	Type	Function
Int GET_TEXTATTR *(PControl, Count, Arg)*	Text (Extended)	Obtains the text rendering attributes. PControl is a pointer to a list of desired attributes. Current attribute values include %a (top left alignment = 0, baseline = 1) and %e (additional intercharacter spacing. Count contains the number of attributes in the control string.

Table 6-123   Continued.

Instruction	Type	Function
Int GET_TRANSP ()	Graphics Attribute Control (Core)	Gets the state of the transparency (T) bit of the control register. Returns 0 if transparency is disabled.
Unsigned Long GET_VECTOR *(TrapNum)*	Communication (Core)	Obtains the address of the trap vector specified by TrapNum.
Int GET_VIDEOMODE ()	Graphics System Initialization (Core)	Returns the current video mode emulation number.
Int GET_WINDOWING ()	Graphics Attribute Control (Core)	Gets the 2-bit windowing code in the control I/O register as shown below.

Code	Function
00	No Windowing
01	Interrupt Request on Write In Window
10	Interrupt Request on Write Outside Window
11	Clip to Window

Instruction	Type	Function
Short GET_WKSP *(Addr, Pitch)*	Workspace (Core)	Returns parameters defining the current offscreen workspace. If the function returns a non-zero value, then Addr and Pitch contain the address and pitch of the workspace area.
Long GSP_CALLOC *(NMemB, Size)*	Pointer-Based Memory Management (Core)	Allocates enough TMS340 memory to contain NMemB objects of Size. Returns 0 if not enough memory remains. Otherwise, returns a pointer to the memory area.
Void GSP_EXECUTE *(Entry Point)*	Graphics System Initialization (Core)	Loads and executes a non-application function. In other words, this function provides a protable COFF loader.
Int GSP_FREE *(PTR)*	Pointer-Based Memory Management (Core)	Deallocates the memory allocated by the GSP_MALLOC, GSP_CALLOC, or GSP_REALLOC functions. PTR points to the beginning of the memory area. Returns 0 if not successful.

Table 6-123   Continued.

Instruction	Type	Function
Long GSP_MALLOC *(Size)*	Pointer-Based Memory Management (Core)	Allocates the amount of TMS340 memory specified by Size. Returns 0 if not enough memory remains. Otherwise, returns a pointer to the memory area.
Long GSP_MAXHEAP ()	Pointer-Based Memory Management (Core)	Returns the largest amount of heap available for allocation.
Void GSP_MINIT *(Stack Size)*	Pointer-Based Memory Management (Core)	Deallocates all dynamically allocated memory in the TMS340 heap. Also changes the size of the stack. Providing a value of -1 allocates the default stack size.
Long GSP_REALLOC *(PTR, Size)*	Pointer-Based Memory Management (Core)	Changes the size of the previously allocated memory block pointed to by PTR. Size determines the new size of memory allocation. Returns 0 if not successful.
Void GSP2COP *(COPID, GSPAddr, COPAddr, Length)*	Communication (Core)	A TMS34020 and above specific function which copies data from the TMS340 address space to the coprocessor address space.
Void GSP2GSP *(Addr1, Addr2, Length)*	Pointer-Based Memory Management (Core)	Copies data within the TMS340 address area. Addr1 contains the source address, Addr2 contains the destination address, and Length contains the length of the data.
Void GSP2HOST *(GPTR, HPTR, Length, Swizzle)*	Communication (Core)	Transfers data from TMS340 memory (GPTR) to host memory (HPTR). Length contains the length of data to transfer. If Swizzle is nonzero, the 34010 reverses the order of the bits in each byte before transfer.
Void GSP2HOSTXY *(SAddr, SPTCH, DAddr, DPTCH, SX, SY, DX, DY, XExt, YExt, PSize, Swizzle)*	Communication (Core)	Transfers a rectangular area of the TMS340 bitmap to the host. SAddr contains the source address; DAddr contains the destination address. The source area starts at SX, SY and is transferred to DX, DY. XExt and YExt define the size of the area to transfer. PSize contains the size of the

Table 6-123   Continued.

Instruction	Type	Function
		pixels transferred. SPTCH and DPTCH contain the source and destination pitch. If Swizzle is nonzero, the 34010 reverses the order of the bits in each byte before transfer.
Void HOST2GSP *(GPTR, HPTR, Length, Swizzle)*	Communication (Core)	Transfers data from host memory (HPTR) to TMS340 memory (GPTR). Length contains the length of data to transfer. If Swizzle is nonzero, the 34010 reverses the order of the bits in each byte before transfer.
Void HOST2GSPXY *(SAddr, SPTCH, DAddr, DPTCH, SX, SY, DX, DY, XExt, YExt, PSize, Swizzle)*	Communication (Core)	Transfers a rectangular area of host memory to the TMS340. SAddr contains the source address; DAddr contains the destination address. The source area starts at SX, SY and transfers to DX, DY. XExt and YExt define the area to transfer. PSize contains the size of the pixels. SPTCH and DPTCH contain source and destination pitch. If Swizzle is nonzero, the 34010 reverses the order of the bits in each byte before transfer.
Void INIT_PALET *()*	Palette (Core)	Initializes the first 16 palette entries to the EGA default palette.
Void INIT_TEXT *()*	Text (Core)	Removes any installed fonts from memory and selects the standard font. Resets all text drawing attributes.
Int INSTALL_ALM *(ALM Name)*	Extensibility (Core)	Installs the absolute load module into the TIGA graphics manager and returns a module identifier. Use the module identifier to invoke the ALM extended functions. Returns a negative number if not successful.
Short INSTALL_FONT *(PFont)*	Text (Extended)	Use this function to install a font into the font table after loading it into TMS340 memory. PFont points to the location of the font file in memory.

Table 6-123   Continued.

Instruction	Type	Function
		The function returns an ID number when successful. Otherwise, it returns 0.
Int INSTALL_PRIMITI VES ()	Graphics System Initialization (Core)	Loads extended graphics primitives in memory. Returns a positive number identifier when successful. Returns a negative number error otherwise.
Int INSTALL_PRIMITI VES ()	Extensibility (Core)	See previous description.
Int INSTALL_RLM *(RLM Name)*	Extensibility (Core)	Installs a relocatable load module into the TIGA graphics manager and returns a module identifier. Use the module identifier to invoke the RLM extended functions. Returns a negative number if not successful.
Void INSTALL_USERERR OR *(Function Name)*	Graphics System Initialization (Core)	Substitutes the default host communication error messages with a user supplied error handling routine.
Int LMO *(N)*	Graphics Utility (Core)	Caculates the position of the leftmost 1 in N. This function treats N as a 32-bit number. Returns -1 if no one found. Otherwise, returns the bit position of the one.
Unsigned Long LOADCOFF *(Filename)*	Graphics System Initialization (Core)	Provides the capability to load portable COFF code into the graphics manager. Not generally used by application programs.
Short PAGE_BUSY ()	Graphics Utility (Core)	Used with the PAGE_FLIP function. Returns a nonzero number while page flipping in progress. Otherwise, it returns 0.
Int PAGE_FLIP *(DIsplay, Drawing)*	Graphics Utility (Core)	Used with multiple frame buffers to set the display page to a particular frame buffer and the drawing page for subsequent drawing operations.

Table 6-123   Continued.

Instruction	Type	Function
Void PATNFILL_CONVEX *(N, Points)*	Graphics Output (Extended)	Fills a covex polygon with a pattern. N defines the number of vertices in the polygon. Points is an array containing the coordinates of each vertice in the polygon. The first and last X,Y coordinate in points should be the same to make sure the polygon is closed. Uses the currently defined pattern for fill.
Void PATNFILL_CONVEX *(N, Points)*	Poly Drawing (Extended)	See previous description.
Void PATNFILL_OVAL *(W, H, XLeft,* *YTop)*	Graphics Output (Extended)	Draws a pattern filled oval on-screen. W contains the width. H contains the height. XLeft and YTop contain the coordinates of the upper left corner of the oval. Uses the currently defined pattern for fill.
Void PATNFILL_PIEARC *(W, H, XLeft,* *YTop, Theta,* *Arc)*	Graphics Output (Extended)	Draws a pattern filled pie-shaped wedge on-screen. W contains the width. H contains the height. XLeft and YTop contain the coordinates of the upper left corner of the oval. Theta contains the start angle. Arc contains the number of degrees of arc. Uses the currently defined pattern for fill.
Void PATNFILL_POLYGO N *(N, Points)*	Graphics Output (Extended)	Draws a pattern filled polygon. N indicates the number of vetices in the polygon. Each point consists of an X and Y coordinate. To draw a closed polygon, use the same coordinates for the first and last set of points. Uses the currently defined pattern for fill.
Void PATNFILL_POLYGO N *(N, Points)*	Poly Drawing (Extended)	See previous description.

Table 6-123 Continued.

Instruction	Type	Function
Void PATNFILL_POLYGO N *(N, Points)*	Workspace (Extended)	See previous description.
Void PATNFILL_RECT *(W, H, XLeft, YTop)*	Graphics Output (Extended)	Draws a pattern filled rectangle on-screen. W contains the width. H contains the height. XLeft and YTop contain the coordinates of the upper left corner. Uses the currently defined pattern for fill.
Void PATNFRAME_OVAL *(W, H, XLeft, Ytop, DX, DY)*	Graphics Output (Extended)	Pattern fills the area between two concentric ovals. W contains the width. H contains the height. XLeft and YTop contain the coordinates of the upper left corner of the oval. DX specifies the horizontal distance between the outer and inner ovals. DY specifies the vertical distance between the two ovals. Uses the currently defined pattern for fill.
Void PATNFRAME_RECT *(W, H, XLeft, YTop, DX, DY)*	Graphics Output (Extended)	Pattern fills the area between two concentric rectangles. W contains the width. H contains the height. XLeft and YTop contain the coordinates of the upper left corner. DX specifies the horizontal distance between the outer and inner rectangles. DY specifies the vertical distance between the two rectangles. Uses the currently defined pattern for fill.
Void PATNPEN_LINE *(X1, Y1, X2, Y2)*	Graphics Output (Extended)	Draws a patterned line on-screen. X1 and Y1 contain the starting coordinate. X2 and Y2 contain the ending coordinate. Uses the currently defined pattern for drawing. Use the SET_PENSIZE function to change pen width and height.
Void PATNPEN_OVALARC *(W, H, XLeft, YTop, Theta, Arc)*	Graphics Output (Extended)	Draws a patterned eliptical arc on-screen. W contains the width. H contains the height. XLeft and YTop contain the coordinates of the upper left

Table 6-123   Continued.

Instruction	Type	Function
		corner. Theta contains the start angle. Arc contains the degrees of arc. Uses the currently defined pattern for drawing. Use the SET_PENSIZE function to change pen width and height.
Void PATNPEN_PIEARC *(W, H, XLeft, YTop, Theta, Arc)*	Graphics Output (Extended)	Draws a patterned eliptical arc on-screen. Two lines emanate from the center of the arc to each end. W contains the width. H contains the height. XLeft and YTop contain the coordinates of the upper left corner. Theta contains the start angle. Arc contains the degrees of arc. Uses the currently defined pattern for drawing. Use the SET_PENSIZE function to change pen width and height.
Void PATNPEN_POINT *(X, Y)*	Graphics Output (Extended)	Draws rectangular set of pixels on-screen (corresponds to pen height and width). The pixel color depends on its position within the currently defined pattern. X and Y contain the coordinate of the pixel. Use the SET_PENSIZE function to change pen width and height.
Void PATNPEN_POLYLINE *(N, Points)*	Graphics Output (Extended)	Draws a group of patterned lines whose end points are supplied as a set of points. N indicates the number of lines to draw. Each point consists of an X and Y coordinate. To draw a closed polygon, use the same coordinates for the first and last set of points. Uses the currently defined pattern for drawing. Use the SET_PENSIZE function to change pen width and height.
Void PATNPEN_POLYLINE *(N, Points)*	Poly Drawing (Extended)	See previous description.

Table 6-123   Continued.

Instruction	Type	Function
Long PEEK_BREG *(BREG)*	Graphics Utility (Core)	Returns a 32-bit number containing the value of a B-file register. BREG contains a number from 0 to 15 corresponding to a file register number.
Void PEN_LINE *(X1, Y1, X2, Y2)*	Graphics Output (Extended)	Draws a line the width and heigth of the current pen on-screen. X1 and Y1 contain the starting coordinate. X2 and Y2 contain the ending coordinate. Use the SET_PENSIZE function to change pen width and height.
Void PEN_OVALARC *(W, H, XLeft, YTop, Theta, Arc)*	Graphics Output (Extended)	Draws an arc the width and heigth of the current pen on-screen. W contains the width. H contains the height. XLeft and YTop contain the coordinates of the upper left corner. Theta contains the start angle. Arc contains the degrees of arc. Use the SET_PENSIZE function to change pen width and height.
Void PEN_PIEARC *(W, H, XLeft, YTop, Theta, Arc)*	Graphics Output (Extended)	Draws an arc the width and heigth of the current pen on-screen. Two lines emanate from the center of the arc to each end. W contains the width. H contains the height. XLeft and YTop contain the coordinates of the upper left corner. Theta contains the start angle. Arc contains the degrees of arc. Use the SET_PENSIZE function to change pen width and height.
Void PEN_POINT *(X, Y)*	Graphics Output (Extended)	Draws rectangular set of pixels on-screen (corresponds to pen height and width). X and Y contain the coordinate of the pixel. Use the SET_PENSIZE function to change pen width and height.
PEN_POLYLINE	Graphics Output (Extended)	Draws a group of lines the width and heigth of the current pen whose end points are suppied as a set of

Table 6-123   Continued.

Instruction	Type	Function
		points. N indicates the number of lines to draw. Each point consists of an X and Y coordinate. To draw a closed polygon, use the same coordinates for the first and last set of points. Use the SET_PENSIZE function to change pen width and height.
PEN_POLYLINE	Poly Drawing (Extended)	See previous description.
Void POKE_BREG *(BREG, Value)*	Graphics Utility (Core)	Writes Value to the B-file register specified by BREG. Value is a 32-bit number.
Int RMO *(N)*	Graphics Utility (Core)	Caculates the position of the rightmost 1 in N. This function treats N as a 32-bit number. Returns -1 if no one found. Otherwise, returns the bit position of the one.
Int SEED_FILL *(XSeed, YSeed, Buffer, Maxbytes)*	Graphics Output (Extended)	Fills a region of connected pixels starting a specified seed pixel. XSeed and YSeed contain the coordinates of the seed pixel. Buffer is an area of memory set aside for working storage. Maxbytes is the number of 8-bit bytes in the storage area.
Int SEED_PATNFILL *(XSeed, YSeed, Buffer, Maxbytes)*	Graphics Output (Extended)	Pattern fills a region of connected pixels starting a specified seed pixel. XSeed and YSeed contain the coordinates of the seed pixel. Buffer is an area of memory set aside for working storage. Maxbytes is the number of 8-bit bytes in the storage area. Uses the currently defined pattern for fill.
Int SELECT_FONT *(ID)*	Text (Extended)	Selects a previously installed font for use. ID is the number returned after font installation.
Void SET_BCOLOR	Graphics	Changes the background color

Table 6-123   Continued.

Instruction	Type	Function
(Color)	Attribute Control (Core)	specified in the COLOR0 B-file register to Color.
Void SET_CLIP_RECT *(W, H, XLeft, YTop)*	Graphics Attribute Control (Core)	Sets the current clipping rectangle by updating the B-file registers WSTART and WEND to match the W and H parameters. XLeft and YTop are relative to the drawing origin.
Void SET_COLORS *(FColor, BColor)*	Graphics Attribute Control (Core)	Changes the foreground color specified in the COLOR1 B-file register to FColor. Also changes the background color specified in the COLOR0 B-file register to BColor.
Int SET_CONFIG *(Graphics Mode, Init Draw)*	Graphics System Initialization (Core)	The SET_CONFIG function changes the mode to match Graphics Mode. If the mode is invalid, returns 0. Otherwise, returns a nonzero result. Init Draw causes the function to reset the following parameters when set true (nonzero)

Transparency is disabled (CONTROL I/O Register).

Window Clipping is set (CONTROL I/O Register).

Pixel Processing is set to replace (CONTROL I/O Register).

PMASK I/O Register is set to 0.

Foreground color is set to light grey and background color to black.

Source and destination bitmaps are set to the screen.

Drawing origin is set to 0, 0.

Pen width and height are set to 1.

Current pattern address is set to 0.

Table 6-123   Continued.

Instruction	Type	Function
		All installed fonts are removed and the current selected font set to the system font.
		Graphics cursor placed in the center of the screen, turned off, and set to the default shape.
		Temporary workspace is initialized.
Void SET_CURS_SHAPE *(Shape)*	Cursor (Core)	Defines the size and shape of the cursor. Shape is a structure containing size, color, and shape bitmaps.
Void SET_CURS_STATE *(Enable)*	Cursor (Core)	Displays the cursor if Enable is nonzero. Removes cursor if Enable is zero.
Void SET_CURS_XY *(X, Y)*	Cursor (Core)	Sets the pixel coordinates of the cursor hotspot. The cursor coordinates are relative to the upper left corner of the screen.
Void SET_DRAW_ORIGIN *(X, Y)*	Graphics Attribute Control (Extended)	Sets the drawing origin for future drawing operations.
Void SET_DSTBM *(Addr, Pitch, XEXT, YEXT, PSize)*	Pixel Array (Extended)	Sets the destination bitmap for future BITBLT operations. An address value of 0 sets the destination to screen.
Void SET_FCOLOR *(Color)*	Graphics Attribute Control (Core)	Changes the foreground color specified in the COLOR1 B-file register to Color.
Void SET_INTERRUPT *(Level, Priority, Enable, Scan Line)*	Extensibility (Core)	Enables or disables a previously installed interrupt service routine. The Scan Line parameter is used for display interrupts only. It sets the scan line at which the interrupt becomes enabled.
Void SET_PALET *(Count, Index, Palet)*	Palette (Core)	Loads an entire palette into memory. Count contains the number of palette entries. Index contains the palette

Table 6-123 **Continued.**

Instruction	Type	Function
		loading start point. Palet contains groups of four values (R, G, B, and I). Each group defines one palette value.
Void SET_PALET_ENTRY *(Index, R, G, B, I)*	Palette (Core)	Loads a single palette into memory. Index contains the palette entry to replace. R, G, B, and I contain the color values for the palette entry.
Void SET_PATN *(P)*	Graphics Attribute Control (Extended)	Defines the pattern used for drawing operations. P is a pointer to a structure containing the height, width, depth, and bit pattern.
Void SET_PENSIZE *(W, H)*	Graphics Attribute Control (Extended)	Sets the width (W) and height (H) of the drawing pen.
Void SET_PMASK *(Mask)*	Graphics Attribute Control (Core)	Defines which plane mask bits are writable. A zero in a bit position enables writing. A one in a bit position disables writing.
Void SET_PPOP *(PPOP Code)*	Graphics Attribute Control (Core)	Defines the pixel processing for future drawing operations

Code	Function
0	Source
1	Source AND Destination
2	Source AND NOT Destination
3	All 0s
4	Source OR NOT Destination
5	Source EQU Destination
6	NOT Destination
7	Source NOR Destination
8	Source OR Destination
9	Destination
10	Source XOR Destination
11	NOT Source AND Destination
12	All 1s
13	NOT Source OR Destination
14	Source NAND Destination
15	NOT Source

Table 6-123   Continued.

Instruction	Type	Function
		16 Source + Destination
		17 ADDS (Source, Destination)
		18 Destination - Source
		19 SUBS (Destination, Source)
		20 MAX (Source, Destination)
		21 MIN (Source, Destination)
Void SET_SRCBM *(Addr, Pitch, XEXT, YEXT, PSize)*	Pixel Array (Extended)	Sets the source bitmap for future BITBLT operations. An address value of 0 sets the source to screen.
Int SET_TEXTATTR *(Control, Count, Arg)*	Text (Extended)	Sets the text rendering attributes. PControl is a pointer to a list of desired attributes. Current attribute values include %a (top left aligment = 0, baseline = 1) and %e (additional intercharacter spacing. Count contains the number of attributes in the control string.
Void SET_TIMEOUT *(Value)*	Graphics System Initialization (Core)	Sets the time in milliseconds that the host waits for a TMS340 function to complete before calling the error function.
Void SET_TRANSP *(Mode)*	Graphics Attribute Control (Core)	Changes the transparency mode (TMS34020 and above only) as shown below. (TMS34010 uses mode 2 only.)

Mode   Function

0	Source transparency = 0.
1	Source transparency = COLOR0
2	Result transparency = 0.
3	Result transparency = COLOR0

Instruction	Type	Function
Unsigned SET_VECTOR *(TrapNum, NewAddr)*	Communication (Core)	Sets the specified trap number to NewAddr. Returns the address of the old interrupt.

Table 6-123   Continued.

Instruction	Type	Function
Int SET_VIDEOMODE *(Mode, Style)*	Graphics System Initialization (Core)	The SET_VIDEOMODE function changes the current video mode and determines how to initialize the new mode. Mode can contain one of the following values: TIGA, MDA, HERCULES, CGA, EGA, VGA, AI_8514, or PREVIOUS. Style determines the initialization method. It can contain one of the following values: NO_INIT, INIT_GLOBALS, INIT, or CLR_SCREEN.
Void SET_WINDOWING *(Enable)*	Graphics Attribute Control (Core)	Sets the 2-bit windowing code in the control I/O register as shown below.

Code   Function

00	No Windowing
01	Interrupt Request on Write In Window
10	Interrupt Request on Write Outside Window
11	Clip to Window

Instruction	Type	Function
Void SET_WKSP *(Addr, Pitch)*	Workspace (Core)	Sets parameters defining the current offscreen workspace. Addr and Pitch contain the address and pitch of the workspace area.
Void STYLED_LINE *(X1, Y1, X2, Y2, Style, Mode)*	Graphics Output (Extended)	Uses Bresenham's algorithm to draw a styled line from X1, Y1 to X2, Y2. Style is a 32-bit value containing a repeating pattern. Mode changes the method used for drawing.

Mode   Function

0	Do not draw background pixels, leave gaps. Load new line-style from style argument.
1	Draw background pixels using COLOR0. Load new line-style from style argument.
2	Do not draw background pixels, leave gaps. Do

Table 6-123   Continued.

Instruction	Type	Function
		not load new line-style from style argument.
	3	Draw background pixels using COLOR0. Do not load new line-style from style argument.
Void SWAP_BM ()	Pixel Array (Extended)	Exchanges pointers to the structures containing the source and destination bitmaps.
Void SYNCHRONIZE ()	Graphics System Initialization (Core)	Synchronizes operations between two processors. Ensures the TMS340 completes an operation before the host CPU tries to manipulate the resulting data.
Int TEXT_OUT (X, Y, PString)	Text (Core)	Sends an ASCII string pointed to by PString to the display using the current font. X and Y specify the starting coordinates for the string.
Int TEXT_WIDTH (PString)	Text (Extended)	Returns the length of the specified string in pixels (using the current font for reference).
Void TRANSP_OFF ()	Graphics Attribute Control (Core)	Disables transparency for future drawing operations.
Void TRANSP_ON ()	Graphics Attribute Control (Core)	Enables transparency for future drawing operations.
Void WAIT_SCAN (Line)	Graphics Utility (Core)	Causes a wait state until the processor scans the specified scan line. Control returns to the calling procedure. Synchronizes drawing operations with the display.
Void ZOOM_RECT (WS, HS, XS, YS, WD, HD, XD, YD, LineBuf)	Pixel Array (Extended)	Expands or shrinks the specified rectangle to fit on the display. WS contains the source width. HS contains the source height. XS and YS contain the coordinates of the upper left corner of the

Table 6-123   Continued.

Instruction	Type	Function
		source screen. WD contains the destination width. HD contains the destination height. XD and YD contain the coordinates of the upper left corner of the destination screen. LineBuf is a buffer large enough to contain one line of the display.

7
ROM Interrupts

This chapter discusses the various interrupt routines contained in ROM and VIDEO BIOS. The first section discusses the ROM extensions for both the EGA and VGA. Whenever possible, this section describes Super VGA extensions accepted by the Video Electronics Standards Association (VESA). Not all manufacturers adhere to these standards. Always check your vendor manual for complete information.

There are four other sections: the diskette, keyboard, printer, and other miscellaneous services. TABLE 7-1 contains a listing of BIOS interrupts in interrupt number order. Because many VIDEO and ROM BIOS manufacturers use non-standard or incompatible functions, always check the vendor reference manuals (when available) for complete information. In most cases the vendor adds to the standard set of routines to allow you to use a specialized feature of the hardware. The routines in this chapter show the generally accepted implementations.

Note: Assume a radix (base) of 10 (decimal) for all example numbers unless a lowercase letter follows the number. Numbers followed by a "b" use base 2 (binary). Numbers followed by an "h" use base 16 (hex).

VIDEO SERVICES

This section contains descriptions for all display adapter-specific ROM interrupts. The EGA and VGA BIOS extension-specific paragraphs identify which adapter uses it. The Super VGA extensions describe standards recently released by VESA. TABLE 7-1 contains a listing of video BIOS interrupts in interrupt number order.

Table 7-1   ROM/Video BIOS Interrupts

Interrupt	Service	Function	Description
5			Print Screen
10h	0		Set Video Mode
10h	1		Set Cursor Size
10h	2		Set Cursor Position
10h	3		Read Cursor Position and Size
10h	4		Read Light Pen Position
10h	5		Select Active Display Page
10h	6		Scroll Window Up
10h	7		Scroll Window Down
10h	8		Read Character and Attribute
10h	9		Write Character and Attribute
10h	Ah		Write Character
10h	Bh		Set Color Palette
10h	Ch		Write Pixel Dot
10h	Dh		Read Pixel Dot
10h	Eh		TTY Character Output
10h	Fh		Get Current Video State
10h	10h	0	Set Individual Palette Register
10h	10h	1	Set Overscan Register
10h	10h	2	Set All Palette Registers
10h	10h	3	Toggle Intensify/Blink
10h	10h	7	Read Individual Palette Register
10h	10h	8	Read Overscan Register
10h	10h	9	Read All Palette Registers
10h	10h	10h	Set Individual DAC Register
10h	10h	12h	Set Block of DAC Registers
10h	10h	13h	Select Color Subset
10h	10h	15h	Read Individual DAC Register
10h	10h	17h	Read Block of DAC Registers
10h	10h	1Ah	Read Color Page State
10h	10h	1Bh	Sum DAC Registers to Gray Shades
10h	11h	0	User Alpha Load
10h	11h	1	ROM Monochrome Set
10h	11h	2	ROM Double Dot Set
10h	11h	3	Set Block Specifier
10h	11h	4	ROM 16 Row Set
10h	11h	10h	User Alpha Load
10h	11h	11h	ROM Monochrome Set
10h	11h	12h	ROM Double Dot Set
10h	11h	14h	ROM 16 Row Set
10h	11h	20h	User Graphics Characters - 8 X 8
10h	11h	21h	User Graphics Characters
10h	11h	22h	ROM 8 X 14 Character Set
10h	11h	23h	ROM 8 X 8 Character Set
10h	11h	24h	ROM 8 X 16 Character Set
10h	11h	30h	Return Character Set Information
10h	12h	10h	Return Memory Allocation Information
10h	12h	20h	Select Alternate Print Screen Routine
10h	12h	30h	Select Scan Lines for Alpha Mode
10h	12h	31h	Select Default Palette Loading
10h	12h	32h	Video Enable/Disable
10h	12h	33h	Summing to Gray Shades
10h	12h	34h	Cursor Emulation

Table 7-1   Continued.

Interrupt	Service	Function	Description
10h	12h	35h	Display Switch
10h	12h	36h	Screen Off/On
10h	13h		Write String
10h	1Ah	0	Read Display Combination Code
10h	1Ah	1	Write Display Combination Code
10h	1Bh		Return Functionality/State Information
10h	1Ch	0	Get Video State Buffer
10h	1Ch	1	Save Video State Buffer
10h	1Ch	2	Restore Video State
10h	4Fh	0	Return Super VGA Information
10h	4Fh	1	Return Super VGA Mode Information
10h	4Fh	2	Set Super VGA Video Mode
10h	4Fh	3	Return Current Video Mode
10h	4Fh	4	Return Save/Restore State Buffer Size
10h	4Fh	4	Save Super VGA Video State
10h	4Fh	4	Restore Super VGA Video State
10h	4Fh	5	Select Super VGA Video Memory Window
10h	4Fh	5	Return Super VGA Video Memory Window
11h			Get Equipment Status
12h			Get Memory Size
13h	0		Reset Disk Drives
13h	1		Get Floppy Disk Status
13h	2		Read Disk Sectors
13h	3		Write Disk Sectors
13h	4		Verify Disk Sectors
13h	5		Format Disk Track
13h	6		Format Bad Track
13h	7		Format Drive
13h	8		Return Disk Parameters
13h	9		Initialize Fixed Disk Table
13h	Ah		Read Long Sectors
13h	Bh		Write Long Sectors
13h	Ch		Seek Cylinder
13h	Dh		Alternate Reset
13h	Eh		Read Sector Buffer
13h	Fh		Write Sector Buffer
13h	10h		Get Drive Status
13h	11h		Recalibrate Drive
13h	12h		Controller RAM Diagnostic
13h	13h		Controller Drive Diagnostic
13h	14h		Controller Internal Diagnostic
13h	15h		Read DASD type
13h	16h		Read Disk Change Line Status
13h	17h		Set DASD Type for Format
13h	18h		Set Media Type for Format
13h	19h		Park Heads
13h	1Ah		Format ESDI Drive
14h	0		Initialize Communications Port
14h	1		Transmit Character
14h	2		Receive Character
14h	3		Get Communications Port Status
14h	4		Extended Initialize Communications Port

Table 7-1   Continued.

Interrupt	Service	Function	Description
14h	5		Extended Communications Port Control
15h	0		Turn On Cassette Motor
15h	1		Turn Off Cassette Motor
15h	2		Read Data Blocks from Cassette
15h	3		Write Data Blocks to Cassette
15h	Fh		Format ESDI Drive Periodic Interrupt
15h	21h	0	Read POST Error Log
15h	21h	1	Write POST Error Log
15h	4Fh		Keyboard Intercept
15h	80h		Device Open
15h	81h		Device Close
15h	82h		Process Termination
15h	83h		Event Wait
15h	84h		Read Joystick
15h	85h		SysReq Key
15h	86h		Delay
15h	87h		Move Extended Memory Block
15h	88h		Get Extended Memory Size
15h	89h		Enter Protected Mode
15h	90h		Device Wait
15h	91h		Device Post
15h	C0h		Get System Environment
15h	C1h		Get Address of Extended BIOS Data Area
15h	C2h	0	Enable/Disable Pointing Device
15h	C2h	1	Reset Pointing Device
15h	C2h	2	Set Sample Rate
15h	C2h	3	Set Resolution
15h	C2h	4	Get Pointing Device Type
15h	C2h	5	Initialize Pointing Device Interface
15h	C2h	6	Set Scaling or Get Status
15h	C2h	7	Set Pointing Device Handler Address
15h	C3h		Set Watchdog Timer Time-Out
15h	C4h		Programmable Option Select
16h	0		Read Keyboard Character
16h	1		Read Keyboard Status
16h	2		Read Keyboard Shift Status
16h	3		Set Repeat Rate
16h	4		Set Keyclick
16h	5		Push Character and Scan Code
16h	10h		Read Character from Enhanced Keyboard
16h	11h		Get Enhanced Keyboard Status
16h	12h		Get Enhanced Keyboard Shift Status
17h	0		Print Character
17h	1		Initialize Printer
17h	2		Get Printer Status
18h			ROM Basic
19h			Warm Boot
1Ah	0		Get Clock Counter
1Ah	1		Set Clock Counter
1Ah	2		Read Real-Time Clock
1Ah	3		Set Real-Time Clock
1Ah	4		Read Date from Real-Time Clock

Table 7-1   Continued.

Interrupt	Service Function	Description
1Ah	5	Set Date of Real-Time Clock
1Ah	6	Set Alarm
1Ah	7	Disable Alarm
1Ah	Ah	Get Day Count
1Ah	Bh	Set Day Count
1Ah	80h	Set Sound Source

Set Video Mode (Interrupt 10h Service 0)

Use With: MDA, CGA, EGA, MCGA, and VGA

This service routine changes the current video mode. TABLE 7-2 contains a listing of applicable video modes. The register contents on service routine entry appear below.

Register Contents:
AH - 0
AL - Desired Video Mode

Example:
```
; Change video mode to 350 by 640 graphics.
XOR    AH,AH
MOV    AL,10h
INT    10h
```

Table 7-2   Video Mode Settings for BIOS Interrupt 10 Service 0

Mode	Type	Colors	Resolution	Glyph Cell
*Enhanced Color Display**				
0h	Text	16/64	350 by 320	8 by 14
1h	Text	16/64	350 by 320	8 by 14
2h	Graphics	16/64	350 by 640	8 by 14
3h	Graphics	16/64	350 by 640	8 by 14
*Standard Display**				
0h	Text	16	200 by 320	8 by 8
1h	Text	16	200 by 320	8 by 8
2h	Graphics	16	200 by 640	8 by 8
3h	Graphics	16	200 by 640	8 by 8
*Enhanced Color and Standard Displays**				
4h	Graphics	4	200 by 320	8 by 8
5h	Graphics	4	200 by 320	8 by 8
6h	Graphics	2	200 by 640	8 by 14

Table 7-2   Continued.

Mode	Type	Colors	Resolution	Glyph Cell
7h	Text	4	350 by 720	9 by 14
Dh	Graphics	16	200 by 320	8 by 8
Eh	Graphics	16	200 by 640	8 by 8
64 KByte Boards*				
Fh	Graphics	4	350 by 640	8 by 14
10h	Graphics	4/64	350 by 640	8 by 14
128 KByte Boards*				
Fh	Graphics	4	350 by 640	8 by 14
10h	Graphics	16/64	350 by 640	8 by 14

---

* Use the standard display settings for CGA; enhanced color
display settings for EGA. The VGA always uses the enhanced color
display and 128 KByte board settings.

Set Cursor Size (Interrupt 10h Service 1)

Use With: MDA, CGA, EGA, MCGA, and VGA

This service changes the cursor size and line position. For example,
when using a CGA display, specifying a starting scan line of 0 and an ending scan line of 7 produces a block cursor. TABLE 7-2 provides a character
size listing for each video mode. The character size minus one specifies
the maximum cursor scan line position.

Register Contents:
AH - 1
CH - Starting Scan Line
CL - Ending Scan Line

Example:

```
; Change to block cursor in mode 7h.
MOV   AH,1
MOV   CH,0
MOV   CL,13
INT   10h
```

Set Cursor Position (Interrupt 10h Service 2)

Use With: MDA, CGA, EGA, MCGA, and VGA

This service changes the cursor position on screen. It therefore affects
where the next text appears. TABLE 7-2 specifies the screen dimensions for
various video modes. Use these values to determine the maximum cursor
row and column position for a particular video mode. TABLE 7-3 shows the

Table 7-3   Video Display Pages

Display Mode	Display Adapter	Pages
0	CGA, EGA, MCGA, VGA	0 - 7
1	CGA, EGA, MCGA, VGA	0 - 7
2	CGA	0 - 3
2	EGA, MCGA, VGA	0 - 7
3	CGA	0 - 3
3	EGA, MCGA, VGA	0 - 7
7	EGA, VGA	0 - 7
Dh	EGA, VGA	0 - 7
Eh	EGA, VGA	0 - 3
Fh	EGA, VGA	0 - 1
10h	EGA, VGA	0 - 1

Note:

Video mode/adapter combinations not listed
use 1 display page.

correlation between video mode, display adapter type, and the number of available pages.

Register Contents:
AH - 2
BH - Video Page Number
DH - Cursor Row
DL - Cursor Column

Example:

```
; Place cursor in upper left corner of page 0.
MOV    AH,2
XOR    BH,BH
XOR    DX,DX
INT    10h
```

Read Cursor Position and Size (Interrupt 10h Service 3)

Use With: MDA, CGA, EGA, MCGA, and VGA

This service reads the current cursor position and size. These values appear in the registers as stated below after interrupt execution. TABLE 7-3 shows the correlation between video mode, display adapter type, and the number of available pages.

Register Contents on Entry:
AH - 3
BH - Video Page Number

Register Contents on Exit:
BH - Video Page Number
CH - Beginning Scan Line of Cursor
CL - Ending Scan Line of Cursor
DH - Cursor Row
DL - Cursor Column

Example:
```
; Get cursor information for page 1.
MOV   AH,3
MOV   BH,1
INT   10h
```

Read Light-Pen Position (Interrupt 10h Service 4)

Use With: CGA and EGA

This service returns the current light-pen position after interrupt execution. TABLE 7-2 specifies the screen dimensions for various video modes. Because the service returns the pixel position of the light pen, use these values to determine light-pen position in relation to total screen size. Only the CGA, MDA, and EGA have light-pen ports.

Register Contents on Entry:
AH - 4

Register Contents on Exit (When AX Equals 1):
AH - Light-Pen Trigger Status (1 When Triggered)
BX - Pixel Column
CX - Pixel Row
DH - Light-Pen Row
DL - Light-Pen Column

Example:
```
; Read current light pen position.
MOV   AH,4
INT   10h
```

Select Active Display Page (Interrupt 10h Service 5)

Use With: MDA, CGA, EGA, MCGA, and VGA

This service selects the active display page. Each adapter allows a different number of display pages depending on the current video mode. TABLE 7-3 shows the correlation between video mode, display adapter type, and the number of available pages. The register contents appear below.

Register Contents on Entry:
AH - 5
AL - Video Page Number

Example:
```
; Select video page number 1.
MOV    AH,5
MOV    AL,1
INT    10h
```

Scroll Window Up (Interrupt 10h Service 6)

Use With: MDA, CGA, EGA, MCGA, and VGA

This service scrolls the window defined by CX and DX up the number of spaces specified in AL. The service does not save any text scrolled past the top of the window. TABLE 7-2 specifies the screen dimensions for various video modes. TABLE 7-4 contains a listing of color combinations and attribute numbers.

Table 7-4   Character Attribute Color Values

Foreground	Background	ex Value	Dec Value
Blue	Black	01h	1
Green	Black	02h	2
Cyan	Black	03h	3
Red	Black	04h	4
Magenta	Black	05h	5
Brown	Black	06h	6
White	Black	07h	7
Gray	Black	08h	8
Light Blue	Black	09h	9
Light Green	Black	0Ah	10
Light Cyan	Black	0Bh	11
Light Red	Black	0Ch	12
Light Magenta	Black	0Dh	13
Yellow	Black	0Eh	14
Bright White	Black	0Fh	15
Black	Blue	10h	16
Green	Blue	12h	18
Cyan	Blue	13h	19
Red	Blue	14h	20
Magenta	Blue	15h	21
Brown	Blue	16h	22
White	Blue	17h	23
Gray	Blue	18h	24
Light Blue	Blue	19h	25
Light Green	Blue	1Ah	26
Light Cyan	Blue	1Bh	27
Light Red	Blue	1Ch	28
Light Magenta	Blue	1Dh	29
Yellow	Blue	1Eh	30
Bright White	Blue	1Fh	31
Black	Green	20h	32
Blue	Green	21h	33
Cyan	Green	23h	35
Red	Green	24h	36

Table 7-4 Continued.

Foreground	Background	ex Value	Dec Value
Magenta	Green	25h	37
Brown	Green	26h	38
White	Green	27h	39
Gray	Green	28h	40
Light Blue	Green	29h	41
Light Green	Green	2Ah	42
Light Cyan	Green	2Bh	43
Light Red	Green	2Ch	44
Light Magenta	Green	2Dh	45
Yellow	Green	2Eh	46
Bright White	Green	2Fh	47
Black	Cyan	30h	48
Blue	Cyan	31h	49
Green	Cyan	32h	50
Red	Cyan	34h	52
Magenta	Cyan	35h	53
Brown	Cyan	36h	54
White	Cyan	37h	55
Gray	Cyan	38h	56
Light Blue	Cyan	39h	57
Light Green	Cyan	3Ah	58
Light Cyan	Cyan	3Bh	59
Light Red	Cyan	3Ch	60
Light Magenta	Cyan	3Dh	61
Yellow	Cyan	3Eh	62
Bright White	Cyan	3Fh	63
Black	Red	40h	64
Blue	Red	41h	65
Green	Red	42h	66
Cyan	Red	43h	67
Magenta	Red	45h	69
Brown	Red	46h	70
White	Red	47h	71
Gray	Red	48h	72
Light Blue	Red	49h	73
Light Green	Red	4Ah	74
Light Cyan	Red	4Bh	75
Light Red	Red	4Ch	76
Light Magenta	Red	4Dh	77
Yellow	Red	4Eh	78
Bright White	Red	4Fh	79
Black	Magenta	50h	80
Blue	Magenta	51h	81
Green	Magenta	52h	82
Cyan	Magenta	53h	83
Red	Magenta	54h	84
Brown	Magenta	56h	86
White	Magenta	57h	87
Gray	Magenta	58h	88
Light Blue	Magenta	59h	89
Light Green	Magenta	5Ah	90
Light Cyan	Magenta	5Bh	91
Light Red	Magenta	5Ch	92

Table 7-4   Continued.

Foreground	Background	ex Value	Dec Value
Light Magenta	Magenta	5Dh	93
Yellow	Magenta	5Eh	94
Bright White	Magenta	5Fh	95
Black	Brown	60h	96
Blue	Brown	61h	97
Green	Brown	62h	98
Cyan	Brown	63h	99
Red	Brown	64h	100
Magenta	Brown	65h	101
White	Brown	67h	103
Gray	Brown	68h	104
Light Blue	Brown	69h	105
Light Green	Brown	6Ah	106
Light Cyan	Brown	6Bh	107
Light Red	Brown	6Ch	108
Light Magenta	Brown	6Dh	109
Yellow	Brown	6Eh	110
Bright White	Brown	6Fh	111
Black	White	70h	112
Blue	White	71h	113
Green	White	72h	114
Cyan	White	73h	115
Red	White	74h	116
Magenta	White	75h	117
Brown	White	76h	118
Gray	White	78h	120
Light Blue	White	79h	121
Light Green	White	7Ah	122
Light Cyan	White	7Bh	123
Light Red	White	7Ch	124
Light Magenta	White	7Dh	125
Yellow	White	7Eh	126
Bright White	White	7Fh	127

Note:

This table lists the default combinations. Both the VGA and EGA allow other possibilities.

Register Contents on Entry:

AH - 6

AL - Number of Lines to Scroll

BH - Attribute to Fill Character

CH - Upper Left Window Row

CL - Upper Left Window Column

DH - Lower Right Window Row

DL - Lower Right Window Column

Example:

; Scroll window up 6 lines starting at row 5, column 0.

```
; Assume a screen size of 25 rows by 80 columns.
MOV     AH,6
MOV     AL,6
XOR     BH,0      ;Black
MOV     CH,5
MOV     CL,0
MOV     DH,25
MOV     DH,80
INT     10h
```

Scroll Window Down (Interrupt 10h Service 7)

Use With: MDA, CGA, EGA, MCGA, and VGA

This service scrolls the window defined by CX and DX down the number of spaces specified in AL. The service does not save any text scrolled past the bottom of the window. TABLE 7-2 specifies the screen dimensions for various video modes. TABLE 7-4 contains a listing of color combinations and attribute numbers.

Register Contents on Entry:
AH - 7
AL - Number of Lines to Scroll
BH - Attribute of Fill Character
CH - Upper Left Window Row
CL - Upper Left Window Column
DH - Lower Right Window Row
DL - Lower Right Window Column

Example:
```
; Scroll window down 5 lines starting at row 0, column 0.
; Assume a screen size of 25 rows by 80 columns.
MOV     AH,7
MOV     AL,5
XOR     BH,0      ;Black
XOR     CX,0
MOV     DH,25
MOV     DH,80
INT     10h
```

Read Character and Attribute (Interrupt 10h Service 8)

Use With: MDA, CGA, EGA, MCGA, and VGA

This service returns the ASCII character number and attribute for the character at the current cursor position. TABLE 7-3 shows the correlation between video mode, display adapter type, and the number of available pages. TABLE 7-4 contains a listing of color combinations and attribute numbers.

Register Contents on Entry:
AH - 8
BH - Video Page Number

Register Contents on Exit:
AH - Character Attribute
AL - Character Number

Example:

```
; Read the character and attribute at row 5, column 20.
MOV    AH,2
XOR    BH,BH
MOV    DH,5
MOV    DL,20
INT    10h
MOV    AH,8
INT    10h
```

Write Character and Attribute (Interrupt 10h Service 9)

Use With: MDA, CGA, EGA, MCGA, and VGA

This service writes the specified character to the display page defined by BH using the color found in BL. TABLE 7-3 shows the correlation between video mode, display adapter type, and the number of available pages. TABLE 7-4 contains a listing of color combinations and attribute numbers.

Register Contents on Entry:
AH - 9
AL - Character
BH - Video Page Number
BL - Character Attribute/Color
CX - Number of Characters

Example:

```
; Write a C in blue at row 5, column 20.
MOV    AH,2
XOR    BH,BH
MOV    DH,5
MOV    DL,20
INT    10h
MOV    AH,9
MOV    AL,'C'
MOV    BL,1
INT    10h
```

Write Character (Interrupt 10h Service Ah)

Use With: MDA, CGA, EGA, MCGA, and VGA

This service writes the number of characters specified in CX at the cursor position. AL contains the character to write. TABLE 7-3 shows the correlation between video mode, display adapter type, and the number of available pages.

Register Contents on Entry:
AH - Ah
AL - Character
BH - Video Page Number
CX - Number of Characters

Example:
```
; Write five *s at the current cursor position.
MOV     AH,0Ah
MOV     AL,'*'
XOR     BH,BH
MOV     CX,5
INT     10h
```

Set Color Palette (Interrupt 10h Service Bh)

Use With: CGA, EGA, MCGA, and VGA

This service changes the palette, background, or border color. In text mode, it selects only the border color. In 320x200 graphics mode, it selects the palette. The colors for palette 0 are green, red, and brown. The colors for palette 1 are cyan, magenta, and white. In all other graphics modes, this service selects the background and border color.

Register Contents on Entry (Color Select):
AH - Bh
BH - 0
BL - Color

Register Contents on Entry (Palette Select):
AH - Bh
BH - 1
BL - Palette

Example:
```
; Select palette number 1.
MOV     AH,0Bh
XOR     BH,BH
MOV     BL,1
INT     10h
```

Write Pixel Dot (Interrupt 10h Service Ch)

Use With: CGA, EGA, MCGA, and VGA

This service draws a dot at the specified graphics coordinate. TABLE 7-2 specifies the screen dimensions for various video modes.

Register Contents on Entry:
AH - Ch
AL - Pixel Color Value
BH - Video Page Number
CX - Column
DX - Row

Example:

```
; Draw a blue dot at coordinates 20, 20 on display page 0.
MOV    Ah,0Ch
MOV    AL,1      ;Blue with black background
XOR    BH,BH
MOV    CX,20
MOV    DX,20
INT    10h
```

Read Pixel Dot (Interrupt 10h Service Dh)

Use With: CGA, EGA, MCGA, and VGA

This service reads the pixel value at a specified graphics coordinate. TABLE 7-2 specifies the screen dimensions for various video modes.

Register Contents on Entry:
AH - Dh
BH - Video Page Number
CX - Column
DX - Row

Register Contents on Exit:
AL - Pixel Color Value

Example:

```
; Get the pixel value at location 20, 20 on display page 1.
MOV    AH,0Dh
MOV    BH,1
MOV    CX,20
MOV    DX,20
INT    10h
```

TTY Character Output (Interrupt 10h Service Eh)

Use With: MDA, CGA, EGA, MCGA, and VGA

This service displays a character at the specified position. TABLE 7-2 specifies the screen dimensions for various video modes.

Register Contents on Entry:
AH - Eh
AL - Character
BH - Video Page Number
BL - Foreground Color (Graphics Modes)

Example:
```
; Output a character to display page 0.
MOV   AH,0Eh
MOV   AL,'C'
XOR   BH,BH
MOV   BL,1Ah     ;Light Green on Blue Background
INT   10h
```

Get Current Video State (Interrupt 10h Service Fh)

Use With: MDA, CGA, EGA, MCGA, and VGA

This service gets the current display mode of the video adapter. TABLE 7-2 provides the parameters for various adapter display modes.

Register Contents on Entry:
AH - Fh

Register Contents on Exit:
AH - Number of Screen Character Columns
AL - Display Mode
BH - Active Display Page

Example:
```
; Get the current display mode.
MOV   AH,0Fh
INT   10h
```

Set Individual Palette Register
(Interrupt 10h Service 10h Function 0)

Use With: EGA, MCGA, and VGA

This service sets the contents of a palette register to a corresponding displayable color. There are 16 palette registers numbered 0 through 15 (0 – 0Fh).

Register Contents on Entry (EGA or VGA):
AH - 10h
AL - 0
BH - Color Value
BL - Palette Register Number

Register Contents on Entry (MCGA):
AH - 10

```
          AL - 0
          BX - 0712h
Example:
    ; This short program shows you the effects of the palette
    ; commands on display appearance.

    .MODEL SMALL

    .STACK  ;Use the default stack of 1024 bytes.

    .DATA

    OldColor    DB    0

    .CODE
    EXAMPLE  PROC FAR

            PUSH    DS              ;Save the original data segment.
            XOR     AX,AX
            PUSH    AX

            MOV     AX,@DATA        ;Point DS & ES to our data segment.
            MOV     DS,AX
            MOV     ES,AX

            MOV     AH,10h          ;Save the original palette color.
            MOV     AL,07h
            MOV     BL,0
            INT     10h
            MOV     OldColor,BH

            MOV     CX,15           ;Number of colors to try.
            MOV     BL,0            ;Black background/gray foreground.
            MOV     BH,19h          ;New color number.
    LoopIt: MOV     AH,10h          ;Change the palette.
            MOV     AL,0
            INT     10h
            INC     BH              ;Get ready for next color.

            XOR     AX,AX           ;Wait for keypress.
            INT     16h

            LOOP    LoopIt          ;Change to next color.

            MOV     AH,10h          ;Restore original color.
            MOV     AL,0
```

```
        MOV    BH,OldColor
        MOV    BL,0
        INT    10h

        RET    ;Return

EXAMPLE ENDP
END     EXAMPLE
```

Set Overscan Register (Interrupt 10h Service 10h Function 1)

Use With: EGA and VGA

This service sets the contents of the overscan register to a corresponding displayable color. This changes the visible border color (normally set to black).

Register Contents on Entry:
AH - 10h
AL - 1
BH - Color Value

Example:

```
; Set the border color to green.
MOV    AH,10h
MOV    AL,1
MOV    BH,1Ah
INT    10h
```

Set All Palette Registers
(Interrupt 10h Service 10h Function 2)

Use With: EGA and VGA

This service sets the contents of all the palette and overscan registers to a corresponding displayable color. Each entry is an 8-bit value. You need 16 color entries plus an overscan entry (17 total bytes) to fill the color correspondence table completely. TABLE 7-4 contains a list of color numbers.

Register Contents on Entry:
AH - 10h
AL - 2
DX - Offset to a Color Correspondence Table
ES - Segment of a Color Correspondence Table

Example:

```
;Change the color of the palette and overscan registers.
MOV    AH,10h
MOV    AL,2
LES    DX,ColorTbl    ;You could use LEA if ES already
INT    10h            ; points to the color table data segment.
```

Toggle Intensify/Blink (Interrupt 10h Service 10h Function 3)

Use With: EGA, MCGA, and VGA

This service changes the bit used to determine whether the most significant bit of a character attribute intensifies or blinks the display. BL contains the intensify bit value. When this value equals 1, the adapter enables blinking.

Register Contents on Entry:
AH - 10h
AL - 3
BL - Blink/Intensify Bit Value

Example:
```
;Turn blinking on.
MOV    AH,10h
MOV    AL,3
MOV    BL,1
INT    10h
```

Read Individual Palette Register (Interrupt 10h Service 10h Function 7)

Use With: VGA

This service reads the color value contained in a single palette register. There are 16 palette registers numbered 0 through 15 (0–0Fh).

Register Contents on Entry:
AH - 10h
AL - 7
BL - Palette Register Number

Register Contents on Exit:
BH - Color Value

Example:
```
;This short program shows you the effects of the palette
;commands on display appearance.

.MODEL SMALL

.STACK ; Use the default stack of 1024 bytes

.DATA

OldColor    DB    0

.CODE
```

```
EXAMPLE  PROC FAR

          PUSH    DS              ;Save the original data segment.
          XOR     AX,AX
          PUSH    AX
          MOV     AX,@DATA        ;Point DS & ES to our data segment.
          MOV     DS,AX
          MOV     ES,AX

          MOV     AH,10h          ;Save the original palette color.
          MOV     AL,07h
          MOV     BL,0
          INT     10h
          MOV     OldColor,BH

          MOV     CX,15           ;Number of colors to try.
          MOV     BL,0            ;Black background/gray foreground.
          MOV     BH,19h          ;New color number.
LoopIt:   MOV     AH,10h          ;Change the palette.
          MOV     AL,0
          INT     10h
          INC     BH              ;Get ready for next color.

          XOR     AX,AX           ;Wait for keypress.
          INT     16h

          LOOP    LoopIt          ;Change to next color.

          MOV     AH,10h          ;Restore original color.
          MOV     AL,0
          MOV     BH,OldColor
          MOV     BL,0
          INT     10h
          RET                     ;Return.
EXAMPLE ENDP
END     EXAMPLE
```

Read Overscan Register
(Interrupt 10h Service 10h Function 8)

Use With: VGA

This service reads the color value contained in the overscan register. The overscan register affects the screen border color.

Register Contents on Entry:

AH - 10h
AL - 8

Register Contents on Exit:
BH - Color Value

Example:
```
MOV    AH,10h
MOV    AL,8
INT    10h
MOV    SaveVal,BH
```

Read All Palette Registers
(Interrupt 10h Service 10h Function 9)

Use With: VGA

This service reads the color value contained in all the palette registers and the overscan register. Use a 17 byte buffer to accept the color correspondence table. TABLE 7-4 contains a list of color table values.

Register Contents on Entry:
AH - 10h
AL - 9
DX - Offset to a Color Correspondence Table
ES - Segment of a Color Correspondence Table

Register Contents on Exit:
DX - Offset to a Color Correspondence Table
ES - Segment of a Color Correspondence Table

Example:
```
;Save the value of the palette and overscan registers.
MOV    AH,10h
MOV    AL,9
LES    DX,ColorTbl    ;You could use LEA if ES already
INT    10h            ; points to the color table data segment.
```

Set Individual DAC Register
(Interrupt 10h Service 10h Function 10h)

Use With: MCGA and VGA

This service programs an individual color register with a red-green-blue color combination. It provides extended control over other means of changing the color table values. There are 16 or 64 colors depending on the color page state. Use Interrupt 10h, Service 10h, Subfunction 1Ah to determine the number of colors. The maximum value of any color is 3Eh (64 colors) for a total of 262,144 color selections.

Register Contents on Entry:
AH - 10h
AL - 10h
BX - Color Register Number
CH - Green Value
CL - Blue Value
DH - Red Value

Example:

```
;Set the blue and green registers to various values.
.MODEL SMALL

.STACK ; Use the default stack of 1024 bytes.

.CODE

EXAMPLE PROC FAR

        PUSH    DS          ;Save the original data segment.
        XOR     AX,AX
        PUSH    AX

        MOV     CH,3Eh      ;Original green value.
        MOV     CL,0        ;Original blue value.
LoopIt: MOV     AH,10h      ;Change the screen colors.
        MOV     AL,10h
        MOV     BX,0
        MOV     DH,0
        INT     10h

        XOR     AX,AX       ;Wait to see effects
        INT     16h

        ADD     CL,2        ;Set new screen colors.
        SUB     CH,2
        CMP     CH,0        ;Exit when we see them all.
        JNE     LoopIt

        RET                 ;Return.

EXAMPLE ENDP
END     EXAMPLE
```

Set Block of DAC Registers (Interrupt 10h Service 10h Function 12h)

Use With: MCGA and VGA

This service programs a group of color registers with the red-green-blue color combinations pointed to by the ES:DX combination. It provides extended control over other means of changing the color table values. There are 16 or 64 colors depending on the color page state. Use Interrupt 10h, Service 10h, Subfunction 1Ah to determine the number of colors. As with the set-all-palette-registers function (Interrupt 10h Service 10h Function 2), you must provide enough values to fill the entire table. However, the size of the table required equals (Number of Color Registers to Program (in CX) − Beginning Color Register Number (in BX)) * 3. For example, if you wanted to program registers 30 through 60 in a 64 color table, you would need (60 − 30) * 3 or a 90-byte table.

Register Contents on Entry:
AH - 10h
AL - 12h
BX - Beginning Color Register Number
CX - Number of Color Registers to Program
DX - Offset to a Color Correspondence Table
ES - Segment to a Color Correspondence Table

Example:
```
;Set the upper 32 colors when using a 64 color set.
MOV    AH,10h
MOV    AL,12h
MOV    BX,32
MOV    CX,32
LES    DX,ColorTbl    ;You could use LEA if ES already
INT    10h            ; points to the color table data segment
```

Select Color Subset (Interrupt 10h Service 10h Function 13h)

Use With: VGA

This service selects the color register paging mode or an individual page of color registers. When in the paging mode, setting BH to 0 selects 4 pages of 64 registers; setting BH to 1 selects 16 pages of 16 registers. This gives you a palette of 64 (BH = 0) or 16 (BH = 1) colors.

Note: You must initialize pages 4 through 15 before using them. The display adapter usually defines pages 0 through 3 when you switch page modes. Pages numbering always begins at 0.

Register Contents on Entry (Paging Mode):
AH - 10h
AL - 13h
BH - Paging Mode
BL - 0

Register Contents on Entry (Color Register Selection):
AH - 10h

```
AL - 13h
BH - Page
BL - 1
```

Example:
```
;Select the 16 color mode, then select color page 15.
MOV    AH,10h  ;Select 16 color mode.
MOV    AL,13h
MOV    BH,1
MOV    BL,0
INT    10h

MOV    AH,10h  ;Select page 15 of 16 pages.
MOV    AL,13h
MOV    BH,14
MOV    BL,1
INT    10h
```

Read Individual DAC Register
(Interrupt 10h Service 10h Function 15h)

Use With: MCGA and VGA

This service reads the contents of an individual color register. There are 16 or 64 total colors depending on the color page state. Use Interrupt 10h, Service 10h, Subfunction 1Ah to determine the number of colors. This function returns an invalid result if you specify a register number higher than the available number of colors.

Register Contents on Entry:
AH - 10h
AL - 15h
BX - Color Register Number

Register Contents on Exit:
CH - Green Value
CL - Blue Value
DH - Red Value

Example:
```
;Get the value for color register 15.
MOV    AH,10h
MOV    AL,15h
MOV    BX,15
INT    10h
```

Read Block of DAC Registers
(Interrupt 10h Service 10h Function 17h)

Use With: MCGA and VGA

This service reads the contents of a group of color registers. The buffer used to hold the color correspondence table must allow three bytes for each register read. There are 16 or 64 colors depending on the color page state. Use Interrupt 10h, Service 10h, Subfunction 1Ah to determine the number of colors. As with the read-all-palette-registers function (Interrupt 10h Service 10h Function 9), you must provide a buffer large enough to contain the entire table. However, the size of the buffer required equals (Number of Color Registers to Program (in CX) – Beginning Color Register Number (in BX)) * 3. For example, if you wanted to get the values of registers 30 through 60 in a 64 color table, you would need (60 – 30) * 3 or a 90 byte table.

Register Contents on Entry:
AH - 10h
AL - 17h
BX - Beginning Color Register Number
CX - Number of Color Registers to Read
DX - Offset to a Color Correspondence Table
ES - Segment to a Color Correspondence Table

Register Contents on Exit:
DX - Offset to a Color Correspondence Table
ES - Segment to a Color Correspondence Table

Example:
```
;Get the values of color registers 32 through 48.
MOV    AH,10h
MOV    AL,17h
MOV    BX,32
MOV    CX,16
LES    DX,ColorTbl    ;You could use LEA if ES already
INT    10h            ; points to the color table data segment.
```

Read Color Page State
(Interrupt 10h Service 10h Function 1Ah)
Use With: VGA

This service returns the current color page and paging mode. The paging mode values equal 4 pages of 64 registers when BL returns 0, and 16 pages of 16 registers when BL returns 1.

Register Contents on Entry:
AH - 10h
AL - 1Ah

Register Contents on Exit:
BH - Color Page
BL - Paging Mode

Example:
```
;Retrieve the color page state.
MOV    AH,10h
MOV    AL,1Ah
INT    10h
```

Sum DAC Registers to Gray Shades (Interrupt 10h Service 10h Function 1Bh)

Use With: MCGA and VGA

This service changes the color values in one or more color registers into their gray scale equivalents. There are 16 or 64 colors depending on the color page state. Use Interrupt 10h, Service 10h, Subfunction 1Ah to determine the number of colors.

Note: You must initialize pages 4 through 15 before using them. Summing and using an undefined page results in a blank or otherwise unreadable display. The display adapter usually defines pages 0 through 3 when you switch page modes. Page numbering always begins at 0.

Register Contents on Entry:
AH - 10h
AL - 1Bh
BX - Beginning Color Register Number
CX - Number of Color Registers to Program

Example:
```
;Sum all the color registers for a 64 color set.
MOV    AH,10h
MOV    AL,1Bh
MOV    BX,0
MOV    CX,64
INT    10h
```

Use Alpha Load (Interrupt 10h Service 11h Function 0)

Use With: EGA, MCGA, and VGA

This service loads a user-defined font into character generator RAM. You must supply at least five pieces of information to use this function. This information includes character size, storage area on the display adapter, number of characters in the font, ASCII code of the first character, and storage area on the host. Character size is the number of bytes used by each character (usually 8, 14, or 16). Each character must use the same amount of memory. You identify the display adapter storage area by its predefined number (block number). There are 4 block areas for fonts on an EGA or 8 areas for a VGA. Block numbers begin at 0 and end at either 3 or 7. Use the set block specifier function (Interrupt 10h Service 11h Function 3) to select the block if you do not use block 0 (default). Point to the host adapter storage area using a combination of ES and BP. Always save BP on the stack.

Note: You must use this function immediately after a mode change. Using the function at any other time produces unpredictable results. Execute the set block specifier function (Interrupt 10h Service 11h Function 3) immediately after this function to load the font on a MCGA display. This function affects alphanumeric modes only, see interrupt 10h service 11h, function 20h-24h for graphics mode functions.

Register Contents on Entry:
AH - 11h
AL - 0
BH - Bytes Per Character
BL - Memory Block
CX - Number of Characters in Font
DX - ASCII Code of First Character in Font
BP - Offset of Font Table
ES - Segment of Font Table

Example:
```
;Load an 8 x 8 font into block 1.
MOV    AH,11
XOR    AL,AL
MOV    BH,8
MOV    BL,1
MOV    CX,94
MOV    DX,' '
PUSH   BP
LES    BP,FontTbl
INT    10h
POP    BP
```

ROM Monochrome Set
(Interrupt 10h Service 11h Function 1)

Use With: EGA and VGA

This service loads the default 8x14 ROM font table into the specified character generator RAM block. There are 4 block areas for fonts on an EGA or 8 areas for a VGA. Block numbers begin at 0 and end at either 3 or 7. Use the set block specifier function (Interrupt 10h Service 11h Function 3) to select the block if you do not use block 0 (default).

Register Contents on Entry:
AH - 11h
AL - 1
BL - Memory Block

Example:
```
;Load the 8 x 14 ROM font into block 0 (default).
MOV    AH,11
MOV    AL,1
MOV    BL,0
INT    10h
```

ROM Double Dot Set (Interrupt 10h Service 11h Function 2)

Use With: EGA, MCGA, and VGA

This service loads the default 8x8 ROM font table into the specified character generator RAM block. There are 4 block areas for fonts on an EGA or 8 areas for a VGA. Block numbers begin at 0 and end at either 3 or 7. Use the set block specifier function (Interrupt 10h Service 11h Function 3) to select the block if you do not use block 0 (default).

Register Contents on Entry:
AH - 11h
AL - 2
BL - Memory Block

Example:
```
;Load the 8 x 8 ROM font into block 0 (default).
MOV    AH,11
MOV    AL,2
MOV    BL,0
INT    10h
```

Set Block Specifier (Interrupt 10h Service 11h Function 3)

Use With: EGA, MCGA, and VGA

This service chooses the character block selected by bit 3 of the character attribute bytes in text display modes. On the EGA and MCGA, bits 0 and 1 of the character generator block select code contain the character block selected when bit 3 equals 0; bits 2 and 3 contain the character block selected when bit 3 equals 1. This provides a selection of four font storage areas. On the VGA, bits 0, 1, and 4 of the character generator block select code containing the character block selected when bit 3 equals 0; bits 2, 3, and 5 contain the character block selected when bit 3 equals 1. This provides a selection of eight font storage areas.

Register Contents on Entry:
AH - 11h
AL - 3
BL - Character Generator Block Select Code

Example:
```
;Select block 7 on a VGA display.
MOV     AH,11
MOV     AL,3
MOV     BL,7
INT     10h
```

ROM 16 Row Set (Interrupt 10h Service 11h Function 4)

Use With: MCGA and VGA

This service loads the default 8x16 ROM font table into the specified character generator RAM block. There are 4 block areas for fonts on an EGA, or 8 areas for a VGA. Block numbers begin at 0 and end at either 3 or 7. Use the set-block-specifier function (Interrupt 10h Service 11h Function 3) to select the block if you do not use block 0 (default).

Register Contents on Entry:
AH - 11h
AL - 4
BL - Memory Block

Example:
```
;Load the 8 x 16 ROM font into block 0 (default).
MOV     AH,11
MOV     AL,4
MOV     BL,0
INT     10h
```

User Alpha Load (Interrupt 10h Service 11h Function 10h)

Use With: EGA, MCGA, and VGA

This service loads a user-defined font into character generator RAM. You must supply at least five pieces of information to use this function. This information includes character size, storage area on the display adapter, number of characters in the font, ASCII code of the first character, and storage area on the host. Character size is the number of bytes used by each character (usually 8, 14, or 16). Each character must use the same amount of memory. You identify the display adapter storage area by its predefined number (block number). There are 4 block areas for fonts on an EGA or 8 areas for a VGA. Block numbers begin at 0 and end at either 3 or 7. Use the set-block-specifier function (Interrupt 10h Service 11h Function 3) to select the block if you do not use block 0 (default). Point to the host adapter storage area using a combination of ES and BP. Always save BP on the stack.

Note: You must use this function immediately after a mode change. Using the function at any other time produces unpredictable results. Never use this function with a MCGA display, use interrupt 10h, service

10h, function 0 instead. The MCGA reserves function 10h for future purpose and automatically defaults to function 0. This function affects alphanumeric modes only, see interrupt 10h service 11h, function 20h-24h for graphics mode functions.

Register Contents on Entry:
AH - 11h
AL - 10h
BH - Bytes Per Character
BL - Memory Block
CX - Number of Characters in Font
DX - ASCII Code of First Character in Font
BP - Offset of Font Table
ES - Segment of Font Table

Example:
```
;Load an 8 x 8 font into block 1.
MOV    AH,11
XOR    AL,AL
MOV    BH,8
MOV    BL,1
MOV    CX,94
MOV    DX,' '
PUSH   BP
LES    BP,FontTbl
INT    10h
POP    BP
```

ROM Monochrome Set
(Interrupt 10h Service 11h Function 11h)

Use With: EGA and VGA

This service loads the default 8x14 ROM font table into the specified character generator RAM block. Use this service only after a mode set with page 0 active. There are 4 block areas for fonts on an EGA or 8 areas for a VGA. Block numbers begin at 0 and end at either 3 or 7. Use the set block specifier function (Interrupt 10h Service 11h Function 3) to select the block if you do not use block 0 (default)

Register Contents on Entry:
AH - 11h
AL - 11h
BL - Memory Block

Example:
```
;Load the 8 x 14 ROM font into block 0 (default).
MOV    AH,11
MOV    AL,11
```

```
MOV    BL,0
INT    10h
```

ROM Double Dot Set
(Interrupt 10h Service 11h Function 12h)

Use With: EGA, MCGA, and VGA

This service loads the default 8x8 ROM font table into the specified character generator RAM block. Use this service only after a mode set with page 0 active. There are 4 block areas for fonts on an EGA or 8 areas for a VGA. Block numbers begin at 0 and end at either 3 or 7. Use the set block specifier function (Interrupt 10h Service 11h Function 3) to select the block if you do not use block 0 (default).

Register Contents on Entry:
AH - 11h
AL - 12h
BL - Memory Block

Example:
```
;Load the 8 x 8 ROM font into block 0 (default)
MOV    AH,11
MOV    AL,4
MOV    BL,0
INT    10h
```

ROM 16 Row Set (Interrupt 10h Service 11h Function 14h)

Use With: MCGA and VGA

This service loads the default 8x16 ROM font table into the specified character generator RAM block. Use this service only after a mode set with page 0 active. There are 4 block areas for fonts on an EGA or 8 areas for a VGA. Block numbers begin at 0 and end at either 3 or 7. Use the set block specifier function (Interrupt 10h Service 11h Function 3) to select the block if you do not use block 0 (default).

Register Contents on Entry:
AH - 11h
AL - 14h
BL - Memory Block

Example:
```
;Load the 8 x 16 ROM font into block 0 (default).
MOV    AH,11
MOV    AL,4
MOV    BL,0
INT    10h
```

User Graphics Characters—8x8
(Interrupt 10h Service 11h Function 20h)

Use With: EGA, MCGA, and VGA

This service sets the interrupt 1Fh pointer to the user font table. The adapter uses the values contained in the table for characters 80h through FFh in graphics modes 4 through 6. These characters provide a compatibility mode extended ASCII character set. Unlike the alphanumeric character set, you may only load one graphics character set at a time. A set consists of both standard and extended ASCII characters. Use this function only after a mode set. Using this function at any other time produces unpredictable results.

Register Contents on Entry:
AH - 11h
AL - 20h
BP - Offset of Font Table
ES - Segment of Font Table

Example:
```
;Load the extended ASCII character set.
MOV    AH,11h
MOV    AL,20h
PUSH   BP
LES    BP,FontTbl
INT    10h
POP    BP
```

User Graphics Characters
(Interrupt 10h Service 11h Function 21h)

Use With: EGA, MCGA, and VGA

This service points the interrupt 43h vector to the user font table and updates the video ROM BIOS data area. The character rows specifier shows the number of character rows per screen. A value of 1 indicates 14 rows, 2 indicates 25 rows, and 3 indicates 43 rows. When the number of rows does not match any of these predefined values, BL contains 0 and DL contains the number of character rows. Unlike the alphanumeric character set, you may only load one graphics character set at a time. A set consists of both standard and extended ASCII characters. Use this function only after a mode set. Using this function at any other time produces unpredictable results.

Register Contents on Entry:
AH - 11h
AL - 21h
BL - Character Rows Specifier

CX - Bytes Per Character
DL - Character Rows Per Screen (When BL = 0)
BP - Offset of User Font Table
ES - Segment of User Font Table

Example:

```
;Load an 8 x 8 character set to provide 43 rows of data
; on screen.
MOV    AH,11h
MOV    AL,21h
MOV    BL,3
MOV    CX,8
PUSH   BP
LES    BP,FontTbl
INT    10h
POP    BP
```

ROM 8x14 Character Set Select
(Interrupt 10h Service 11h Function 22h)

Use With: EGA, MCGA, and VGA

This service points the interrupt 43h vector to the default 8x14 ROM font and updates the video ROM BIOS data area. The character rows specifier shows the number of character rows per screen. A value of 1 indicates 14 rows, 2 indicates 25 rows, and 3 indicates 43 rows. When the number of rows does not match any of these predefined values, BL contains 0 and DL contains the number of character rows. Unlike the alphanumeric character set, you may only load one graphics character set at a time. A set consists of both standard and extended ASCII characters. Use this function only after a mode set. Using this function at any other time produces unpredictable results.

Register Contents on Entry:
AH - 11h
AL - 22h
BL - Character Rows Specifier
DL - Character Rows Per Screen (When BL = 0)

Example:

```
; Load an 8 x 14 character set to provide 25 rows of
; data on screen.
MOV    AH,11h
MOV    AL,22h
MOV    BL,2
INT    10h
```

ROM 8x8 Character Set Select
(Interrupt 10h Service 11h Function 23h)

Use With: EGA, MCGA, and VGA

This service points the interrupt 43h vector to the default 8x8 ROM font and updates the video ROM BIOS data area. The character rows specifier shows the number of character rows per screen. A value of 1 indicates 14 rows, 2 indicates 25 rows, and 3 indicates 43 rows. When the number of rows does not match any of these predefined values, BL contains 0 and DL contains the number of character rows. Unlike the alphanumeric character set, you may only load one graphics character set at a time. A set consists of both standard and extended ASCII characters. Use this function only after a mode set. Using this function at any other time produces unpredictable results.

    Register Contents on Entry:
    AH - 11h
    AL - 23h
    BL - Character Rows Specifier
    DL - Character Rows Per Screen (When BL = 0)

Example:

```
;Load an 8 x 8 character set to provide 43 rows of
; data on screen.
MOV    AH,11h
MOV    AL,23h
MOV    BL,3
INT    10h
```

ROM 8x16 Character Set Select
(Interrupt 10h Service 11h Function 24h)

Use With: EGA, MCGA, and VGA

This service points the interrupt 43h vector to the default 8x16 ROM font and updates the video ROM BIOS data area. The character rows specifier shows the number of character rows per screen. A value of 1 indicates 14 rows, 2 indicates 25 rows, and 3 indicates 43 rows. When the number of rows does not match any of these predefined values, BL contains 0 and DL contains the number of character rows. Unlike the alphanumeric character set, you may only load one graphics character set at a time. A set consists of both standard and extended ASCII characters. Use this function only after a mode set. Using this function at any other time produces unpredictable results.

    Register Contents on Entry:
    AH - 11h

AL - 24h
BL - Character Rows Specifier
DL - Character Rows Per Screen (When BL = 0)

Example:
```
; Load an 8 x 16 character set to provide 25 rows of
; data on screen.
MOV   AH,11h
MOV   AL,24h
MOV   BL,2
INT   10h
```

Return Character Set Information
(Interrupt 10h Service 11h Function 30h)

Use With: EGA, MCGA, and VGA

This service returns a pointer to the font character definition table. It also returns the number of bytes per character for that font. Because this function destroys the contents of BP, always push BP on the stack. Restore BP before you perform any other operations.

Register Contents on Entry:
AH - 11h
AL - 30h
BH - Font Code
   0 - Current Interrupt 1Fh Contents
   1 - Current Interrupt 43h Contents
   2 - 8x14 ROM Font
   3 - 8x8 ROM Font (Characters 00h - 7Fh)
   4 - 8x8 ROM Font (Characters 80h - FFh)
   5 - Alternate 9x14 ROM Font
   6 - 8x16 ROM Font
   7 - Alternate 9x16 ROM Font

Register Contents on Exit:
CX - Bytes Per Character
DL - Character Rows on Screen
BP - Offset of Font Table
ES - Segment of Font Table

Example: ; Get the 8 x 8 ROM Font characteristics.
```
MOV    AH,11h
MOV    AL,30h
MOV    BH,3
PUSH   BP
INT    10h
             ; Look at data.
```

```
POP    BP          ;Before performing any other operations.
```

Return Memory Allocation Information
(Interrupt 10h Service 12h Function 10h)

Use With: EGA and VGA

This service returns the active subsystem memory and display configuration information.

Register Contents on Entry:
AH - 12h
BL - 10h

Register Contents on Exit:
BH - Display Type
    0 - Color
    1 - Monochrome
BL - Memory Installed (EGA Only)
    0 - 64K
    1 - 128K
    2 - 192K
    3 - 256K
CH - Feature Control Register Bits
    0 - Output Bit 0, Input Status Bit 5
    1 - Output Bit 0, Input Status Bit 6
    2 - Output Bit 1, Input Status Bit 5
    3 - Output Bit 1, Input Status Bit 6
    4 through 7 - Not Used
CL - Switch Settings (One Bit Per Switch)
    0 - Configuration Switch 1
    1 - Configuration Switch 2
    2 - Configuration Switch 3
    3 - Configuration Switch 4
    4 through 7 - Not Used

Example:

```
;Get the current subsystem memory and display
; configuration information.
MOV    AH,12h
MOV    BL,10h
INT    10h
```

Select Alternate Print Screen Routine
(Interrupt 10h Service 12h Function 20h)

Use With: EGA and VGA

This service selects an alternate print screen routine. Use this service when the screen length is not 25 lines. This routine will not print graphics screens.

Register Contents on Entry:
AH - 12h
BL - 20h

Example:
```
;Output the current display to the printer.
MOV   AH,12h
MOV   BL,20h
INT   21h
```

Select Scan Lines for Alpha Mode
(Interrupt 10h Service 12h Function 30h)

Use With: EGA and VGA

This service selects the number of scan lines used for text modes. The selection takes effect only after a display selection interrupt (10h function 0).

Register Contents on Entry:
AH - 12h
AL - Scan Line Code
     0 - 200 Lines
     1 - 350 Lines
     2 - 400 Lines
BL - 30h

Register Contents on Exit:
AL - 12h When VGA is Active
AL - 0 When VGA is Not Active

Example:
```
;Set the display to 350 lines (Standard EGA).
MOV   AH,12h
MOV   AL,1
MOV   BL,30h
INT   21h
```

Select Default Palette Loading
(Interrupt 10h Service 12h Function 31h)

Use With: MCGA and VGA

This service enables/disables default palette loading when a video mode change occurs. An EGA display adapter always resets the palette after a mode change or reset. Disabling default palette loading allows a

VGA or MCGA display adapter to retain special palette settings. Unsuccessful completion of this function means the display adapter is not VGA or MCGA. Failure also occurs with incompatible or failed-display adapters.

Register Contents on Entry:
AH - 12h
AL - 0 to Enable/1 to Disable Default Palette Loading
BL - 31h

Register Contents on Exit:
AL - 12h For Successful Completion

Example:
```
;Disable default palette loading.
MOV     AH,12h
MOV     AL,1
MOV     BL,31h
INT     10h
```

Video Enable/Disable
(Interrupt 10h Service 12h Function 32h)

Use With: MCGA and VGA

This service enables/disables CPU access to the video adapters I/O ports and video refresh buffer. Use this service to protect the display adapter memory and registers from accidental overwrite during critical drawing operations. Both areas are accessible as a default. This also prevents memory resident programs from interfering with normal display adapter functions. The EGA always allows access to the video adapters I/O ports and video refresh buffer. Unsuccessful completion of this function means the display adapter is not VGA or MCGA. Failure also occurs with incompatible or failed-display adapters.

Register Contents on Entry:
AH - 12h
AL - 0 to Enable/1 to Disable Access
BL - 32h

Register Contents on Exit:
AL - 12h For Successful Completion

Example:
```
;Enable CPU access to the video adapters I/O ports and
; video refresh buffer.
MOV     AH,12h
XOR     AL,AL
MOV     BL,32
INT     10h
```

Summing to Gray Shades
(Interrupt 10h Service 12h Function 33h)

Use With: MCGA and VGA

This service enables/disables grayscale summing for the active display. This prevents memory resident programs from interfering with normal display adapter functions. When you enable summing, the display adapter uses a combination of 30% red, 59% green, and 11% blue intensity to simulate gray scales. Unsuccessful completion of this function means the display adapter is not VGA or MCGA. Failure also occurs with incompatible or failed-display adapters.

Register Contents on Entry:
AH - 12h
AL - 0 to Enable/1 to Disable Gray-Scale Summing
BL - 33h

Register Contents on Exit:
AL - 12h For Successful Completion

Example:

```
;Disable gray-scale summing.
MOV    AH,12h
MOV    AL,1
MOV    BL,33h
INT    10h
```

Cursor Emulation (Interrupt 10h Service 12h Function 34h)

Use With: VGA

This service enables/disables cursor emulation. When enabled, cursor emulation automatically re-sizes the cursor to correspond to current character dimensions. When disabled, allows you to use actual VGA lines for cursor size settings. Unsuccessful completion of this function means the display adapter is not VGA. Failure also occurs with incompatible or failed display adapters.

Register Contents on Entry:
AH - 12h
AL - 0 to Enable/1 to Disable Cursor Emulation
BL - 34h

Register Contents on Exit:
AL - 12h For Successful Completion

Example:

```
;Enable cursor emulation.
MOV    AH,12h
XOR    AL,AL
```

```
MOV    BL,34h
INT    10h
```

Display Switch (Interrupt 10h Service 12h Function 35h)

Use With: MCGA and VGA

This service allows selection of one or two video adapters when port addresses or memory usage conflicts occur. Use this function to switch between an adapter installed on the motherboard and a high-resolution adapter installed in an expansion slot. To use this function correctly, you must set up a 128 KByte video buffer. The function reroutes all calls to the expansion slot display adapter video RAM to this buffer. Unsuccessful completion of this function means the display adapter is not VGA or MCGA. Failure also occurs with incompatible or failed display adapters.

Register Contents on Entry:
AH - 12h
AL - Switching Function
    0 - Disable Initial Video Adapter
    1 - Enable System Board Video Adapter
    2 - Disable Active Video Adapter
    3 - Enable Inactive Video Adapter
BL - 35h
DX - Offset of 128 KByte Buffer (Function 0, 2, or 3)
ES - Segment of 128 KByte Buffer (Function 0, 2, or 3)

Register Contents on Exit:
AL - 12h For Successful Completion
DX - Offset of 128 KByte Buffer (Function 0, 2, or 3)
ES - Segment of 128 KByte Buffer (Function 0, 2, or 3)

Example:
```
;Select the system board video adapter.
MOV    AH,12h
MOV    AL,1
MOV    BL,35h
LES    DX,VideoBuf
INT    10h
```

Screen Off/On (Interrupt 10h Service 12h Function 36h)

Use With: VGA

This service enables/disables video refresh for the active display. This allows the host adapter to update video memory without distorting the display. Unsuccessful completion of this function means the display adapter is not VGA. Failure also occurs with incompatible or failed display adapters.

Register Contents on Entry:
AH - 12h
AL - 0 to Enable/1 to Disable Video Refresh
BL - 36h

Register Contents on Exit:
AL - 12h for Successful Completion

Example:
```
;Disable, then enable video refresh.
MOV   AH,12h   ;Disable video refresh.
MOV   AL,1
MOV   BL,36h
INT   10h
      .                ;Perform any video updates.
      .
      .
MOV   AH,12h   ;Enable video refresh.
MOV   AL,0
MOV   BL,36h
INT   10h
```

Write String (Interrupt 10h Service 13h)

Use With: MDA, CGA, EGA, MCGA, and VGA

This service transfers a string to the active display video buffer, starting at a specified position. TABLE 7-3 shows the correlation between video mode, display adapter type, and the number of available pages. Because this function changes the contents of BP, you must save BP on the stack before using this function.

Register Contents on Entry:
AH - 13h
AL - Write Mode
        0 - Attribute in BL. String contains character codes only. Cursor position does not update after write.
        1 - Attribute in BL. String contains character codes only. Cursor position updates after write (1 position).
        2 - String contains alternating character codes and attribute bytes. Cursor position does not update after write.
        3 - String contains alternating character codes and attribute bytes. Cursor position updates after write (2 positions).
BH - Video Page Number
BL - Attribute (Write Modes 0 and 1)
CX - Length of Character String
DH - Starting Row
DL - Starting Column

BP - Offset of String
ES - Segment of String

Example:

```
;Display a string using special formatting attributes.
MOV    AH,13h
MOV    AL,3
XOR    BX,BX
MOV    CX,20        ;String 20 characters long.
MOV    DH,12
MOV    DL,29        ;Center the string.
PUSH   BP
LES    BP,DispSTR
INT    10h
POP    BP
```

Read Display Combination Code
(Interrupt 10h Service 1Ah Function 0)

Use With: PS/2

This service returns a code describing the installed video display adapter(s). TABLE 7-5 contains a list of applicable display adapters. If this function fails (does not return 1Ah in AL), then the host machine is not a PS/2 or a hardware failure occurred.

Table 7-5   PS/2 Display Adapter Codes

Code	Video Subsystem Type
00h	No Display
01h	MDA with 5151 Monitor
02h	CGA with 5153 or 5154 Monitor
03h	Reserved
04h	EGA with 5153 or 5154 Monitor
05h	EGA with 5151 Monitor
06h	PGA with 5175 Monitor
07h	VGA with Analog Monochrome Monitor
08h	VGA with Analog Color Monitor
09h	Reserved
0Ah	MCGA with Digital Color Monitor
0Bh	MCGA with Analog Monochrome Monitor
0Ch	MCGA with Analog Color Monitor
0Dh - FEh	Reserved

Register Contents on Entry:
AH - 1Ah
AL - 0

Register Contents on Exit:
AL - 1Ah For Successful Completion
BH - Inactive Display Code
BL - Active Display Code

Example:
```
;Get the installed video adapter configuration.
MOV    AH,1Ah
XOR    AL,AL
INT    10h
```

Write Display Combination Code
(Interrupt 10h Service 1Ah Function 1)

Use With: PS/2

This service writes a code describing the installed video display adapter(s) to the ROM BIOS. TABLE 7-5 contains a list of applicable display adapters. If this function fails (does not return 1Ah in AL), then the host machine is not a PS/2 or a hardware failure occurred.

Register Contents on Entry:
AH - 1Ah
AL - 1
BH - Inactive Display Code
BL - Active Display Code

Register Contents on Exit:
AL - 1Ah For Successful Completion

Example:
```
;Set a VGA with an analog color monitor active, and
; no monitor inactive.
MOV    AH, 1Ah
MOV    AL,1
XOR    BH,BH
MOV    BL,8
INT    10h
```

Return Functionality/State Information
(Interrupt 10h Service 1Bh)

Use With: PS/2

This service obtains information about the current display mode in a 64-byte buffer. TABLE 7-6 contains a listing of the data returned in the buffer. Bytes 0 through 3 contain a DWORD pointer to a table containing the video adapter and monitor capabilities. TABLE 7-7 contains a listing of the functionality data. If this function fails (does not return 1Bh in AL), then the host machine is not a PS/2 or a hardware failure occurred.

Table 7-6   PS/2 Video Display Mode Data

Byte	Contents
00h - 03h	Pointer to Functionality Information (Table 14-7)
04h	Current Video Mode
05h - 06h	Number of Character Columns
07h - 08h	Length of Video Refresh Buffer
09h - 0Ah	Display Upper Left Corner Starting Address
0Bh - 1Ah	Cursor position for video pages 0 - 7. First byte contains X coordinate. Second byte contains Y coordinate.
1Bh	Cursor Starting Line
1Ch	Cursor Ending Line
1Dh	Active Video Page Number
1Eh - 1Fh	Adapter Base Port Address
20h	Current Setting of Register 3B8h (Monochrome) or 3D8h (Color)
21h	Current Setting of Register 3B9h (Monochrome) or 3D9h (Color)
22h	Number of Character Rows
23h - 24h	Character Height in Scan Lines
25h	Active Display Code (Table 14-5)
26h	Inactive Display Code (Table 14-5)
27h - 28h	Number of Displayable Colors
29h	Number of Display Pages
2Ah	Number of Scan Lines
	00h - 200 Scan Lines
	01h - 350 Scan Lines
	02h - 400 Scan Lines
	03h - 480 Scan Lines
	04h through FFh - Reserved
2Bh	Primary Character Block
2Ch	Secondary Character Block
2Dh	Miscellaneous State Information (Bits)
	0 - 1 when all modes on all displays active.
	1 - 1 if gray-scale summing active.
	2 - 1 if monochrome display attached.
	3 - 1 when default palette loading disabled.
	4 - 1 if cursor emulation active.
	5 - 1 for Intensity/0 for Blink
	6 through 7 - Reserved
2Eh - 30h	Reserved
31h	Video Memory Available (EGA Only)
	0 - 64K
	1 - 128K
	2 - 192K
	3 - 256K
32h	Save Pointer State Information (Bits)
	0 - 1 when 512 character set active.
	1 - 1 when dynamic save area active.
	2 - 1 when alpha font override active.
	3 - 1 when graphics font override active.
	4 - 1 when palette override active.
	5 - 1 when DCC extension active.
	6 through 7 - Reserved
33h - 3Fh	Reserved

Table 7-7   PS/2 Display Adapter Functionality Information

Byte	Bit	Meanings
00h	0	1 when video mode 0 supported
	1	1 when video mode 1 supported
	2	1 when video mode 2 supported
	3	1 when video mode 3 supported
	4	1 when video mode 4 supported
	5	1 when video mode 5 supported
	6	1 when video mode 6 supported
	7	1 when video mode 7 supported
01h	0	1 when video mode 8 supported
	1	1 when video mode 9 supported
	2	1 when video mode Ah supported
	3	1 when video mode Bh supported
	4	1 when video mode Ch supported
	5	1 when video mode Dh supported
	6	1 when video mode Eh supported
	7	1 when video mode Fh supported
02h	0	1 when video mode 10h supported
	1	1 when video mode 11h supported
	2	1 when video mode 12h supported
	3	1 when video mode 13h supported
	4 - 7	Reserved
03h - 06h		Reserved
07h	0	1 if 200 text mode scan lines available
	1	1 if 350 text mode scan lines available
	2	1 if 400 text mode scan lines available
	3	Reserved
08h		Character Blocks Available in Text Modes
09h		Maximum Number of Active Character Blocks in Text Modes
0Ah	0	1 when all modes on all displays active.
	1	1 if gray-scale summing active.
	2	1 if character font loading available.
	3	1 when default palette loading available.
	4	1 if cursor emulation active.
	5	1 if EGA 64 color palette available.
	6	1 if color register loading available.
	7	1 if color register paging mode select available.
0Bh	0	1 if light pen available.
	1	1 if save/restore video state available.
	2	1 if background intensity/blinking control available.

Table 7-7   Continued.

Byte	Bit	Meanings
	3	1 if get/set display combination code available.
	4 - 7	Reserved
OCh - ODh		Reserved
OEh	0	1 if display adapter support 512 character sets.
	1	1 when dynamic save area available.
	2	1 if alpha font override available.
	3	1 if graphics font override available.
	4	1 if palette override available.
	5	1 if display combination code extension available.
	6 - 7	Reserved
OFh		Reserved

Register Contents on Entry:
AH - 1Bh
BX - 0 (Implementation Type)
DI - Offset to a 64-byte Buffer
ES - Segment of a 64-byte Buffer

Register Contents on Exit:
AL - 1Bh For Successful Completion

Example:
```
;Get the functionality and state information.
MOV   AH,1Bh
XOR   BX,BX
LES   DI,VBuff
```

Get Video State Buffer
(Interrupt 10h Service 1Ch Function 0)

Use With: PS/2 VGA

This service obtains the memory requirements to save the current digital-to-analog (DAC) state and color registers, ROM BIOS video driver area, or video hardware state to RAM (as requested below). If this function fails (does not return 1Ch in AL), then the host machine is not a PS/2 with a VGA or a hardware failure occurred.

Register Contents on Entry:
AH - 1Ch
AL - 0

CX - Requested States (Bits)
   0 - Save Video Hardware State
   1 - Save Video BIOS Data Area
   2 - Save Video DAC State and Color Registers
   3 through 15 - Reserved
BX - Offset of Buffer
ES - Segment of Buffer

Register Contents on Exit:
AL - 1Ch For Successful Completion
BX - Number of Required 64-byte Blocks

Example:

```
;Obtain the amount of memory required to save the DAC
; state and color registers.
MOV    AH,1Ch
XOR    AL,AL
MOV    CX,2
LES    BX,VBuff
INT    10h
```

Save Video State (Interrupt 10h Service 1Ch Function 1)

Use With: PS/2 VGA

This service saves the current digital-to-analog (DAC) state and color registers, ROM BIOS video driver area, or video hardware state to RAM. If this function fails (does not return 1Ch in AL), then the host machine is not a PS/2 with a VGA or a hardware failure occurred.

Register Contents on Entry:
AH - 1Ch
AL - 1
CX - Requested States (Bits)
   0 - Save Video Hardware State
   1 - Save Video BIOS Data Area
   2 - Save Video DAC State and Color Registers
   3 through 15 - Reserved
BX - Offset of Buffer
ES - Segment of Buffer

Register Contents on Exit:
AL - 1Ch For Successful Completion

Example:

```
;Save the current BIOS data area information.
MOV    AH,1Ch
MOV    AL,1
MOV    CX,1
LES    BX,VBuff
INT    10h
```

Restore Video State (Interrupt 10h Service 1Ch Function 2)

Use With: PS/2 VGA

This service restores the current digital-to-analog (DAC) state and color registers, ROM BIOS video driver area, or video hardware state to RAM. If this function fails (does not return 1Ch in AL), then the host machine is not a PS/2 with a VGA or a hardware failure occurred.

Register Contents on Entry:
AH - 1Ch
AL - 2
CX - Requested States (Bits)
　　0 - Restore Video Hardware State
　　1 - Restore Video BIOS Data Area
　　2 - Restore Video DAC State and Color Registers
　　3 through 15 - Reserved
BX - Offset of Buffer
ES - Segment of Buffer

Register Contents on Exit:
AL - 1Ch For Successful Completion

Example:
```
;Restore the current BIOS data area information.
MOV    AH,1Ch
MOV    AL,2
MOV    CS,1
LES    BX,VBuff
INT    10h
```

Note: The following functions show you how to implement the VESA standard for Super VGA functions. Not all manufacturers adhere to these standards. Always check your manufacturer manual before assuming you can use these functions. Another compatibility check is using function 0 to return Super VGA information. Every Super VGA function returns the following status information in AX upon return from the interrupt. If AL equals 4Fh, the display adapter supports the specified function. Otherwise, the display adapter does not support the function. If AH contains 0, then the function was successful. If AH contains 1, then the function was not successful.

Return Super VGA Information
(Interrupt 10h, Service 4Fh, Function 0)

This function returns information about the capabilities of the Super VGA environment supported by the manufacturer. The function returns this information in a 256-byte buffer. TABLE 7-16 at the end of this chapter contains a complete description of this buffer. If a VGA with extended capability fails to provide this information, it does not adhere to the VESA standard.

Register Contents on Entry:
AH - 4Fh
AL - 0
DI - Offset of Data Buffer
ES - Segment of Data Buffer

Register Contents on Exit:
AX - Status

Example:
```
;Get the Super VGA capability information.
MOV    AH, 4Fh
XOR    AL,AL
LES    DI,VBuff
INT    10h
```

Return Super VGA Mode Information (Interrupt 10h, Service 4Fh, Function 1)

This function returns information about a specific Super VGA mode. Because some manufacturers add modes not directly supported by the Super VGA specification, you can use this function to obtain programming information for the extended mode. The function returns this information in a 256-byte buffer. TABLE 7-17 at the end of this chapter contains a complete description of this buffer. If a VGA with extended capability fails to provide this information, it does not adhere to the VESA standard.

Register Contents on Entry:
AH - 4Fh
AL - 1
CX - Mode Number
DI - Offset of Data Buffer
ES - Segment of Data Buffer

Register Contents on Exit:
AX - Status

Example:
```
;Get information about Super VGA mode 101h.
MOV    AH,4Fh
MOV    AL,1
MOV    CX,101h
LES    DI,VBuff
INT    10h
```

Set Super VGA Video Mode
(Interrupt 10h, Service 4Fh, Function 2)

This function performs all the setup required to use a Super VGA mode. It initializes all registers and memory required to use the specified mode. If the mode change fails, the function leaves the environment unchanged and exits with an error code.

Register Contents on Entry:
AH - 4Fh
AL - 2
BX - Video Mode
    Bits 0-14 - Video Mode Number
    Bit 15 - Clear Memory Flag (0 = Clear Memory)

Register Contents on Exit:
AX - Status

Example:
```
;Set Super VGA video mode 102h without clearing memory.
MOV    AH,4Fh
MOV    AL,2
MOV    BX,102h
INT    10h
```

Return Current Video Mode
(Interrupt 10h, Service 4Fh, Function 3)

Returns the VESA standard or OEM defined Super VGA mode number. Unlike the standard video mode read function, this function does not return the status of the memory clear bit. Use the get-current-video-state function (Interrupt 10h Service Fh) to obtain this information.

Register Contents on Entry:
AH - 4Fh
AL - 3

Register Contents on Exit:
AX - Status
BX - Current Video Mode

Example:
```
;Get the current Super VGA video mode.
MOV    AH,4Fh
MOV    AL,3
INT    10h
```

Note: The services provided by function 4 are a superset of the standard VGA BIOS function 1Ch described previously. The following paragraphs describe all three subfunctions.

Return Save/Restore State Buffer Size
(Interrupt 10h, Service 4Fh, Function 4, Subfunction 0)

This function obtains the size buffer required to store any of four types of information. Each state occupies a separate bit of the request register (CX). You can, therefore, request the buffer size required to store any or all states. Always allocate buffer memory in blocks of 64 bytes.

Register Contents on Entry:
AH - 4Fh
AL - 4
DL - 0
CX - Requested States
    Bit 0 - Video Hardware State
    Bit 1 - Video BIOS State
    Bit 2 - Video DAC State
    Bit 3 - Super VGA State
    Bits 4 through 15 - Set to Zero

Register Contents on Exit:
AX - Status
BX - Number of 64-byte Blocks Required

Example:

```
;Get the memory required to store the hardware and DAC states.
MOV     AH,4Fh
MOV     AL,4
MOV     DL,0
MOV     CX,0000000000000101b
INT     10h
```

Save Super VGA Video State
(Interrupt 10h, Service 4Fh, Function 4, Subfunction 1)

This function stores the requested states in a buffer. Use subfunction 0 to determine the size buffer required to save the required state information.

Register Contents on Entry:
AH - 4Fh
AL - 4
DL - 1
CX - Requested States
    Bit 0 - Video Hardware State
    Bit 1 - Video BIOS State

Bit 2 - Video DAC State
Bit 3 - Super VGA State
Bits 4 through 15 - Set to Zero
BX - State Buffer Offset
ES - State Buffer Segment

Register Contents on Exit:
AX - Status

Example:

```
;Save the current hardware and BIOS states.
MOV    AH,4Fh
MOV    AL,4
MOV    DL,1
MOV    CX,0000000000000011b
LES    BX,VBuff
INT    10h
```

Restore Super VGA Video State
(Interrupt 10h, Service 4Fh, Function 4, Subfunction 2)

This function restores one or more previously saved states. When using this function you must specify the same state information as you saved. The function will not allow you to skip over unneeded data.

Register Contents on Entry:
AH - 4Fh
AL - 4
DL - 2
CX - Requested States
    Bit 0 - Video Hardware State
    Bit 1 - Video BIOS State
    Bit 2 - Video DAC State
    Bit 3 - Super VGA State
    Bits 4 through 15 - Set to Zero
BX - State Buffer Offset
ES - State Buffer Segment

Register Contents on Exit:
AX - Status

Example:

```
;Restore the current hardware and BIOS states.
MOV    AH,4Fh
MOV    AL,4
MOV    DL,2
MOV    CX,0000000000000011b
LES    BX,VBuff
INT    10h
```

Select Super VGA Memory Window
(Interrupt 10h, Service 4Fh, Function 5, Subfunction 0)

This function sets the position of the specified window in memory. Before using this function, you should obtain the window data using interrupt 10h, service 4Fh, function 1 (explained previously). You may also execute this function using the far call address obtained using function 1. However, the far call method destroys the contents of AX and DX. In addition, you do not receive any return information from the far call method. The far call method does execute quicker than the BIOS function.

Register Contents on Entry:
AH - 4Fh
AL - 5
BH - 0
BL - Window Number
    0 - Window A
    1 - Window B
DX - Window Position in Video Memory (in Window Granularity Units)

Register Contents on Exit:
AX - Status

Example:
```
;Set the position of Window A.
MOV    AH,4Fh
MOV    AL,5
MOV    BH,0
MOV    BL,0
MOV    DX,15
INT    10h
```

Return Super VGA Memory Window
(Interrupt 10h, Service 4Fh, Function 5, Subfunction 1)

This function gets the position of the specified window in memory. Before using this function, you should obtain the window data using interrupt 10h, service 4Fh, function 1 (explained previously). You may also execute this function using the far call address obtained using function 1. However, the far call method destroys the contents of AX and DX. In addition, you do not receive any return information from the far call method. The far call method does execute quicker than the BIOS function.

Register Contents on Entry:
AH - 4Fh
AL - 5
BH - 1
BL - Window Number

                    0 - Window A
                    1 - Window B

Register Contents on Exit:
AX - Status
DX - Window Position in Video Memory (in Window Granularity Units)

Example:
```
;Get the position of Window A.
MOV    AH,4Fh
MOV    AL,5
MOV    BH,1
MOV    BL,0
INT    10h
```

HARD DISK DRIVE/FLOPPY DISKETTE SERVICES

This section contains a complete listing of all standard hard and floppy disk related BIOS function calls. TABLE 7-1 contains a listing of BIOS interrupts in interrupt number order. Some vendors provide additional functions in ROM. Refer to your vendor manual if you wish to use these extended functions.

Reset Disk Drives (Interrupt 13h Service 0)

Use With: PC, AT, and PS/2
This service resets the disk controller, re-calibrates any attached disk drives, and prepares the disk for I/O. If the drive fails to perform any of these tasks, AH contains an error message on return from the interrupt. TABLE 7-8 at the end of this chapter contains a listing of the disk drive error codes returned in AH.

Register Contents on Entry:
AH - 0
DL - Drive (0 - 7Fh for Floppy, 80h - FFh Hard Disk)

Register Contents on Exit:
AH - 0 if Successful, Error Code if not Successful
CF - 0 if Successful, 1 if not Successful

Example:
```
;Reset the first hard drive
MOV    AH,0
MOV    DL,80h
INT    13h
```

Get Disk Drive Status (Interrupt 13h Service 1)

Use With: PC, AT, and PS/2
This service returns the status of the most recent disk operation. If the

drive was unable to write or read information, AH contains an error message on return from the interrupt. TABLE 7-8 at the end of this chapter contains a listing of the disk drive error codes returned in AH.

Register Contents on Entry:
AH - 1
DL - Drive (0 - 7Fh for Floppy, 80h - FFh Hard Disk)

Register Contents on Exit:
AH - 0
AL - Status of Previous Disk Operation

Example:
```
;Get the status of floppy drive A.
MOV    AH,1
MOV    DL,0
INT    13h
```

Read Disk Sectors (Interrupt 13h Service 2)

Use With: PC, AT, and PS/2

This service reads one or more sectors from disk. You must provide a buffer large enough to receive any information from the drive. Using a buffer too small to hold the information could result in damaged data. If the drive experiences a failure during a read, write, or seek, AH contains an error number on return from the interrupt. TABLE 7-8 at the end of this chapter contains a listing of the disk drive error codes returned in AH.

Register Contents on Entry:
AH - 2
AL - Number of Sectors
CH - Cylinder
CL - Sector
DH - Head
DL - Drive (0 - 7Fh for Floppy, 80h - FFh Hard Disk)
BX - Offset of Buffer
ES - Segment of Buffer

Register Contents on Exit:
AH - 0 if Successful, Error Code if not Successful
AL - Number of Sectors Transferred
CF - 0 if Successful, 1 if not Successful

Example:
```
;Read 1024 bytes of data from a floppy disk.
MOV    AH,2
MOV    AL,2
MOV    CH,1
MOV    CL,7
```

```
MOV    DH,1
MOV    DL,0
LES    BX,DBuff
INT    13h
```

Write Disk Sectors (Interrupt 13h Service 3)

Use With: PC, AT, and PS/2

This service writes one or more sectors to disk. You must supply a buffer containing enough data to write to the drive. If the buffer is too small, you could write garbage to the drive, resulting in damaged data. If the drive experiences a failure during a read, write, or seek, AH contains an error number on return from the interrupt. TABLE 7-8 at the end of this chapter contains a listing of the disk drive error codes returned in AH.

Register Contents on Entry:
AH - 3
AL - Number of Sectors
CH - Cylinder
CL - Sector
DH - Head
DL - Drive (0 - 7Fh for Floppy, 80h - FFh Hard Disk)
BX - Offset of Buffer
ES - Segment of Buffer

Register Contents on Exit:
AH - 0 if Successful, Error Code if not Successful
AL - Number of Sectors Transferred
CF - 0 if Successful, 1 if not Successful

Example:
```
;Write 1024 bytes of data to a floppy disk.
MOV    AH,3
MOV    AL,2
MOV    CH,1
MOV    CL,7
MOV    DH,1
MOV    DL,0
LES    BX,DBuff
INT    13h
```

Verify Disk Sectors (Interrupt 13h Service 4)

Use With: PC, AT, and PS/2

This service verifies one or more disk sector addresses. It does not transfer information between the drive and the host. It does make sure the drive is ready to receive data. If the disk contains errors or the drive fails to perform correctly, AH contains an error message on return from the interrupt. TABLE 7-8 at the end of this chapter contains a listing of the disk drive error codes returned in AH.

Register Contents on Entry:
AH - 4
AL - Number of Sectors
CH - Cylinder
CL - Sector
DH - Head
DL - Drive (0 - 7Fh for Floppy, 80h - FFh Hard Disk)
BX - Offset of Buffer
ES - Segment of Buffer

Register Contents on Exit:
AH - 0 if Successful, Error Code if not Successful
AL - Number of Sectors Verified
CF - 0 if Successful, 1 if not Successful

Example:

```
;Verify the first head of a hard disk with 614
; cylinders, 4 heads, and 26 sectors per track.
MOV    AH,4
MOV    AL,15964    ;614 cylinders x 25 sectors/track
XOR    CX,CX
MOV    DH,0
MOV    DL,80h
LES    BX,DBuff
INT    13h
```

Format Disk Track (Interrupt 13h Service 5)

Use With: PC, AT, and PS/2

This service formats one or more disk tracks. If a disk track contains a flaw or the drive fails to perform as expected, AH contains an error code on return from the interrupt. TABLE 7-8 at the end of this chapter contains a listing of the disk drive error codes returned in AH.

Note: PC/XT floppy disks receive the sector per track value from the BIOS floppy parameter table. Always use interrupt 13h, service 17h to select the media type for floppy disks on an AT or PS/2. Fixed disks place the upper 2-bits of the 10-bit cylinder number in the upper 2-bits of CL.

Register Contents on Entry:
AH - 5
AL - Interleave
CH - Cylinder
DH - Head
DL - Drive (0 - 7Fh for Floppy, 80h - FFh Hard Disk)
BX - Offset of Address Field List (Except PC/XT). The Field Address

List contains the following 4-byte entries for each sector of a disk.

> Byte 0 - Cylinder
> Byte 1 - Head
> Byte 2 - Sector
> Byte 3 - Sector Size Code
>> 00 - 128 Bytes/Sector
>> 01 - 256 Bytes/Sector
>> 02 - 512 Bytes/Sector
>> 13 - 1024 Bytes/Sector

ES - Segment of Address Field List (Except PC/XT)

Register Contents on Exit:
AH - 0 if Successful, Error Code if not Successful
CF - 0 if Successful, 1 if not Successful

Example:

```
;Format a floppy disk with 40 tracks and 9 sectors per track.
          MOV   AH,5            ;Set initial parameters
          MOV   AL,1
          MOV   CH,0
          MOV   DH,0
          MOV   DL,0
          LES   BX,DBuff
NextTrk:  INT   10h             ;Format a track
          INC   DH              ;Next head.
          CMP   DH,2            ;No more heads, go to next
          JNE   NextTrk         ; cylinder.
          MOV   DH,0            ;First head.
          INC   CH              ;Next cylinder.
          CMP   CH,40           ;No more cylinders, format
          JNE   NextTrk         ; finished.
```

Format Bad Track (Interrupt 13h Service 6)

Use With: PC

This service formats one or more disk tracks. If the function finds a flawed disk track, it sets the bad sector flag for that track. However, if the drive fails to perform as expected, AH contains an error code on return from the interrupt. TABLE 7-8 at the end of this chapter contains a listing of the disk drive error codes returned in AH.

Note: This function is defined for PC/XT hard disk drives only. You cannot use it on floppy disk drives at any time. Some AT hard drives perform erratically or not at all when using this function.

Register Contents on Entry:
AH - 6
AL - Interleave

CH - Cylinder
DH - Head
DL - Drive (80h - FFh Hard Disk)

Register Contents on Exit:
AH - 0 if Successful, Error Code if not Successful
CF - 0 if Successful, 1 if not Successful

Example:

```
;Format a hard disk with 614 tracks, 4 heads, and 26 sectors per track.
                MOV    AH,6        ;Set initial parameters.
                MOV    AL,3        ;Many hard drives use an
                MOV    CH,0        ; interleave of 3.
                MOV    DH,0
                MOV    DL,80h
NextTrk:        INT    10h         ;Format a track
                INC    DH          ;Next head.
                CMP    DH,4        ;No more heads, go to next
                JNE    NextTrk     ; cylinder.
                MOV    DH,0        ;First head.
                INC    CH          ;Next cylinder.
                CMP    CH,614      ;No more cylinders, format
                JNE    NextTrk     ; finished.
```

Format Drive (Interrupt 13h Service 7)

Use With: PC

This service formats an entire disk drive. It provides the least code-intensive method of formatting a hard drive. Notice you cannot use it for floppy disk drive formatting. If a disk track contains a flaw or the drive fails to perform as expected, AH contains an error code on return from the interrupt. TABLE 7-8 at the end of this chapter contains a listing of the disk drive error codes returned in AH.

Note: This function is defined for PC/XT hard disk drives only. You cannot use it on floppy disk drives at any time. Some AT hard drives perform erratically or not at all when using this function.

Register Contents on Entry:
AH - 7
AL - Interleave
CH - Cylinder
DL - Drive (80h - FFh Hard Disk)

Register Contents on Exit:
AH - 0 if Successful, Error Code if not Successful
CF - 0 if Successful, 1 if not Successful

Example:
```
;Format a hard disk with 614 tracks, 4 heads, and 26 sectors per track.
MOV     AH,7        ;Set initial parameters
MOV     AL,3        ;Many hard drives use an
MOV     CH,0        ; interleave of 3.
MOV     DL,80h
INT     10h         ;Format the disk.
```

Return Disk Parameters (Interrupt 13h Service 8)

Use With: PC, AT, and PS/2

This service returns the parameters of the requested drive. If a drive fails to perform as expected, AH contains an error code on return from the interrupt. TABLE 7-8 at the end of this chapter contains a listing of the disk drive error codes returned in AH.

Note: Do not use this function for PC/XT floppy disk drives. You may use it on PC/XT hard disk drives.

Register Contents on Entry:
AH - 8
DL - Drive (0 - 7Fh for Floppy, 80h - FFh Hard Disk)

Register Contents on Exit:
AH - 0 if Successful, Error Code if not Successful
CF - 0 if Successful, 1 if not Successful
BH - Floppy Disk Drive Type
    1 - 360 KB, 40 Track, 5.25"
    2 - 1.2 MB, 80 Track, 5.25"
    3 - 720 KB, 80 Track, 3.5"
    4 - 1.44 MB, 80 Track, 3.5"
CH - Low 8 Bits of Maximum Cylinder Number
CL - Bits 6 and 7 - High 2 Bits of Maximum Cylinder
    Bits 0 through 5 - Maximum Sector Number
DH - Maximum Head Number
DL - Number of Drives (Counts physical, not logical drives.)
DI - Offset of Disk Parameter Table
ES - Segment of Disk Parameter Table

Example:
```
;Get the parameters for floppy drive B.
MOV     AH,8
MOV     DL,1
INT     13h
```

Initialize Fixed Disk Table (Interrupt 13h Service 9)

Use With: PC, AT, and PS/2

This service initializes the fixed disk controller before performing I/O using the ROM BIOS disk parameter block(s) values. You need to perform this low-level initialization to prepare the drive for use. While a floppy disk drive uses standard parameters, a hard disk controller could attach to a wide variety of hard disks.

When using this service on a PC, the interrupt 41h vector must point to the disk parameter block. This block is 15 bytes long. Bytes 0 and 1 contain the maximum number of cylinders. Byte 2 contains the maximum number of heads. Bytes 3 and 4 contain the cylinder number where reduced write current starts. Bytes 5 and 6 contain the cylinder number where write precompensation starts. Byte 7 contains the maximum ECC burst length. Byte 8 contains the drive options including drive option (bits 0-2), disable ECC retries (bit 6), and disable disk access retries (bit 7). The standard time-out value appears in byte 9. The time-out value for drive formatting appears in byte 10. Finally, byte 11 contains the time-out value for drive checking. Most controllers reserve bytes 12 through 15 for future use.

When using this service on an AT or PS/2, the interrupt 41h vector must point to the drive 0 disk parameter block; the interrupt 46h vector must point to the drive 1 disk parameter block. The disk parameter block is 15 bytes long. Bytes 0 and 1 contain the maximum number of cylinders. Byte 2 contains the maximum number of heads. Most controllers reserve bytes 3 and 4 for future use. Bytes 5 and 6 contain the cylinder number where write precompensation starts. Byte 7 contains the maximum ECC burst length. Byte 8 contains the drive options including more than 8 heads flag (bit 3), manufacturer's defect map present at maximum cylinder + 1 flag (bit 5), and a nonzero value for bits 6 and 7. Most controllers reserve bytes 9 through 11 for future use. The landing zone cylinder appears in bytes 12 and 13. The sectors per track value appears in byte 14. Most controllers reserve byte 15 for future use.

If the drive controller fails to initialize properly or the disk drive fails to provide the information required for initialization, AH returns with an error number. Table 7-8 at the end of this chapter contains a listing of the disk drive error codes returned in AH.

Note: Never use this function on a floppy disk drive. Floppy drives do not require the low-level initialization required by hard disk drives.

Register Contents on Entry:
AH - 9
DL - Drive (80h - FFh Hard Disk)

Register Contents on Exit:
AH - 0 if Successful, Error Code if not Successful
CF - 0 if Successful, 1 if not Successful

Example:

```
; Initialize hard disk drive D.
MOV    AH,9
MOV    DL,81h
INT    13h
```

Read Long Sectors (Interrupt 13h Service Ah)

Use With: PC, AT, and PS/2

This service reads the requested sectors into memory with their associated 4-byte ECC codes. You must provide a buffer large enough to receive any information from the drive. Include one extra word per sector of information for the ECC code. Using a buffer too small to hold the information could result in damaged data. Unlike the read disk sectors function (interrupt 13h service 2), this function does not automatically correct ECC errors. Transfers stop with any sector containing a read error. If the drive experiences a failure during a read, write, or seek, AH contains an error number on return from the interrupt. TABLE 7-8 at the end of this chapter contains a listing of the disk drive error codes returned in AH.

Note: Never use this function on floppy disk drives.

Register Contents on Entry:
AH - Ah
AL - Number of Sectors
CH - Cylinder
CL - Sector
DH - Head
DL - Drive (80h - FFh Hard Disk)
BX - Offset of Buffer
ES - Segment of Buffer

Register Contents on Exit:
AH - 0 if Successful, Error Code if not Successful
AL - Number of Sectors Transferred
CF - 0 if Successful, 1 if not Successful

Example:
```
;Read 5 sectors starting at cylinder 20, sector 15,
; head 3 of hard disk drive C.
MOV    AH,Ah
MOV    AL,5
MOV    CH,20
MOV    CL,15
MOV    DH,3
MOV    DL,80h
LES    BX,DBuff
INT    13h
```

Write Long Sectors (Interrupt 13h Service Bh)

Use With: PC, AT, and PS/2

This service writes the requested sectors into memory with their associated 4-byte ECC codes. You must supply a buffer containing enough data to write to the drive. Include one extra word per sector of information for the ECC code. If the buffer is too small, you could write garbage to the drive, resulting in damaged data. Unlike the write disk sectors function (interrupt 13h service 3), this function does not automatically correct ECC errors. Transfers stop with any sector containing a write error. If the drive experiences a failure during a read, write, or seek, AH contains an error number on return from the interrupt. TABLE 7-8 at the end of this chapter contains a listing of the disk drive error codes returned to AH.

Note: Never use this function on floppy disk drives.

Register Contents on Entry:
AH - Bh
AL - Number of Sectors
CH - Cylinder
CL - Sector
DH - Head
DL - Drive (80h - FFh Hard Disk)
BX - Offset of Buffer
ES - Segment of Buffer

Register Contents on Exit:
AH - 0 if Successful, Error Code if not Successful
AL - Number of Sectors Transferred
CF - 0 if Successful, 1 if not Successful

Example:

```
;Write 5 sectors starting at cylinder 20, sector 15,
; head 3 of hard disk drive C.
MOV    AH,Bh
MOV    AL,5
MOV    CH,20
MOV    CL,15
MOV    DH,3
MOV    DL,80h
LES    BX,DBuff
INT    13h
```

Seek Cylinder (Interrupt 13h Service Ch)

Use With: PC, AT, and PS/2

This service positions the hard disk read/write head to the desired position. It does not transfer any data. The four functions read sector (service 2), read sector long (service Ah), write sector (service 3), and write sector long (service Bh) contain an implied seek. You do not need to position the head manually before reading or writing with these functions. If the drive experiences a failure during a read, write, or seek, AH contains an error number on return from the interrupt. TABLE 7-8 at the end of this chapter contains a listing of the disk drive error codes returned in AH.

Note: Never use this function on floppy disk drives.

Register Contents on Entry:
AH - Ch
CH - Low 8 Bits of Maximum Cylinder Number
CL - High 2 Bits of Maximum Cylinder in Bits 6 and 7
DH - Head Number
DL - Drive (80h - FFh Hard Disk)

Register Contents on Exit:
AH - 0 if Successful, Error Code if not Successful
CF - 0 if Successful, 1 if not Successful

Example:
```
;Position the head 4 to cylinder 108 of drive C.
MOV    AH, Ch
MOV    CH, 108
XOR    CL,CL
MOV    DH,4
MOV    DL,80h
INT    13h
```

Alternate Reset (Interrupt 13h Service Dh)

Use With: PC, AT, and PS/2

This service resets the disk controller, re-calibrates any attached disk drives, and prepares the disk for I/O. If the drive experiences a failure during a read, write, or seek or the drive controller fails to initialize, AH contains an error number on return from the interrupt. TABLE 7-8 at the end of this chapter contains a listing of the disk drive error codes returned in AH.

Note: Never use this function on floppy disk drives. It differs from the reset performed by interrupt 13 service 0.

Register Contents on Entry:
AH - Dh
DL - Drive (80h - FFh Hard Disk)

Register Contents on Exit:
AH - 0 if Successful, Error Code if not Successful
CF - 0 if Successful, 1 if not Successful

Example:
```
;Reset drive C and prepare if for use.
MOV    AH,Dh
MOV    DL,80h
INT    13h
```

Read Sector Buffer (Interrupt 13h Service Eh)

Use With: PC

This service reads the contents of the fixed disk adapter's internal sector buffer to system memory. It does not read any data from the fixed disk itself. You must provide a buffer large enough to receive any information from the drive buffer. This buffer is normally 512 bytes long. However, some drives use a sector length of 1,024 bytes. Using a buffer too small to hold the information could result in damaged data. If the fixed disk drive adapter experiences a failure during a read or write, AH contains an error number on return from the interrupt. TABLE 7-8 at the end of this chapter contains a listing of the disk drive error codes returned in AH.

Note: Never use this function on floppy disk, or PC/AT or PS/2 hard disk drives.

Register Contents on Entry:
AH - Eh
BX - Offset of Buffer
ES - Segment of Buffer

Register Contents on Exit:
AH - 0 if Successful, Error Code if not Successful
CF - 0 if Successful, 1 if not Successful

Example:

```
;Read hard disk sector buffer.
MOV    AH,Eh
LES    BX,DBuff
INT    13h
```

Write Sector Buffer (Interrupt 13h Service Fh)

Use With: PC

This service writes the contents of system memory to the fixed disk adapter's internal sector buffer. Use the write sector buffer function to initialize the hard disk drive sector buffer before using the format disk track function (interrupt 13h service 5) to format the drive. This function does not write any data to the fixed disk itself. You must supply a buffer containing enough data to write to the drive buffer. This buffer is normally 512 bytes long. However, some drives use a sector length of 1,024 bytes. If the buffer is too small, you could write garbage to the drive, resulting in damaged data. If the fixed disk drive adapter experiences a failure during a read or write, AH contains an error number on return from the interrupt. TABLE 7-8 at the end of this chapter contains a listing of the disk drive error codes returned in AH.

Note: Never use this function on floppy disk, or PC/AT or PS/2 hard disk drives.

Register Contents on Entry:
AH - Fh
BX - Offset of Buffer
ES - Segment of Buffer

Register Contents on Exit:
AH - 0 if Successful, Error Code if not Successful
CF - 0 if Successful, 1 if not Successful

Example:
```
;Write to the hard disk drive buffer.
MOV    AH,Fh
LES    BX,DBuff
INT    13h
```

Get Drive Status (Interrupt 13h Service 10h)

Use With: PC, AT, and PS/2

This service tests to see if the specified hard disk is operational, then returns the drive status. If the drive or drive adapter experiences a failure during a read, write, or seek, AH contains an error number on return from the interrupt. TABLE 7-8 at the end of this chapter contains a listing of the disk drive error codes returned in AH.

Note: Never use this function on floppy disk drives.

Register Contents on Entry:
AH - 10h
DL - Drive (80h - FFh Hard Disk)

Register Contents on Exit:
AH - 0 if Successful, Error Code if not Successful
CF - 0 if Successful, 1 if not Successful

Example:
```
;Test hard disk drive D.
MOV    AH,10h
MOV    DL,81h
INT    13h
```

Re-calibrate Drive (Interrupt 13h Service 11h)

Use With: PC, AT, and PS/2

This service causes a re-calibration of the hard disk adapter. It positions the hard disk read/write head at cylinder 0 and returns the drive's operational status. If the drive or drive adapter experiences a failure during a read, write, or seek, AH contains an error number on return from the interrupt. TABLE 7-8 at the end of this chapter contains a listing of the disk drive error codes returned in AH.

Note: Never use this function on floppy disk drives.

Register Contents on Entry:
AH - 11h
DL - Drive (80h - FFh Hard Disk)

Register Contents on Exit:
AH - 0 if Successful, Error Code if not Successful
CF - 0 if Successful, 1 if not Successful

Example:
```
;Test and recalibrate hard disk drive C.
MOV    AH,11h
MOV    DL,80h
INT    13h
```

Controller RAM Diagnostic (Interrupt 13h Service 12h)

Use With: PC

This service starts a test of the hard disk adapter internal sector buffer. Always test the drive controller using this test before testing the drive using service 13h. A faulty controller always results in the failure of service 13h. If the drive adapter experiences a failure during a read or write, AH contains an error number on return from the interrupt. TABLE 7-8 at the end of this chapter contains a listing of the disk drive error codes returned in AH.

Note: Never use this function on floppy disk, or PC/AT or PS/2 hard disk drives. Use the controller internal diagnostic function (interrupt 13h service 14h) to test PC/AT or PS/2 drives instead.

Register Contents on Entry:
AH - 12h

Register Contents on Exit:
AH - 0 if Successful, Error Code if not Successful
CF - 0 if Successful, 1 if not Successful

Example:
```
;Test the hard disk drive controller.
MOV    AH,12h
INT    13h
```

Controller Drive Diagnostic (Interrupt 13h Service 13h)

Use With: PC

This service starts a test of a hard disk drive using adapter built-in diagnostic routines. Always test the drive controller using this test before testing the drive using service 13h. A faulty controller always results in the failure of service 13h. If the drive or drive adapter experiences a failure during a read, write, or seek, AH contains an error number on return from the interrupt. TABLE 7-8 at the end of this chapter contains a listing of the disk drive error codes returned in AH.

Note: Never use this function on floppy disk, or PC/AT or PS/2 hard disk drives. Use the controller internal diagnostic function (interrupt 13h service 14h) to test PC/AT or PS/2 drives instead.

Register Contents on Entry:
AH - 13h

Register Contents on Exit:
AH - 0 if Successful, Error Code if not Successful
CF - 0 if Successful, 1 if not Successful

Example:
```
;Test the hard disk drive after testing the drive controller.
MOV    AH,12h   ;Test the drive controller.
INT    13h
CMP    AH,0     ;See if it failed.
JNE    ErrMsg   ;If so, display an error message.
MOV    AH,13h   ;Test the hard disk drive.
INT    13h
```

Controller Internal Diagnostic (Interrupt 13h Service 14h)

Use With: PC, AT, and PS/2

This service starts a hard disk drive adapter built-in test sequence. If the drive or drive adapter experiences a failure during a read, write, or seek, AH contains an error number on return from the interrupt. TABLE 7-8 at the end of this chapter contains a listing of the disk drive error codes returned in AH.

Note: Never use this function on floppy disk drives.

Register Contents on Entry:
AH - 14h

Register Contents on Exit:
AH - 0 if Successful, Error Code if not Successful
CF - 0 if Successful, 1 if not Successful

Example:
```
;Perform the disk drive controller internal diagnostic.
MOV    AH,14h
INT    13h
```

Read DASD Type (Interrupt 13h Service 15h)

Use With: AT and PS/2

This service retrieves a code indicating the referenced floppy or hard disk drive type. If the drive or drive adapter fails to provide this information, AH contains an error number on return from the interrupt. TABLE 7-8 at the end of this chapter contains a listing of the disk drive error codes returned in AH. In some extreme cases, the computer will report that no drive exists instead of reporting an error code.

Register Contents on Entry:
AH - 15h
DL - Drive (0 - 7Fh for Floppy, 80h - FFh Hard Disk)

Register Contents on Exit:
AH   0 - No Drive Present (if Successful)
          1 - Floppy Disk Drive Without Change-Line Support
          2 - Floppy Disk Drive With Change-Line Support
          3 - Fixed Disk
          Error Code (if not Successful)
CX:DX - Number of 512-Byte Sectors (Fixed Disk Only)
CF - 0 if Successful, 1 if not Successful

Example:

```
;See if the computer contains a hard drive.
MOV    AH,15h
MOV    DL,80h
INT    13h
CMP    AH,0        ;Check for drive existence.
JE     NoDrive
CMP    AH,3        ;Check for drive error.
JG     ErrMsg
```

Read Disk Change Line Status (Interrupt 13h Service 16h)

Use With: AT and PS/2

This service returns the status of the floppy disk change line. It checks the status of the door switch. When the user opens and then closes the door, this function returns with the carry flag set. However, even if the function detects the door open and close, it does not mean that the user actually changed the floppy disk. If the drive or drive adapter experiences a failure during a read, write or seek, AH contains an error number on return from the interrupt. TABLE 7-8 at the end of this chapter contains a listing of the disk drive error codes returned in AH.

Note: Never use this function on a PC/XT floppy disk, or any type of hard disk drive.

Register Contents on Entry:
AH - 16h
DL - Drive (0 - 7Fh for Floppy)

Register Contents on Exit:

AH - 0 if Change Line Inactive (No Disk Change)
      6 if Change Line Active (Disk Change)
CF - 0 if Successful, 1 if not Successful

Example:

```
;Wait for the user to change the floppy disk in drive A.
LoopIt:    MOV    AH,16h ;Get change status.
           MOV    DL,0
           INT    13h
           JNC    LoopIt ;If not changed, try again.
```

Set DASD Type for Format (Interrupt 13h Service 17h)

Use With: AT and PS/2

This service selects the floppy disk type of the requested drive. It also resets the drive change line, if set. If the drive or drive adapter experiences a failure during a read, write, or seek, AH contains an error number on return from the interrupt. This function always fails if you try to set the drive for an incompatible disk format. TABLE 7-8 at the end of this chapter contains a listing of the disk drive error codes returned in AH.

Note: Never use this function on a PC/XT floppy disk, or any type of hard disk drive.

Register Contents on Entry:
AH - 17h
AL - Floppy Disk Type Code
      0 - Not Used
      1 - 360 KB Floppy, 360 KB Drive
      2 - 360 KB Floppy, 1.2 MB Drive
      3 - 1.2 MB Floppy, 1.2 MB Drive
      4 - 720 KB Floppy, 720 KB Drive
DL - Drive (0 - 7Fh for Floppy)

Register Contents on Exit:
AH - 0 if Successful, Error Code if not Successful
CF - 0 if Successful, 1 if not Successful

Example:

```
;Set drive A for 1.2 MB floppies.
MOV    AH,17h
MOV    AL,3
MOV    DL,0
INT    13h
```

Set Media Type for Format (Interrupt 13h Service 18h)

Use With: AT and PS/2

This service selects media characteristics for the specified drive. If the drive or drive adapter experiences a failure during a read, write, or seek, AH contains an error number on return from the interrupt. This function normally fails if you try to set the drive for an incompatible disk format. TABLE 7-8 at the end of this chapter contains a listing of the disk drive error codes returned in AH.

Note: Never use this function on a PC/XT floppy disk, or any type of hard disk drive.

Register Contents on Entry:
AH - 18h
CH - Number of Cylinders
CL - Sectors Per Track
DL - Drive (0 - 7Fh for Floppy)

Register Contents on Exit:
AH - 0 if Successful, Error Code if not Successful
CF - 0 if Successful, 1 if not Successful
DI - Offset of Disk Parameter Table for Media Type
ES - Segment of Disk Parameter Table for Media Type

Example:
```
;Set drive A for 360 KByte format (40 tracks, 9 sectors/track).
MOV    AH,18h
MOV    CH,40
MOV    CL,9
MOV    DL,0
INT    13h
```

Park Heads (Interrupt 13h Service 19h)

Use With: PS/2

This service moves the read/write arm to a storage position. This prevents damage to media data areas when the drive loses power. If the drive or drive adapter experiences a failure during a seek, AH contains an error number on return from the interrupt. TABLE 7-8 at the end of this chapter contains a listing of the disk drive error codes returned in AH.

Note: Never use this function on any type of floppy disk, or PC/XT or PC/AT hard disk drive.

Register Contents on Entry:
AH - 19h
DL - Drive (80h - FFh Hard Disk)

Register Contents on Exit:
AH - 0 if Successful, Error Code if not Successful
CF - 0 if Successful, 1 if not Successful

Example:
```
;Park the drive D hard disk heads.
MOV    AH,19h
MOV    DL,81h
INT    13h
```

Format ESDI Drive (Interrupt 13h Service 1Ah)

Use With: PS/2

This service initializes sector and track address fields on a hard disk drive attached to the enhanced small device interface (ESDI) fixed disk drive adapter A. You must perform a partition of the disk after using the low-level format routine provided by this function. If the drive or drive adapter experiences a failure during a read, write, or seek, AH contains an error number on return from the interrupt. TABLE 7-8 at the end of this chapter contains a listing of the disk drive error codes returned in AH.

Note: Never use this function on any type of floppy disk, or PC/XT or PC/AT hard disk drive.

Register Contents on Entry:
AH - 1Ah
AL - Relative Block Address (RBA) Defect Table Count
    0 - No RBA Table
    >0 - RBA Table Used
CL - Format Modifier Bits (True When Set)
    0 - Ignore Primary Defect Map
    1 - Ignore Secondary Defect Map
    2 - Update Secondary Defect Map
    3 - Perform Extended Surface Analysis
    4 - Generate Periodic Interrupt
    5 through 7 - Reserved (Set to 0)
DL - Drive (80h - FFh Hard Disk)
BX - Offset of RBA Table
ES - Segment of RBA Table

Register Contents on Exit:
AH - 0 if Successful, Error Code if not Successful
CF - 0 if Successful, 1 if not Successful

Example:
```
;Format ESDI drive C, with an RBA defect table of 1 (1
; error more than the original manufacturer error map),
; use secondary defect map, and perform extended
; surface analysis.
MOV    AH,1Ah
MOV    AL,1
```

```
MOV    CL,
MOV    DL,80h
LES    BX,RBATbl
INT    13h
```

KEYBOARD SERVICES

This section contains a complete listing of all standard keyboard-related BIOS function calls. Some keyboards provide extended or non-standard BIOS functions in addition to the standard BIOS calls. Refer to your manufacturer manual for details on these extended or non-standard functions. This section assumes you are using a full-size 84 or 101 key keyboard. Some portable computer keyboards do not adhere to these standards. TABLE 7-1 contains a listing of BIOS interrupts in interrupt number order.

Read Keyboard Character (Interrupt 16h Service 0)

Use With: PC, AT, and PS/2

This service reads a character from the keyboard. It also returns the associated scan code. TABLE 7-9 at the end of this chapter shows the BIOS keyboard routine scan codes and ASCII character returned. TABLE 7-10 at the end of this chapter shows the scan code obtained from port 60h for each character.

Register Contents on Entry:
AH - 0

Register Contents on Exit:
AH - Keyboard Scan Code
AL - ASCII Character

Example:
```
;This short program shows you the effects of the palette
; commands on display appearance.

.MODEL SMALL

.STACK  ; Use the default stack of 1024 bytes.

.DATA

OldColor       DB    0

.CODE

EXAMPLE PROC FAR
```

```
        PUSH    DS              ;Save the original data segment.
        XOR     AX,AX
        PUSH    AX

        MOV     AX,@DATA        ;Point DS & ES to our data segment.
        MOV     DS,AX
        MOV     ES,AX

        MOV     AH,10h          ;Save the original palette color.
        MOV     AL,07h
        MOV     BL,0
        INT     10h
        MOV     OldColor,BH

        MOV     CX,15           ;Number of colors to try.
        MOV     BL,0            ;Black background/gray foreground.
        MOV     BH,19h          ;New color number.
LoopIt: MOV     AH,10h          ;Change the palette.
        MOV     AL,0
        INT     10h
        INC     BH              ;Get ready for next color.

        XOR     AX,AX           ;Wait for keypress.
        INT     16h

        LOOP    LoopIt          ;Change to next color.

        MOV     AH,10h          ;Restore original color.
        MOV     AL,0
        MOV     BH,OldColor
        MOV     BL,0
        INT     10h

        RET                     ;Return.

EXAMPLE ENDP
END     EXAMPLE
```

Read Keyboard Status (Interrupt 16h Service 1)

Use With: PC, AT, and PS/2

This service checks the keyboard for a character. If the buffer contains a character, it sets a flag and reads the character from the keyboard. It also returns the associated scan code. TABLE 7-9 at the end of this chapter shows the BIOS keyboard routine scan codes and ASCII character returned. TABLE 7-10 at the end of this chapter shows the scan code obtained from port 60h for each character.

Register Contents on Entry:
AH - 1

Register Contents on Exit:
AH - Keyboard Scan Code
AL - ASCII Character
ZF - 0 for key input, 1 for no key input

Example:

```
;Wait for the user to press a key.
LoopIt:   MOV   AH,1
          INT   16h
          JZ    LoopIt
```

Read Keyboard Shift Status (Interrupt 16h Service 2)

Use With: PC, AT, and PS/2

This service returns the ROM BIOS flag byte that describes the current keyboard toggle and shift key status.

Register Contents on Entry:
AH - 2

Register Contents on Exit:
AL - Flags (True When Bit Set)
      0 - Right Shift Key Depressed
      1 - Left Shift Key Depressed
      2 - Ctrl Key Depressed
      3 - Alt Key Depressed
      4 - Scroll Key On
      5 - Num Lock Key On
      6 - Caps Lock Key On
      7 - Insert Key On

Example:

```
;Check the status of the insert key.
MOV   AH,2
INT   16h
AND   AL,10000000b
CMP   AL,80h
JNE   InsertOff
```

Set Repeat Rate (Interrupt 16h Service 3)

Use With: AT and PS/2

This service changes ROM BIOS key repeat rate and delay. The repeat rate affects how fast the computer replicates a keystroke when you hold the key down. The delay affects how long you must hold the key down before the computer replicates it.

Note: Do not use this function with PC-only keyboards. These keyboards lack the additional chips required to program the repeat rate and delay parameters.

Register Contents on Entry:
AH - 3
AL - 5
BH - Repeat Delay (msec.)

    00h - 250
    01h - 500
    02h - 750
    03h - 1000

BL - Repeat Rate (Characters per Second)

    00h - 30.0
    01h - 26.7
    02h - 24.0
    03h - 21.8
    04h - 20.0
    05h - 18.5
    06h - 17.1
    07h - 16.0
    08h - 15.0
    09h - 13.3
    0Ah - 12.0
    0Bh - 10.9
    0Ch - 10.0
    0Dh - 9.2
    0Eh - 8.6
    0Fh - 8.0
    10h - 7.5
    11h - 6.7
    12h - 6.0
    13h - 5.5
    14h - 5.0
    15h - 4.6
    16h - 4.3
    17h - 4.0
    18h - 3.7
    19h - 3.3
    1Ah - 3.0
    1Bh - 2.7
    1Ch - 2.5
    1Dh - 2.3
    1Eh - 2.1
    1Fh - 2.0

Example:
```
;Change the repeat rate 10 characters per second and
; the delay to 500 milliseconds.
MOV     AH,3
MOV     AL,5
MOV     BH,1
MOV     BL,0Ch
INT     16h
```

Set Keyclick (Interrupt 16h Service 4)

Use With: PC, AT, and PS/2

This service sets the keyboard click on or off. Keyclick is the ticking noise produced by the computer speaker as you type. It simulates the noise produced by some mechanical keyboards.

Register Contents on Entry:
AH - 4
AL - Sub-function
     0 - Set Click Off
     1 - Set Click On

Example:
```
;Turn keyclick on.
MOV     AH,4
MOV     AL,1
INT     16h
```

Push Character and Scan Code (Interrupt 16h Service 5)

Use With: AT and PS/2

This service places a character and scan code in the keyboard typeahead buffer. This allows you to simulate user keystrokes. TABLE 7-9 at the end of this chapter shows the BIOS keyboard routine scan codes and ASCII character returned. TABLE 7-10 at the end of this chapter shows the scan code obtained from port 60h for each character.

Note: Do not use this function with PC-only keyboards. These keyboards lack the additional chips required to program the typeahead buffer.

Register Contents on Entry:
AH - 5
CH - Scan Code
CL - Character

Register Contents on Exit:
AL - 0 if Successful, 1 if not Successful
CF - 0 if Successful, 1 if not Successful

Example:
```
;Place an A in the keyboard typeahead buffer.
MOV    AH,5
MOV    CH,1Eh
MOV    CL,'A'
INT    16h
```

Read Character from Enhanced Keyboard (Interrupt 16h Service 10h)

Use With: AT and PS/2

This service reads a character and scan code from the keyboard typeahead buffer. TABLE 7-9 at the end of this chapter shows the BIOS keyboard routine scan codes and ASCII character returned. TABLE 7-10 at the end of this chapter shows the scan code obtained from port 60h for each character.

Note: Do not use this function with PC-only keyboards. These keyboards do not provide the extended services of an enhanced keyboard.

Register Contents on Entry:
AH - 5

Register Contents on Exit:
AH - Scan Code
AL - Character

Example:
```
;Read a character from the keyboard.
MOV    AH,5
INT    16h
```

Get Enhanced Keyboard Status (Interrupt 16h Service 11h)

Use With: AT and PS/2

This service checks the keyboard for a character. If the buffer contains a character, it sets a flag and reads the character from the keyboard. It also returns the associated scan code. TABLE 7-9 at the end of this chapter shows the BIOS keyboard routine scan codes and ASCII character returned. TABLE 7-10 at the end of this chapter shows the scan code obtained from port 60h for each character.

Note: Do not use this function with PC-only keyboards. These keyboards do not provide the extended services provided by an enhanced keyboard.

Register Contents on Entry:
AH - 11h

Register Contents on Exit:
AH - Keyboard Scan Code
AL - ASCII Character
ZF - 0 for key input, 1 for no key input

Example:

```
;Wait for the user to press a key.
LoopIt:   MOV   Ah,11h
          INT   16h
          JZ    LoopIt
```

Get Enhanced Keyboard Shift Status
(Interrupt 16h Service 12h)

Use With: AT and PS/2

This service returns the ROM BIOS flag byte that describes the current keyboard toggle and shift key status.

Note: Do not use this function with PC-only keyboards. These keyboards do not provide the extended services provided by an enhanced keyboard.

Register Contents on Entry:
AH - 12h

Register Contents on Exit:
AX - Flags (True When Bit Set)
      0 - Right Shift Key Depressed
      1 - Left Shift Key Depressed
      2 - Either Ctrl Key Depressed
      3 - Either Alt Key Depressed
      4 - Scroll Key On
      5 - Num Lock Key On
      6 - Caps Lock Key On
      7 - Insert Key On
      8 - Left Ctrl Key Depressed

Example:

```
;Check the status of the insert key.
MOV   AH,12h
INT   16h
AND   AX,0000000010000000b
CMP   AX,80h
JNE   InsertOff
```

PRINTER SERVICES

This section contains a complete listing of all standard printer-related BIOS function calls. Most machines do not provide any extended printer services. TABLE 7-1 contains a listing of BIOS interrupts in interrupt number order.

Print Screen (Interrupt 5)

Use With: PC, AT, and PS/2

This service sends the contents of the video buffer (without attributes) to the printer port. You cannot use this service on graphics screens. There are no specific register contents required on entry, and no register output on exit.

Print Character (Interrupt 17h Service 0)

Use With: PC, AT, and PS/2

This service sends a character to the printer port and returns the current printer status. The printer status includes error status bits, but not an error code.

Register Contents on Entry:
AH - 0
AL - Character
DX - Printer Number (0 = LPT1, 1 = LPT2, 2 = LPT3)

Register Contents on Exit:
AH - Printer Status (Bits True When set)
    0 - Printer Timed Out
    1 - Unused
    2 - Unused
    3 - I/O Error
    4 - Printer Selected
    5 - Out of Paper
    6 - Printer Acknowledge
    7 - Printer Not Busy

Example:

```
;Send the letter A to LPT1.
MOV    AH,0
MOV    AL,'A'
MOV    DX,0
INT    17h
```

Initialize Printer (Interrupt 17h Service 1)

Use With: PC, AT, and PS/2

This service initializes the printer port and returns the current printer status. The printer status includes error status bits, but not an error code. Initialization includes setting top of form, performing any printer internal diagnostics, and moving the print head to the left-hand margin.

Register Contents on Entry:
AH - 1
DX - Printer Number (0 = LPT1, 1 = LPT2, 2 = LPT3)

Register Contents on Exit:
AH - Printer Status (Bits True When Set)
    0 - Printer Timed Out
    1 - Unused
    2 - Unused
    3 - I/O Error
    4 - Printer Selected
    5 - Out of Paper
    6 - Printer Acknowledge
    7 - Printer Not Busy

Example:
```
; Initialize the printer on LPT1.
MOV   AH,1
MOV   DX,0
INT   17h
```

Get Printer Status (Interrupt 17h Service 2)

Use With: PC, AT, and PS/2

This service returns the current printer status. It does not output any data or initialize the printer. The printer status includes error status bits, but not an error code.

Register Contents on Entry:
AH - 2
DX - Printer Number (0 = LPT1, 1 = LPT2, 2 = LPT3)

Register Contents on Exit:
AH - Printer Status (Bits True When Set)
    0 - Printer Timed Out
    1 - Unused
    2 - Unused
    3 - I/O Error
    4 - Printer Selected
    5 - Out of Paper
    6 - Printer Acknowledge
    7 - Printer Not Busy

Example:
```
;Get the printer status of LPT2.
```

```
MOV   AH,2
MOV   DX,1
INT   17h
```

MISCELLANEOUS SERVICES

This section contains a complete listing of all standard miscellaneous BIOS function calls. Depending on the peripheral devices you install, the manufacturer of your computer BIOS, and any software-based ROM extensions, you may have access to extended functions. Check your vendor manuals for details on any extended functions. In addition, some noncompatible computers fail to implement the miscellaneous ROM BIOS functions properly. Always test these functions on the computer with which you intend to use them. TABLE 7-1 contains a listing of BIOS interrupts in interrupt number order.

Get Equipment Status (Interrupt 11h)

Use With: PC, AT, and PS/2

This service obtains the equipment list code word contained in ROM BIOS.

Register Contents on Exit:
AX - Equipment List Code Word (Bits)

Bits	Description
0	1 if floppy disk drive installed.
1	1 if math co-processor installed.
2 - 3	System Board RAM Size
	00b - 16KB
	01b - 32KB
	10b - 48KB
	11b - 64KB
4 - 5	Initial Video Mode
	00b - Reserved
	01b - 40x25 Color Text
	10b - 80x25 Color Text
	11b - 80x25 Monochrome
6 - 7	Number of Floppy Disk Drives
	00b - 1
	01b - 2
	10b - 3
	11b - 4
8	Reserved
9 - 11	Number of RS-232 Ports Installed
12	1 if game adapter installed.
13	1 if internal MODEM installed (PC only)
14 - 15	Number of Installed Printers

Get Memory Size (Interrupt 12h)

Use With: PC, AT, and PS/2

This service obtains the amount of conventional memory available to DOS. This number does not include any extended or expanded memory installed. Use the get-extended-memory-size function (interrupt 15h, service 88h) to obtain extended memory size. Use the get-number-of-pages function (interrupt 67h, service 42h) to determine the amount of expanded memory present.

Register Contents on Exit:
AX - Conventional Memory Size in KBytes

Initialize Communications Port (Interrupt 14h Service 0)

Use With: PC, AT, and PS/2

This service initializes a communications port for use. See interrupt 14h service 4h and 5h for baud rates greater than 9600 baud on PS/2 machines. TABLE 7-11 at the end of this chapter shows the initialization parameter byte definitions. Notice that the port status bits show error conditions as well as data status information.

Register Contents on Entry:
AH - 0
AL - Initialization Parameter
DX - Communications Port Number (0 = COM1:, 1 = COM2:)

Register Contents on Exit:
AH - Port Status (Bits True When Set)
    0 - Receive Data Ready
    1 - Overrun Error Detected
    2 - Parity Error Detected
    3 - Framing Error Detected
    4 - Break Detected
    5 - Transmit Holding Register Empty
    6 - Transmit Shift Register Empty
    7 - Timed-Out
AL - Modem Status (Bits True When Set)
    0 - Change in Clear-To-Send Status
    1 - Change in Data-Set-Ready Status
    2 - Trailing Edge Ring Indicator
    3 - Change in Receive Line Signal Detect
    4 - Clear-To-Send
    5 - Data-Set-Ready
    6 - Ring Indicator
    7 - Receive Line Signal Detect

Example:
```
;Initialize COM2 for use.
MOV    AH,0
MOV    AL,10011011b  ;8 data bits, 1 stop bit, even parity, 1200 baud.
MOV    DX,1
INT    14h
```

Transmit Character (Interrupt 14h Service 1)

Use With: PC, AT, and PS/2

This service writes a character to the specified communications port. Notice the port status bits show error conditions as well as data status information.

Register Contents on Entry:
AH - 1
AL - Character
DX - Communications Port Number (0 = COM1:, 1 = COM2:)

Register Contents on Exit:
AH - Port Status (Bits True When Set)
    0 - Receive Data Ready
    1 - Overrun Error Detected
    2 - Parity Error Detected
    3 - Framing Error Detected
    4 - Break Detected
    5 - Transmit Holding Register Empty
    6 - Transmit Shift Register Empty
    7 - 0 if successful, 1 if not successful
AL - Character

Example:
```
;Transmit an A through COM1.
MOV    AH,1
MOV    AL,'A'
MOV    DX,0
INT    14h
```

Receive Character (Interrupt 14h Service 2)

Use With: PC, AT, and PS/2

This service reads a character from the specified communications port. Notice the port status bits show error conditions as well as data status information.

Register Contents on Entry:
Ah - 2

DX - Communications Port Number (0 = COM1:, 1 = COM2:)

Register Contents on Exit:
AH - Port Status (Bits True When Set)
     1 - Overrun Error Detected
     2 - Parity Error Detected
     3 - Framing Error Detected
     4 - Break Detected
     7 - 0 if successful, 1 if not successful
AL - Character

Example:
```
;Receive a character from COM2.
MOV    AH,2
MOV    DX,1
INT    14h
```

Get Communications Port Status (Interrupt 14h Service 3)

Use With: PC, AT, and PS/2

This service returns the status of the specified communications port. AH returns the port status bits showing error conditions as well as data status information. AL returns the MODEM status information which shows not only MODEM specific information, but also telephone line information.

Register Contents on Entry:
AH - 3
DX - Communications Port Number (0 = COM1:, 1 = COM2:)

Register Contents on Exit:
AH - Port Status (Bits True When Set)
     0 - Receive Data Ready
     1 - Overrun Error Detected
     2 - Parity Error Detected
     3 - Framing Error Detected
     4 - Break Detected
     5 - Transmit Holding Register Empty
     6 - Transmit Shift Register Empty
     7 - Timed-Out
AL - Modem Status (Bits True When Set)
     0 - Change in Clear-To-Send Status
     1 - Change in Data-Set-Ready Status
     2 - Trailing Edge Ring Indicator
     3 - Change in Receive Line Signal Detect
     4 - Clear-To-Send
     5 - Data-Set-Ready

6 - Ring Indicator
7 - Receive Line Signal Detect

Example:
```
;Get the port status of COM1.
MOV    AH,3
MOV    DX,0
INT    14h
```

Extended Initialize Communications Port (Interrupt 14h Service 4)

Use With: PS/2

This service initializes a communications port for use. It provides a superset of the service 0 functions for PS/2 machines. Do not use this function with the PC/XT or PC/AT. AH returns the port status bits showing error conditions as well as data status information. AL returns the MODEM status information that shows not only MODEM specific information, but also telephone line information.

Register Contents on Entry:
AH - 4
AL - Break Flag
    0 - No Break
    1 - Break
BH - Parity
    0 - None
    1 - Odd
    2 - Even
    3 - Stack Parity Odd
    4 - Stack Parity Even
BL - Stop Bits
    0 - 1 Bit
    1 - 2 Bits if Word Length 6 - 8 bits
    1 - 1.5 Bits if Word Length 5 Bits
CH - Word Length
    0 - 5 Bits
    1 - 6 Bits
    2 - 7 Bits
    3 - 8 Bits
CL - Baud Rate
    0 - 110 Baud
    1 - 150 Baud
    2 - 300 Baud
    3 - 600 Baud
    4 - 1,200 Baud
    5 - 2,400 Baud

6 - 4,800 Baud
7 - 9,600 Baud
8 - 19,200 Baud
DX - Communications Port Number (0 = COM1:, 1 = COM2:)

Register Contents on Exit:
AH - Port Status (Bits True When Set)
    0 - Receive Data Ready
    1 - Overrun Error Detected
    2 - Parity Error Detected
    3 - Framing Error Detected
    4 - Break Detected
    5 - Transmit Holding Register Empty
    6 - Transmit Shift Register Empty
    7 - Timed-Out
AL - Modem Status (Bits True When Set)
    0 - Change in Clear-To-Send Status
    1 - Change in Data-Set-Ready Status
    2 - Trailing Edge Ring Indicator
    3 - Change in Receive Line Signal Detect
    4 - Clear-To-Send
    5 - Data-Set-Ready
    6 - Ring Indicator
    7 - Receive Line Signal Detect

Example:

```
; Initialize COM1.
MOV     AH,4
MOV     AL,0        ;Break Enabled
MOV     BH,2        ;Even Parity
MOV     BL,1        ;2 Stop Bits
MOV     CH,8        ;8 Data Bits
MOV     CL,6        ;4,800 Baud
MOV     DX,0
INT     14h
```

Extended Communications Port Control
(Interrupt 14h Service 5)

Use With: PS/2

This service reads or sets the modem control register (MCR) for the specified serial communications port. Do not use this function with the PC/XT or PC/AT. If you set AL to write the MCR (value of 1), AH returns the port status bits showing error conditions as well as data status information. AL returns the MODEM status information which shows not only

MODEM specific information, but also telephone line information. If you set AL to read the MCR (value of 0), you do not need to enter anything into BL. The function returns with the MCR settings in BL.

Register Contents on Entry:

AH - 5

AL - Sub-function

    0 - Read Modem Control Register

    1 - Write Modem Control Register

BL - MCR Contents (Bits True When Set)

    0 - Data-Terminal Ready

    1 - Request-To-Send

    2 - Output 1

    3 - Output 2

    4 - Loop (Testing)

    5 through 7 - Reserved

DX - Communications Port Number (0 = COM1:, 1 = COM2:)

Register Contents on Exit (AL = 0):

BL - Modem Control Register Contents (see above)

Register Contents on Exit (AL = 1):

AH - Port Status (Bits True When Set)

    0 - Receive Data Ready

    1 - Overrun Error Detected

    2 - Parity Error Detected

    3 - Framing Error Detected

    4 - Break Detected

    5 - Transmit Holding Register Empty

    6 - Transmit Shift Register Empty

    7 - Timed-Out

AL - Modem Status (Bits True When Set)

    0 - Change in Clear-To-Send Status

    1 - Change in Data-Set-Ready Status

    2 - Trailing Edge Ring Indicator

    3 - Change in Receive Line Signal Detect

    4 - Clear-To-Send

    5 - Data-Set-Ready

    6 - Ring Indicator

    7 - Receive Line Signal Detect

Example:

```
;Read the COM2 MCR.
MOV    AH,5
MOV    AL,0
XOR    BL,BL
```

```
MOV    DX,1
INT    14h
```

Turn On Cassette Motor (Interrupt 15h Service 0)

Use With: PC

This service sets the cassette tape motor on. This function does not read data from or write data to the cassette. Use service 3 to read data and service 4 to write data. You must turn the cassette on before reading data and off after reading data. Do not use this function on a PC/AT or PS/2.

Register Contents on Entry:
AH - 0

Register Contents on Exit:
AH - 0 if Successful, 86h if Not Successful
CF - 0 if Successful, 1 if Not Successful

Turn Off Cassette Motor (Interrupt 15h Service 1)

Use With: PC

This service sets the cassette tape motor off. This function does not read data from or write data to the cassette. Use service 3 to read data and service 4 to write data. You must turn the cassette on before reading data and off after reading data. Do not use this function on a PC/AT or PS/2.

Register Contents on Entry:
AH - 1

Register Contents on Exit:
AH - 0 if Successful, 86h if Not Successful
CF - 0 if Successful, 1 if Not Successful

Read Data Blocks from Cassette (Interrupt 15h Service 2)

Use With: PC

This service reads one or more 256-byte blocks from the cassette tape into system memory. You must turn the cassette on before reading data and off after reading data. If the cassette fails to operate, AH returns with an error number. If the cassette does not contain the requested number of data blocks, DX will not match CX on return from the interrupt. Do not use this function on a PC/AT or PS/2.

Register Contents on Entry:
AH - 2
CX - Number of 256-Byte Blocks
BX - Offset of Data Buffer
ES - Segment of Data Buffer

Register Contents on Exit:
AH - Status (if not successful)
      01h - CRC Error
      02h - Bit Signals Scrambled
      04h - No Data Found
      80h - Invalid Command
      86h - Cassette Not Present
DX - Number of Bytes Read
BX - Offset of Last Byte Read
ES - Segment of Last Byte Read
CF - 0 if Successful, 1 if Not Successful

Example:
```
;Read 2 KBytes from the cassette.
MOV   AH,2
MOV   CX,8
LES   BX,CBuff
INT   15h
```

Write Data Blocks to Cassette (Interrupt 15h Service 3)

Use With: PC

This service writes one or more 256-byte blocks from the cassette tape into system memory. You must turn the cassette on before writing data and off after writing data. If the cassette fails to operate, AH returns with an error number. Do not use this function on a PC/AT or PS/2.

Register Contents on Entry:
AH - 3
CS - Number of 256-Byte Blocks
BX - Offset of Data Buffer
ES - Segment of Data Buffer

Register Contents on Exit:
AH - Status (if not successful)
      80h - Invalid Command
      86h - Cassette Not Present
CX - 0
BX - Offset of Last Byte Written + 1
ES - Segment of Last Byte Written
CF - 0 if Successful, 1 if Not Successful

Example:
```
;Write 4 KBytes to the cassette.
MOV   AH,2
MOV   CX,16
LES   BX,CBuff
INT   15h
```

Format ESDI Drive Periodic Interrupt (Interrupt 15h Service Fh)

Use With: PS/2

This ROM BIOS invokes this function on the drive adapter after each ESDI fixed disk cylinder operation completes during a format or surface analysis. A program can trap the interrupt and determine the current cylinder number. Do not use this function on the PC/XT or PC/AT. The BIOS on these machines do not provide this extended function.

Register Contents on Entry:
AH - 0Fh
AL - Phase Code
    0 - Reserved
    1 - Surface Analysis
    2 - Format

Register Contents on Exit:
CF - 0 if Successful, 1 if Not Successful

Example:
```
;Format an ESDI drive.
MOV    AH,0Fh
MOV    AL,2
INT    15h
```

Read POST Error Log (Interrupt 15h Service 21h Function 0)

Use With: PS/2

This service reads the error information collected during power-on self-test (POST). The error log consists of single word entries. The first byte contains the error code and the second byte contains the device code. Do not use this function on the PC/XT, PC/AT, or PS/2 Model 25/30. The BIOS on these machines do not provide this extended function.

Register Contents on Entry:
AH - 21h
AL - 0

Register Contents on Exit:
AH - 0 (if successful)
AH - Status (if not successful)
    80h - Invalid Command
    86h - Function Not Supported
BX - Number of POST Errors Found
DI - Offset of POST Error Log
ES - Segment of POST Error Log
CF - 0 if Successful, 1 if Not Successful

Write POST Error Log (Interrupt 15h Service 21h Function 1)

Use With: PS/2

This service writes the error information collected during power-on self-test (POST). The error log consists of single-word entries. The first byte contains the error code and the second byte contains the device code. Each device uses a unique identifier and produces unique codes. Obtain the identifier and codes from the manufacturer manuals. Application programs do not normally use this interrupt. Do not use this function on the PC/XT, PC/AT, or PS/2 Model 25/30. The BIOS on these machines do not provide this extended function.

Register Contents on Entry:
AH - 21h
AL - 1
BH - Device Identifier
BL - Device Error Code

Register Contents on Exit:
AH - 0 (if successful)
AH - Status (if not successful)
    01h - Error List Full
    80h - Invalid Command
    86h - Function Not Supported
CF - 0 if Successful, 1 if Not Successful

Keyboard Intercept (Interrupt 15h Service 4Fh)

Use With: PS/2

The ROM BIOS interrupt 09h interrupt handler invokes this service for every keystroke. An operating system or memory resident program can capture this service to filter the raw keyboard input. It can then return the character changed or unchanged. TABLE 7-9 at the end of this chapter shows the BIOS keyboard routine scan codes and ASCII character returned. TABLE 7-10 at the end of this chapter shows the scan code obtained from port 60h for each character. Do not use this function on the PC/XT or PC/AT. The BIOS on these machines do not provide this extended function.

Register Contents on Entry:
AH - 4Fh
AL - Scan Code

Register Contents on Exit:
CF - 0 if Successful, 1 if Not Successful
AL - New Scan Code if Successful

Example:
```
;Get a scan code from the keyboard.
MOV    AH,4Fh
MOV    AL,65  ;Letter A
INT    15h
```

Device Open (Interrupt 15h Service 80h)

Use With: AT and PS/2

This service obtains the ownership of a logical device for a process. A multitasking operating system could capture this interrupt and use it to arbitrate device usage among more than one program. Use this service with services 81h and 82h to provide a simple device arbitration environment. The standard BIOS routine always returns with the carry flag clear and AH containing 0. The multitasking operating system would determine the device and process identification codes specified below.

Register Contents on Entry:
AH - 80h
BX - Device Identification
CX - Process Identification

Register Contents on Exit:
AH - 0 if Successful, Status if Not Successful
CF - 0 if Successful, 1 if Not Successful

Device Close (Interrupt 15h Service 81h)

Use With: AT and PS/2

This service releases ownership of a logical device for a process. A multitasking operating system could capture this interrupt and use it to arbitrate device usage among more than one program. Use this service with services 80h and 82h to provide a simple device arbitration environment. The standard BIOS routine always returns with the carry flag clear and AH containing 0. The multitasking operating system would determine the device and process identification codes specified below.

Register Contents on Entry:
AH - 81h
BX - Device Identification
CX - Process Identification

Register Contents on Exit:
AH - 0 if Successful, Status if Not Successful
CF - 0 if Successful, 1 if Not Successful

Process Termination (Interrupt 15h Service 82h)

Use With: AT and PS/2

This service releases ownership of all logical devices for a process about to end. A multitasking operating system could capture this interrupt and use it to arbitrate device usage among more than on program. Use this service with services 80h and 81h to provide a simple device arbitration environment. The standard BIOS routine always returns with the carry flag clear and AH containing 0. The multitasking operating system would determine the process identification code specified below.

Register Contents on Entry:
AH - 82h
BX - Process Identification

Register Contents on Exit:
AH - 0 if Successful, Status if Not Successful
CF - 0 if Successful, 1 if Not Successful

Event Wait (Interrupt 15h Service 83h)

Use With: AT and PS/2

This service requests a setting of a semaphore after a specified period of time. It also cancels previous requests. If this function is successful, it sets bit 7 of the semaphore byte after the requested time elapses. The calling program must clear the semaphore before it calls this function again. The actual time interval used for this function revolves around the 976 microsecond ($1/1024$ second) interrupt of the CMOS clock. This provides finer timing control than the $1/100$ second resolution of the get time function (interrupt 21H function 2Ch). Do not use this function on the PC/XT or PS/2 Models 25/30.

Register Contents on Entry:
AH   - 83h
AL   - 0 (Event Wait Request)
AL   - 1 (Event Wait Cancel)
CX:DX - Microseconds
BX   - Offset of Semaphore Byte
ES   - Segment of Semaphore Byte

Register Contents on Exit (AL = 0):
CF   - 0 if Successful, 1 if Not Successful

Example:
```
;Wait for 1/1000 second before performing a task.
            MOV    AH,83h
            MOV    AL,0
            XOR    CX,CX
            MOV    DX,1000
            LES    BX,SByte
            INT    15h
LoopIt:   BTSByte,7 ;Bit test bit 7.
            JNC    LoopIt      ;Wait if zero, time not elapsed.
```

Read Joystick (Interrupt 15h Service 84h)

Use With: AT and PS/2

This service reads the joystick switch settings or potentiometer values. You can use the first function (DX = 0) to see if the machine has a joystick installed. If the machine does not have a joystick, this function returns 0 in AL. In addition, it returns with AX, BX, CX, and DX containing 0 if you execute function 1 with no joystick attached. When using a 250 KΩ joystick, the potentiometer values range between 0 and 416 (0-1A0h).

Register Contents on Entry:
AH - 84h
DX - 0 Read Switches, 1 Read Potentiometers.

Register Contents on Exit (CX = 0):
AL - Switch Settings (Bits 4 - 7)
CF - 0 if Successful, 1 if Not Successful

Register Contents on Exit (DX = 1):
AX - Joystick-A X Value
BX - Joystick-A Y Value
CX - Joystick-B X Value
DX - Joystick-B Y Value
CF - 0 if Successful, 1 if Not Successful

Example:

```
;Read the joystick switch settings.
MOV    AH,84h
MOV    DX,0
INT    15h
```

SysReq Key (Interrupt 15h Service 85h)

Use With: AT and PS/2

The ROM BIOS keyboard handler invokes this service when it detects a SysReq key press. The standard routine always returns a success code for this function because it contains a dummy routine. A multitasking operating system could use this interrupt to detect a user need for operating system assistance.

Register Contents on Entry:
AH - 85h
AL - 0 if Depressed, 1 if Released

Register Contents on Exit:
AH - 0 Successful, Status if Not Successful
CF - 0 if Successful, 1 if Not Successful

Delay (Interrupt 15h Service 86h)

Use With: AT and PS/2

This service suspends the calling program for a specified interval. Use it to create clock speed independent, timed programs. The actual time interval used for this function revolves around the 976 microsecond ($1/1024$ second) interrupt of the CMOS clock. This provides finer timing control than the $1/100$ second resolution of the get time function (interrupt 21H function 2Ch). Do not use this function on the PC/XT or PS/2 Models 25/30.

Register Contents on Entry:
AH - 86h
CX:DX - Microseconds to Wait

Register Contents on Exit:
CF - 0 if Successful, 1 if Not Successful

Example:
```
;Wait 1.0001 seconds to perform a task.
MOV    AH,86h
MOV    CX,000Fh    ;Use combination of CX and DX to
MOV    DX,4254h    ; convert time to hex. First bit of
INT    15h         ; CX equals 65,536 microseconds.
```

Move Extended Memory Block (Interrupt 15h Service 87h)

Use With: AT and PS/2

This service transfers data between conventional and extended memory. Extended memory lies above the 1 MB addressing capability of the 8088/8086 processor. To use extended memory the processor must switch to protected mode. To switch to protected mode, the CPU needs a global descriptor table. TABLE 7-12 at the end of this chapter contains a listing of the GDT format required to use this service. The ROM BIOS fills in the values of offsets 00h–0Fh and 20h–2Fh of the GDT before switching the processor to protected mode. All addresses in protected mode refer to 24- or 32-bit linear (physical) addresses, not the segment and offset format normally used in real mode. This service executes with interrupts disabled. It might interfere with communications programs and network drivers. Programs that use this function will not execute in the compatibility window of OS/2.

Register Contents on Entry:
AH - 87h
CX - Number of Words to Move
SI - Offset of Global Descriptor Table
ES - Segment of Global Descriptor Table

Register Contents on Exit:
AH - Status
    0 - Successful
    1 - RAM Parity Error
    2 - Exception Interrupt Error
    3 - Gate Address Line 20 Failed
CF - 0 if Successful, 1 if Not Successful

Get Extended Memory Size (Interrupt 15h Service 88h)

Use With: AT and PS/2

This service retrieves the amount of extended memory in an 80286/80386/80486 equipped machine. Extended memory lies above the 1 MB addressing capability of the 8088/8086 processor. Programs that use this function will not execute in the compatibility window of OS/2.

Register Contents on Entry:
AH - 88h

Register Contents on Exit:
AX - Amount of Extended Memory in KBytes

Enter Protected Mode (Interrupt 15h Service 89h)

Use With: AT and PS/2

This service switches the CPU into protected mode operation. Extended memory lies above the 1 MB addressing capability of the 8088/8086 processor. To use extended memory the processor must switch to protected mode. To switch to protected mode, the CPU needs a global descriptor table. TABLE 7-13 at the end of this chapter contains a listing of the global descriptor table (GDT) format required to use this service. The ROM BIOS fills in the values for offsets 00h–0Fh and 20h–2Fh of the GDT before switching the processor to protected mode. All addresses in protected mode refer to 24- or 32-bit linear (physical) addresses, not the segment and offset format normally used in real mode. This service executes with interrupts disabled. It might interfere with communications programs and network drivers. Programs that use this function will not execute in the compatibility window of OS/2.

Register Contents on Entry:
AH - 89h
BH - Interrupt Number for IRQ0 Written to ICW2 of PIC#1
BL - Interrupt Number for IRQ8 Written to ICW2 of PIC#2
SI   - Offset of Global Descriptor Table
ES - Segment of Global Descriptor Table

Register Contents on Exit:
AX - 0 if Successful, FFh if Not Successful
CF - 0 if Successful, 1 if Not Successful

CS - User Defined Selector
DS - User Defined Selector
ES - User Defined Selector
SS - User Defined Selector

Device Wait (Interrupt 15h Service 90h)

Use With: AT and PS/2

The ROM BIOS fixed disk, floppy disk, printer, network, and keyboard handlers invoke this service before performing a programmed wait for I/O completion. When using this function with network devices, ES:BX point to a network control block (NCB). A multitasking operating system could use this function to dispatch other tasks while the requesting process waits for I/O to complete.

Register Contents on Entry:
AH - 90h
AL - Device Type
    Not Defined:
    00h - 7Fh Serially Reusable Devices
    80h - BFh Re-entrant Devices
    C0h - FFh Wait-Only Calls, No POST Function
    Predefined:
    00h - Disk
    01h - Floppy Disk
    02h - Keyboard
    03h - Pointing Device
    80h - Network
    FCh - Fixed Disk Reset
    FDh - Floppy Disk Drive Motor Start
    FEh - Printer
BX - Offset of Request Block (Device Types 80h - FFh)
ES - Segment of Request Block (Device Types 80h - FFh)

Register Contents on Exit:
AH - 0 if Successful
CF - 0 if Successful, 1 if Not Successful

Example:
```
;Wait until a floppy disk drive completes a write.
;No request block required for a floppy drive.
MOV    AH,90h
MOV    AL,1
INT    15h
```

Device Post (Interrupt 15h Service 91h)

Use With: AT and PS/2

The ROM BIOS fixed disk, floppy disk, network, and keyboard handlers invoke this service to show I/O operation completion and/or device ready. When using this function with network devices, ES:BX point to a network control block (NCB). A multitasking operating system could use this function to restart a halted process upon completion of I/O.

Register Contents on Entry:
AH - 91h
AL - Device Type
    Not Defined:
    00h - 7Fh Serially Reusable Devices
    80h - BFh Re-entrant Devices
    Predefined:
    00h - Disk
    01h - Floppy Disk
    02h - Keyboard
    03h - Pointing Device
    80h - Network
BX - Offset of Request Block (Device Types 80h - FFh)
ES - Segment of Request Block (Device Types 80h - FFh)

Register Contents on Exit:
AH - 0 if Successful

Example:
```
;Restart a program after a network hard disk write.
MOV    AH,91h
MOV    AL,80h
LES    BX,NRB
INT    15h
```

Get System Environment (Interrupt 15h Service C0h)

Use With: AT and PS/2

This service obtains system configuration data. TABLE 7-14 at the end of this chapter contains a listing of the configuration table contents.

Register Contents on Entry:
AH - C0h

Register Contents on Exit:
BX - Offset of Configuration Table
ES - Segment of Configuration Table

Example:
```
;Get the system environment.
MOV    AH,0C0h
INT    15h
```

Get Address of Extended BIOS Data Area
(Interrupt 15h Service C1h)

Use With: PS/2

This service obtains the segment of the extended BIOS data area. Never use this function with a PC/XT or PC/AT. You may use it on PS/2 Models 25/30.

Register Contents on Entry:
AH - C1h

Register Contents on Exit:
ES - Segment of Extended BIOS Data Area
CF - 0 if Successful, 1 if Not Successful

Example:
```
;Get the extended BIOS segment address.
MOV    AH,0C1h
INT    15h
```

Enable/Disable Pointing Device
(Interrupt 15h Service C2h Function 0)

Use With: PS/2

This service enables/disables the mouse or other system pointing device. Never use this function with a PC/XT or PC/AT. Use the DOS interrupt 33h functions to control the PC/XT or PC/AT mouse. You may use this function on PS/2 Models 25/30.

Register Contents on Entry:
AH - C2h
AL - 0
BH - 0 to Disable/1 to Enable Pointing Device

Register Contents on Exit:
AH - Status
    0 - Successful
    1 - Invalid Function Call
    2 - Invalid Input
    3 - Interface Error
    4 - Re-send
    5 - No Far Call Installed
CF - 0 if Successful, 1 if Not Successful

Example:
```
;Enable the pointing device.
MOV    AH,0C2h
MOV    AL,0
```

```
MOV    BH,1
INT    15h
```

Reset Pointing Device
(Interrupt 15h Service C2h Function 1)

Use With: PS/2

This service resets the mouse or other system pointing device. Never use this function with a PC/XT or PC/AT. Use the DOS interrupt 33h functions to control the PC/XT and PC/AT mouse. You may use this function on PS/2 Models 25/30.

Register Contents on Entry:
AH - 2hC
AL - 1

Register Contents on Exit:
AH - Status
    0 - Successful
    1 - Invalid Function Call
    2 - Invalid Input
    3 - Interface Error
    4 - Re-send
    5 - No Far Call Installed
BH - Device Identification
CF - 0 if Successful, 1 if Not Successful

Example:
```
;Reset the pointing device.
MOV    AH,C2h
MOV    AL,1
INT    15h
```

Set Sample Rate (Interrupt 15h Service C2h Function 2)

Use With: PS/2

This service sets the mouse or other system pointing device sampling rate. The sampling rate determines how often the system updates the mouse or other pointer position data. Never use this function with a PC/XT or PC/AT. Use the DOS interrupt 33h functions to control the PC/XT and PC/AT mouse. You may use this function on PS/2 Models 25/30.

Register Contents on Entry:
AH - C2h
AL - 2
BH - Sample Rate Value
    0 - 10 Reports Per Second

1 - 20 Reports Per Second
2 - 40 Reports Per Second
3 - 60 Reports Per Second
4 - 80 Reports Per Second
5 - 100 Reports Per Second
6 - 200 Reports Per Second

Register Contents on Exit:
AH - Status
    0 - Successful
    1 - Invalid Function Call
    2 - Invalid Input
    3 - Interface Error
    4 - Re-send
    5 - No Far Call Installed
CF - 0 if Successful, 1 if Not Successful

Example:
```
;Set the mouse sampling rate for 60 reports/second.
MOV    AH,C2h
MOV    AL,2
MOV    BH,3
INT    15h
```

Set Resolution (Interrupt 15h Service C2h Function 3)

Use With: PS/2

This service sets the mouse or other system pointing device resolution. The resolution determines how far you must move the pointing device to change its position data by one millimeter. Some programmers refer to this as the pointing device sensitivity. Never use this function with a PC/XT or PC/AT. Use the DOS interrupt 33h functions to control the PC/XT and PC/AT mouse. You may use this function on PS/2 Models 25/30.

Register Contents on Entry:
AH - C2h
AL - 3
BH - Resolution Value
    0 - 1 Count Per Millimeter
    1 - 2 Counts Per Millimeter
    2 - 4 Counts Per Millimeter
    3 - 8 Counts Per Millimeter

Register Contents on Exit:
AH - Status
    0 - Successful
    1 - Invalid Function Call

2 - Invalid Input
3 - Interface Error
4 - Re-send
5 - No Far Call Installed
CF - 0 if Successful, 1 if Not Successful

Example:
```
;Set the mouse resolution to 4 counts/millimeter.
MOV    AH,C2h
MOV    AL,3
MOV    BH,2
INT    15h
```

Get Pointing Device Type
(Interrupt 15h Service C2h Function 4)

Use With: PS/2

This service returns the mouse or other system pointing device identification code. Never use this function with a PC/XT or PC/AT. Use the DOS interrupt 33h functions to control the PC/XT and PC/AT mouse. You may use this function on PS/2 Models 25/30.

Register Contents on Entry:
AH - C2h
AL - 4

Register Contents on Exit:
AH - Status
    0 - Successful
    1 - Invalid Function Call
    2 - Invalid Input
    3 - Interface Error
    4 - Re-send
    5 - No Far Call Installed
BH - Device Identification
CF - 0 if Successful, 1 if Not Successful

Example:
```
;Get the device identification code.
MOV    AH,C2h
MOV    AL,4
INT    15h
```

Initialize Pointing Device Interface
(Interrupt 15h Service C2h Function 5)

Use With: PS/2

This service sets the data package size for the mouse or other system pointing device. It also resets the resolution, sampling rate, and scaling to their default values. Use this function at the start of a program to place the pointing device in a known state. Never use this function with a PC/XT or PC/AT. Use the DOS interrupt 33h functions to control the PC/XT and PC/AT mouse. You may use this function on PS/2 Models 25/30.

Register Contents on Entry:
AH - C2h
AL - 5
BH - Data Package Size in Bytes (1 - 8)

Register Contents on Exit:
AH - Status
    0 - Successful
    1 - Invalid Function Call
    2 - Invalid Input
    3 - Interface Error
    4 - Re-send
    5 - No Far Call Installed
CF - 0 if Successful, 1 if Not Successful

Example:

```
;Set the mouse data package size to 8 bytes.
MOV    AH,C2h
MOV    AL,5
MOV    BH,8
INT    15h
```

Set Scaling or Get Status
(Interrupt 15h Service C2h Function 6)

Use With: PS/2

This service returns the mouse or other system pointing device status. It also sets the device scaling factor. Never use this function with a PC/XT or PC/AT. Use the DOS interrupt 33h functions to control the PC/XT and PC/AT mouse. You may use this function on PS/2 Models 25/30.

Register Contents on Entry:
AH - C2h
AL - 6
BH - Extended Command
    0 - Return Device Status
    1 - Set Scaling at 1:1
    2 - Set Scaling at 2:1

Register Contents on Exit:
AH - Status
    0 - Successful
    1 - Invalid Function Call

2 - Invalid Input
3 - Interface Error
4 - Re-send
5 - No Far Call Installed

BH - Status Byte (if BH = 0) (Bits True When Set)
    0 - Right Button Pressed
    1 - Reserved
    2 - Left Button Pressed
    3 - Reserved
    4 - 1:1 Scaling When Clear, 2:1 Scaling When Set
    5 - Device Enabled
    6 - Stream Mode When Clear, Remote Mode When Set
    7 - Reserved

CL - Resolution
    0 - 1 Count Per Millimeter
    1 - 2 Counts Per Millimeter
    2 - 4 Counts Per Millimeter
    3 - 8 Counts Per Millimeter

DL - Sample Rate
    0 - 10 Reports Per Second
    1 - 20 Reports Per Second
    2 - 40 Reports Per Second
    3 - 60 Reports Per Second
    4 - 80 Reports Per Second
    5 - 100 Reports Per Second
    6 - 200 Reports Per Second

CF - 0 if Successful, 1 if Not Successful

Example:

```
;Get the pointing device status.
MOV   AH,C2h
MOV   AL,6
MOV   BH,0
INT   15h
```

Set Pointing Device Handler Address
(Interrupt 15h Service C2h Function 7)

Use With: PS/2

This service sets the mouse or other system pointing device driver address. You could use this function to install a special driver (for a non-standard device) or add extended functions to the current driver. Never use this function with a PC/XT or PC/AT. You may use it on PS/2 Models 25/30.

Register Contents on Entry:
AH - C2h
AL - 7

BX - Offset of User Routine
ES - Segment of User Routine

Register Contents on Exit:
AH - Status
     0 - Successful
     1 - Invalid Function Call
     2 - Invalid Input
     3 - Interface Error
     4 - Re-send
     5 - No Far Call Installed
CF - 0 if Successful, 1 if Not Successful

Example:
```
;Point the pointing device address to a special device handler.
MOV    AH,C2h
MOV    AL,7
LES    BX,DAddress
INT    15h
```

Set Watchdog Timer Time-Out (Interrupt 15h Service C3h)

Use With: PS/2

This service enables/disables the watchdog timer. The watchdog automatically reboots the machine after processor activity stops for a defined period. It does this using the nonmaskable interrupt (NMI) line of the processor then executing a special routine. Enable the watchdog when programming or during time-critical operations. Disable the timer during I/O or when using interrupt driven programs. Never use this function with a PC/XT, PC/AT, or PS/2 Models 25/30.

Register Contents on Entry:
AH - C3h
AL - 0 to Disable/1 to Enable Watchdog Time-Out
BH - Watchdog Timer Counter

Register Contents on Exit:
CF - 0 if Successful, 1 if Not Successful

Example:
```
;Enable the watchdog.
MOV    AH,C3h
MOV    AL,1
MOV    BH,80h
INT    15h
```

Programmable Option Select (Interrupt 15h Service C4h)

Use With: PS/2

This service returns the base POS register address, enables a slot for setup, or enables an adapter. Obtain specific slot data using port input instructions after enabling the slot using this service. TABLE 7-15 at the end of this chapter contains the port addresses available to all slots. Never use this function with a PC/XT or PC/AT. You may use it on PS/2 Models 25/30. Future versions of EISA-based (extended industry standard architecture) machines may use this function.

Register Contents on Entry:
AH - C3h
AL - Sub-function
    0 - Return Base POS Adapter Register Address
    1 - Enable Slot
    2 - Enable Adapter
BH - Slot Number if AL = 1

Register Contents on Exit:
CF - 0 if Successful, 1 if Not Successful
DX - Base POS Adapter Register Address (if AL = 0)

Example:

```
;Enable slot number 2.
MOV    AH,C3h
MOV    AL,1
MOV    BH,2
INT    15h
```

ROM Basic (Interrupt 18h)

Use With: PC, AT, and PS/2

This service transfers system control to ROM BASIC. It requires no input and provides no output. Most non-IBM machines do not provide a copy of BASIC in ROM. Therefore, you cannot use this interrupt to invoke BASIC.

Warm Boot (Interrupt 19h)

Use With: PC, AT, and PS/2

This service starts the reboot sequence from a floppy or fixed disk. It requires no input and provides no output. A warm boot does not perform a complete POST. It does perform a partial memory check and reset the processor registers.

Get Clock Counter (Interrupt 1Ah Service 0)

Use With: AT and PS/2

This service gets the current contents of the clock tick counter. Do not confuse this counter with the system or CMOS clock. The original PC does not support this function, however many versions of the PC/XT do.

Register Contents on Entry:
AH - 0

Register Contents on Exit:
AL - Rolled Over Flag
     0   - Past Midnight Since Last Read

    < >0 - Not Past Midnight Since Last Read
CX:DX - Tick Count (1,573,040 Maximum)

Example:
```
;Get the current clock tick count.
MOV    AH,0
INT    1Ah
```

Set Clock Counter (Interrupt 1Ah Service 1)

Use With: AT and PS/2
    This service sets the current contents of the clock counter. Do not confuse this counter with the system or CMOS clock. The original PC does not support this function, however many versions of the PC/XT do.

Register Contents on Entry:
Ah - 1
CX:DX - Tick Count (1,573,040 Maximum)

Example:
```
;Reset the clock tick counter to 0.
MOV    AH,1
XOR    CX,CX
XOR    DX,DX
INT    1Ah
```

Read Real-Time Clock (Interrupt 1Ah Service 2)

Use With: AT and PS/2
    This service reads the current time from the CMOS time/date chip. This function is not available on the PC/XT.

Register Contents on Entry:
AH - 2

Register Contents on Exit:
CH - Hours in Binary Coded Decimal (BCD) Format
CL - Minutes in BCD Format
DH - Seconds in BCD Format
DL - 0 if Standard Time, 1 if Daylight Saving Time
CF - 0 if Clock Running, 1 if Clock Stopped

Example:
```
;Get the current system time.
MOV    AH,2
INT    1Ah
```

Set Real-Time Clock (Interrupt 1Ah Service 3)

Use With: AT and PS/2

This service sets the current time of the CMOS time/date chip. This function is not available on the PC/XT.

Register Contents on Entry:
AH - 3
CH - Hours in Binary Coded Decimal (BCD) Format
CL - Minutes in BCD Format
DH - Seconds in BCD Format
DL - 0 if Standard Time, 1 if Daylight Saving Time

Example:
```
;Set the system time to 09:28:37 standard time.
MOV    AH,3
MOV    CH,09h
MOV    CL,28h
MOV    DH,37h
MOV    DL,0
INT    1Ah
```

Read Date from Real-Time Clock (Interrupt 1Ah Service 4)

Use With: AT and PS/2

This service reads the current date from the CMOS time/date chip. This function is not available on the PC/XT.

Register Contents on Entry:
AH - 4

Register Contents on Entry:
AH - 4

Register Contents on Exit:
CH - Century in Binary Coded Decimal (BCD) Format
CL - Year in BCD Format
DH - Month in BCD Format
DL - Day in BCD Format
CF - 0 if Clock Running, 1 if Clock Stopped

Example:
```
;Get the current date.
MOV    AH,4
INT    1Ah
```

Set Date of Real-Time Clock (Interrupt 1Ah Service 5)

Use With: AT and PS/2

This service sets the current date of the CMOS time/date chip. This function is not available on the PC/XT.

Register Contents on Entry:
AH - 5
CH - Century in Binary Coded Decimal (BCD) Format
CL - Year in BCD Format
DH - Month in BCD Format
DL - Day in BCD Format

Example:

```
;Set the current date to 07/04/90.
MOV    AH,5
MOV    CH,19h
MOV    CL,90h
MOV    DH,07h
MOV    DL,04h
INT    1Ah
```

Set Alarm (Interrupt 1Ah Service 6)

Use With: AT and PS/2

This service sets an alarm using the CMOS time/date chip. It automatically enables the clock chip interrupt level (IRQ8). You may only specify one alarm at a time. The alarm remains in effect until you disable it with function 7. Place the alarm interrupt handler at interrupt vector 4Ah. This function is not available on the PC/XT.

Register Contents on Entry:
AH - 6
CH - Hours in Binary Coded Decimal (BCD) Format
CL - Minutes in BCD Format
DH - Seconds in BCD Format

Register Contents on Exit:
CF - 0 if Successful, 1 if Not Successful

Example:

```
;Set an alarm for 14:23:50.
MOV    AH,6
MOV    CH,14h
MOV    CL,23h
MOV    DH,50h
INT    1Ah
```

Disable Alarm (Interrupt 1Ah Service 7)

Use With: AT and PS/2

This service disables a pending CMOS time/date chip alarm. It does not disable the clock chip interrupt level (IRQ8). This function is not available on the PC/XT.

Register Contents on Entry:
AH - 7

Example:
```
;Disable the CMOS alarm.
MOV   AH,7
INT   1Ah
```

Get Day Count (Interrupt 1Ah Service Ah)

Use With: PS/2

This service gets the contents of the system day counter. This function is not available on the PC/XT or PC/AT. You may use it on PS/2 Models 25/30.

Register Contents on Entry:
AH - Ah

Register Contents on Exit:
CF - 0 if Successful, 1 if Not Successful
CX - Count of Days Since January 1, 1980

Example:
```
;Get the number of days since 01/01/1980
MOV   AH,Ah
INT   1Ah
```

Set Day Count (Interrupt 1Ah Service Bh)

Use With: PS/2

This service sets the contents of the system day counter. This function is not available on the PC/XT or PC/AT. You may use it on PS/2 Models 25/30.

Register Contents on Entry:
AH - Bh
CX - Count of Days since January 1, 1980

Register Contents on Exit:
CF - 0 if Successful, 1 if Not Successful

Example:
```
;Set the number of days since 01/01/1980
MOV   AH,Bh
MOV   CX,3742  ;03/31/1990
INT   1Ah
```

Set Sound Source (Interrupt 1Ah Service 80h)

Use With: PCjr

Sets the source of tones used by the PCjrs "Audio Out" or RF modulator. Do not use this function with the PC, PC/XT, PC/AT, or PS/2.

Register Contents on Entry:
AH - 80h
AL - Sound Source
    0 - 8253 Programmable Timer

1 - Cassette Input
2 - Audio In Line on I/O Channel
3 - Sound Generator Chip

Example:

```
;Set the PCjr sound source to the sound generator chip.
MOV    AH,80h
MOV    AL,3
INT  . 1Ah
```

Table 7-8   Floppy/Hard Disk Drive Error Codes

Code	Hard	Floppy	Description
00h	Yes	Yes	No Error
01h	Yes	Yes	Invalid Command
02h	Yes	Yes	Address Mark Not Found
03h	Yes	No	Disk Write Protected
04h	Yes	Yes	Sector Not Found
05h	No	Yes	Reset Failed
06h	Yes	No	Floppy Disk Removed
07h	No	Yes	Bad Parameter Table
08h	Yes	No	DMA Overrun
09h	Yes	Yes	DMA Crossed 64 KByte Boundary
0Ah	No	Yes	Bad Sector Flag
0Bh	No	Yes	Bad Track Flag
0Ch	Yes	No	Media Type Not Found
0Dh	No	Yes	Invalid Number of Sectors on Format
0Eh	No	Yes	Control Data Address Mark Detected
0Fh	No	Yes	DMA Arbitration Level Out of Range
10h	Yes	Yes	Uncorrectable CRC or ECC Data Error
11h	No	Yes	ECC Corrected Data Error
20h	Yes	Yes	Controller Failure
40h	Yes	Yes	Seek Failed
80h	Yes	Yes	Disk Timed-Out
AAh	No	Yes	Disk Not Ready
BBh	No	Yes	Undefined Error
CCh	No	Yes	Write Fault
E0h	No	Yes	Status Register Error
FFh	No	Yes	Sense Operation Failed

Table 7-9   BIOS Keyboard Routine Output

Scan Code		ASCII Value		
Decimal	Hex	Decimal	Hex	Keystroke
0	00h	0	00h	Break
1	01h	27	1Bh	Esc
2	02h	49	31h	1
		33	21h	!

Table 7-9   Continued.

Scan Code		ASCII Value		
Decimal	Hex	Decimal	Hex	Keystroke
3	03h	50	32h	2
		64	40h	@
		0	00h	Ctrl-@
4	04h	51	33h	3
		35	23h	#
5	05h	52	34h	4
		36	24h	$
6	06h	53	35h	5
		37	25h	%
7	07h	54	36h	6
		94	5Eh	^
8	08h	55	37h	7
		38	26h	&
9	09h	56	38h	8
		42	2Ah	* (Shift-8)
10	0Ah	57	39h	9
		40	28h	(
11	0Bh	48	30h	0
		41	29h	)
12	0Ch	45	2Dh	-
		95	5Fh	_
		31	1Fh	Ctrl-_
13	0Dh	61	3Dh	=
		43	2Bh	+
14	0Eh	8	08h	Backspace
		127	7Fh	Ctrl-Backspace
15	0Fh	9	09h	Tab
		0	00h	Back Tab
16	10h	113	71h	q
		81	51h	Q
		0	00h	Alt-Q
		17	11h	Ctrl-Q
17	11h	119	77h	w
		87	57h	W
		0	00h	Alt-W
		23	17h	Ctrl-W
18	12h	101	65h	e
		69	45h	E
		0	00h	Alt-E
		5	05h	Ctrl-E
19	13h	114	72h	r
		82	52h	R
		0	00h	Alt-R
		18	12h	Ctrl-R
20	14h	116	74h	t
		84	54h	T
		0	00h	Alt-T
		20	14h	Ctrl-T
21	15h	121	79h	y
		89	59h	Y

Table 7-9   Continued.

Scan Code		ASCII Value		
Decimal	Hex	Decimal	Hex	Keystroke
		0	00h	Alt-Y
		25	19h	Ctrl-Y
22	16h	117	75h	u
		85	59h	U
		0	00h	Alt-U
		21	15h	Ctrl-U
23	17h	105	69h	i
		73	49h	I
		0	00h	Alt-I
		9	09h	Ctrl-I
24	18h	111	6Fh	o
		79	4Fh	O
		0	00h	Alt-O
		15	0Fh	Ctrl-O
25	19h	112	70h	p
		80	50h	P
		0	00h	Alt-P
		16	10h	Ctrl-P
26	1Ah	91	5Bh	[
		123	7Bh	{
		27	1Bh	Ctrl-[
27	1Bh	93	5Dh	]
		125	7Dh	}
		29	1Dh	Ctrl-]
28	1Ch	13	0Dh	Return
30	1Eh	97	61h	a
		65	41h	A
		0	00h	Alt-A
		1	01h	Ctrl-A
31	1Fh	115	73h	s
		83	53h	S
		0	00h	Alt-S
		19	13h	Ctrl-S
32	20h	100	64h	d
		68	44h	D
		0	00h	Alt-D
		4	04h	Ctrl-D
33	21h	102	66h	f
		70	46h	F
		0	00h	Alt-F
		6	06h	Ctrl-F
34	22h	103	67h	g
		71	47h	G
		0	00h	Alt-G
		7	07h	Ctrl-G
35	23h	104	68h	h
		72	48h	H
		0	00h	Alt-H
		8	08h	Ctrl-H
36	24h	106	6Ah	j
		74	4Ah	J
		0	00h	Alt-J
		10	0Ah	Ctrl-J

Table 7-9 Continued.

Scan Code		ASCII Value		
Decimal	Hex	Decimal	Hex	Keystroke
37	25h	107	6Bh	k
		75	4Bh	K
		0	00h	Alt-K
		11	0Bh	Ctrl-K
38	26h	108	6Ch	l
		76	4Ch	L
		0	00h	Alt-L
		12	0Ch	Ctrl-L
39	27h	59	3Bh	;
		58	3Ah	:
40	28h	39	27h	'
		34	22h	"
41	29h	96	60h	`
		126	7Eh	
43	2Bh	92	5Ch	\
		124	7Ch		
		28	1Ch	Ctrl-\
44	2Ch	122	7Ah	z
		90	5Ah	Z
		0	00h	Alt-Z
		26	1Ah	Ctrl-Z
45	2Dh	120	78h	x
		88	58h	X
		0	00h	Alt-X
		24	18h	Ctrl-X
46	2Eh	99	63h	c
		67	43h	C
		0	00h	Alt-C
		3	03h	Ctrl-C
47	2Fh	118	76h	v
		86	56h	V
		0	00h	Alt-V
		22	16h	Ctrl-V
48	30h	98	62h	b
		66	42h	B
		0	00h	Alt-B
		2	02h	Ctrl-B
49	31h	110	6Eh	n
		78	4Eh	N
		0	00h	Alt-N
		14	0Eh	Ctrl-N
50	32h	109	6Dh	m
		77	4Dh	M
		0	00h	Alt-M
		13	0Dh	Ctrl-M
51	33h	44	2Ch	,
		60	3Ch	<
52	34h	46	2Eh	.
		62	3Eh	>
53	35h	47	2Fh	/
		63	3Fh	?

Table 7-9   Continued.

Scan Code		ASCII Value		
Decimal	Hex	Decimal	Hex	Keystroke
55	37h	42	2Ah	*
		0	00h	Alt-Pause
56	38h	0	00h	Alt-Break
57	39h	32	20h	Space
58	3Ah	0	00h	Caps Lock
59	3Bh	0	00h	F1
60	3Ch	0	00h	F2
61	3Dh	0	00h	F3
62	3Eh	0	00h	F4
63	3Fh	0	00h	F5
64	40h	0	00h	F6
65	41h	0	00h	F7
66	42h	0	00h	F8
67	43h	0	00h	F9
68	44h	0	00h	F10
69	45h	0	00h	Num Lock
70	46h	0	00h	Scroll Lock
71	47h	0	00h	Home
		55	37h	7 (Keypad)
72	48h	0	00h	Up-Arrow
		56	38h	8 (Keypad)
73	49h	0	00h	PgUp
		57	39h	9 (Keypad)
74	4Ah	45	2Dh	- (Next to Keypad)
75	4Bh	0	00h	Left-Arrow
		52	34h	4 (Keypad)
76	4Ch	0	00h	Keypad Middle Key
		53	35h	5 (Keypad)
77	4Dh	0	00h	Right-Arrow
		54	36h	6 (Keypad)
78	4Eh	43	2Bh	+ (Next to Keypad)
79	4Fh	0	00h	End
		49	31h	1 (Keypad)
80	50h	0	00h	Down-Arrow
		50	32h	2 (Keypad)
81	51h	0	00h	PgDn
		51	33h	3 (Keypad)
82	52h	0	00h	Ins
		48	30h	0 (Keypad)
83	53h	0	00h	Del
		46	2Eh	. (Keypad)
84	54h	0	00h	Shift-F1
85	55h	0	00h	Shift-F2
86	56h	0	00h	Shift-F3
87	57h	0	00h	Shift-F4
88	58h	0	00h	Shift-F5
89	59h	0	00h	Shift-F6
90	5Ah	0	00h	Shift-F7
91	5Bh	0	00h	Shift-F8
92	5Ch	0	00h	Shift-F9
93	5Dh	0	00h	Shift-F10
94	5Eh	0	00h	Ctrl-F1
95	5Fh	0	00h	Ctrl-F2

Table 7-9   Continued.

Scan Code		ASCII Value		
Decimal	Hex	Decimal	Hex	Keystroke
96	60h	0	00h	Ctrl-F3
97	61h	0	00h	Ctrl-F4
98	62h	0	00h	Ctrl-F5
99	63h	0	00h	Ctrl-F6
100	64h	0	00h	Ctrl-F7
101	65h	0	00h	Ctrl-F8
102	66h	0	00h	Ctrl-F9
103	67h	0	00h	Ctrl-F10
104	68h	0	00h	Alt-F1
105	69h	0	00h	Alt-F2
106	6Ah	0	00h	Alt-F3
107	6Bh	0	00h	Alt-F4
108	6Ch	0	00h	Alt-F5
109	6Dh	0	00h	Alt-F6
110	6Eh	0	00h	Alt-F7
111	6Fh	0	00h	Alt-F8
112	70h	0	00h	Alt-F9
113	71h	0	00h	Alt-F10
114	72h	0	00h	Ctrl-PrtSc
115	73h	0	00h	Ctrl-Left-Arrow
116	74h	0	00h	Ctrl-Right-Arrow
117	75h	0	00h	Ctrl-End
118	76h	0	00h	Ctrl-PgDn
119	77h	0	00h	Ctrl-Home
120	78h	0	00h	Alt-1 (Keyboard)
121	79h	0	00h	Alt-2 (Keyboard)
122	7Ah	0	00h	Alt-3 (Keyboard)
123	7Bh	0	00h	Alt-4 (Keyboard)
124	7Ch	0	00h	Alt-5 (Keyboard)
125	7Dh	0	00h	Alt-6 (Keyboard)
126	7Eh	0	00h	Alt-7 (Keyboard)
127	7Fh	0	00h	Alt-8 (Keyboard)
128	80h	0	00h	Alt-9 (Keyboard)
129	81h	0	00h	Alt-0 (Keyboard)
130	82h	0	00h	Alt-- (Keyboard)
131	83h	0	00h	Alt-= (Keyboard)
132	84h	0	00h	Ctrl-PgUp

Table 7-10   Port 60h Keyboard Scan Codes

Key Code		
Decimal	Hex	Keystroke
1	01h	Esc
2	02h	1
3	03h	2
4	04h	3

Table 7-10   Continued.

Key Code

Decimal	Hex	Keystroke
5	05h	4
6	06h	5
7	07h	6
8	08h	7
9	09h	8
10	0Ah	9
11	0Bh	0
12	0Ch	-
13	0Dh	=
14	0Eh	Backspace
15	0Fh	Tab
16	10h	q
17	11h	w
18	12h	e
19	13h	r
20	14h	t
21	15h	y
22	16h	u
23	17h	i
24	18h	o
25	19h	p
26	1Ah	[
27	1Bh	]
28	1Ch	Enter
29	1Dh	Ctrl
29/69	1Dh/45h	Pause
30	1Eh	a
31	1Fh	s
32	20h	d
33	21h	f
34	22h	g
35	23h	h
36	24h	j
37	25h	k
38	26h	l
39	27h	;
40	28h	'
41	29h	`
42	2Ah	Left Shift
42/52	2Ah/34h	PrtSc (Middle)
42/71	2Ah/47h	Home (Middle)
42/72	2Ah/48h	Up-Arrow (Middle)
42/73	2Ah/49h	PgUp (Middle)
42/75	2Ah/4Bh	Lt-Arrow (Middle)
42/77	2Ah/4Dh	Rt-Arrow (Middle)
42/79	2Ah/4Fh	End (Middle)
42/80	2Ah/50h	Dn-Arrow (Middle)
42/81	2Ah/51h	PgDn (Middle)
42/82	2Ah/52h	Insert (Middle)
42/83	2Ah/53h	Delete (Middle)
43	2Bh	\
44	2Ch	z

Table 7-10   Continued.

Key Code

Decimal	Hex	Keystroke
45	2Dh	x
46	2Eh	c
47	2Fh	v
48	30h	b
49	31h	n
50	32h	m
51	33h	,
52	34h	.
53	35h	/
54	36h	Right Shift
55	37h	* (Next to Keypad)
56	38h	Alt
57	39h	Space
58	3Ah	Caps Lock
59	3Bh	F1
60	3Ch	F2
61	3Dh	F3
62	3Eh	F4
63	3Fh	F5
64	40h	F6
65	41h	F7
66	42h	F8
67	43h	F9
68	44h	F10
69	45h	Num Lock
70	46h	Scroll Lock
71	47h	Home (Keypad)
72	48h	Up-Arrow (Keypad)
73	49h	PgUp (Keypad)
74	4Ah	- (Keypad)
75	4Bh	Lt-Arrow (Keypad)
76	4Ch	5 (Keypad)
77	4Dh	Rt-Arrow (Keypad)
78	4Eh	+ (Keypad)
79	4Fh	End (Keypad)
80	50h	Dn-Arrow (Keypad)
81	51h	PgDn (Keypad)
82	52h	Ins (Keypad)
83	53h	Del (Keypad)
84	54h	Unused
85	55h	Unused
86	56h	Unused
87	57h	F11
88	58h	F12

Table 7-11   Communications Port Initialization Byte

Bit	Function
0 - 1	Word Length 10b = 7 bits 11b = 8 bits
2	Stop Bits 0 = 1 bit 1 = 2 bits
3 - 4	Parity 00b = None 01b = Odd 10b = None 11b = Even
5 - 7	Baud Rate 000b = 110 001b = 150 010b = 300 011b = 600 100b = 1200 101b = 2400 110b = 4800 111b = 9600

Table 7-12   Global Descriptor Table Format for Interrupt 15h Service 87h

Byte	Contents
00h - 0Fh	Reserved
10h - 11h	Segment Length in Bytes (2 * CX - 1 or Greater)
12h - 14h	24-bit Source Address
15h	Access Rights Byte (always 93h)
16h - 17h	Reserved
18h - 19h	Segment Length in Bytes (2 * CX - 1 or Greater)
1Ah - 1Ch	24-bit Destination Address
1Dh	Access Rights Byte (always 93h)
1Eh - 2Fh	Reserved

Table 7-13   Global Descriptor Table Format for Interrupt 15h Service 89h

Byte	Contents
00h	Dummy Descriptor (Initialized to 0)
08h	Global Descriptor Table (GDT)
10h	Interrupt Descriptor Table (IDT)

Table 7-13   Continued.

Byte	Contents
18h	User Data Segment (DS)
20h	User Data Segment (ES)
28h	User Data Segment (SS)
30h	User Data Segment (CS)
38h	BIOS Code Segment

Note: The table described above contains eight
      8-byte descriptors. The user fills in the
      first 7, the ROM BIOS fills in the eighth.

Table 7-14   Equipment Configuration Table Contents

Byte	Contents
00h - 01h	Table Length in Bytes
02h	System Model
	FFh - PC
	FEh - PC/XT
	FBh - PC/XT (See Submodel Byte)
	FDh - PCjr
	FCh - PC/AT (See Submodel Byte)
	FCh - PC/XT-286 (See Submodel Byte)
	FAh - PS/2 Model 30 (See Submodel Byte)
	FCh - PS/2 Model 50 (See Submodel Byte)
	FCh - PS/2 Model 60 (See Submodel Byte)
	F8h - PS/2 Model 70 (See Submodel Byte)
	F8h - PS/2 Model 80 (See Submodel Byte)
03h	System Submodel
	00h or 01h - PC/XT
	00h or 01h - PC/AT
	02h - PC/XT-286
	00h - PS/2 Model 30
	04h - PS/2 Model 50
	05h - PS/2 Model 60
	04h or 09h - PS/2 Model 70
	00h or 01h - PS/2 Model 80
04h	BIOS Revision Level
05h	Configuration Flags (Bits True When Set)
	0 - Reserved
	1 - Micro Channel Implemented
	2 - Extended BIOS Area Allocated
	3 - Wait for Enternal Event Available
	4 - Keyboard Intercept Available
	5 - Real-Time Clock Available

Table 7-14   Continued.

Byte	Contents
05h	Configuration Flags (Bits True When Set)
	6 - Slave 8259 Present 7 - DMA Channel 3 Used
06h - 09h	Reserved

Table 7-15   POS Slot Ports

Port	Function
100h	MCA ID Low Byte
101h	MCA ID High Byte
102h	Option Select Byte 1
103h	Option Select Byte 2
104h	Option Select Byte 3
105h	Option Select Byte 4
106h	Subaddress Extension Low Byte
107h	Subaddress Extension High Byte

Table 7-16   Super VGA Information Block Format

Byte	Function
0 - 3 (Byte)	VESA Signature - Contains 'VESA'
4 - 5 (Word)	VESA Version Number - High byte is the major revision number. Low byte is the minor revision number. VESA capabilities are upward compatible.
6 - 9 (Double Word)	Pointer to OEM String - Null terminated string identifying the manufacturer. The string may contain other information.
10 - 13 (Byte)	Video Equipment Capabilities (Reserved)
14 - 17 (Double Word)	Pointer to a list of mode numbers supported by display adapter. Each number is 16-bits long. The last number in the series is -1 (0FFFFh).
18 - 256	Reserved

Table 7-17   Super VGA Mode Information Block Format

Byte	Function

0 - 1 (Word)   Mode Attributes - Defines the characteristics of the video mode as shown below. A value of 1 in the bit position makes the statement true. Hardware support for the mode infers that the display adapter is configured correctly and that the correct display adapter is attached. Extended mode support is provided to define the resolution, number of bit planes, and pixel format of non-VESA supported modes.

Bit	Function
0	Mode Supported in Hardware
1	Extended Mode Information Available
2	Output Functions Supported by BIOS
3	Color (True)/Monochrome (False)
4	Graphics Mode (True)/Text Mode (False)
5 - 15	Reserved

2 (Byte)   Window A Attributes - Describes if the mode supports CPU windowing. It also describes how the windowing scheme is implemented as shown below. A value of 1 in the bit position makes the statement true.

Bit	Function
0	Window is Supported
1	Window is Readable
2	Window is Writable
3 - 7	Reserved

3 (Byte)   Window B Attributes - Describes if the mode supports CPU windowing. It also describes how the windowing scheme is implemented as shown below. A value of 1 in the bit position makes the statement true.

Bit	Function
0	Window is Supported
1	Window is Readable
2	Window is Writable
3 - 7	Reserved

4 - 5 (Word)   Window Granularity - Defines the smallest window boundry size in KBytes.

6 - 7 (Word)   Window Size - Defines the window size in KBytes.

8 - 9 (Word)   Window A Segment - Specifies the window segment location in CPU address space.

Table 7-17   Continued.

Byte	Function
10 - 11 (Word)	Window B Segment - Specifies the window segment location in CPU address space.
12 - 15 (Double Word)	Window Function Address - Pointer to the CPU video memory windowing function. This pointer allows you to call the windowing function directly. You may also access this function through interrupt 10h, service 4Fh, function 5.
16 - 17 (Word)	Bytes Per Scan Line - Defines the length of a logical scan line. A logical scan line may equal or exceed the size of the physical scan line.

Extended Information for Non-VESA Supported Video Modes

18 - 19 (Word)	X Axis Resolution - The width of the display. Value is in pixels for graphics mode and characters for text mode.
20 - 21 (Word)	Y Axis Resolution - The height of the display. Values is in pixels for graphics mode and characters for text mode.
22 (Byte)	X Character Cell Size - Width of characters in pixels.
23 (Byte)	Y Character Cell Size - Heigth of characters in pixels.
24 (Byte)	Number of Planes - Number of memory planes available for use. This value is set to one for standard packed pixel modes.
25 (Byte)	Bits per Pixel - Number of bit planes available for color display. Four bit planes provide 16 on-screen colors. Bit planes normally assume even values (except for monochrome with a single bit plane). You may also use this field to describe packed pixel modes. For example, a 16 color packed pixel mode would use 4 bits per pixel in one plane.
26 (Byte)	Number of Banks - Defines the number of scan line banks. For example, CGA uses two banks and Hercules uses four banks. This value is set to one for modes that do not use banks (for example VGA).
27 (Byte)	Memory Model - Specifies the memory model used for the mode as shown below.

Value	Function
00h	Text Mode
01h	CGA Graphics

Table 7-17   Continued.

Byte	Function
	Bit *Function*
	02h Hercules Graphics
	03h 4-Plane Planar
	04h Packed Pixel
	05h Non-Chain 4, 256 Color
	06h-0Fh Reserved, Defined by VESA
	10h-FFh Reserved, Defined by OEM
28 (Byte)	Bank Size - The size of a scan line bank in KBytes. For example, CGA and Hercules graphics use a bank size of 8 KBytes. This value is set to zero for modes that do not use banks (for example VGA).
29 - 256	Reserved

8

DOS Program Control Interrupts

This chapter discusses the DOS program control interrupt routines, including several undocumented services. Program control interrupts determine how a program deallocates memory and returns control to DOS. Each interrupt description contains the first DOS version to provide the service, the required register contents on routine entry, and a code fragment showing usage. TABLE 8-1 at the end of this chapter lists the interrupts in numeric order. Use this table to identify the interrupts described in other chapters.

TERMINATE PROGRAM (INTERRUPT 20h)

DOS 1.0

This service ends the current process and returns control to DOS. When a process uses this interrupt, DOS restores the termination-handler, Ctrl–C, and critical-error handler vectors from the Program Segment Prefix (PSP). The PSP contains the addresses of the original interrupts. DOS then returns control to the resident portion of COMMAND.COM. This interrupt requires no special register contents on entry.

For DOS 1.0, this interrupt is the usual method to end a program. For versions of DOS greater than 1.0, you can use services 31h (Terminate-and-Stay-Resident) or 4Ch (Terminate Process with Return Code) instead. These services offer greater flexibility and greater reliability than this service.

TERMINATE PROGRAM (INTERRUPT 21h SERVICE 0)

DOS 1.0

This service ends the current process and returns control to DOS.

When a process uses this interrupt, DOS restores the termination-handler, Ctrl–C, and critical error handler vectors. DOS then returns control to the resident portion of COMMAND.COM.

You can use this service for .COM programs and .EXE programs with less than 64 KBytes of code. However, because you must provide the PSP segment address and programs with more than 64 KBytes of code change the value in CS, you could experience problems with larger .EXE programs. As an alternative, you can use services 31h (Terminate-and-Stay-Resident) or 4Ch (Terminate Process with Return Code) instead.

Register Contents on Entry:
AH - 0
CS - Segment Address of Program Segment Prefix

Example:
```
;Terminate program
MOV   AH,0
MOV   CS,PSP
INT   21h
```

SET INTERRUPT VECTOR (INTERRUPT 21h SERVICE 25h)

DOS 1.0

This service changes the address of an interrupt vector to a new address defined by the user. Always use this function in place of direct editing of the interrupt vector table. Using this function permits you to change the interrupt address without disrupting an on-going process. Always save the old interrupt vector address before changing it. You can obtain the old address using interrupt 21h service 35h.

Register Contents on Entry:
AH - 25h
AL - Interrupt Number
DX - Offset of Interrupt Handling Routine
DS - Segment of Interrupt Handling Routine

Example:
```
;Set the Ctrl-C interrupt vector
MOV   AH,25h
MOV   AL,23h
LDS   DX,CHandler
INT   21h
```

CREATE NEW PSP (INTERRUPT 21h SERVICE 26h)

DOS 1.0

This service copies the PSP of the currently executing program to a specific memory location, defined by the user. It then updates the PSP copy to make it usable by other programs. After this service copies the executing program PSP, it updates the memory size information of the new PSP. This service also saves the contents of the termination (interrupt 22h), Ctrl–C handler (interrupt 23h), and critical error handler (interrupt 24h) at offset 0Ah.

Note: This interrupt requires you to perform a three step process to execute a program. For DOS versions 2.0 and greater, use service 4Bh (Execute Program) to load and execute a program in a single step.

Register Contents on Entry:
AH - 26h
DX - Segment of New Program Segment Prefix (PSP)

Example:
```
;Create new PSP
MOV    AH,26h
MOV    DX,SET PSP
INT    21h
```

TERMINATE-AND-STAY-RESIDENT (INTERRUPT 21h SERVICE 31h)

DOS 2.0

This service ends the current process and returns control to the parent process. DOS reserves the memory used by the child process. It does not overlay the memory when loading other transient programs. Any memory allocated using interrupt 21h service 48h (Allocate Memory Block) remains allocated. Because the memory does remain allocated, you must provide some method of activating the program through some hardware or software interrupt or event. Otherwise, the memory remains unavailable for any use.

When a process uses this interrupt, DOS restores the termination-handler, Ctrl–C, and critical error handler vectors. DOS also flushes all buffers and closes any devices or files opened by the process.

Some programs use COMMAND.COM as the parent process. If this happens, DOS returns control to the resident portion of COMMAND.COM. It also loads the transient portion, if necessary. Once control returns to COMMAND.COM, it displays the DOS prompt or executes the next line of the current batch file.

When the program terminates, the parent process receives a return code from the child process. The parent process retrieves this return code using interrupt 21h service 4Dh. You can also test for the return code using the IF ERRORLEVEL statement in a batch file. The standard return code protocol uses a zero for successful execution and a non-zero number to indicate an error.

Note: Never use this interrupt with a program loaded into high DOS memory (linked with the /HIGH switch). Doing so halts the system because DOS cannot load the transient portion of COMMAND.COM.

Register Contents on Entry:
AH - 31h
AL - Return Code
DX - Memory Requirements in Paragraphs

Example:
```
;Terminate and stay resident
MOV    AH,4Dh    ;Get return code
INT    21h
MOV    AH,31h
MOV    DX,4      ;Allocate 4 memory blocks
INT    21h
```

GET INDOS FLAG ADDRESS
(INTERRUPT 21h SERVICE 34h)

DOS 3.1

This service increments the DOS flag for each occurrence of an interrupt 21h service, and decrements it after each return. A value of 0 shows that no interrupt 21h service routines are in progress. The byte preceding the InDOS flag contains the critical error handler flag. Both bytes are essential for memory resident programs. Because DOS is not reentrant and a memory resident program might require a DOS service, you need to know if the application program is using a DOS interrupt.

Note: This is an undocumented feature. DOS might not support it in future upgrades. However, this feature is valid with versions of DOS from 3.1 to 4.01.

Register Contents on Entry:
AH - 34h

Register Contents on Exit:
DI - InDOS Flag Offset
ES - InDOS Flag Segment

Example:
```
;Get InDos flag address
MOV    AH,34h
INT    21h
```

GET INTERRUPT
VECTOR (INTERRUPT 21h SERVICE 35h)

DOS 2.0

This service is the only approved way to get the current address for a specified interrupt vector. Use this service instead of reading an interrupt vector from the interrupt vector table. This ensures compatibility with future versions of DOS. You may use interrupt 21h service 25h to set an interrupt vector once you save the old one using this service.

Register Contents on Entry:
AH - 39h
AL - Interrupt Number

Register Contents on Exit:
BX - Offset of Interrupt Handler
ES - Segment of Interrupt Handler

Example:
```
;Get Ctrl-C interrupt vector
MOV    AH,39h
MOV    AL,23h
INT    21h
```

EXECUTE PROGRAM (INTERRUPT 21h SERVICE 4Bh)

DOS 2.0

This service runs a program under control of another program. DOS returns control to the originating program upon program completion. This service can also load overlays requested by the calling process. However, this is an unusual use for this service. Most programs use other, more efficient methods of loading overlays.

Note that overlays load into memory already allocated by the program calling the overlay function. Programs, on the other hand, load into unused memory. Therefore the originating program should release all available memory before running another program. This step is optional for running .EXE programs but necessary for running .COM programs.

When you load a program, DOS requires information about certain aspects of the current program. Pointers to this information appear in a parameter block. TABLE 8-2 at the end of this chapter contains a listing of the parameter block format. An overlay requires a much simpler form of the parameter block. TABLE 8-2 contains a description of these requirements as well.

The environment block contains a listing of common program parameters. This includes the location of the command processor, the current prompt, and the path. Many programs use additional parameters stored in the environment block. The environment block is a paragraph aligned set of ASCIIZ strings. Each parameter in the block ends with a zero. The block ends with a double null (00h) byte.

The command tail contains all the parameters passed on the command line to the parent program. Some programs modify the command tail before passing it to the child process. The command tail begins with a count byte. This tells the program how many letters appear in the command tail. The next byte contains a space (20h). The command tail ends with a carriage return. The count byte does not include this extra byte.

The child process inherits all file handles held by the parent process. DOS version 3.0 and above allows the parent process to prevent this by setting the inheritance bit. The child process also inherits any file or device redirection used by the parent process.

Register Contents on Entry:
AH - 4Bh
AL - Subfunction
    0- Load and Execute Program
    3- Load Overlay
BX - Offset of Parameter Block
DX - Offset of ASCIIZ Program Pathname
ES - Segment of Parameter Block
DS - Offset of ASCIIZ Program Pathname

Register Contents on Exit:
AX - Error Code (If Unsuccessful)
CF - Clear if Successful, Set if Unsuccessful

Example:
```
;Execute program
MOV    AH,4Bh
MOV    AL,0
LDS    DX,PNAME
LES    BX,BLOCK
INT    21h
```

TERMINATE PROCESS WITH RETURN CODE (INTERRUPT 21h SERVICE 4Ch)

DOS 2.0

This service ends the current process and passes a return code to the parent process. If the program uses COMMAND.COM as the parent process, DOS transfers control to the resident portion. If necessary, DOS also loads the transient portion of the command processor. Once control returns to COMMAND.COM, it displays the DOS prompt or executes the next line of the current batch file.

When a process uses this interrupt, DOS restores the termination handler, Ctrl–C, and critical error handler vectors. DOS also flushes the file buffers and transfers control to the termination-handler.

When the program terminates, the parent process receives a return code from the child process. The parent process retrieves this return code using interrupt 21h service 4Dh. You can also test for the return code using the IF ERRORLEVEL statement in a batch file. The standard return code protocol uses a zero for successful execution and a non-zero number to indicate an error.

Note: DOS does not close files opened with file control blocks (FCBs). The program must close any open files before it calls this service. Otherwise, the file might lose data.

Register Contents on Entry:
AH - 4Ch
AL - Return Code

Example:
```
;Terminate process with return code
MOV    AH,4Dh      ;Get return code
INT    21h
MOV    AH,4Ch
INT    21h
```

GET RETURN CODE (INTERRUPT 21h SERVICE 4Dh)

DOS 2.0

This service obtains the return code and termination type of a child process upon successful completion of interrupt 21h service 4Bh (Execute Program). You can also use this service to obtain the return code of a terminate-and-stay-resident program (interrupt 21h service 31h or interrupt 27h). This service returns valid information one time. Later calls return invalid return codes.

Register Contents on Entry:
AH - 4Dh

Register Contents on Exit:
AH - Exit Type
    0 - Normal Exit Through Int 20h, Int 21h Service 0, Int 21h
      Service 4Ch
    1 - User Entered Ctrl–C to Terminate Program
    2 - Critical Error Handler Terminated Program
    3 - Normal Exit Through Int 21h Service 31h or Int 27h
AL - Return Code Passed by Child Process

Example:
```
;Get return code
MOV    AH,4Dh
INT    21h
```

SET PSP ADDRESS (INTERRUPT 21h SERVICE 50h)

DOS 3.1

This service works with terminate-and-stay-resident programs (TSRs) by switching DOS from using the PSP address of the current program to the PSP address of the TSR program. You call this service with the PSP segment address stored in BX.

Note: This is an undocumented feature. DOS might not support it in future upgrades. However, this feature is valid with versions of DOS from 3.1 to 4.01.

Register Contents on Entry:
AH - 50h
BX - PSP Segment

Example:
```
;Set PSP Address
MOV    AH,50h
MOV    BX,PSP
INT    21h
```

GET PSP ADDRESS (INTERRUPT 21h SERVICE 51h)

DOS 3.1

This service gets the PSP address of the currently running program. You can use this service with terminate-and-stay-resident (TSR) programs. The TSR can save the PSP address of the non-TSR program and tell DOS to use the PSP address of the TSR program instead. Because this is an undocumented feature, you should use the documented service 62h (Get PSP Address) instead.

Note: This is an undocumented feature. DOS might not support it in future upgrades. However, this feature is valid with versions of DOS from 3.1 to 4.01.

Register Contents on Entry:
AH - 51h

Register Contents on Exit:
BX - PSP Segment

Example:
```
;Get PSP Address
MOV    AH, 15h
INT    21h
```

GET PSP ADDRESS (INTERRUPT 21h SERVICE 62h)

DOS 3.0

This service gets the program segment prefix (PSP) address of the currently running program. DOS passes the PSP address in the DS and ES registers when the program begins execution. This function provides a convenient method of returning the PSP address without saving it.

You can use this service with terminate-and-stay-resident (TSR) programs. The TSR can save the PSP address of the non-TSR program and tell DOS to use the PSP address of the TSR program instead. Because this service performs the same functions as service 51h (Get PSP Address), you should use this documented service instead.

The PSP contains several important pieces of program information. This information includes the environment block, command line block, terminate, Ctrl–C, and critical error handler vectors, and the top address of available RAM.

Register Contents on Entry:
AH - 62h

Register Contents on Exit:
BX - PSP Segment Address

Example:
```
;Get PSP Address
MOV   AH,62h
INT   21h
```

TERMINATE ADDRESS (INTERRUPT 22h)

DOS 1.0

This interrupt vector contains the address of the program that receives control when the currently executing program ends. Its address appears at offsets 0Ah through 0Dh of the PSP. You should never issue this interrupt directly.

CTRL – BREAK HANDLER ADDRESS (INTERRUPT 23h)

DOS 1.0

This interrupt vector contains the address of the routine that receives control when DOS detects a Ctrl–Break or Ctrl–C (unless an application program or device driver modifies the interrupt routine). Its address appears at offsets 0Eh through 11h of the PSP. You should never issue this interrupt directly.

CRITICAL ERROR HANDLER ADDRESS (INTERRUPT 24h)

DOS 1.0

This interrupt vector contains the address of the routine that receives control when DOS detects a critical error. On entry to the error handling routine, the DI register contains an error code. TABLE 8-3 at the end of this chapter contains a listing of critical error codes. The address of this service appears at offsets 12h through 15h of the PSP. You should never issue this interrupt directly.

TERMINATE-AND-STAY-RESIDENT (INTERRUPT 27h)

DOS 1.0

This service ends the current process and returns control to DOS. When DOS receives control, it reserves the memory used by the program. This includes any memory requested using interrupt 21h service 48h. DOS normally uses the value returned in DX as the amount of memory to reserve for the application. If DX contains a value in the range of 0FFF1h to 0FFFFh, DOS discards the high bit. This results in an allocation 32 KBytes less than the original request.

When a process uses this interrupt, DOS restores the termination, Ctrl–C, and critical error handler vectors. DOS then returns control to the resident portion of COMMAND.COM. It loads the transient portion of the command processor, if necessary. Once control returns to COMMAND .COM, it displays the DOS prompt or executes the next line of the current batch file.

Use this service only for DOS 1.0. For DOS 2.0 or later, use service 31h (Terminate-and-Stay-Resident) instead because this is an improved TSR termination handler. One improvement includes a larger memory reservation. This service allows you to reserve a maximum of 65,520 bytes.

Note: DOS does not close files opened with file control blocks (FCBs). The program must close any open files before it calls this service. Otherwise, the file might lose data.

Never use this interrupt with a program loaded into high DOS memory (linked with the /HIGH switch). Doing so halts the system because DOS cannot load the transient portion of COMMAND.COM.

Register Contents on Entry:
DX - Offset of Last Program Byte + 1
CS - Segment of PSP

STANDARD TERMINATE-AND-STAY-RESIDENT HANDLER (INTERRUPT 28h)

DOS 2.0

This service normally contains only an IRET instruction. DOS calls it at each iteration of services 01h through 0Ch. A TSR can use this interrupt to determine the appropriate times for performing work. For instance, a print spooler could print the contents of a file while an application program waits for keyboard input. The TSR interrupt handler substituted for interrupt 28h determines any required register contents on entry and any register contents on exit.

Note: This is an undocumented feature. DOS might not support it in future upgrades. However, this feature is valid with versions of DOS from 2.0 to 4.01.

Note: The multiplex interrupt 2Fh provides a method of interprocess communication between DOS extensions. The following services list the standard DOS extensions. The service number appears in AH upon entry to the multiplex interrupt. DOS reserves service numbers 00h through 0BFh for its own use. Application programs may use service numbers 0C0h through 0FFh. Always use these services carefully. They vary from software vendor to software vendor because they are DOS extensions.

PRINT SPOOLER (INTERRUPT 2Fh SERVICE 01h)

DOS 3.0

This service sends a file to the print spooler and gets the print spooler status.

Register Contents on Entry:
AH - 1
AL - Subfunction
    0 - Get Installed State
    1 - Submit File For Printing
    2 - Remove File From Print Queue
    3 - Cancel All Files in Queue
    4 - Hold Print Jobs for Status Read
    5 - Release Hold
DX - Offset of Packet (Subfunction 1)
    Offset of ASCIIZ Pathname (Subfunction 2)
DS - Segment of Packet (Subfunction 1)
    Segment of ASCIIZ Pathname (Subfunction 2)

Register Contents on Exit (If Successful):
CF - 0
AL - Print Spooler State (Subfunction 0)
    00h - OK to Install
    01h - Do Not Install
    FFh - Installed
DX - Error Count (Subfunction 4)
SI - Offset of Print Queue File List (Subfunction 4)
DS - Segment of Print Queue File List (Subfunction 4)

Register Contents on Exit (If Not Successful):
CF - 1
AX - Error Code

Example:
```
;Cancel all files in print spooler queue
MOV     AH,1
MOV     AL,3
LDS     DX,PATHNAME
INT     21h
```

ASSIGN (INTERRUPT 2Fh SERVICE 02h)

DOS 3.2

This service returns a code showing the status of the resident portion of the ASSIGN.EXE or ASSIGN.COM program. AL returns with the status information.

Register Contents on Entry:
AH - 2
AL - 0

Register Contents on Exit (If Successful):
CF - 0
AL - Assign Installed Status
    00h - OK to Install
    01h - Do Not Install
    FFh - Installed

Register Contents on Exit (If Not Successful):
CF - 1
AX - Error Code

Example:
```
;Assign
MOV   AH,2
MOV   AL,0
INT   21h
```

SHARE (INTERRUPT 2Fh SERVICE 10h)

DOS 3.2

This service returns a code showing the status of the resident portion of the SHARE.EXE program. AL returns with the status information.

Register Contents on Entry:

AH - 10h
AL - 0

Register Contents on Exit (If Successful):
CF - 0
AL - Share Installed Status
    00h - OK to Install
    01h - Do Not Install
    FFh - Installed

Register Contents on Exit (If Not Successful):
CF - 1
AX - Error Code

Example:
```
;Share
MOV    AH,10h
MOV    AL,0
INT    21h
```

APPEND (INTERRUPT 2Fh SERVICE B7h)

DOS 3.3

This service returns the APPEND DOS command installed state, version, and file search path.

Register Contents on Entry:

AH - B7h

AL - Subfunction

00h - Get Installed State

02h - Get Append Version (DOS 4.0)

04h - Get Append Path Pointer (DOS 4.0)

06h - Get Append Function State (DOS 4.0)

07h - Set Append Function State (DOS 4.0)

11h - Set Return Found Name State (DOS 4.0)

BX - Append State (Bits, Subfunction 07h)

0   Append Enabled

1 - 12 Reserved (0)

13   /Path Switch Active

14   /E Switch Active

15   /X Switch Active

Register Contents on Exit (If Successful):

CF - 0

AL - Append Status (Subfunction 0)

00h - OK to Install

01h - Do Not Install

FFh - Installed

AX - FFFFh (Subfunction 2)

DI - Offset of Active Append Path (Subfunction 4)

ES - Segment of Active Append Path (Subfunction 4)

BX - Append State (Subfunction 6, See Above)

Register Contents on Exit (If Not Successful):

CF - 1

AX - Error Code

Example:
```
;Get Append version in DOS 4.0
MOV    AH,B7h
MOV    AL,02h
MOV    BX,0        ;Append enabled
INT    21h
```

Table 8-1   DOS Interrupt Listing in Numeric Order

Interrupt	Service	Function	Page	Description
20h			535	Terminate Program
21h	0		535	Terminate Program
21h	1		615	Character Input with Echo
21h	2		562	Character Output
21h	3		644	Auxiliary Input
21h	4		645	Auxiliary Output
21h	5		629	Printer Output
21h	6		623	Direct Console I/O
21h	7		624	Unfiltered Character Input Without Echo
21h	8		624	Character Input Without Echo
21h	9		562	Display String
21h	Ah		625	Buffered Keyboard Input
21h	Bh		626	Check Input Status
21h	Ch		627	Flush Input Buffer Then Input
21h	Dh		563	Disk Reset
21h	Eh		564	Select Disk
21h	Fh		564	Open File
21h	10h		565	Close File
21h	11h		566	Find First File
21h	12h		566	Find Next File
21h	13h		567	Delete File
21h	14h		568	Sequential Read
21h	15h		568	Sequential Write
21h	16h		569	Create File
21h	17h		570	Rename File
21h	18h			Reserved
21h	19h		571	Get Current Disk
21h	1Ah		571	Set DTA Address
21h	1Bh		572	Get Default Drive Data
21h	1Ch		573	Get Drive Data
21h	1Dh			Reserved
21h	1Eh			Reserved
21h	1Fh			Reserved
21h	20h			Reserved
21h	21h		573	Random Read
21h	22h		574	Random Write
21h	23h		575	Get File Size
21h	24h		576	Set Relative Record Number
21h	25h		536	Set Interrupt Vector
21h	26h		536	Create New PSP
21h	27h		576	Random Block Read
21h	28h		577	Random Block Write
21h	29h		578	Parse Filename
21h	2Ah		779	Get Date
21h	2Bh		791	Set Date
21h	2Ch		791	Get Time

Table 8-1 Continued.

Interrupt	Service	Function	Page	Description
21h	2Dh		791	Set Time
21h	2Eh		579	Set Verify Flag
21h	2Fh		580	Get DTA Address
21h	30h		792	Get DOS Version Number
21h	31h		537	Terminate and Stay Resident
21h	32h		580	Get DOS Disk Parameter Block
21h	33h		793	Get/Set Break Flag, Get Boot Drive
21h	34h		538	Get InDOS Flag Address
21h	35h		538	Get Interrupt Vector
21h	36h		581	Get Drive Allocation Information
21h	37h			Reserved
21h	38h		794	Get/Set Country Information
21h	39h		582	Create Directory
21h	3Ah		582	Delete Directory
21h	3Bh		583	Set Current Directory
21h	3Ch		583	Create File
21h	3Dh		584	Open File
21h	3Eh		585	Close File
21h	3Fh		586	Read File/Device
21h	40h		587	Write File/Device
21h	41h		587	Delete File
21h	42h		588	Set File Pointer
21h	43h		588	Get/Set File Attributes
21h	44h	0	762	IOCTL:Get Device Information
21h	44h	1	763	IOCTL:Set Device Information
21h	44h	2	765	IOCTL:Read Control Data From Character Device
21h	44h	3	765	IOCTL:Write Control Data To Character Device
21h	44h	4	766	IOCTL:Read Control Data From Block Device
21h	44h	5	767	IOCTL:Write Control Data To Block Device
21h	44h	6	767	IOCTL:Check Input Status
21h	44h	7	768	IOCTL:Check Output Status
21h	44h	8	769	IOCTL:Check if Block Device is Removable
21h	44h	9	769	IOCTL:Check if Block Device is Remote
21h	44h	Ah	770	IOCTL:Check if Handle is Remote
21h	44h	Bh	771	IOCTL:Change Sharing Retry Count

Interrupt	Service	Function	Page	Description
21h	44h	Ch	771	IOCTL:Generic I/O Control for Character Devices
21h	44h	Dh	774	IOCTL:Generic I/O Control for Block Devices
21h	44h	Eh	777	IOCTL:Get Logical Drive Map
21h	44h	Fh	777	IOCTL:Set Logical Drive Map
21h	45h		797	Duplicate Handle
21h	46h		798	Redirect Handle
21h	47h		589	Get Current Directory
21h	48h		798	Allocate Memory Block
21h	49h		799	Release Memory Block
21h	4Ah		800	Resize Memory Block
21h	4Bh		539	Execute Program
21h	4Ch		540	Terminate Process with Return Code
21h	4Dh		541	Get Return Code
21h	4Eh		590	Find First File
21h	4Fh		591	Find Next File
21h	50h		541	Set PSP Address
21h	51h		542	Get PSP Address
21h	52h			Reserved
21h	53h			Reserved
21h	54h		592	Get Verify Flag
21h	55h			Reserved
21h	56h		592	Rename File
21h	57h		593	Get/Set File Date and Time
21h	58h		800	Get/Set Allocation Strategy
21h	59h		801	Get Extended Error Information
21h	5Ah		594	Create Temporary File
21h	5Bh		594	Create New File
21h	5Ch		595	Lock/Unlock File Region
21h	5Dh		804	Set Extended Error Information
21h	5Eh	0	805	Get Machine Name
21h	5Eh	2	634	Set Printer Setup String
21h	5Eh	3	635	Get Printer Setup String
21h	5Fh	2	806	Get Redirection List Entry
21h	5Fh	3	806	Redirect Device
21h	5Fh	4	807	Cancel Device Redirection
21h	60h			Reserved
21h	61h			Reserved
21h	62h		542	Get PSP Address
21h	63h		627	Get DBCS Lead Byte Table
21h	64h			Reserved
21h	65h		808	Get Extended Country Information
21h	66h		809	Get/Set Code Page

Interrupt	Service	Function	Page	Description
33h	15h		680	Get Mouse Save State Buffer Size
33h	16h		681	Save Mouse Driver State
33h	17h		681	Restore Mouse Driver State
33h	18h		682	Set Alternate Mouse Event Handler
33h	19h		683	Get Address of Alternate Mouse Event Handler
33h	1Ah		684	Set Mouse Sensitivity
33h	1Bh		684	Get Mouse Sensitivity
33h	1Ch		685	Set Mouse Interrupt Rate
33h	1Dh		685	Select Pointer
33h	1Eh		686	Get Pointer Page
33h	1Fh		686	Disable Mouse Driver
33h	20h		687	Enable Mouse Driver
33h	21h		687	Reset Mouse Driver
33h	22h		687	Set Language for Mouse Driver Messages
33h	23h		688	Get Language Number
33h	24h		689	Get Mouse Information
67h	40h		708	Get Status
67h	41h		708	Get Page Frame Address
67h	42h		709	Get Number of Pages
67h	43h		709	Allocate Handle and Pages
67h	44h		710	Map Extended Memory
67h	45h		711	Release Handle and Extended Memory
67h	46h		711	Get Version
67h	47h		712	Save Page Map
67h	48h		712	Restore Page Map
67h	49h			Reserved
67h	4Ah			Reserved
67h	4Bh		713	Get Handle Count
67h	4Ch		713	Get Handle Pages
67h	4Dh		714	Get Handles for All Pages
67h	4Eh	0	714	Save Page Map
67h	4Eh	1	715	Restore Page Map
67h	4Eh	2	715	Save and Restore Page Map
67h	4Eh	3	716	Get Size of Page Map Information
67h	4Fh	0	716	Save Partial Page Map
67h	4Fh	1	717	Restore Partial Page Map
67h	4Fh	2	718	Get Size of Partial Page Map Information
67h	50h	0	718	Map Multiple Pages by Number
67h	50h	1	719	Map Multiple Pages by Address
67h	51h		720	Reallocate Pages for Handle
67h	52h	0	720	Get Handle Attribute
67h	52h	1	721	Set Handle Attribute

Interrupt	Service	Function	Page	Description
67h	52h	2	721	Get Attribute Capability
67h	53h	0	722	Get Handle Name
67h	53h	1	722	Set Handle Name
67h	54h	0	723	Get All Handle Names
67h	54h	1	724	Search for Handle Name
67h	54h	2	724	Get Total Handles
67h	55h	0	725	Map Page Numbers and Jump
67h	55h	1	725	Map Page Segments and Jump
67h	56h	0	726	Map Page Numbers and Call
67h	56h	1	727	Map Page Segments and Call
67h	56h	2	727	Get Stack Space for Map Page and Call
67h	57h	0	728	Move Memory Region
67h	57h	1	729	Exchange Memory Regions
67h	58h	0	730	Get Addresses of Mappable Pages
67h	58h	1	730	Get Number of Mappable Pages
67h	59h	0	731	Get Hardware Configuration
67h	59h	1	731	Get Number of Raw Pages
67h	5Ah	0	732	Allocate Handle and Standard Pages
67h	5Ah	1	732	Allocate Handle and Raw Pages
67h	5Bh	0	733	Get Alternate Map Registers
67h	5Bh	1	734	Set Alternate Map Registers
67h	5Bh	2	734	Get Size of Alternate Map Register Save Area
67h	5Bh	3	735	Allocate Alternate Map Register Set
67h	5Bh	4	735	Deallocate Alternate Map Register Set
67h	5Bh	5	736	Allocate DMA Register Set
67h	5Bh	6	736	Enable DMA on Alternate Map Register Set
67h	5Bh	7	737	Disable DMA on Alternate Map Register Set
67h	5Bh	8	737	Deallocate DMA Register Set
67h	5Ch		737	Prepare Extended Memory Manager for Warm Boot
67h	5Dh	0	738	Enable EMM Operating System Functions
67h	5Dh	1	738	Disable EMM Operating System Functions
67h	5Dh	2	739	Release Access Key

Table 8-2   Interrupt 21h Service 4Bh Parameter Block Format

Byte	Contents
Subfunction 0	
00h - 01h	Segment Pointer to Environment Block
02h - 03h	Offset of Command Line Call
04h - 05h	Segment of Command Line Call
06h - 07h	Offset of First FCB Copied Into New PSP + 5Ch
08h - 09h	Segment of First FCB
0Ah - 0Bh	Offset of Second FCB Copied Into New PSP + 6Ch
0Ch - 0Dh	Segment of Second FCB
Subfunction 3	
00h - 01h	Segment Address to Load Overlay
02h - 03h	Relocation Factor to Apply to Loaded Image

Table 8-3   Critical Error Codes

Code	Error
00h	Write Protect Error
01h	Unknown Unit
02h	Drive Not Ready
03h	Unknown Command
04h	Data Error (CRC)
05h	Bad Request Structure Length
06h	Seek Error
07h	Unknown Media Type
08h	Sector Not Found
09h	Printer Out of Paper
0Ah	Write Fault
0Bh	Read Fault
0Ch	General Failure
0Dh	Reserved
0Eh	Reserved
0Fh	Invalid Disk Change (DOS 3.0)

9

DOS Video Service Interrupts

This chapter discusses the DOS video service interrupt routines. Each interrupt description contains the first DOS version to provide the service, the required register contents on routine entry, and a code fragment showing usage. This chapter describes only the standard DOS input. Device drivers like ANSI.SYS may enhance the number of parameters allowed for each interrupt. TABLE 8-1 lists the interrupts in numeric order. Appendix A provides you with a complete listing of the ASCII character codes. Refer to your DOS manual for a listing of applicable ANSI.SYS escape sequences.

Besides the standard methods shown below, many programs choose to directly access the display adapter or use ROM interrupt supplements. Chapter 6 describes direct access to the most common types of video display adapters.

Chapter 7 describes the ROM interrupts available for manipulating the display. Both sections describe the current standards for MDA, CGA, Hercules, EGA, VGA, Super VGA, 8514/A, and 34010-based display adapters. You must use either a direct interface or ROM interrupts to manipulate the displays in graphics mode. The following DOS interrupts are valid in character mode only.

DOS does provide another method of sending output to the display. It assigns file handle 0001h to the display (CON device). Use interrupt 21h service 40h to open the display as a file. You may then send strings directly to the display. This method only works with non-redirected displays. You can also output characters using interrupt 21h service 6. This method uses direct console I/O, with no interference from the operating system. Figure 9-1 shows a typical example of how to use the DOS video display interrupts.

9-1A Assembly language sample programs for DOS video service interrupts.

```
;***************************************************************************************************
;* Sample Program 16, DOS Video Service Interrupts                *
;* This program shows you how to use the two DOS video service interrupts.  The first interrupt (21h service  *
;* 02h) sends a single character to the screen.  The second interrupt (21h service 09h) sends an entire *
;* string to the display.  Notice that you must provide a "$" (dollar sign) as the string terminator.  You      *
;* do not need any special equipment to use this program.               *
;*                            *
;* Copyright 1989 John Mueller & Wallace Wang - Tab Books. *
;***************************************************************************************************


;***************************************************************************************************
;* Perform the program setup.                   *
;***************************************************************************************************

.MODEL MEDIUM   ; Use a medum model size.

.STACK  ; Use the defalt stack of 1024 bytes.

;***************************************************************************************************
;* Begin the data area.  Declare all variables.          *
;***************************************************************************************************
.DATA

;Standard equates.

LF       EQU     10
CR       EQU     13
StrEnd EQU     36

;Program variables.

readme  DB       2 DUP (' ')
message DB       80 DUP (' '),StrEnd
Msg1     DB       'Typing a character will echo it back on'
            DB       ' the screen: ',StrEnd
Msg2     DB       CR,LF,'Type a string of characters to see'
            DB       ' it echo back on screen: ',StrEnd
LineFeed        DB       CR,LF,StrEnd

;***************************************************************************************************
;* Begin the code segment.                   *
;***************************************************************************************************
.CODE

Example PROC     FAR
Start:  MOV      AX,@DATA        ;Point DS & ES to our data segment.
            MOV      DS,AX
            MOV      ES,AX

            CALL     ClearScr        ;Clear the display.
```

```
        LEA     DX,Msg1 ;Load the first message and
        CALL    displaystring   ;display it.

        LEA     DI,readme       ;Get the first input of a
        MOV     CX,2    ; single character plus
        CALL    GetChar ; carriage return.

        MOV     DL,readme       ;Display the character.
        CALL    characteroutput
        LEA     DX,Msg2 ;Load the second message and
        CALL    displaystring   ;display it.

        LEA     DI,message      ;Get the second input of a
        MOV     CX,80   ; string plus a carriage
        CALL    GetChar ; return.

        LEA     DX,message      ;Display the string.
        CALL    displaystring

Exit:   MOV     AX,4C00h        ;Exit to DOS.
        INT     21h
        RET

Example ENDP
```

```
;***************************************************************************************
;* This procedure clears the display and places the cursor at coordinates 0,0.  *
;***************************************************************************************

ClearScr        PROC    NEAR

        MOV     AX,0619h         ;Scroll 25 lines.
        MOV     BH,7    ;Use gray.
        XOR     CX,CX   ;Start at coordinate 0,0.
        MOV     DX,1950h         ;End at coordinate 25,80.
        INT     10h

        MOV     AX,0200h         ;Set cursor position.
        XOR     BH,BH   ;Use page 0.
        XOR     DX,DX   ;Use coordinate 0,0.
        INT     10h

        RET

ClearScr        ENDP
```

```
;***************************************************************************************
;* This procedure gets one or more characters from the keyboard.  It displays the characters as it      *
;* retrieves them.  You need to place the following values in the specified registers to use this procedure.   *
;*      CX - Number of Characters                 *
;*      DI - Offset of String Storage             *
;***************************************************************************************
```

9-1A Continued.

```
GetChar PROC    NEAR

MoreChar:       MOV     AX,0100h        ;Get the input and echo it to
        INT     21h     ; the display.
        CMP     AL,CR   ;See if user pressed enter.
        JE      Exit1   ;If so, exit.
        MOV     [DI],AL ;Save the input in storage.
        INC     DI      ;Point to next storage position.
        LOOP    MoreChar        ;Get next character.

Exit1:  LEA     DX,LineFeed     ;Display the line feed.
        MOV     AX,0900h
        INT     21h

        RET
GetChar ENDP

;****************************************************************************
;* This procedure sends a single character to the screen.  You need to place the following values in the    *
;* specified registers to use this procedure.      *
;*      DL - 8 bit Character        *
;****************************************************************************

characteroutput PROC    NEAR

        MOV     AX,0200h
        INT     21h

        RET

characteroutput ENDP

;****************************************************************************
;* This procedure sends a string of characters to the display.  Notice that the string must end with a "$"   *
;* (dollar) sign.  DOS displays characters (even code) until it encounters the correct termination character.   *
;* You need to place the following values in the specified registers to use this procedure.       *
;*      DX - String Offset      *
;*      DS - String Segment      *
;****************************************************************************

displaystring   PROC    NEAR

        MOV     AX,0900h
        INT     21h

        RET

displaystring   ENDP

END     Start
```

9-1B BASIC language program for DOS video service interrupts.

```
REM Sample Program 16, DOS Video Service Interrupts Demonstration
REM This program shows you how to send output to your display using DOS services 2 and 9.  Unfortunately,
REM the number of output methods provided by DOS is limited to a single character and string character mode
REM output.  You do not need any special equipment to use this program.
REM
REM Copyright 1989, 1990 John Mueller & Wallace Wang - Tab Books.


' $INCLUDE: 'qbx.bi'

DIM InRegs AS RegType
DIM OutRegs AS RegType


DEFINT A-Z

DECLARE SUB CharacterOutput (Character$)
DECLARE SUB DisplayString (Message$)


' ******************************

CLS
PRINT "Typing a character will echo it back on screen: "
INPUT Character$
CALL CharacterOutput(Character$)


PRINT
PRINT "Type a string of characters to see it echo back on screen: "
INPUT Message$
CALL DisplayString(Message$)



SUB CharacterOutput (Character$)
  DIM InRegs AS RegType
  DIM OutRegs AS RegType
  InRegs.ax = &H200
  InRegs.dx = ASC(Character$)
  CALL Interrupt(&H21, InRegs, OutRegs)
END SUB

SUB DisplayString (Message$)
  DIM InRegs AS RegTypeX
  DIM OutRegs AS RegTypeX

  Message$ = Message$ + "$"

  InRegs.ax = &H900
  InRegs.ds = SSEG(Message$)
  InRegs.dx = SADD(Message$)

  CALL InterruptX(&H21, InRegs, OutRegs)
END SUB
```

9-1C C language program for DOS video service interrupts.

```
/* Sample Program 16, DOS Video Service Interrupts
   This program shows you how to use the two DOS video service
   interrupts.  The first interrupt (21h service 02h) sends a
   single character to the screen.  The second interrupt (21h
   service 09h) sends an entire string to the display.  Notice
   that you must provide a "$" (dollar sign) as the string
   terminator.  You do not need any special equipment to use
   this program.
   Copyright 1989,1990 John Mueller & Wallace Wang - Tab Books, /

#include <dos.h>
#include <conio.h>
#include <ctype.h>
#include <string.h>

union   REGS    iReg, oReg;
struct  SREGS   segregs;
char    readme;
char    message[80];

void characteroutput (char *character)
        {
        iReg.h.ah = 0x02;
        iReg.h.dl = *character;
        intdos (&iReg, &oReg);
        }


void displaystring (char *message)
        {
        strcat (message, "$");
        /* printf ("%s", message); */

        iReg.h.ah = 0x09;
        iReg.x.dx = message;
        intdos (&iReg, &oReg);
        }

main ()
        {
        void characteroutput (char*);
        void displaystring (char*);

        clrscr();
        printf ("Typing a character will echo it back on screen: ");
        scanf ("%c", &readme);
        characteroutput (&readme);

        printf ("\nType a string of characters to see it echo back on screen: ");
        scanf ("%s", message);
        displaystring (message);
        return 0;
        }
```

9-1D Pascal language program for DOS video service interrupts.

```
(*******************************************************************************************************)
(* Sample Program 16, DOS Video Service Interrupts Demonstration        *)
(* This program shows you how to send output to your display using DOS services 2 and 9.  Unfortunately,   *)
(* the number of output methods provided by DOS is limited to a single character and string character mode   *)
(* output.  You do not need any special equipment to use this program.  *)
(*                               *)
(* Copyright 1989, 1990 John Mueller & Wallace Wang - Tab Books.   *)
(*******************************************************************************************************)

PROGRAM Video;

USES
  Dos;
VAR
  Regs : Registers;
  ReadMe : char;
  Message : string;

  PROCEDURE CharacterOutput (Character : integer);
  BEGIN
    Regs.AH := $02;
    Regs.DL := Character;
    MsDos (Regs);
  END; (* CharacterOutput *)

  PROCEDURE DisplayString (Message : string);
  BEGIN
    Message := Message + '$';
    WITH Regs DO
      BEGIN
        ax := $0900;
        ds := Seg (Message);
        dx := Ofs (Message[1]);
        MsDos (Regs);
      END;
  END; (* DisplayString *)

BEGIN
  Write ('Typing a character will echo it back on screen: ');
  Readln (ReadMe);
  CharacterOutput (Ord(ReadMe));

  Writeln;
  Write ('Type a string of characters to see it echo back on screen: ');
  Readln (Message);
  DisplayString (Message);
END.
```

CHARACTER OUTPUT (INTERRUPT 21h SERVICE 2)

DOS 1.0

This service outputs a character to the standard output device (display only for DOS 1.0). Backspace characters work as a nondestructive backspace on the screen. However, if the user redirects the display to a file or device, then the backspace character receives no special treatment. If this service detects a Ctrl–C or Ctrl–Break, it calls interrupt 23h (Ctrl–Break Handler Address).

You can redirect the display when using DOS 2.0 and later. For example, you could redirect output from the video display to a disk file. Because this service does not test if there is enough space on a disk, it continues writing characters to the disk without telling you of an error condition.

Register Contents on Entry:
AH - 02h
DL - 8-bit Output Data

Example:
```
;Character output
MOV    AH,02h
MOV    DL,DATA
INT    21h
```

DISPLAY STRING (INTERRUPT 21h SERVICE 9)

DOS 1.0

This service sends a '$' terminated character string to the standard console device (display only for DOS 1.0). It does not print the dollar sign ($). Always use service 2h for single character output because this service requires more time to output a single character. If this service detects a Ctrl–C or Ctrl–Break, it calls interrupt 23h (Ctrl–Break Handler Address).

With DOS 2.0 and later, you can redirect the output from the video display to a disk file. Because this service does not test if there is enough space on a disk, it continues writing characters to the disk without telling you of an error condition.

Register Contents on Entry:
AH - 9
DX - Offset of Character String
DS - Segment of Character String

Example:
```
;Display string
MOV    AH,9
LDS    DX,BUFF
INT    21h
```

10
DOS Hard Disk/Floppy Diskette Service Interrupts

This chapter discusses the DOS hard disk/floppy diskette service interrupt routines. Each interrupt description contains the first DOS version to provide the service, the required register contents on routine entry, and a code fragment showing usage. TABLE 8-1 lists the interrupts in order.

Because DOS provides a wide variety of disk interface services and most device drivers modify DOS to handle special devices, you should avoid using ROM interrupts for a disk interface. In many cases the ROM calls do not adequately service non-standard devices. This results in data loss. Direct access of the disk drive is even more dangerous. Never access a disk directly. See Fig. 10-1 for programs demonstrating DOS disk services.

DISK RESET (INTERRUPT 21h SERVICE Dh)
DOS 1.0

This service writes all buffered data to disk and clears the file buffers. You must close any open files before using this service. It does not automatically update the disk directory to reflect changes to open files. When using DOS version 3.0 or above, use service 68h in place of the service. Service 68h provides advanced functions including automatic directory updates.

Register Contents on Entry:
AH - 0Dh

Example:
```
;Reset disk
    MOV   AH,0Dh
    INT   21h
```

SELECT DISK (INTERRUPT 21h SERVICE Eh)

DOS 1.0

This service changes the default drive to the drive requested in DL. In addition, it returns the number of available logical drives in AL. The number of logical drives includes hard disk partitions, floppy disks, RAM drives, and any other special block device. The number returned in AL depends on the version of DOS in use. Versions 1 through 2 return a value of 2 in single drive IBM PCs. Version 3 and above returns 5 or the value contained in the LASTDRIVE entry of CONFIG.SYS. To determine the actual number of attached drives use ROM interrupt 11h.

The maximum number of drives available for use depends on the version of DOS installed. Version 1.0 allows up to 16 drive designators (0Fh). Version 2.0 allows up to 63 drive designators (3Fh). Version 3.0 and above allows up to 26 drive designators (19h). Always assume a maximum limit of 26 drives for compatibility reasons.

Register Contents on Entry:
AH - 0Eh
DL - Drive Number (0 = A, 1 = B)

Register Contents on Exit:
AL - Number of Logical System Drives

Example:
```
;Set default drive to A
MOV    AH,0Eh
MOV    DL,0
INT    21h
```

OPEN FILE (INTERRUPT 21h SERVICE Fh)

DOS 1.0

This service opens the requested file from the current directory. To use this service you must create a file control block (FCB) structure to tell DOS

Table 10-1   DOS File Control Block Structure

Offset	Length	Contents
00h	Byte	Drive Number
01h	8 Bytes	Filename
09h	3 Bytes	Extension
0Ch	Word	Current Block Field
0Eh	Word	Record Size Field
10h	DWord	File Size from Directory
14h	Word	Date Stamp from Directory
16h	Word	Time Stamp from Directory

about the device. TABLE 10-1 contains a listing of the FCB structure. If you want to use a record size other than 128 bytes for the block device, then change offset 0Eh after you open the file and before you read/write to it. In addition, you must set the FCB relative-record field, offset 21h, if you intend to perform random file access.

The date field of the FCB uses the following structure: Bits 0 through 4 contain the day, bits 5 through 8 contain the month, and bits 9 through 15 contain the year. The time field of the FCB uses the following structure: Bits 0 through 4 contain the seconds in 2 second increments, bits 5 through 10 contain the minutes, and bits 11 through 15 contain the hours.

Use service 3Dh in place of this service when using DOS versions above 2.0. This service allows you full access to the hierarchical directory structure. If you choose not to use service 3Dh, you cannot access files outside the current directory.

Register Contents on Entry:
AH - 0Fh
DX - Offset of File Control Block (FCB)
DS - Segment of File Control Block (FCB)

Register Contents on Exit:
AL - 00h if Successful, FFh if Unsuccessful
FCB - All Data Blanks Filled-In

Example:
```
;Open a file
MOV    AH,0Fh
LDS    DX,FCB
INT    21h
```

CLOSE FILE (INTERRUPT 21h SERVICE 10h)

DOS 1.0

This service closes the requested file, flushes all associated disk buffers, and updates the file size, date, and time of last modification as required. TABLE 10-1 contains a listing of the file control block (FCB) structure.

Caution: Use interrupt 21h service 3Eh in place of this service whenever possible. Versions of DOS above 2.0 support service 3Eh. This function does not reliably detect a floppy disk change. In a worst-case scenario, this could result in damage to the floppy disk file allocation table and directory.

Register Contents on Entry:
AH - 10h
DX - Offset of File Control Block (FCB)
DS - Segment of File Control Block (FCB)

Register Contents on Exit:
AL - 00h if Successful, FFh if Unsuccessful

Example:
```
;Open a file
MOV    AH,10h
LDS    DX,FCB
INT    21h
```

FIND FIRST FILE (INTERRUPT 21h SERVICE 11h)

DOS 1.0

This service finds the first occurrence of the requested file in the current directory. With DOS 1.0 and later, you can use the question mark (?) as a wild-card character. With DOS 3.0 and later, you can use asterisks (*) as wild cards. When using DOS 2.0 or above, use interrupt 21h service 4Eh in place of this service. DOS allows you full access to the hierarchical structure of the disk directory when you use service 4Eh. This service does not support paths.

Use a standard file control block (FCB) structure to search for files without any attributes (except archive) set. However, you must use an extended FCB to search for files with the system, hidden, read-only, directory, or volume label attributes set. The attribute byte of the extended FCB determines the attributes of the files returned. For example, to search for files with the system or read-only bits set, you set the system and read-only bits of the FCB attribute. TABLE 10-1 contains a listing of the FCB structure.

You must use interrupt 21h service 1Ah to point to a disk transfer area (DTA) buffer before using this service. DOS uses this buffer as an area in which to place the disk directory.

Register Contents on Entry:
AH - 11h
DX - Offset of File Control Block (FCB)
DS - Segment of File Control Block (FCB)

Register Contents on Exit:
AL - 00h if Successful, FFh if Unsuccessful

Example:
```
;Find first file
MOV    AH,11h
LDS    DX,FCB
INT    21h
```

FIND NEXT FILE (INTERRUPT 21h SERVICE 12h)

DOS 1.0

This service finds the next occurrence of the requested file. You must use service 11h (Find First File) to find the first occurrence of a file before using this service. When using DOS 2.0 or above, use interrupt 21h service 4Fh in place of this service. DOS allows you full access to the hierarchical structure of the disk directory when you use service 4Fh. This service does not support paths.

Use a standard file control block (FCB) structure to search for files without any attributes (except archive) set. However, you must use an extended FCB to search for files with the system, hidden, read-only, directory, or volume label attributes set. The attribute byte of the extended FCB determines the attributes of the files returned. For example, to search for files with the system or read-only bits set, you set the system and read-only bits of the FCB attribute. TABLE 10-1 contains a listing of the FCB structure.

You must use interrupt 21h service 1Ah to point to a disk transfer area (DTA) buffer before using this service. DOS uses this buffer as an area in which to place the disk directory. If you want to use the same buffer used for service 11h, you do not need to reestablish the DTA address.

Register Contents on Entry:
AH - 12h
DX - Offset of File Control Block (FCB)
DS - Segment of File Control Block (FCB)

Register Contents on Exit:
AL - 00h if Successful, FFh if Unsuccessful

Example:
```
;Find next file
MOV    AH,12h
LDS    DX,FCB
INT    21h
```

DELETE FILE (INTERRUPT 21h SERVICE 13h)

DOS 1.0

This service deletes the requested file in the current directory. With DOS 1.0 and later, you can use the question mark (?) as a wild-card character. With DOS 3.0 and later, you can use asterisks (*) as wild cards. TABLE 10-1 contains a listing of the file control block (FCB) structure. When using DOS 2.0 or above, use interrupt 21h service 41h in place of this service. DOS allows you full access to the hierarchical structure of the disk directory when you use service 41h. This service does not support paths.

Register Contents on Entry:
AH - 13h
DX - Offset of File Control Block (FCB)
DS - Segment of File Control Block (FCB)

Register Contents on Exit:
AL - 00h if Successful, FFh if Unsuccessful

Example:
```
;Delete a file
MOV   AH,13h
LDS   DX,FCB
INT   21h
```

SEQUENTIAL READ (INTERRUPT 21h SERVICE 14h)

DOS 1.0

This service reads the next sequential data block from the requested file and updates the file pointer. In addition, DOS updates offsets 0Ch (current block field) and 20h (current record field) of the file control block (FCB). DOS places the data read from the file in the disk transfer area (DTA). You must use interrupt 21h service 1Ah to point to a DTA buffer before using this service. If you specify a DTA smaller than the record size, DOS might overwrite code or other data with the file contents. If the DTA appears on a segment (64 KByte boundary), and writing to the buffer would cause a segment overflow or wraparound, then this service returns with an error code of 02h. It does not read the specified file contents. DOS automatically pads partial reads (due to end of file) with zeros.

Offset 0Eh of the FCB structure determines the number of bytes read from the file. DOS uses a default record size of 128 bytes. TABLE 10-1 contains a listing of the FCB.

Register Contents on Entry:
AH - 14h
DX - Offset of Previously Opened FCB
DS - Segment of Previously Opened FCB

Register Contents on Exit:
AL - Status
    00h - Read Successful
    01h - End of File
    02h - Segment Wrap
    03h - Partial Record Read at End of File

Example:
```
;Sequential read
MOV   AH,14h
LDS   DX,FCB
INT   21h
```

SEQUENTIAL WRITE (INTERRUPT 21h SERVICE 15h)

DOS 1.0

This service writes the next sequential data block from the disk transfer area (DTA) to the specified file. It then updates the file pointer (only after a successful write). In addition, DOS updates offsets 0Ch (current block field) and 20h (current record field) of the file control block (FCB). You must use interrupt 21h service 1Ah to point to a DTA buffer before using this service. If you specify a DTA smaller than the record size, DOS sends garbage data to the file. If the DTA appears on a segment (64 KByte boundary) and writing to the buffer would cause a segment overflow or wraparound, then this service returns with an error code of 02h. It does not write the specified file contents.

Offset 0Eh of the FCB structure determines the number of bytes written to the file. DOS uses a default record size of 128 bytes. TABLE 10-1 contains a listing of the FCB.

Register Contents on Entry:
AH - 15h
DX - Offset of Previously Opened FCB
DS - Segment of Previously Opened FCB

Register Contents on Exit:
AL - Status
    00h - Write Successful
    01h - Disk is Full
    02h - Segment Wrap

Example:
```
;Sequential write
MOV   AH,15h
LDS   DX,FCB
INT   21h
```

CREATE FILE (INTERRUPT 21h SERVICE 16h)

DOS 1.0

This service creates the requested file. If a file with the same name already exists in the directory structure, DOS truncates the old entry and enters a new one. Because this function automatically opens the file it creates, you do not need to call service 0Fh.

Caution: This service could irretrievably damage data on your disk. When using DOS 2.0 or above, use interrupt 21h services 3Ch, 5Ah, 5Bh, or 6Ch in place of this service. In addition to better file protection, DOS allows you full access to the hierarchical structure of the disk directory when you use services 3Ch, 5Ah, 5Bh, or 6Ch. This service does not support paths.

Use a standard file control block (FCB) structure to create files without any attributes (except archive) set. However, you must use an extended FCB to create files with the system, hidden, read-only, directory, or volume label attributes set. The attribute byte of the extended FCB determines the attributes of the files created. For example, to create files with the system or read-only bits set, you set the system and read-only bits of the FCB attribute. TABLE 10-1 contains a listing of the file control block (FCB) structure.

The date field of the FCB uses the following structure. Bits 0 through 4 contain the day, bits 5 through 8 contain the month, and bits 9 through 15 contain the year. The time field of the FCB uses the following structure. Bits 0 through 4 contain the seconds in 2 second increments, bits 5 through 10 contain the minutes, and bits 11 through 15 contain the hours.

Register Contents on Entry:
AH - 16h
DX - Offset of Unopened File Control Block (FCB)
DS - Segment of Unopened File Control Block (FCB)

Register Contents on Exit:
AL   - 00h if Successful, FFh if Unsuccessful
FCB - All Data Blanks Filled-In

Example:
```
;Create a file
MOV    AH,16h
LDS    DX,FCB
INT    21h
```

RENAME FILE (INTERRUPT 21h SERVICE 17h)

DOS 1.0

This service alters the name of the requested file in the current directory. It uses a special file control block (FCB). TABLE 10-1 contains a listing of the standard FCB structure. To modify a standard FCB, place the source filename including drive number and extension in bytes 0 through 0Bh. Do not include the period between the filename and extension. Place the new filename at offset 11h. The new extension appears at offset 19h. You may use the ? wildcard character. Whenever DOS sees the wildcard character, it matches every occurrence of the source filename that equals the remaining letters. If you use the wildcard character in the new filename, DOS leaves those characters unchanged in the resulting filename. If you use an extended FCB, DOS allows you to change the name of files with the system, hidden, read-only, directory, or volume label attributes set. This function fails if it finds a file with the new filename in the current directory.

When using DOS 2.0 or above, use interrupt 21h service 56h in place of this service. DOS allows you full access to the hierarchical structure of the disk directory when you use service 56h. This service does not support paths.

Register Contents on Entry:
AH - 17h
DX - Offset of Unopened File Control Block (FCB)
DS - Segment of Unopened File Control Block (FCB)

Register Contents on Exit:
AL - 00h if Successful, FFh if Unsuccessful

Example:
```
;Rename File
MOV    AH,17h
LDS    DX,FCB
INT    21h
```

GET CURRENT DISK (INTERRUPT 21h SERVICE 19h)

DOS 1.0

This service returns the drive code of the current default drive where drive A is 0, drive B is 1, etc. Use interrupt 21h service 0Eh to set the default drive.

Register Contents on Entry:
AH - 19h

Register Contents on Exit:
AL - Drive Code (A = 0, B = 1, etc.)

Example:
```
;Get the drive code
MOV    AH,19h
INT    21h
```

SET DTA ADDRESS (INTERRUPT 21h SERVICE 1Ah)

DOS 1.0

This service changes the address used as a disk transfer area (DTA) for subsequent file control block (FCB) operations. DOS uses a default DTA of 128 bytes located at offset 0080h of the program segment prefix (PSP). The programmer must make sure the DTA buffer is large enough for any disk operations. Therefore, if the DTA is not large enough, you must create a new buffer and set the DTA to point to it using this function. Use interrupt 21h service 2Fh to determine the address of the DTA.

Most FCB oriented DOS block device functions rely on the DTA as a buffer. The only handle oriented (DOS 2.0 and above) functions that rely on the DTA are services 4Eh (find first file) and 4Fh (find next file).

Register Contents on Entry:
AH - 1Ah
DX - Offset of DTA
DS - Segment of DTA

Example:
```
;Set DTA Address
MOV    AH,1Ah
LDS    DX,DTA
INT    21h
```

GET DEFAULT DRIVE DATA
(INTERRUPT 21h SERVICE 1Bh)

DOS 1.0

This service gets the format information about the default disk drive. Use service 1Ch or 36h to obtain information about disk drives other than the default drive. This service also retrieves the media identification byte from the file allocation table (FAT). TABLE 10-2 contains a listing of media

Table 10-2   Media Identification Byte Values

Code	Drive Type
F0h	3.5-inch, Double Sided, 18 Sectors or Other
F8h	Fixed Disk
F9h	5.25-inch, Double Sided, 15 Sectors or 3.5-inch, Double Sided, 9 Sectors
FCh	5.25-inch, Single Sided, 9 Sectors
FDh	5.25-inch, Double Sided, 9 Sectors
FEh	5.25-inch, Single Sided, 8 Sectors
FFh	5.25-inch, Double Sided, 8 Sectors

identification code values. This service retrieves a copy of the media identification code. If you need to read the media identification code and FAT, use interrupt 25h.

Register Contents on Entry:
AH - 1Bh

Register Contents on Exit:
AL - Sectors per Cluster (FFh if Unsuccessful)
BX - Offset of Media ID Byte
CX - Size of Physical Sector
DX - Number of Clusters
DS - Segment of Media ID Byte

Example:
```
;Get default drive data
MOV    AH,1Bh
INT    21h
```

GET DRIVE DATA (INTERRUPT 21h SERVICE 1Ch)

DOS 1.0

This service gets format information about the specified disk drive. It also retrieves the media identification byte from the file allocation table (FAT). TABLE 10-2 contains a listing of media identification code values. The only difference between this service and service 1Bh is that you can select a specific drive. This service retrieves a copy of the media identification code. If you need to read the media identification code and FAT, use interrupt 25h.

Register Contents on Entry:
AH - 1Ch
DL - Drive Code (0 = A, 1 = B, etc.)

Register Contents on Exit:
AL - Sectors per Cluster (FFh if Unsuccessful)
BX - Offset of Media ID Byte
CX - Size of Physical Sector
DX - Number of Clusters
DS - Segment of Media ID Byte

Example:

```
;Get data from drive B
MOV    AH, 1Ch
MOV    DL,1
INT    21h
```

RANDOM READ (INTERRUPT 21h SERVICE 21h)

DOS 1.0

This service reads the selected data block from the requested file. DOS uses a combination of the relative record field (offset 21h) and record size field (offset 0Eh) of the file control block (FCB) to determine the data read location. It updates the current block field (offset 0Ch) and current record field (offset 20h) to match the relative record field. The relative record field remains the same. The application program must update this field to read a different sector. TABLE 10-1 contains a listing of the FCB structure. DOS uses a default record length of 128 bytes (stored in the record size field). To change the record length, update the value stored at offset 0Eh of the FCB.

DOS places the data read from the file in the disk transfer area (DTA). You must use interrupt 21h service 1Ah to point to a DTA buffer before using this service. If you specify a DTA smaller than the record size, DOS may overwrite code or other data with the file contents. If the DTA appears on a segment (64 KByte boundary) and writing to the buffer would cause a segment overflow or wraparound, then this service returns with an error code of 02h. It does not read the specified file contents. DOS automatically pads partial reads (due to end of file) with zeros.

Register Contents on Entry:
AH - 21h
DX - Offset of Previously Opened FCB
DS - Segment of Previously Opened FCB

Register Contents on Exit:
AL - Status
    00h - Read Successful
    01h - End of File *
    02h - Segment Wrap
    03h - Partial Record Read at End of File

Example:
```
;Random read
MOV    AH,21h
LDS    DX,FCB
INT    21h
```

RANDOM WRITE (INTERRUPT 21h SERVICE 22h)

DOS 1.0

This service writes the selected data block from the disk transfer area (DTA) to the requested file. DOS uses a combination of the relative record field (offset 21h) and record size field (offset 0Eh) of the file control block (FCB) to determine the data write location. It updates the current block field (offset 0Ch) and current record field (offset 20h) to match the relative record field. The relative record field remains the same. The application program must update this field to write to a different sector. TABLE 10-1 contains a listing of the FCB structure. DOS uses a default record length of 128 bytes (stored in the record size field). To change the record length, update the value stored at offset 0Eh of the FCB.

This service uses the DTA as a buffer to hold data until written to the drive. You must use interrupt 21h service 1Ah to point to a DTA buffer before using this service. If you specify a DTA smaller than the record size, DOS writes garbage data to the file. If the DTA appears on a segment (64 KByte boundary) and reading from the buffer would cause a segment overflow or wraparound, then this service returns with an error code of 02h. It does not write the specified file contents. DOS always writes files containing whole numbers of records. You cannot write a partial record to a file.

Note: This function performs a logical, not physical data write. You must close the file and flush the DOS buffers to make sure DOS actually writes all records to the file. If you reset the drive or flush the buffers before you close the file, then the file may lose some data.

Register Contents on Entry:
Ah - 22h

DX - Offset of Previously Opened FCB
DS - Segment of Previously Opened FCB

Register Contents on Exit:
AL - Status
    00h - Write Successful
    01h - Disk Full
    02h - Segment Wrap

Example:
```
;Random write
MOV    AH,22h
LDS    DX,FCB
INT    21h
```

GET FILE SIZE (INTERRUPT 21h SERVICE 23h)

DOS 1.0

This service searches for the requested file in the current directory. If it finds the file, it updates the FCB file size parameter in terms of number of records. To determine the actual file size in bytes, multiply the record size parameter (offset 0Eh) by the number of records. You can also set the record size to one to get the file size in bytes. Do not use wildcard characters (? and *) with this service.

Use a standard file control block (FCB) structure to search for files without any attributes (except archive) set. However, you must use an extended FCB to search for files with the system, hidden, read-only, directory, or volume label attributes set. The attribute byte of the extended FCB determines the attributes of the files searched for. For example, to search for files with the system or read-only bits set, you set the system and read-only bits of the FCB attribute. TABLE 10-1 contains a listing of the file control block (FCB) structure.

Register Contents on Entry:
AH - 23h
DX - Offset of Unopened File Control Block (FCB)
DS - Segment of Unopened File Control Block (FCB)

Register Contents on Exit:
AL - 00h if Successful, FFh if Unsuccessful
FCB - Relative Record Field Updated With Number of Records

Example:
```
;Get file size
MOV    AH,23h
LDS    DX,FCB
INT    21h
```

SET RELATIVE RECORD NUMBER
(INTERRUPT 21h SERVICE 24h)

DOS 1.0

This service sets the file control block (FCB) relative record field to match the position pointed to by the current FCB. Use this function to switch from sequential to random file I/O. This service derives the relative record field contents (offset 21h) from the record size (offset 0Eh), current block (offset 0Ch), and current record fields (offset 20h) of the FCB. Always initialize the relative record field to zero before calling the service. TABLE 10-1 contains a listing of the file control block (FCB) structure.

Register Contents on Entry:
AH - 24h
DX - Offset of Unopened File Control Block (FCB)
DS - Segment of Unopened File Control Block (FCB)

Register Contents on Exit:
AL   - Indeterminate
FCB - Relative Record Field Updated

Example:

```
;Set relative record number
MOV    AH,24h
LDS    DX,FCB
INT    21h
```

RANDOM BLOCK READ (INTERRUPT 21h SERVICE 27h)

DOS 1.0

This service reads the specified number of records from the requested file. Unlike service 21h you can read more than one record at a time. DOS places the data read from the file in the disk transfer area (DTA). You must use interrupt 21h service 1Ah to point to a DTA buffer before using this service. If you specify a DTA smaller than the record size, DOS may over-write code or other data with the file contents. If the DTA appears on a segment (64 KByte boundary) and writing to the buffer would cause a segment overflow or wraparound, then this service returns with an error code of 02h. It does not read the specified file contents. DOS automatically pads partial reads (due to end-of-file) with zeros.

The file position read depends on the value stored in the relative record (offset 21h) and record size (offset 0Eh) fields of the file control block (FCB). This service uses a default record size of 128 bytes. Change the value of the record size field after you open the file, but before you perform any I/O to change the size of the records read from the file. DOS automatically updates the current block (offset 0Ch), current record (offset 20h), and relative record fields after each read. TABLE 10-1 contains a listing of the FCB structure.

Register Contents on Entry:
AH - 27h
CX - Number of Records to Read
DX - Offset of Previously Opened FCB
DS - Segment of Previously Opened FCB

Register Contents on Exit:
AL - Status
    00h - Read Successful
    01h - End of File
    02h - Segment Wrap
    03h - Partial Record Read at End of File
CX - Actual Number of Records Read

Example:

```
;Random block read of 4 records
MOV    AH,27h
MOV    CX,4
LDS    DX,FCB
INT    21h
```

RANDOM BLOCK WRITE (INTERRUPT 21h SERVICE 28h)

DOS 1.0

This service writes the specified number of records from the disk transfer area (DTA) to the requested file. Unlike service 22h you can write more than one record at a time. You must use interrupt 21h service 1Ah to point to a DTA buffer before using this service. If you specify a DTA smaller than the record size, DOS will write garbage data to the file. If the DTA appears on a segment (64 KByte boundary), and writing to the buffer would cause a segment overflow or wraparound, then this service returns with an error code of 02h. It does not write the specified data to the file.

The file position written to depends on the value stored in the relative record (offset 21h) and record size (offset 0Eh) fields of the file control block (FCB). This service uses a default record size of 128 bytes. Change the value of the record size field after you open the file, but before you perform any I/O to change the size of the records written to the file. DOS automatically updates the current block (offset 0Ch), current record (offset 20h), and relative record fields after each write. TABLE 10-1 contains a listing of the FCB structure.

Register Contents on Entry:
AH - 28h
CX - Number of Records
DX - Offset of Previously Opened FCB
DS - Segment of Previously Opened FCB

Register Contents on Exit:
AL - Status
　　　00h - Write Successful
　　　01h - Disk Full
　　　02h - Segment Wrap
CX - Actual Number of Records Written

Example:
```
;Random block write of 4 records
MOV    AH,28h
MOV    CX,4
LDS    DX,FCB
INT    21h
```

PARSE FILENAME (INTERRUPT 21h SERVICE 29h)

DOS 1.0

This service parses a filename into various file control block (FCB) fields. The filename variable can contain a drive specifier, filename, and file extension. Always end the filename variable with a zero (ASCIIZ format). This service does not support a path specifier. If the variable used to contain the filename does not contain a valid string, ES:DI + 1 points to an ASCII blank upon return from this service. You may use the ? and * wildcard characters as part of the filename or extension. TABLE 10-1 contains a listing of the file control block (FCB) structure. TABLE 10-3 contains a listing of the parsing control flag entries.

Table 10-3　Parsing Control Flag Values

Bit	Value	Description
0	0	Leading Separators Not Scanned Off
	1	Leading Separators Scanned Off
1	0	FCB drive ID byte set to 0 if no drive specifier present in the parsed string.
	1	FCB drive ID byte not modified if the parsed string does not contain a drive specifier.
2	0	FCB filename field set to ASCII blanks if no filename present in the parsed string.
	1	FCB filename field not modified if the parsed string does not contain a filename specifier.
3	0	FCB extension field set to ASCII blanks if no extension present in the parsed string.
	1	FCB extension field not modified if the parsed string does not contain an extension specifier.

Register Contents on Entry:
AH - 29h
AL - Parsing Control Flags
SI - Offset of String
DI - Offset of File Control Block
DS - Segment of String
ES - Segment of File Control Block

Register Contents on Exit:
AL - Status
    00h - No Wildcard Characters Encountered
    01h - Wildcard Characters Encountered
    FFh - Drive Specifier Invalid
SI - Offset of String End + 1
DI - Offset of Formatted File Control Block
DS - Segment of String
ES - Segment of Formatted File Control Block

Example:

```
;Parse file name
MOV    AH,29h
MOV    AL,0          ;Leading separators not scanned off
LDS    SI,SBUFF
LES    DI,FBUFF
INT    21h
```

SET VERIFY FLAG (INTERRUPT 21h SERVICE 2Eh)

DOS 1.0

This service sets the system verify flag to the specified condition. If you set the verify flag, DOS reads each record after it writes it to disk. Because this adds extra overhead to the write process, DOS normally clears the verify flag. Using this service on a device that does not support read after write verification does not produce an error (or any other effect). You can obtain the state of the verify flag using service 54h. DOS provides the VERIFY ON and VERIFY OFF commands as an alternate method of controlling the verify flag state.

AH - 2Eh
AL - Verify Flag Condition
    0 - On
    1 - Off
DL - 0 (DOS Versions 1.0 and 2.0)

Example:

```
;Set verify flag on
MOV    AH,2Eh
MOV    AL,0
MOV    DL,0
INT    21h
```

GET DTA ADDRESS (INTERRUPT 21h SERVICE 2Fh)

DOS 2.0

This service obtains the position of the current disk transfer address (DTA). DOS creates a default DTA of 128 bytes at offset 80h of the program segment prefix (PSP). You can change the DTA address using interrupt 21h service 1Ah.

Register Contents on Entry:
AH - 2Fh

Register Contents on Exit:
BX - Offset of DTA
ES - Segment of DTA

Example:

```
;Get DTA Address
MOV    AH,2Fh
INT    21h
```

GET DOS DISK PARAMETER BLOCK (INTERRUPT 21h SERVICE 32h)

DOS 2.0

This service gets the disk parameter block for the requested drive where 0 is the default drive, 1 is drive A, etc. TABLE 10-4 lists the contents

Table 10-4   DOS Disk Parameter Block

Offset	Length	Contents
DOS Versions 2.X and 3.X		
00h	Byte	Drive Number
01h	Byte	Logical Unit Within Driver
02h	Word	Bytes Per Sector
04h	Byte	Sectors Per Cluster - 1
05h	Byte	Shift Count of Sectors Per Cluster
06h	Word	Number of Reserved Boot Sectors
08h	Byte	Copies of the File Allocation Table (FAT)
09h	Word	Maximum Root Directory Entries
0Bh	Word	First Data Sector
0Dh	Word	Highest Cluster Number
0Fh	Byte	Sectors Per FAT
10h	Word	First Directory Sector
12h	DWord	Address of Device Driver
16h	Byte	Media Descriptor Byte
17h	Byte	Access Flag
18h	DWord	Pointer to Next Parameter Block
1Ch	DWord	Reserved (Usually FFFF:0000)

Table 10-4   Continued.

Offset	Length	Contents
DOS Versions 4.X		
00h	Byte	Drive Number
01h	Byte	Logical Unit Within Driver
02h	Word	Bytes Per Sector
04h	Byte	Sectors Per Cluster - 1
05h	Byte	Shift Count of Sectors Per Cluster
06h	Word	Number of Reserved Boot Sectors
08h	Byte	Copies of the File Allocation Table (FAT)
09h	Word	Maximum Root Directory Entries
0Bh	Word	First Data Sector
0Dh	Word	Highest Cluster Number
0Fh	Word	Sectors Per FAT
11h	Word	First Directory Sector
13h	DWord	Address of Device Driver
17h	Byte	Media Descriptor Byte
18h	Byte	Access Flag
19h	DWord	Pointer to Next Parameter Block
1Dh	DWord	Reserved (Usually FFFF:0000)

of the disk parameter block. Note that the parameter block for DOS 4.0 is 1 byte longer than previous versions. This change reflects the increased volume size allowed by DOS 4.0.

Note: This is an undocumented feature. DOS might not support it in future upgrades. However, this feature is valid with versions of DOS from 2.0 to 4.01.

Register Contents on Entry:
AH - 32h
DX - Drive Number

Register Contents on Exit:
BX - Offset of Disk Parameter Block
DS - Segment of Disk Parameter Block

Example:
```
;Get DOS disk parameter block for drive B
MOV   AH,32h
MOV   DX,2
INT   21h
```

GET DRIVE ALLOCATION INFORMATION (INTERRUPT 21h SERVICE 36h)

DOS 2.0

This service obtains the specified disk drive parameters. These parameters allow calculation of drive capacity and remaining free space.

To calculate drive capacity multiply CX∗AX∗DX on interrupt return. To calculate remaining disk space multiply CX∗AX∗BX on interrupt return. This service subtracts lost clusters from the total number of clusters available.

Register Contents on Entry:
AH - 36h
DL - Drive Code (0 = A, 1 = B, etc.)

Register Contents on Exit:
AX - Sectors Per Cluster (FFFFh if Drive Invalid)
BX - Number of Available Clusters
CX - Bytes Per Sector
DX - Clusters Per Drive

Example:
```
;Get drive allocation information for drive B
MOV   AH,36h
MOV   DL,1
INT   21h
```

CREATE DIRECTORY (INTERRUPT 21h SERVICE 39h)

DOS 2.0

This service creates a directory using the specified drive and path. There are several reasons why this service fails to create a directory. These reasons include nonexistent path elements, directory name already exists, and full root or parent directory. When using DOS 3.0 or above this function fails on a network if the calling program has insufficient access rights.

Register Contents on Entry:
AH - 39h
DX - Offset of ASCIIZ Path Name
DS - Segment of ASCIIZ Path Name

Register Contents on Exit:
AX - Error Code if Unsuccessful
CF - 0 if Successful, 1 if Unsuccessful

Example:
```
;Create Directory
MOV   AH,39h
LDS   DX,BUFF
INT   21h
```

DELETE DIRECTORY (INTERRUPT 21h SERVICE 3Ah)

DOS 2.0

This service deletes a directory using the specified drive and path.

There are several reasons why this service fails to delete a directory. These reasons include: nonexistent path elements, requested directory is also the current directory, and the directory contains files or subdirectory entries. When using DOS 3.0 or above this function fails on a network if the calling program has insufficient access rights.

Register Contents on Entry:
AH - 3Ah
DX - Offset of ASCIIZ Path Name
DS - Segment of ASCIIZ Path Name

Register Contents on Exit:
AX - Error Code if Unsuccessful
CF - 0 if Successful, 1 if Unsuccessful

Example:
```
;Delete directory
MOV    AH,3Ah
LDS    DX,BUFF
INT    21h
```

SET CURRENT DIRECTORY (INTERRUPT 21h SERVICE 3Bh)

DOS 2.0

This service sets the default directory using the specified drive and path. This function fails if the requested directory path does not exist. Use interrupt 21h service 47h returns the current directory name and path. You can use this information to reset the directory to its original default.

Register Contents on Entry:
AH - 3Bh
DX - Offset of ASCIIZ Path Name
DS - Segment of ASCIIZ Path Name

Register Contents on Exit:
AX - Error Code if Unsuccessful
CF - 0 if Successful, 1 if Unsuccessful

Example:
```
;Set current directory
MOV    AH,3Bh
LDS    DX,BUFF
INT    21h
```

CREATE FILE (INTERRUPT 21h SERVICE 3Ch)

DOS 2.0

This service creates a new file using the default drive and path. You can use a drive and path specifier to modify the location of the new file. If the file already exists, this service truncates its length to 0 and opens it for use. The filename variable contains a drive, path, filename, and extension. You end the filename with a zero to create an ASCIIZ string. DOS normally creates a file without any attributes set. If you use DOS version 3.0 or above, you can create a volume label by specifying an attribute of 0008h. Otherwise, you should always keep bit 3 of the attribute specification clear.

There are several reasons why this service fails to create a new file. These reasons include nonexistent path elements, the root or requested directory is full, and a file with the same name and its read-only attribute set already exists. When using DOS 3.0 or above, this function fails on a network if the calling program has insufficient access rights.

AH - 3Ch
CX - File Attributes (Bits True When Set)
    0 - Ready-Only
    1 - Hidden
    2 - System
    3 - Volume Label
    4 - Reserved (0)
    5 - Archive
    6 through 15 - Reserved (0)
DX - Offset of ASCIIZ Filename
DS - Segment of ASCIIZ Filename

Register Contents on Exit:
AX - Handle if Successful, Error Code if Unsuccessful
CF - 0 if Successful, 1 if Unsuccessful

Example:
```
;Create file
MOV    AH,3Ch
MOV    CX,0        ;Read-only
LDS    DX,BUFF
INT    21h
```

OPEN FILE (INTERRUPT 21h SERVICE 3Dh)

DOS 2.0

This service opens a file using the default drive and path. You can use a drive and path specifier to modify the location of the new file. The filename variable contains a drive, path, filename, and extension. You end the filename with a zero to create an ASCIIZ string. DOS always sets the file pointer to the beginning of the file.

You may open any normal, system, or hidden file with any access mode setting. To open a read-only file, use the read-only access mode setting. TABLE 10-5 contains a listing of the access mode entry parameters.

Table 10-5   Access Mode Entry Parameters

Bit	Value	Description
0 - 2	000	Read Access
	001	Write Access
	010	Read/Write Access
3		Reserved (0)
4 - 6	000	Compatibility Mode
	001	Deny All
	010	Deny Write
	011	Deny Read
	100	Deny None
7	0	Child Process Does Not Inherit Handle
	1	Child Process Inherits Handle

There are several reasons why this service fails to open a file. These reasons include nonexistent path elements or the access mode entry contains an incorrect access mode parameter. When using DOS 3.0 or above this function fails on a network if the calling program has insufficient access rights. It also fails if DOS loads SHARE.EXE and the program tries to open the file with an incompatible access mode entry.

AH - 3Ch
AL - Access Mode
DX - Offset of ASCIIZ Filename
DS - Segment of ASCIIZ Filename

Register Contents on Exit:
AX - Handle if Successful, Error Code if Unsuccessful
CF - 0 if Successful, 1 if Unsuccessful

Example:
```
;Open file
MOV   AH,3Ch
MOV   AL,010      ;Read/Write Access
LDS   DX,BUFF
INT   21h
```

CLOSE FILE (INTERRUPT 21h SERVICE 3Eh)

DOS 2.0

This service closes a file using the handle supplied upon completion of the file create or open services. DOS also flushes all buffers associated with the file to disk, releases the handle for reuse, and updates the time and date entries if a program changed the file.

Register Contents on Entry:
AH - 3Eh
BX - Handle

Register Contents on Exit:
AX - Error Code if Unsuccessful
CF - 0 if Successful, 1 if Unsuccessful

Example:
```
;Close file
MOV    AH,3Eh
MOV    BX,FHandle
INT    21h
```

READ FILE/DEVICE (INTERRUPT 21h SERVICE 3Fh)

DOS 2.0

This service uses the handle obtained during a previous create or open process to read the contents of a file or device. After each read, DOS automatically updates the file pointer to reflect the number of bytes read. If you want to read a character device in cooked mode, DOS reads up to the number of bytes requested or a carriage return, whichever comes first. When you try to read a file with the file pointer at the end-of-file, AX returns with zero and the carry flag returns clear. AX returns with a value less than CX if an error occurs or the service reaches end-of-file before it reads the requested number of bytes. When using DOS 3.0 or above, the user must possess read access rights to the file and directory.

Register Contents on Entry:
AH - 3Fh
BX - Handle
CX - Number of Bytes
DX - Offset of Buffer
DS - Segment of Buffer

Register Contents on Exit:
AX - Number of Bytes Transferred, Error Code if Unsuccessful
CF - 0 if Successful, 1 if Unsuccessful

Example:
```
;Read file/device
MOV    AH,3Fh
MOV    BX,FHandle
MOV    CX,256
LDS    DX,BUFF
INT    21h
```

WRITE FILE/DEVICE (INTERRUPT 21h SERVICE 40h)

DOS 2.0

This service uses the handle obtained during a previous create or open process to write the contents of a buffer to a file or device. After each write, DOS automatically updates the file pointer to reflect the number of bytes read. If you want to write to a character device in cooked mode, the output string must not contain a Ctrl–Z (1Ah) character. Otherwise, DOS stops writing when it reaches the character. A write error also occurs when DOS attempts to write data to a full disk. If you set CX to zero, DOS extends or truncates the file to the current file pointer position. When using DOS 3.0 or above the user must possess write access rights to the file and directory.

Register Contents on Entry:
AH - 40h
BX - Handle
CX - Number of Bytes
DX - Offset of Buffer
DS - Segment of Buffer

Register Contents on Exit:
AX - Number of Bytes Transferred, Error Code if Unsuccessful
CF - 0 if Successful, 1 if Unsuccessful

DELETE FILE (INTERRUPT 21h SERVICE 41h)

DOS 2.0

This service deletes a file using the default drive and path. You can use a drive and path specifier to modify the location of the deleted file. DOS deletes the file by replacing the first letter of the filename entry in the directory with a ⌟ (E5h) character. It also marks the clusters owned by the file as free. DOS does not overwrite the file data. Unlike the file control block (FCB) oriented services, you cannot use the ? or * wildcard characters with this function.

There are several reasons why this service fails to delete a file. These reasons include nonexistent path elements or the file has its read-only attribute set. When using DOS 3.0 or above, this function fails on a network if the calling program has insufficient access rights.

Register Contents on Entry:
AH - 14h
DX - Offset of ASCIIZ Filename
DS - Segment of ASCIIZ Filename

Register Contents on Exit:
AX - Error Code if Unsuccessful
CF - 0 if Successful, 1 if Unsuccessful

Example:
```
;Delete file
MOV    AH,41h
LDS    DX,BUFF
INT    21h
```

SET FILE POINTER (INTERRUPT 21h SERVICE 42h)

DOS 2.0

This service changes the relative offset of the file pointer to the position specified. It allows you to specify a 32-bit pointer position and a positioning method. However, DX:AX always returns the file pointer position from the start of the file. DOS uses the new file position for all subsequent input/output. You can use interrupt 21h service 42h to determine the file size. If you set the file pointer before the start or after the end of file, DOS returns an error on any following input/output operations.

Register Contents on Entry:
AH - 42h
AL - Method Code
      00h - Absolute Offset From Start of File
      01h - Signed Offset From Current Position
      02h - Signed Offset From End of File
BX - Handle
CX - Most Significant Half of Offset
DX - Least Significant Half of Offset

Register Contents on Exit:
AX - Least Significant Half of Resulting File Pointer if Successful,
      Error Code if Not Successful
DX - Most Significant Half of Resulting File Pointer
CF - 0 if Successful, 1 if Unsuccessful

GET/SET FILE ATTRIBUTES
(INTERRUPT 21h SERVICE 43h)

DOS 2.0

This service gets or sets the attributes of a directory or file. You must clear bits 3 and 4 of the CX register when changing the attributes of a file. DOS does not allow you to change a file into a directory or volume label. You may assign a hidden attribute to a directory using this function. When using DOS version 3.0 or above, the user must possess CREATE access rights to the directory containing a file on a network.

Register Contents on Entry:
AH - 43h
AL - 0 to Get Attributes, 1 to Set Attributes

CX - Attributes (Bits True When Set)
  0 - Read-Only
  1 - Hidden
  2 - System
  3 - Volume Label
  4 - Directory
  5 - Archive
  6 through 15 - Reserved (0)
DX - Offset of ASCIIZ File/Path Name
DS - Segment of ASCIIZ File/Path Name

Register Contents on Exit:
AX - Error Code if Unsuccessful
CX - Attributes (Bits True When Set)
  0 - Read-Only
  1 - Hidden
  2 - System
  3 - Volume Label
  4 - Reserved (0)
  5 - Archive
  6 through 15 - Reserved (0)
CF - 0 if Successful, 1 if Unsuccessful

Example:
```
;Get file attributes
MOV    AH,43h
MOV    AL,0        ;Get file attributes
MOV    CX,0        ;Read-only
LDS    DX,BUFF
INT    21h
```

GET CURRENT DIRECTORY
(INTERRUPT 21h SERVICE 47h)

DOS 2.0

This service obtains a string describing the path from the root directory to the current directory. The string returned by this function does not contain a drive identifier or leading backslash (\). DOS terminates the string with a double null byte (00h). This service fails if you specify an invalid drive. Use interrupt 21h service 3Bh to set the current directory.

Register Contents on Entry:
AH - 47h
DL - Drive Code (0 = A, 1 = B, etc.)
SI - Offset of a 64-Byte Buffer
DS - Segment of a 64-Byte Buffer

Register Contents on Exit:
AX - Error Code if Unsuccessful
CF - 0 if Successful, 1 if Unsuccessful

FIND FIRST FILE (INTERRUPT 21h SERVICE 4Eh)

DOS 2.0

This service finds the first file matching the filename parameter using the default drive and path. You can use a drive and path specifier to modify the file search path. TABLE 10-6 contains a listing of the disk transfer area

Table 10-6   Service 4Eh/4Fh Returned File Parameters

Byte	Bit	Contents
00h-14h		Reserved
15h		Attributes of Matched File
16h-17h		File Time
	00h-04h	2-Second Increments
	05h-0Ah	Minutes
	0Bh-0Fh	Hours
18h-19h		File Date
	00h-04h	Day
	05h-0Ah	Month
	0Bh-0Fh	Year (Relative to 1980)
1Ah-1Dh		File Size
1Eh-2Ah		ASCIIZ File Name and Extension

contents upon exit from this routine. You can use the question mark (?) or asterisk (*) as wildcard characters.

You must use interrupt 21h service 1Ah to point to a disk transfer area (DTA) buffer before using this service. DOS uses this buffer as an area to place the disk directory.

Use the attribute entry to specify the file attributes to accept during the search. DOS always searches for files with the normal attribute set. In addition to normal files, you can search for files with the hidden, system, and directory attributes set.

Register Contents on Entry:

AH - 4Eh

CX - Attributes (Bits True When Set)

    0 - Read-Only

    1 - Hidden

    2 - System

    3 - Volume Label

    4 - Reserved (0)

    5 - Archive

    6 through 15 - Reserved (0)

DX - Offset of ASCIIZ File/Path Name

DS - Segment of ASCIIZ File/Path Name

Register Contents on Exit:

AX - Error Code if Unsuccessful

CF - 0 if Successful, 1 if Unsuccessful

Example:

```
;Find first file
MOV   AH,4Eh
MOV   CX,0        ;Read-only
LDS   DX,BUFF
INT   21h
```

FIND NEXT FILE (INTERRUPT 21h SERVICE 4Fh)

DOS 2.0

This service finds the next file matching the filename parameter using the default drive and path. You can use a drive and path specifier to modify the file search path. Service 4Eh must successfully execute before using this service. You cannot change the contents of the disk transfer area (DTA) before using the service. TABLE 10-6 contains a listing of the DTA contents upon exit from this routine. You can use the question mark (?) or asterisk (*) as wildcard characters.

You must use interrupt 21h service 1Ah to point to a DTA buffer before using this service. DOS uses this buffer as an area in which to place the disk directory.

Use the attribute entry to specify the file attributes to accept during the search. DOS always searches for files with the normal attribute set. In addition to normal files, you can search for files with the hidden, system, and directory attributes set.

Register Contents on Entry:

AH   - 4Fh

DTA - Contains Information From Previous Search

Register Contents on Exit:

AX   - Error Code if Unsuccessful

CF   - 0 if Successful, 1 if Unsuccessful

GET VERIFY FLAG (INTERRUPT 21h SERVICE 54h)

DOS 2.0

This service obtains the value of the verify flag. If you set the verify flag, DOS reads each record after it writes it to disk. Because this adds extra overhead to the write process, DOS normally clears the verify flag. You can set the state of the verify flag using interrupt 21h service 2Eh. DOS provides the VERIFY ON and VERIFY OFF commands as an alternate method of controlling the verify flag state.

> Register Contents on Entry:
> AH - 54h
>
> Register Contents on Exit:
> AL - Current Verify Flag Value
>   0 - Verify Off
>   1 - Verify On

Example:
```
;Get verify flag
MOV   AH,54h
INT   21h
```

RENAME FILE (INTERRUPT 21h SERVICE 56h)

DOS 2.0

This service renames either a directory (DOS 3.0 and later only) or filename entry. In addition to renaming a file, DOS 3.0 allows you to move the file to a different directory on the same drive. You can use a drive and path specifier to modify the file search path. Do not use the question mark (?) or asterisk (*) as wildcard characters in either the old or new filenames.

There are several reasons why this service fails to rename or move a file. These reasons include: nonexistent path elements, a file with the new filename already exists in the specified directory, the old and new filenames specify different drives, or the root or other directory is full. When using DOS 3.0 or above, this function fails on a network if the calling program has insufficient access rights.

> Register Contents on Entry:
> AH - 56h
> DX - Offset of current ASCIIZ File/Path Name
> DI - Offset of New ASCIIZ File/Path Name
> DS - Segment of current ASCIIZ File/Path Name
> ES - Segment of New ASCIIZ File/Path Name
>
> Register Contents on Exit:
> AX - Error Code if Unsuccessful
> CF - 0 if Successful, 1 if Unsuccessful

Example:
```
;Rename file
MOV   AH,56h
LDS   SI,BUFF
LES   DI,BUFF
INT   21h
```

GET/SET FILE DATE AND TIME (INTERRUPT 21h SERVICE 57h)

DOS 2.0

This service obtains or modifies the time and date stamp of a file's directory entry. To use this function, you must create or open the file using services 3Ch, 3Dh, 5Ah, 5Bh, or 6Ch. The directory command will not display the file and time stamp of a file with a time and date stamp of zero. The effects of this service remain in effect until you close the file. Modifications to the file do not affect the time and date stamp.

Register Contents on Entry (Get Time):
AH - 57h
AL - 0
BX - Handle

Register Contents on Entry (Set Time):
AH - 57h
AL - 1
BX - Handle
CX - Time (Formatted as Shown in TABLE 10-6)
DX - Date (Formatted as Shown in TABLE 10-6)

Register Contents on Exit:
AX - Error Code if Unsuccessful
CX - Time (AL = 0)
DX - Date (AL = 0)
CF - 0 if Successful, 1 if Unsuccessful

Example:
```
; Get file date
MOV   AH,57h
MOV   AL,0
MOV   BX,FHandle
INT   21h

; Set file time
MOV   AH,57h
MOV   AL,1
MOV   BX,FHandle
```

```
MOV
MOV
INT    21h
```

CREATE TEMPORARY FILE
(INTERRUPT 21h SERVICE 5Ah)

DOS 3.0

This service creates a temporary file using the default drive and path. You can use a drive and path specifier to modify the file creation path. Always add at least 13 bytes of space to the ASCIIZ path you supply to DOS. This path contains the name of the file upon interrupt return. DOS does not automatically delete files created with this service when the program ends. This service fails if the root directory is full or the path supplied does not exist.

Register Contents on Entry:

AH - 5Ah

CX - Attributes (Bits True When Set)

    0 - Read-Only

    1 - Hidden

    2 - System

    3 - Volume Label

    4 - Reserved (0)

    5 - Archive

    6 through 15 - Reserved (0)

DX - Offset of ASCIIZ Path Name

DS - Segment of ASCIIZ Path Name

Register Contents on Exit:

AX - Handle if Successful, Error Code if Unsuccessful

DX - Offset of Complete ASCII Path and Filename

DS - Segment of Complete ASCIIZ Path and Filename

CF - 0 if Successful, 1 if Unsuccessful

Example:

```
;Create temporary file
MOV    AH,5Ah
MOV    CX,0        ;Read-only
LDS    DX,BUFF
INT    21h
```

CREATE NEW FILE (INTERRUPT 21h SERVICE 5Bh)

DOS 3.0

This service creates a new file using the default drive and path. You can use a drive and path specifier to modify the location of the new file. If the file already exists, this service fails and does not overwrite it. The filename variable contains a drive, path, filename, and extension. You end the filename with a zero to create an ASCIIZ string. DOS normally creates a file without any attributes set. You can create a volume label by specifying an attribute of 0008h. Otherwise, you should always keep bit 3 of the attribute specification clear.

There are several reasons why this service fails to create a new file. These reasons include nonexistent path elements, the root or requested directory is full, and a file with the same name already exists. This function fails on a network if the calling program has insufficient access rights.

Register Contents on Entry:
AH - 5Bh
CX - Attributes (Bits True When Set)
    0 - Read-Only
    1 - Hidden
    2 - System
    3 - Volume Label
    4 - Reserved (0)
    5 - Archive
    6 through 15 - Reserved (0)
DX - Offset of ASCIIZ Filename
DS - Segment of ASCIIZ Filename

Register Contents on Exit:
AX - Handle if Successful, Error Code if Unsuccessful
CF - 0 if Successful, 1 if Unsuccessful

Example:
```
;Create new file
MOV    AH,5Bh
MOV    CX,0        ;Read-only
LDS    DX,BUFF
INT    21h
```

LOCK/UNLOCK FILE REGION (INTERRUPT 21h SERVICE 5Ch)

DOS 3.0

This service locks/unlocks a region of the specified file. Use this service in a networking or multitasking environment to make sure two programs do not use the same part of a file at the same time. Always specify the starting position of the lock as a 32-bit number referenced to the beginning of the file. You use a 32-bit number to specify the locked region length.

DOS does not automatically unlock a file region when a program terminates. The program is responsible for unlocking the regions it locks. To remedy the results of an unexpected termination, a program using region locks should install their own interrupt 23h and 24h handlers.

In addition to locking the actual file, an application can lock an area beyond the end-of-file. This allows the program to add records to the end of a file (for example, append in a database program).

Note: You must load SHARE to use this function. DOS returns an error if it does not find SHARE loaded in memory.

Register Contents on Entry:
AH - 5Ch
AL - 0 Lock Region, 1 Unlock Region
BX - Handle
CX - High Part of Region Offset
DX - Low Part of Region Offset
SI - High Part of Region Length
DI - Low Part of Region Length

Register Contents on Exit:
AX - Error Code if Unsuccessful
CF - 0 if Successful, 1 if Unsuccessful

Example:

```
;Lock file region
MOV    AH,4Ch
MOV    AL,0
MOV    BX,FHandle
MOV    CX
MOV    DX,
********
INT    21h
```

SET HANDLE COUNT (INTERRUPT 21h SERVICE 67h)

DOS 3.3

This service sets the maximum number of handles available to open files and devices simultaneously. It does this by controlling the size of the table used to store file handles. DOS uses a default table capable of storing 20 file handles. This service fails if an application requests more than 20 handles and there is not enough system memory to support the enlarged table.

Register Contents on Entry:
AH - 67h
BX - Number of Handles

Register Contents on Exit:
AX - Error Code if Unsuccessful
CF - 0 if Successful, 1 if Unsuccessful

Example:
```
;Set number of handles to 3
MOV   AH,67h
MOV   BX,3
INT   21h
```

COMMIT FILE (INTERRUPT 21h SERVICE 68h)

DOS 3.3

This service writes any data currently contained in DOS buffers to the specified handle. If the handle refers to a file, DOS updates the time and date stamp. This service is more reliable in multitasking and networking environments than closing and reopening a file.

Register Contents on Entry:
AH - 68h
BX - Handle

Register Contents on Exit:
AX - Error Code if Unsuccessful
CF - 0 if Successful, 1 if Unsuccessful

Example:
```
;Commit file
MOV   AH,68h
MOV   BX,FHandle
INT   21h
```

EXTENDED OPEN FILE (INTERRUPT 21h SERVICE 6Ch)

DOS 4.0

This service opens, creates, or replaces a file using the default drive and path. You can use a drive and path specifier to modify the location of the new file. TABLE 10-7 contains a listing of the extended access mode

Table 10-7   Extended Access Mode Entry Parameters

Bit	Value	Description
0 - 2	000	Read Access
	001	Write Access
	010	Read/Write Access
3		Reserved (0)
4 - 6	000	Compatibility Mode
	001	Deny All
	010	Deny Write
	011	Deny Read
	100	Deny None

Table 10-7   Continued.

Bit	Value	Description
7	0	Child Process Does Not Inherit Handle
	1	Child Process Inherits Handle
8-12		Reserved (0)
13	0	Execute Interrupt 24h
	1	Return Error to Process
14	0	Writes Buffered and Deferred
	1	Physical Write at Request Time
15		Reserved (0)

entry parameters. TABLE 10-8 contains a listing of the open flag parameters.

Table 10-8   Open Flag Parameters

Bit	Value	Description
0-3		Action if File Exists
	0000	Fail
	0001	Open File
	0010	Replace File
4-7		Action if File Doesn't Exist
	0000	Fail
	0001	Create File
8-15		Reserved (0)

There are several reasons why this service fails to open a file. These reasons include: nonexistent path elements, the root directory or subdirectory is full, another file using the read-only attribute and the same filename exists, or the calling program has insufficient access rights.

Use the attribute entry to specify the file attributes to accept during the search. DOS always searches for files with the normal attribute set. In addition to normal files, you can search for files with the hidden, system, and directory attributes set.

Register Contents on Entry:
AH - 6Ch
AL - 0
BX - Access Mode
CX - Attributes (Bits True When Set)
    0 - Read-Only
    1 - Hidden
    2 - System
    3 - Volume Label
    4 - Reserved (0)
    5 - Archive
    6 through 15 - Reserved (0)
DX - Open Flag
SI - Offset of ASCIIZ Filename
DS - Segment of ASCIIZ Filename

Register Contents on Exit:
AX - Handle if Successful, Error Code if Unsuccessful
CX - Action Taken
    1 - Opened Existing File
    2 - Created New File
    3 - Replaced Existing File
CF - 0 if Successful, 1 if Unsuccessful

ABSOLUTE DISK READ (INTERRUPT 25h)

DOS 1.0

This service directly reads logical disk sectors into memory. TABLE 10-9 contains a listing of error codes. TABLE 10-10 contains a listing of parameter block requirements.

Table 10-9   Absolute Disk Read/Write Error Codes

Code	Error
01h	Bad Command
02h	Bad Address Mark
04h	Requested Sector Not Found
08h	Direct Memory Access (DMA) Failure
10h	Data Error (Bad CRC)
20h	Controller Failed
40h	Seek Operation Failed
80h	Attachment Failed to Respond

Upon return from the interrupt, the stack still contains the CPU flags. Use the POPF and ADD SP,2 instructions to control stack growth. Both instructions remove the flags from the stack.

Table 10-10   Absolute Disk Read/Write Parameter Block

Byte	Contents
00h-03h	32-Bit Sector Number
04h-05h	Number of Sectors to Read
06h-07h	Offset of Buffer
08h-09h	Segment of Buffer

Logical sector numbers begin at head 0, cylinder 0, sector 1 and continue to the last sector. DOS always updates the head number before the cylinder number. Logical sectors might not appear physically adjacent due to the effects of interleaving.

Caution: This service can and will destroy data on your disk if used incorrectly. Always use this service with extreme care.

Register Contents on Entry (>32 MB Partitions):
AL - Drive Number (0 = A, 1 = B, etc.)
CX - Number of Sectors to Read
DX - Starting Sector Number
BX - Offset of Buffer
DS - Segment of Buffer

Register Contents on Entry (>32 MB Partitions):
AL - Drive Number (0 = A, 1 = B, etc.)
CX - -1
BX - Offset of Parameter Block
DS - Segment of Parameter Block

Register Contents on Exit:
AX - Error Code if Unsuccessful
CF - 0 if Successful, 1 if Unsuccessful

ABSOLUTE DISK WRITE (INTERRUPT 26h)

DOS 1.0

This service directly writes data contained in memory to logical disk sectors. TABLE 10-9 contains a listing of error codes. TABLE 10-10 contains a listing of parameter block requirements.

Upon return from the interrupt, the stack still contains the CPU flags. Use the POPF or ADD SP,2 instructions to control stack growth. Both instructions remove the flags from the stack.

Logical sector numbers begin at head 0, cylinder 0, sector 1 and continue to the last sector. DOS always updates the head number before the cylinder number. Logical sectors might not appear physically adjacent due to the effects of interleaving.

Caution: This service can and will destroy data on your disk if used incorrectly. Always use this service with extreme care.

Register Contents on Entry (>32 MB Partitions):
AL - Drive Number (0 = A, 1 = B, etc.)
CX - Number of Sectors to Write
DX - Starting Sector Number
BX - Offset of Buffer
DS - Segment of Buffer

Register Contents on Entry (>32 MB Partitions):
Al - Drive Number (0 = A, 1 = B, etc.)
CX - −1
BX - Offset of Parameter Block
DS - Segment of Parameter Block

Register Contents on Exit:
AX - Error Code if Unsuccessful
CF - 0 if Successful, 1 if Unsuccessful

10-1A Assembly language program for DOS disk services.

```
;****************************************************************************************************
;* Sample Program 17, DOS DOS Hard Disk Drive/Floppy Diskette Services  *
;* This program shows you how to use some of the floppy and hard disk services provided by DOS.  First, the   *
;* program displays the parameters for the current drive.  It then asks if you want to change to another      *
;* directory.  If you do not want to change directories, press enter without typing anything.  Once the *
;* programs changes to the requested directory, it asks you for a file name to delete.  If you do not want to  *
;* delete a file, press enter without typing anything.  If you do want to test the delete feature, make sure   *
;* you create a non-usable file.  You do not need any special equipment to use this program.    *
;*                          *
;* Copyright 1989 John Mueller & Wallace Wang - Tab Books *
;****************************************************************************************************


;****************************************************************************************************
;* Perform the program setup.                    *
;****************************************************************************************************

.MODEL MEDIUM   ; Use a medum model size.

.STACK  ; Use the defalt stack of 1024 bytes.

;****************************************************************************************************
;* Begin the data area.  Declare all variables.          *
;****************************************************************************************************
.DATA

;Standard equates.

LF        EQU     10
CR        EQU     13
StrEnd   EQU     36
attribute          EQU        27h

;Program variables.

directoryname    DB       20 DUP (' '),0
filename         DB       13 DUP (' '),0
error    DW      0
drive    DB      0
Msg1     DB      'Drive    = '
driveletter      DB       5 DUP (0),LF,CR,'Sectors  = '
sectors DB      5 DUP (0),LF,CR,'Offset   = '
offs     DB      5 DUP (0),LF,CR,'Size     = '
csize    DB      5 DUP (0),LF,CR,'Clusters = '
clusters         DB       5 DUP (0),LF,CR,'Segment  = '
segmnt  DB      5 DUP (0),LF,CR,StrEnd
Msg2     DB      'Change to which directory: ',StrEnd
Msg3     DB      'Enter a file to delete: ',StrEnd
LineFeed          DB        CR,LF,StrEnd
```

10-1A Continued.

```
;*************************************************************************************************
;* Begin the code segment.                                 *
;*************************************************************************************************
.CODE

Example PROC    FAR
Start:  MOV     AX,@DATA         ;Point DS & ES to our data segment.
        MOV     DS,AX
        MOV     ES,AX

        CALL    ClearScr         ;Clear the display.
        CALL    getcurrentdisk   ;Get the disk number.
        CALL    getdrivedata     ;Use it to get parameters.
        MOV     AL,drive         ;Convert the drive number to
        ADD     AL,65   ; a letter.
        LEA     DI,driveletter   ;Save the drive letter.
        ADD     DI,4
        MOV     [DI],AL
        MOV     AX,0900h         ;Display the drive parameters.
        LEA     DX,Msg1
        INT     21h

        MOV     AX,0900h         ;Display the change directory
        LEA     DX,Msg2 ; message.
        INT     21h
        MOV     CX,21   ;Get the new directory name.
        LEA     DI,directoryname
        CALL    GetChar
        CALL    setcurrentdirectory      ;Change directories.

        MOV     AX,0900h         ;Display an extra space
        LEA     DX,LineFeed      ; between questions.
        INT     21h

        MOV     AX,0900h         ;Display the delete file
        LEA     DX,Msg3 ; message.
        INT     21h
        MOV     CX,14   ;Get the filename.
        LEA     DI,filename
        CALL    GetChar
        CALL    findfile         ;See if the file exists.
        CMP     AX,0
        JNE     Exit    ;If not, exit.
        CALL    deletefile       ;Otherwise, delete the file.

Exit:   MOV     AX,4C00h         ;Exit to DOS.
        INT     21h
        RET

Example ENDP
```

10-1A Continued.

```
;********************************************************************************************
;* This procedure clears the display and places the cursor at coordinates 0,0.  *
;********************************************************************************************

ClearScr      PROC     NEAR

        MOV      AX,0619h       ;Scroll 25 lines.
        MOV      BH,7     ;Use gray.
        XOR      CX,CX    ;Start at coordinate 0,0.
        MOV      DX,1950h        ;End at coordinate 25,80.
        INT      10h

        MOV      AX,0200h        ;Set cursor position.
        XOR      BH,BH    ;Use page 0.
        XOR      DX,DX    ;Use coordinate 0,0.
        INT      10h

        RET
ClearScr      ENDP


;********************************************************************************************
;* This procedure gets one or more characters from the keyboard.  It displays the characters as it      *
;* retrieves them.  You need to place the following values in the specified registers to use this procedure.    *
;*      CX - Number of Characters            *
;*      DI - Offset of String Storage        *
;********************************************************************************************

GetChar PROC    NEAR

MoreChar:       MOV      AX,0100h        ;Get the input and echo it to
        INT      21h      ; the display.
        CMP      AL,CR    ;See if user pressed enter.
        JE       Exit1    ;If so, exit.
        MOV      [DI],AL  ;Save the input in storage.
        INC      DI       ;Point to next storage position.
        LOOP     MoreChar         ;Get next character.

Exit1:  LEA      DX,LineFeed      ;Display the line feed.
        MOV      AX,0900h
        INT      21h

        RET

GetChar ENDP


;********************************************************************************************
;* This procedure converts an integer to a character representation.      *
;********************************************************************************************

HexConv PROC    NEAR
```

```
        MOV     CX,10    ;Load the divisor.
NextChar:       XOR     DX,DX    ;Clear DX.
        DIV     CX       ;Place first number in DX.
        ADD     DL,30h   ;Convert to a character.
        MOV     [DI],DL  ;Move to string location.
        DEC     DI       ;Update string pointer.
        CMP     AX,10    ;See if we need to divide.
        JGE     NextChar
        ADD     AL,30h   ;If not, AX less than 10.
        MOV     [DI],AL  ;Convert to character and store.

        RET

HexConv ENDP
```

```
;******************************************************************************************************
;* This procedure selects the specified disk drive.  DL contains the drive number you want selected (0 = A,   *
;* 1 = B, etc.).                                    *
;******************************************************************************************************

selectdisk      PROC    NEAR

        MOV     AX,0E00h
        MOV     DL,drive
        INT     21h
        MOV     drive,AL
        RET

selectdisk      ENDP
```

```
;******************************************************************************************************
;* This procedure gets the number of the current disk drive.  The interrupt returns with the drive number   *
;* (0 = A, 1 = B, etc.) in AL.                      *
;******************************************************************************************************

getcurrentdisk  PROC    NEAR

        MOV     AX,1900h
        INT     21h
        MOV     drive,AL

        RET

getcurrentdisk  ENDP
```

```
;******************************************************************************************************
;* This procedure gets various parameters for the selected drive.  In the case of this program, it gets the  *
;* parameters for the default drive.  However, you could place the number of any drive in DL and obtain *
;* information for that drive.  The information returned includes: sectors per cluster, segment and offset    *
;* of the media descriptor byte, size of the physical sector in bytes, and number of clusters.  *
;******************************************************************************************************
```

```
getdrivedata    PROC    NEAR

        MOV     AX,1B00h
        MOV     DL,drive
        INT     21h
        PUSH    DS      ;Save segment.
        PUSH    BX      ;Save offset.
        PUSH    CX      ;Save sector size.
        PUSH    DX      ;Save number of clusters.

        MOV     BX,@DATA        ;Restore DS.
        MOV     DS,BX

        XOR     AH,AH   ;Remove unneeded data.
        LEA     DI,sectors      ;Convert number of sectors/
        ADD     DI,4    ; cluster to a number.
        CALL    HexConv

        POP     AX      ;Get number of clusters.
        LEA     DI,clusters     ;Convert number of clusters
        ADD     DI,4    ; to a number.
        CALL    HexConv

        POP     AX      ;Get sector size.
        LEA     DI,csize        ;Convert sector size to a
        ADD     DI,4    ; number.
        CALL    HexConv

        POP     AX      ;Get offset.
        LEA     DI,offs ;Convert offset to a number.
        ADD     DI,4
        CALL    HexConv

        POP     AX      ;Get segment.
        LEA     DI,segmnt       ;Convert segment to a number.
        ADD     DI,4
        CALL    HexConv

        RET

getdrivedata    ENDP

;******************************************************************************************************
;* This procedure sets the directory to the ASCIIZ string pointed to by DS:DX.  If the directory does not    *
;* exist, DOS retains the current directory and returns an error message.       *
;******************************************************************************************************

setcurrentdirectory     PROC    NEAR

        MOV     AX,3B00h
```

```
        LEA     DX,directoryname
        INT     21h
        MOV     error,AX

        RET


setcurrentdirectory     ENDP


;************************************************************************************************************
;* This procedure determines if the selected file with the desired attributes exists in the specified    *
;* directory.  If the ASCIIZ string containing the filename does not include a directory, then DOS looks in   *
;* the current directory.  Even if the file exists, DOS must match both the filename and file attribute *
;* before returning a true condition.                          *
;************************************************************************************************************


findfile        PROC    NEAR

        MOV     AX,4E00h
        LEA     DX,filename
        MOV     CX,attribute
        INT     21h

        RET


findfile        ENDP


;************************************************************************************************************
;* This procedure deletes the specified file.  If the ASCIIZ string containing the filename does not include   *
;* a directory, then DOS looks for the file in the current directory.  If DOS does find the file, it returns   *
;* with an error code.                   *
;************************************************************************************************************


deletefile      PROC    NEAR

        MOV     AX,4100h
        LEA     DX,filename
        INT     21h
        MOV     error,AX

        RET


deletefile      ENDP

END     Start
```

10-1B BASIC language program for DOS disk services.

```
REM Sample Program 17, DOS Floppy Diskette/Hard Disk Service Interrupts Demonstration
REM This program shows you how to use the DOS floppy diskette/hard disk drive services.  This program
REM concentrates on showing the you the procedures for changing directories, finding a file, and manipulating
REM it (in this case by deleting it).  These are the three most common functions you need to perform using a
```

10-1B Continued.

```
REM disk drive.  To take full advantage of this program you should use a hard disk drive.  However, it will
REM work with a floppy disk only system as well.  You do not need any special equipment to use this program.
REM
REM Copyright 1989, 1990 John Mueller & Wallace Wang - Tab Books.


' $INCLUDE: 'qbx.bi'

DEFINT A-Z

DECLARE SUB GetCurrentDisk (Drive)
DECLARE SUB GetDriveData (Drive, Sectors, Offset, Size, Clusters, Segment)
DECLARE SUB SetCurrentDirectory (Directory$, ErrorNote)
DECLARE FUNCTION FindFile (FileName$, Attribute)
DECLARE SUB DeleteFile (FileName$, ErrorNote)


' ********************************************

CLS
CALL GetCurrentDisk(Drive)

' Find the current drive and get information on it
CALL GetDriveData(Drive, Sectors, Offset, Size, Clusters, Segment)
DriveLetter$ = CHR$(Drive + 65)
PRINT "Drive    = ", DriveLetter$
PRINT "Sectors  = ", Sectors
PRINT "Offset   = ", Offset
PRINT "Size     = ", Size
PRINT "Clusters = ", Clusters
PRINT "Segment  = ", Segment

' Set current directory
PRINT "Change to which directory: "
INPUT Directory$
CALL SetCurrentDirectory(Directory$, ErrorNote)
PRINT ErrorNote

' Search if a file exists, then delete it
PRINT "Enter a file to delete: "
INPUT FileName$

IF FindFile(FileName$, 0) = 1 THEN
  CALL DeleteFile(FileName$, ErrorNote)
ELSE
  PRINT "File not found"
END IF

SUB DeleteFile (FileName$, ErrorNote)
  DIM InRegs AS RegTypeX
  DIM OutRegs AS RegTypeX
```

10-1B Continued.

```
      InRegs.ax = &H4100
      InRegs.ds = SSEG(FileName$)
      InRegs.dx = SADD(FileName$)
      CALL InterruptX(&H21, InRegs, OutRegs)
      ErrorNote = OutRegs.ax
   END SUB


   FUNCTION FindFile (FileName$, Attribute)
      DIM InRegs AS RegTypeX
      DIM OutRegs AS RegTypeX

      InRegs.ax = &H4E00
      InRegs.ds = SSEG(FileName$)
      InRegs.dx = SADD(FileName$)
      InRegs.cx = Attribute
      CALL InterruptX(&H21, InRegs, OutRegs)
      PRINT "*** = "; OutRegs.ax
      IF OutRegs.ax = 0 THEN
         FindFile = 1         ' TRUE
      ELSE
         FindFile = 0         ' FALSE
      END IF
   END FUNCTION


   SUB GetCurrentDisk (Drive)
      DIM InRegs AS RegTypeX
      DIM OutRegs AS RegTypeX
      InRegs.ax = &H1900
      CALL InterruptX(&H21, InRegs, OutRegs)
      Drive = OutRegs.ax AND &HFF
   END SUB


   SUB GetDriveData (Drive, Sectors, Offset, Size, Clusters, Segment)
      DIM InRegs AS RegTypeX
      DIM OutRegs AS RegTypeX

      InRegs.ax = &H1B00
      InRegs.dx = Drive
      CALL InterruptX(&H21, InRegs, OutRegs)
      Sectors = OutRegs.ax AND &HFF
      Offset = OutRegs.bx
      Size = OutRegs.cx
      Clusters = OutRegs.dx
      Segment = OutRegs.ds
   END SUB


   SUB SetCurrentDirectory (Directory$, ErrorNote)
      DIM InRegs AS RegTypeX
      DIM OutRegs AS RegTypeX
      InRegs.ax = &H3B00
```

10-1B Continued.

```
   InRegs.dx = SADD(Directory$)
   InRegs.ds = SSEG(Directory$)
   CALL InterruptX(&H21, InRegs, OutRegs)
   ErrorNote = OutRegs.ax
END SUB
```

10-1C C language program for DOS disk services.

```
        /* Sample Program 17, DOS Hard Disk Drive/Floppy Diskette Services
This program shows you how to use some of the floppy and
hard disk services provided by DOS.  First, the program
displays the parameters for the current drive.  It then asks
if you want to change to another directory.  If you do not
want to change directories, press enter without typing
anything.  Once the programs changes to the requested
directory, it asks you for a file name to delete.  If you do
not want to delete a file, press enter without typing
anything.  If you do want to test the delete feature, make
sure you create a non-usable file.  You do not need any
special equipment to use this program.
Copyright 1989,1990 John Mueller & Wallace Wang - Tab Books */


#include <dos.h>
#include <conio.h>
#include <ctype.h>

union  REGS     iReg, oReg;
struct SREGS    segregs;
char   directoryname[10], filename[10];
int    error;

void selectdisk (int *drive)
       {
       iReg.h.ah = 0xE;
       iReg.h.dl = *drive;
       intdos (&iReg, &oReg);
       *drive = oReg.h.al;
       }


void getcurrentdisk (int *drive)
       {
       iReg.h.ah = 0x19;
       intdos (&iReg, &oReg);
       *drive = oReg.h.al;
       }


void getdrivedata (int *drive, int *sectors, int *offs, int *csize, int *clusters, int *segmnt)
       {
       iReg.h.ah = 0x1B;
       iReg.h.dl = *drive;
       int86x (0x21,&iReg, &oReg, &segregs);
```

```
         *sectors = oReg.h.al;
         *offs = oReg.x.bx;
         *csize = oReg.x.cx;
         *clusters = oReg.x.dx;
         segread (&segregs);
         *segmnt = segregs.ds;
         }


void setcurrentdirectory (char *directoryname, int *error)
         {
         iReg.h.ah = 0x3B;
         iReg.x.dx = directoryname;
         intdos (&iReg, &oReg);
         *error = oReg.x.ax;
         }


int findfile (char *filename, int attribute)
         {
         iReg.h.ah = 0x4E;
         iReg.x.dx = filename;
         iReg.x.cx = attribute;
         intdos (&iReg, &oReg);
         if (oReg.x.ax == 0)
           return 1;  /* TRUE */
         else
           return 0;  /* FALSE */
         }


void deletefile (char *filename, int *error)
         {
         iReg.h.ah = 0x41;
         iReg.x.dx = filename;
         intdos (&iReg, &oReg);
         *error = oReg.x.ax;
         }


main ()
         {
         void selectdisk (int*);
         void getcurrentdisk (int*);
         void setcurrentdirectory (char*, int*);
         int findfile (char*, int*);
         void deletefile (char*, int*);

         unsigned int drive, driveletter, sectors, offs, csize, clusters, segmnt;

         getcurrentdisk (&drive);
         getdrivedata (&drive, &sectors, &offs, &csize, &clusters, &segmnt);

         driveletter = toascii (drive+65);
```

10-1C Continued.

```
      printf ("Drive     = %c\n", driveletter);
      printf ("Sectors = %d\n", sectors);
      printf ("Offset    = %d\n", offs);
      printf ("Size      = %d\n", csize);
      printf ("Clusters = %u\n", clusters);
      printf ("Segment = %d\n", segmnt);

      /* Set current directory */
      printf ("Change to which directory: ");
      gets (directoryname);
      setcurrentdirectory (&directoryname, &error);

      /* Search if a file exists, then delete it */
      printf ("\nEnter a file to delete: ");
      gets (filename);
      if (findfile (filename, 0x0027) == 1)
        deletefile (&filename, &error);

      return 0;
      }
```

10-1D Pascal language program for DOS disk services.

```
(*********************************************************************************************)
(* Sample Program 17, DOS Floppy Diskette/Hard Disk Service Interrupts Demonstration     *)
(* This program shows you how to use the DOS floppy diskette/hard disk drive services.  This program    *)
(* concentrates on showing the you the procedures for changing directories, finding a file, and manipulating    *)
(* it (in this case by deleting it).  These are the three most common functions you need to perform using a    *)
(* disk drive.  To take full advantage of this program you should use a hard disk drive.  However, it will    *)
(* work with a floppy disk only system as well.  You do not need any special equipment to use this program.    *)
(*                                *)
(* Copyright 1989, 1990 John Mueller & Wallace Wang - Tab Books*)
(*********************************************************************************************)


PROGRAM Disks;

(* Copyright 1989,1990 John Mueller & Wallace Wang - Tab Books *)

USES
  Dos;
VAR
  Regs : Registers;
  Drive, Sectors, Offset, Size, Clusters, Segment,
    DTASeg, DTAOfs, Error : integer;
  DriveLetter : char;
  Filename, DirectoryName : string;

  PROCEDURE SelectDisk (VAR Drive : integer);
  BEGIN
    Regs.ah := $E;
```

```
  Regs.dl := Drive;
  MsDos (Regs);
  Drive := Regs.al;
END;  (* SelectDisk *)


PROCEDURE GetCurrentDisk (VAR Drive : integer);
BEGIN
  Regs.ah := $19;
  MsDos (Regs);
  Drive := Regs.al;
END;  (* GetCurrentDisk *)


PROCEDURE GetDefaultDriveData (VAR Sectors, Offset, Size, Clusters, Segment : integer);
BEGIN
  Regs.ah := $1B;
  MsDos (Regs);
  Sectors := Regs.al;
  Offset := Regs.bx;
  Size := Regs.cx;
  Clusters := Regs.dx;
  Segment := Regs.ds;
END;  (* GetDefaultDriveData *)


PROCEDURE GetDriveData (VAR Drive, Sectors, Offset, Size, Clusters, Segment : integer);
BEGIN
  Regs.ah := $1B;
  Regs.dl := Drive;
  MsDos (Regs);
  Sectors := Regs.al;
  Offset := Regs.bx;
  Size := Regs.cx;
  Clusters := Regs.dx;
  Segment := Regs.ds;
END;  (* GetDriveData *)


FUNCTION FindFile (ASCIIZ : string; Attribute : integer) : boolean;
BEGIN
  Regs.ah := $4E;
  Regs.ds := Seg (ASCIIZ);
  Regs.dx := Ofs (ASCIIZ)+1;
  Regs.cx := Attribute;
  MsDos (Regs);
  IF Regs.ax = 0 THEN
    FindFile := TRUE
  ELSE
    FindFile := FALSE;
END;  (* FindFile *)


PROCEDURE DeleteFile (FileName : string;
                      VAR Error : integer);
```

```
BEGIN
  Regs.ah := $41;
  Regs.dx := Ofs (FileName)+1;
  Regs.ds := Seg (FileName);
  MsDos (Regs);
  Error := Regs.ax;
END;  (* DeleteFile *)


PROCEDURE SetCurrentDirectory (VAR DirectoryName : string;
                                VAR Error : integer);
BEGIN
  Regs.ah := $3B;
  Regs.dx := Ofs (DirectoryName)+1;
  Regs.ds := Seg (DirectoryName);
  MsDos (Regs);
  Error := Regs.ax;
END;  (* SetCurrentDirectory *)

BEGIN
  GetCurrentDisk (Drive);

  (* Find the current drive and get information on it *)

  GetDriveData (Drive, Sectors, Offset, Size, Clusters, Segment);
  DriveLetter := Chr(Drive+65);
  Writeln ('Drive    = ', DriveLetter);
  Writeln ('Sectors  = ', Sectors);
  Writeln ('Offset   = ', Offset);
  Writeln ('Size     = ', Size);
  Writeln ('Clusters = ', Clusters);
  Writeln ('Segment  = ', Segment);

  (* Set current directory *)
  Write ('Change to which directory: ');
  Readln (DirectoryName);
  SetCurrentDirectory (DirectoryName, Error);

  (* Search if a file exists, then delete it *)
  Write ('Enter a file to delete: ');
  Readln (FileName);
  IF FindFile (FileName, 0) = TRUE THEN
    DeleteFile (FileName, Error);

END.
```

11
DOS Keyboard Interrupts

This chapter discusses the DOS keyboard interrupt routines. Each interrupt description contains the first DOS version to provide the service, the required register contents on routine entry, and a code fragment showing usage. TABLE 8-1 lists the DOS interrupts in numeric order. Figure 11-1 shows you how to use the DOS keyboard interrupts. In addition, almost every example program throughout this book shows you other methods of using the keyboard interrupts. The DOS keyboard interrupts allow you to access non-standard keyboard configurations. Always use a DOS interrupt when you want to use a keyboard requiring the use of a device driver.

In addition to the methods described below, DOS provides an alternate keyboard input method. You can use interrupt 21h service 3Fh to read the keyboard as a file. Use the standard DOS handle of 0 as input to the service. Of course, you can always use the ROM interrupts described in Chapter 7. Appendix A contains a listing of the ASCII values returned by DOS and ROM keyboard interrupts.

CHARACTER INPUT WITH ECHO
(INTERRUPT 21h SERVICE 1)

DOS 1.0

This service reads a character from the standard input device (keyboard only when using DOS 1.X) and outputs it to the standard output device (monitor only when using DOS 1.X). If the keyboard buffer is empty, it waits until the user presses a key.

With DOS 2.0 or later, this service can read a character from an input device other than the keyboard. DOS can send the character to an output device other than the screen (for example, a disk file). When reading characters from a redirected device, this service cannot detect the logical end

11-1A Assembly language program for keyboard service interrupts.

```
;*******************************************************************************************
;* Sample Program 18, DOS Keyboard Service Interrupts          *
;* This program shows you how to use the keyboard service routines provided by DOS.  It starts by asking the  *
;* user to input a character.  The program reads the character and converts it to its ASCII equivalent.  You  *
;* do not need any special equipment to use this program.          *
;*                         *
;* Copyright 1989 John Mueller & Wallace Wang - Tab Books *
;*******************************************************************************************


;*******************************************************************************************
;* Perform the program setup.              *
;*******************************************************************************************

.MODEL MEDIUM   ; Use a medum model size.

.STACK  ; Use the defalt stack of 1024 bytes.

;*******************************************************************************************
;* Begin the data area.  Declare all variables.          *
;*******************************************************************************************
.DATA

;Standard equates.

LF       EQU     10
CR       EQU     13
StrEnd   EQU     36

;Program variables.

Msg1     DB       'Press an alphanumeric key and the'
         DB       ' following procedure',LF,CR,'returns the'
         DB       ' ASCII code equivalent',LF,CR,StrEnd
readme   DB       3 DUP (' '),LF,CR,StrEnd

;*******************************************************************************************
;* Begin the code segment.              *
;*******************************************************************************************
.CODE

Example PROC     FAR
Start:   MOV      AX,@DATA        ;Point DS & ES to our data segment.
         MOV      DS,AX
         MOV      ES,AX

         CALL     ClearScr        ;Clear the display.

         MOV      AX,0900h        ;Display initial message.
         LEA      DX,Msg1
         INT      21h
```

11-1A Continued.

```
        CALL    inputwithecho   ;Get an input character and
                                ; display its ASCII
                                ; equivalent in decimal form.

Exit:   MOV     AX,4C00h        ;Exit to DOS.
        INT     21h
        RET

Example ENDP
```

```
;**********************************************************************************************************
;* This procedure clears the display and places the cursor at coordinates 0,0.  *
;**********************************************************************************************************
;

ClearScr        PROC    NEAR

        MOV     AX,0619h        ;Scroll 25 lines.
        MOV     BH,7    ;Use gray.
        XOR     CX,CX   ;Start at coordinate 0,0.
        MOV     DX,1950h        ;End at coordinate 25,80.
        INT     10h

        MOV     AX,0200h        ;Set cursor position.
        XOR     BH,BH   ;Use page 0.
        XOR     DX,DX   ;Use coordinate 0,0.
        INT     10h

        RET

ClearScr        ENDP
```

```
;**********************************************************************************************************
;* This procedure gets a character from the display.  The DOS service routine automatically displays the     *
;* character.  The procedure then converts the character to a decimal equivalent and displays it.       *
;**********************************************************************************************************
;

inputwithecho   PROC    NEAR

        MOV     AX,0100h        ;Returns keystroke in AL.
        INT     21h
        XOR     AH,AH   ;Zero the upper portion of AX.
        LEA     DI,readme       ;Load the storage variable
        ADD     DI,2    ; and point to the end.
        CALL    HexConv ;Convert AL to a character.

        MOV     AX,0900h        ;Print the result
        LEA     DX,readme
        INT     21h

        RET
```

11-1A Continued.

```
inputwithecho    ENDP

;*****************************************************************************************************
;* This procedure converts an integer to a character representation.      *
;*****************************************************************************************************

HexConv PROC     NEAR

          MOV     CX,10    ;Load the divisor.
NextChar:         XOR     DX,DX    ;Clear DX.
          DIV     CX       ;Place first number in DX.
          ADD     DL,30h   ;Convert to a character.
          MOV     [DI],DL  ;Move to string location.
          DEC     DI       ;Update string pointer.
          CMP     AX,10    ;See if we need to divide.
          JGE     NextChar
          ADD     AL,30h   ;If not, AX less than 10.
          MOV     [DI],AL  ;Convert to character and store.
          RET


HexConv ENDP

END     Start
```

11-1B BASIC language program for keyboard service interrupts.

```
REM Sample Program 18, DOS Keyboard Service Interrupts Demonstration
REM This program shows you how to directly access the keyboard services provided by DOS.  In addition, it
REM shows you one technique of recovering the value of all flags stored in the flag register.  You do not
REM need any special equipment to use this program.
REM
REM Copyright 1989, 1990 John Mueller & Wallace Wang - Tab Books

' $INCLUDE: 'qbx.bi'
DIM InRegs AS RegType
DIM OutRegs AS RegType

DEFINT A-Z

DECLARE SUB InputWithEcho ()
DECLARE SUB DirectConsole ()
DECLARE SUB UnfilteredInput ()
DECLARE SUB InputWithoutEcho ()

' ************************************************

PRINT "Press an alphanumeric key and the following procedure"
PRINT "returns the ASCII code equivalent"
InputWithEcho
```

11-1B Continued.

```
SUB DirectConsole
  DIM InRegs AS RegType
  DIM OutRegs AS RegType
  InRegs.ax = &H600
  InRegs.dx = &HFF
  CALL Interrupt(&H21, InRegs, OutRegs)
  ReadMe = OutRegs.ax AND &HFF
  PRINT ReadMe
END SUB


SUB InputWithEcho
  DIM InRegs AS RegType
  DIM OutRegs AS RegType

  InRegs.ax = &H100
  CALL Interrupt(&H21, InRegs, OutRegs)
  ReadMe = OutRegs.ax AND &HFF
  PRINT ReadMe
END SUB


SUB InputWithoutEcho
  DIM InRegs AS RegType
  DIM OutRegs AS RegType
  InRegs.ax = &H800
  CALL Interrupt(&H21, InRegs, OutRegs)
  ReadMe = OutRegs.ax AND &HFF
END SUB


SUB UnfilteredInput
  DIM InRegs AS RegType
  DIM OutRegs AS RegType
  InRegs.ax = &H700
  CALL Interrupt(&H21, InRegs, OutRegs)
END SUB
```

11-1C C language program for keyboard service interrupts.

```
        /* Sample Program 18, DOS Keyboard Service Interrupts
This program shows you how to use the keyboard service
routines provided by DOS.  It starts by asking the user to
input a character.  The program reads the character and
converts it to its ASCII equivalent.  You do not need any
special equipment to use this program.
Copyright 1989,1990 John Mueller & Wallace Wang - Tab Books */


#include <dos.h>
#include <conio.h>
#include <ctype.h>


union   REGS    iReg, oReg;
struct  SREGS   segregs;
```

```
void inputwithecho (void)
      {
      int readme;

      iReg.h.ah = 1;
      intdos (&iReg, &oReg);
      readme = oReg.h.al;
      printf ("%d", readme);
      }


void directconsole (void)
      {
      iReg.h.ah = 6;
      iReg.h.dl = 0xFF;
      intdos (&iReg, &oReg);
      printf ("%d", oReg.h.al);
      }


void unfilteredinput (void)
      {
      iReg.h.ah = 7;
      intdos (&iReg, &oReg);
      }


void inputwithoutecho (void)
      {
      iReg.h.ah = 8;
      intdos (&iReg, &oReg);
      }


main ()
      {
      void inputwithecho ();
      void directconsole ();
      void unfilteredinput ();
      void inputwithoutecho ();
      void checkinputstatus ();

      printf ("Press an alphanumeric key and the following procedure\n");
      printf ("returns the ASCII code equivalent\n");
      inputwithecho ();
      }
```

11-1D Pascal language program for keyboard service interrupts.

```
(*********************************************************************************************************)
(* Sample Program 18, DOS Keyboard Service Interrupts Demonstration    *)
(* This program shows you how to directly access the keyboard services provided by DOS.  In addition, it    *)
(* shows you one technique of recovering the value of all flags stored in the flag register.  You do not    *)
```

11-1D Continued.

```
(* need any special equipment to use this program.        *)
(*                          *)
(* Copyright 1989, 1990 John Mueller & Wallace Wang - Tab Books   *)
(*************************************************************************)

PROGRAM Keyboard;

(* 9F loads all flags in AH, bit 6 has zero flag *)

USES
  Dos;
VAR
  Regs : Registers;

  PROCEDURE InputWithEcho;
  VAR
    ReadMe : integer;
  BEGIN
    Regs.ah := 1;
    MsDos (Regs);
    ReadMe := Regs.al;
    Writeln (ReadMe);
  END; (* InputWithEcho *)

  PROCEDURE DirectConsole;
  BEGIN
    Regs.ah := 6;
    Regs.dl := $FF;
    MsDos (Regs);
    Writeln (Regs.al);
  END;  (* DirectConsole *)

  PROCEDURE UnfilteredInput;
  BEGIN
    Regs.ah := 7;
    MsDos (Regs);
  END;  (* UnfilteredInput *)

  PROCEDURE InputWithoutEcho;
  BEGIN
    Regs.ah := 8;
    MsDos (Regs);
  END;  (* InputWithoutEcho *)

  PROCEDURE BufferedInput (CharIn : byte);
  BEGIN
    Regs.ah := $A;
    Regs.dx := Ofs (CharIn);
    Regs.ds := Seg (CharIn);
  END; (* BufferedInput *)
```

11-1D Continued.

```
FUNCTION CheckInputStatus : boolean;
BEGIN
  Regs.ah := $B;
  MsDos (Regs);
  IF Regs.al = 0 THEN
    CheckInputStatus := FALSE;
  IF Regs.al = $FF THEN
    CheckInputStatus := TRUE;
END;  (* CheckInputStatus *)

PROCEDURE FlushInputBuffer (NumIn : byte);
BEGIN
  Regs.ah := $C;
  Regs.al := NumIn;
  IF Regs.al = $A THEN
    BEGIN
      Regs.dx := Ofs (NumIn);
      Regs.ds := Seg (NumIn);
    END;
  MsDos (Regs);
END;  (* FlushInputBuffer *)

PROCEDURE GetDBCS;
BEGIN
  Regs.ah := $63;
  Regs.al := 1;
  Regs.dl := 1;
  MsDos (Regs);
END;  (* GetDBCS *)

BEGIN
 { InputWithEcho;
  DirectConsole;
  UnfilteredInput;
  InputWithoutEcho;
  REPEAT
  UNTIL CheckInputStatus;
  FlushInputBuffer (1);
  GetDBCS;
  BufferedInput (1);  }
  DirectConsole;
END.
```

of file character (Ctrl–Z). It continues reading to the physical end of the file. When writing to a disk, this service cannot determine if the disk is already full.

If the keyboard buffer contains an extended ASCII character, this service returns a zero (0) on the first call. Call the service a second time to determine the scan code of the key pressed. DOS requires a second call if the key pressed is a non-alphanumeric key such as the function or cursor keys. If this service reads a Ctrl – C character (ASCII code 3) and the user did not redirect the keyboard output, it calls interrupt 23h (Ctrl – Break Handler Address). This service always calls interrupt 23h if it detects Ctrl – C with BREAK set on.

Register Contents on Entry:
AH - 1

Register Contents on Exit:
AL - 8-Bit Input Data

Example:
```
;Character input with echo
MOV   AH,1
INT   21h
```

DIRECT CONSOLE I/O (INTERRUPT 21h SERVICE 6)

DOS 1.0

This service reads a character from the standard input device (keyboard only when using DOS 1.X) and outputs it to the standard output device (monitor only when using DOS 1.X). This service outputs all characters and control characters without operating system interpretation. It does not call interrupt 23h (Ctrl – C Handler) when the user enters a Ctrl – C combination at the keyboard. The setting of BREAK does not affect the output of this service.

With DOS 2.0 or later, this service can read a character from an input device other than the keyboard. DOS can send the character to an output device other than the screen (for example, a disk file). When reading characters from a redirected device, this service cannot detect the logical end-of-file character (Ctrl – Z). It continues reading to the physical end of the file. When writing to a disk, this service cannot determine if the disk is already full.

If the keyboard buffer contains an extended ASCII character, this service returns a zero (0) on the first call. Call the service a second time to determine the scan code of the key pressed. DOS requires a second call if the key pressed is a non-alphanumeric key such as the function or cursor keys.

Register Contents on Entry:
AH - 6
DL - Function
      00h through FEh - Output Request
      FFh - Input Request

Register Contents on Exit (DL = FFh):

ZF - Clear if Character Ready, Set if Character Not Ready
AL - 8-Bit Input Data

Example:
```
;Direct console I/O
MOV    AH,6
MOV    DL,FFh      ;Input request
INT    21h
```

UNFILTERED CHARACTER INPUT WITHOUT ECHO (INTERRUPT 21h SERVICE 7)

DOS 1.0

This service waits until the keyboard detects an input, then reads a character from the standard input device (keyboard only when using DOS 1.X). It does not send the input data to the output device. This service ignores the Ctrl–C or Ctrl–Break keys.

With DOS 2.0 or later, this service can read a character from an input device other than the keyboard (for example, a disk file). When reading characters from a redirected device, this service cannot detect the logical end of file character (Ctrl–Z). It continues reading to the physical end of the file. You cannot redirect the output of this service.

If the keyboard buffer contains an extended ASCII character, this service will return a zero (0) on the first call. Call the service a second time to determine the scan code of the key pressed. DOS requires a second call if the key pressed is a non-alphanumeric key such as the function or cursor keys.

Register Contents on Entry:
AH - 7

Register Contents on Exit:
AL - 8-Bit Input Data

Example:
```
;Unfiltered character input without echo
MOV    AH,7
INT    21h
```

CHARACTER INPUT WITHOUT ECHO (INTERRUPT 21h SERVICE 8)

DOS 1.0

This service waits until the keyboard detects an input, then reads a character from the standard input device (keyboard only when using DOS 1.X). It does not send the input data to the output device.

If the keyboard buffer contains an extended ASCII character, this service returns a zero (0) on the first call. Call the service a second time to determine the scan code of the key pressed. DOS requires a second call if the key pressed is a non-alphanumeric key such as the function or cursor keys. If this service reads a Ctrl–C character (ASCII code 3) and the user did not redirect the keyboard output, it calls interrupt 23h (Ctrl–Break Handler Address). This service always calls interrupt 23h if it detects Ctrl–C with BREAK set on.

With DOS 2.0 or later, this service can read a character from an input device other than the keyboard (for example, a disk file). When reading characters from a redirected device, this service cannot detect the logical end-of-file character (Ctrl–Z). It continues reading to the physical end of the file. You cannot redirect the output of this service.

Register Contents on Entry:
AH - 8

Register Contents on Exit:
AL - 8-Bit Input Data

Example:
```
;Character input without echo
MOV    AH,8
INT    21h
```

BUFFERED KEYBOARD INPUT (INTERRUPT 21h SERVICE Ah)

DOS 1.0

This service reads a character from the standard input device (keyboard only when using DOS 1.X) and stores the characters in a buffer. It continues reading data from the keyboard until the user presses Enter or the buffer fills to one character less than its maximum capacity. DOS outputs the bell character to the speaker if the user continues to input data after filling the buffer. The user must press Enter to end the input. DOS places the carriage return as the last character in the buffer. The minimum buffer size is 2 bytes (1 byte for the input character and 1 byte for the ending carriage return). The maximum buffer size is 255 bytes. The buffer uses the following format: byte 0 contains the maximum characters to read and byte 1 contains the number of characters returned by DOS, Bytes 2 and above contain user input from the keyboard or redirected device. TABLE 11-1 shows the buffer format.

With DOS 2.0 or later, this service can read a character from an input device other than the keyboard (for example, a disk file). When reading characters from a redirected device, this service cannot detect the logical end of file character (Ctrl–Z). It continues reading to the physical end of the file. You cannot redirect the output of this service.

If this service reads a Ctrl–C character (ASCII code 3) and the user did not redirect the keyboard output, it calls interrupt 23h (Ctrl–Break Handler Address). This service always calls interrupt 23h if it detects Ctrl–C with BREAK set on.

This service implements full keyboard buffering with typeahead capability. DOS allows you to use any of the standard keyboard editing commands.

Register Contents on Entry:
AH - Ah
DX - Buffer Offset
DS - Buffer Segment

Example:
```
;Buffered keyboard input
MOV   AH,Ah
LDS   DX,BUFF
INT   21h
```

Table 11-1   Keyboard Input Buffer Format

Byte	Contents
0	Maximum Number of Characters to Read
1	Number of Characters Read
2+	String Read From Keyboard

CHECK INPUT STATUS (INTERRUPT 21h SERVICE Bh)

DOS 1.0

This service checks the standard input device (keyboard only for DOS 1.X) to determine if the keyboard buffer contains a character. It does not identify the actual character. The flag returned remains true until another service retrieves the character. If this service reads a Ctrl–C character (ASCII code 3) and the user did not redirect the keyboard output, it calls interrupt 23h (Ctrl–Break Handler Address). This service always calls interrupt 23h if it detects Ctrl–C with BREAK set on. Interrupt 21h service 44h function 06h performs the same task as this service.

Register Contents on Entry:
AH - Bh

Register Contents on Exit:
AL - 00h if No Character Available
       FFh if Character Available

Example:
```
;Check input status
MOV   AH,Bh
INT   21h
```

FLUSH INPUT BUFFER THEN INPUT (INTERRUPT 21h SERVICE Ch)

DOS 1.0

This service clears the input buffer and then calls a character input service. You use this service to prevent typeahead errors that occur when the user types characters before your program is ready to accept any input.

With DOS 2.0 or later, this service can read a character from an input device other than the keyboard (for example, a disk file). When reading characters from a redirected device, this service cannot detect the logical end-of-file character (Ctrl – Z). It continues reading to the physical end of the file. You cannot redirect the output of this service.

You can use this service as an alternative to the earlier DOS service 1 (Character Input with Echo), service 6 (Direct Console I/O), service 7 (Unfiltered Character Input without Echo), service 8 (Character Input without Echo), and service Ah (Buffered Keyboard Input). Always enter one of these numbers in AL before calling this service.

The input service number placed in AL determines if this service acts on Ctrl – C. See the previous descriptions to find out how this service handles Ctrl – C input.

Register Contents on Entry:
AH - Ch
AL - Input Service Number (1, 6, 7, 8, or Ah)
DX - Buffer Offset (if AL = Ah)
DS - Buffer Segment (if AL = Ah)

Example:
```
;Flush input buffer then input
MOV    AH,Ch
MOV    AL,1
LDS    DX,BUFF
INT    21h
```

GET DBCS LEAD BYTE TABLE (INTERRUPT 21h SERVICE 63h)

DOS 2.25 Only

This service gets the address of lead-byte ranges for double-byte character sets (DBCS) system table. It also sets or gets the interim console flag. You may use this service with DOS version 2.25 only. DOS version 3.0 and above do not support this service. Interrupt 21h service 65h replaces this service for DOS versions 3.3 and above.

Register Contents on Entry:
AH - 63h

AL - Function
  0 - Get DBCS Lead-Byte Table Address
  1 - Set/Clear Interim Console Flag
  2 - Obtain Interim Console Flag Value
DL - Console Flag Status (AL = 1)
  0 - Clear Flag
  1 - Set Flag

Register Contents on Exit:
AX - Error Code if Unsuccessful
DL - Interim Console Flag Value (Function 2)
SI - Offset of DBCS Lead-Byte Table (Function 0)
DS - Segment of DBCS Lead-Byte Table (Function 0)
CF - 0 if Successful, 1 if Unsuccessful

Example:

```
;Get DBCS Lead Byte Table
MOV    AH,63h
MOV    AL,1     ;Set/Clear interim console flag
MOV    DL,1
INT    21h
```

12
DOS Printer Service Interrupts

This chapter discusses the DOS printer service interrupt routines. Each interrupt description contains the first DOS version to provide the service, the required register contents on routine entry, and a code fragment showing usage. TABLE 8-1 lists the interrupts in numeric order. Figure 12-1 shows you how to use the DOS printer service interrupts. You cannot use these services for graphics output. When using DOS version 2.0 or above, you can output data to the printer using interrupt 21h service 40. Use the predefined DOS handle 4 or a handle obtained by opening the device for output for this purpose. This alternate print method allows you to send graphics to the printer. Although using a DOS service might provide you with an easier output method, using a ROM interrupt provides faster output. In addition, a DOS interrupt does not provide access to the advanced features of some printers.

PRINTER OUTPUT (INTERRUPT 21h SERVICE 5)
DOS 1.0

This service sends a character to the standard list device (LPT1 only for DOS 1.0). When using DOS version 2.0 or above, use the MODE command to redirect printer output from LPT1 to another port. If the printer is busy, this service waits until the printer can accept input. Because this service does not check if the printer is on, calling this service when a printer is off or not connected will place the computer in an infinite wait. There is no standard method of checking the printer status under DOS. If this service detects a Ctrl–C or Ctrl–Break, it calls Interrupt 23h (Ctrl–Break Handler).

12-1A Assembly language program for keyboard service interrupts.

```
;***********************************************************************************************
;* Sample Program 19, DOS Printer Service Interrupts          *
;* This program shows you how to use the printer service routines provided by DOS.  It starts by asking the    *
;* user to input a character.  The program reads the character and sends it to the printer.  The program then  *
;* sends a carriage return to the printer.  After the printer recieves the carriage return, it outputs the     *
;* user character and advances to the next line.  You do not need any special equipment to use this program.   *
;*                        *
;* Copyright 1989 John Mueller & Wallace Wang - Tab Books *
;***********************************************************************************************


;***********************************************************************************************
;* Perform the program setup.                   *
;***********************************************************************************************

.MODEL MEDIUM   ; Use a medum model size.

.STACK  ; Use the defalt stack of 1024 bytes.

;***********************************************************************************************
;* Begin the data area.  Declare all variables.          *
;***********************************************************************************************
.DATA

;Standard equates.

LF      EQU     10
CR      EQU     13
StrEnd  EQU     36

;Program variables.

Msg1    DB      'Type a letter to print:',CR,LF,StrEnd
Printer DB      'PRN',0
Handle  DW      0
PrntChar        DB      ' '
LineFeed        DB      LF,CR,StrEnd

;***********************************************************************************************
;* Begin the code segment.                    *
;***********************************************************************************************
.CODE

Example PROC    FAR
Start:  MOV     AX,@DATA        ;Point DS & ES to our data segment.
        MOV     DS,AX
        MOV     ES,AX

        CALL    ClearScr        ;Clear the display.

        MOV     AX,3D01h        ;Open the printer for
```

```
        LEA     DX,Printer       ; writing.
        INT     21h
        JC      Exit      ;Exit on error.
        MOV     Handle,AX

        MOV     AX,0900h         ;Display initial message.
        LEA     DX,Msg1
        INT     21h

        MOV     CX,1      ;Get a single character.
        LEA     DI,PrntChar
        CALL    GetChar

        MOV     AX,0500h         ;Send the character to the
        MOV     DL,PrntChar      ; printer.
        INT     21h

        MOV     AX,4000h         ;Send a carriage return to
        MOV     BX,Handle        ; the printer.
        MOV     CX,2
        LEA     DX,LineFeed
        INT     21h

        MOV     AX,3E00h         ;Close the printer as an
        MOV     BX,Handle        ; output device.
        INT     21h

Exit:   MOV     AX,4C00h         ;Exit to DOS.
        INT     21h
        RET

Example ENDP
```

```
;**********************************************************************************************************
;* This procedure clears the display and places the cursor at coordinates 0,0.  *
;**********************************************************************************************************

ClearScr        PROC    NEAR

        MOV     AX,0619h         ;Scroll 25 lines.
        MOV     BH,7      ;Use gray.
        XOR     CX,CX     ;Start at coordinate 0,0.
        MOV     DX,1950h         ;End at coordinate 25,80.
        INT     10h

        MOV     AX,0200h         ;Set cursor position.
        XOR     BH,BH     ;Use page 0.
        XOR     DX,DX     ;Use coordinate 0,0.
        INT     10h

        RET
```

12-1A Continued.

```
ClearScr        ENDP


;*****************************************************************************************************
;* This procedure gets one or more characters from the keyboard.  It displays the characters as it        *
;* retrieves them.  You need to place the following values in the specified registers to use this procedure.  *
;*      CX - Number of Characters          *
;*      DI - Offset of String Storage      *
;*****************************************************************************************************
;

GetChar PROC    NEAR

MoreChar:       MOV     AX,0100h        ;Get the input and echo it to
        INT     21h     ; the display.
        CMP     AL,CR   ;See if user pressed enter.
        JE      Exit1   ;If so, exit.
        MOV     [DI],AL ;Save the input in storage.
        INC     DI      ;Point to next storage position.
        LOOP    MoreChar        ;Get next character.
Exit1:  LEA     DX,LineFeed     ;Display the line feed.
        MOV     AX,0900h
        INT     21h

        RET

GetChar ENDP

END     Start
```

12-1B BASIC language program for keyboard service interrupts.

```
REM Sample Program 19, DOS Printer Service Interrupts
REM This program shows you how to use the printer service routines provided by DOS.  It starts by asking the
REM user to input a character.  The program reads the character and sends it to the printer.  The program then
REM sends a carriage return to the printer.  After the printer recieves the carriage return, it outputs the
REM user character and advances to the next line.  You do not need any special equipment to use this program.
REM
REM Copyright 1989 John Mueller & Wallace Wang - Tab Books

' $INCLUDE: 'qbx.bi'

DIM InRegs AS RegType
DIM OutRegs AS RegType

DEFINT A-Z

' *****************************

CLS
OPEN "LPT1:BIN" FOR OUTPUT AS #1
```

12-1B Continued.

```
InRegs.ax = &H500
PRINT "Type a letter to print"
INPUT Letter$
InRegs.dx = ASC(Letter$)

CALL Interrupt(&H21, InRegs, OutRegs)
LPRINT CHR$(10)
LPRINT CHR$(13)
CLOSE #1
```

12-1C C language program for keyboard service interrupts.

```
/* Sample Program 19, DOS Printer Service Interrupts
This program shows you how to use the printer service routines
provided by DOS.  It starts by asking the user to input a
character.  The program reads the character and sends it to
the printer.  The program then sends a carriage return to the
printer.  After the printer recieves the carriage return, it
outputs the user character and advances to the next line.  You
do not need any special equipment to use this program.

Copyright 1989,1990 John Mueller & Wallace Wang - Tab Books */

#include <dos.h>
#include <stdio.h>
#include <ctype.h>

union   REGS    iReg, oReg;
FILE    *printer;
char    letter;
int     makeme;

main ()
        {
        printer = fopen("prn", "w");

        iReg.h.ah = 5;

        printf ("Type a letter to print:\n");
        letter = fgetchar ();
        iReg.h.dl = letter;

        intdos (&iReg, &oReg);
        fputs ("\n", printer);
        fclose (printer);
        return 0;
        }
```

12-1D Pascal language for keyboard service interrupts.

```
(*********************************************************************************************************)
(* Sample Program 19, DOS Printer Service Interrupts          *)
(* This program shows you how to use the printer service routines provided by DOS.  It starts by asking the   *)
(* user to input a character.  The program reads the character and sends it to the printer.  The program then *)
(* sends a carriage return to the printer.  After the printer recieves the carriage return, it outputs the    *)
(* user character and advances to the next line.  You do not need any special equipment to use this program.  *)
(*                              *)
(* Copyright 1989 John Mueller & Wallace Wang - Tab Books *)
(*********************************************************************************************************)

PROGRAM Printer;
USES
  Dos;
VAR
  Regs : Registers;
  F : text;
  Letter : char;
BEGIN
  Assign (F, 'PRN');
  Rewrite (F);
  Regs.ah := 5;

  Writeln ('Type a letter to print');
  Readln (Letter);
  Regs.dl := Ord(Letter);

  MsDos (Regs);
  Writeln (F, ^J);
  Writeln (F, ^M);
  Close (F);
END.
```

Register Contents on Entry:
AH - 5
DL - 8-Bit Data for Output

Example:
```
;Printer output
MOV   AH,5
MOV   DL,DATA
INT   21h
```

SET PRINTER SETUP STRING
(INTERRUPT 21h SERVICE 5Eh FUNCTION 2)

DOS 3.1

This service specified a printer initialization string so network users can assign individual printing parameters to a shared network printer. You get the redirection list index using interrupt 21h service 5Fh function 2 (Get Redirection List). Use service 5Eh function 3 to get the existing printer setup string. This allows you to modify a correctly formatted string.

Note: This service is available only when Microsoft Networks is running.

Register Contents on Entry:
AH - 5Eh
AL - 2
BX - Redirection List Index
CX - Length of Setup String
SI - Offset of Setup String
DS - Segment of Setup String

Register Contents on Exit:
AX - Error Code if Unsuccessful
CF - 0 if Successful, 1 if Unsuccessful

Example:

```
;Set printer setup string
MOV    AH,5Eh
MOV    AL,2
???
```

GET PRINTER SETUP STRING
(INTERRUPT 21h SERVICE 5Eh FUNCTION 3)

DOS 3.1

This service retrieves the printer initialization string defined by service 5Eh function 2 (Set Printer Setup String). You get the redirection list index using interrupt 21h service 5Fh function 2 (Get Redirection List).

Note: This service is available only when Microsoft Networks is running.

Register Contents on Entry:
AH - 5Eh
AL - 3
BX - Redirection List Index
DI - Offset of Receive Setup String
ES - Segment of Receive Setup String

Register Contents on Exit:
AX - Error Code if Unsuccessful
CX - Length of Setup String
DI - Offset of Buffer Holding Setup String
ES - Segment of Buffer Holding Setup String
CF - 0 if Successful, 1 if Unsuccessful

Example:

```
;Get printer setup string
MOV    AH,5Eh
MOV    AL,3
???
LES    DI,STRING
```

13

DOS Serial Port Service Interrupts

This chapter discusses the DOS serial port service interrupt routines. Each interrupt description contains the first DOS version to provide the service, the required register contents on routine entry, and a code fragment showing usage. TABLE 8-1 lists the interrupts in numeric order. Figure 13-1 shows you how to use the DOS serial port interrupts. Notice that the DOS services provide very few functions.

There are several disadvantages to using DOS interrupts to control serial port input and output. First, DOS does not support interrupt-driven serial communications. This means that any software using the DOS serial port services require all the computer's resources. The disadvantage of this approach is that you cannot perform background communications. The only method of using interrupt-driven communications with the serial port is direct register manipulation. You must write your own serial driver because even the ROM services (interrupt 14h) do not provide this feature.

In addition to the cost of convenience, the DOS serial port services are slower than direct chip access or ROM services (interrupt 14h). This means that you could lose information by using the DOS services for higher speed communications (faster than 9,600 baud on some computers). In addition, because DOS does not detect serial port errors, your application would not realize that DOS lost the characters. DOS uses a standard setup of 2,400 baud, no parity, 1 stop bit, and 8 data bits.

Finally, you cannot directly control the port parameters (registers) using the DOS services. You must directly manipulate the chip registers or use the limited controls provided by ROM services (interrupt 14h) to set the port parameters. These parameters include transmission speed in baud, parity, number of stop bits, and number of data bits.

13-1A Assembly language program for serial port service interrupts.

```
;********************************************************************************************
;* Sample Program 20, DOS Serial Port Service Interrupts Demonstration  *
;* This program shows you how to use the DOS serial port services.  It begins by asking if you want to send      *
;* or receive a character through the serial port.  Once you make a selection, the program sends or receives     *
;* a character.  To use this program you need to connect two computers through their serial ports.  You do       *
;* not need any additional special equipment to use this program.      *
;*                                *
;* Copyright 1989 John Mueller & Wallace Wang - Tab Books *
;********************************************************************************************
;

;********************************************************************************************
;* Perform the program setup.                      *
;********************************************************************************************
;

.MODEL MEDIUM   ; Use a medum model size.

.STACK  ; Use the defalt stack of 1024 bytes.

;********************************************************************************************
;* Begin the data area.  Declare all variables.        *
;********************************************************************************************
;
.DATA

;Standard equates.

LF      EQU     10
CR      EQU     13
StrEnd  EQU     36

;Program variables.

Msg1    DB      'Send or Receive a character?',LF,CR,StrEnd
Msg2    DB      'Enter a character: ',StrEnd
Msg3    DB      'Received '
Reply   DB      2 DUP (' ')
        DB      'through the serial port.',LF,CR,StrEnd
Answer  DB      2 DUP (' ')
LineFeed        DB      CR,LF,StrEnd


;********************************************************************************************
;* Begin the code segment.                         *
;********************************************************************************************
;
.CODE

Example PROC    FAR
Start:  MOV     AX,@DATA        ;Point DS & ES to our data segment.
        MOV     DS,AX
        MOV     ES,AX

        CALL    ClearScr        ;Clear the display.
```

```
        MOV     AX,0900h        ;Display initial message.
        LEA     DX,Msg1
        INT     21h

        LEA     DI,Answer       ;Get a single character from
        MOV     CX,1    ; the user.
        CALL    GetChar

        LEA     DI,Answer       ;Convert the character to
        MOV     CX,1    ; uppercase, if required.
        CALL    UpCase

        CMP     BYTE PTR [Answer],'S'   ;See if the user wants
        JNE     Receive ; to send a character.

        MOV     AX,0900h        ;Ask user to enter a
        LEA     DX,Msg2 ; character.
        INT     21h

        LEA     DI,Answer       ;Get a single character from
        MOV     CX,1    ; the user.
        CALL    GetChar

        CALL    AuxOutput       ;Send it to the serial port.
        JMP     Exit    ;Leave the program.

Receive:        CALL    AuxInput        ;Wait for a character.

        MOV     AX,0900h        ;Display the result.
        LEA     DX,Msg3
        INT     21h

Exit:   MOV     AX,4C00h        ;Exit to DOS.
        INT     21h
        RET

Example ENDP
;***************************************************************************************************************
;* This procedure gets a character from the serial port.  It then stores the character in Reply.         *
;***************************************************************************************************************

AuxInput        PROC    NEAR

        MOV     AH,3
        INT     21h
        MOV     Reply,AL

        RET

AuxInput        ENDP
```

13-1A Continued.

```
;********************************************************************************
;* This procedure sends the contents of Answer to the serial port.      *
;********************************************************************************

AuxOutput       PROC    NEAR

        MOV     AH,4
        MOV     AL,Answer
        INT     21h

        RET

AuxOutput       ENDP

;********************************************************************************
;* This procedure clears the display and places the cursor at coordinates 0,0.  *
;********************************************************************************

ClearScr        PROC    NEAR

        MOV     AX,0619h         ;Scroll 25 lines.
        MOV     BH,7     ;Use gray.
        XOR     CX,CX    ;Start at coordinate 0,0.
        MOV     DX,1950h         ;End at coordinate 25,80.
        INT     10h

        MOV     AX,0200h         ;Set cursor position.
        XOR     BH,BH    ;Use page 0.
        XOR     DX,DX    ;Use coordinate 0,0.
        INT     10h

        RET

ClearScr        ENDP

;********************************************************************************
;* This procedure gets one or more characters from the keyboard.  It displays the characters as it      *
;* retrieves them.  You need to place the following values in the specified registers to use this procedure.   *
;*      CX - Number of Characters              *
;*      DI - Offset of String Storage          *
;********************************************************************************

GetChar PROC    NEAR

MoreChar:       MOV     AX,0100h         ;Get the input and echo it to
        INT     21h      ; the display.
        CMP     AL,CR    ;See if user pressed enter.
        JE      Exit1    ;If so, exit.
        MOV     [DI],AL  ;Save the input in storage.
        INC     DI       ;Point to next storage position.
        LOOP    MoreChar         ;Get next character.
```

13-1A Continued.

```
Exit1:  LEA     DX,LineFeed     ;Display the line feed.
        MOV     AX,0900h
        INT     21h

        RET

GetChar ENDP

;********************************************************************************************************
;* This procedure converts a lowercase letter to an uppercase letter.  You need to place the following values  *
;* in the specified registers to use this procedure.            *
;*      CX - Number of Characters             *
;*      DI - Offset of String Storage          *
;********************************************************************************************************

UpCase  PROC    NEAR

NewLetter:      MOV     AL,[DI] ;Store the current letter in
        CMP     AL,97   ; AX and see if its a
        JL      LoopIt  ; lowercase letter.
        CMP     AL,122
        JG      LoopIt

        SUB     AL,32   ;Convert the character to
        MOV     [DI],AL ; uppercase.

LoopIt: INC     DI      ;Point to the next character.
        LOOP    NewLetter       ;Convert it.

        RET

UpCase  ENDP

END     Start
```

13-1B BASIC language program for serial port service interrupts.

```
REM Sample Program 20, DOS Serial Port Service Interrupts Demonstration
REM This program shows you how to use the DOS serial port services.  It begins by asking if you want to send
REM or receive a character through the serial port.  Once you make a selection, the program sends or receives
REM a character.  To use this program you need to connect two computers through their serial ports.  You do
REM not need any additional special equipment to use this program.
REM
REM Copyright 1989, 1990 John Mueller & Wallace Wang - Tab Books

' $INCLUDE: 'qbx.bi'

DEFINT A-Z

DECLARE SUB AuxInput (Serial)
DECLARE SUB AuxOutput (Serial)
```

13-1B   Continued.

```
' ****************************************

PRINT "Send or Receive a character?"
INPUT Answer$
IF UCASE$(Answer$) = "S" THEN
  PRINT "Enter a character"
  INPUT Answer$
  AuxOutput (ASC(Answer$))
ELSE
  AuxInput (Reply)
  PRINT "Received "; Reply; " through the serial port."
END IF

SUB AuxInput (Serial)
  DIM InRegs AS RegType
  DIM OutRegs AS RegType

  InRegs.ax = &H300
  CALL Interrupt(&H21, InRegs, OutRegs)
  Serial = OutRegs.ax AND &HFF
END SUB

SUB AuxOutput (Serial)
  DIM InRegs AS RegType
  DIM OutRegs AS RegType

  InRegs.ax = &H400
END SUB
```

13-1C   C language program for serial port service interrupts.

```
      /*  Sample Program 20, DOS Serial Port Service Interrupts Demonstration
This program shows you how to use the DOS serial port services.  It begins by asking if you want to send
or receive a character through the serial port.  Once you make a selection, the program sends or receives
a character.  To use this program you need to connect two computers through their serial ports.  You do
not need any additional special equipment to use this program.

Copyright 1989, 1990 John Mueller & Wallace Wang - Tab Books */

#include <dos.h>
#include <conio.h>
#include <ctype.h>

union  REGS    iReg, oReg;

void auxinput (int *serial)
     {
     iReg.h.ah = 3;
     intdos (&iReg, &oReg);
     *serial = oReg.h.al;
     }
```

13-1C Continued.

```
void auxoutput (int *serial)
        {
        iReg.h.ah = 4;
        iReg.h.al = *serial;
        intdos (&iReg, &oReg);
        }


main ()
        {
        char    *answer, reply, in;
        int     number, result;

        void auxinput (int*);
        void auxoutput (int*);

        printf ("Send or Receive a character?\n");
        scanf ("%c", &reply);
        if (reply == 's')
          {
          printf ("Enter a character:  ");
          scanf ("%c%*c", &answer);
          printf ("%c %d", answer, answer);
          auxoutput (&answer);
          }
        else
          {
          auxinput (&reply);
          printf ("Received %c through the serial port.", reply);
          }
        return 0;
        }
```

13-1D Pascal program for serial port service interrupts.

```
(*****************************************************************************************)
(* Sample Program 20, DOS Serial Port Service Interrupts Demonstration  *)
(* This program shows you how to use the DOS serial port services.  It begins by asking if you want to send    *)
(* or receive a character through the serial port.  Once you make a selection, the program sends or receives   *)
(* a character.  To use this program you need to connect two computers through their serial ports.  You do     *)
(* not need any additional special equipment to use this program.        *)
(*                                *)
(* Copyright 1989, 1990 John Mueller & Wallace Wang - Tab Books *)
(*****************************************************************************************)


PROGRAM Serial;

USES
  Dos;
VAR
  Regs : Registers;
  Answer : char;
```

```
 Reply : integer;

 PROCEDURE AuxInput (VAR Serial : integer);
 BEGIN
   Regs.ah := 3;
   MsDos (Regs);
   Serial := Regs.al;
 END;  (* AuxInput *)

 PROCEDURE AuxOutput (Serial : integer);
 BEGIN
   Regs.ah := 4;
   Regs.al := Serial;
   MsDos (Regs);
 END;  (* AuxOutput *)

BEGIN
 Writeln ('Send or Receive a character?');
 Readln (Answer);
 IF UpCase (Answer) = 'S' THEN
   BEGIN
     Write ('Enter a character: ');
     Readln (Answer);
     AuxOutput (Ord(Answer));
   END
 ELSE
   BEGIN
     AuxInput (Reply);
     Writeln ('Received ', Reply, 'through the serial port.');
   END;
END.  (* Serial *)
```

DOS provides an alternate method of performing serial port input/output. Use interrupt 21h service 3Fh with the DOS predefined handle of 3 as an alternate communication method. You can also open the AUX device to use a handle other than the standard DOS handle. This method of input/output is slightly faster than the standard DOS serial port service routines.

AUXILIARY INPUT (INTERRUPT 21h SERVICE 3)

DOS 1.0

This service reads a character from the standard auxiliary device (COM1: only for DOS 1.0). When using DOS version 2.0 or above, you can use the mode command to change the port used as the standard auxiliary device. If the serial port buffer does not contain a character when DOS checks it, this service waits until one is available. The serial port buffer holds a single character. If characters arrive faster than your program can handle, the serial port loses these extra characters. If the user presses Ctrl–C while using this service, DOS transfers control to the Ctrl–C handler (interrupt 23h).

Register Contents on Entry:
AH - 3

Register Contents on Exit:
AL - 8-Bit Input Data

Example:
```
;Auxiliary input
MOV    AH,3
INT    21h
```

AUXILIARY OUTPUT (INTERRUPT 21h SERVICE 4)

DOS 1.0

This service outputs a character to the standard auxiliary device (COM1: only for DOS 1.0). When using DOS version 2.0 or above, you can use the mode command to change the port used as the standard auxiliary device. If the output device is busy, DOS waits to output the character. Before calling this service, you must define the communications parameters (baud rate, stop bits, data bits, etc.). Use the ROM interrupt 14h services for this purpose. If the user presses Ctrl–C while using this service, DOS transfers control to the Ctrl–C handler (interrupt 23h).

Register Contents on Entry:
AH - 4
AL - 8-Bit Input Data

Example:
```
;Auxiliary output
MOV    AH,4
MOV    AL,BUFF
INT    21h
```

14

DOS Mouse Extensions

DOS provides support for a mouse through mouse service routines. Each mouse routine lists the required register contents on entry, the register contents on exit, the purpose of each routine, and a code fragment showing how to use the routine. TABLE 8-1 lists the interrupts in numeric order.

There are three standards used for the mouse interface. These standards include Microsoft, Logitech, and Mouse Systems. All three standards use the same general principles of mouse operation. Differences between them include physical differences (like the number of buttons) and minor software differences. Often, the software differences are small or nonexistent. The following paragraphs apply specifically to the Microsoft standard for mice. However, these paragraphs apply to the other two standards as well. We tested each function using both a Microsoft and Logitech mouse. Figure 14-1 shows how to use the DOS mouse extensions to initialize and control a mouse.

DIFFERENCES BETWEEN TWO-BUTTON AND THREE-BUTTON MICE

The main difference between most mice is the number of buttons they support. Some mice support five or six buttons. However, most mice in use today provide two or three buttons. Most programs use only two-button operations. However, some programs allow you to assign extended functions to the extra combinations provided by a three-button mouse.

The only difference in programming a three-button rather than a two-button mouse is the number of possible button push combinations. A two-button mouse provides three combinations of button presses. Many software vendors make the right button equivalent to the Enter key, the

14-1A Assembly language program for mouse service interrupt extensions.

```
;***********************************************************************************************
;* Sample Program 21, DOS Mouse Service Interrupt Extensions Demonstration      *
;* This program shows you how to use the DOS mouse service extensions.  The mouse driver supplied with your      *
;* mouse usually provides these extensions.  Most mice install the extensions as a terminate and stay   *
;* resident program or a device driver.  The program begins by showing you how to initialize the mouse.  It     *
;* then shows you how to obtain mouse button and movement information.  You need the following special  *
;* equipment to use this program.                          *
;*                              *
;*      Mouse (2 or 3 button)            *
;*      Appropriate Mouse Driver                 *
;*                          *
;* Copyright 1989 John Mueller & Wallace Wang - Tab Books *
;***********************************************************************************************


;***********************************************************************************************
;* Perform the program setup.                 *
;***********************************************************************************************

.MODEL MEDIUM    ; Use a medum model size.

.STACK   ; Use the defalt stack of 1024 bytes.


;***********************************************************************************************
;* Begin the data area.  Declare all variables.          *
;***********************************************************************************************
.DATA

;Standard equates.

True     EQU     01
LF       EQU     10
CR       EQU     13
StrEnd   EQU     36


;Program variables.

ButtonType1      DB      'Left          ',StrEnd
ButtonType2      DB      'Right         ',StrEnd
ButtonType3      DB      'Left & Right  ',StrEnd
ButtonType4      DB      'Center        ',StrEnd
ButtonType5      DB      'Left & Center ',StrEnd
ButtonType6      DB      'Center & Right',StrEnd
ButtonType7      DB      'None          ',StrEnd
PortType1        DB      'Bus mouse',LF,CR,StrEnd
PortType2        DB      'Serial mouse',LF,CR,StrEnd
PortType3        DB      'InPort mouse',LF,CR,StrEnd
PortType4        DB      'PS/2 mouse',LF,CR,StrEnd
PortType5        DB      'HP mouse',LF,CR,StrEnd
NumButtons       DW      0
MouseType        DB      0
OldX     DW      0
```

14-1A Continued.

```
OldY      DW      0
MovX      DW      0
MovY      DW      0
X         DB      4 DUP (' ')
Y         DB      3 DUP (' '),StrEnd
Msg1      DB      'Mouse driver version: '
Version DB        5 DUP (' '),LF,CR,StrEnd
MouseThere      DB      0

;***************************************************************************************************
;* Begin the code segment.                          *
;***************************************************************************************************
;
.CODE

Example PROC      FAR
Start:  MOV       AX,@DATA        ;Point DS & ES to our data segment.
        MOV       DS,AX
        MOV       ES,AX

        CALL      ClearScr        ;Clear the display.

        CALL      InitializeMouse ;Detect mouse pressence.
        CMP       MouseThere,True ;See if it is present.
        JNE       Exit    ;If not, exit.

        CALL      ShowMousePointer        ;Display the mouse pointer.

        CALL      GetMouseInfo    ;Get the version number.
        MOV       AX,0900h        ;Display version number.
        LEA       DX,Msg1
        INT       21h

NextLoop:       CALL    GetMousePosition        ;Display mouse position.

        PUSH      DX      ;Save the string address.
        MOV       AX,0200h        ;Position the cursor.
        XOR       BX,BX
        MOV       DH,3
        MOV       DL,0
        INT       10h
        POP       DX      ;Restore the string address.
        MOV       AX,0900h        ;Display the mouse key press
        INT       21h     ; string.

        LEA       DI,OldX ;Read the motion counters.
        LEA       SI,OldY
        CALL      ReadMouseMotionCounters

        MOV       AX,MovX
        CMP       AX,OldX ;See if the user moved the
        JNE       DispXY  ; mouse.  If so, then display
```

```
        MOV     AX,MovY
        CMP     AX,OldY ; the new position.
        JNE     DispXY  ; Otherwise, go to next step.
        JMP     StoreNew

DispXY: MOV     AX,0200h         ;Position the cursor.
        XOR     BX,BX
        MOV     DH,2
        MOV     DL,0
        INT     10h
        MOV     AX,0900h         ;Display the X and Y mouse
        LEA     DX,X    ; coordinates.
        INT     21h

StoreNew:       LEA     DI,MovX ;Read the motion counters.
        LEA     SI,MovY
        CALL    ReadMouseMotionCounters
        MOV     AX,0B00h         ;See if user pressed a key.
        INT     21h
        CMP     AL,0
        JNE     KeyPressed      ;Exit if a key was pressed.
        JMP     NextLoop        ;Otherwise, continue
                        ; processing mouse input.

KeyPressed:     CALL    HideMousePointer        ;Hide the mouse pointer.

Exit:   MOV     AX,4C00h        ;Exit to DOS.
        INT     21h
        RET

Example ENDP


;********************************************************************************************************
;* This procedure clears the display and places the cursor at coordinates 0,0.  *
;********************************************************************************************************
;

ClearScr        PROC    NEAR

        MOV     AX,0619h         ;Scroll 25 lines.
        MOV     BH,7    ;Use gray.
        XOR     CX,CX   ;Start at coordinate 0,0.
        MOV     DX,1950h         ;End at coordinate 25,80.
        INT     10h

        MOV     AX,0200h         ;Set cursor position.
        XOR     BH,BH   ;Use page 0.
        XOR     DX,DX   ;Use coordinate 0,0.
        INT     10h

        RET
```

```
ClearScr        ENDP

;*********************************************************************************************
;* This procedure gets the mouse version and port connection type.  It converts the version number to a *
;* numeric string.  It interprets the port type and selects an appropriate display string.        *
;*********************************************************************************************

GetMouseInfo    PROC    NEAR

        MOV     AX,0024h        ;Get the mouse information.
        INT     33h

        PUSH    CX      ;Save the port type and
        PUSH    BX      ; minor version number.
        LEA     DI,Version      ;Convert the major version
        INC     DI      ; number to a string.
        XOR     AH,AH
        MOV     AL,BH
        CALL    HexConv

        LEA     DI,Version      ;Place a period between the
        INC     DI      ; major and minor version
        INC     DI      ; numbers.
        MOV     BYTE PTR [DI],'.'

        INC     DI      ;Restore the minor version
        INC     DI      ; number and convert it to
        POP     AX      ; a string.
        XOR     AH,AH
        CALL    HexConv

        POP     CX      ;Restore the port connection
        CMP     CH,1    ; type and load the address
        JNE     Type2   ; of the appropriate
        LEA     DX,PortType1    ; connection string in DX.
        JMP     PrintIt
Type2:  CMP     CH,2
        JNE     Type3
        LEA     DX,PortType2
        JMP     PrintIt
Type3:  CMP     CH,3
        JNE     Type4
        LEA     DX,PortType3
        JMP     PrintIt
Type4:  CMP     CH,4
        JNE     Type5
        LEA     DX,PortType4
        JMP     PrintIt
Type5:  LEA     DX,PortType5
PrintIt:        MOV     AX,0900h        ;Display the port connection
        INT     21h     ; string.
```

14-1A Continued.

```
        RET

GetMouseInfo    ENDP

;********************************************************************************************************
;* This procedure obtains the current mouse position and the button press information.  It places the mouse    *
;* position in two variables, X and Y.  It loads the address of the appropriate button press string in DX.     *
;********************************************************************************************************
;

GetMousePosition        PROC    NEAR

        MOV     AX,0003h        ;Get the mouse data.
        INT     33h

        MOV     AX,CX   ;Divide the X position data
        MOV     CX,3    ; by 8 to convert it to a
        SHR     AX,CL   ; character position.  Then
        LEA     DI,X    ; convert the number to a
        ADD     DI,2    ; string for display.
        PUSH    DX
        CALL    HexConv

        POP     AX      ;Restore the Y position data.
        MOV     CX,3    ;Divide it by 8 to convert it
        SHR     AX,CL   ; to a character position.
        LEA     DI,Y    ;Convert the number to a
        ADD     DI,2    ; string for display.
        CALL    HexConv

        CMP     BX,1    ;Determine which buttons are
        JNE     BType1  ; pressed and load the
        LEA     DX,ButtonType1  ; appropriate message
        JMP     Exit2   ; address.
BType1: CMP     BX,2
        JNE     BType2
        LEA     DX,ButtonType2
        JMP     Exit2
BType2: CMP     BX,3
        JNE     BType3
        LEA     DX,ButtonType3
        JMP     Exit2
BType3: CMP     BX,4
        JNE     BType4
        LEA     DX,ButtonType4
        JMP     Exit2
BType4: CMP     BX,5
        JNE     BType5
        LEA     DX,ButtonType5
        JMP     Exit2
BType5: CMP     BX,6
```

```
        JNE     BType6
        LEA     DX,ButtonType6
        JMP     Exit2
BType6: LEA     DX,ButtonType7


Exit2:  RET


GetMousePosition        ENDP
```

```
;*********************************************************************************************************
;* This procedure converts an integer to a character representation.    *
;*********************************************************************************************************
```

```
HexConv PROC    NEAR

        MOV     CX,10   ;Load the divisor.
NextChar:       XOR     DX,DX   ;Clear DX.
        DIV     CX      ;Place first number in DX.
        ADD     DL,30h  ;Convert to a character.
        MOV     [DI],DL ;Move to string location.
        DEC     DI      ;Update string pointer.
        CMP     AX,10   ;See if we need to divide.
        JGE     NextChar
        ADD     AL,30h  ;If not, AX less than 10.
        MOV     [DI],AL ;Convert to character and store.

        RET

HexConv ENDP
```

```
;*********************************************************************************************************
;* This procedure hides the mouse pointer.              *
;*********************************************************************************************************
```

```
HideMousePointer        PROC    NEAR

        MOV     AX,0002h
        INT     33h

        RET

HideMousePointer        ENDP
```

```
;*********************************************************************************************************
;* This procedure initializes the mouse driver to a know state.  If the interrupt cannot find a mouse on the    *
;* current machine, it does not return OFFFFh in AX upon return.  If it does find a mouse, the interrupt         *
;* places the number of mouse buttons in BX.            *
;*********************************************************************************************************
```

```
InitializeMouse PROC    NEAR
```

```
        MOV     AX,0000h        ;Initialize the mouse.
        INT     33h
        CMP     AX,0FFFFh       ;Check for pressence of mouse.
        JNE     Exit1   ;If no mouse present, exit.
        MOV     MouseThere,True ;Otherwise, report that a
        MOV     NumButtons,BX   ; mouse is present and save
                                ; the number of buttons.

Exit1:  RET

InitializeMouse ENDP

;****************************************************************************************************
;* This procedure gets the amount of movement since the last reading of the mouse motion registers.  To use    *
;* this procedure, you must place the following information in the specified registers. *
;*      DI - X Axis Storage Variable Address            *
;*      SI - Y Axis Storage Variable Address            *
;****************************************************************************************************

ReadMouseMotionCounters PROC    NEAR

        MOV     AX,000Bh        ;Read the motion registers.
        INT     33h

        MOV     [DI],CX ;Save the X Axis Value.
        MOV     [SI],DX ;Save the Y Axis Value.

        RET

ReadMouseMotionCounters ENDP

;****************************************************************************************************
;* This procedure displays the mouse pointer.          *
;****************************************************************************************************

ShowMousePointer        PROC    NEAR

        MOV     AX,0001h
        INT     33h

        RET

ShowMousePointer        ENDP

END     Start
```

14-1B BASIC language program for mouse service interrupt extensions.

```
REM Sample Program 21, DOS Mouse Service Interrupt Extensions Demonstration
REM This program shows you how to use the DOS mouse service extensions.  The mouse driver supplied with your
REM mouse usually provides these extensions.  Most mice install the extensions as a terminate and stay
```

14-1B Continued.

```
REM resident program or a device driver.  The program begins by showing you how to initialize the mouse.  It
REM then shows you how to obtain mouse button and movement information.  You need the following special
REM equipment to use this program.
REM      Mouse (2 or 3 button)
REM      Appropriate Mouse Driver
REM
REM Copyright 1989, 1990 John Mueller & Wallace Wang - Tab Books


' $INCLUDE: 'qbx.bi'

DEFINT A-Z

DECLARE SUB InitializeMouse (MouseHere)
DECLARE SUB ShowMousePointer ()
DECLARE SUB HideMousePointer ()
DECLARE SUB GetMousePosition (X, Y, Button$)
DECLARE SUB SetMousePosition (X, Y)
DECLARE SUB ReadMouseMotionCounters (X, Y)
DECLARE SUB GetMouseInfo (Version!, MouseType$)

'****************************************************
CLS
EVENT ON
CALL InitializeMouse(NumButtons)
IF NumButtons <> 0 THEN

  CALL ShowMousePointer
  CALL GetMouseInfo(Version!, MouseType$)
  PRINT "Mouse driver version:"; Version!

  DO
    CALL GetMousePosition(X, Y, Button$)
    LOCATE 3, 1
    IF OldButton$ <> Button$ THEN
      PRINT "                "
    END IF
    LOCATE 3, 1
    PRINT Button$
    OldButton$ = Button$

    CALL ReadMouseMotionCounters(OldX, OldY)
    IF (OldX <> MovX) AND (OldY <> MovY) THEN
      LOCATE 4, 1
      PRINT "                "
      LOCATE 4, 1
      PRINT X; Y
    END IF
    CALL ReadMouseMotionCounters(MovX, MovY)

  LOOP WHILE INKEY$ = ""
```

```
   CALL HideMousePointer

END IF

SUB GetMouseInfo (Version!, MouseType$)
   DIM InRegs AS RegType
   DIM OutRegs AS RegType
   InRegs.ax = &H24
   CALL Interrupt(&H33, InRegs, OutRegs)
   TotalVersion$ = RIGHT$("000" + HEX$(OutRegs.bx), 4)
   MajorVersion% = VAL(LEFT$(TotalVersion$, 2))
   MinorVersion% = VAL(RIGHT$(TotalVersion$, 2))
   Version! = MajorVersion% + (MinorVersion% / 10)
   MouseType% = OutRegs.cx \ 256
   SELECT CASE MouseType%
     CASE 1
       PRINT "Bus mouse"
     CASE 2
       PRINT "Serial mouse"
     CASE 3
       PRINT "InPort mouse"
     CASE 4
       PRINT "PS/2 mouse"
     CASE 5
       PRINT "HP mouse"
   END SELECT
END SUB

SUB GetMousePosition (X, Y, Button$)
   DIM InRegs AS RegType
   DIM OutRegs AS RegType

   InRegs.ax = 3
   CALL Interrupt(&H33, InRegs, OutRegs)
   X = OutRegs.cx / 8
   Y = OutRegs.dx / 8
   SELECT CASE OutRegs.bx
     CASE 0
       Button$ = "None"
     CASE 1
       Button$ = "Left"
     CASE 2
       Button$ = "Right"
     CASE 3
       Button$ = "Left_Right"
     CASE 4
       Button$ = "Center"
     CASE 5
       Button$ = "Left_Center"
     CASE 6
```

```
      Button$ = "Center_Right"
  END SELECT
END SUB


SUB HideMousePointer
  DIM InRegs AS RegType
  DIM OutRegs AS RegType
  InRegs.ax = 2
  CALL Interrupt(&H33, InRegs, OutRegs)
END SUB


SUB InitializeMouse (NumButtons)
  DIM InRegs AS RegType
  DIM OutRegs AS RegType

  InRegs.ax = 0
  CALL Interrupt(&H33, InRegs, OutRegs)

  IF OutRegs.ax = &HFFFF THEN
    NumButtons = OutRegs.bx
  ELSE
    PRINT "Mouse not found"
    NumButtons = 0
  END IF
END SUB


SUB ReadMouseMotionCounters (X, Y)
  DIM InRegs AS RegType
  DIM OutRegs AS RegType
  InRegs.ax = &HB
  CALL Interrupt(&H33, InRegs, OutRegs)
  X = OutRegs.cx
  Y = OutRegs.dx
END SUB

SUB SetMousePosition (X, Y)
  DIM InRegs AS RegType
  DIM OutRegs AS RegType

  InRegs.ax = 4
  InRegs.cx = X
  InRegs.dx = Y
  CALL Interrupt(&H33, InRegs, OutRegs)
END SUB


SUB ShowMousePointer
 .DIM InRegs AS RegType
  DIM OutRegs AS RegType
  InRegs.ax = 1
  CALL Interrupt(&H33, InRegs, OutRegs)
END SUB
```

14-1C C language program for mouse service interrupt extensions.

```
        /* Sample Program 21, DOS Mouse Service Interrupt Extensions Demonstration
This program shows you how to use the DOS mouse service extensions.  The mouse driver supplied with your
mouse usually provides these extensions.  Most mice install the extensions as a terminate and stay
resident program or a device driver.  The program begins by showing you how to initialize the mouse.  It
then shows you how to obtain mouse button and movement information.  You need the following special
equipment to use this program.
        Mouse (2 or 3 button)
        Appropriate Mouse Driver


Copyright 1989, 1990 John Mueller & Wallace Wang - Tab Books */


#include <dos.h>
#include <conio.h>

union REGS iReg, oReg;
struct SREGS segregs;
int c, numbuttons, x, y, oldmouse, mousebutton, oldx, oldy, movx, movy;
float mouseversion;

void msub ()
        {
        iReg.x.ax = 4;
        iReg.x.cx = 0;
        iReg.x.dx = 0;
        int86 (0x33, &iReg, &oReg);
        }


int initializemouse ()
        {
        iReg.x.ax = 0;
        int86 (0x33, &iReg, &oReg);
        if (oReg.x.ax == 0xFFFF)
          return (oReg.x.bx);
        else
          return (0);
        }


void resetmouse ()
        {
        iReg.x.ax = 0;
        int86 (0x33, &iReg, &oReg);
        }


void showmousepointer ()
        {
        iReg.x.ax = 1;
        int86 (0x33, &iReg, &oReg);
        }


void hidemousepointer ()
        {
```

14-1C Continued.

```
        iReg.x.ax = 2;
        int86 (0x33, &iReg, &oReg);
        }


void getmouseposition (int *x, int *y, int *mousebutton)
        {
        iReg.x.ax = 3;
        int86 (0x33, &iReg, &oReg);
        *x = oReg.x.cx / 8;
        *y = oReg.x.dx / 8;
        *mousebutton = oReg.x.bx;
        }


void readmousemotioncounters (int *x, int *y)
        {
        iReg.x.ax = 0xB;
        int86 (0x33, &iReg, &oReg);
        *x = oReg.x.cx;
        *y = oReg.x.dx;
        }


float getmouseinfo ()
        {
        int mousetype;
        int majorver;
        float minorver;

        iReg.x.ax = 0x24;
        int86 (0x33, &iReg, &oReg);
        mousetype = oReg.h.ch;
        switch (mousetype)
          {
          case 1 : printf ("Bus mouse\n"); break;
          case 2 : printf ("Serial mouse\n"); break;
          case 3 : printf ("InPort mouse\n"); break;
          case 4 : printf ("PS/2 mouse\n"); break;
          case 5 : printf ("HP mouse\n"); break;
          }
        majorver = oReg.h.bh;
        minorver = oReg.h.bl;
        minorver = minorver/10;
        return (majorver + minorver);
        }


main ()
        {
        void msub (void);
        void resetmouse (void);
        void showmousepointer (void);
        void hidemousepointer (void);
        void getmouseposition (int*, int*, int*);
```

```
void readmousemotioncounters (int*, int*);
int initializemouse ();
float getmouseinfo ();

clrscr ();
numbuttons = initializemouse ();

if (numbuttons != 0)   /* Mouse found */
  {
  showmousepointer ();
  mouseversion = getmouseinfo ();
  printf ("Mouse driver version: %3.1f\n", mouseversion);

  do
    {
    c = kbhit ();
    getmouseposition (&x, &y, &mousebutton);
    window (1,1,80,25);

    gotoxy (1,4);

    if (oldmouse != mousebutton)
      {
        switch (mousebutton)
          {
          case 0 : clreol(); printf ("None"); break;
          case 1 : clreol(); printf ("Left"); break;
          case 2 : clreol(); printf ("Right"); break;
          case 3 : clreol(); printf ("Left & Right"); break;
          case 4 : clreol(); printf ("Center"); break;
          case 5 : clreol(); printf ("Left & Center"); break;
          case 6 : clreol(); printf ("Center & Right"); break;
          }
      }
    oldmouse = mousebutton;
    readmousemotioncounters (&oldx, &oldy);

    if ((oldx != movx) && (oldy != movy))
      {
      window (1,3,20,4);
      clreol();
      gotoxy (1,3);
      printf ("%d   %d", x, y);
      }
    readmousemotioncounters (&movx, &movy);
    }
  while (c == 0);

  hidemousepointer ();
  }
}
```

14-1C Continued.

```
/*
        iReg.x.ax = 12;
        iReg.x.cx = 8;
        iReg.x.dx = (int) msub;
        segregs.es = ((long) msub) >> 16;
        int86x(0x33, &iReg, &oReg, &segregs);
*/
```

14-1D Pascal program for mouse service interrupt extensions.

```
(*******************************************************************************************)
(* Sample Program 21, DOS Mouse Service Interrupt Extensions Demonstration     *)
(* This program shows you how to use the DOS mouse service extensions.  The mouse driver supplied with your     *)
(* mouse usually provides these extensions.  Most mice install the extensions as a terminate and stay    *)
(* resident program or a device driver.  The program begins by showing you how to initialize the mouse.  It      *)
(* then shows you how to obtain mouse button and movement information.  You need the following special  *)
(* equipment to use this program.                            *)
(*       Mouse (2 or 3 button)            *)
(*       Appropriate Mouse Driver                 *)
(*                        *)
(* Copyright 1989, 1990 John Mueller & Wallace Wang - Tab Books *)
(*******************************************************************************************)

PROGRAM Mouse;
USES
  Dos, Crt;
TYPE
  CursorType = (Hardware, Software);
  ButtonType = (Left, Right, Left_Right, Center, Left_Center, Center_Right, None);
  MouseAddress = longint;
  MouseRecord = RECORD
                    Ofs : word;
                    Seg : word;
                END;  (* RECORD *)
VAR
  Regs : Registers;
  Answer : char;
  NumButtons, MouseType : byte;
  OldX, OldY, MovX, MovY, X, Y, Count : integer;
  Button : ButtonType;
  Version : real;

  FUNCTION InitializeMouse (VAR NumButtons : byte) : boolean;
  (* Works *)
  BEGIN
    Regs.ax := 0;
    Intr ($33, Regs);
    InitializeMouse := FALSE;
    NumButtons := 0;
    IF Regs.ax = $FFFF THEN   (* Mouse found *)
      BEGIN
        InitializeMouse := TRUE;
        NumButtons := Regs.bx;
```

```
    END;
END; (* InitializeMouse *)

PROCEDURE ShowMousePointer;
(* Works *)
BEGIN
  Regs.ax := 1;
  Intr ($33, Regs);
END; (* ShowMousePointer *)

PROCEDURE HideMousePointer;
(* Works *)
BEGIN
  Regs.ax := 2;
  Intr ($33, Regs);
END; (* HideMousePointer *)

PROCEDURE GetMousePosition (VAR X, Y : integer;
                           VAR Button : ButtonType);
(* Works *)
BEGIN
  Regs.ax := $3;
  Intr ($33, Regs);
  X := Regs.cx shr 3;
  Y := Regs.dx shr 3;
  CASE Regs.bx OF
    0 : Button := None;
    1 : Button := Left;
    2 : Button := Right;
    3 : Button := Left_Right;
    4 : Button := Center;
    5 : Button := Left_Center;
    6 : Button := Center_Right;
  END;  (* CASE *)
END;  (* GetMousePosition *)

FUNCTION MouseButtonPressed (VAR Button : ButtonType) : boolean;
(* Works *)
BEGIN
  Regs.ax := $3;
  Intr ($33, Regs);
  IF Regs.bx > 0 THEN
    MouseButtonPressed := TRUE
  ELSE
    MouseButtonPressed := FALSE;
  CASE Regs.bx OF
    0 : Button := None;
    1 : Button := Left;
    2 : Button := Right;
    3 : Button := Left_Right;
    4 : Button := Center;
```

```
      5 : Button := Left_Center;
      6 : Button := Center_Right;
  END;  (* CASE *)
END;  (* MouseButtonPressed *)


PROCEDURE SetMousePosition (X, Y : integer);
(* Works *)
BEGIN
  Regs.ax := $4;
  Regs.cx := X shl 3;
  Regs.dx := Y shl 3;
  Intr ($33, Regs);
END;  (* SetMousePosition *)


PROCEDURE GetButtonPressInfo (VAR Button : ButtonType;
                              VAR Count : integer;
                              VAR Last_X, Last_Y : integer);
(* Works *)
BEGIN
  Regs.ax := 5;
  CASE Button OF
    None         : Regs.bx := 0;
    Left         : Regs.bx := 1;
    Right        : Regs.bx := 2;
    Left_Right   : Regs.bx := 3;
    Center       : Regs.bx := 4;
    Left_Center  : Regs.bx := 5;
    Center_Right : Regs.bx := 6;
  END;  (* CASE *)
  Intr ($33, Regs);
  Count := Regs.bx;
  Last_X := Regs.cx;
  Last_Y := Regs.dx;
  CASE Regs.ax OF
    0 : Button := None;
    1 : Button := Left;
    2 : Button := Right;
    3 : Button := Left_Right;
    4 : Button := Center;
    5 : Button := Left_Center;
    6 : Button := Center_Right;
  END;  (* CASE *)
END;  (* GetButtonPressInfo *)


PROCEDURE GetButtonReleaseInfo (VAR Button : ButtonType;
                                VAR Count : integer;
                                VAR Last_X, Last_Y : integer);
(* Works *)
BEGIN
  Regs.ax := 6;
  Intr ($33, Regs);
```

```
CASE Button OF
   None          : Regs.bx := 0;
   Left          : Regs.bx := 1;
   Right         : Regs.bx := 2;
   Left_Right    : Regs.bx := 3;
   Center        : Regs.bx := 4;
   Left_Center   : Regs.bx := 5;
   Center_Right  : Regs.bx := 6;
END;  (* CASE *)
Intr ($33, Regs);
Count := Regs.bx;
Last_X := Regs.cx;
Last_Y := Regs.dx;
CASE Regs.ax OF
   0 : Button := None;
   1 : Button := Left;
   2 : Button := Right;
   3 : Button := Left_Right;
   4 : Button := Center;
   5 : Button := Left_Center;
   6 : Button := Center_Right;
  END;  (* CASE *)
END;  (* GetButtonReleaseInfo *)


PROCEDURE SetHorizontalLimitsForPointer (MinX, MaxX : integer);
(* Works *)
BEGIN
  Regs.ax := 7;
  Regs.cx := MinX shl 3;
  Regs.dx := MaxX shl 3;
  Intr ($33, Regs);
END;  (* SetHorizontalLimitsForPointer *)


PROCEDURE SetVerticalLimitsForPointer (MinY, MaxY : integer);
(* Works *)
BEGIN
  Regs.ax := 8;
  Regs.cx := MinY shl 3;
  Regs.dx := MaxY shl 3;
  Intr ($33, Regs);
END;  (* SetVerticalLimitsForPointer *)


PROCEDURE SetMousePointerExclusionArea (UpperLeftX, UpperLeftY,
                                        LowerRightX, LowerRightY : integer);
(* Works *)
BEGIN
  Regs.cx := UpperLeftX shl 3;
  Regs.dx := UpperLeftY shl 3;
  Regs.si := LowerRightX shl 3;
  Regs.di := LowerRightY shl 3;
```

```
  Regs.ax := $10;
  Intr ($33, Regs);
END;  (* SetMousePointerExclusionArea *)


PROCEDURE ReadMouseMotionCounters (VAR Horizontal, Vertical : integer);
(* Works *)
BEGIN
  Regs.ax := $B;
  Intr ($33, Regs);
  Horizontal := Regs.cx;
  Vertical := Regs.dx;
END;  (* ReadMouseMotionCounters *)

PROCEDURE SetMickeystoPixelsRatio (XRatio, YRatio : integer);
(* Works *)
BEGIN
  Regs.ax := $F;
  Regs.cx := XRatio;
  Regs.dx := YRatio;
  Intr ($33, Regs);
END;  (* SetMickeystoPixelsRatio *)

PROCEDURE SetDoubleSpeedThreshold (Speed : byte);
(* Works *)
BEGIN
  Regs.ax := $13;
  Regs.dx := Speed;
  Intr ($33, Regs);
END;  (* SetDoubleSpeedThreshold *)

FUNCTION GetMouseBufferSize : integer;
(* Works *)
BEGIN
  Regs.ax := $15;
  Intr ($33, Regs);
  GetMouseBufferSize := Regs.bx;
END;  (* GetMouseBufferSize *)

PROCEDURE RestoreMouseDriverState;
VAR
  DriverState : integer;
BEGIN
  DriverState := GetMouseBufferSize;
  Regs.ax := $17;
  Regs.dx := Ofs (DriverState);
  Regs.es := Seg (DriverState);
  Intr ($33, Regs);
END;  (* RestoreMouseDriverState *)


PROCEDURE SelectPointerPage (PageNum : byte);
```

14-1D Continued.

```
(* Works *)
BEGIN
  Regs.ax := $1D;
  Regs.bx := PageNum;
  Intr ($33, Regs);
END;  (* SelectPointerPage *)


PROCEDURE GetPointerPage (VAR PointerPage : byte);
(* Works *)
BEGIN
  Regs.ax := $1E;
  Intr ($33, Regs);
  PointerPage := Regs.bx;
END;  (* GetPointerPage *)


PROCEDURE SetMouseSensitivity (HMickey, VMickey : byte);
(* Works *)
BEGIN
  Regs.ax := $1A;
  Regs.bx := HMickey;
  Regs.cx := VMickey;
  Intr ($33, Regs);
END;  (* SetMouseSensitivity *)

PROCEDURE GetMouseSensitivity (VAR HMickey, VMickey, Speed : byte);
(* Works *)
BEGIN
  Regs.ax := $1B;
  Intr ($33, Regs);
  HMickey := Regs.bx;
  VMickey := Regs.cx;
  Speed := Regs.dx;
END;  (* GetMouseSensitivity *)


FUNCTION GetLanguageNumber : byte;
(* Works *)
BEGIN
  Regs.ax := $23;
  Intr ($33, Regs);
  GetLanguageNumber := Regs.bx;
  CASE GetLanguageNumber OF
    0 : Writeln ('English');
    1 : Writeln ('French');
    2 : Writeln ('Dutch');
    3 : Writeln ('German');
    4 : Writeln ('Swedish');
    5 : Writeln ('Finnish');
    6 : Writeln ('Spanish');
    7 : Writeln ('Portuguese');
    8 : Writeln ('Italian');
  END;  (* CASE *)
```

14-1D Continued

```
END;   (* GetLanguageNumber *)


PROCEDURE GetMouseInfo (VAR MouseVersion : real;
                        VAR MouseType : byte);
(* Works *)
BEGIN
  Regs.ax := $24;
  Intr ($33, Regs);
  MouseVersion := Regs.bh + (Regs.bl/10);
  MouseType := Regs.ch;

  CASE Regs.ch OF
    1 : Writeln ('Bus mouse');
    2 : Writeln ('Serial mouse');
    3 : Writeln ('InPort mouse');
    4 : Writeln ('PS/2 mouse');
    5 : Writeln ('HP mouse');
  END;   (* CASE *)


END;   (* GetMouseInfo *)


BEGIN
  ClrScr;
  IF InitializeMouse (NumButtons) = TRUE THEN  (* Mouse is found *)
    BEGIN
      ShowMousePointer;

        GetMouseInfo (Version, MouseType);
        Writeln ('Mouse driver version: ', Version:2:1);
        REPEAT
          GetMousePosition (X, Y, Button);
          GotoXY (1,2);
          CASE Button OF
            Left : BEGIN
                     ClrEol;
                     Write ('Left');
                   END;
            Right : BEGIN
                      ClrEol;
                      Write ('Right');
                    END;
            Center : BEGIN
                       ClrEol;
                       Write ('Center');
                     END;
            Left_Right : BEGIN
                           ClrEol;
                           Write ('Left & Right');
                         END;
            Left_Center : BEGIN
                            ClrEol;
```

```
                Write ('Left & Center');
              END;
  Center_Right : BEGIN
                   ClrEol;
                   Write ('Right & Center');
                 END;
END;  (* CASE *)

ReadMouseMotionCounters (OldX, OldY);

IF (OldX <> MovX) AND (OldY <> MovY) THEN
  BEGIN

             Window (1,3,20,4);
             ClrEol;
             GotoXY (1,1);
             Write (X, ' ', Y);
           END;

       ReadMouseMotionCounters (MovX, MovY);

     UNTIL KeyPressed;

   HideMousePointer;
  END;
END.  (* Mouse *)
```

left button equivalent to a selection key code, and the left-right button chord equivalent to the escape key. Most users find that these are the three most commonly used keyboard selections. Placing these selections on the mouse enhances ease of use.

A three-button mouse allows you seven button combinations. This means you can add four functions to the semi-standard mouse selections. Some standard added functions include help select, file save, and menu select. Most vendors that support only two-button mice use the middle button of a three-button mouse to emulate the left-right button chord of the two-button mouse.

RESET MOUSE AND GET STATUS (INTERRUPT 33h SERVICE 00h)

This service checks for the existence of a mouse. If the mouse exists, it identifies the number of mouse buttons and disables any memory resident user handlers for mouse events. In addition, it initializes the mouse as follows.

- Places the mouse in the center of the display.
- Sets the mouse pointer display page to zero.

- Hides the mouse pointer.
- Sets the mouse pointer shape to an arrow for graphics mode and a block cursor for text mode.
- Disables the user mouse event handler.
- Enables mouse emulation of a light pen.
- Sets the horizontal mickeys to pixels ratio at 8 to 8. Sets the vertical mickeys to pixels ratio at 16 to 8.
- Sets the double speed threshold to 64 mickeys/second.
- Sets the minimum and maximum horizontal and vertical pointer position limits to include the entire screen in the current display mode.

You must use this service before using any of the other mouse services. Failing to use this service can result in program failure because the mouse is not in a known state.

Register Contents on Entry:
AX - 0

Register Contents on Exit:
AX - Status

    0000h - Mouse Not Available
    FFFFh - Mouse Available
BX - Number of Mouse Buttons

Example:
```
;Reset Mouse and Get Status
MOV    AX,0
INT    33h
```

SHOW MOUSE POINTER (INTERRUPT 33h SERVICE 01h)

This service displays the mouse pointer on screen. The mouse driver maintains a counter for the mouse pointer. Each time you hide the mouse, the driver decrements the counter by one. If the counter is negative, the driver increments the pointer each time you use this service. The mouse driver displays the mouse pointer when the counter contains a value of zero.

If you used services 07h or 08h (Set Horizontal Limits for Pointer or Set Vertical Limits for Pointer) to change the pointer limits, the mouse driver displays the mouse pointer within this defined area. If you used service 10h (Set Mouse Pointer Exclusion Area) to hide the mouse pointer, calling this service displays the mouse pointer.

Register Contents on Entry:
AX - 1

Example:
```
;Show Mouse Pointer
MOV    AX,1
INT    33h
```

HIDE MOUSE POINTER (INTERRUPT 33h SERVICE 02h)

This service removes the mouse pointer from the screen. The mouse driver continues to track the mouse position and performs any other requested mouse function. The mouse driver maintains a counter for the mouse pointer. Each time you hide the mouse, the driver decrements the counter by one. If the pointer is negative, the driver increments the counter each time you use service 01h to display the mouse. The mouse driver displays the mouse pointer when the counter contains a value of zero.

Use this service before changing any area of the screen that contains the mouse pointer. This prevents the mouse pointer from interfering with a newly displayed screen. In some cases, the mouse driver leaves a gap where the mouse pointer appeared when you move the mouse.

Register Contents on Entry:
AX - 2

Example:
```
;Hide Mouse Pointer
MOV    AX,2
INT    33h
```

GET MOUSE POSITION AND BUTTON STATUS (INTERRUPT 33h SERVICE 03h)

This service returns the current horizontal and vertical coordinates of the mouse position along with the status of the left, right, and center mouse buttons for a three-button mouse. It returns the status of only the left and right mouse buttons for a two-button mouse. For example, if BX contains 4 on return, then the user pressed the center mouse button.

This service always returns the mouse position in pixels. It uses the upper-left corner of the display as a reference point (0, 0). The CX and DX coordinates refer to the virtual mouse screen and NOT the text screen. To convert the virtual mouse screen coordinates to text screen coordinates, divide the coordinates by the character block size. For example, if CX returns 18, DX returns 64, and the character block size is 9 by 16, then the character position is 2, 4.

Register Contents on Entry:
AX - 3

Register Contents on Exit:

BX - Mouse Button Status (Bits True When set)

    0 - Left Button Down

    1 - Right Button Down

    2 - Center Button down

    3 through 15 - Reserved (0)

CX - Horizontal (X) Coordinate in Pixels

DX - Vertical (Y) Coordinate in Pixels

Example:

```
;Get Mouse Position and Button Status
MOV   AX,3
INT   33h
```

SET MOUSE POINTER POSITION
(INTERRUPT 33h SERVICE 04h)

This service displays the mouse at a new horizontal and vertical position. The limits defined by services 07h and 08h (Set Horizontal Limits for Pointer and Set Vertical Limits for Pointer) affect the mouse position. If you specify a mouse position outside the defined limits, the mouse driver automatically adjusts the requested position to the nearest limit. For example, if you set the maximum horizontal position to 85, then use this service to place the mouse pointer at a horizontal position of 90, the mouse pointer appears at the maximum horizontal position of 85.

Always provide the mouse position in pixels. The mouse driver uses the upper-left corner of the display as a reference pointer (0, 0). The coordinates refer to the virtual screen mouse coordinates and NOT to the text screen coordinates. To convert the text screen coordinates to the virtual mouse screen coordinates multiply the character position by the character block size. For example, if you want to position the mouse at row 8 column 20 and the display uses a character block size of 8 by 16, then CX contains 160 and DX contains 128.

The only time this service fails is if you don't reset the mouse using service 00h (Reset Mouse and Get Status) or call service 21h (Reset Mouse Driver). You cannot see the results of this service if you have not called service 01h (Show Mouse Pointer), if you hid the cursor using service 02h (Hide Mouse Pointer), or if you position the mouse pointer in an area defined by service 10h (Set Mouse Pointer Exclusion Area).

Register Contents on Entry:

AX - 4

CX - Horizontal (X) Coordinate in Pixels

DX - Vertical (Y) Coordinate in Pixels

Example:

```
;Set Mouse Pointer Position to (50,60)
```

```
MOV    AX,4
MOV    CX,50
MOV    DX,60
INT    33h
```

GET BUTTON PRESS INFORMATION
(INTERRUPT 33h SERVICE 05h)

This service returns the status of the mouse buttons. In addition, it returns the number of presses and last position for the requested mouse button. BX determines which button this service checks. If BX is 0, then this service checks the left button. If BX is 1 or 2, this service checks the right or center buttons. The button press value can range from 0 to 65,535. This service will not detect the overflow if you press the mouse button more than 65,535 times. The values for the horizontal and vertical coordinates refer to the mouse pointer's position at the time the user pressed a mouse button, not the current location of the mouse pointer. This service automatically resets the number of button presses for the requested button to zero. Use this service to detect user double clicks on menu items or other areas of the display.

Register Contents on Entry:
AX - 5
BX - Button
    0- Left Button
    1 - Right Button
    2 - Center Button

Register Contents on Exit:
AX - Mouse Button Status (Bits True When set)
    0 - Left Button Down
    1 - Right Button Down
    2 - Center Button down
    3 through 15 - Reserved (0)
BX - Button Press Counter
CX - Horizontal (X) Coordinate in Pixels
DX - Vertical (Y) Coordinate in Pixels

Example:
```
;Get Button Press Information
MOV    AX,5
MOV    BX,1     ;Right button
INT    33h
```

GET BUTTON RELEASE INFORMATION
(INTERRUPT 33h SERVICE 06h)

This service returns the status of the mouse buttons. In addition, it returns the number of releases and last position for the requested mouse button. BX determines which button this service checks. If BX is 0, then this service checks the left button. If BX is 1 or 2, this service checks the right or center buttons. The button press value can range from 0 to 65,535. This service will not detect the overflow if you press the mouse button more than 65,535 times. The values for the horizontal and vertical coordinates refer to the mouse pointer's position at the time the user pressed a mouse button, not the current location of the mouse pointer. This service automatically resets the number of button releases for the requested button to zero. Use this service to detect user double clicks on menu items or other areas of the display.

Register Contents on Entry:
AX - 6
BX - Button
    0 - Left Button
    1 - Right Button
    2 - Center Button

Register Contents on Exit:
AX - Mouse Button Status (Bits True When Set)
    0 - Left Button Down
    1 - Right Button Down
    2 - Center Button down
    3 through 15 - Reserved (0)
BX - Button Release Counter
CX - Horizontal (X) Coordinate in Pixels
DX - Vertical (Y) Coordinate in Pixels

Example:

```
;Get Button Release Information
MOV    AX,6
MOV    BX,1     ;Right button
INT    33h
```

SET HORIZONTAL LIMITS FOR POINTER (INTERRUPT 33h SERVICE 07h)

This service sets the minimum and maximum horizontal limits of mouse movement within the display area. If you specify a minimum limit greater than the maximum limit, this service interchanges the two values. The mouse driver automatically repositions the mouse pointer to fall within the specified horizontal limits. Use this service to provide windowing capabilities for the mouse.

Register Contents on Entry:
AX - 7
CX - Minimum (X) Coordinate in Pixels
DX - Maximum (Y) Coordinate in Pixels

Example:
```
;Set Horizontal Limits for Pointer
MOV    AX,7
MOV    CX,45    ;Minimum X-coordinate
MOV    DX,60    ;Maximum X-coordinate
INT    33h
```

SET VERTICAL LIMITS FOR POINTER
(INTERRUPT 33h SERVICE 08h)

This service sets the minimum and maximum vertical limits of mouse movement within the display area. If you specify a minimum limit greater than the maximum limit, this service interchanges the two values. The mouse driver automatically repositions the mouse pointer to fall within the specified vertical limits. Use this service to provide windowing capabilities for the mouse.

Register Contents on Entry:
AX - 8
CX - Minimum (Y) Coordinate in Pixels
DX - Maximum (Y) Coordinate in Pixels

Example:
```
;Set Vertical Limits For Pointer
MOV    AX,8
MOV    CX,10    ;Minimum Y-coordinate
MOV    DX,70    ;Maximum Y-coordinate
INT    33h
```

SET GRAPHICS POINTER SHAPE
(INTERRUPT 33h SERVICE 09h)

This service defines the mouse pointer shape and hot spot in graphics mode. It does not affect the text mode pointer. To display the mouse pointer, you need to use service 01h (Show Mouse Pointer).

The image pointer buffer consists of two 32-byte sections for a total length of 64 bytes. The first 32-byte section contains a bit image that the mouse driver ANDs with the screen image. The second 32-byte section contains a bit image that the mouse driver XORs with the screen image.

The mouse driver uses the hot spot to determine mouse position during a button press. The mouse pointer hot spot values can range from 16 to – 16. The mouse driver uses the upper-left corner (0, 0) of the mouse pointer bit map as the reference point for the hot spot. You must use an even value for the horizontal hot spot offset in display modes 4 and 5.

Register Contents on Entry:
AX - 9

BX - Hot Spot Offset From Left
CX - Hot Spot Offset From Top
DX - Offset of Pointer Image Buffer
DS - Segment of Pointer Image Buffer

Example:

```
;Set Graphics Pointer Shape and Hot Spot.
.DATA.
;Create the AND pointer bit image. Use a diamond shaped pointer.
MousePtr    DB    0000000000000000b
            DB    0000000110000000b
            DB    0000000110000000b
            DB    0000001111000000b
            DB    0000001111000000b
            DB    0000011111100000b
            DB    0000011111100000b
            DB    0000111111110000b
            DB    0000111111110000b
            DB    0001111111111000b
            DB    0001111111111000b
            DB    0011111111111100b
            DB    0011111111111100b
            DB    0111111111111110b
            DB    0111111111111110b
            DB    1111111111111111b
            DB    1111111111111111b
            DB    0111111111111110b
            DB    0111111111111110b
            DB    0011111111111100b
            DB    0011111111111100b
            DB    0001111111111000b
            DB    0001111111111000b
            DB    0000111111110000b
            DB    0000111111110000b
            DB    0000011111100000b
            DB    0000011111100000b
            DB    0000001111000000b
            DB    0000001111000000b
            DB    0000000110000000b
            DB    0000000110000000b
            DB    0000000000000000b
            DB    32 DUP (0)      ;Clear the XOR bit image.
.CODE
Example PROC    FAR
            MOV    AX,0009h
            MOV    BX,8               ;Place the hot spot in the
```

```
        MOV     CX,16           ; center of the diamond.
        LES     DX,MousePtr
        INT     33h
```

SET TEXT POINTER TYPE
(INTERRUPT 33h SERVICE 0Ah)

This service defines the mouse pointer shape and attributes in text mode. It does not affect the graphics mode cursor. You can choose two types of text cursors: software and hardware.

The software cursor does not have a shape of its own. Instead, the software cursor uses one of the 256 ASCII characters to define its shape. Just like the graphics cursor, you define both AND and XOR mask values. In addition to shape, you define the foreground and background colors, intensity, and underscoring. The mask values in CX and DX use bits 0-7 for the character value, 8-10 for the foreground color, 11 for intensity, 12-14 for the background color, and 15 for blink.

The hardware cursor appears as a block. The block width depends on the display mode you use. The block height and position on the display line depend on the value contained in the CX and DX registers. CX contains the starting scan line. DX contains the ending scan line. The maximum scan line value depends on the display mode. For example, if the current display mode uses a 9 by 16 character, and you wanted to center a block cursor on the display, you could set CX to 1 and DX to 14. The scan line count always begins with zero for the bottom line.

Register Contents on Entry:
AX - Ah
BX - Pointer Type
     0 - Software Cursor
     1 - Hardware Cursor
CX - AND Mask Value (BX = 0), Start Line (BX = 1)
DX - XOR Mask Value (BX = 0), End Line (BX = 1)

Example:
```
        Set Text Pointer Type (Software cursor)
        MOV     AX,Ah
        MOV     BX,0
        MOV     CX,21B1h        ;Blue fore, Green back, Char 178.
        MOV     DX,F4DBh        ;Red fore, Blinking White back, Char 219.
        INT     33h
```

READ MOUSE MOTION COUNTERS
(INTERRUPT 33h SERVICE 0Bh)

This service returns the horizontal and vertical movement of the mouse movement (measured in mickeys) since the last call. A positive value shows movement right or downwards; a negative value shows movement left or upwards. The mickey count always ranges from −32768 to 32767. This service will not detect an overflow if the mickey count exceeds these values. One mickey represents 1/200-inch mouse movement.

Register Contents on Entry:
AX - Bh

Register Contents on Exit:
CX - Horizontal (X) Mickey Count
DX - Vertical (Y) Mickey Count

Example:

```
;Read Mouse Motion Counters
MOV     AX,Bh
INT     33h
```

SET USER-DEFINED MOUSE EVENT HANDLER (INTERRUPT 33h SERVICE 0Ch)

This service changes the address and event mask used by the mouse driver each time a mouse event occurs. The mask points to the user-defined handler for the specified mouse events. For example, if CX contains 1, then the mouse driver calls the user-defined handler every time the user moves the mouse. The mouse driver still reports events not handled by the user-defined handler. You must use service 0 to disable the user-defined handler.

When the mouse driver passes control to the user-defined handler, it makes a far call. Therefore, the user-defined handler must contain procedures using far returns. The mouse driver also fills the registers with specific information before it calls the user-defined handler. AX contains the mouse event flags. The flags appear in the same order as the event mask used to set up the user-defined handler. BX contains the button state. Bit 0 defines the left button, bit 1 defines the right button, and bit 2 defines the center button. CX contains the horizontal (X) pointer coordinate. DX contains the vertical (Y) pointer coordinate. SI contains the last raw vertical mickey count. DI contains the last raw horizontal mickey count. Finally, DS contains the mouse driver data segment.

Note: You must know how to create interrupt-driven programs before using this service. The user-defined handler uses the same techniques applied to memory resident interrupt-driven programs.

Register Contents on Entry:
AX - Ch
CX - Event Mask (Bit Selected if Set)
        0 - Mouse Movement
        1 - Left Button Press
        2 - Left Button Release

3 - Right Button Press
4 - Right Button Release
5 - Middle Button Press
6 - Middle Button Release
7 through 15 - Reserved (0)
DX - Offset of User Defined Handler
ES - Segment of User Defined Handler

Example:

```
;Set User-Defined Mouse Event Handler
MOV    AX,Ch
MOV    CX,6     ;Middle button release
LES    DX,Handle
INT    33h
```

TURN ON LIGHT-PEN EMULATION
(INTERRUPT 33h SERVICE 0Dh)

This service lets the mouse emulate a light pen. You simulate pushing the pen against the screen by pressing both the left and right mouse buttons (for a three-button mouse) or both buttons (for a two-button mouse). When you release either mouse button, the pen is off the screen.

Register Contents on Entry:
AX - Dh

Example:

```
;Turn On Light-Pen Emulation
MOV    AX,Dh
INT    33h
```

TURN OFF LIGHT-PEN EMULATION
(INTERRUPT 33h SERVICE 0Eh)

This service disables light-pen emulation. If a program can use both a light pen and a mouse, you must disable the light-pen emulation for the program to work correctly.

Register Contents on Entry:
AX - Eh

Example:

```
;Turn Off Light-Pen Emulation
MOV    AX,Eh
INT    33h
```

SET MICKEYS-TO-PIXELS RATIO
(INTERRUPT 33h SERVICE 0Fh)

This service sets the mickey-to-pixel ratio for horizontal and vertical mouse movement. The ratio determines the number of mickeys for every 8 virtual-screen pixels. One mickey represents $1/200$-inch of mouse travel.

The default value for the horizontal ratio is 8 mickeys to 8 virtual-screen pixels. The default value for the vertical ratio is 16 mickeys to 8 virtual-screen pixels. The mickey-to-pixel ratio can range from 1 to 32767. You can also set the mickey-to-pixel ratio using service 1Ah (Set Mouse Sensitivity).

Register Contents on Entry:
AX - Fh
CX - Horizontal Mickeys (Range 1 - 32,767, Default 8)
DX - Vertical Mickeys (Range 1 - 32,767, Default 16)

Example:

```
;Set Mickeys to Pixels Ratio
MOV     AX,Fh
MOV     CX,8
MOV     DX,16
INT     33h
```

SET MOUSE POINTER EXCLUSION AREA
(INTERRUPT 33h SERVICE 10h)

This service defines an area where the mouse pointer will not appear on the screen. To redisplay the mouse pointer in the area defined by this service, you need to call service 00h (Reset Mouse and Get Status) or 01h (Show Cursor). You can disable the exclusion area by making a second call to this service. One use for this service is to help determine the availability of menu selections or usability of a screen area.

Register Contents on Entry:
AX - 10h
CX - Upper Left X Coordinate
DX - Upper Left Y Coordinate
SI - Lower Right X Coordinate
DI - Lower Right Y Coordinate

Example:

```
;Set Mouse Pointer Exclusion Area (10,15) to (70,65)
MOV     AX,10h
MOV     CX,10
MOV     DX,15
MOV     SI,70
MOV     DI,65
INT     33h
```

SET DOUBLE SPEED THRESHOLD
(INTERRUPT 33h SERVICE 13h)

This service sets the threshold speed for doubling the movement of the mouse pointer. The threshold lets you define how fast you can move the mouse before the speed of the mouse pointer doubles. The default threshold is 64 mickeys/second.

This service makes it easier for you to move the mouse pointer long distances across the screen. You can also set the threshold speed using service 1Ah (Set Mouse Sensitivity).

Register Contents on Entry:
AX - 13h
DX - Threshold Speed in Mickeys/Second

Example:
```
;Set Double Speed Threshold
MOV    AX,13h
MOV    DX,64
INT    33h
```

SWAP USER-DEFINED MOUSE EVENT HANDLERS
(INTERRUPT 33h SERVICE 14h)

This service changes the address and event mask used by the mouse driver each time a mouse event occurs. It returns the address of the previous event handler. The mask points to the user-defined handler for the specified mouse events. For example, if CX contains 1, then the mouse driver calls the user-defined handler every time the user moves the mouse. The mouse driver still reports events not handled by the user-defined handler. You must use service 0 to disable the user-defined handler. In essence, this service allows you to use more than one user-defined event handler, even though you can use only one at a time.

When the mouse driver passes control to the user-defined handler, it makes a far call. Therefore, the user-defined handler must contain procedures using far returns. The mouse driver also fills the registers with specific information before it calls the user-defined handler. AX contains the mouse event flags. The flags appear in the same order as the event mask used to set up the user-defined handler. BX contains the button state. Bit 0 defines the left button, bit 1 defines the right button, and bit 2 defines the center button. CX contains the horizontal (X) pointer coordinate. DX contains the vertical (Y) pointer coordinate. SI contains the last raw vertical mickey count. DI contains the last raw horizontal mickey count. Finally, DS contains the mouse driver data segment.

Register Contents on Entry:
AX - 14h
CX - Event Mask (Bit Selected if Set)

0 - Mouse Movement
1 - Left Button Press
2 - Left Button Release
3 - Right Button Press
4 - Right Button Release
5 - Middle Button Press
6 - Middle Button Release
7 through 15 - Reserved (0)
DX - Offset of User Defined Handler
ES - Segment of User Defined Handler

Register Contents on Exit:
CX - Previous Event Mask
DX - Offset of Previous User Defined Handler
ES - Segment of Previous User Defined Handler

Example:

```
;Swap User-Defined Mouse Event Handlers
MOV    AX,14h
MOV    CX,1    ;Left button press
LES    DX,Handle
INT    33h
```

GET MOUSE SAVE STATE BUFFER SIZE (INTERRUPT 33h SERVICE 15h)

This service gets the buffer size required to store the current mouse driver state. You would use this service with service 16h (Save Mouse Driver State) and service 17h (Restore Mouse Driver State).

These three services let you temporarily interrupt your program and run another program that also uses a mouse. If you temporarily exit a program and run another program that uses a mouse, the mouse might not work correctly with the second program.

Using these three services involves a two-step process. First, use service 15h (Get Mouse Save State Buffer Size) to determine if you have enough space to store the mouse driver state. Next, use service 16h (Save Mouse Driver State) to place the mouse driver state in the buffer.

You then turn control of the mouse over to the other program. Once the second program returns control to the first program, you would use service 17h (Restore Mouse Driver State) to regain control of the mouse again.

Register Contents on Entry:
AX - 15h

Register Contents on Exit:
BX - Buffer Size in Bytes

Example:
```
;Get Mouse Save State Buffer Size
MOV    AX,15h
INT    33h
```

SAVE MOUSE DRIVER STATE
(INTERRUPT 33h SERVICE 16h)

This service stores the current mouse driver state. You would use this service with service 15h (Get Mouse Save State Buffer Size) and service 17h (Restore Mouse Driver State). Always call this service before you execute a child process using interrupt 21h service 4Bh.

These three services let you temporarily interrupt your program and run another program that also uses a mouse. If you temporarily exit a program and run another program that uses a mouse, the mouse might not work correctly with the second program.

Using these three services involves a two-step process. First, use service 15h (Get Mouse Save State Buffer Size) to determine if you have enough space to store the mouse driver state. Next, use service 16h (Save Mouse Driver State) to place the mouse driver state in the buffer.

You then turn control of the mouse over to the other program. Once the second program returns control to the first program, you would use service 17h (Restore Mouse Driver State) to regain control of the mouse again.

Note: No documented standard exists for the format of the buffer used to store the mouse data. In fact, its format varies from vendor to vendor.

Register Contents on Entry:
AX - 16h
DX - Buffer Offset
ES - Buffer Segment

Example:
```
;Save Mouse Driver State
MOV    AX,16h
LES    DX,BUFF
INT    33h
```

RESTORE MOUSE DRIVER STATE
(INTERRUPT 33h SERVICE 17h)

This service restores the current mouse driver state. You would use this service with service 15h (Get Mouse Save State Buffer Size) and service 16h (Save Mouse Driver State). Always use this service immediately after a child process returns control of the mouse to the parent process.

These three services let you temporarily interrupt your program and run another program that also uses a mouse. If you temporarily exit a program and run another program that uses a mouse, the mouse might not work correctly with the second program.

Using these three services involves a two-step process. First, use service 15h (Get Mouse Save State Buffer Size) to determine if you have enough space to store the mouse driver state. Next, use service 16h (Save Mouse Driver State) to place the mouse driver state in the buffer.

You then turn control of the mouse over to the other program. Once the second program returns control to the first program, you would use service 17h (Restore Mouse Driver State) to regain control of the mouse again.

Note: No documented standard exists for the format of the buffer used to store the mouse data. In fact, its format varies from vendor to vendor.

Register Contents on Entry:
AX - 17h
DX - Buffer Offset
ES - Buffer Segment

Example:
```
;Restore Mouse Driver State
MOV    AX,17h
LES    DX,BUFF
INT    33h
```

SET ALTERNATE MOUSE EVENT HANDLER (INTERRUPT 33h SERVICE 18h)

This service changes the mouse event handler address for the specified event mask. It allows you to use three simultaneous event handlers. Whenever a mouse event occurs, the mouse driver calls the event handler matching the mask conditions. For example, if CX contains 1, then the mouse driver calls the user-defined handler every time the user moves the mouse. If two drivers define the same mouse event, then the driver uses the shift key state to determine which handler to call. The mouse driver still reports events not handled by the user-defined handler. You must use service 0 to disable the user-defined handler. Every handler defined with this service must use one of the shift state keys (Shift, Ctrl, or Alt) defined in CX. The mouse driver uses these shift state keys (bits 5, 6, and 7) to determine which driver to call. Make sure each driver uses a different shift state key mask.

When the mouse driver passes control to the user-defined handler, it makes a far call. Therefore, the user-defined handler must contain procedures using far returns. The mouse driver also fills the registers with specific information before it calls the user-defined handler. AX contains the mouse event flags. The flags appear in the same order as the event mask used to set up the user-defined handler. BX contains the button state. Bit 0 defines the left button, bit 1 defines the right button, and bit 2 defines the center button. CX contains the horizontal (X) pointer coordinate. DX contains the vertical (Y) pointer coordinate. SI contains the last raw vertical mickey count. DI contains the last raw horizontal mickey count. Finally, DS contains the mouse driver data segment.

Register Contents on Entry:
AX - 18h
CX - Event Mask (Bit Selected if Set)
    0 - Mouse Movement
    1 - Left Button Press
    2 - Left Button Release
    3 - Right Button Press
    4 - Right Button Release
    5 - Shift Key Pressed During Button Press or Release
    6 - Ctrl Key Pressed During Button Press or Release
    7 - Alt Key Pressed During Button Press or Release
    8 through 15 - Reserved (0)
DX - Offset of User Defined Handler
ES - Segment of User Defined Handler

Register Contents on Exit:
AX - 18h if Successful, FFFFh if Unsuccessful

Example:
```
;Set Alternate Mouse Event Handler
MOV    AX,18h
MOV    CX,2    ;Left button release
LES    DX,Handle
INT    33h
```

GET ADDRESS OF ALTERNATE MOUSE
EVENT HANDLER (INTERRUPT 33h SERVICE 19h)

This service gets the address for the mouse event handler matching the event mask. Use this service with event handlers installed using service 18h. Because service 18h allows you to install multiple event handlers, this service allows you to find the handler you want to replace or disable.

Register Contents on Entry:
AX - 19h
CX - Event Mask (Bit Selected if Set)
    0 - Mouse Movement
    1 - Left Button Press
    2 - Left Button Release
    3 - Right Button Press
    4 - Right Button Release

5 - Middle Button Press
6 - Middle Button Release
7 through 15 - Reserved (0)

Register Contents on Exit:
CX - 0 if Not Successful, Event Mask if Successful
DX - Offset of User Defined Handler
ES - Segment of User Defined Handler

Example:
```
;Get Address of Alternate Mouse Event Handler
MOV    AX,19h
MOV    CX,1     ;Left button press
INT    33h
```

SET MOUSE SENSITIVITY
(INTERRUPT 33h SERVICE 1Ah)

The mouse sensitivity defines how hard or easy the mouse pointer moves when you move the mouse. The higher the sensitivity, the faster the mouse pointer moves with little actual movement of the mouse.

The sensitivity numbers can range between 1 and 100, where 50 specifies the default mickey factor of 1. This service also lets you specify the double-speed threshold ratio. One mickey equals $1/200$-inch of mouse travel.

Register Contents on Entry:
AX - 1Ah
BX - Horizontal Mickeys (Range 1 - 32,767, Default 8)
CX - Vertical Mickeys (Range 1 - 32,767, Default 16)
DX - Double Speed Threshold in Mickeys/Second

Example:
```
;Set Mouse Sensitivity
MOV    AX,1Ah
MOV    BX,8
MOV    CX,16
MOV    DX,64
INT    33h
```

GET MOUSE SENSITIVITY
(INTERRUPT 33h SERVICE 1Bh)

This service gets the current number of mickeys per 8 pixels of horizontal or 16 pixels of vertical movement, plus the threshold for doubling the mouse pointer motion. One mickey equals $1/200$-inch of mouse travel.

Register Contents on Entry:
AX - 1Bh

Register Contents on Exit:
BX - Horizontal Mickeys (Range 1 - 32,767, Default 8)
CX - Vertical Mickeys (Range 1 - 32,767, Default 16)
DX - Double Speed Threshold in Mickeys/Second

Example:
```
;Get Mouse Sensitivity
    MOV   AX,1Bh
    INT   33h
```

SET MOUSE INTERRUPT RATE (INTERRUPT 33h SERVICE 1Ch)

This service only works with the Microsoft InPort bus mouse that uses the InPort programmable chip. Calling this service will set the number of times per second the mouse driver polls the mouse for status information. For better resolution while displaying graphics, faster interrupt rates provide better resolution. However, slower interrupt rates sometimes let the program run faster. If BX contains more than one bit set, the mouse driver selects the lower interrupt rate.

Note: Most mouse drivers allow you to set the mouse interrupt rate. Some bus mice also support an interrupt rate feature in hardware. Refer to your vendor technical manual for details on changing this feature.

Register Contents on Entry:
AX - 1Ch
BX - Interrupt Rate Flags (Bits True When Set)
    0 - No Interrupts Allowed
    1 - 30 Interrupts/Second
    2 - 50 Interrupts/Second
    3 - 100 Interrupts/Second
    4 - 200 Interrupts/Second
    5 through 15 - Reserved (0)

Example:
```
;Set Mouse Interrupt Rate
    MOV   AX,1Ch
    MOV   BX,1     ;30 interrupts/second
    INT   33h
```

SELECT POINTER PAGE (INTERRUPT 33h SERVICE 1Dh)

This service selects on which display page the mouse pointer appears. Valid page numbers range from 0 to 7, depending on the display adapter used (CGA, MCGA, EGA, or VGA) and the current display mode. Chapter 6 provides a description of each display adapter and provides tables listing the number of pages available for various display modes.

Register Contents on Entry:
AX - 1Dh
BX - Page

Example:
```
;Select Pointer Page
MOV    AX,1Dh
MOV    BX,1    ;Page 1
INT    33h
```

GET POINTER PAGE (INTERRUPT 33h SERVICE 1Eh)

This service retrieves the current mouse pointer display page number.
Service 1Dh (Select Pointer Page) selects the mouse pointer display page.

Register Contents on Entry:
AX - 1Eh

Register Contents on Exit:
BX - Page

Example:
```
;Get Pointer Page
MOV    AX,1Eh
INT    33h
```

DISABLE MOUSE DRIVER
(INTERRUPT 33h SERVICE 1Fh)

This service disables the mouse and returns the address of the previous interrupt 33h handler. When you call this service, the mouse driver releases any interrupt vectors it captured (except interrupt 33h). The application program can complete the process of logically removing the mouse driver by restoring the original interrupt 33h vector. Use interrupt 21h service 25h to perform this task. Logically removing the driver does not remove the mouse driver from memory or allow other programs to allocate memory held by the mouse driver.

Register Contents on Entry:
AX - 1Fh

Register Contents on Exit:
AX - 001Fh if Successful, FFFFh if Not Successful
BX - Offset of Previous Interrupt 33h Handler
ES - Segment of Previous Interrupt 33h Handler

Example:
```
;Disable Mouse Driver
MOV    AX,1Fh
INT    33h
```

ENABLE MOUSE DRIVER
(INTERRUPT 33h SERVICE 20h)

This service enables the mouse driver and sets the Interrupt 33h vector to the mouse-interrupt vector.

Register Contents on Entry:
AX - 20h

Example:
```
;Enable Mouse Driver
MOV    AX,20h
INT    33h
```

RESET MOUSE DRIVER (INTERRUPT 33h SERVICE 21h)

This service resets the mouse driver. It does not perform any initialization of the mouse hardware. This allows you to reset the driver without losing any hardware-specific changes. When you use this service, the mouse driver removes the pointer from the screen, disables any user installed interrupt handlers, and sets the following default values.

Horizontal mickey-to-pixels ratio	8
Vertical mickey-to-pixels ratio	16
Double-speed threshold	64 mickeys/second
Minimum horizontal cursor position	0
Maximum horizontal cursor position	Maximum X value − 1
Minimum vertical cursor position	0
Maximum vertical cursor position	Maximum Y value − 1

Register Contents on Entry:
AX - 21h

Register Contents on Exit:
AX - 0021h if Successful, FFFFh if Not Successful
BX - Number of Mouse Buttons

Example:
```
;Reset Mouse Driver
MOV    AX,21h
INT    33h
```

SET LANGUAGE FOR MOUSE DRIVER MESSAGES
(INTERRUPT 33h SERVICE 22h)

This service selects the language used for mouse driver prompts and error messages This interrupt only works with special international mouse driver software.

Register Contents on Entry:
AX - 22h
BX - Language Number
    0 - English
    1 - French
    2 - Dutch
    3 - German
    4 - Swedish
    5 - Finnish
    6 - Spanish
    7 - Portuguese
    8 - Italian

Example:
```
;Set Language for Mouse Driver Messages
MOV   AX,22h
MOV   BX,1    ;French
INT   33h
```

GET LANGUAGE NUMBER
(INTERRUPT 33h SERVICE 23h)

This service retrieves the current language used for mouse driver prompts and error messages. This interrupt only works with special international mouse driver software.

Register Contents on Entry:
AX - 23h

Register Contents on Exit:
BX - Language Number
    0 - English
    1 - French
    2 - Dutch
    3 - German
    4 - Swedish
    5 - Finnish
    6 - Spanish
    7 - Portuguese
    8 - Italian

Example:
```
;Get Language Number
MOV   AX,23h
INT   33h
```

GET MOUSE INFORMATION
(INTERRUPT 33h SERVICE 24h)

This service retrieves the mouse driver version, the mouse type, and mouse adapter interrupt IRQ number. The CH register identifies the mouse type as follows:

A value of 1 identifies a bus mouse
A value of 2 identifies a serial mouse
A value of 3 identifies a Microsoft InPort mouse
A value of 4 identifies a PS/2 mouse
A value of 5 identifies a Hewlett-Packard mouse

Register Contents on Entry:
AX - 24h

Register Contents on Exit:
BH - Major Version Number
BL - Minor Version Number
CH - Mouse Type
     1 - Bus Mouse
     2 - Serial Mouse
     3 - InPort Mouse
     4 - PS/2 Mouse
     5 - HP Mouse
CL - IRQ Number
     0 - PS/2
     2, 3, 4, 5, or 7 - PC, PC/XT, and PC/AT

Example:
```
;Get Mouse Information
MOV    AX, 24h
INT    33h
```

15
DOS Expanded Memory
Support Interrupts

Expanded memory lies outside the normal address range of an 8088/8086 processor. You access it using an expanded memory manager (EMM). The manager uses windowing techniques to place 16 KByte sections of this memory in an area above the 640 KByte address limit of DOS, but below the 1 MByte barrier of the processor. Each window is called a page. Most EMM functions operate on one page of data at a time. In fact, most status information uses the page as a standard unit of measure. Expanded memory does not lie in a processor-protected mode address range like extended memory. In fact, you can use expanded memory in an 8088/8086 equipped machine. These machines cannot use extended memory because they cannot go into protected mode. Some books call expanded memory EMS memory. This book uses both terms interchangeably.

This chapter discusses the DOS expanded memory support interrupt routines. If you use DOS version 4.0 or above, you have access to all LIM 4.0 expanded memory interrupts (although you still need the appropriate hardware to use them). DOS 4.0 provides its own EMM driver. If you use any other version of DOS, you need an expanded memory driver from the manufacturer of your expanded memory board. You can still use an off-the-shelf EMM with DOS 4.0. Some drivers provide better handling of expanded memory.

The following paragraphs describe the EMS interrupts in numeric order. Each interrupt description contains the first EMS version to provide the service, the required register contents on routine entry, and a code fragment showing usage. TABLE 8-1 lists the interrupts in numeric order. Figure15-1 shows you how to use the interrupts to create a simple EMS program.

15-1A Assembly language program for expanded memory.

```
;********************************************************************************************************
;* Sample Program 22, Expanded Memory Manager Demonstration        *
;* This program shows you how to detect expanded memory using DOS interrupt 21h, service 3Dh.  It then shows   *
;* you how to manipulate expanded memory using Interrupt 67h.  Some of the expanded memory features it shows   *
;* you include obtaining the amount of expanded memory, allocating pages, and testing it for errors.  You      *
;* must have the following equipment to use this program.          *
;*       Expanded Memory Board            *
;*       Expanded Memory Manager Comptible With LIM 3.0 or Above.        *
;*       EMS 4.0 or Above Recommended for Best Results.  *
;*                         *
;* Copyright 1989,1990 John Mueller & Wallace Wang - Tab Books *
;********************************************************************************************************


;********************************************************************************************************
;* Perform the program setup.                  *
;********************************************************************************************************

.MODEL MEDIUM

.STACK ; Use the defalt stack of 1024 bytes.


;********************************************************************************************************
;* Begin the data area.  Declare all variables.          *
;********************************************************************************************************


.DATA

LF      EQU     10
CR      EQU     13
StrEnd  EQU     36
Msg1    DB      'Expanded Memory Not Installed'
        DB      CR,LF,StrEnd
Msg2    DB      'Expanded Memory Installed',CR,LF,StrEnd
Msg3    DB      'EMS Version: '
Version DB      3 DUP (' '),CR,LF,LF,'Unallocated Pages: '
UPages  DB      3 DUP (' '),' Pages'
UMem    DB      6 DUP (' '),' KBytes',CR,LF
        DB      'Total EMS Pages:   '
TPages  DB      3 DUP (' '),' Pages'
TMem    DB      6 DUP (' '),' KBytes',CR,LF,StrEnd
Msg4    DB      CR,LF,'Raw Pages:        '
RUPages DB      3 DUP (' '),' Pages',CR,LF
        DB      'Total Raw Pages:   '
RTPages DB      3 DUP (' '),' Pages',CR,LF,LF,StrEnd
Msg5    DB      'Open EMS Handles:',CR,LF
        DB      'Handle Name',CR,LF,StrEnd
Device  DB      'EMMXXXX0',0
Handle  DW      0
GVersion        DB      '4.0'
HandBuff        DB      255 DUP ('         '),0,0
DispHand        DB      15 DUP (' '),CR,LF,StrEnd
```

15-1A Continued.

```
;*****************************************************************************************************
;* Begin the code segment.                        *
;*****************************************************************************************************

  .CODE

EXAMPLE PROC FAR
        PUSH    DS      ;Save the original data segment.
        XOR     AX,AX
        PUSH    AX

        MOV     AX,@DATA        ;Point DS & ES to our data segment.
        MOV     DS,AX
        MOV     ES,AX

;*****************************************************************************************************
;* This part of the program checks the for the existence of the expanded memory manager.  If the manager is   *
;* installed, it gets the EMS status.                     *
;*****************************************************************************************************

        MOV     AH,3Dh  ;Check for EMS memory by
        MOV     AL,01000010b    ; opening EMM manager using
        LEA     DX,Device       ; Open File function.
        INT     21h
        JNC     Success ;File exit?

        MOV     AX,0900h        ;Print not installed message.
        LEA     DX,Msg1
        INT     21h
        JMP     Exit    ;Return to DOS.

Success:        MOV     Handle,AX       ;Save the file handle.

        MOV     AX,0900h        ;Print installed message.
        LEA     DX,Msg2
        INT     21h

        MOV     AH,3Eh  ;Close the file.
        MOV     BX,handle
        INT     21h

        MOV     AH,40h  ;Get EMS Status.
        INT     67h
        CMP     AH,0    ;If OK, start processing.
        JE      EMSGood
        JMP     Exit    ;Otherwise, leave program.

;*****************************************************************************************************
;* This part of the program begins by getting the version number and displaying the number of standard EMS    *
;* pages and memory.  If the EMS version is 4.0 or above, the program continues by displaying the number of    *
```

```
;* raw pages, raw page size, and memory.                     *
;*************************************************************************************************

EMSGood:        CALL    GetVersion      ;Get the EMS version, store it, and display it.

        CALL    GetPages        ;Get number of EMS pages.
        PUSH    BX      ;Save unallocated pages.
        PUSH    DX      ;Save total pages.
        PUSH    DX      ;Save total pages.
        MOV     AX,BX   ;Put unallocated pages in AX.
        LEA     DI,UPages       ;Point to end of buffer.
        INC     DI
        INC     DI
        CALL    HexConv ;Convert UPages to a number.

        POP     AX      ;Retrieve total pages.
        MOV     CX,16   ;Multiply by 16 to get KBytes.
        MUL     CX
        LEA     DI,TMem ;Point to end of buffer.
        ADD     DI,5
        CALL    HexConv

        POP     AX      ;Retrieve total pages.
        LEA     DI,TPages       ;Point to end of buffer.
        INC     DI
        INC     DI
        CALL    HexConv ;Convert TPages to a number.

        POP     AX      ;Retrieve unallocated pages.
        MOV     CX,16   ;Multiply by 16 to get KBytes.
        MUL     CX
        LEA     DI,UMem ;Point to end of buffer.
        ADD     DI,5
        CALL    HexConv

        MOV     AX,0900h        ;Display the page totals.
        LEA     DX,Msg3
        INT     21h

        LEA     DI,Version      ;See if we are using version
        LEA     SI,GVersion     ; 4.0 or greater.
        MOV     CX,3
        REP     CMPSB
        JE      Ver4_0  ;If so, display extended info.
        JMP     Exit    ;Otherwise, exit.


;*************************************************************************************************
;* This section of the program deals specifically with LIM versions 4.0 and above.  If your machines does not  *
;* contain this level of EMS, then it exits after the previous section.  This section displays the         *
;* unallocated and total number of raw pages.  A raw page does not necessarily have a size of 16 KBytes;        *
```

15-1A Continued.

```
;* therefore the number of pages may differ.  Finally, this section displays the EMS handles and any    *
;* associated name.                                        *
;********************************************************************************************************

Ver4_0: CALL    GetRPages       ;Get number of raw EMS pages.
        PUSH    DX      ;Save total pages.
        MOV     AX,BX   ;Put unallocated pages in AX.
        LEA     DI,RUPages      ;Point to end of buffer.
        INC     DI
        INC     DI
        CALL    HexConv ;Convert UPages to a number.

        POP     AX      ;Retrieve total pages.
        LEA     DI,RTPages      ;Point to end of buffer.
        INC     DI
        INC     DI
        CALL    HexConv ;Convert TPages to a number.

        MOV     AX,0900h        ;Display the raw page totals.
        LEA     DX,Msg4
        INT     21h

        MOV     AX,0900h        ;Display the handles heading.
        LEA     DX,Msg5
        INT     21h

        CALL    GetHandles      ;Fill a buffer with the handle names.
        LEA     SI,HandBuff     ;Point to the beginning of the buffer.
        MOV     AX,[SI] ;Load the handle number.
ListBuff:       LEA     DI,DispHand     ;Load the display string.
        ADD     DI,5    ;Point to end of number area.
        CALL    HexConv ;Convert to characters.
        INC     SI      ;Point to handle name.
        INC     SI
        LEA     DI,DispHand     ;Add space for handle name.
        ADD     DI,7
        MOV     CX,8    ;Number of characters.
        REP     MOVSB   ;Move from buffer to string.
        MOV     AX,0900h        ;Display the handle number
        LEA     DX,DispHand     ; and name.
        INT     21h
        MOV     AX,[SI] ;Load the handle number.
        CMP     AX,0    ;Last one?
        JNE     ListBuff        ;If not, display next handle.

Exit:   RET             ;Return.

EXAMPLE ENDP

;********************************************************************************************************
;* This procedure fills a buffer with the EMS handle numbers (actual number, not characters) and names.  It    *
```

15-1A Continued.

```
;* marks the end of the buffer with a double zero.                                    *
;**********************************************************************************************

GetHandles      PROC    NEAR

        MOV     AX,5400h        ;Load the service number.
        LEA     DI,HandBuff     ;Load the buffer address.
        INT     67h     ;Fill the buffer.

        MOV     CL,10   ;Multiply number of handles
        XOR     AH,AH   ; by field size and add one.
        MUL     CL
        ADD     DI,AX   ;Point to last buffer entry.
        MOV     WORD PTR [DI],0 ;Add an end of string character.

        RET

GetHandles      ENDP

;**********************************************************************************************
;* This procedure obtains the number of standard 16 KByte pages.  This includes both total and unallocated  *
;* pages.  It returns the unallocated pages in BX and the total pages in DX.    *
;**********************************************************************************************

GetPages        PROC    NEAR

        MOV     AH,42h
        INT     67h

        RET

GetPages        ENDP

;**********************************************************************************************
;* This procedure obtains the number of raw EMS pages.  Raw pages can be sizes other than the standard 16   *
;* KByte size.  This number includes both total and unallocated pages.  It returns the unallocated pages in  *
;* BX and the total pages in DX.    *
;**********************************************************************************************

GetRPages       PROC    NEAR

        MOV     AX,5901h
        INT     67h

        RET

GetRPages       ENDP

;**********************************************************************************************
;* This procedure gets the EMS version number from the driver and places it in a buffer area.  Notice the   *
```

15-1A Continued.

```
;* version number is in BCD format.  The upper four bits of AL contain the major revision number and the        *
;* lower four bits contain the minor revision number.                    *
;**********************************************************************************************************************
;

GetVersion      PROC    NEAR

        MOV     AH,46h  ;Get the version number.
        INT     67h

        LEA     DI,Version      ;Load the buffer address.
        PUSH    AX      ;Save the minor number.
        MOV     CX,4    ;Shift the major version
        SHR     AX,CL   ; number to the lower 4-bits.
        ADD     AL,30h  ;Convert it to a character.
        MOV     [DI],AL ;Place it in the buffer.

        INC     DI      ;Place a decimal point between
        MOV     AL,'.'  ; the major and minor version
        MOV     [DI],AL ; numbers.

        INC     DI      ;Point to the minor number.
        POP     AX      ;Restore the minor number.
        SHL     AX,CL   ;Push the major number in AH.
        XOR     AH,AH   ;Zero out the major number.
        SHL     AX,CL   ;Place the minor number in the
        ADD     AH,30h  ; lower 4-bits of AH and
        MOV     [DI],AH ; convert it to a character.

        RET

GetVersion      ENDP

;**********************************************************************************************************************
;* This procedure converts a hexidecimal number to a decimal character equivalent.  AX contains the number      *
;* to convert and DI the address of the end of a storage buffer on entry.  The procedure does not return a       *
;* value.                        *
;**********************************************************************************************************************
;

HexConv PROC    NEAR

        MOV     CX,10   ;Load divisor.
DoDiv:  XOR     DX,DX   ;Clear DX.
        DIV     CX      ;Divide AX by 10
        ADD     DX,30h  ;Change remainder to char.
        MOV     [DI],DL ;Store the number.
        DEC     DI      ;Point to next number.
        CMP     AX,9    ;See if we need to divide.
        JG      DoDiv
        ADD     AX,30h  ;Change quotient to char.
        MOV     [DI],AL ;Store the number.
```

15-1A Continued.

```
        RET

HexConv ENDP

END     EXAMPLE
```

15-1B BASIC language program for expanded memory.

```
REM Sample Program 22, Expanded Memory Manager Demonstration
REM This program shows you how to detect expanded memory using DOS interrupt 21h, service 3Dh.  It then shows
REM you how to manipulate expanded memory using Interrupt 67h.  Some of the expanded memory features it shows
REM you include obtaining the amount of expanded memory, allocating pages, and testing it for errors.  You
REM must have the following equipment to use this program.
REM     Expanded Memory Board
REM     Expanded Memory Manager Comptible With LIM 3.0 or Above.
REM     EMS 4.0 or Above Recommended for Best Results.
REM
REM Copyright 1989,1990 John Mueller & Wallace Wang - Tab Books

' $INCLUDE: 'qbx.bi'

DEFINT A-Z

DECLARE FUNCTION GetStatus ()
DECLARE SUB GetVersion (ErrorMsg, Version)
DECLARE SUB GetPages (ErrorMsg, UPages, TPages)
DECLARE SUB GetRPages (ErrorMsg, UPages, TPages)
DECLARE SUB GetHandles (ErrorMsg, Number)

' *****************************************

Msg1$ = "Expanded Memory Not Installed"
Msg2$ = "Expanded Memory Installed"
Msg3$ = "EMS Version: "
Msg4$ = "Unallocated Pages:   "
Msg5$ = "Total EMS Pages:     "
Msg6$ = "Raw Pages:           "
Msg7$ = "Total Raw Pages:     "
Msg8$ = "Open EMS Handles:    "
Msg9$ = "Handle Name"
Device$ = "EMMXXXX0"
Pages$ = " Pages "
KBytes$ = " KBytes "
UMem$ = "      "
TMem$ = "      "
GVersion = 4

EMMHandle = 0
Count = 1

PRINT "Here we go!"
```

15-1B Continued.

```
IF GetStatus THEN
  CALL GetVersion(ErrorMsg, Version)
  PRINT
  PRINT
  PRINT Msg3$; Version
  CALL GetPages(ErrorMsg, UPages, TPages)
  PRINT
  PRINT Msg4$; UPages; Pages; UMem$; KBytes
  PRINT Msg5$; TPages; Pages; TMem$; KBytes
  IF Version = GVersion THEN
    CALL GetRPages(ErrorMsg, RUPages, RTPages)
    PRINT
    PRINT Msg6$; RUPages; Pages
    PRINT Msg7$; RTPages; Pages
    CALL GetHandles(ErrorMsg, Number)
    PRINT
    PRINT Msg8$; Msg9$
    END IF

ELSE
  PRINT Msg1$
END IF

SUB GetHandles (ErrorMsg, Number)
  DIM InRegs AS RegType
  DIM OutRegs AS RegType

  InRegs.ax = &H5402
  CALL Interrupt(&H67, InRegs, OutRegs)
  ErrorMsg = OutRegs.ax \ &HFF
  Number = OutRegs.bx
END SUB

SUB GetPages (ErrorMsg, UPages, TPages)
  DIM InRegs AS RegType
  DIM OutRegs AS RegType

  InRegs.ax = &H42
  CALL Interrupt(&H67, InRegs, OutRegs)
  ErrorMsg = OutRegs.ax \ &HFF
  UPages = OutRegs.bx * 16
  TPages = OutRegs.dx * 16
END SUB

SUB GetRPages (ErrorMsg, RUPages, RTPages)
  DIM InRegs AS RegType
  DIM OutRegs AS RegType

  InRegs.ax = &H5900
  CALL Interrupt(&H67, InRegs, OutRegs)
  ErrorMsg = OutRegs.ax \ &HFF
```

15-1B Continued.

```
  RUPages = OutRegs.bx
  RTPages = OutRegs.dx
END SUB

FUNCTION GetStatus
  DIM InRegs AS RegType
  DIM OutRegs AS RegType

  InRegs.ax = &H40
  CALL Interrupt(&H67, InRegs, OutRegs)
  IF OutRegs.ax = 0 THEN
    GetStatus = True
  ELSE
    GetStatus = False
  END IF
END FUNCTION

SUB GetVersion (ErrorMsg, Version)
  DIM InRegs AS RegType
  DIM OutRegs AS RegType

  InRegs.ax = &H46
  CALL Interrupt(&H67, InRegs, OutRegs)
  ErrorMsg = OutRegs.ax \ &HFF
  Version = OutRegs.ax AND &HFF
END SUB
```

15-1C C language program for expanded memory.

```
/* Sample Program 22, Expanded Memory Manager Demonstration
   This program shows you how to detect expanded memory using DOS interrupt 21h, service 3Dh.  It then shows
   you how to manipulate expanded memory using Interrupt 67h.  Some of the expanded memory features it shows
   you include obtaining the amount of expanded memory, allocating pages, and testing it for errors.  You
   must have the following equipment to use this program.
        Expanded Memory Board
        Expanded Memory Manager Compatible With LIM 3.0 or Above.
        EMS 4.0 or Above Recommended for Best Results.

   Copyright 1989,1990 John Mueller & Wallace Wang - Tab Books
*/

#include <dos.h>
#include <graph.h>
#include <stdio.h>
#include <stdlib.h>
#include <string.h>

char *Msg1 = "Expanded Memory Not Installed";
char *Msg2 = "Expanded Memory Installed";
char *Msg3 = "EMS Version: ";
```

```
char *Msg4 = "Unallocated Pages: ";
char *Msg5 = "Total EMS Pages:   ";
char *Msg6 = "Raw Pages:         ";
char *Msg7 = "Total Raw Pages:   ";
char *Msg8 = "Open EMS Handles:";
char *Msg9 = "Handle Name";
char *Device = "EMMXXXX0";
char *Pages = " Pages ";
char *KBytes = " KBytes";
char *Version = " . ";
char *GVersion = "4.0";
char *UPages = "    ";
char *UMem = "        ";
char *TPages = "    ";
char *TMem = "        ";
char *RUPages = "    ";
char *RTPages = "    ";
char *Temp = "  ";

unsigned int EMMHandle = 0;
unsigned int Count = 0;

struct HBuff {
                int HNum;
                char HName[7];
           } HandBuff[255];

union REGS inregs, outregs;

main()
{
        inregs.x.ax=0x3D42;             /* Load service and function. */
        inregs.x.dx=Device;             /* Point to ASCIIZ filename. */
        intdos(&inregs,&outregs);       /* Perform interrupt. */

        /* Perform following steps if successful. */

        if (!outregs.x.cflag)
        {
        EMMHandle = outregs.x.ax;       /* Save file handle. */
        printf("%s\n", Msg2);   /* Print installed message. */
        inregs.x.ax = 0x3E00;   /* Close the handle. */
        inregs.x.bx = EMMHandle;
        intdos(&inregs,&outregs);

/* Start processing the EMS parameters. */

        inregs.h.ah = 0x40;             /* Get EMM status. */
        int86(0x67,&inregs,&outregs);
        if (!outregs.x.ax)              /* If EMM is working correctly. */
        {
```

15-1C Continued.

```
            /*
               This section gets the values available to all versions
               of EMS above version 3.0.
            */

                    GetVersion();
                    printf("%s%s\n\n", Msg3, Version);
                    GetPages();
                    printf("%s%3s%s%6s%s\n", Msg4, UPages, Pages, UMem, KBytes);
                    printf("%s%3s%s%6s%s\n", Msg5, TPages, Pages, TMem, KBytes);

                    /* This section first checks if the EMM is version
                       4.0.  If so, then it gets additional information
                       about EMM status.
                    */

                    if (!strncmp(Version,GVersion,3))
                    {
                            GetRPages();
                            printf("\n%s%3s%s\n", Msg6, RUPages, Pages);
                            printf("%s%3s%s\n\n", Msg7, RTPages, Pages);
                            GetHandles();
                            printf("%s\n%s\n", Msg8, Msg9);
                            for (Count=0; Count<=outregs.x.bx-2; Count++)
                                    printf("%6i %8s\n", HandBuff[Count].HNum, HandBuff[Count].HName);
                    }
            }
    }
    else                                    /* If EMM isn't installed, then */
            printf("%s", Msg1);             /* print not installed message. */
}


GetVersion()

/* This function uses service 46h of interrupt 67h to determine
   the version number of the EMM.  You need this value to decide
   which EMS services you can and cannot use.
*/

{
        inregs.h.ah = 0x46;                             /* Get version number. */
        int86(0x67,&inregs,&outregs);

        outregs.h.ah = 0x00;                            /* Zero upper half of AX. */
        outregs.x.ax = _rotr(outregs.x.ax,4);   /* Shift Major Version Number */
        Temp = outregs.h.al+0x30;                       /* Convert to a Character */
        Version[0] = Temp;                              /* Store in Version String. */
        outregs.x.ax = _rotr(outregs.x.ax,8);   /* Shift Major Version to AH */
                                                        /* and Minor Version in AL */
        outregs.h.ah = 0x00;                            /* Zero upper half of AX. */
```

```
        outregs.x.ax = _rotr(outregs.x.ax,4);   /* Shift Minor Version Number */
        Temp = outregs.h.al+0x30;                    /* Convert to a Character */
        Version[2] = Temp;                           /* Store in Version String. */

}


GetPages()


/* This function uses service 42h of interrupt 67h to determine
   the amount of memory available.  It returns not only the total
   amount available, but the amount not in use.  The interrupt
   returns a value in EMS pages of 16 KBytes.  You must multiply
   the pages by 16 to determine the actual memory available.
*/


{

        inregs.h.ah = 0x42;                          /* Get page totals. */
        int86(0x67,&inregs,&outregs);

        itoa(outregs.x.bx,UPages,10);         /* Convert number of pages. */
        itoa(outregs.x.dx,TPages,10);

        outregs.x.bx = outregs.x.bx * 16;         /* Convert to memory in KBytes. */
        outregs.x.dx = outregs.x.dx * 16;
        itoa(outregs.x.bx,UMem,10);
        itoa(outregs.x.dx,TMem,10);
}


GetRPages()


/* This procedure determines the total and available number of raw
   pages provided by the EMS card.  A raw page may contain more or
   less than the standard 16 KByte pages.  For example, some drivers
   may provide 64 KByte raw memory pages.
*/


{

        inregs.x.ax = 0x5901;                /* Get the number of raw pages. */
        int86(0x67,&inregs,&outregs);

        itoa(outregs.x.bx,RUPages,10);       /* Convert both the unallocated */
        itoa(outregs.x.dx,RTPages,10);       /* and total raw pages to characters. */
}


GetHandles()


/* This procedure fills an array structure with the handle numbers
   and names allocated by the EMM driver.  Each allocation uses a
   unique number.  Each handle number does not necessarily have an
   associated handle name.
```

15-1C Continued.

```
*/

{
        inregs.x.ax = 0x5400;              /* Get the number and name of all */
        inregs.x.di = HandBuff;            /* handles recognized by the EMM. */
        int86(0x67,&inregs,&outregs);      /* BX contains the total number of */
                                            /* of handles on return. */
}
```

15-1D Pascal program for expanded memory.

```
(*********************************************************************************************)
(* Sample Program 22, DOS Expanded Memory Service Interrupt Extensions Demonstration    *)
(* This program shows you how to detect expanded memory using DOS interrupt 21h, service 3Dh.  It then shows    *)
(* you how to manipulate expanded memory using Interrupt 67h.  Some of the expanded memory features it shows    *)
(* you include obtaining the amount of expanded memory, allocating pages, and testing it for errors.  You       *)
(* must have the following equipment to use this program.              *)
(*      Expanded Memory Board            *)
(*      Expanded Memory Manager Comptible With LIM 3.0 or Above.          *)
(*      EMS 4.0 or Above Recommended for Best Results.  *)
(*                                *)
(* Copyright 1989, 1990 John Mueller & Wallace Wang - Tab Books *)
(*********************************************************************************************)


PROGRAM EMM_Demo;
(* This program shows you how to manipulate expanded memory using
   Interrupt 67h. Some of the expanded memory features it shows you
   include obtaining the amount of expanded memory, allocating pages,
   and testing it for errors. You must have the following equipment
   to use this program.

   Expanded Memory Board
   Expanded Memory Manager compatible with LIM 3.0 or above
   EMS 4.0 or Above recommended for best results

   Copyright 1898,1990 John Mueller & Wallace Wang - Tab Books *)

USES
  Dos;
CONST
  Msg1 = 'Expanded Memory Not Installed';
  Msg2 = 'Expanded Memory Installed';
  Msg3 = 'EMS Version: ';
  Msg4 = 'Unallocated Pages:    ';
  Msg5 = 'Total EMS Pages:      ';
  Msg6 = 'Raw Pages:            ';
  Msg7 = 'Total Raw Pages:      ';
  Msg8 = 'Open EMS Handles:     ';
  Msg9 = 'Handle Name';
  Device = 'EMMXXXX0';
```

```
  Pages = ' Pages ';
  KBytes = ' KBytes ';
  GVersion = 4.0;

  EMMHandle : integer = 0;
  Count : integer = 1;
TYPE
  HandBuffRecord = RECORD
    HNum : integer;
    HName : string[7];
  END;  (* RECORD *)
VAR
  HandBuff : ARRAY [1..255] OF HandBuffRecord;
  Regs : Registers;
  Error, UPages, TPages, RUPages, RTPages, Number, UMem, TMem : integer;
  Version : real;

  FUNCTION GetStatus : boolean;
  BEGIN
    Regs.ah := $40;
    Intr ($67, Regs);
  IF Regs.ah = 0 THEN
    GetStatus := TRUE
  ELSE
    GetStatus := FALSE;
END;  (* GetStatus *)


PROCEDURE GetVersion (VAR Error : integer;
                      VAR Version : real);

BEGIN
  Regs.ah := $46;
  Intr ($67, Regs);
  Error := Regs.ah;
  Version := Regs.al;
END;  (* GetVersion *)


PROCEDURE GetPages (VAR Error, UPages, TPages : integer);
BEGIN
  Regs.ah := $42;        (* Get page totals *)
  Intr ($67, Regs);
  Error := Regs.ah;
  UPages := Regs.bx * 16;
  TPages := Regs.dx * 16;
END;  (* GetPages *)


PROCEDURE GetRPages (VAR Error, RUPages, RTPages : integer);
BEGIN
  Regs.ah := $59;        (* Get the number of raw pages *)
  Regs.al := 0;
  Intr ($67, Regs);
  Error := Regs.ah;
```

```
   RUPages := Regs.bx;
   RTPages := Regs.dx;
 END;  (* GetRPages *)

 PROCEDURE GetHandles (VAR Error, Number : integer);
 BEGIN
   Regs.ah := $54;
   Regs.al := 2;
   Intr ($67, Regs);
   Error := Regs.ah;
   Number := Regs.bx;
 END;  (* GetHandles *)

BEGIN
 IF GetStatus = TRUE THEN
   BEGIN
     GetVersion (Error, Version);
     Writeln;
     Writeln;
     Writeln (Msg3, Version);
     GetPages (Error, UPages, TPages);
     Writeln;
     Writeln (Msg4, UPages, Pages, UMem, KBytes);
     Writeln (Msg5, TPages, Pages, TMem, KBytes);
     IF Version = GVersion THEN
       BEGIN
         GetRPages (Error, RUPages, RTPages);
         Writeln;
         Writeln (Msg6, RUPages, Pages);
         Writeln;
         Writeln (Msg7, RTPages, Pages);
         GetHandles (Error, Number);
         Writeln;
         Writeln (Msg8, Msg9);
       END
   END
 ELSE
   Writeln (Msg1);
END.
```

CHECKING EXPANDED MEMORY STATUS

You must make sure your machine contains expanded memory before attempting to use the following functions. There are two methods of determining if your machine contains EMS. The first method uses a DOS interrupt to attempt to open the EMM driver using the guaranteed filename of 'EMMXXXX0'. If this function succeeds, then your machine contains expanded memory. There is one problem with using this method. If your machine happens to have a file in the current directory with the same name as the EMM driver, then this method might return incorrect results. The following example program shows how to use this method of determining the presence of expanded memory.

```
.MODEL      SMALL
.STACK                      ;Use the default stack of 1024 bytes.
.DATA
LF          EQU     10
CR          EQU     13
StrEnd      EQU     36
Msg1        DB      'Expanded Memory Not Installed',CR,LF,StrEnd
Msg2        DB      'Expanded Memory Installed',CR,LF,StrEnd
Device      DB      'EMMXXXX0',0
Handle      DW      0

.CODE
EXAMPLE     PROC FAR

            PUSH    DS              ;Save the original data segment.
            XOR     AX,AX
            PUSH    AX
            MOV     AX,@DATA        ;Point DS & ES to our data segment.
            MOV     DS,AX
            MOV     ES,AX

            MOV     AH,3Dh          ;Check for EMS memory by opening EMM.
            MOV     AL,01000010b    ; manager using Open File function.
            LEA     DX,Device
            INT     21h
            JNC     Success         ;File exit?
            MOV     AX,0900h        ;Print not installed message.
            LEA     DX,Msg1
            INT     21h
            JMP     Exit            ;Return to DOS.

Success:    MOV     Handle,AX       ;Save the file handle.
            MOV     AX,0900h        ;Print installed message.
            LEA     DX,Msg2
            INT     21h
            MOV     AH,3Eh          ;Close the file.
            MOV     BX,handle
            INT     21h

Exit:       RET             Return.
EXAMPLE     ENDP
END         EXAMPLE
```

If you want a foolproof method of determining the presence of EMS memory, use this second method. The only problem with this method is that you directly examine memory that does not belong to your program. This can produce incompatibilities between your program and other memory-resident programs or device drivers. Using this method, you get the address of the EMM driver. Once you obtain this address, look at offset 0Ah of the device header. If your machine contains expanded memory you see the string 'EMMXXXX0'. The following example program shows how to use this method of determining the presence of expanded memory.

```
.MODEL    SMALL
.STACK                    ;Use the default stack of 1024 bytes.
.DATA
LF        EQU    10
CR        EQU    13
StrEnd    EQU    36
Msg1      DB     'Expanded Memory Not Installed',CR,LF,StrEnd
Msg2      DB     'Expanded Memory Installed',CR,LF,StrEnd
Device    DB     'EMMXXXX0',0
Handle    DW     0
.CODE
EXAMPLE   PROC FAR

          PUSH     DS              ;Save the original data segment.
          XOR      AX,AX
          PUSH     AX
          MOV      AX,@DATA        ;Point DS & ES to our data segment.
          MOV      DS,AX
          MOV      ES,AX
          MOV      AH,35h          ;Get the location of interrupt
                                   ;   vector 67h.
          MOV      AL,67h          ;This is the EMM interrupt vector.
          INT      21h
          MOV      DI,0Ah          ;Point to device name offset.
          MOV      CX,8            ;Compare the device name to the
                                   ;   standard name.
          LEA      SI,Device       ;load the standard name address.
          REP      CMPSB
          JE       Success         ;Jump if string compare.

          MOV      AX,0900h        ;Print not installed message.
          LEA      DX,Msg1
          INT      21h
          JMP      Exit            ;Return to DOS.

Success:
          MOV AX,0900h             ;Print installed message.
          LEA      DX,Msg2
```

```
       INT          21h

EXIT:    RET                          ;Return
EXAMPLE  ENDP
END      EXAMPLE
```

GET STATUS (INTERRUPT 67h SERVICE 40h)

EMS 3.0

This service tests to see if an expanded memory board is available and whether the computer can use it. You should always use this service first before calling any other service, to verify that expanded memory exists.

Note: Always verify the presence of the expanded memory manager by using one of the two methods described in the checking expanded memory status section before using this function. This function only checks the viability of the installed software and hardware.

Register Contents on Entry:
AH - 40h

Register Contents on Exit:
AH - 00h if Successful, Error Code if Unsuccessful

Example:
```
;Determine if expanded memory is available.
MOV   AH,40h
INT   67h
CMP   AH,0
JNE   ErrMsg
```

GET PAGE FRAME ADDRESS
(INTERRUPT 67h SERVICE 41h)

EMS 3.0

This service returns the EMM page frame segment address. Once you use service 40h (Get Status) to verify that expanded memory exists, use this service to determine its location in memory. A page frame contains four 16 KByte pages. These pages contain data mapped from expanded memory into DOS conventional memory. Your EMM might not limit you to a page frame of 64 KBytes if you use EMS version 4.0 or above. See service 58 function 0 for enhanced function information.

Note: You do not need to get an EMS handle before using this function.

Register Contents on Entry:
AH - 41h

Register Contents on Exit:
AH - 00h if Successful, Error Code if Unsuccessful
BX - Segment Base of Page Frame

Example:
```
;Get the EMM segment address.
MOV    AH,41h
INT    67h
```

GET NUMBER OF PAGES
(INTERRUPT 67h SERVICE 42h)

EMS 3.0

This service returns the total number of logic expanded memory pages and the number of pages not already allocated. You can use this service to determine if there is enough memory for your program. To obtain the total memory available, multiply the number of available pages by 16. This value equals the total available memory in KBytes. If you use EMS version 4.0 or above, see service 59 function 1 for enhanced function information.

Note: You do not need to get an EMS handle before using this function.

Register Contents on Entry:
AH - 42h

Register Contents on Exit:
AH - 00h if Successful, Error Code if Unsuccessful
BX - Unallocated Pages
DX - Total Pages

Example:
```
;Get the unallocated and total number of expanded memory pages.
MOV    AH,42h
INT    67h
```

ALLOCATE HANDLE AND PAGES
(INTERRUPT 67h SERVICE 43h)

EMS 3.0

This service obtains an EMM handle, then allocates memory pages controlled by that handle. Every EMM mapping, release, and close function requires you to provide the handle returned with this function. There are two main reasons this function fails: lack of available handles, or lack of EMS memory. In the first case, you must wait until another application releases a handle. In the second case, use service 42h to determine the total number of available pages. You may then use this value to allocate memory. Each page you allocate contains 16 KBytes of memory. If your application requires you to allocate memory in other than 16 KByte pages, then use the raw page allocation service 5Ah, function 1. In addition to lack of handles or memory, a hardware or software failure will cause this service to fail.

Note: The operating system always reserves EMS handle 0000 for its own use.

Register Contents on Entry:
AH - 43h
BX - Number of Pages to Allocate

Register Contents on Exit:
AH - 00h if Successful, Error Code if Unsuccessful
DX - EMM handle

Example:
```
;Allocate 64 KBytes of EMS memory.
MOV     AH,43h
MOV     BX,4
INT     67h
CMP     AH,0
JNE     ERRMsg
MOV     EMSHandle,DX
```

MAP EXPANDED MEMORY (INTERRUPT 67h SERVICE 44h)

EMS 3.0

This service maps one of the logical pages assigned to an EMM handle to physical memory accessible to the CPU. Service 43h (Allocates Handles and Pages) assigns standard 16 KByte logical pages to the EMM handle. Service 5Ah assigns raw logical pages to the EMM handle. A raw page can contain more or less than the standard 16 KBytes. A logical page uses the range from 0 to n – 1, where n is the number of pages allocated to the EMM handle. Specify a logical page number in BX. The physical page is in the range of 0 to 3 and begins at the base address obtained using service 41h. Specify the physical page number in AL. You may use service 58 function 0 to obtain a listing of available physical pages and their addresses.

Register Contents on Entry:
AH - 44h
AL - Physical Page
BX - Logical Page
DX - EMM Handle

Register Contents on Exit:
AH - 00h if Successful, Error Code if Unsuccessful

Example:
```
;Map page 2 of EMM handle 1 to physical page 3.
MOV     AH,44h
MOV     AL,3
```

```
MOV    BX,2
MOV    DX,Handle1
INT    67h
```

RELEASE HANDLE AND EXPANDED MEMORY (INTERRUPT 67h SERVICE 45h)

EMS 3.0

This service deallocates memory pages assigned to a handle, then releases the handle. If a program fails to call this service before terminating, the pages remain allocated and unavailable for use by other programs. An application using expanded memory should install its own Ctrl – C and critical error handler to prevent unexpected program termination. EMS version 4.0 automatically sets the handle name to ASCII nulls when this function releases it.

Register Contents on Entry:
AH - 45h
DX - EMM Handle

Register Contents on Exit:
AH - 00h if Successful, Error Code if Unsuccessful

Example:
```
;Release an EMM handle.
MOV    AH,45h
MOV    DX,EMMHandle
INT    67h
```

GET VERSION (INTERRUPT 67h SERVICE 46h)

EMS 3.0

This service returns the EMS version number in binary coded decimal (BCD) format. The upper four bits of AL contain the major release number (0–9). The lower four bits contain the minor version number (0–9). For example, if the version number is 4.0, then AL returns 40h. The version number allows you to determine the services supported by the EMM.

Register Contents on Entry:
AH - 46h

Register Contents on Exit:
AH - 00h if Successful, Error Code if Unsuccessful
AL - Version Number

Example:
```
;Get the version number.
MOV    AH,46h
INT    67h
```

SAVE PAGE MAP (INTERRUPT 67h SERVICE 47h)

EMS 3.0

This service saves the contents of the expanded memory hardware page mapping registers. It then associates those contents with an EMM handle. You can use this service for writing terminate-and-stay-resident (TSR) programs that use expanded memory. Programs that take advantage of the advanced capabilities of EMS version 4.0 should use services 4Eh or 4Fh. This service saves the mapping state for a 64 KByte page frame only. You must use service 48h to restore page maps saved with this service.

Note: Although application programs may safely use this service, its purpose is to provide interrupt handler and device drivers a safe method of using EMS memory. The EMM handle always refers to the handle assigned to the device driver or interrupt handler during bootup. The EMM handle never refers to the handle owned by another program.

Register Contents on Entry:

AH - 47h
DX - EMM Handle

Register Contents on Exit:
AH - 00h if Successful, Error Code if Unsuccessful

Example:
```
;Save the page map for a device driver.
MOV    AH,47h
MOV    DX,DDHandle
INT    67h
```

RESTORE PAGE MAP (INTERRUPT 67h SERVICE 48h)

EMS 3.0

This service restores the previously saved contents of the expanded memory hardware page mapping registers. You can use this service with service 47h (Save Map Page) to save the memory registers before loading a TSR program, then restoring the map registers after the TSR program is finished. Programs that take advantage of the advanced capabilities of EMS version 4.0 should use services 4Eh or 4Fh. This service restores the mapping state for a 64 KByte page frame only. You must use service 47h to save page maps restored with this service.

Note: Although application programs may safely use this service, its purpose is to provide interrupt handler and device drivers a safe method of using EMS memory. The EMM handle always refers to the handle assigned to the device driver or interrupt handler during bootup. The EMM handle never refers to the handle owned by another program.

Register Contents on Entry:
AH - 48h
DX - EMM Handle

Register Contents on Exit:
AH - 00h if Successful, Error Code if Unsuccessful

Example:
```
;Restore the page map for a device driver.
MOV   AH,48h
MOV   DX,DDHandle
INT   67h
```

GET HANDLE COUNT (INTERRUPT 67h SERVICE 4Bh)

EMS 3.0

This service returns the number of active EMS pages, which can range from 0 to 255. If it returns a value of zero, none of the expanded memory is in use and the EMM is idle. The value returned does not reflect the number of programs using expanded memory. One program may obtain more than one handle.

Register Contents on Entry:
AH - 4Bh

Register Contents on Exit:
AH - 00h if Successful, Error Code if Unsuccessful
BX - Number of Active EMM Handles

Example:
```
;Get the number of active EMS handles.
MOV   AH,4Bh
INT   67h
```

GET HANDLE PAGES (INTERRUPT 67h SERVICE 4Ch)

EMS 3.0

This service returns the number of active EMS pages associated with a particular handle. This number can range from 1 to 512 for versions before LIM EMS 4.0. In addition, these versions of EMM may not have handles with zero pages. LIM 4.0 and above allows a range of 0 to 2,048 pages per handle.

Register Contents on Entry:
AH - 4Ch
DX - EMM Handle

Register Contents on Exit:
AH - 00h if Successful, Error Code if Unsuccessful
BX - Number of Active EMM Pages

Example:
```
;Get the number of pages assigned to handle 1.
MOV    AH,4Ch
MOV    DX,Handle1
INT    67h
```

GET HANDLES FOR ALL PAGES
(INTERRUPT 67h SERVICE 4Dh)

EMS 3.0

This service returns the number of active EMS pages associated with all EMM handles in an array. The maximum number of EMM handles is 256. This includes the operating system handle (0). Each handle uses a 32-bit array entry. The first word of the array entry contains the handle number. The second word of the array entry contains the number of pages associated with that handle.

Register Contents on Entry:
AH - 4Dh
DI - Offset of a 1024 Byte Buffer
ES - Segment of a 1024 Byte Buffer

Register Contents on Exit:
AH - 00h if Successful, Error Code if Unsuccessful
BX - Number of Active EMM Handles

Example:
```
;Get the number of pages associated with each handle
; in use.
MOV    AH,4Dh
LEA    DI,HandBuff
INT    67h
```

SAVE PAGE MAP
(INTERRUPT 67h SERVICE 4Eh FUNCTION 00h)

EMS 3.2

This service saves the current expanded memory hardware page mapping state in the specified buffer. Use interrupt 67h service 4Eh function 3 to determine the buffer size. The size and format of the buffer varies. This service does not require you to provide a handle to associate with the page map. You must use service 4Eh function 1 to restore the information placed in the buffer.

Register Contents on Entry:
AH - 4Eh
AL - 0

DI - Offset of Buffer
ES - Segment of Buffer

Register Contents on Exit:
AH - 00h if Successful, Error Code if Unsuccessful

Example:
```
; Save the page map.
MOV    AX,4E00h
LEA    DI,HandBuff
INT    67h
```

RESTORE PAGE MAP
(INTERRUPT 67h SERVICE 4Eh FUNCTION 01h)
EMS 3.2

This service restores the previously saved expanded memory hardware page mapping state. This service does not require you to provide a handle to associate with the page map. You must use service 4Eh function 0 or 2 to save the information placed in the buffer.

Register Contents on Entry:
AH - 4Eh
AL - 1
DI - Offset of Buffer
ES - Segment of Buffer

Register Contents on Exit:
AH - 00h if Successful, Error Code if Unsuccessful

Example:
```
; Restore a previously saved page state.
MOV    AX,4E01h
LEA    DI,HandBuff
INT    67h
```

SAVE AND RESTORE PAGE MAP
(INTERRUPT 67h SERVICE 4Eh FUNCTION 02h)
EMS 3.2

This service saves the current expanded memory hardware page mapping state in the specified buffer. It then sets the expanded memory page mapping state using information contained in a different buffer. Therefore, it performs the duties of both service 4Eh functions 0 and 1. Use interrupt 67h service 4Eh function 3 to determine the buffer size. The size and format of the buffer varies. This service does not require you provide a handle to associate with the page map. Use service 4Eh function 1 if you want to restore a previously saved page map without saving the current page map first.

Register Contents on Entry:
AH - 4Eh
AL - 2
SI   - Offset of Restore Buffer
DI   - Offset of Receiving Buffer
DS - Segment of Restore Buffer
ES - Segment of Receiving Buffer

Register Contents on Exit:
AH - 00h if Successful, Error Code if Unsuccessful

Example:
```
;Save the current page map, then restore a previously
; saved page map.
MOV    AX,4E02h
LEA    DI,HandBuff1
LEA    SI,HandBuff2
INT    67h
```

GET SIZE OF PAGE MAP INFORMATION (INTERRUPT 67h SERVICE 4Eh FUNCTION 03h)

EMS 3.2

This service returns the buffer size required to store the expanded memory hardware page mapping state.

Register Contents on Entry:
AH - 4Eh
AL - 3

Register Contents on Exit:
AH - 00h if Successful, Error Code if Unsuccessful
AL - Size of Buffer in Bytes

Example:
```
;Get the page map buffer size.
MOV    AX,4E03h
INT    67h
```

SAVE PARTIAL PAGE MAP (INTERRUPT 67h SERVICE 4Fh FUNCTION 00h)

EMS 4.0

This service saves a subset of the expanded memory page mapping registers in the specified buffer. The map list contains two word sets. The first word contains the number of mappable segments, followed by a list of the segment addresses of the mappable memory region. You must provide a one-word segment address for each mappable memory region. Use interrupt 67h service 4Fh function 2 to determine the size of the buffer required to store the partial page map.

Register Contents on Entry:
AH - 4Fh
AL - 0
SI - Offset of the Map List
DI - Offset of Receiving Buffer
DS - Segment of the Map List
ES - Segment of Receiving Buffer

Register Contents on Exit:
AH - 00h if Successful, Error Code if Unsuccessful

Example:
```
;Save a partial page map.
MOV    AX,4F00h
LDS    SI,MapList
LES    DI,MapBuffer
INT    67h
```

RESTORE PARTIAL PAGE MAP
(INTERRUPT 67h SERVICE 4Fh FUNCTION 01h)

EMS 4.0

This service restores a previously saved subset of the expanded memory page mapping registers. Use this service only after saving the subset of the expanded memory page mapping registers with function 00h (Save Partial Page Map).

Register Contents on Entry:
AH - 4Fh
AL - 1
SI - Offset of the Buffer
DS - Segment of the Buffer

Register Contents on Exit:
AH - 00h if Successful, Error Code if Unsuccessful

Example:
```
;Restore a saved partial page map.
MOV    AX,4F01h
LDS    SI,MapBuffer
INT    67h
```

GET SIZE OF PARTIAL PAGE MAP INFORMATION (INTERRUPT 67h SERVICE 4Fh FUNCTION 02h)

EMS 4.0

This service returns the memory requirement (in bytes) to store a subset of the expanded memory page mapping registers. Always make sure you create a buffer large enough to store the partial page map. Failure to do this will result in overwritten data or code. Often, a programmer creates a buffer large enough to store the entire page map instead of the partial page map. This is especially true if you intend to save and restore page maps of various sizes throughout the execution of a program.

Register Contents on Entry:
AH - 4Fh
AL - 2
BX - Number of Pages

Register Contents on Exit:
AH - 00h if Successful, Error Code if Unsuccessful
AL - Size of Array in Bytes

Example:
```
;Get the memory required to store 4 map pages.
MOV    AX,4F02h
MOV    BX,4
INT    67h
```

MAP MULTIPLE PAGES BY NUMBER (INTERRUPT 67h SERVICE 50h FUNCTION 00h)

EMS 4.0

This service maps one or more logical expanded memory pages onto physical pages accessible by the CPU. You reference the physical pages by number.

The buffer contains 32-bit entries. Use one entry for each page you want to map. The first word of each entry contains the logical expanded memory page. The second word contains the physical page number to which you want to map the logical expanded memory page. If you use a logical page number of -1, the physical page becomes inaccessible.

Register Contents on Entry:
AH - 50h
AL - 0
CX - Number of Pages to Map
DX - EMM Handle
SI - Offset of the Buffer
DS - Segment of the Buffer

Register Contents on Exit:
AH - 00h if Successful, Error Code if Unsuccessful

Example:
```
; Map 5 pages.
MOV    AX,5000h
MOV    CX,5
MOV    DX,EMMHandle
LDS    SI,EMMBuffer
INT    67h
```

MAP MULTIPLE PAGES BY ADDRESS (INTERRUPT 67h SERVICE 50h FUNCTION 01h)

EMS 4.0

This service maps one or more logical expanded memory pages onto physical pages accessible by the CPU. You reference the physical pages by segment address. Get the mappable segment address using interrupt 67h service 58h function 0.

The buffer contains 32-bit entries. Use one entry for each page you want to map. The first word of each entry contains the logical expanded memory page. The second word contains the physical page segment address to which you want to map the logical expanded memory page. If you use a logical page number of − 1, the physical page becomes inaccessible.

Register Contents on Entry:
AH - 50h
AL - 1
CX - Number of Pages to Map
DX - EMM Handle
SI - Offset of the Buffer
DS - Segment of the Buffer

Register Contents on Exit:
AH - 00h if Successful, Error Code if Unsuccessful

Example:
```
; Map 2 pages.
MOV    AX,5001h
MOV    CX,2
MOV    DX,EMMHandle
LDS    SI,EMMBuffer
INT    67h
```

REALLOCATE PAGES FOR HANDLE
(INTERRUPT 67h SERVICE 51h)

EMS 4.0

This service lets a program increase or decrease the number of pages allocated to an EMM handle. The size of the pages depends on whether the pages were allocated using service 43h (Allocate Handle and Pages) or 5Ah (Allocate Handle and Standard Pages).

If they were allocated using service 43h, the pages are 16K in size. If they were allocated with service 5Ah, the EMS software determines their size.

You can allocate zero pages to an EMS handle. The handle remains active and you can reallocate pages to it later. You must still use service 45h to deallocate the EMS handle.

Register Contents on Entry:
AX - 51h
BX - New Number of Pages
DX - EMM Handle

Register Contents on Exit:
AH - 00h if Successful, Error Code if Unsuccessful
BX - Logical Pages Owned by EMM Handle

Example:
```
;Allocate zero EMS pages to an EMM handle.
MOV    AX,5100h
MOV    BX,0
MOV    DX,EMMHandle
INT    67h
```

GET HANDLE ATTRIBUTE
(INTERRUPT 67h SERVICE 52h FUNCTION 00h)

EMS 4.0

This service gets the attribute of an EMM handle. The EMM maintains non-volatile handles and associated memory pages across a warm boot.

Register Contents on Entry:
AX - 52h
AL - 0
DX - EMM Handle

Register Contents on Exit:
AH - 00h if Successful, Error Code if Unsuccessful
AL - Attribute
    0 - Volatile
    1 - Non-Volatile

Example:
```
;Get the handle attribute of the operating system handle.
MOV    AX,5200h
MOV    DX,0
INT    67h
```

SET HANDLE ATTRIBUTE
(INTERRUPT 67h SERVICE 52h FUNCTION 01h)

EMS 4.0

This service sets the attribute of an EMM handle. The EMM maintains non-volatile handles and associated memory pages across a warm boot. If the EMS hardware does not support non-volatile pages, this service returns an error.

Register Contents on Entry:
AX - 52h
AL - 1
BL - Attribute
    0 - Volatile
    1 - Non-Volatile
DX - EMM Handle

Register Contents on Exit:
AH - 00h if Successful, Error Code if Unsuccessful

Example:
```
;Set the handle attribute of the operating system
; handle to non-volatile.
MOV    AX,5201h
MOV    BL,1
MOV    DX,0
INT    67h
```

GET ATTRIBUTE CAPABILITY
(INTERRUPT 67h SERVICE 52h FUNCTION 02h)

EMS 4.0

This service gets the attribute support capability of the EMM. The EMM maintains non-volatile handles and associated memory pages across a warm boot.

Register Contents on Entry:
AX - 52h
AL - 2

Register Contents on Exit:
AH - 00h if Successful, Error Code if Unsuccessful

AL - Attribute Capability
    0 - Only Volatile Handles Supported
    1 - Volatile and Non-Volatile Handles Supported

Example:

```
;Get the attribute capability of the EMM.
MOV    AX,5202h
INT    67h
```

GET HANDLE NAME
(INTERRUPT 67h SERVICE 53h FUNCTION 00h)

EMS 4.0

This service gets the eight-character name assigned to an EMM handle. The name length is always eight characters. You can assign a new name to the handle using interrupt 67h service 53 function 1. You need not use ASCII characters for the handle name.

Register Contents on Entry:
AH - 53h
AL - 0
DX - EMM Handle
DI - Offset of 8 Byte Buffer
ES - Segment of 8 Byte Buffer

Register Contents on Exit:
AH - 00h if Successful, Error Code if Unsuccessful

Example:

```
;Get the name of the operating system handle.
.DATA
EMMHandle    DW      0
EMMName DB       8 DUP (0)
.CODE
MOV    AX,5300h
MOV    DX,EMMHandle
LEA    DI,EMMName
INT    67h
```

SET HANDLE NAME
(INTERRUPT 67h SERVICE 53h FUNCTION 01h)

EMS 4.0

This service assigns an eight-character name to an EMM handle. The name length is always eight characters. You do not need to use ASCII characters for the handle name, but the name you supply must contain exactly eight characters. Pad the end of a name less than eight characters long with zeros. The EMS manager always initializes a handle name to eight zero bytes. It preserves the name of non-volatile handles across a warm boot.

Register Contents on Entry:
AH - 53h
AL - 1
DX - EMM Handle
DI - Offset of 8 Byte Name
ES - Segment of 8 Byte Name

Register Contents on Exit:
AH - 00h if Successful, Error Code if Unsuccessful

Example:

```
;Set the name of the operating system handle to OSHANDLE.
.DATA
EMMHandle       DW      0
EMMName DB      'OSHANDLE'
.CODE
MOV     AX,5301h
MOV     DX,EMMHandle
LEA     DI,EMMName
INT     67h
```

GET ALL HANDLE NAMES
(INTERRUPT 67h SERVICE 54h FUNCTION 00h)

EMS 4.0

This service gets the eight-character name assigned to all active EMM handles. The EMM allows a maximum of 255 handles. This function fills the buffer with a 10-byte entry for each active handle. The first two bytes of the buffer contain the handle number. The last eight bytes contain the handle name. The maximum size buffer required by this service is 2,550 bytes.

Register Contents on Entry:
AH - 53h
AL - 3
DI - Offset of a 2550 Byte Buffer
ES - Segment of a 2550 Byte Buffer

Register Contents on Exit:
AH - 00h if Successful, Error Code if Unsuccessful
AL - Number of Active Handles

Example:

```
;Get the names of all the EMM handles.
MOV     AX,5303h
LEA     DI,EMMNBuff
INT     67h
```

SEARCH FOR HANDLE NAME
(INTERRUPT 67h SERVICE 54h FUNCTION 01h)

EMS 4.0

This service searches for the EMM handle associated with an eight-character name.

> Register Contents on Entry:
> AH - 54h
> AL - 0
> DI - Offset of 8 Byte Name
> ES - Segment of 8 Byte Name
>
> Register Contents on Exit:
> AH - 00h if Successful, Error Code if Unsuccessful
> DX - EMM Handle

Example:

```
;Search for a specific EMM handle.
MOV    AX,5400h
LEA    DI,EMMName
INT    67h
```

GET TOTAL HANDLES
(INTERRUPT 67h SERVICE 54h FUNCTION 02h)

EMS 4.0

This service returns the total number of handles supported by the expanded memory manager (EMM). This includes the operating system handle (0).

> Register Contents on Entry:
> AH - 54h
> AL - 2
>
> Register Contents on Exit:
> AH - 00h if Successful, Error Code if Unsuccessful
> BX - Number of Handles

Example:

```
;Get the total number of handles.
MOV    AX,5402h
INT    67h
```

MAP PAGE NUMBERS AND JUMP
(INTERRUPT 67h SERVICE 55h FUNCTION 00h)

EMS 4.0

This service alters the method used to map expanded memory pages to physical page numbers, then jumps to the specified address. A request for zero pages with a valid far jump address results in a simple far jump. TABLE 15-1 contains a description of the buffer contents.

Table 15-1   Map Pages and Jump Buffer Format

Offset	Length	Contents
00h	4 Bytes	Far Pointer to Jump Target
04h	1 Byte	Number of Pages to Map Before Jump
05h	4 Bytes	Far Pointer to Map List

Register Contents on Entry:
AH - 55h
AL - 0
DX - EMM Handle
SI - Buffer Offset
DS - Buffer Segment

Register Contents on Exit:
AH - 00h if Successful, Error Code if Unsuccessful

Example:
```
;Map the page numbers for EMM handle number 1.
MOV    AX,5500h
MOV    DX,1
LDS    SI,EMMBuff
INT    67h
```

MAP PAGE SEGMENTS AND JUMP
(INTERRUPT 67h SERVICE 55h FUNCTION 01h)

EMS 4.0

This service alters the method used to map expanded memory pages to physical page segments, then jumps to the specified address. A request for zero pages with a valid far jump address results in a simple far jump. TABLE 15-1 contains a description of the buffer contents.

Register Contents on Entry:
AH - 55h
AL - 1
DX - EMM Handle

SI - Buffer Offset
DS - Buffer Segment

Register Contents on Exit:
AH - 00h if Successful, Error Code if Unsuccessful

Example:
```
;Map the page segments for EMM handle number 1.
MOV    AX,5501h
MOV    DX,1
LDS    SI,EMMBuff
INT    67h
```

MAP PAGE NUMBERS AND CALL (INTERRUPT 67h SERVICE 56h FUNCTION 00h)

EMS 4.0

This service alters the method used to map expanded memory pages to physical page numbers, then calls the specified address. When the EMM regains control, it again modifies the method used to map expanded memory pages to physical pages. A request for zero pages with a valid far jump address results in a simple far jump. TABLE 15-2 contains a descrip-

Table 15-2   Map Pages and Call Buffer Format

Offset	Length	Contents
00h	4 Bytes	Far Pointer to Call Target
04h	1 Byte	Number of Pages to Map Before Call
05h	4 Bytes	Far Pointer to List of Pages to Map Before Call
09h	1 Byte	Number of Pages to Map Before Return
0Ah	4 Bytes	Far Pointer to List of Pages to Map Before Return
0Eh	8 Bytes	Reserved (0)

tion of the buffer contents. This service requires extra stack space to save the mapping context. Use interrupt 67h service 56h function 2 to determine the amount of stack space required.

Register Contents on Entry:
AH - 56h

AL - 0
DX - EMM Handle
SI - Buffer Offset
DS - Buffer Segment

Register Contents on Exit:
AH - 00h if Successful, Error Code if Unsuccessful

Example:
```
;Map the page numbers for EMM handle number 1.
MOV    AX,5600h
MOV    DX,1
LDS    SI,EMMBuff
INT    67h
```

MAP PAGE SEGMENTS AND CALL
(INTERRUPT 67h SERVICE 56h FUNCTION 01h)

EMS 4.0

This service alters the method used to map expanded memory pages to physical page segments, then calls the specified address. When the EMM regains control, it again modifies the method used to map expanded memory pages to physical pages. A request for zero pages with a valid far jump address results in a simple far jump. TABLE 15-2 contains a description of the buffer contents. This service requires extra stack space to save the mapping context. Use interrupt 67h service 56h function 2 to determine the amount of stack space required.

Register Contents on Entry:
AH - 56h
AL - 1
DX - EMM Handle
SI - Buffer Offset
DS - Buffer Segment

Register Contents on Exit:
AH - 00h if Successful, Error Code if Unsuccessful

Example:
```
;Map the page segments for EMM handle number 1.
MOV    AX,5601h
MOV    DX,1
LDS    SI,EMMBuff
INT    67h
```

GET STACK SPACE FOR MAP PAGE AND CALL
(INTERRUPT 67h SERVICE 56h FUNCTION 02h)

EMS 4.0

This service returns the amount of stack space required by interrupt

67h service 56h functions 0 (Map Page Numbers and call) and 1 (Map Page Segments and Call).

Register Contents on Entry:
AH - 56h
AL - 2

Register Contents on Exit:
AH - 00h if Successful, Error Code if Unsuccessful
BX - Stack Space Required in Bytes

Example:
```
;Get the amount of stack space required for the Map
; Page Segments and Call service.
MOV    AX,5602h
INT    67h
```

MOVE MEMORY REGION
(INTERRUPT 67h SERVICE 57h FUNCTION 00h)

EMS 4.0

This service moves memory between conventional or expanded memory to any other memory location without disturbing the current expanded memory mapping context. TABLE 15-3 contains a description of the buffer contents.

Table 15-3   Move Memory Region Buffer Format

Offset	Length	Contents
00h	4 Bytes	Region in Bytes
04h	1 Byte	Source Memory Type (0 Conventional, 1 Expanded)
05h	2 Bytes	Source Memory Handle
07h	2 Bytes	Source Memory Offset
09h	2 Bytes	Source Memory Segment or Physical Page Number
0Bh	1 Byte	Destination Memory Type (0 Conventional, 1 Expanded)
0Ch	2 Bytes	Destination Memory Handle
0Eh	2 Bytes	Destination Memory Offset
10h	2 Bytes	Destination Memory Segment or Physical Page Number

You can specify a memory region length of zero bytes with this service. The maximum length of a move is 1 MByte. If you specify a length longer than one expanded memory page, the EMM uses the page required to supply or receive the data.

If the source and destination ranges overlap, the EMM moves data in such a manner that the destination range contains an intact copy of the original data. The EMM then returns a nonzero status.

Register Contents on Entry:
AH - 57h
AL - 0
SI - Offset of Buffer
DS - Segment of Buffer

Register Contents on Exit:
AH - 00h if Successful, Error Code if Unsuccessful

Example:
```
;Move the memory regions specified in EMMBuff.
MOV    AX,5700h
LDS    SI,EMMBuff
INT    67h
```

EXCHANGE MEMORY REGIONS (INTERRUPT 67h SERVICE 57h FUNCTION 01h)

EMS 4.0

This service exchanges memory between conventional or expanded memory locations without disturbing the current expanded memory mapping context. TABLE 15-3 contains a description of the buffer contents.

You can specify a memory region length of zero bytes with this service. The maximum length of a move is 1 MByte. If you specify a length longer than one expanded memory page, the EMM uses the page required to supply or receive the data.

If the source and destination ranges overlap, the EMM does not perform the exchange. It does return an error code.

Register Contents on Entry:
AH - 57h
AL - 1
SI - Offset of Buffer
DS - Segment of Buffer

Register Contents on Exit:
AH - 00h if Successful, Error Code if Unsuccessful

Example:
```
;Exchange the memory regions specified in EMMBuff.
MOV    AX,5701h
```

```
LDS   SI,EMMBuff
INT   67h
```

GET ADDRESSES OF MAPPABLE PAGES
(INTERRUPT 67h SERVICE 58h FUNCTION 00h)

EMS 4.0

This service obtains the segment base address and physical page number of each expandable memory page. Each entry uses one double-word entry. The first word contains the page segment base address. The second word contains the physical page number. You can determine the buffer size in bytes by multiplying the number of mappable pages (obtained using interrupt 67h service 58h function 1) by 4.

Register Contents on Entry:
AH - 58h
AL - 0
DI - Offset of Buffer
ES - Segment of Buffer

Register Contents on Exit:
AH - 00h if Successful, Error Code if Unsuccessful
CX - Number of Buffer Entries

Example:
```
;Get the addresses of the mappable pages listed in EMMBuff.
MOV   AX,5800h
LES   DI,EMMBuff
INT   67h
```

GET NUMBER OF MAPPABLE PAGES
(INTERRUPT 67h SERVICE 58h FUNCTION 01h)

EMS 4.0

This service returns the number of mappable pages.

Register Contents on Entry:
AH - 58h
AL - 1

Register Contents on Exit:
AH - 00h if Successful, Error Code if Unsuccessful
CX - Number of Mappable Physical Pages

Example:
```
;Get the total number of mappable pages.
MOV   AX,5801h
INT   67h
```

GET HARDWARE CONFIGURATION
(INTERRUPT 67h SERVICE 59h FUNCTION 00h)

EMS 4.0

This service retrieves the expanded memory hardware configuration. TABLE 15-4 contains a listing of the parameters returned in the buffer. Use

Table 15-4   EMS Hardware Configuration Parameters

Offset	Length	Contents
00h	2 Bytes	Size of Raw Expanded Memory in Paragraphs
02h	2 Bytes	Number of Alternate Register Sets
04h	2 Bytes	Size of Mapping Context Save Area in Bytes
06h	2 Bytes	Number of Register Sets Assignable to DMA Channels
08h	2 Bytes	DMA Operation Type 0 - DMA Usable With Alternate Register Sets 1 - Only One DMA Register Set Available

interrupt 67h service 4Eh function 3 to determine the memory required to store the buffer.

Note: This is an operating system-specific function. The operating system can refuse an application program access to its features.

Register Contents on Entry:
AH - 59h
AL - 0
DI - Offset of Buffer
ES - Segment of Buffer

Register Contents on Exit:
AH - 00h if Successful, Error Code if Unsuccessful

Example:
```
;Get the hardware configuration.
MOV    AX,5900h
LES    DI,EMMBuff
INT    67h
```

GET NUMBER OF RAW PAGES
(INTERRUPT 67h SERVICE 59h FUNCTION 01h)

EMS 4.0

This service obtains the total number of raw pages and the number of unallocated raw pages present in the system. Raw pages can contain more or less than 16 KBytes of data. This service returns the same value as interrupt 67h service 42h if the EMM does not support raw pages.

Register Contents on Entry:
AH - 59h
AL - 1

Register Contents on Exit:
AH - 00h if Successful, Error Code if Unsuccessful
BX - Unallocated Raw Pages
DX - Total Raw Pages

Example:
```
;Get the number of raw pages.
MOV    AH,5901h
INT    67h
```

ALLOCATE HANDLE AND STANDARD PAGES (INTERRUPT 67h SERVICE 5Ah FUNCTION 00h)

EMS 4.0

This service allocates an EMM handle and associated 16K pages. You can allocate zero pages with this service.

Register Contents on Entry:
AH - 5Ah
AL - 0
BX - Number of Pages

Register Contents on Exit:
AH - 00h if Successful, Error Code if Unsuccessful
DX - Handle

Example:
```
;Allocate 4 standard pages (64 KBytes).
MOV    AX,5A00h
MOV    BX,4
INT    67h
```

ALLOCATE HANDLE AND RAW PAGES (INTERRUPT 67h SERVICE 5Ah FUNCTION 01h)

EMS 4.0

This service allocates an EMM handle and associated raw pages. Raw pages can contain more or less than 16 KBytes of data. You may allocate zero pages with this service.

Register Contents on Entry:
AH - 5Ah
AL - 1
BX - Number of Pages

Register Contents on Exit:
AH - 00h if Successful, Error Code if Unsuccessful
DX - Handle

Example:
```
;Allocate 4 raw pages of 32 KBytes (128 KBytes).
MOV    AX,5A01h
MOV    BX,4
INT    67h
```

GET ALTERNATE MAP REGISTERS
(INTERRUPT 67h SERVICE 5Bh FUNCTION 00h)

EMS 4.0

This service returns the number of the active alternate register set. If no active alternate register set exists, it saves the state of the mapping registers in a buffer and returns the buffer address. You must specify the address of a save area using service 5Bh function 1 and initialize it with service 4Eh function 0 before using this service. If you fail to perform these two tasks, this service returns an address of zero and does not save the registers.

Note: This is an operating system-specific function. The operating system can refuse an application program access to its features.

Register Contents on Entry:
AH - 5Bh
AL - 0

Register Contents on Exit:
AH - 00h if Successful, Error Code if Unsuccessful
BL - Current Active Alternate Map Register Set if Active,
     0 if Not Active
DI - Offset of Alternate Map Register Set Buffer
ES - Segment of Alternate Map Register Set Buffer

Example:
```
;Get the alternate map registers.
MOV    AX,5B00h
INT    67h
```

SET ALTERNATE MAP REGISTERS
(INTERRUPT 67h SERVICE 5Bh FUNCTION 01h)

EMS 4.0

This service selects an alternate map register set. If hardware does not support alternate register sets, it restores the mapping state from the specified buffer. You must initialize the save area using service 4Eh function 0 before using this service.

Note: This is an operating system-specific function. The operating system can refuse an application program access to its features.

Register Contents on Entry:
AH - 5Bh
AL - 1
BL - Current Active Alternate Map Register Set if Active,
    0 if Not Active
DI - Offset of Alternate Map Register Set Buffer (if BL = 0)
ES - Segment of Alternate Map Register Set Buffer (if BL = 0)

Register Contents on Exit:
AH - 00h if Successful, Error Code if Unsuccessful

Example:
```
;Set the alternate map registers.
MOV    AX,5B01h
XOR    BL,BL
LES    DI,MapRBuff
INT    67h
```

GET SIZE OF ALTERNATE MAP REGISTER SAVE AREA
(INTERRUPT 67h SERVICE 5Bh FUNCTION 02h)

EMS 4.0

This service returns the amount of memory required by interrupt 67h service 5Bh functions 0 (Get Alternate Map Registers) and 1 (Set Alternate Map Registers).

Note: This is an operating system-specific function. The operating system can refuse an application program access to its features.

Register Contents on Entry:
AH - 5Bh
AL - 2

Register Contents on Exit:
AH - 00h if Successful, Error Code if Unsuccessful
DX - Size of Buffer in Bytes

Example:
```
;Get the size of the alternate map register save area.
```

```
MOV   AX,5B02h
INT   67h
```

ALLOCATE ALTERNATE MAP REGISTER SET (INTERRUPT 67h SERVICE 5Bh FUNCTION 03h)

EMS 4.0

This service allocates an alternate map register set for use with interrupt 67h service 5Bh functions 0 and 1. The device driver copies contents of the map register set into the newly allocated alternate map register set.

Note: This is an operating system-specific function. The operating system can refuse an application program access to its features.

Register Contents on Entry:
AH - 5Bh
AL - 3

Register Contents on Exit:
AH - 00h if Successful, Error Code if Unsuccessful
BL - Alternate Map Register Set if Successful,
    0 if No Alternate Sets Available.

Example:
```
;Allocate an alternate map register set.
MOV   AX,5B03h
INT   67h
```

DEALLOCATE ALTERNATE MAP REGISTER SET (INTERRUPT 67h SERVICE 5Bh FUNCTION 04h)

EMS 4.0

This service releases an alternate map register set allocated using interrupt 67h service 5Bh function 3 (Allocate Alternate Map Register Set). You cannot deallocate the current alternate map register set.

Note: This is an operating system-specific function. The operating system can refuse an application program access to its features.

Register Contents on Entry:
AH - 5Bh
AL - 4
BL - Alternate Map Register Set Number

Register Contents on Exit:
AH - 00h if Successful, Error Code if Unsuccessful

Example:
```
;Deallocate alternate map register set 2.
MOV   AX,5B04h
MOV   BL,2
INT   67h
```

ALLOCATE DMA REGISTER SET
(INTERRUPT 67h SERVICE 5Bh FUNCTION 05h)

EMS 4.0

This service allocates a DMA register set.

Note: This is an operating system-specific function. The operating system can refuse an application program access to its features.

Register Contents on Entry:
AH - 5Bh
AL - 5

Register Contents on Exit:
AH - 00h if Successful, Error Code if Unsuccessful
BL - DMA Register Set Number if Successful, 0
    if No DMA Sets Available

Example:
```
;Allocate a DMA register set.
MOV     AX,5B05h
INT     67h
```

ENABLE DMA ON ALTERNATE MAP REGISTER SET
(INTERRUPT 67h SERVICE 5Bh FUNCTION 06h)

EMS 4.0

This service associates a DMA channel with an alternate map register set. If you do not assign a DMA channel to an alternate map register set, the EMM maps DMA for that register set through the current register set. The EMM does not associate a DMA channel with alternate map register set zero.

Note: This is an operating system-specific function. The operating system can refuse an application program access to its features.

Register Contents on Entry:
AH - 5Bh
AL - 6
BL - Alternate Map Register Set Number
DL - DMA Channel Number

Register Contents on Exit:
AH - 00h if Successful, Error Code if Unsuccessful

Example:
```
;Associate DMA channel 2 with alternate map register
; set number 5.
MOV     AX,5B06h
MOV     BL,5
MOV     DL,2
INT     67h
```

DISABLE DMA ON ALTERNATE MAP REGISTER SET (INTERRUPT 67h SERVICE 5Bh FUNCTION 07h)

EMS 4.0

This service disables DMA accesses for all DMA channels associated with an alternate map register set.

Note: This is an operating system-specific function. The operating system can refuse an application program access to its features.

Register Contents on Entry:
AH - 5Bh
AL - 7
BL - Alternate Map Register Set Number

Register Contents on Exit:
AH - 00h if Successful, Error Code if Unsuccessful

Example:

```
;Disable all DMA access for alternate map register set 5.
MOV    AX,5B07h
MOV    BL,5
INT    67h
```

DEALLOCATE DMA REGISTER SET (INTERRUPT 67h SERVICE 5Bh FUNCTION 08h)

EMS 4.0

This service releases a DMA register set.

Note: This is an operating system-specific function. The operating system can refuse an application program access to its features.

Register Contents on Entry:
AH - 5Bh
AL - 8
BL - DMA Register Set Number

Register Contents on Exit:
AH - 00h if Successful, Error Code if Unsuccessful

Example:

```
;Release DMA register set number 1.
MOV    AX,5B08h
MOV    BL,1
INT    67h
```

PREPARE EXTENDED MEMORY MANAGER FOR WARM BOOT (INTERRUPT 67h SERVICE 5Ch)

EMS 4.0

This service prepares the expanded memory manager for a warm boot. It saves any non-volatile pages, alternate map register sets, current mapping context, and any other hardware dependencies normally initialized at start-up. However, this service cannot save expanded memory mapped below the DOS 640 KByte boundary. Therefore, an application that maps expanded memory below this boundary must trap all error conditions that could lead to an unexpected system reboot.

Register Contents on Entry:
AH - 5Ch

Register Contents on Exit:
AH - 00h if Successful, Error Code if Unsuccessful

Example:
```
;Prepare the system for a warm boot.
MOV   AH,5Ch
INT   67h
```

ENABLE EMM OPERATING SYSTEM FUNCTIONS (INTERRUPT 67h SERVICE 5Dh FUNCTION 00h)

EMS 4.0

This service enables operating system-specific EMM functions for use by other programs. The operating system always calls this function immediately after EMM initialization. This service returns an access key the first time the operating system calls it. All future calls to this service require that you supply the access key.

Note: This is an operating system-specific function. The operating system can refuse an application program access to its features.

Register Contents on Entry:
AH   - 5Dh
AL   - 0
BX:CX - Access Key (If Not First Call to Service)

Register Contents on Exit:
AH   - 00h if Successful, Error Code if Unsuccessful
BX:CX - Access Key (If First Call to Service)

DISABLE EMM OPERATING SYSTEM FUNCTIONS (INTERRUPT 67h SERVICE 5Dh FUNCTION 01h)

EMS 4.0

This service disables operating system specific EMM functions for use by other programs, allowing operating system-only access. The operating system always calls this function immediately after EMM initialization. This service returns an access key the first time the operating system calls it. All future calls to this service require that you supply the access key.

Note: This is an operating system-specific function. The operating system can refuse an application program access to its features.

Register Contents on Entry:
AH   - 5Dh
AL   - 1
BX:CX - Access Key (If Not First Call to Service)

Register Contents on Exit:
AH   - 00h if Successful, Error Code if Unsuccessful
BX:CX - Access Key (If First Call to Service)

RELEASE ACCESS KEY
(INTERRUPT 67h SERVICE 5Dh FUNCTION 02h)

EMS 4.0

This service releases the access key previously obtained by interrupt 67h service 5Dh functions 0 (Enable EMM Operating System Functions) and 1 (Disable EMM Operating System Functions). Releasing the access key has the same effect as initializing the EMM. The EMM returns to its initial start-up state. The operating system retrieves a new key the next time it calls interrupt 67h service 5Dh functions 0 or 1.

Note: This is an operating system-specific function. The operating system can refuse an application program access to its features.

Register Contents on Entry:
AH   - 5Dh
AL   - 2
BX:CX - Access Key

Register Contents on Exit:
AH   - 00h if Successful, Error Code if Unsuccessful

16
DOS Input/Output
Control Interrupts

This chapter discusses the DOS input/output control interrupt routines. It includes several undocumented services. Always test these undocumented services with the device you intend to support before using it in a program. Each function description contains the first DOS version to provide the service, the required register contents on routine entry, and a code fragment showing usage. TABLE 8-1 lists the interrupts in numeric order. Figure 16-1 shows an example of how to use these services.

The input/output control services provide you with the means to access and control both standard and non-standard input/output devices. For example, you could use these services to create a special device driver for a tape backup system without resorting to low-level or ROM routines. You can also change how DOS provides access to a device. For example, you could change output to a printer from ASCII to binary mode. This improves print speed because DOS does not monitor the character stream.

There are two types of devices handled by these services: character and block. A character device differs from a block device in the way it handles data. Character devices accept data one character at a time. For example, a printer is a character device. Block devices accept data one record at a time. A record always contains the same number of characters throughout a data transfer. Often, the record is also a function 2. For example, most floppy disk drives accept data in 512-byte blocks.

Note: These services provide support for a variety of environments including local devices, files, and networks. You may use functions 00h, 06h, and 07h with file handles. You may not use functions 00h through 08h for network devices. Failure to observe these limitations might result in unpredictable operation or damage to the device or files.

16-1A Assembly language program for Input/Output interrupt.

```
;******************************************************************************************************
;* Sample Program 23, DOS Input/Ouput Interrupt Demonstration   *
;* This program gets the BIOS parameter block (BPB) data for a disk drive and places it in a special    *
;* structure.  It then displays this information in a usable format.  To use this procedure type PROGRM23    *
;* <DRIVE LETTER>.  If you do not provide a drive letter, the program automatically assumes a value of  *
;* drive A.  You must have DOS version 3.0 or above to use this program.         *
;*                          *
;* Copyright 1989,1990 John Mueller & Wallace Wang - Tab Books*
;******************************************************************************************************
;


;******************************************************************************************************
;* Perform the program setup.               *
;******************************************************************************************************
;

.MODEL MEDIUM

.STACK  ; Use the defalt stack of 1024 bytes.


;******************************************************************************************************
;* Begin the data area.  Declare all variables.         *
;******************************************************************************************************
;

.DATA

LF      EQU     10
CR      EQU     13
StrEnd  EQU     36

;BPB is a special structure defining the information returned by
; interrupt 21h service 44h function 0Dh subfunction 60h.  BPBVar
; is a variable instance of the BPB structure.

BPB     STRUC
        SFunc   DB      0
        DType   DB      0
        DAttr   DW      0
        NumCyl  DW      0
        MType   DB      0
        ;Start of Device BPB Field.
        BPS     DW      0
        SPAU    DB      0
        ResSect DW      0
        NFats   DB      0
        RDirEnt DW      0
        TSect   DW      0
        MedDesc DB      0
        SectPFat        DW      0
        SectPTrk        DW      0
        NHeads  DW      0
```

```
        HSect   DQ      0
                DB      11 DUP (0)
        ;End of Device BPB Field.
        Track   DW      0
BPB     ENDS
BPBVar  BPB     <>


;MSG1 displays all the applicable parameters for drive A.  All
; subprocedures use these variables as a repository for character
; conversions of BPB table entries.
MSG1    DB      'Drive '
DLtr    DB      'A has the following parameters:',CR,LF,LF
        DB      'Type: '
DriveT  DB      24 DUP (' '),CR,LF,'Attributes: '
DAttrT  DB      65 DUP (' '),CR,LF,'Media Descriptor:   '
MTypeT  DB      4 DUP (' '),CR,LF,'Number of Cylinders: '
NCylsT  DB      4 DUP (' '),CR,LF,LF,'Track Layout:',CR,LF
        DB      'Bytes/Sector:                    '
BPST    DB      4 DUP (' '),CR,LF,'Sectors/Allocation Unit:       '
SPAUT   DB      4 DUP (' '),CR,LF,'Reserved Sectors:              '
RST     DB      4 DUP (' '),CR,LF,'Number of File Allocation Tables: '
FATS    DB      4 DUP (' '),CR,LF,'Root Directory Entry Maximum:   '
RDirEntT   DB   4 DUP (' '),CR,LF,'Total Sectors:              '
SectT   DB      8 DUP (' '),CR,LF,'Sectors/Track:          '
SPTT    DB      4 DUP (' '),CR,LF,'Sectors/FAT:            '
SPFT    DB      4 DUP (' '),CR,LF,'Number of Heads:        '
HeadsT  DB      4 DUP (' '),CR,LF,StrEnd


;These strings define the drive sizes recognized by DOS.

Drive1  DB      '320/360 KByte, 5.25-inch'
Drive2  DB      '1.2 MByte, 5.25-inch   '
Drive3  DB      '720 KByte, 3.5-inch    '
Drive4  DB      'Single-Density 8-inch  '
Drive5  DB      'Double-Density 8-inch  '
Drive6  DB      'Fixed Disk             '
Drive7  DB      'Tape Drive             '
Drive8  DB      'Other                  '
DriveE  DB      'ERROR IN GETTING TYPE!!',07


;These strings define the drive attributes recognized by DOS.

DAttr1  DB      'Removable Storage Medium   ',CR,LF
DAttr2  DB      'Nonremovable Storage Medium',CR,LF
DAttr3  DB      '            Door Lock Not Supported'
DAttr4  DB      '            Door Lock Supported    '


;************************************************************************************************
;* Begin the code segment.                           *
;************************************************************************************************
```

16-1A Continued.

```
.CODE

EXAMPLE PROC FAR

        MOV     AX,@DATA        ;Point DS to our data segment.
        MOV     DS,AX   ; Leave PSP address in ES.

;*********************************************************************************************
;* This part of the program performs four basic tasks related to determining the statistics for drive A.  The  *
;* first section uses the DOS Get Device Parameters routine of the Generic I/O Control for Block Devices      *
;* function.  The second section interprets the results of this interrupt.  The third section clears the      *
;* display.  And the fourth section displays the statistics.    *
;*********************************************************************************************
;
        MOV     AL,BYTE PTR ES:0082h    ;Get the drive letter.
        CMP     AL,'A'  ;Start of alphabet.
        JL      NoChar  ;No input drive.
        CMP     AL,'Z'  ;Upper case character.
        JL      UpCase
        CMP     AL,'a'  ;Start of lower case.
        JL      NoChar  ;No input drive.
        CMP     AL,'z'  ;End of lower case.
        JG      NoChar  ;No input drive.
        MOV     DLtr,AL ;Save the drive letter.
        SUB     AL,96   ;Convert to drive number.
        MOV     BL,AL   ;Move to BL then get info.
        JMP     FillBPB
UpCase: MOV     DLtr,AL ;Save the drive letter.
        SUB     AL,64   ;Convert to drive number.
        MOV     BL,AL   ;Move to BL then get info.
        JMP     FillBPB
NoChar: MOV     BL,1    ;Use default of drive A.
FillBPB:        MOV     AX,440Dh        ;Fill BPBVar with drive A
        MOV     CX,0860h        ; statistics.
        LEA     DX,BPBVar
        INT     21h

        MOV     AX,@DATA        ;Point ES to our data segment.
        MOV     ES,AX

        CALL    GetType ;Define disk type.
        CALL    GetAttr ;Define disk attributes.
        CALL    GetMType        ;Convert media type number.
        CALL    GetCyls ;Convert number of cylinders.
        CALL    GetTracks       ;Convert track field.

        MOV     AX,0619h        ;Clear the display.
        MOV     BH,7h
        XOR     CX,CX
        MOV     DX,1950h
```

```
          INT     10h

          MOV     AX,0200h        ;Set cursor position.
          XOR     BH,BH    ;Use page 0.
          XOR     DX,DX    ;Use coordinate 0,0.
          INT     10h

          MOV     AX,0900h        ;Display disk statistics.
          LEA     DX,MSG1
          INT     21h

Exit:     MOV     AX,4C00h
          INT     21h
          RET             ;Return.

EXAMPLE ENDP


;*******************************************************************************************************
;* This procedure determines the type drive listed in BPBVar and places a suitable text string in MSG1. *
;*******************************************************************************************************

GetType PROC    NEAR

          XOR     AH,AH    ;Load the drive type.
          MOV     AL,BPBVar.DType
          CMP     AX,0     ;See if 320/360 KB, 5.25-inch
          JNE     Type1    ;If not, check next type.
          LEA     SI,Drive1       ;Otherwise, load the string.
          LEA     DI,DriveT
          MOV     CX,24
          REP     MOVSB
          JMP     GTExit

Type1:    CMP     AX,1     ;See if 1.2 MB, 5.25-inch
          JNE     Type2    ;If not, check next type.
          LEA     SI,Drive2       ;Otherwise, load the string.
          LEA     DI,DriveT
          MOV     CX,24
          REP     MOVSB
          JMP     GTExit

Type2:    CMP     AX,2     ;See if 720 KB, 3.5-inch
          JNE     Type3    ;If not, check next type.
          LEA     SI,Drive3       ;Otherwise, load the string.
          LEA     DI,DriveT
          MOV     CX,24
          REP     MOVSB
          JMP     GTExit

Type3:    CMP     AX,3     ;See if Single Density, 8-inch
```

```
        JNE     Type4   ;If not, check next type.
        LEA     SI,Drive4       ;Otherwise, load the string.
        LEA     DI,DriveT
        MOV     CX,24
        REP     MOVSB
        JMP     GTExit


Type4:  CMP     AX,4    ;See if Double Density, 8-inch
        JNE     Type5   ;If not, check next type.
        LEA     SI,Drive5       ;Otherwise, load the string.
        LEA     DI,DriveT
        MOV     CX,24
        REP     MOVSB
        JMP     GTExit


Type5:  CMP     AX,5    ;See if Fixed Disk
        JNE     Type6   ;If not, check next type.
        LEA     SI,Drive6       ;Otherwise, load the string.
        LEA     DI,DriveT
        MOV     CX,24
        REP     MOVSB
        JMP     GTExit


Type6:  CMP     AX,6    ;See if Tape Drive
        JNE     Type7   ;If not, check next type.
        LEA     SI,Drive7       ;Otherwise, load the string.
        LEA     DI,DriveT
        MOV     CX,24
        REP     MOVSB
        JMP     GTExit


Type7:  CMP     AX,7    ;See if Other Type
        JNE     Type8   ;If not, error in type.
        LEA     SI,Drive8       ;Otherwise, load the string.
        LEA     DI,DriveT
        MOV     CX,24
        REP     MOVSB
        JMP     GTExit
Type8:  LEA     SI,DriveE       ;Load error message.
        LEA     DI,DriveT
        MOV     CX,24
        REP     MOVSB


GTExit: RET


GetType ENDP

;************************************************************************************************
;* This procedure takes the disk drive attribute word and bit tests the defined bit locations.  Each bit     *
;* defines a different drive attribute.  At present, only the first two bits contain relevant information.    *
;************************************************************************************************
;
```

```
GetAttr PROC    NEAR


        MOV     AX,BPBVar.DAttr ;Load the disk attributes.
        MOV     CX,1    ;Test for storage type.
        TEST    AX,CX
        JNZ     NRemov  ;If bits match, nonremovable.
        LEA     SI,DAttr1       ;Load attribute string.
        LEA     DI,DAttrT
        MOV     CX,29
        REP     MOVSB
        JMP     DoorType        ;Get next attribute.

NRemov: LEA     SI,DAttr2       ;Load attribute string.
        LEA     DI,DAttrT
        MOV     CX,29
        REP     MOVSB
        JMP     DoorType        ;Get next attribute.

DoorType:       MOV     CX,2    ;Test for door type.
        TEST    AX,CX
        JNZ     DLSupp  ;If bits match, door lock supported.
        LEA     SI,DAttr3       ;Load attribute string.
        MOV     CX,35
        REP     MOVSB
        JMP     Exit3   ;Exit routine.

DLSupp: LEA     SI,DAttr4       ;Load attribute string.
        MOV     CX,35
        REP     MOVSB

Exit3:  RET


GetAttr ENDP
```

;***
;* This procedure gets the media descriptor type for drive A. This number appears as a hex number in the BPB *
;* structure. All this procedure does is load the correct information and addresses. Procedure HexConv   *
;* performs the rest of the task.   *
;***

```
GetMType        PROC    NEAR

        XOR     AH,AH   ;Get the media descriptor number.
        MOV     AL,BPBVar.MType
        LEA     DI,MTypeT       ;Load the character storage
        ADD     DI,3    ; address and point to end.
        CALL    HexConv ;Convert number to characters

        RET


GetMType        ENDP
```

16-1A Continued.

```
;***************************************************************************************************
;* This procedure gets the number of cylinders supported by drive A.  This number appears as a hex number in    *
;* the BPB structure.  All this procedure does is load the correct information and addresses.  Procedure        *
;* HexConv performs the rest of the task.                     *
;***************************************************************************************************

GetCyls PROC    NEAR

        MOV     AX,BPBVar.NumCyl        ;Get the media descriptor number.
        LEA     DI,NCylsT       ;Load the character storage
        ADD     DI,3    ; address and point to end.
        CALL    HexConv ;Convert number to characters

        RET

GetCyls ENDP


;***************************************************************************************************
;* This procedure gets the track data supported by drive A.  This number appears as a hex number in the BPB    *
;* structure.  All this procedure does is load the correct information and addresses.  Procedure HexConv        *
;* performs the rest of the task.  However, since each parameter appears in a separate variable, this    *
;* procedure makes multiple calls to HexConv.                 *
;***************************************************************************************************

GetTracks       PROC    NEAR

        MOV     AX,BPBVar.BPS   ;Get the bytes/sector value.
        LEA     DI,BPST ;Load the character storage
        ADD     DI,3    ; address and point to end.
        CALL    HexConv ;Convert number to characters

        XOR     AH,AH   ;Get the sectors/allocation
        MOV     AL,BPBVar.SPAU  ; unit value.
        LEA     DI,SPAUT        ;Load the character storage
        ADD     DI,3    ; address and point to end.
        CALL    HexConv ;Convert number to characters

        MOV     AX,BPBVar.ResSect       ;Get the number of reserved sectors.
        LEA     DI,RST  ;Load the character storage
        ADD     DI,3    ; address and point to end.
        CALL    HexConv ;Convert number to characters

        XOR     AH,AH   ;Get the number of FATS.
        MOV     AL,BPBVar.NFats
        LEA     DI,FATS ;Load the character storage
        ADD     DI,3    ; address and point to end.
        CALL    HexConv ;Convert number to characters

        MOV     AX,BPBVar.RDirEnt       ;Get the maximum number of
                        ; root directory entries.
        LEA     DI,RDirEntT     ;Load the character storage
```

```
          ADD      DI,3     ; address and point to end.
          CALL     HexConv ;Convert number to characters
          MOV      AX,BPBVar.TSect ;Get the total number of sectors.
          LEA      DI,SectT        ;Load the character storage
          ADD      DI,7     ; address and point to end.
          CALL     HexConv ;Convert number to characters

          MOV      AX,BPBVar.SectPFat      ;Get the number of sectors per FAT.
          LEA      DI,SPFT ;Load the character storage
          ADD      DI,3     ; address and point to end.
          CALL     HexConv ;Convert number to characters

          MOV      AX,BPBVar.SectPTrk      ;Get the number of sectors per track.
          LEA      DI,SPTT ;Load the character storage
          ADD      DI,3     ; address and point to end.
          CALL     HexConv ;Convert number to characters

          MOV      AX,BPBVar.NHeads
          LEA      DI,HeadsT       ;Load the character storage
          ADD      DI,3     ; address and point to end.
          CALL     HexConv ;Convert number to characters

          RET

GetTracks      ENDP


;********************************************************************************************************
;
;* This procedure converts a hexidecimal number to a decimal character equivalent.  AX contains the number    *
;* to convert and DI the address of the end of a storage buffer on entry.  The procedure does not return a     *
;* value.                                            *
;********************************************************************************************************
;

HexConv PROC    NEAR

          MOV      CX,10   ;Load divisor.
DoDiv:    XOR      DX,DX   ;Clear DX.
          DIV      CX      ;Divide AX by 10
          ADD      DX,30h  ;Change remainder to char.
          MOV      [DI],DL ;Store the number.
          DEC      DI      ;Point to next number.
          CMP      AX,9    ;See if we need to divide.
          JG       DoDiv
          ADD      AX,30h  ;Change quotient to char.
          MOV      [DI],AL ;Store the number.

          RET

HexConv ENDP

END     EXAMPLE
```

16-1B BASIC language program for Input/Output interrupt.

```
REM Sample Program 23, DOS Input/Ouput Interrupt Demonstration
REM This program gets the BIOS parameter block (BPB) data for a disk drive and places it in a special
REM structure.  It then displays this information in a usable format.  To use this procedure type PROGRM23
REM <DRIVE LETTER>.  If you do not provide a drive letter, the program automatically assumes a value of
REM drive A.  You must have DOS version 3.0 or above to use this program.
REM
REM Copyright 1989,1990 John Mueller & Wallace Wang - Tab Books

' $INCLUDE: 'qbx.bi'

DEFINT A-Z
DIM InRegs AS RegTypeX
DIM OutRegs AS RegTypeX

TYPE BPB
   SFunc AS STRING * 1
   DType AS STRING * 1
   DAttr AS INTEGER
   NumCyl AS INTEGER
   MType AS STRING * 1
   BPS AS INTEGER
   SPAU AS STRING * 1
   ResSect AS INTEGER
   NFats AS STRING * 1
   RDirEnt AS INTEGER
   TSect AS INTEGER
   MedDesc AS STRING * 1
   SectPFat AS INTEGER
   SectPtrk AS INTEGER
   NHeads AS INTEGER
   HSect AS LONG
END TYPE

DIM SHARED BPBVar AS BPB

DECLARE SUB GetCyls (NCylsT)
DECLARE SUB GetType (DriveT$)
DECLARE SUB GetAttr (DAttrT1$, DAttrT2$)
DECLARE SUB GetMType (MType$)
DECLARE SUB GetTracks (BPS, SPAU$, ResSect, NFats$, RDirEnt, TSect, SectPtrk, SectPFat, NHeads)

' *****************************************

Msg1$ = "Drive "
Dltr$ = "A has the following parameters"
Msg2$ = "Type: "
Msg3$ = "Attributes: "
Msg4$ = "Media Descriptor:        "
Msg5$ = "Number of cylinders:      "
Msg6$ = "Track Layout:                "
Msg7$ = "Bytes/Sector:                "
```

```
Msg8$ = "Sectors/Allocation Unit:                "
Msg9$ = "Reserved Sectors:                        "
Msg10$ = "Number of File Allocation Tables:    "
Msg11$ = "Root Directory Entry Maximum:        "
Msg12$ = "Total Sectors:                        "
Msg13$ = "Sectors/Track:                        "
Msg14$ = "Sectors/FAT:                          "
Msg15$ = "Number of Heads:                      "

CLS
InRegs.bx = 1
InDrive$ = COMMAND$
IF (InDrive$ >= "A") AND (InDrive$ <= "Z") THEN
  InRegs.bx = ASC(InDrive$) - 64
END IF


InRegs.ax = &H440D
InRegs.cx = &H860
InRegs.dx = VARPTR(BPBVar)
InRegs.ds = VARSEG(BPBVar)
CALL InterruptX(&H21, InRegs, OutRegs)

CALL GetType(DriveT$)
CALL GetAttr(DAttrT1$, DAttrT2$)
CALL GetMType(MType$)
CALL GetCyls(NCylsT)
CALL GetTracks(BPS, SPAU$, ResSect, NFats$, RDirEnt, TSect, SectPtrk, SectPFat, NHeads)

PRINT Msg1$ + Dltr$
PRINT Msg2$ + " " + DriveT$
PRINT Msg3$ + " " + DAttrT1$
PRINT "   " + DAttrT2$
PRINT Msg4$ + MType$
PRINT Msg5$; NCylsT
PRINT
PRINT Msg6$
PRINT Msg7$; BPS
PRINT Msg8$; SPAU
PRINT Msg9$; ResSect
PRINT Msg10$; ASC(NFats$)
PRINT Msg11$; RDirEnt
PRINT Msg12$; TSect
PRINT Msg13$; SectPtrk
PRINT Msg14$; SectPFat
PRINT Msg15$; NHeads


SUB GetAttr (DAttrT1$, DAttrT2$)

  ' These strings define the drive attributes reocgnized by DOS.

  DAttr1$ = "Removable Storage Medium"
```

```
DAttr2$ = "Nonremovable Storage Medium"
DAttr3$ = "          Door Lock Not Supported"
DAttr4$ = "          Door Lock Supported"

SELECT CASE BPBVar.DAttr
CASE 0
  DAttrT1$ = DAttr1$
  DAttrT2$ = DAttr3$
CASE 1
  DAttrT1$ = DAttr2$
  DAttrT2$ = DAttr3$
CASE 2
  DAttrT1$ = DAttr1$
  DAttrT2$ = DAttr4$
CASE 3
  DAttrT1$ = DAttr2$
  DAttrT2$ = DAttr4$
END SELECT
END SUB


SUB GetCyls (NCylsT)
  NCylsT = BPBVar.NumCyl
END SUB


SUB GetMType (MType$)
  MType$ = BPBVar.MType
END SUB


SUB GetTracks (BPS, SPAU$, ResSect, NFats$, RDirEnt, TSect, SectPtrk, SectPFat, NHeads)
  BPS = BPBVar.BPS
  SPAU$ = BPBVar.SPAU
  ResSect = BPBVar.ResSect
  NFats$ = BPBVar.NFats
  RDirEnt = BPBVar.RDirEnt
  TSect = BPBVar.TSect
  SectPtrk = BPBVar.SectPtrk
  SectPFat = BPBVar.SectPFat
  NHeads = BPBVar.NHeads
END SUB


SUB GetType (DriveT$)
  ' These strings define the drive sizes recognized by DOS.

  Drive1$ = "320/360 KByte, 5.25-inch"
  Drive2$ = "1.2 MByte, 5.25-inch"
  Drive3$ = "720 KByte, 3.5-inch"
  Drive4$ = "Single-Density 8-inch"
  Drive5$ = "Double-Density 8-inch"
  Drive6$ = "Fixed disk"
  Drive7$ = "Tape drive"
  Drive8$ = "Other"
```

```
  DriveE$ = "ERROR IN GETTING TYPE!!"

  SELECT CASE ASC(BPBVar.DType)
    CASE 0
        DriveT$ = Drive1$
    CASE 1
        DriveT$ = Drive2$
    CASE 2
        DriveT$ = Drive3$
    CASE 3
        DriveT$ = Drive4$
    CASE 4
        DriveT$ = Drive5$
    CASE 5
        DriveT$ = Drive6$
    CASE 6
        DriveT$ = Drive7$
    CASE 7
        DriveT$ = Drive8$
    CASE ELSE
        DriveT$ = DriveE$
  END SELECT
END SUB
```

16-1C C language program for Input/Output interrupt.

```
/* Sample Program 23, DOS Input/Ouput Interrupt Demonstration
   This program gets the BIOS parameter block (BPB) data for a disk drive and places it in a special
   structure.  It then displays this information in a usable format.  To use this procedure type PROGRM23
   <DRIVE LETTER>.  If you do not provide a drive letter, the program automatically assumes a value of
   drive A.  You must have DOS version 3.0 or above to use this program.  Always compile this program
   using the /Zp option to pack the BPB structure.  Failure to use this option will result in a
   non-functional program since the compiler always word aligns integers.

   Copyright 1989,1990 John Mueller & Wallace Wang - Tab Books
*/

#include <dos.h>
#include <graph.h>
#include <stdio.h>
#include <stdlib.h>
#include <string.h>

/* Program Control and Execution Variables. */

char InDrive = " ";
union REGS inregs, outregs;

/* BPB is a special structure defining the information returned
   by interrupt 21h service 44h function 0Dh subfunction 60h.
```

16-1C Continued.

```
    BPBVar is a variable instance of the BPB structure.
*/

struct BPB {
            unsigned char SFunc;
            unsigned char DType;
            unsigned short DAttr;
            unsigned short NumCyl;
            unsigned char MType;
            unsigned short BPS;            /* Start of Device BPB Field */
            unsigned char SPAU;
            unsigned short ResSect;
            unsigned char NFats;
            unsigned short RDirEnt;
            unsigned short TSect;
            unsigned char MedDesc;
            unsigned short SectPFat;
            unsigned short SectPTrk;
            unsigned short NHeads;
            unsigned long HSect;
            unsigned char Reserved[10];        /* End of Device BPB Field */
            unsigned short Track;
         } BPBVar;

/* These messages display all the applicable parameters for the
   selected drive.  All subprocedures use these variables as a
   repository for character conversions of the BPB table entries.
*/

char *Msg1  = "Drive ";
char *DLtr  = "A has the following parameters:";
char *Msg2  = "Type: ";
char *Msg3  = "Attributes: ";
char *Msg4  = "Media Descriptor:     ";
char *Msg5  = "Number of Cylinders: ";
char *Msg6  = "Track Layout:         ";
char *Msg7  = "Bytes/Sector:                 ";
char *Msg8  = "Sectors/Allocation Unit:      ";
char *Msg9  = "Reserved Sectors:             ";
char *Msg10 = "Number of File Allocation Tables: ";
char *Msg11 = "Root Directory Entry Maximum:     ";
char *Msg12 = "Total Sectors:                ";
char *Msg13 = "Sectors/Track:              ";
char *Msg14 = "Sectors/FAT:                  ";
char *Msg15 = "Number of Heads:              ";
char *DriveT = "                        ";
char *DAttrT1 = "                           ";
char *DAttrT2 = "                                  ";
char *MTypeT  = "     ";
char *NCylsT  = "     ";
char *BPST    = "     ";
```

```
char *SPAUT    = "      ";
char *RST      = "      ";
char *FATS     = "      ";
char *RDirEntT = "      ";
char *SectT    = "         ";
char *SPTT     = "      ";
char *SPFT     = "      ";
char *HeadsT   = "      ";


/* These strings define the drive sizes recognized by DOS. */


char *Drive1 = "320/360 KByte, 5.25-inch";
char *Drive2 = "1.2 MByte, 5.25-inch    ";
char *Drive3 = "720 KByte, 3.5-inch     ";
char *Drive4 = "Single-Density 8-inch   ";
char *Drive5 = "Double-Density 8-inch   ";
char *Drive6 = "Fixed Disk              ";
char *Drive7 = "Tape Drive              ";
char *Drive8 = "Other                   ";
char *DriveE = "ERROR IN GETTING TYPE!! ";


/* These strings define the drive attributes recognized by DOS. */

char *DAttr1 = "Removable Storage Medium    ";
char *DAttr2 = "Nonremovable Storage Medium";
char *DAttr3 = "          Door Lock Not Supported";
char *DAttr4 = "          Door Lock Supported    ";

main(int argc, char *argv[10])
      {

      inregs.x.bx=1;                       /* Store number for drive A in BX. */


      InDrive = *argv[1];              /* Save the Drive Letter */
      if ((InDrive >= 'A' && InDrive <= 'Z') || (InDrive >= 'a' && InDrive <= 'z'))
      {
             InDrive = toupper(InDrive);    /* Convert InDrive to upper case. */
             DLtr[0] = InDrive;             /* If user input letter, replace display letter. */
             inregs.x.bx = InDrive;  /* Replace bx drive number. */
             inregs.x.bx = inregs.x.bx - 64;
      }

      inregs.x.ax = 0x440D;          /* Load service and function. */
      inregs.x.cx = 0x0860;          /* Load subfunction value. */
      inregs.x.dx = &BPBVar;         /* Load BIOS Parameter Block address. */
      intdos(&inregs,&outregs);              /* Perform interrupt. */

      GetType();                       /* Define disk type. */
      GetAttr();                       /* Define disk attributes. */
      GetMType();                      /* Convert media type number. */
      GetCyls();                       /* Convert number of cylinders. */
```

16-1C Continued.

```
    GetTracks();                              /* Convert track field. */

    _clearscreen(_GCLEARSCREEN);    /* Clear the Display. */

    printf("%s\n", argc);
    printf("%s%s\n\n", Msg1, DLtr); /* Display Disk Statistics */
    printf("%s%s\n", Msg2, DriveT);
    printf("%s%s\n%s\n", Msg3, DAttrT1, DAttrT2);
    printf("%s%s\n", Msg4, MTypeT);
    printf("%s%s\n\n", Msg5, NCylsT);
    printf("%s\n", Msg6);
    printf("%s%4s\n", Msg7, BPST);
    printf("%s%4s\n", Msg8, SPAUT);
    printf("%s%4s\n", Msg9, RST);
    printf("%s%4s\n", Msg10, FATS);
    printf("%s%4s\n", Msg11, RDirEntT);
    printf("%s%4s\n", Msg12, SectT);
    printf("%s%8s\n", Msg13, SPTT);
    printf("%s%4s\n", Msg14, SPFT);
    printf("%s%4s\n", Msg15, HeadsT);
    }


GetType()

/* This procedure determines the type drive listed in BPBVar and
   places a suitable text string in MSG1.  Each drive type uses a
   unique number that allows the use of a case statement.
*/

{

    switch (BPBVar.DType)
        {
        case 0:                          /* 320/360 KByte, 5.25-inch */
            strncpy(DriveT,Drive1,23);
            break;
        case 1:                          /* 1.2 MByte, 5.25-inch */
            strncpy(DriveT,Drive2,23);
            break;
        case 2:                          /* 720 KByte, 3.5-inch */
            strncpy(DriveT,Drive3,23);
            break;
        case 3:                          /* Single-Density, 8-inch */
            strncpy(DriveT,Drive4,23);
            break;
        case 4:                          /* Double Density, 8-inch */
            strncpy(DriveT,Drive5,23);
            break;
        case 5:                          /* Fixed Disk */
            strncpy(DriveT,Drive6,23);
            break;
```

```
                case 6:                        /* Tape Drive */
                        strncpy(DriveT,Drive7,23);
                        break;
                case 7:                        /* Other */
                        strncpy(DriveT,Drive8,23);
                        break;
                default:
                        strncpy(DriveT,DriveE,23);
                }
}


GetAttr()

/* This procedure takes the disk drive attribute word and bit
   tests the defined bit locations.  Each bit defines a different
   drive attribute.  At present, only the first two bits contain
   relevant information.  This allows use a simple switch
   statement to test the individual bit values.
*/

{
        switch (BPBVar.DAttr)
                {
                case 0:
                        strncpy(DAttrT1,DAttr1,27);
                        strncpy(DAttrT2,DAttr3,40);
                        break;
                case 1:
                        strncpy(DAttrT1,DAttr2,27);
                        strncpy(DAttrT2,DAttr3,40);
                        break;
                case 2:
                        strncpy(DAttrT1,DAttr1,27);
                        strncpy(DAttrT2,DAttr4,40);
                        break;
                case 3:
                        strncpy(DAttrT1,DAttr2,27);
                        strncpy(DAttrT2,DAttr4,40);
                }
}


GetMType()

/* This procedure gets the media descriptor type for drive A.
   This number appears as a hex number in the BPB structure.  All
   this procedure does is load the correct information and
   addresses.  Procedure itoa performs the rest of the task.
*/

{
```

16-1C   Continued.

```
        itoa(BPBVar.MType,MTypeT,10);

}

GetCyls()

/* This procedure gets the number of cylinders supported by drive
   A.  This number appears as a hex number in the BPB structure.
   All this procedure does is load the correct information and
   addresses.  Procedure itoa performs the rest of the task.
*/

{

        itoa(BPBVar.NumCyl,NCylsT,10);

}

GetTracks()

/* This procedure gets the track data supported by drive A.  This
   number appears as a hex number in the BPB structure.  All this
   procedure does is load the correct information and addresses.
   Procedure itoa performs the rest of the task.  However,
   since each parameter appears in a separate variable, this
   procedure makes multiple calls to itoa.
*/

{

        itoa(BPBVar.BPS, BPST, 10);              /* Bytes per Sector */
        itoa(BPBVar.SPAU, SPAUT, 10);       /* Sectors per Allocation Unit */
        itoa(BPBVar.ResSect, RST, 10);      /* Number of Reserved Sectors */
        itoa(BPBVar.NFats, FATS, 10);       /* Number of FATS */
        itoa(BPBVar.RDirEnt, RDirEntT, 10); /* Number of Root Directory Entries */
        itoa(BPBVar.TSect, SectT, 10);      /* Total Number of Sectors (Standard Volume) */
        itoa(BPBVar.SectPTrk, SPTT, 10);         /* Sectors per Track */
        itoa(BPBVar.SectPFat, SPFT, 10);         /* Sectors per FAT */
        itoa(BPBVar.NHeads, HeadsT, 10);         /* Number of Heads */

}
```

16-1D   Pascal program for Input/Output interrupt.

```
    PROGRAM Input_Output;

(* Sample Program 23, DOS Input/Output Interrupt Demonstration
   This program gets the BIOS parameter block (BPB) data for a disk
   drive and places it in an array. It then displays this information
   in a usable format. To use this program, type PROGRM23 <Drive Letter>.
   If you do not provide a drive letter, the program automatically assumes
```

a value of drive A. You must have DOS version 3.2 or above to use
this program.

Copyright 1989,1990 John Mueller & Wallace Wang - Tab Books
*)

```
USES
  Dos, Crt;
CONST
  ArrayLength = 45;

  Msg1  = 'Drive ';
  Dltr  = 'A has the following parameters:';
  Msg2  = 'Type: ';
  Msg3  = 'Attributes: ';
  Msg4  = 'Media Descriptor:        ';
  Msg5  = 'Number of cylinders:     ';
  Msg6  = 'Track Layout:               ';
  Msg7  = 'Bytes/Sector:               ';
  Msg8  = 'Sectors/Allocation Unit:    ';
  Msg9  = 'Reserved Sectors:           ';
  Msg10 = 'Number of File Allocation Tables: ';
  Msg11 = 'Root Directory Entry Maximum:    ';
  Msg12 = 'Total Sectors:              ';
  Msg13 = 'Sectors/Track:              ';
  Msg14 = 'Sectors/FAT:                ';
  Msg15 = 'Number of Heads:            ';

  (* These strings define the drive sizes recognized by DOS. *)

  Drive1 = '320/360 KByte, 5.25-inch';
  Drive2 = '1.2 MByte, 5.25-inch';
  Drive3 = '720 KByte, 3.5-inch';
  Drive4 = 'Single-Density 8-inch';
  Drive5 = 'Double-Density 8-inch';
  Drive6 = 'Fixed disk';
  Drive7 = 'Tape drive';
  Drive8 = 'Other';
  DriveE = 'ERROR IN GETTING TYPE!!';

  (* These strings define the drive attributes recognized by DOS. *)

  DAttr1 = 'Removable Storage Medium';
  DAttr2 = 'Nonremovable Storage Medium';
  DAttr3 = '            Door Lock Not Supported';
  DAttr4 = '            Door Lock Supported';
  (
TYPE
  BPB = RECORD
    SFunc  : char;      1
```

16-1D Continued.

```
   DType   : char;       2
   DAttr   : integer;    3,4
   NumCyl  : integer;    5,6
   MType   : char;       7
   BPS     : integer;    8,9
   SPAU    : char;       10
   ResSect : integer;    11,12
   NFats   : char;       13
   RDirEnt : integer;    14,15
   TSect   : integer;    16,17
   MedDesc : char;       18
   SectPFat: integer;    19,20
   SectPTrk: integer;    21,22
   NHeads  : integer;    23,24
   HSect   : longint;    25,26,27,28
   Reserved:string[10];  29,30,31,32,33,34,35,36,37,38
   Track   : integer;    39,40
 END;  (* RECORD *)
 }


VAR
  Regs : Registers;
  BPBVar : ARRAY [1..ArrayLength] OF Byte;
  InDrive, DriveT, DAttrT1, DAttrT2 : string;
  BPS, SPAU, ResSect, NFats, RDirEnt, TSect, SectPTrk, SectPFat,
    NHeads, MTypeT, NumCyl : integer;


PROCEDURE GetType;

(* This procedure determiens the type drive listed in BPBVar and
   places a suitable text string in MSG1. Each drive type uses a
   unique number that allows the use of a case statement. *)


BEGIN
  CASE BPBVar[2] OF
    0 : DriveT := Drive1;
    1 : DriveT := Drive2;
    2 : DriveT := Drive3;
    3 : DriveT := Drive4;
    4 : DriveT := Drive5;
    5 : DriveT := Drive6;
    6 : DriveT := Drive7;
    7 : DriveT := Drive8;
  ELSE
    DriveT := DriveE;
  END;  (* CASE *)
END;  (* GetType *)


PROCEDURE GetAttr;

(* This procedure takes the disk drive attribute word and bit
```

tests the defined bit locations. Each bit defines a different
drive attribute. At present, only the first two bits contain
relevant information. This allows use of a simple CASE
statement to test the individual bit values. *)

```
BEGIN
  CASE BPBVar[3] OF
    0 : BEGIN
          DAttrT1 := DAttr1;
          DAttrT2 := DAttr3;
        END;
    1 : BEGIN
          DAttrT1 := DAttr2;
          DAttrT2 := DAttr3;
        END;
    2 : BEGIN
          DAttrT1 := DAttr1;
          DAttrT2 := DAttr4;
        END;
    3 : BEGIN
          DAttrT1 := DAttr2;
          DAttrT2 := DAttr4;
        END;
  END;  (* CASE *)
END;  (* GetAttr *)


PROCEDURE GetMType;

(* This procedure gets the media descriptor type for drive A.
   This number appears as a hex number in the BPB structure. All
   this procedure does is load the correct information and addresses. *)


BEGIN
  MTypeT := BPBVar[7];
END;  (* GetMType *)


PROCEDURE GetCyls;

(* This procedure gets the number of cylinders supported by drive
   A. This number appears as a hex number in the BPB structure. All
   this procedure does is load the correct information and addresses. *)


BEGIN
  NumCyl := (BPBVar[6] * 256) + BPBVar[5];
END;  (* GetCyls *)


PROCEDURE GetTracks;

(* This procedure gets the track data supported by drive A.
   This number appears as a hex number in the BPB structure. All
```

16-1D Continued.

```
  this procedure does is load the correct information and
  addresses. *)

BEGIN
  BPS := (BPBVar[9] * 256) + BPBVar[8];
  SPAU := BPBVar[10];
  ResSect := (BPBVar[12] * 256) + BPBVar[11];
  NFats := BPBVar[13];
  RDirEnt := (BPBVar[15] * 256) + BPBVar[14];
  TSect := (BPBVar[17] * 256) + BPBVar[16];
  SectPTrk := (BPBVar[22] * 256) + BPBVar[21];
  SectPFat := (BPBVar[20] * 256) + BPBVar[19];
  NHeads := (BPBVar[24] * 256) + BPBVar[23];
END;  (* GetTracks *)

PROCEDURE InitArray;
VAR
  I : byte;
BEGIN
  FOR I := 1 to ArrayLength DO
    BPBVar[I] := 0;
END;

BEGIN
  ClrScr;
  InitArray;
  Regs.bx := 1;
  InDrive := ParamStr (1);
  IF ((InDrive >= 'A') AND (InDrive <= 'Z')) OR
     ((InDrive >= 'a') AND (InDrive <= 'z')) THEN
    BEGIN
      InDrive := UpCase (InDrive[1]);
      Regs.bx := Ord (InDrive[1]) - 64;
    END;
  Regs.ah := $44;
  Regs.al := $D;
  Regs.ch := $08;
  Regs.cl := $60;
  Regs.dx := Ofs (BPBVar);
  Regs.ds := Seg (BPBVar);
  MsDos (Regs);

  GetType;
  GetAttr;
  GetMType;
  GetCyls;
  GetTracks;
  ClrScr;

  Writeln (Msg1, ' ', DLtr);
  Writeln;
```

```
Writeln (Msg2, DriveT);
Writeln (Msg3, DAttrT1);
Writeln (DAttrT2);
Writeln (Msg4, MTypeT);
Writeln (Msg5, NumCyl);
Writeln;
Writeln (Msg6);
Writeln (Msg7, BPS);
Writeln (Msg8, SPAU);
Writeln (Msg9, ResSect);
Writeln (Msg10, NFats);
Writeln (Msg11, RDirEnt);
Writeln (Msg12, TSect);
Writeln (Msg13, SectPTrk);
Writeln (Msg14, SectPFat);
Writeln (Msg15, NHeads);
END.
```

IOCTL: GET DEVICE INFORMATION
(INTERRUPT 21h SERVICE 44h FUNCTION 0)

DOS 2.0

This service gets a device information word for the specified handle. TABLE 16-1 outlines the contents of the device information word. When you

Table 16-1   Device Information Word Format

Bit	Contents
For Files	
0 - 5	Drive Number (0 = A, 1 = B, etc.)
6	0 - File Has Been Written 1 - File Has Not Been Written
7	0 - Indicates File
8 - 15	Reserved
For Devices	
0	1 - Standard Input
1	1 - Standard Output
2	1 - NUL Device
3	1 - Clock Device

Table 16-1 Continued.

Bit	Contents
4	Reserved
5	0 - Handle in ASCII Mode 1 - Handle in Binary Mode
6	0 - End of File on Input
7	1 - Indicates Device
8 - 13	Reserved
14	0 - IOCTL Subfunctions 02h and 03h Supported 1 - IOCTL Subfunctions 02h and 03h Not Supported
15	Reserved

get device information for a device, the upper eight bits of DX correspond to the device driver attribute word.

If you use this service to get device information about a file, bit 5 tells you if DOS accessed the file in binary or ASCII mode. When DOS accesses a file in ASCII mode, it filters the character stream. If the character stream contains the characters Ctrl–C, Ctrl–S, Ctrl–P, Ctrl–Z, or carriage return, DOS processes the character rather than passing it to the application. DOs always treats all characters in a binary file as data.

Register Contents on Entry:
AH - 44h
AL - 0
BX - Handle

Register Contents on Exit:
AX - Error Code if Not Successful
DX - Device Information Word
CF - 0 if Successful, 1 if Not Successful

Example:
```
;Get device information
MOV   AH,44h
MOV   AL,0
MOV   BX,Handle
INT   21h
```

IOCTL: SET DEVICE INFORMATION (INTERRUPT 21h SERVICE 44h FUNCTION 1)

DOS 2.0

This service changes device settings associated with character devices. Do not use this function with a file handle. You must set the upper eight bits of DX to zero. Otherwise, this function does not change the device information. It returns with an error code of 0001h (invalid function) in AX. TABLE 16-2 outlines the device information word format.

Table 16-2   Device Information Word Output Format

Bit	Contents
0	1 - Standard Input
1	1 - Standard Output
2	1 - NUL Device
3	1 - Clock Device
4	Reserved (0)
5	0 - Select ASCII Mode 1 - Select Binary Mode
6	Reserved (0)
7	1 - Indicates Device
8 - 15	Reserved (0)

Bit 5 of the device information determines if DOS accesses the device in binary or ASCII mode. When DOS accesses a file in ASCII mode, it filters the character stream. If the character stream contains the characters Ctrl–C, Ctrl–S, Ctrl–P, Ctrl–Z, or carriage return, DOS processes the character rather than passing it to the application. DOS always treats all characters in a binary file as data.

Register Contents on Entry:
AH - 44h
AL - 1
BX - Handle
DX - Device Information Word

Example:
```
;Set device information
MOV    AH,44h
MOV    AL,1
MOV    BX,Handle
MOV    DX,WORD
INT    21h
```

IOCTL: READ CONTROL DATA FROM CHARACTER DEVICE DRIVER (INTERRUPT 21h SERVICE 44h FUNCTION 2)

DOS 2.0

This service reads device control data from a character device driver. The format and size of control data for each device varies because each device requires different control data. This function does not always retrieve input data from the physical device. When supported, this function also obtains hardware-dependent status and availability information. DOS might not provide a special service to get this information.

DOS does not require that character device drivers support this function. To determine if a device supports this function, test bit 14 of the device information word returned by function 00h. If the device driver does not support this function, DOS returns AX with error code 0001h (invalid function) and the carry flag set.

Register Contents on Entry:
AH - 44h
AL - 2
BX - Handle
CX - Number of Byte to Read
DX - Offset of Buffer
DS - Segment of Buffer

Register Contents on Exit:
AX - Bytes Read if Successful, Error Code if Not Successful
CF - 0 if Successful, 1 if Not Successful

Example:

```
; Read Control Data From Character Device Driver
MOV     AH,44h
MOV     AL,2
MOV     BX,Handle
MOV     CX,5        ;Number of byte to read
LDS     DX,BUFF
INT     21h
```

IOCTL: WRITE CONTROL DATA TO CHARACTER DEVICE DRIVER (INTERRUPT 21h SERVICE 44h FUNCTION 3)

DOS 2.0

This service writes device control data. The format and size of control data for each device varies because each device requires different control data. This function does not always result in output to the physical device. When supported, this function also requests hardware-dependent operations. It does this by setting parameters in the buffer. For example, you could set up the characteristics of a serial port or other hardware. DOS might not provide a special service to set these characteristics.

DOS does not require that character device drivers support this function. To determine if a device supports this function, test bit 14 of the device information word returned by function 00h. If the device driver does not support this function, DOS returns AX with error code 0001h (invalid function) and the carry flag set.

Register Contents on Entry:
AH - 44h
AL - 3
BX - Handle
CX - Number of Byte to Transfer
DX - Offset of Buffer
DS - Segment of Buffer

Register Contents on Exit:
AX - Bytes Transferred if Successful, Error Code if Not Successful
CF - 0 if Successful, 1 if Not Successful

IOCTL: READ CONTROL DATA FROM BLOCK DEVICE DRIVER (INTERRUPT 21h SERVICE 44h FUNCTION 4)

DOS 2.0

This service inputs block device control data directly to an application program buffer. The format and size of this data changes from driver to driver because each device requires different control data. This function does not always result in input to the application program. When supported, this function also obtains hardware-dependent status and availability information. DOS might not provide a special service to get this information.

DOS does not require that block device drivers support this function. To determine if a device supports this function, test bit 14 of the device information word returned by function 00h. Unfortunately, not all block devices report this status accurately. If the device driver does not support this function, DOS returns AX with error code 0001h (invalid function) and the carry flag set.

Register Contents on Entry:
AH - 44h
AL - 4
Bl - Drive Code (0 = Default, 1 = A, 2 = B, etc.)
CX - Number of Bytes to Transfer
DX - Offset of Buffer
DS - Segment of Buffer

Register Contents on Exit:

AX - Bytes Transferred if Successful, Error Code if Not Successful
CF - 0 if Successful, 1 if Not Successful

Example:
```
;Read Control Data From Block Device Driver
MOV   AH,44h
MOV   AL,3
MOV   BX,Handle
MOV   CX,256        ;Number of bytes to transfer
LDS   DX,BUFF
INT   21h
```

IOCTL: WRITE CONTROL DATA TO BLOCK DEVICE DRIVER (INTERRUPT 21h SERVICE 44h FUNCTION 5)

DOS 2.0

This service outputs block device control data directly from an application program buffer to a device. The format and size of this data changes from application to application because each device requires different control data. This function does not always result in output to the block device driver. When supported, this function also requests hardware-dependent operations. It does this by setting parameters in the buffer. For example, you could tell a tape drive to rewind or change the interface characteristics of a hard drive. DOS might not provide a special service to set these characteristics.

DOS does not require that block device drivers support this function. To determine if a device supports this function, test bit 14 of the device information word returned by function 00h. Unfortunately, not all block devices report this status accurately. If the device driver does not support this function, DOS returns AX with error code 0001h (invalid function) and the carry flag set.

Register Contents on Entry:
AH - 44h
AL - 5
BL - Drive Code (0 = Default, 1 = A, 2 = B, etc.)
CX - Number of Bytes to Transfer
DX - Offset of Buffer
DS - Segment of Buffer

Register Contents on Exit:
AX - Bytes Transferred if Successful, Error Code if Not Successful
CF - 0 if Successful, 1 if Not Successful

IOCTL: CHECK INPUT STATUS (INTERRUPT 21h SERVICE 44h FUNCTION 6)

DOS 2.0

This function checks if a device or file is ready for input. You can use this function to determine the ready state of the device. For example, because DOS does not provide the means to check the status of the serial port, you could use this function to check it.

Register Contents on Entry:
AH - 44h
AL - 6
BX - Handle

Register Contents on Exit:
AL - Status if Successful
    00h if Device Not Ready or File Pointer at EOF
    FFh if Device Ready or File Pointer Not at EOF
AX - Error Code if Not Successful
CF - 0 if Successful, 1 if Not Successful

Example:
```
;Write Control Data To Block Device Driver
MOV    AH,44h
MOV    AL,6
MOV    BX,Handle
INT    21h
```

IOCTL: CHECK OUTPUT STATUS
(INTERRUPT 21h SERVICE 44h FUNCTION 7)

DOS 2.0

This function checks if a device is ready for output. Never use this function to check the ready state of a device. If you use this function with the handle for a file, it always returns a ready status. It does not check for drive errors or full disks.

Register Contents on Entry:
AH - 44h
AL - 7
BX - Handle

Register Contents on Exit:
AL - Status if Successful
    00h if Device Not Ready
    FFh if Device Ready
AX - Error Code if Not Successful
CF - 0 if Successful, 1 if Not Successful

Example:
```
;Check Output Status
MOV    AH,44h
MOV    AL,7
```

```
MOV    BX,Handle
INT    21h
```

IOCTL: CHECK IF BLOCK DEVICE IS REMOVABLE (INTERRUPT 21h SERVICE 44h FUNCTION 8)

DOS 3.0

This service checks if the block device contains a removable storage medium. One way to use this function is to check for the existence of a floppy in a disk drive. Using this service, you could detect disk changes during a backup or installation routine. Never use this function on a network drive.

DOS does not require that block device drivers support this function. To determine if a device supports this function, test bit 14 of the device information word returned by function 00h. Unfortunately, not all block devices report this status accurately. If the device driver does not support this function, DOS returns AX with error code 0001h (invalid function) and the carry flag set.

Register Contents on Entry:
AH - 44h
AL - 8
BL - Drive Code (0 = Default, 1 = A, 2 = B, etc.)

Register Contents on Exit:
AL - Status if Successful
    0 - Medium Removable
    1 - Medium Not Removable
AX - Error Code if Not Successful
CF - 0 if Successful, 1 if Not Successful

Example:
```
;Check If Block Device is Removable
MOV    AH,44h
MOV    AL,8
MOV    BL,1        ;Drive A
INT    21h
```

IOCTL: CHECK IF BLOCK DEVICE IS REMOTE (INTERRUPT 21h SERVICE 44h FUNCTION 9)

DOS 3.1

This service checks if the block device resides at the computer running the program or redirected to a network server. You could use this service to aid in error detection. However, avoid using it to determine the location of a device. An application program should treat reads and writes to both local and remote devices as the same. The network software provides the services required to redirect output to the proper location.

Register Contents on Entry:
AH - 44h
AL - 9
BL - Drive Code (0 = Default, 1 = A, 2 = B, etc.)

Register Contents on Exit:
AX - Error Code if Not Successful
DX - Device Attribute Bit 12
    0 - Drive is Local
    1 - Drive is Remote
CF - 0 if Successful, 1 if Not Successful

Example:

```
;Check If Block Device Is Remote
MOV    AH,44h
MOV    AL,9
MOV    BL,1        ;Drive A
INT    21h
```

IOCTL: CHECK IF HANDLE IS REMOTE (INTERRUPT 21h SERVICE 44h FUNCTION Ah)

DOS 3.1

This service checks if the handle refers to a file or device that resides at the computer running the program, or redirected to a network server. You could use this service to aid in error detection. However, avoid using it to determine the location of a file. An application program should treat reads and writes to both local and remote devices as the same. The network software provides the services required to redirect output to the proper location. This service always returns an error if a network connection does not exist on the computer. It returns with carry flag set. AX contains 0001h (invalid function).

Register Contents on Entry:
AH - 44h
AL - Ah
BX - Handle

Register Contents on Exit:
AX - Error Code if Not Successful
DX - Device Attribute Bit 15
    0 - Drive is Local
    1 - Drive is Remote
CF - 0 if Successful, 1 if Not Successful

Example:
```
;Check if Handle Is Remote
MOV    AH,44h
MOV    AL,Ah
MOV    BX,Handle
INT    21h
```

IOCTL: CHANGE SHARING RETRY COUNT (INTERRUPT 21h SERVICE 44h FUNCTION Bh)

DOS 3.1

This service sets the number of times DOS retries a disk operation caused by a file-sharing violation failure before it returns an error to the requesting process. You must load SHARE to use this function.

Note: Avoid using this service on any machine other than the file server. It affects the operation of the entire network, not the local machine. Always restore the default sharing retry count before a program ends.

Register Contents on Entry:
AH - 44h
AL - Bh
CX - Delays per Retry (Default = 1)
DX - Number of Retries (Default = 7)

Register Contents on Exit:
AX - Error Code if Not Successful
CF - 0 if Successful, 1 if Not Successful

Example:
```
;Change Sharing Retry Count
MOV    AH,44h
MOV    AL,Bh
MOV    CX,1
MOV    DX,7
INT    21h
```

IOCTL: GENERIC I/O CONTROL FOR CHARACTER DEVICES (INTERRUPT 21h SERVICE 44H FUNCTION Ch)

DOS 3.2

This service provides a general purpose communications manager between application programs and character devices. TABLE 16-3 contains a listing of parameter block formats for various function codes.

Register Contents on Entry:
AH - 44h
AL - Ch

Table 16-3   Character Device Parameter Block Formats

Size	Contents	Description
45h and 65h		
Word	?	Printer Iteration Count
4Ah and 6Ah DOS 3.3 and 4.0		
Word	2	Length of Following Data
Word	?	Code Page ID
4Ah and 6Ah DOS 4.0 - DBCS Lead Byte Table		
Word	?	Use This Equation (N + 2) * 2 + 1 to Determine the Length of Following Data
Word	?	Code Page ID
Byte	Strt,End	DBCS Lead Byte Range 1
.		
.		
.		
Byte	Strt,End	DBCS Lead Byte Range N
Byte	0,0	
4Ch		
Word	0	Font Type Bit 0
		0 - Downloaded
		1 - Cartridge
Word	?	Use This Equation (N + 1) * 2 to Determine the Length of Following Data
Word	N	Number of Code Pages in Following List
Word	?	Code Page 1
.		
.		
.		
Word	?	Code Page N
4Dh		
Word	2	Length of Following Data
Word	0	Reserved
5Fh and 7Fh		
Byte	0	Level
Byte	0	Reserved
Word	14	Length of Following Data
Word	?	Control Flags (Bit 0)
		0 - Intensity
		1 - Blink

Table 16-3   Continued.

Size	Contents	Description
Byte	?	Mode Type (1 = Text, 2 = APA)
Byte	0	Reserved
Word	?	Colors
		0 - Monochrome
		1 - 2 Colors
		2 - 4 Colors
		4 - 16 Colors
		8 - 256 Colors
Word	?	Pixel Columns
Word	?	Pixel Rows
Word	?	Character Columns
Word	?	Character Rows
6Bh		
Word	?	Use This Equation (N + M + 2) * 2 to Determine the Length of Following Da
Word	N	Number of Hardware Code Pages
Word	?	Hardware Code Page 1
.		
.		
.		
Word	?	Hardware Code Page N
Word	M	Number of Prepared Code Pages
Word	?	Prepared Code Page 1
.		
.		
.		
Word	?	Prepared Code Page M

BX - Handle

CH - Category Code:

    00h - Unknown

    01h - COM1, COM2, COM3, or COM4

    03h - CON

    05h - LPT1, LPT2, or LPT3

CL - Function Code

    45h - Set Iteration

    4Ah - Select Code Page

    4Ch - Start Code Page Preparation

    4Dh - End Code Page Preparation

    5Fh - Set Display Information

    65h - Get Iteration Count

    6Ah - Query Selected Code Page

    6Bh - Query Prepare

    7Fh - Get Display Information

DX - Offset of Parameter Block
DS - Segment of Parameter Block

Register Contents on Exit:
AX - Error Code if Not Successful
DX - Offset of Parameter Block (CL = 65h, 6Ah, 6Bh, or 7Fh)
DS - Segment of Parameter Block (CL = 65h, 6Ah, 6Bh, or 7Fh)
CF - 0 if Successful, 1 if Not Successful

Example:
```
;Generic I/O Control For Character Devices
MOV    AH,44h
MOV    AL,Ch
MOV    BX,Handle
MOV    CH,03h
MOV    CL,5Fh
LDS    DX,BUFF
INT    21h
```

IOCTL: GENERIC I/O CONTROL FOR BLOCK DEVICES (INTERRUPT 21h SERVICE 44h FUNCTION Dh)

DOS 3.2

This service provides a general purpose communications medium between an application program and a block write device. TABLE 16-4 contains a listing of parameter block formats for various function codes.

Table 16-4   Block Device Parameter Block Formats

Byte	Bit	Description
40h and 60h		
00h	0	0 - Device BPB Field Contains a New Default BPB
		1 - Use Current BPB
	1	0 - Use All Fields in Parameter Block
		1 - Use Only Track Field Layout
	2	0 - Sectors in Track May Be Different Sizes
		1 - Sectors in Track Are All The Same Size; Sector Numbers Range From 1 to The Maximum Number of Sectors
	3 - 7	Reserved
01h		Device Type
		0 - 320/360 KB, 5.25-inch Disk
		1 - 1.2 MB, 5.25-inch Disk
		2 - 720 KB, 3.5-inch Disk
		3 - Single Density, 8-inch Disk
		4 - Double Density, 8-inch Disk
		5 - Fixed Disk

Table 16-4   Continued.

Byte	Bit	Description
		6 - Tape Drive
		7 - Other Type of Block Device
02h	0	0 - Removable Storage Medium
		1 - Non-Removable Storage Medium
	1	0 - Door Lock Not Supported
		1 - Door Lock Supported
	2 - 15	Reserved
04h		Number of Cylinders
06h		Media Type
		0 - 1.2 MB, 5.25-inch Disk
		1 - 320/360 KB, 5.25-inch Disk
07h		Device BPB
07h-08h		Bytes per Sector
09h		Sectors per Cluster
0Ah-0Bh		Reserved Sectors
0Ch		Number of File Allocation Tables
0Dh-0Eh		Maximum Number of Root Directory Entries
0Fh-10h		Number of Sectors
11h		Media Descriptor
12h-13h		Sectors per FAT
14h-15h		Sectors per Track
16h-17h		Number of Heads
18h-1Bh		Number of Hidden Sectors
1Ch-1Fh		Large Number of Sectors (if Bytes 08h-09h = 0)
20h-25h		Reserved
26h		Varible Length Table
26h-27h		Number of Sectors in Track
28h-29h		Number of First Sector in Track
2Ah-2Bh		Size of First Sector in Track

.
.
.

Table 16-4   Continued.

Byte	Bit	Description
NN		Number of Last Sector in Track
MM		Size of Last Sector in Track
41h and 61h		
00h		Special-Functions Field (Set to 0)
01h-02h		Head
03h-04h		Cylinder
05h-06h		Starting Sector
07h-08h		Sectors to Transfer
09h-0Ch		Transfer Buffer Address
42h and 62h		
00h		Special-Functions Field
	0	0 - Format/Verify Track
		1 - Format Status Call (DOS 4.0 Only)
	1 - 7	Reserved
01h-02h		Head
03h-04h		Cylinder
47h and 67h		
00h		Special-Functions Field (Set to 0)
01h		Disk Access Flag

Register Contents on Entry:
AH - 44h
AL - Dh
BL - Drive Code (0 = Default, 1 = A, 2 = B, etc.)
CH - 8 (Category Code = Disk Drive)
Cl - Function Code
    40h - Set Device Parameters
    41h - Write Track
    42h - Format and Verify Track
    47h - Set Access Flag
    60h - Get Device Parameters
    61h - Read Track
    62h - Verify Track
    67h - Get Access Flag

Register Contents on Exit:
AX - Error Code if Not Successful
DX - Offset of Parameter Block (CL = 60h or 61h)
DS - Segment of Parameter Block (CL = 60h or 61h)
CF - 0 if Successful, 1 if Not Successful

Example:

```
;Generic I/O Control For Block Devices
MOV    AH,44h
MOV    AL,Dh
MOV    BL,2        ;Drive B
MOV    CH,8
MOV    CL,62h      ;Verify track
INT    21h
```

IOCTL: GET LOGICAL DRIVE MAP
(INTERRUPT 21h SERVICE 44h FUNCTION Eh)

DOS 3.2

This service returns the logical drive code most recently used to access the specified block device. If you do not assign a logical drive code to a drive using function 0Fh, then the logical and physical drive codes are the same.

Register Contents on Entry:
AH - 44h
AL - Eh
BL - Drive Code (0 = Default, 1 = A, 2 = B, etc.)

Register Contents on Exit:
AL - Drive (if Successful)
    00h - Only One Logical Drive Code Assigned to Block Device
    01h through 1Ah - Logical Drive Number (1 = A, 2 = B, etc.)
                Mapped to Block Device
AX - Error Code if Not Successful
CF - 0 if Successful, 1 if Not Successful

Example:

```
;Get Logical Drive Map
MOV    AH,44h
MOV    AL,Eh
MOV    BL,2        ;Drive B
INT    21h
```

IOCTL: SET LOGICAL DRIVE MAP
(INTERRUPT 21h SERVICE 44h FUNCTION Fh)

DOS 3.2

This service sets the next logical drive used to access a block device. If a physical drive contains more than one logical drive, use this service to inform the drive device driver which logical drive you intend to access next.

Register Contents on Entry:
AH - 44h
AL - Fh
BL - Drive Code (0 = Default, 1 = A, 2 = B, etc.

Register Contents on Exit:
AL - Drive (if Successful)
    00h - Only One Logical Drive Code Assigned to Block Device
    01h through 1Ah - Logical Drive Number (1 = A, 2 = B, etc.)
          Mapped to Block Device
AX - Error Code if Not Successful
CF - 0 if Successful, 1 if Not Successful

Example:
```
;Set Logical Drive Map
MOV    AH,44h
MOV    AL,Fh
MOV    BL,2        ;Drive B
INT    21h
```

17

DOS Miscellaneous Interrupts

This chapter discusses the DOS miscellaneous interrupt routines. These services provide access to housekeeping or other functions like time and date. This chapter includes an undocumented service. Always test this service with your application, version of DOS, and machine configuration before using it. Each interrupt description contains the first DOS version to provide the service, the required register contents on routine entry, and a code fragment showing usage. TABLE 8-1 lists the interrupts in numeric order. Figure 17-1 shows you how to use some of the DOS miscellaneous services.

GET DATE (INTERRUPT 21h SERVICE 2Ah)

DOS 1.0

This service gets the system date from the DOS internal clock, NOT from the real-time clock/calendar if one exists. The registers contain the same information required to use service 2Bh. You can use this function with service 2Bh to find information about an arbitrary date. For example, you could find the day of week.

Register Contents on Entry:
AH - 2Ah

Register Contents on Exit:
CX - Year (1980 - 2099)
DH - Month (1 - 12)
DL - Day (1 - 31)
AL - Day of Week (0 = Sunday, 1 = Monday, etc.)

17-1A Assembly language program for miscellaneous interrupts.

```
;******************************************************************************************************
;* Sample Program 24, DOS Miscellaneous Interrupt Demonstration *
;* This program shows you how to use the DOS miscellaneous service interrupts to display the system time        *
;* and date.  You do not need any special equipment to use this program.        *
;*                                *
;* Copyright 1989 John Mueller & Wallace Wang - Tab Books *
;******************************************************************************************************


;******************************************************************************************************
;* Perform the program setup.                    *
;******************************************************************************************************

.MODEL MEDIUM    ; Use a medum model size.

.STACK  ; Use the defalt stack of 1024 bytes.

;******************************************************************************************************
;* Begin the data area.  Declare all variables.           *
;******************************************************************************************************
.DATA

;Standard equates.

LF        EQU     10
CR        EQU     13
StrEnd  EQU     36


;Program variables.

hours     DB      2 DUP (' '),':'
minutes DB      2 DUP (' '),':'
seconds DB      3 DUP (' ')
noon      DB      4 DUP (' '),StrEnd
dayweekname      DB      10 DUP (' ')
monthname        DB      10 DUP (' ')
day       DB      2 DUP (' '),', '
year      DW      3 DUP (' '),LF,CR,StrEnd
month     DB      0
dayweek DB      0
AM        DB      'am'
PM        DB      'pm'
Sunday    DB      'Sunday    '
Monday    DB      'Monday    '
Tuesday DB      'Tuesday   '
Wednesday        DB      'Wednesday'
Thursday         DB      'Thursday '
Friday  DB      'Friday    '
Saturday         DB      'Saturday '
January DB      'January   '
February         DB      'February '
March     DB      'March     '
```

17-1A Continued.

```
April     DB      'April    '
May       DB      'May      '
June      DB      'June     '
July      DB      'July     '
August    DB      'August   '
September         DB       'September'
October DB        'October  '
November          DB       'November '
December          DB       'December '

Msg1      DB      'DT Program - Copyright (C) 1990 by TAB'
          DB      ' Books',LF,CR,StrEnd


;***************************************************************************************************
;* Begin the code segment.                              *
;***************************************************************************************************
.CODE


Example PROC      FAR
Start:    MOV     AX,@DATA          ;Point DS & ES to our data segment.
          MOV     DS,AX
          MOV     ES,AX

          CALL    ClearScr          ;Clear the display.

          MOV     AX,2C00h          ;Get the time.
          INT     21h

          MOV     hours,CH          ;Save the values.
          MOV     minutes,CL
          MOV     seconds,DH

          CMP     hours,12          ;See if its AM or PM.
          JL      NotPM
          JE      NoonTime
          SUB     hours,12          ;Convert to standard time.
NoonTime:         LEA      DI,noon ;Move appropriate designator
          LEA     SI,PM    ; to the variable noon.
          MOV     CX,2
          REP     MOVSB
          JMP     GotTime
NotPM:    LEA     DI,noon
          LEA     SI,AM
          MOV     CX,2
          REP     MOVSB

GotTime:          MOV      AL,hours          ;Convert hours to a string.
          XOR     AH,AH
          LEA     DI,hours
          INC     DI
          CALL    HexConv
```

```
          MOV     AL,minutes      ;Convert minutes to a string.
          XOR     AH,AH
          LEA     DI,minutes
          INC     DI
          CALL    HexConv

          MOV     AL,seconds      ;Convert seconds to a string.
          XOR     AH,AH
          LEA     DI,seconds
          INC     DI
          CALL    HexConv

          MOV     AX,0900h        ;Display the time.
          LEA     DX,hours
          INT     21h

          MOV     AX,2A00h        ;Get the date.
          INT     21h
          MOV     year,CX ;Save the values.
          MOV     month,DH
          MOV     day,DL
          MOV     dayweek,AL

          CMP     dayweek,0       ;Determine the day of the
          JNE     DW1     ; week and store a string
          LEA     SI,Sunday       ;  in dayweekname.
          JMP     MoveDW
DW1:      CMP     dayweek,1
          JNE     DW2
          LEA     SI,Monday
          JMP     MoveDW
DW2:      CMP     dayweek,2
          JNE     DW3
          LEA     SI,Tuesday
          JMP     MoveDW
DW3:      CMP     dayweek,3
          JNE     DW4
          LEA     SI,Wednesday
          JMP     MoveDW
DW4:      CMP     dayweek,4
          JNE     DW5
          LEA     SI,Thursday
          JMP     MoveDW
DW5:      CMP     dayweek,5
          JNE     DW6
          LEA     SI,Friday
          JMP     MoveDW
DW6:      LEA     SI,Saturday
MoveDW:   MOV     CX,9    ;Store the day name string.
          LEA     DI,dayweekname
          REP     MOVSB
```

```
          CMP      month,1  ;Determine the month of the
          JNE      MN01     ; year and store the correct
          LEA      SI,January      ; string in monthname.
          JMP      MoveMN
MN01:     CMP      month,2
          JNE      MN02
          LEA      SI,February
          JMP      MoveMN
MN02:     CMP      month,3
          JNE      MN03
          LEA      SI,March
          JMP      MoveMN
MN03:     CMP      month,4
          JNE      MN04
          LEA      SI,April
          JMP      MoveMN
MN04:     CMP      month,5
          JNE      MN05
          LEA      SI,May
          JMP      MoveMN
MN05:     CMP      month,6
          JNE      MN06
          LEA      SI,June
          JMP      MoveMN
MN06:     CMP      month,7
          JNE      MN07
          LEA      SI,July
          JMP      MoveMN
MN07:     CMP      month,8
          JNE      MN08
          LEA      SI,August
          JMP      MoveMN
MN08:     CMP      month,9
          JNE      MN09
          LEA      SI,September
          JMP      MoveMN
MN09:     CMP      month,10
          JNE      MN10
          LEA      SI,October
          JMP      MoveMN
MN10:     CMP      month,11
          JNE      MN11
          LEA      SI,November
          JMP      MoveMN
MN11:     LEA      SI,December
MoveMN:   MOV      CX,9     ;Store the month name string.
          LEA      DI,monthname
          REP      MOVSB
          MOV      AL,day   ;Convert the day value into
          XOR      AH,AH    ; a string.
```

```
        LEA     DI,day
        INC     DI
        CALL    HexConv

        MOV     AX,year ;Convert the year value into
        LEA     DI,year ; a string.
        INC     DI
        INC     DI
        INC     DI
        CALL    HexConv

        MOV     AX,0900h        ;Display the date.
        LEA     DX,dayweekname
        INT     21h

        MOV     AX,0900h        ;Display copywrite message.
        LEA     DX,Msg1
        INT     21h

Exit:   MOV     AX,4C00h        ;Exit to DOS.
        INT     21h
        RET

Example ENDP

;************************************************************************
;* This procedure clears the display and places the cursor at coordinates 0,0.  *
;************************************************************************

ClearScr        PROC    NEAR

        MOV     AX,0619h        ;Scroll 25 lines.
        MOV     BH,7    ;Use gray.
        XOR     CX,CX   ;Start at coordinate 0,0.
        MOV     DX,1950h        ;End at coordinate 25,80.
        INT     10h

        MOV     AX,0200h        ;Set cursor position.
        XOR     BH,BH   ;Use page 0.
        XOR     DX,DX   ;Use coordinate 0,0.
        INT     10h

        RET

ClearScr        ENDP

;************************************************************************
;* This procedure converts an integer to a character representation.    *
;************************************************************************

HexConv PROC    NEAR
```

```
        MOV     CX,10    ;Load the divisor.
NextChar:       XOR     DX,DX    ;Clear DX.
        DIV     CX       ;Place first number in DX.
        ADD     DL,30h   ;Convert to a character.
        MOV     [DI],DL  ;Move to string location.
        DEC     DI       ;Update string pointer.
        CMP     AX,10    ;See if we need to divide.
        JGE     NextChar
        ADD     AL,30h   ;If not, AX less than 10.
        MOV     [DI],AL  ;Convert to character and store.

        RET

HexConv ENDP

END     Start
```

17-1B BASIC language program for miscellaneous interrupts.

```
' Sample Program 24, DOS Miscellaneous Interrupt Demonstration
' This program shows you how to use the DOS miscellaneous
' service interrupts to display the system time and date.  You
' do not need any special equipment to use this program.
' Copyright 1989 John Mueller & Wallace Wang - Tab Books

' $INCLUDE: 'qbx.bi'
DIM InRegs AS RegType
DIM OutRegs AS RegType

InRegs.ax = &H2A00

CALL Interrupt(&H21, InRegs, OutRegs)

Year = OutRegs.cx
Month = (OutRegs.dx \ &HFF)

SELECT CASE Month
CASE 1
  Month$ = "January"
CASE 2
  Month$ = "February"
CASE 3
  Month$ = "March"
CASE 4
  Month$ = "April"
CASE 5
  Month$ = "May"
CASE 6
  Month$ = "June"
CASE 7
  Month$ = "July"
```

```
CASE 8
  Month$ = "August"
CASE 9
  Month$ = "September"
CASE 10
  Month$ = "October"
CASE 11
  Month$ = "November"
CASE 12
  Month$ = "December"
END SELECT

Day = (OutRegs.dx AND &HFF)
Dayname = OutRegs.ax AND &HFF

SELECT CASE Dayname
CASE 0
  Day$ = "Sunday"
CASE 1
  Day$ = "Monday"
CASE 2
  Day$ = "Tuesday"
CASE 3
  Day$ = "Wednesday"
CASE 4
  Day$ = "Thursday"
CASE 5
  Day$ = "Friday"
CASE 6
  Day$ = "Saturday"
END SELECT

InRegs.ax = &H2C00

CALL Interrupt(&H21, InRegs, OutRegs)

Hour = (OutRegs.cx \ &HFF)
Minutes = (OutRegs.cx AND &HFF)
Seconds = (OutRegs.dx \ &HFF)
IF (Hour > 12) THEN
  Hour = Hour - 12
  Noon$ = " pm"
ELSE
  IF (Hour = 12) THEN
    Noon$ = " pm"
  ELSE
    Noon$ = " am"
  END IF
END IF
IF (Hour > 9) THEN
```

17-1B Continued.

```
  PRINT USING "##"; Hour;
ELSE
  PRINT USING "#"; Hour;
END IF
PRINT ":";

IF (Minutes < 10) THEN
  PRINT USING "0#"; Minutes;
ELSE
  PRINT USING "##"; Minutes;
END IF

PRINT ":";

IF (Seconds < 10) THEN
  PRINT USING "0#"; Seconds;
ELSE
  PRINT USING "##"; Seconds;
END IF

PRINT Noon$;
PRINT "   ";

PRINT Day$; "  "; Month$;
PRINT USING " ##"; Day;
PRINT ","; Year

PRINT "(DT) Date and Time Program - Copyright (C) 1990 by TAB Books"
```

17-1C C language program for miscellaneous interrupts.

```
/* Sample Program 24, DOS Miscellaneous Interrupt Demonstration
   This program shows you how to use the DOS miscellaneous service interrupts to display the system time and
   date.  You do not need any special equipment to use this program.

   Copyright 1989,1990 John Mueller & Wallace Wang - Tab Books
*/

#include <dos.h>

int     hours, minutes, seconds;
char    *noon;
int     year, month, day, dayweek;
char    *dayweekname, *monthname;
union   REGS regs;

main ()
        {
        regs.h.ah = 0x2C;
        intdos (&regs,&regs);
```

17-1C Continued.

```
hours = regs.h.ch;
minutes = regs.h.cl;
seconds = regs.h.dh;

noon = "am";
if (hours >= 12)
  if (hours > 12)
    hours = hours - 12;
  noon = "pm";

printf ("%d:", hours);
if (minutes < 10)
  printf ("0%d", minutes);
else
  printf ("%d", minutes);

if (seconds < 10)
  printf (":0%d", seconds);
else
  printf (":%d", seconds);

printf (" %s", noon);

/* Get date here */
regs.h.ah = 0x2A;
intdos (&regs,&regs);

year = regs.x.cx;
month = regs.h.dh;
day = regs.h.dl;
dayweek = regs.h.al;

switch (dayweek)
        {
        case 0 : dayweekname = "Sunday"; break;
        case 1 : dayweekname = "Monday"; break;
        case 2 : dayweekname = "Tuesday"; break;
        case 3 : dayweekname = "Wednesday"; break;
        case 4 : dayweekname = "Thursday"; break;
        case 5 : dayweekname = "Friday"; break;
        case 6 : dayweekname = "Saturday"; break;
        }
printf ("   %s   ", dayweekname);

switch (month)
        {
        case 1 : monthname = "January"; break;
        case 2 : monthname = "February"; break;
        case 3 : monthname = "March"; break;
        case 4 : monthname = "April"; break;
        case 5 : monthname = "May"; break;
```

17-1C Continued.

```
        case 6 : monthname = "June"; break;
        case 7 : monthname = "July"; break;
        case 8 : monthname = "August"; break;
        case 9 : monthname = "September"; break;
        case 10: monthname = "October"; break;
        case 11: monthname = "November"; break;
        case 12: monthname = "December"; break;
        }
printf ("%s %d, %d\n", monthname, day, year);
printf ("DT Program - Copyright (C) 1990 by TAB Books\n");
}
```

17-1D Pascal program for miscellaneous interrupts.

```
    (*******************************************************************************************************)
(* Sample Program 24, DOS Miscellaneous Interrupt Demonstration *)
(* This program shows you how to use the DOS miscellaneous service interrupts to display the system time and    *)
(* date.  You do not need any special equipment to use this program.    *)
(*                              *)
(* Copyright 1989,1990 John Mueller & Wallace Wang - Tab Books *)
    (*******************************************************************************************************)

PROGRAM DateAndTime;
USES
  Dos;
VAR
  Regs : Registers;

  PROCEDURE GetTime;
  VAR
    Hours, Minutes, Seconds : byte;
    Noon : string[2];
  BEGIN
    Regs.ah := $2C;
    MsDos (Regs);
    Hours := Regs.ch;
    Minutes := Regs.cl;
    Seconds := Regs.dh;

    Noon := 'am';
    IF (Hours >= 12) THEN
      BEGIN
        IF (Hours > 12) THEN
          Hours := Hours - 12;
        Noon := 'pm';
      END;

    Write (Hours, ':');
    IF (Minutes < 10) THEN
      Write ('0', Minutes)
    ELSE
```

17-1D Continued.

```
   Write (Minutes);

  IF (Seconds < 10) THEN
    Write (':0', Seconds)
  ELSE
    Write (':', Seconds);

  Write (' ', Noon);
END;  (* GetTime *)


PROCEDURE GetDate;
VAR
  Year : word;
  Month, Day, DayWeek : byte;
  DayWeekName, MonthName : string [11];
BEGIN
  Regs.ah := $2A;
  MsDos (Regs);
  Year := Regs.cx;
  Month := Regs.dh;
  Day := Regs.dl;
  DayWeek := Regs.al;
  CASE DayWeek OF
    0 : DayWeekName := 'Sunday';
    1 : DayWeekName := 'Monday';
    2 : DayWeekName := 'Tuesday';
    3 : DayWeekName := 'Wednesday';
    4 : DayWeekName := 'Thursday';
    5 : DayWeekName := 'Friday';
    6 : DayWeekName := 'Saturday';
  END;  (* CASE *)
  Write ('   ', DayWeekName, '   ');

  CASE Month OF
    1 : MonthName := 'January';
    2 : MonthName := 'February';
    3 : MonthName := 'March';
    4 : MonthName := 'April';
    5 : MonthName := 'May';
    6 : MonthName := 'June';
    7 : MonthName := 'July';
    8 : MonthName := 'August';
    9 : MonthName := 'September';
    10: MonthName := 'October';
    11: MonthName := 'November';
    12: MonthName := 'December';
  END;  (* CASE *)
  Writeln (MonthName, ' ', Day, ', ', Year);

  Writeln ('DT Program - Copyright (C) 1990 by TAB Books');
END;  (* GetDate *)
```

17-1D Continued.

```
BEGIN
  GetTime;
  GetDate;
END.
```

Example:
```
;Get current date from DOS internal clock
MOV    AH,2Ah
INT    21h
```

SET DATE (INTERRUPT 21h SERVICE 2Bh)

DOS 1.0

This service sets the system date of the DOS internal clock. The registers contain the same information required to use service 2Ah. You can use this function with service 2Bh to find information about an arbitrary date. For example, you could find the day of week. You cannot use this service to set your computer CMOS clock. If you type an incorrect date, this service retains the previous date and ignores the incorrect date entry.

Register Contents on Entry:
AH - 2Bh
CX - Year
DH - Month
DL - Day

Register Contents on Exit:
AL - 00h if Successful, FFh if Not Successful

Example:
```
;Sets the date of the DOS internal clock to 12-5-91
MOV    AH,2Bh
MOV    CX,1991
MOV    DH,12
MOV    DL,5
INT    21h
```

GET TIME (INTERRUPT 21h SERVICE 2Ch)

DOS 1.0

This service gets the system time from the DOS internal clock, NOT from the real-time clock/calendar if one exists. It does not affect the system date. The register format of this service is the same as service 2Dh. On most IBM PC compatible systems, the real time clock does not output time in single hundredth-second values. Ignore the hundredth-second output of DL when using this type of machine.

Register Contents on Entry:
AH - 2Ch

Register Contents on Exit:
CH - Hours
CL - Minutes
DH - Seconds
DL - Hundredths of Seconds

Example:
```
;Reads the current time from the DOS internal clock
MOV   AH,2Ch
INT   21h
```

SET TIME (INTERRUPT 21h SERVICE 2Dh)

DOS 1.0

This service sets the system time. It does not affect the system date. The register format of this service is the same as service 2Ch. You cannot use this service to set your computer's CMOS clock. If you type an incorrect time, this service retains the previous time and ignores the incorrect time entry.

Register Contents on Entry:
AH - 2Dh
CH - Hours
CL - Minutes
DH - Seconds
DL - Hundredths of Seconds

Register Contents on Exit:
AL - 00h if Successful, FFh if Not Successful

Example:
```
;Sets the time as 3:30:25:04 am
MOV   AH,2Ch
MOV   CH,3      ;Hours
MOV   CL,30     ;Minutes
MOV   DH,25     ;Seconds
MOV   DL,4      ;Hundredths of Seconds
INT   21h
```

GET DOS VERSION NUMBER
(INTERRUPT 21h SERVICE 30h)

DOS 2.0

This service gets the version number, OEM serial number, and software serial number of your computer's DOS. If you use a version of DOS below 2.0, this service returns a 0 for both the major and minor version numbers (registers AL and AH).

The main use for this service is so your program can identify which DOS functions are available. For example, if your program needs functions only available in DOS 3.0 or higher, and someone runs your program using DOS 2.0 or lower, this service lets your program display an error message. Always exit using a service appropriate for the version of DOS installed on the machine, not the version your program uses.

Register Contents on Entry:
AH - 30h
AL - 0

Register Contents on Exit:
AL - Major Version Number
AH - Minor Version Number
BH - OEM's Serial Number
BL:CX - 14-Bit Software Serial Number

Example:
```
;Gets the DOS version number
MOV     AH,30h
MOV     AL,0
INT     21h
```

GET/SET BREAK FLAG, GET BOOT DRIVE (INTERRUPT 21h SERVICE 33h)

DOS 2.0

This service performs three different tasks. The first two tasks include getting or setting the Ctrl–Break flag. This determines whether DOS checks for the Ctrl–C or Ctrl–Break keys. When set on, if the user enters Ctrl–C or Ctrl–Break, control passes from the application to interrupt 23h (Ctrl–C Handler). Controlling the Ctrl–C or Ctrl–Break keys by installing your own version of interrupt 23h is an alternative to disabling the Ctrl–C or Ctrl–Break keys.

If you use DOS version 4.0, this service also gets the system boot drive. Most versions of DOS return the COMSPEC drive, not the actual boot drive.

Note: This service affects all programs that test for the Ctrl–C or Ctrl–Break keys. Make sure that using this service does not affect other programs. Always restore the Ctrl–C handler and status flag to its original state when your program exits.

Register Contents on Entry (Get Break Flag):
AH - 33h
AL - 0

Example:
```
;Get the break flag
MOV    AH,33h
MOV    AL,0
INT    21h
```

Register Contents on Exit (Set Break Flag):
AH - 33h
AL - 1
DL - Status
    0 - Break Flag Off
    1 - Break Flag On

Register Contents on Exit (Get Break Flag):
DL - Status
    0 - Break Flag Off
    1 - Break Flag On

Example:
```
;Set break flag on
MOV    AH,33h
MOV    AL,1
MOV    DL,1
INT    21h
```

Register Contents on Entry (Get Boot Drive):
AH - 33h
AL - 5

Register Contents on Exit (Get Boot Drive):
DL - Drive Number (1 = A, 2 = B, etc.)

Example:
```
;Get boot drive
MOV    AH,33h
MOV    AL,5
INT    21h
```

GET/SET COUNTRY INFORMATION (INTERRUPT 21h SERVICE 38h)

DOS 2.0

This service gets or sets country-dependent information. TABLE 17-1 contains a listing of country information returned in a specified buffer upon completion of the get function. In most cases, the country code is the three digits corresponding to the international code for the telephone system. TABLE 17-2 contains a listing of some supported country codes (the codes supported vary from version to version, and from manufacturer to manufacturer).

Table 17-1   Country Information Buffer Format

Byte	Bit	Contents
PC-DOS Versions 2.0 and 2.1		
00h-01h		Date Format 0 - USA (M-D-Y) 1 - Europe (D-M-Y) 2 - Japan (Y-M-D)
02h-03h		ASCIIZ Currency Symbol
04h-05h		ASCIIZ Thousands Separator
06h-07h		ASCIIZ Decimal Separator
08h-1Fh		Reserved (0)
MS-DOS Versions 2.0 and Later, PC-DOS Versions 3.0 and Later		
00h-01h		Date Format 0 - USA (M-D-Y) 1 - Europe (D-M-Y) 2 - Japan (Y-M-D)
02h-06h		ASCIIZ Currency Symbol String
07h-08h		ASCIIZ Thousands Separator
09h-0Ah		ASCIIZ Decimal Separator
0Bh-0Ch		ASCIIZ Date Separator Character
0Dh-0Eh		ASCIIZ Time Separator Character
0Fh		Currency Format
	0	0 - Currency Format Precedes Value 1 - Currency Format Follows Value
	1	0 - No Space Between Value and Currency Symbol 1 - One Space Between Value and Currency Symbol
	2	0 - Currency Symbol and Decimal are Separate 1 - Currency Symbol Replaces Decimal
10h		Number of Digits After Decimal in Currency
11h		Time Format
	0	0 - 12 Hour Clock 1 - 24 Hour Clock
12h-15h		Case Map Call Address
16h-17h		ASCIIZ Data-List Separator
18h-21h		Reserved (0)

Table 17-2   Common Country Codes

Code	Country
001	United States
002	Canada (French Speaking)
003	Latin America
031	Netherlands
032	Belgium
033	France
034	Spain
039	Italy
041	Switzerland
044	United Kingdom
045	Denmark
046	Sweden
047	Norway
049	Germany
061	Australia
081	Japan
082	Korea
086	Simplified Chinese
088	Traditional Chinese
351	Portugal
358	Finland
785	Arabic Speaking
972	Hebrew Speaking

The country-specific parameters are set in the CONFIG.SYS file using the DOS COUNTRY.SYS command. The country-specific parameters this service can set include the date format (USA mm-dd-yy, Europe dd-mm-yy, Japan yy-mm-dd), currency symbol ($, £, ¥), time format (12 or 24 hour clock), and decimal character (period or comma).

The case map call address returned by DOS version 3.0 or above is the segment of a far procedure used to map the extended ASCII characters (values 128–255). You call the procedure with the character you wish to map in AL. If an alternate value for the character exists, the procedure returns its value in AL. Otherwise, AL returns unchanged.

Note: You can get information for a requested (rather than the current) country when using DOS 3.0 or above. Only DOS 3.0 or above supports setting the country information. You must change the CONFIG.SYS entry when using DOS 2.0 or below. Use interrupt 21h service 65h to retrieve a superset of the data provided by this service when using DOS 3.3 and above.

Register Contents on Entry (Getting Country DOS 2.0):
AH - 38h
AL - 0 (Current Country Information)
DX - Offset of Buffer for Returned Information
DS - Segment of Buffer for Returned Information

Example:
```
;Get country information with DOS 2.0
MOV    AH,38h
MOV    AL,0
LDS    DX,BUFF·
INT    21h
```

Register Contents on Entry (Getting Country DOS 3.0 or Later):
AH - 38h
AL - Return Type
    0 - Current Country
    1 through FEh - Countries With Codes < 255
    FFh - Countries With Codes > 255
BX - Country Code if Al = FFh

Example:
```
;Get country information for DOS 3.0 or later
MOV    AH,38h
MOV    AL,0
INT    21h
```

Register Contents on Entry (Setting Country DOS 3.0 or Later):
AH - 38h
AL - Set Type
    1 through FEh - Countries With Codes < 255
    FFh - Countries With Codes > 255
BX - Country Code if AL = FFh
DX - FFFFh

Register Contents on Exit:
AX - Error Code if Not Successful
BX - Country Code
DX - Offset of Buffer
DS - Segment of Buffer
CF - 0 if Successful, 1 if Not Successful

Example:
```
;Set country information for United States
MOV    AH,38h
MOV    AL,1
MOV    DX,FFFFh
INT    21h
```

DUPLICATE HANDLE (INTERRUPT 21h SERVICE 45h)

DOS 2.0

This service creates a handle that references the same device or file as the specified handle. In versions earlier than DOS 3.3, you could use this service to force an update to a file's directory entry without opening and closing the file. In DOS 3.3 or later, you can use Interrupt 21h Service 68h (Commit File) instead.

The handle returned by this service remains linked to the original handle. If you move the file pointer of one handle by reading or writing, DOS automatically updates the file pointer of the second handle.

Register Contents on Entry:
AH - 45h
BX - Handle to Duplicate

Register Contents on Exit:
AX - New Handle if Successful, Error Code if Not Successful
CF - 0 if Successful, 1 if Not Successful

Example:
```
;Duplicate handle
MOV     AH,45h
MOV     BX,FHandle
INT     21h
```

REDIRECT HANDLE (INTERRUPT 21h SERVICE 46h)

DOS 2.0

This service redirects the handle in CX to point to the same file or device as the handle in BX. If the file pointer of one of the handles in CX or BX changes position, the other file pointer changes automatically. If you pass a handle pointing to an open file in CX, DOS closes the file before redirecting the handle.

Register Contents on Entry:
AH - 46h
BX - Handle for File or Device
CX - Handle to Redirect

Register Contents on Exit:
AX - Error Code if Not Successful
CF - 0 if Successful, 1 if Not Successful

Example:
```
;Redirect handle
MOV     AH,46h
MOV     BX,FHandle
MOV     CX,FHandle2
INT     21h
```

ALLOCATE MEMORY BLOCK (INTERRUPT 21h SERVICE 48h)

DOS 2.0

This service allocates a block of memory and returns a pointer to the beginning of the memory block. You access the new block of memory using the segment and offset combination AX:0000. When DOS loads a COM program, it allocates all available memory to the program, leaving none for dynamic allocation. The memory allocated to an EXE program depends on the MINALLOC and MAXALLOC values in the EXE header.

Register Contents on Entry:
AH - 48h
BX - Number of Paragraphs to Allocate

Register Contents on Exit:
AX - Base Segment Address of Allocated Block,
     Error Code if Not Successful
CF - 0 if Successful, 1 if Not Successful

Example:
```
;Allocate three memory blocks
MOV    AH,48h
MOV    BX,3
```

RELEASE MEMORY BLOCK
(INTERRUPT 21h SERVICE 49h)

DOS 2.0

This service releases a previously allocated block of memory defined by service 48h (Allocate Memory Block). This function causes a system failure if the application program attempts to release a memory block owned by another process. In addition, a program can cause a system or function failure if it passes an invalid base address (memory block does not exist) in ES.

Register Contents on Entry:
AH - 49h
ES - Memory Block to Release

Register Contents on Exit:
AX - Error Code if Not Successful
CF - 0 if Successful, 1 if Not Successful

Example:
```
;Release memory block
MOV    AH,48h
MOV    BX,3
INT    21h
MOV    AH,49h
MOV    ES,AX
INT    21h
```

RESIZE MEMORY BLOCK
(INTERRUPT 21h SERVICE 4Ah)

DOS 1.0

This service changes the size of a memory block defined by service 48h (Allocate Memory Block). All COM programs must use this service before using service 4Bh (Execute Program) because COM programs use all available RAM. The memory initially allocated to an EXE program depends on the MINALLOC and MAXALLOC values in the EXE header.

If this function fails because of a lack of available memory (program tries to increase the block size) BX returns with the amount of available memory. A program can look at this value to determine the maximum memory available. The program should end immediately if there is not enough memory available for it to execute.

Register Contents on Entry:
AH - 4Ah
BX - New Number of Paragraphs to Allocate
ES - Memory Block to Resize

Register Contents on Exit:
AX - Error Code if Not Successful
CF - 0 if Successful, 1 if Not Successful
BX - Maximum Paragraphs Available if Not Successful

Example:

```
;Resize memory block
MOV     AH,48h
MOV     BX,3
INT     21h
MOV     AH,4Ah
MOV     BX,3
MOV     ES,AX
```

GET/SET ALLOCATION STRATEGY
(INTERRUPT 21h SERVICE 58h)

DOS 3.0

This service gets or changes the method DOS uses to allocate memory blocks: first fit, best fit, and last fit. DOS uses a default strategy of first fit.

First fit allocates memory starting at the beginning of the memory block. *Best fit* searches for the best-fitting memory block which is the most efficient method, but also the slowest. *Last fit* allocates memory starting at the end of the memory block.

In DOS version 2.0, this service only exists in Microsoft and IBM versions. If you have a version of DOS from a third-party vendor that has modified DOS, this service might not exist or might perform a different function.

Register Contents on Entry (Get Strategy):
AH - 58h
AL - 0

Example:
```
;Get Strategy
MOV    AH,58h
MOV    AL,0
INT    21h
```

Register Contents on Entry (Set Strategy):
AH - 58h
AL - 1
BX - Desired Strategy Code
    0 - First Fit
    1 - Best Fit
    2 - Last Fit

Register Contents on Exit:
AX - Current Strategy Code if AL = 0, Error Code if Not Successful
CF - 0 if Successful, 1 if Not Successful

Example:
```
;Set Strategy for Best Fit
MOV    AH,58h
MOV  · AL,0
MOV    BX,1
INT    21h
```

GET EXTENDED ERROR INFORMATION (INTERRUPT 21h SERVICE 59h)

DOS 1.0

This service obtains an extended error code, error class, recommended action, and point of failure each time an interrupt 21h or 24h service call fails. The four types of error information include a description of the error (AX), the cause of the error (BH), recommended action (BL), and the source of the error (CH). TABLE 17-3 contains a listing of all four groups

Table 17-3   Extended Error Information

Code	Description
Extended Error Code	
00h	No Error
01h	Function Number Invalid
02h	File Not Found
03h	Path Not Found

Table 17-3   Continued.

Code	Description
04h	Too Many Open Files
05h	Access Denied
06h	Handle Invalid
07h	Memory Control Block Destroyed
08h	Insufficient Memory
09h	Memory Block Address Invalid
0Ah	Environment Invalid
0Bh	Format Invalid
0Ch	Access Code Invalid
0Dh	Data Invalid
0Eh	Unknown Unit
0Fh	Disk Drive Invalid
10h	Attempted to Remove Current Directory
11h	Not Same Device
12h	No More Files
13h	Disk Write-Protected
14h	Unknown Unit
15h	Drive Not Ready
16h	Unknown Command
17h	Data Error (CRC)
18h	Bad Request Structure Length
19h	Seek Error
1Ah	Unknown Media Type
1Bh	Sector Not Found
1Ch	Printer Out of Paper
1Dh	Write Fault
1Eh	Read Fault
1Fh	General Failure
20h	Sharing Violation
21h	Lock Violation
22h	Disk Change Invalid
23h	FCB Unavailable
24h	Sharing Buffer Exceeded
25h - 31h	Reserved
32h	Unsupported Network Request
33h	Remote Machine Not Listening
34h	Duplicate Name on Network
35h	Network Name Not Found
36h	Network Busy
37h	Device No Longer Exists on Network
38h	NetBIOS Command Limit Exceeded
39h	Error in Network Adapter Hardware
3Ah	Incorrect Response From Network
3Bh	Unexpected Network Error
3Ch	Remote Adapter Incompatible
3Dh	Print Queue Full
3Eh	Not Enough Space for Print File
3Fh	Print File Canceled
40h	Network Name Deleted
41h	Network Access Denied
42h	Incorrect Network Device Type
43h	Network Name Not Found

Table 17-3   Continued.

Code	Description
44h	Network Name Limit Exceeded
45h	NetBIOS Session Limit Exceeded
46h	File Sharing Temporarily Paused
47h	Network Request Not Accepted
48h	Print or Disk Redirection Paused
49h - 4Fh	Reserved
50h	File Already Exists
51h	Reserved
52h	Cannot Make Directory
53h	Fail on Int 24h
54h	Too Many Redirections
55h	Duplicate Redirection
56h	Invalid Password
57h	Invalid Parameter
58h	Network Device Fault
59h	Function Not Supported by Network
5Ah	Required System Component Not Installed

Error Class

Code	Description
01h	Out of Resource
02h	Not Error, Temporary Situation Expected to End
03h	Authorization Problem
04h	Internal Error in System Software
05h	Hardware Failure
06h	System Software Failure, Active Process Not at Fault
07h	Application Program Error
08h	File or Item Not Found
09h	File or Item of Invalid Type or Format
0Ah	File or Item Locked
0Bh	Wrong Disk in Drive, Bad Spot on Disk, or Storage Medium Problem
0Ch	Item Already Exists
0Dh	Unknown Error

Recommended Action

Code	Description
01h	Retry Reasonable Number of Times, Then Prompt User to Select Abort or Ignore
02h	Retry Reasonable Number of Times With Delay Between Retries, Then Prompt User to Select Abort or Ignore
03h	Get Corrected Information From User
04h	Abort Application With Cleanup
05h	Perform Immediate Exit Without Cleanup
06h	Ignore Error
07h	Retry After User Intervention to Remove Cause of Error

Error Locus

Code	Description
01h	Unknown
02h	Block Device (Disk or Disk Emulator)
03h	Network

Table 17-3   Continued.

```
Code            Description
04h             Serial Device
05h             Memory
```

of information. Never code your program to recognize a specific set of error messages. Each new version of DOS updates and adds to the existing list of error types.

Register Contents on Entry:
AH - 59h
BX - 0

Register Contents on Exit:
AX - Extended Error Code
BH - Error Class
BL - Recommended Action
CH - Error Locus
DI - Offset of ASCIIZ Volume Label to Insert
ES - Segment of ASCIIZ Volume Label to Insert

Example:
```
;Get extended error information
MOV    AH,59h
MOV    BX,0
INT    21h
```

SET EXTENDED ERROR INFORMATION (INTERRUPT 21h SERVICE 5Dh)

DOS 3.1

This service sets the information returned by the next call to interrupt 21h service 59h. The combination of DS:DX contains an 11-word data structure. DOS returns the first eight bytes of this structure in AX, BX, CX, DX, SI, DI, DS, and ES respectively using interrupt 21h service 59h. The last three bytes remain set at zero.

This extended error information consists of an extended error code, error class, recommend action, and point of failure. The four types of error information include a description of the error (AX), the cause of the error (BH), recommend action (BL), and the source of the error (CH). TABLE 17-3 contains a listing of all four groups of information. Never code your program to recognize a specific set of error messages. Each new version of DOS updates and adds to the existing list of error types.

Note: This is an undocumented feature. DOS might not support it in future upgrades. However, most versions of DOS from version 3.1 to 4.01 support this service.

Register Contents on Entry:
AX - 5D0Ah
DX - Offset of 11 Word Data Structure
DS - Segment of 11 Word Data Structure

Example:
```
;Set extended error information
MOV    AX,5D0h
LDS    DX,BUFF
INT    21h
```

GET MACHINE NAME
(INTERRUPT 21h SERVICE 5Eh FUNCTION 0)
DOS 3.1

This service returns a 15-character, null terminated (00h) ASCIIZ string identifying the local computer. It pads the end of the string with spaces as required. This function is available only when using Microsoft Networks. It produces unpredictable results if you use it without a network running.

Register Contents on Entry:
AH - 5Eh
AL - 0
DX - Offset of Buffer
DS - Segment of Buffer

Register Contents on Exit:
AX - Error Code if Not Successful
CH - Status
    0 - Name Not Defined
    < >0 - Name Defined
CL - NetBIOS Name Number
DX - Offset of Identifier
DS - Segment of Identifier
CF - 0 if Successful, 1 if Not Successful

Example:
```
;Get machine name
MOV    AH,5Eh
MOV    AL,0
LDS    DX,BUFF
INT    21h
```

GET REDIRECTION LIST ENTRY
(INTERRUPT 21h SERVICE 5Fh FUNCTION 2)

DOS 3.1

This service gets the system redirection list. The redirection list provides the names of network printers, files, or directories for ease of use. It is only available when using both Microsoft Networks and SHARE.

Register Contents on Entry:
AH - 5Fh
AL - 02h
BX - Redirection Index
SI - Offset of 16-Byte Buffer to Receive Local Device Name
DI - Offset of 128-Byte Buffer to Receive Network Name
DS - Segment of 16-Byte Buffer to Receive Local Device Name
ES - Segment of 128-Byte Buffer to Receive Network Name

Register Contents on Exit:
AX - Error Code if Not Successful
BH - Device Status Flag (Bit 0)
    0 - Device Valid
    1 - Device Not Valid
BL - Device Type
    3 - Printer
    4 - Drive
CX - Stored Parameter Value
SI - Offset of Local Device Name
DI - Offset of Network Name
DS - Segment of Local Device Name
ES - Segment of Network Name
CF - 0 if Successful, 1 if Not Successful

Example:

```
;Get redirection list entry
MOV    AH,5Fh
MOV    AL,02h
MOV    BX,0
LDS    SI,LBUFF
LES    DI,NBUFF
INT    21h
```

REDIRECT DEVICE
(INTERRUPT 21h SERVICE 5Fh FUNCTION 3)

DOS 3.1

This service changes the redirection list entries across a network by associating a local device name with a network name. It is only available when using both Microsoft Networks and SHARE. You can use a local name consisting of a drive specifier followed by a colon with this function (for example, D:). You must use PRN, LPT1, LPT2, or LPT3 when redirecting a printer. If you pass a null string followed by a password, DOS tries to grant access to the network directory.

Register Contents on Entry:
AH - 5Fh
AL - 3
BL - Device Type
    3 - Printer
    4 - Drive
CX - Stored Parameter Value
SI - Offset of ASCIIZ Local Device Name
DI - Offset of ASCIIZ Network Name, Followed by ASCIIZ Password
DS - Segment of ASCIIZ Local Device Name
ES - Segment of ASCIIZ Network Name, Followed by ASCIIZ Password

Register Contents on Exit:
AX - Error Code if Not Successful
CF - 0 if Successful, 1 if Not Successful

Example:
```
;Redirect device to printer
MOV    AH,5Fh
MOV    AL,3
MOV    BL,3
LDS    SI,LBUFF
LES    DI,NBUFF
```

CANCEL DEVICE REDIRECTION (INTERRUPT 21h SERVICE 5Fh FUNCTION 4)

DOS 3.1

This service cancels a previous redirection request. It is only available when using both Microsoft Networks and SHARE. You can use a local name consisting of a drive specifier followed by a colon with this function (for example, D:). You must use PRN, LPT1, LPT2, or LPT3 when redirecting a printer. Passing a string containing a double backslash (\ \ ) cuts the connection between the local machine and the network.

Register Contents on Entry:
AH - 5Fh
AL - 4
SI - Offset of ASCIIZ Local Device Name
DS - Segment of ASCIIZ Local Device Name

Register Contents on Exit:
AX - Error Code if Not Successful
CF - 0 if Successful, 1 if Not Successful

Example:
```
;Cancel device redirection
MOV    AH,5F
MOV    AL,4
LDS    SI,LBUFF
INT    21h
```

GET EXTENDED COUNTRY INFORMATION
(INTERRUPT 21h SERVICE 65h)
DOS 3.3

This service returns extended country information in more detail than service 38h (Get/Set Country Information). TABLE 17-4 lists the return buffer information.

Table 17-4   Extended Country Information

Byte	Bit	Description
Data Returned by Function 01h		
00h		Information ID
01h-02h		Length of Following Buffer
03h-04h		Country ID
05h-06h		Code Page Number
07h-08h		Date Format
		0 - USA (M-D-Y)
		1 - Europe (D-M-Y)
		2 - Japan (Y-M-D)
09h-0Dh		ASCIIZ Currency Symbol
0Eh-0Fh		ASCIIZ Thousands Separator
10h-11h		ASCIIZ Decimal Separator
12h-13h		ASCIIZ Date Separator
14h-15h		ASCIIZ Time Separator
16h	0	0 - Currency Symbol Precedes Value
		1 - Currency Symbol Follows Value
	1	0 - No Space Between Value and Currency Symbol
		1 - One Space Between Value and Currency Symbol
	2	0 - Currency Symbol and Decimal are Separate
		1 - Currency Symbol Replaces Decimal Separator
17h		Number of Digits After Decimal in Currency
18h		Time Format (Bit 0)
		0 - 12 Hour Clock
		1 - 24 Hour Clock
19h-1Ch		Case Map Routine Call Address
1Dh-1Eh		ASCIIZ Data List Separator
1Fh-28h		Reserved
Data Returned by Functions 02h, 04h, and 06h		
00h		Information ID Code
01h-05h		Double-Word Pointer to Table

The uppercase and filename uppercase tables contain 130 or less bytes. The first two bytes tell you the length of the table. The remaining bytes contain equivalent characters for extended ASCII characters 128 to 255. This allows you to substitute plain characters for accented characters used in filenames and documents. Using these tables with filenames allows you to access the files without the aid of a special keyboard. You can also use this table to translate output to a printer, because some printers do not support the IBM extended ASCII character set.

The collating table contains a maximum of 258 bytes. The first two bytes tell you the length of the table. The rest of the table contains the characters you should substitute for ASCII characters 0 through 255 during sort operations. This allows you to perform case-insensitive sorts or place accented characters in their correct positions.

Register Contents on Entry:
AH - 65h
AL - Function
      1 - Get General Internationalization Information
      2 - Get Pointer to Uppercase Table
      4 - Get Pointer to Filename Uppercase Table
      6 - Get Pointer to Collating Table
      7 - Get Pointer to Double-Byte Character Set (DBCS) Vector
BX - Code Page of Interest
CX - Length of Buffer to Receive Information (> = 5 Bytes)
DX - Country ID (– 1 Default)
DI - Offset of Buffer to Receive Information
ES - Segment of Buffer to Receive Information

Register Contents on Exit:
AX - Error Code if Not Successful
CF - 0 if Successful, 1 if Not Successful

Example:

```
;Get extended country information
MOV    AH,65h
MOV    AL,1      ;Get general internationalization information
MOV    BX,-1     ;Active CON device
MOV    CX,5      ;Buffer length
MOV    DX,-1     ;Country ID
LES    DI,BUFF
INT    21h
```

GET/SET CODE PAGE (INTERRUPT 21h SERVICE 66h)

DOS 3.3

This service gets or selects the current code page. When you use this service, DOS gets a new code page from the COUNTRY.SYS file. You must prepare a device to use code pages before calling the service. This includes adding the appropriate DEVICE= statement to CONFIG.SYS and adding the NLSFUNC and MODE CP PREPARE commands to AUTOEXEC.BAT.

Register Contents on Entry:
AH - 66h
AL - Subfunction
    1 - Get Code Page
    2 - Select Code Page
BC - Code Page to Select (AL = 2)

Register Contents on Exit:
AX - Error Code if Not Successful
BX - Active Code Page (AL = 1)
DX - Default Code Page (AL = 1)
CF - 0 if Successful, 1 if Not Successful

Example:
```
;Get code page
MOV    AH,66h
MOV    AL,1
INT    21h
```

18
Memory-Resident Programming

The first memory-resident or terminate-and-stay-resident program was the DOS print spooler that let you use your computer and printer at the same time. The first popular terminate-and-stay-resident (TSR) program came from Borland International with the introduction of Sidekick. Sidekick provided a notepad, calendar, and calculator available from within any program. Unlike conventional programs that load in memory and then terminate when you are through with the program, TSR programs remain in memory even after you exit from them. To run a conventional program, you type the proper command to load it into memory. To run a TSR program, you load the program in memory once. From that point on, you press a certain keystroke combination called a *hotkey* that begins running the TSR program. When you leave the TSR program, the TSR remains in memory, ready to call again.

Figure 18-1 shows a typical TSR programming example. Notice that unlike most TSRs, this program shows you how to create an EXE format program. In many cases you need more than the 64 Kbytes provided by the COM format. This programming example shows you how to get the extra memory you require. (Only Assembly and Pascal shown).

TYPES OF TSR PROGRAMS

There are two types of TSR programs: active and passive. *Passive* TSR programs perform a task without requiring user input. Examples of passive TSR programs are print spoolers or programs that display the time on the screen. These programs very seldom take control of the keyboard interrupt. However, every TSR controls one or more interrupts. In most cases a passive TSR tries to control an event interrupt. For example, an

```
;*****************************************************************************************************
;* Sample Program 25, Terminate and Stay Resident Programming Techniques Demonstration  *
;* This program shows you how to create terminate and stay resident programs.  This includes the special      *
;* routines required to make the program resident.  The Pascal version of this program uses TSRUNIT library   *
;* to provide the special routines required to make this program operate correctly.  This library also  *
;* contains an assortment of other TSR related routines.                    *
;* Notice that a TSR unit consists of two sections.  The first section contains the interrupt handler code    *
;* required to pass control to a program after you install the TSR.  The second section contains the    *
;* initialization code required to install the program.  You do not need any special equipment to use this   *
;* program.                                   *
;*                        *
;* Copyright 1989 John Mueller & Wallace Wang - Tab Books *
;*****************************************************************************************************


;*****************************************************************************************************
;* Perform the program setup.                         *
;*****************************************************************************************************


.MODEL MEDIUM   ; Use a medum model size.

.STACK  ; Use the defalt stack of 1024 bytes.


;*****************************************************************************************************
;* Begin the data area.  Declare all variables.             *
;*****************************************************************************************************
.DATA

;Standard equates.

LF      EQU     10
CR      EQU     13
StrEnd  EQU     36
CharPort        EQU     60h


;Program variables.

Msg1    DB      'èèëëëëëëëëëëëëëëëëëëëë£'
Msg2    DB      'ø  TSR Test Program   ø'
Msg3    DB      'àëëëëëëëëëëëëëëëëëëëëë¥'
Msg4    DB      'Installing PROGRM25 as a TSR.',LF,CR
        DB      'Press Alt-A to see message.',LF,CR,StrEnd
Msg5    DB      'Press any key when ready...'
DoOld9  LABEL   DWORD
Old9    DW      2 DUP (0)
VBuff   DB      4000 DUP (0)
CurParm DW      0
CurPos  DW      0


;These two entries help the program determine the amount of
; memory required by the data segment.  It uses this value
; during TSR installation.
```

```
DataEnd  EQU     $
DataSize         DW      DataEnd


;**************************************************************************************************
;* Begin the code segment.                                *
;**************************************************************************************************
;
.CODE
Example PROC    FAR
Start:  PUSHF           ;Save flags and registers.
        PUSH    AX
        PUSH    BX
        PUSH    CX
        PUSH    DX
        PUSH    BP
        PUSH    DS
        PUSH    ES
        PUSH    DI
        PUSH    SI

        IN      AL,CharPort     ;Check for the control key
        CMP     AL,30   ; combination.
        JNE     QExit
        MOV     AH,2    ;Check shift keys.
        INT     16h
        AND     AL,0fh
        CMP     AL,8    ;Check Alt key.
        JE      DoIt    ;If key code pressed, then
                        ; display message.

QExit:  POP     SI      ;Restore flags and registers.
        POP     DI
        POP     ES
        POP     DS
        POP     BP
        POP     DX
        POP     CX
        POP     BX
        POP     AX
        POPF
        JMP     CS:DoOld9       ;Otherwise, call interrupt 16.

DoIt:   CLI             ;Reset the interrupt
        MOV     AL,20h  ; controller.
        OUT     20h,AL
        STI

        MOV     AX,@DATA        ;Point DS & ES to our data segment.
        MOV     DS,AX
        MOV     ES,AX

        CALL    GetCPosit       ;Save the cursor position.
```

```
        CALL    SaveScrn        ;Save the screen contents.
        CALL    ClearScr        ;Clear the display.
        CALL    Message ;Display the message.
        CALL    RestScrn        ;Restore the screen contents.
        CALL    SetCPosit       ;Restore the cursor position.

        POP     SI      ;Restore flags and registers.
        POP     DI
        POP     ES
        POP     DS
        POP     BP
        POP     DX
        POP     CX
        POP     BX
        POP     AX
        POPF
        IRET

Example ENDP


;*****************************************************************************************************
;* This procedure clears the display and places the cursor at coordinates 0,0.  *
;*****************************************************************************************************

ClearScr        PROC    NEAR

        MOV     AX,0619h        ;Scroll 25 lines.
        MOV     BH,7    ;Use gray.
        XOR     CX,CX   ;Start at coordinate 0,0.
        MOV     DX,1950h        ;End at coordinate 25,80.
        INT     10h

        MOV     AX,0200h        ;Set cursor position.
        XOR     BH,BH   ;Use page 0.
        XOR     DX,DX   ;Use coordinate 0,0.
        INT     10h
        RET

ClearScr        ENDP


;*****************************************************************************************************
;* This procedure gets the coordinates of the cursor and places both the cursor size and coordinates in *
;* variables.  The program uses the contents of the variables to restore the cursor to its original position    *
;* on program exit.                              *
;*****************************************************************************************************

GetCPosit       PROC    NEAR

        MOV     AX,0300h
        XOR     BX,BX
        INT     10h
```

```
        MOV     CurParm,CX
        MOV     CurPos,DX
        RET

GetCPosit       ENDP

;************************************************************************************************
;* This procedure displays a message when the user presses the required control key combination.    *
;************************************************************************************************

Message PROC    NEAR

        MOV     AX,1300h        ;Display the first line of
        MOV     BX,0007h        ; the message.
        MOV     CX,23
        MOV     DX,0A14h
        PUSH    BP
        LEA     BP,Msg1
        INT     10h
        POP     BP

        MOV     AX,1300h        ;Display the second line of
        MOV     BX,0007h        ; the message.
        MOV     CX,23
        MOV     DX,0B14h
        PUSH    BP
        LEA     BP,Msg2
        INT     10h
        POP     BP

        MOV     AX,1300h        ;Display the third line of
        MOV     BX,0007h        ; the message.
        MOV     CX,23
        MOV     DX,0C14h
        PUSH    BP
        LEA     BP,Msg3
        INT     10h
        POP     BP

        MOV     AX,1301h        ;Display the completed
        MOV     BX,0007h        ; message.
        MOV     CX,27
        MOV     DX,1400h
        PUSH    BP
        LEA     BP,Msg5
        INT     10h
        POP     BP

        XOR     AX,AX   ;Wait for a keypress.
        INT     16h
```

18-1A Continued.

```
          RET

Message ENDP

;****************************************************************************************
;* This procedure restores the screen buffer to its original state on program exit.   *
;****************************************************************************************

RestScrn        PROC    NEAR

        PUSH    ES      ;Save ES.
        MOV     AX,0B800h       ;Load the video segment.
        MOV     ES,AX
        MOV     DI,0    ;Load the starting position.
        LEA     SI,VBuff        ;Load the storage buffer offset.
        MOV     CX,4000 ;80 characters * 25 lines.
        REP     MOVSB   ;Restore the buffer.
        POP     ES      ;Restore ES.

        RET

RestScrn        ENDP

;****************************************************************************************
;* This procedure saves the contents of the video buffer to a storage location within program memory.  The   *
;* program uses the contents of the storage location to restore the display to its original appearance upon   *
;* program exit.                                         *
;****************************************************************************************

SaveScrn        PROC    NEAR

        PUSH    DS      ;Save DS.
        MOV     AX,0B800h       ;Load the video segment.
        MOV     DS,AX
        MOV     SI,0    ;Load the starting position.
        LEA     DI,VBuff        ;Load the storage buffer offset.
        MOV     CX,4000 ;80 characters * 25 lines.
        REP     MOVSB   ;Save the buffer.
        POP     DS      ;Restore DS.

        RET

SaveScrn        ENDP

;****************************************************************************************
;* This procedure restores the cursor to its original position upon program exit.      *
;****************************************************************************************

SetCPosit       PROC    NEAR

        MOV     AX,0200h
```

18-1A Continued.

```
        XOR     BX,BX
        MOV     DX,CurPos
        INT     10h

        RET

SetCPosit       ENDP

;********************************************************************************************************
;* This is the second half of the TSR.  It installs the TSR in memory then exits.  The installation consists  *
;* of three parts.  The first part retrieves the current interrupt 9 vector, saves it, and points interrupt 9  *
;* to our procedure.  The second part calculates the amount of memory used by the program.  The memory  *
;* allocation calculation discludes the installation portion of the program since it is no longer required.    *
;* The final part exits back to DOS after telling DOS how much memory to reserve for the resident part of the  *
;* program.                                  *
;********************************************************************************************************

Install PROC    FAR

ProgSize        EQU     $ - Start       ;End of the resident part of
                        ; the program.

TSRInstall:     MOV     AX,@DATA        ;Point DS & ES to our data segment.
        MOV     DS,AX
        MOV     ES,AX

        MOV     AX,3509h        ;Get interrupt 16 vector.
        INT     21h
        MOV     WORD PTR Old9,BX        ;Save the vector.
        MOV     WORD PTR [Old9+2],ES

        MOV     AX,2509h        ;Point interrupt 16 to our
        PUSH    DS      ; procedure
        PUSH    CS
        POP     DS
        LEA     DX,Start
        INT     21h
        POP     DS      ;Restore DS.

        MOV     AX,0900h
        LEA     DX,Msg4
        INT     21h
        MOV     AX,ProgSize     ;Calculate the amount of
        MOV     CX,16   ; memory to reserve.  First,
        XOR     DX,DX   ; calculate the number of
        DIV     CX      ; paragraphs used by the code
        INC     AX      ; segment.  Then, calculate
        MOV     BX,AX   ; the number of paragraphs
        MOV     AX,DataSize     ; used by the data segment.
        XOR     DX,DX   ; Add the two values together
        DIV     CX      ; and store the result in DX.
```

```
        INC     AX
        ADD     AX,BX
        MOV     DX,AX

        MOV     AX,3100h        ;Terminate and Stay Resident.
        INT     21h
        RET

Install ENDP

END     TSRInstall
```

18-1D Pascal TSR demonstration.

```
    (***********************************************************************************************************)
(* Sample Program 25, Terminate and Stay Resident Programming Techniques Demonstration  *)
(* This program shows you how to create terminate and stay residen programs.  The TSRUNIT library provides      *)
(* special routines required to make this program operate correctly.  You must compile the TSRUNIT program      *)
(* first, then this program.  You do not need any special equipment to use this program.          *)
(*                              *)
(* Copyright 1989,1990 John Mueller & Wallace Wang - Tab Books *)
    (***********************************************************************************************************)


PROGRAM TSRTest;

{$M 1024, 5120, 10240}
USES
  TSRUnit, Crt;
TYPE
  Buffer = string[255];
  Proc = PROCEDURE;
  BufPtr = ^Buffer;
  ProcPtr = ^Proc;
VAR
  PrtBit : BufPtr;
  Next : ProcPtr;

  {$F+}
  PROCEDURE Message;
  BEGIN
    GotoXY (20,10);
    Writeln ('èëëëëëëëëëëëëëëëëëëëë£');
    GotoXY (20,11);
    Writeln ('¤  TSR Test Program   ¤');
    GotoXY (20,12);
    Writeln ('àëëëëëëëëëëëëëëëëëëëë¥');
    Readln;
  END;  (* Message *)
  {$F-}
```

```
BEGIN
  Next := Addr(Message);
  PrtBit^ := 'The DOS 4.0 program';
  TSRInstall (PrtBit, Next, AltKey, 'A');
END.
```

event may consist of a program sending output to the printer. These event driven interrupts activate the TSR. If the TSR cannot control the required interrupt, then it uses memory without performing useful work.

Active TSR programs expect user input. Examples of active TSR programs include calculators or simple word processors. Of the two types of TSR programs, active TSRs are more complicated to program. You not only need to track events, but user input as well. As a result, active TSRs always take control of more interrupts than passive TSRs of the same capability. An active TSR always keeps track of the keyboard interrupt so it can monitor user input. When the user types standard input, the TSR passes the input to the standard keyboard interrupt. Otherwise, the TSR processes the keystroke, saves any required registers and memory locations, and makes itself active.

HOW TSR PROGRAMS BEGIN

The following steps show you how a typical TSR activates itself. You can look for these steps within the source code listing of FIG. 18-2. Not every TSR performs every step listed below. For example, passive TSRs skip the first part of step 3 because they do not need to take control of the keyboard interrupt. However, every TSR should perform step 2. Failure to save the contents of registers or memory could prevent the application that the TSR interrupted from working correctly.

1. Check for identical ID string: The first time a TSR program loads itself in memory, it should also install a unique ID string. By checking to see if its ID string already appears in memory, a TSR program prevents multiple copies of itself from loading. Loading multiple copies of a TSR uses memory and reduces the efficiency of your computer without performing any useful work.
2. Save pointer to top of memory stack: The pointer designates the stack address where the TSR program begins. Creating a stack frame prevents the TSR from overwriting any data saved by an application on the stack. C programs always use a stack frame when calling another function. Other programming languages use a stack frame by convention. If you create a TSR specifically for 80286 and above computers, then you can use the ENTER command to create a stack frame and the LEAVE command to restore the stack.

18-2 TSR library source code listing.

```
(*****************************************************************************************************)
(* Terminate and Stay Resident (TSR) Unit for Program 25          *)
(* This unit contains the procedures required to create a terminate and stay resident (TSR) interface   *)
(* with Turbo Pascal 5.5.  Notice that a TSR unit consists of two sections.  The first section contains the    *)
(* interrupt handler code required to pass control to a program after you install the TSR.  The second *)
(* section contains the initialization code required to install the program.  You do not need any special      *)
(* equipment to use this program.                    *)
(*                          *)
(* Copyright 1989, 1990 John Mueller & Wallace Wang - Tab Books*)
(*****************************************************************************************************)


UNIT TSRUnit; {Create TSR programs with Turbo Pascal 5.0 & TSRUnit}
(*
The author and any distributor of this software assume no responsi-
bility for damages resulting from this software or its use due to
errors, omissions, incompatibility with other software or with
hardware, or misuse; and specifically disclaim any implied warranty
of fitness for any particular purpose or application.
*)


{$B-,F-,I+,R-,S+} {Set compiler directives to normal values.}


INTERFACE {=========================================================}
USES DOS, CRT;
CONST
(*** Shift key combination codes.                    }
  AltKey = 8;  CtrlKey = 4;  LeftKey = 2;  RightKey = 1;

  TSRVersion : WORD = $0202;       {Low byte.High byte = 2.02     }

TYPE
  String80  = STRING[80];
  ChrWords  = RECORD CASE INTEGER OF
                  1: ( W: WORD );
                  2: ( C: CHAR; A: BYTE );
              END;
  LineWords = ARRAY[1..80] OF ChrWords;

VAR
  TSRScrPtr : POINTER; {Pointer to saved screen image.          }
  TSRChrPtr : POINTER; {Pointer to first character to insert.    }
  TSRMode   : BYTE;       {Video mode --------- before TSR popped up.}
  TSRWidth  : BYTE;       {Number of screen columns-- "  "    "    " .}
  TSRPage   : BYTE;       {Active video page number-- "  "    "    " .}
  TSRColumn : BYTE;       {Cursor column number ----- "  "    "    " .}
  TSRRow    : BYTE;       {Cursor row number -------- "  "    "    " .}
{
** Procedure for installing the TSR program.               }
PROCEDURE TSRInstall( PgmName,              {Ptr to a char. string. }
                      PgmPtr  : POINTER; {Ptr to FUNCTION to call}
                      ShiftComb: BYTE;    {Hot key--shift key comb}
```

```
                      KeyChr   : CHAR );  {Hot Key--character key.}
{
  ShiftComb and KeyChr specify the default hot keys for the TSR.
  ShiftComb may be created by adding or ORing the constants AltKey,
  CtrlKey, LeftKey, and RightKey together.  KeyChr may be
  characters 0-9 and A-Z.

  The default hot keys may be overridden when the TSR is installed
  by specifying optional parameters on the command line.  The
  parameter format is:
                      [/A] [/C] [/R] [/L] [/"[K["]]]
  The square brackets surround optional items--do not include them.
  Any characters between parameters are ignored. The order of the
  characters does not matter; however, the shift keys specified are
  cumulative and the last character key "K" specified is the used.
}
{
** Functions for checking status of printer LPT1.               }
FUNCTION PrinterStatus: BYTE;    {Returns status of printer.     }
FUNCTION PrinterOkay:   BOOLEAN; {Returns TRUE if printer is okay.}


{
** Routines for obtaining one row of screen characters.         }
FUNCTION ScreenLineStr( Row: BYTE ): String80; {Returns char. str.}
PROCEDURE ScreenLine( Row: BYTE; VAR Line: LineWords; {Returns    }
                                 VAR Words: BYTE );   {chr & color}

IMPLEMENTATION {==================================================}
VAR
  BuffSize, InitCMode : WORD;
  NpxFlag             : BOOLEAN;
  Buffer              : ARRAY[0..8191] OF WORD;
  NpxState            : ARRAY[0..93] OF BYTE;
  RetrnVal, InitVideo : BYTE;

CONST   {Offsets to items contained in PROCEDURE Asm.            }
  UnSafe = 0;    Flg  = 1;     Key    = 2;     Shft = 3;
  StkOfs = 4;    StkSs = 6;    DosSp  = 8;     DosSs = 10;
  Prev  = 12;    Flg9 = 13;    InsNumb = 14;
  Dos21 = $10;        Dos25  = Dos21+4;     Dos26  = Dos25+4;
  Bios9 = Dos26+4;    Bios16 = Bios9+4;     DosTab = Bios16+4;
  Our21 = DosTab+99;  Our25  = Our21+51;    Our26  = Our25+24;
  Our09 = Our26+24;   Our16  = Our09+127+8; InsChr = Our16+180-8;
  PopUp = InsChr+4;   Pgm    = PopUp+4;

PROCEDURE Asm; {Inline code--data storage and intercept routines. }
INTERRUPT;
BEGIN
INLINE(
{*** Storage for interrupt vectors.                             }
     {Dos21: }  >0/>0/    {DOS func. intr vector.                }
```

```
{Dos25:  }  >0/>0/      {DOS abs. disk read intr. vector.    }
{Dos26:  }  >0/>0/      {DOS abs. sector write intr.vector.  }
{Bios9:  }  >0/>0/      {BIOS key stroke intr. vector.       }
{Bios16: }  >0/>0/      {BIOS buffered keybd. input intr.vect.}

{DosTab: ARRAY[0..98] OF BYTE = {Non-reetrant DOS functions.}
0/0/0/0/0/0/0/  0/0/0/0/0/1/1/1/  1/1/1/1/1/1/1/1/
1/1/1/1/1/1/1/1/  1/1/1/1/1/1/0/1/  1/1/1/1/1/1/1/0/
1/0/0/0/0/0/1/1/  1/1/1/1/1/1/1/1/  1/1/1/1/1/1/1/1/
0/0/0/0/0/0/1/1/  0/0/0/1/0/1/1/  0/1/1/1/1/0/0/0/  0/0/0/
```

```
{*** OurIntr21 ******* Intercept routine for DOS Function Intr.***}
(  0} $9C/                { PUSHF            ;Save flags.             }
(  1} $FB/                { STI              ;Enable interrupts.      }
(  2} $80/$FC/$63/        { CMP   AH,63H     ;Assume unsafe if new    }
(  5} $73/<22-7/          { JNB   IncF       ;function--skip table.}
(  7} $50/                { PUSH  AX         ;Save registers.         }
(  8} $53/                { PUSH  BX         ;Load offset to table.}
(  9} $BB/>DosTab/        { MOV   BX,[DosTab]                         }
( 12} $8A/$C4/            { MOV   AL,AH      ;Load table entry        }
( 14} $2E/                { CS:              ;index.                  }
( 15} $D7/                { XLAT             ;Get value from table.}
( 16} $3C/$00/            { CMP   AL,0       ;If TRUE then set flag}
( 18} $5B/                { POP   BX         ;Restore registers.      }
( 19} $58/                { POP   AX         ;                        }
( 20} $74/$17/            { JZ    JmpDos21   ;Jump to orig. intr.     }
( 22} $2E/        {IncF:  CS:              ;                        }
( 23} $FE/$06/>UnSafe/    { INC   [UnSafe]   ;Set UnSafe flag.        }
( 27} $9D/                { POPF             ;Restore flags.          }
( 28} $9C/                { PUSHF            ;                        }
( 29} $2E/                { CS:              ;                        }
( 30} $FF/$1E/>Dos21/     { CALL FAR [Dos21] ;Call orig. intr.        }
( 34} $FB/                { STI              ;Enable interrupts.      }
( 35} $9C/                { PUSHF            ;Save flags.             }
( 36} $2E/                { CS:              ;                        }
( 37} $FE/$0E/>UnSafe/    { DEC   [UnSafe]   ;Clear UnSafe flag.      }
( 41} $9D/                { POPF             ;Restore flags.          }
( 42} $CA/$02/$00/        { RETF  2          ;Return & remove flag.}

( 45} $9D/        {JmpDos21: POPF            ;Restore flags.          }
( 46} $2E/                { CS:              ;                        }
( 47} $FF/$2E/>Dos21/     { JMP FAR [Dos21]  ;Jump to orig. intr.     }
( 51}
{*** OurIntr25 ********** Intercept routine for DOS Abs. Read *** }
(  0} $9C/                { PUSHF            ;Save flags.             }
(  1} $2E/                { CS:              ;                        }
(  2} $FE/$06/>UnSafe/    { INC   [UnSafe]   ;Set UnSafe flag.        }
(  6} $9D/                { POPF             ;Restore flags.          }
(  7} $9C/                { PUSHF            ;                        }
(  8} $2E/                { CS:              ;                        }
(  9} $FF/$1E/>Dos25/     { CALL FAR [Dos25] ;Call DOS abs. read.     }
```

18-2 Continued.

```
( 13) $83/$C4/$02/       ( ADD   SP,2        ;Clean up stack.      )
( 16) $9C/               ( PUSHF             ;Save flags.          )
( 17) $2E/               ( CS:               ;                     )
( 18) $FE/$0E/>UnSafe/    ( DEC   [UnSafe]    ;Clear UnSafe flag.   )
( 22) $9D/               ( POPF              ;Restore flags.  Leave)
( 23) $CB/               ( RETF              ;old flags on the stk.)
( 24)

(*** OurIntr26 ********** Intercept routine for DOS Abs. Write ***)
(  0) $9C/               ( PUSHF             ;Save flags.          )
(  1) $2E/               ( CS:               ;                     )
(  2) $FE/$06/>UnSafe/    ( INC   [UnSafe]    ;Set UnSafe flag.     )
(  6) $9D/               ( POPF              ;Restore flags.       )
(  7) $9C/               ( PUSHF             ;                     )
(  8) $2E/               ( CS:               ;                     )
(  9) $FF/$1E/>Dos26/     ( CALL  FAR [Dos26] ;Call DOS abs. write. )
( 13) $83/$C4/$02/       ( ADD   SP,2        ;Clean up stack.      )
( 16) $9C/               ( PUSHF             ;Save flags.          )
( 17) $2E/               ( CS:               ;                     )
( 18) $FE/$0E/>UnSafe/    ( DEC   [UnSafe]    ;Clear UnSafe flag.   )
( 22) $9D/               ( POPF              ;Restore flags.  Leave)
( 23) $CB/               ( RETF              ;old flags on the stk.)
( 24)


(*** OurIntr9 ********** Intercept for BIOS Hardware Keyboard Intr)
(  0) $9C/               ( PUSHF             ;Entry point.         )
(  1) $FB/               ( STI               ;Enable interrupts.   )
(  2) $1E/               ( PUSH DS            ;                     )
(  3) $0E/               ( PUSH CS            ;DS := CS;            )
(  4) $1F/               ( POP  DS            ;                     )
(  5) $50/               ( PUSH AX            ;Preserve AX on stack.)
(  6) $31/$C0/           ( XOR   AX,AX        ;Set AH to 0.         )
(  8) $E4/$60/           ( IN    AL,60h       ;Read byte from keybd )
( 10) $3C/$E0/           ( CMP   AL,0E0h      ;If multi-byte codes, )
( 12) $74/<75-14/        ( JE    Sfx          ;then jump and set    )
( 14) $3C/$F0/           ( CMP   AL,0F0h      ;multi-byte flag, Flg9)
( 16) $74/<75-18/        ( JE    Sfx          ;                     )
( 18) $80/$3E/>Flg9/$00/ ( CMP   [Flg9],0     ;Exit if part of      )
( 23) $75/<77-25/        ( JNZ   Cfx          ;multi-byte code.     )
( 25) $3A/$06/>Key/      ( CMP   AL,[Key]     ;Exit if key pressed  )
( 29) $75/<88-31/        ( JNE   PreExit      ;is not hot key.      )

( 31) $50/               ( PUSH AX            ;Hot key was pressed, )
( 32) $06/               ( PUSH ES            ;check shift key      )
( 33) $B8/$40/$00/       ( MOV   AX,0040h     ;status byte.  First  )
( 36) $8E/$C0/           ( MOV   ES,AX        ;load BIOS segment.   )
( 38) $26/               ( ES:               ;                     )
( 39) $A0/>$0017/        ( MOV   AL,[0017h]   ;AL:= Shift key status)
( 42) $07/               ( POP   ES           ;Restore ES register. )
( 43) $24/$0F/           ( AND   AL,0Fh       ;Clear unwanted bits. )
( 45) $3A/$06/>Shft/     ( CMP   AL,[Shft]    ;Exit if not hot key  )
( 49) $58/               ( POP   AX           ;shift key combination)
```

```
( 50) $75/<88-52/           ( JNE  PreExit      ;(Restore AX first).  )

                            (                   ;Hot Keys encountered.)
( 52) $3A/$06/>Prev/        ( CMP  AL,[Prev]    ;Discard repeated hot )
( 56) $74/<107-58/          ( JE   Discard      ;key codes.           )
( 58) $A2/>Prev/            ( MOV  [Prev],AL    ;Update Prev.         )
( 61) $F6/$06/>Flg/3/       ( TEST [Flg],3      ;If Flg set, keep key )
( 66) $75/<99-68/           ( JNZ  JmpBios9     ;& exit to orig. BIOS )
( 68) $80/$0E/>Flg/1/       ( OR   [Flg],1      ;9. Else set flag and)
( 73) $EB/<107-75/          ( JMP  SHORT Discard;discard key stroke.  )

( 75) $B4/$01/        {Sfx: MOV  AH,1           ;Load AH with set flag)
( 77) $88/$26/>Flg9/  {Cfx: MOV  [Flg9],AH      ;Save multi-byte flag.)
( 81) $C6/$06/>Prev/$FF/ ( MOV  [Prev],0FFh     ;Change prev key byte.)
( 86) $EB/<99-88/           ( JMP  SHORT JmpBios9                      )

( 88) $3C/$FF/        {PreExit: CMP AL,0FFh     ;Update previous key   )
( 90) $74/<99-92/           ( JE   JmpBios9      ;unless key is buffer-)
( 92) $3C/$00/              ( CMP  AL,0          ;full code--a 00h     )
( 94) $74/<99-96/           ( JZ   JmpBios9      ;0FFh                 )
( 96) $A2/>Prev/            ( MOV  [Prev],AL     ;Update previous key. )

( 99) $58/    {JmpBios9: POP  AX               ;Restore registers and)
(100) $1F/                  ( POP  DS            ;flags.               )
(101) $9D/                  ( POPF               ;                     )
(102) $2E/                  ( CS:                ;                     )
(103) $FF/$2E/>Bios9/       ( JMP  [Bios9]       ;Exit to orig. intr 9.)

(107) $E4/$61/        {Discard: IN  AL,61h      ;Clear key from buffer)
(109) $8A/$E0/              ( MOV  AH,AL         ;by resetting keyboard)
(111) $0C/$80/              ( OR   AL,80h        ;port and sending EOI )
(113) $E6/$61/              ( OUT  61h,AL        ;to intr. handler     )
(115) $86/$E0/              ( XCHG AH,AL         ;telling it that the  )
(117) $E6/$61/              ( OUT  61h,AL        ;key has been         )
(119) $B0/$20/              ( MOV  AL,20h        ;processed.           )
(121) $E6/$20/              ( OUT  20h,AL        ;                     )
(123) $58/                  ( POP  AX            ;Restore registers and)
(124) $1F/                  ( POP  DS            ;flags.               )
(125) $9D/                  ( POPF               ;                     )
(126) $CF/                  ( IRET               ;Return from interrupt)
(127)

{*** OurIntr16 ***** Intercept routine for Buffered Keyboard Input)
(  0) $58/    {JmpBios16: POP  AX               ;Restore AX, DS, and  )
(  1) $1F/                  ( POP  DS            ;FLAGS registers then )
(  2) $9D/                  ( POPF               ;exit to orig. BIOS   )
(  3) $2E/                  ( CS:                ;intr. 16h routine.   )
(  4) $FF/$2E/>Bios16/      ( JMP  [Bios16]      ;                     )

(  8) $9C/    {OurIntr16: PUSHF                  ;Preserve FLAGS.       )
(  9) $FB/                  ( STI                ;Enable interrupts.   )
```

18-2 Continued.

```
(  10) $1E/          ( PUSH DS          ;Preserve DS and AX   )
(  11) $50/          ( PUSH AX          ;registers.           )
(  12) $0E/          ( PUSH CS          ;DS := CS;            )
(  13) $1F/          ( POP  DS          ;                     )
(  14) $F6/$C4/$EF/  ( TEST AH,EFh      ;Jmp if not read char.)
(  17) $75/<48-19/   ( JNZ  C3          ;request.             )

                     (*** Intercept loop for Read Key service.)
(  19) $F6/$06/>Flg/1/ (C1: TEST [Flg],1   ;If pop up Flg bit is )
(  24) $74/<29-26/   ( JZ   C2          ;set then call INLINE )
(  26) $E8/>122-29/  ( CALL ToPopUp     ;pop up routine.      )
(  29) $F6/$06/>Flg/16/(C2: TEST [Flg],10h ;Jmp if insert flg set)
(  34) $75/<48-36/   ( JNZ  C3          ;                     )
(  36) $FE/$C4/      ( INC  AH          ;Use orig. BIOS       )
(  38) $9C/          ( PUSHF            ;service to check for )
(  39) $FA/          ( CLI              ;character ready.     )
(  40) $FF/$1E/>Bios16/ ( CALL FAR [Bios16];Disable interrupts.  )
(  44) $58/          ( POP  AX          ;Restore AX and save  )
(  45) $50/          ( PUSH AX          ;it again.            )
(  46) $74/<19-48/   ( JZ   C1          ;Loop until chr. ready)

(  48) $F6/$06/>Flg/17/(C3: TEST [Flg],11h ;Exit if neither bit  )
(  53) $74/<-55/     ( JZ   JmpBios16   ;of Flg is set.       )
(  55) $F6/$06/>Flg/$01/ ( TEST [Flg],1   ;If pop up Flg bit is )
(  60) $74/<65-62/   ( JZ   C4          ;set then call INLINE )
(  62) $E8/>122-65/  ( CALL ToPopUp     ;pop up routine.      )
(  65) $F6/$06/>Flg/$10/(C4:TEST [Flg],10h ;Exit unless have     )
(  70) $74/<-72/     ( JZ   JmpBios16   ;characters to insert.)
(  72) $F6/$C4/$EE/  ( TEST AH,0EEh     ;If request is not a  )
(  75) $75/<-77/     ( JNZ  JmpBios16   ;chr. request, exit.  )

                     (*** Insert a character.                 )
(  77) $58/          ( POP  AX          ;AX := BIOS service no)
(  78) $53/          ( PUSH BX          ;Save BX and ES.      )
(  79) $06/          ( PUSH ES          ;                     )
(  80) $C4/$1E/>InsChr/ ( LES  BX,[InsChr] ;PTR(ES,BX) := InsChr;)
(  84) $26/          ( ES:              ;AL := InsChr^;       )
(  85) $8A/$07/      ( MOV  AL,[BX]     ;                     )
(  87) $07/          ( POP  ES          ;Restore ES and BX.   )
(  88) $5B/          ( POP  BX          ;                     )
(  89) $F6/$C4/$01/  ( TEST AH,01h      ;IF AH IN [$01,$11]   )
(  92) $B4/$00/      ( MOV  AH,00h      ;   THEN ReportOnly;  )
(  94) $75/<114-96/  ( JNZ  ReportOnly  ;Set Scan code to 0.  )
(  96) $FE/$06/>InsChr/ ( INC  [InsChr]  ;Inc( InsChr );       )
( 100) $FF/$0E/>InsNumb/ ( DEC  [InsNumb] ;Dec( InsNumb );      )
( 104) $75/<111-106/ ( JNZ  SkipReset   ;IF InsNumb = 0 THEN  )
( 106) $80/$26/>Flg/$EF/ ( AND  [Flg],0EFh ; Clear insert chr flg)
( 111) $1F/    (SkipReset: POP  DS       ;Restore BX, DS, and  )
( 112) $9D/          ( POPF             ;FLAGS, then return   )
( 113) $CF/          ( IRET             ;from interrupt.      )
```

18-2 Continued.

```
{114} $1F/      {ReportOnly: POP  DS          ;Report char. ready.  }
{115} $9D/      {           POPF              ;Restore DS and FLAGS.}
{116} $50/      {           PUSH AX           ;Clear zero flag bit   }
{117} $40/      {           INC  AX           ;to indicate a         }
{118} $58/      {           POP  AX           ;character ready.      }
{119} $CA/>0002/ {          RETF 2            ;Exit & discard FLAGS }

                           {*** Interface to PopUpCode Routine.     }
{122} $50/      {ToPopUp: PUSH AX             ;Save AX.              }
{123} $FA/      {        CLI                  ;Disable interrupts.   }
{124} $F6/$06/>UnSafe/$FF/{TEST [UnSafe],0FFh ;IF UnSafe <> 0        }
{129} $75/<177-131/ {     JNZ  PP2            ;      THEN Return.    }
{131} $A0/>Flg/ {        MOV  AL,[Flg]        ;Set in-use bit; clear}
{134} $24/$FE/  {        AND  AL,0FEh         ;pop up bit of Flg.    }
{136} $0C/$02/  {        OR   AL,2            ;Flg := (Flg AND $FE)  }
{138} $A2/>Flg/ {        MOV  [Flg],AL        ;       OR 2;          }
                {                             ;**Switch to our stack}
{141} $A1/>StkOfs/ {     MOV  AX,[StkOfs]     ;Load top of our stack}
{144} $87/$C4/  {        XCHG AX,SP           ;Exchange it with      }
{146} $A3/>DosSp/ {      MOV  [DosSp],AX      ;stk.ptr, save old SP.}
{149} $8C/$16/>DosSs/ {  MOV  [DosSs],SS      ;Save old SS.          }
{153} $8E/$16/>StkSs/ {  MOV  SS,[StkSs]      ;Replace SS with our   }
{157} $FB/      {        STI                  ;SS. Enable interrupts}

{158} $9C/      {        PUSHF                ;Interrupt call to pop}
{159} $FF/$1E/>PopUp/ {  CALL FAR [PopUp]     ;up TSR routine.       }

{163} $FA/      {        CLI                  ;Disable interrupts.   }
{164} $8B/$26/>DosSp/ {  MOV  SP,[DosSp]      ;Restore stack ptr     }
{168} $8E/$16/>DosSs/ {  MOV  SS,[DosSs]      ;SS:SP.  Clear in-use  }
{172} $80/$26/>Flg/$FD/ { AND [Flg],0FDh      ;bit of Flg.           }

{177} $FB/      {PP2: STI                     ;Enable interrupts.    }
{178} $58/      {     POP  AX                 ;Restore AX.           }
{179} $C3 );    {     RET                     ;Return.               }
{180}
END; {Asm.} {END corresponds to 12 bytes of code--used for storage}

PROCEDURE PopUpCode; {Interface between the BIOS intercept      }
INTERRUPT;           {routines and your TSR function.           }
CONST  BSeg = $0040;   VBiosOfs = $49;
TYPE
  VideoRecs = RECORD
            VideoMode                      : BYTE;
            NumbCol, ScreenSize, MemoryOfs : WORD;
            CursorArea        : ARRAY[0..7] OF WORD;
            CursorMode                     : WORD;
            CurrentPage                    : BYTE;
            VideoBoardAddr                 : WORD;
            CurrentMode, CurrentColor      : BYTE;
        END;
```

18-2 Continued.

```
VAR
  Regs        : Registers;
  VideoRec    : VideoRecs;
  KeyLock     : BYTE;
  ScrnSeg     : WORD;
BEGIN
  SwapVectors;                              {Set T.P. intr. vectors.}
  Move( Ptr(BSeg,VBiosOfs)^, VideoRec,      {Get Video BIOS info.   }
       SizeOf(VideoRec) );
  WITH VideoRec, Regs DO BEGIN
    IF (VideoMode > 7) OR                   {Abort pop up if unable}
       (ScreenSize > BuffSize) THEN BEGIN   {to save screen image. }
      SwapVectors;                          {Restore intr. vectors.}
      Exit;
    END;
    KeyLock := Mem[BSeg:$0017];             {Save lock key states. }
    IF VideoMode = 7 THEN ScrnSeg := $B000  {Save screen--supports }
    ELSE ScrnSeg := $B800;                  {text, MGA & CGA modes.}
    Move( PTR( ScrnSeg, MemoryOfs )^, Buffer, ScreenSize );
    AX := InitVideo;                        {If in graphics mode,  }
    IF (VideoMode >=4)                      {switch to text mode.  }
       AND (VideoMode <= 6) THEN Intr( $10, Regs );
    AX := $0500;                            {Select display page 0.}
    Intr( $10, Regs );
    CX := InitCMode;                        {Set cursor size.      }
    AH := 1;
    Intr( $10, Regs );


    TSRMode   := VideoMode;                 {Fill global variables  }
    TSRWidth  := NumbCol;                   {with current information}
    TSRPage   := CurrentPage;
    TSRColumn := Succ( Lo( CursorArea[CurrentPage] ) );
    TSRRow    := Succ( Hi( CursorArea[CurrentPage] ) );


    IF NpxFlag THEN                         {Save co-processor state.}
      INLINE( $98/ $DD/$36/>NpxState );     {WAIT FSAVE [NpxState]  }
{
*** Call user's program and save return code--no. char. to insert.
}
    INLINE( $2E/$FF/$1E/>Pgm/     { CALL FAR CS:[Pgm]   }
            $2E/$A3/>InsNumb );   { MOV CS:[InsNumb],AX }

    IF Mem[CSeg:InsNumb] > 0 THEN BEGIN     {Have char. to insert.  }
      MemL[CSeg:InsChr] := LONGINT( TSRChrPtr );
      Mem[CSeg:Flg]     := Mem[CSeg:Flg] OR $10;
    END;
{
*** Pop TSR back down--Restore computer to previous state.
}
    IF NpxFlag THEN                         {Restore co-prcssr state.}
      INLINE( $98/ $DD/$36/>NpxState );     {WAIT FSAVE [NpxState]  }
```

```
      Mem[BSeg:$17] :=                      {Restore key lock status.}
        (Mem[BSeg:$17] AND $0F) OR (KeyLock AND $F0);

      IF Mem[BSeg:VBiosOfs] <> VideoMode THEN BEGIN
        AX := VideoMode;                    {Restore video mode.    }
        Intr( $10, Regs );
      END;
      AH := 1;  CX := CursorMode;           {Restore cursor size.   }
      Intr( $10, Regs );
      AH := 5;  AL := CurrentPage;          {Restore active page.   }
      Intr( $10, Regs );
      AH := 2;  BH := CurrentPage;          {Restore cursor positon. }
      DX := CursorArea[CurrentPage];
      Intr( $10, Regs );                    {Restore screen image.   }
      Move( Buffer, PTR( ScrnSeg, MemoryOfs )^, ScreenSize );

      SwapVectors;                          {Restore non-T.P. vectors.}
    END;
END; {PopUp.}
{
***** Printer Functions:
}
FUNCTION PrinterStatus: BYTE;              {Returns status of LPT1.}
{ Definition of status byte bits (1 & 2 are not used), if set then:
 Bit: -- 7 ---  ---- 6 ----  -- 5 ---  -- 4 ---  -- 3 --  --- 0 ---
        Not busy  Acknowledge  No paper  Selected  I/O Err. Timed-out
}
VAR Regs  : Registers;
BEGIN
  WITH Regs DO BEGIN
    AH := 2;  DX := 0;     {Load BIOS function and printer number. }
    Intr( $17, Regs );     {Call BIOS printer services.            }
    PrinterStatus := AH;   {Return with printer status byte.       }
  END;
END; {PrinterStatus.}


FUNCTION PrinterOkay: BOOLEAN;  {Returns TRUE if printer is okay. }
VAR  S : BYTE;
BEGIN
  S := PrinterStatus;
  IF ((S AND $10) <> 0) AND ((S AND $29) = 0) THEN
    PrinterOkay := TRUE
  ELSE PrinterOkay := FALSE;
END;  {PrinterOkay.}
{
***** Procedures to obtain contents of saved screen image.
}
PROCEDURE ScreenLine( Row: BYTE; VAR Line: LineWords;
                                 VAR Words: BYTE );
BEGIN
  Words := 40;                            {Determine screen line size.}
```

```
  IF TSRMode > 1 THEN  Words := Words*2;              {Get line's       }
  Move( Buffer[Pred(Row)*Words], Line, Words*2 );  {characters and }
END; {ScreenLine.}                                    {colors.          }


FUNCTION ScreenLineStr( Row: BYTE ): String80; {Returns just chars}
VAR
  Words, i   : BYTE;
  LineWord   : LineWords;
  Line       : String80;
BEGIN
  ScreenLine( Row, LineWord, Words );    {Get chars & attributes.  }
  Line := '';                            {Move characters to string}
  FOR i := 1 TO Words DO Insert( LineWord[i].C, Line, i );
  ScreenLineStr := Line;
END; {ScreenString.}
{
***** TSR Installation procedure.
}
PROCEDURE TSRInstall( PgmName, PgmPtr: POINTER;
                      ShiftComb: BYTE; KeyChr: CHAR );
CONST
  ScanChr = '+1234567890++++QWERTYUIOP++++ASDFGHJKL+++++ZXCVBNM';
  CombChr = 'RLCA"';
VAR
  PgmNamePtr, PlistPtr: ^STRING;
  i, j, k              : WORD;
  Regs                 : Registers;
  Comb, ScanCode       : BYTE;
BEGIN
  IF Ofs( Asm ) <> 0 THEN EXIT;          {Offset of Asm must be 0}
  MemW[CSeg:StkSs]  := SSeg;             {Save pointer to top of }
  MemW[CSeg:StkOfs] := Sptr + 308;       {TSR's stack.           }
  MemL[CSeg:PopUp]  := LONGINT(@PopUpCode); {Save PopUpCode addr. }
  MemL[CSeg:Pgm]    := LONGINT(PgmPtr);  {Save PgmPtr.           }
  PgmNamePtr        := PgmName;          {Convert ptr to string ptr.}

  Writeln('Installing Stay-Resident program: ',PgmNamePtr^);
{
*****  Save intercepted interrupt vectors: $09, $16, $21, $25, $26.
}
  GetIntVec( $09, POINTER( MemL[CSeg:Bios9] ) );
  GetIntVec( $16, POINTER( MemL[CSeg:Bios16] ) );
  GetIntVec( $21, POINTER( MemL[CSeg:Dos21] ) );
  GetIntVec( $25, POINTER( MemL[CSeg:Dos25] ) );
  GetIntVec( $26, POINTER( MemL[CSeg:Dos26] ) );
{
***** Get equipment list and video mode.
}
  WITH Regs DO BEGIN
    Intr( $11, Regs );                   {Check equipment list for }
    NpxFlag := (AL AND 2) = 2;           {math co-processor.       }
```

```
  AH       := 15;                    {Get current video mode   }
  Intr( $10, Regs );                 {and save it for when TSR }
  InitVideo := AL;                   {is activated.            }
  AH := 3; BH := 0;                  {Get current cursor size  }
  Intr( $10, Regs );                 {and save it for when TSR }
  InitCMode := CX;                   {is activated.            }
END; {WITH Regs}
{
***** Get info. on buffer for saving screen image.
}
  BuffSize := SizeOf( Buffer );
  TSRScrPtr := @Buffer;
{
*** Determine activation key combination.
}
  Comb := 0;  i := 1;                {Create ptr to            }
  PlistPtr := Ptr( PrefixSeg, $80 ); {parameter list.          }
  WHILE i < Length( PlistPtr^ ) DO BEGIN  {Check for parameters.}
    IF PlistPtr^[i] = '/' THEN BEGIN      {Process parameter.   }
      Inc( i );
      j := Pos( UpCase( PlistPtr^[i] ), CombChr );
      IF (j > 0) AND (j < 5) THEN Comb := Comb OR (1 SHL Pred(j))
      ELSE IF j <> 0 THEN BEGIN           {New activation char. }
        Inc( i );   k := Succ( i );
        IF i > Length(PlistPtr^) THEN KeyChr := #0
        ELSE BEGIN
          IF ((k <= Length(PlistPtr^)) AND (PlistPtr^[k] = '"'))
             OR (PlistPtr^[i] <> '"') THEN KeyChr := PlistPtr^[i]
          ELSE KeyChr := #0;
        END; {ELSE BEGIN}
      END; {ELSE IF ... BEGIN}
    END; {IF PlistPtr^[i] = '/'}
    Inc( i );
  END; {WHILE ...}
  IF Comb = 0 THEN Comb := ShiftComb;  {Use default combination.  }
  IF Comb = 0 THEN Comb := AltKey;     {No default, use [Alt] key.}
  ScanCode := Pos( UpCase( KeyChr ), ScanChr );  {Convert char. to}
  IF ScanCode < 2 THEN BEGIN                     {scan code.      }
    ScanCode := 2;  KeyChr := '1';
  END;
  Mem[CSeg:Shft] := Comb;              {Store shift key combination}
  Mem[CSeg:Key]  := ScanCode;          {and scan code.             }
{
*** Output an installation message:  Memory used & activation code.
}
  Writeln( 'Memory used is approximately ',
    ( ($1000 + Seg(FreePtr^) - PrefixSeg)/64.0):7:1,' K (K=1024).');
  Writeln(
'Activate program by pressing the following keys simultaneously:');
  IF (Comb AND 1) <> 0 THEN Write(' [Right Shift]');
  IF (Comb AND 2) <> 0 THEN Write(' [Left Shift]');
```

```
  IF (Comb AND 4) <> 0 THEN Write(' [Ctrl]');
  IF (Comb AND 8) <> 0 THEN Write(' [Alt]');
  Writeln(' and "', KeyChr, '".');
(
*** Intercept orig. interrupt vectors; Then exit and stay-resident.
)
  SetIntVec( $21, Ptr( CSeg, Our21 ) );
  SetIntVec( $25, Ptr( CSeg, Our25 ) );
  SetIntVec( $26, Ptr( CSeg, Our26 ) );
  SetIntVec( $16, Ptr( CSeg, Our16 ) );
  SetIntVec( $09, Ptr( CSeg, Our09 ) );
  SwapVectors;                            {Save turbo intr.vectors.}
  MemW[CSeg:UnSafe] := 0;                 {Allow TSR to pop up.    }
  Keep( 0 );                              {Exit and stay-resident. }
END; {TSRInstall.}
END. {TSRUnit.}
```

3. Save interrupt vector table addresses: Perform the following sequence before installing the TSR vector in the interrupt vector table. You can use DOS service 35h to get the address of an interrupt vector. Use DOS service 25h to set the value in the interrupt vector table to point to your program. Only save and set the interrupt vectors your program needs to operate correctly. The following list shows the most common interrupts:

> Save 09h keyboard input interrupt
> Save 16h keyboard driver
> Save 21h MS-DOS function caller
> Save 25h absolute disk read
> Save 26h absolute disk write

The preceding steps save the original interrupt vectors. When you remove the TSR memory, restore the interrupt vector table to its original state. The computer can use the original interrupt vectors as if the TSR program never existed.

4. Save screen image for when TSR quits: This allows the TSR program to "pop-up" over the currently running program. After exiting, the TSR program needs to replace the original image back on the screen. Make sure your TSR can handle both text and graphics displays. The programs in Chapter 6 show you how to detect and manipulate various types of displays. Detection of display adapter type, current mode, and attached monitor type are the three essentials to creating a pop-up that works well. Of course, you always need to tailor the capabilities of your TSR to the needs of the user. If memory is more important than functionality, you might need to limit the TSR to text-only or graphics-only displays.

5. Redirect essential interrupt vectors: Once you save all the values required to restore the application program environment, you need

to install the TSR. The first step in installing the TSR is to point the interrupt vector addresses to your routines. You must make certain that the TSR is capable of handling the interrupt correctly. This means that you must handle both expected and unexpected situations. This is the last step your program performs before going resident (quitting without removing itself from memory). The following list shows the most common interrupts.

Intercept $21 MS-DOS function caller
Intercept $25 absolute disk read
Intercept $26 absolute disk write
Intercept $16 keyboard driver
Intercept $09 keyboard input interrupt

6. Run and quit the TSR program: This step is where your TSR program does its work. A passive program monitors equipment events while an active program monitors the keyboard. Remember to save the application display each time the user presses the proper key combination to activate your program.
7. Redisplay the screen image saved in step 4.

PARTS OF A TSR

Every TSR program has two parts (some have many more). The first part installs the TSR in memory. You do not need to keep this portion resident. Its only purpose is to save the interrupt vectors your program needs to work and point these vectors to the appropriate start points in your program. Normally, this part of the program also displays some type of installation message. This message usually contains the program name, copyright notice, and instructions for program activation.

The second part of a TSR is the resident program. This is the part of the program that performs useful work for the user. You must include routines for handling the interrupts—performing whatever work the TSR is supposed to do—and error correction routines. If your TSR does not include these three minimal functions, then you will have problems using it.

A
ASCII Table

Dec	Hex	Character		Dec	Hex	Character
0	0			28	1C	
1	1			29	1D	
2	2			30	1E	
3	3			31	1F	
4	4			32	20	
5	5			33	21	!
6	6			34	22	"
7	7			35	23	#
8	8			36	24	$
9	9			37	25	%
10	A			38	26	&
11	B			39	27	'
12	C			40	28	(
13	D			41	29	)
14	E			42	2A	*
15	F			43	2B	+
16	10			44	2C	,
17	11			45	2D	–
18	12			46	2E	.
19	13			47	2F	/
20	14			48	30	0
21	15	§		49	31	1
22	16			50	32	2
23	17			51	33	3
24	18			52	34	4
25	19			53	35	5
26	1A			54	36	6
27	1B	P		55	37	7

833

Dec	Hex	Character		Dec	Hex	Character
56	38	8		104	68	h
57	39	9		105	69	i
58	3A	:		106	6A	j
59	3B	;		107	6B	k
60	3C	<		108	6C	l
61	3D	=		109	6D	m
62	3E	>		110	6E	n
63	3F	?		111	6F	o
64	40	@		112	70	p
65	41	A		113	71	q
66	42	B		114	72	r
67	43	C		115	73	s
68	44	D		116	74	t
69	45	E		117	75	u
70	46	F		118	76	v
71	47	G		119	77	w
72	48	H		120	78	x
73	49	I		121	79	y
74	4A	J		122	7A	z
75	4B	K		123	7B	{
76	4C	L		124	7C	¦
77	4D	M		125	7D	}
78	4E	N		126	7E	~
79	4F	O		127	7F	Δ
80	50	P		128	80	Ç
81	51	Q		129	81	ü
82	52	R		130	82	é
83	53	S		131	83	â
84	54	T		132	84	ä
85	55	U		133	85	à
86	56	V		134	86	å
87	57	W		135	87	ç
88	58	X		136	88	ê
89	59	Y		137	89	ë
90	5A	Z		138	8A	è
91	5B	[		139	8B	ï
92	5C	\		140	8C	î
93	5D	]		141	8D	ì
94	5E	^		142	8E	Ä
95	5F	__		143	8F	Å
96	60	`		144	90	É
97	61	a		145	91	æ
98	62	b		146	92	Æ
99	63	c		147	93	ô
100	64	d		148	94	ö
101	65	e		149	95	ò
102	66	f		150	96	û
103	67	g		151	97	ù

Dec	Hex	Character	Dec	Hex	Character
152	98	ÿ	200	C8	╚
153	99	Ö	201	C9	╔
154	9A	Ü	202	CA	╩
155	9B	¢	203	CB	╦
156	9C	£	204	CC	╠
157	9D	¥	205	CD	═
158	9E	₧	206	CE	╬
159	9F	ƒ	207	CF	╧
160	A0	á	208	D0	╨
161	A1	í	209	D1	╤
162	A2	ó	210	D2	╥
163	A3	ú	211	D3	╙
164	A4	ñ	212	D4	╘
165	A5	Ñ	213	D5	╒
166	A6	ª	214	D6	╓
167	A7	º	215	D7	╫
168	A8	¿	216	D8	╪
169	A9	⌐	217	D9	┘
170	AA	¬	218	DA	┌
171	AB	1/2	219	DB	█
172	AC	1/4	220	DC	▄
173	AD	¡	221	DD	▌
174	AE	<<	222	DE	▐
175	AF	>>	223	DF	▀
176	B0	░	224	E0	α
177	B1	▒	225	E1	β
178	B2	▓	226	E2	Γ
179	B3	│	227	E3	π
180	B4	┤	228	E4	Σ
181	B5	╡	229	E5	σ
182	B6	╢	230	E6	μ
183	B7	╖	231	E7	τ
184	B8	╕	232	E8	Φ
185	B9	╣	233	EA	8
186	BA	║	234	EB	Ω
187	BB	╗	235	EC	δ
188	BC	╝	236	ED	∞
189	BD	╜	237	ED	θ
190	BE	╛	238	EE	ϵ
191	BF	┐	239	EF	∩
192	C0	└	240	F0	≡
193	C1	┴	241	F1	±
194	C2	┬	242	F2	≥
195	C3	├	243	F3	≤
196	C4	─	244	F4	⌠
197	C5	┼	245	F5	⌡
198	C6	╞	246	F6	÷
199	C7	╟	247	F7	≈

Dec	Hex	Character		Dec	Hex	Character
248	F8	°		252	FC	n
249	F9	●		253	FD	$_2$
250	FA	.		254	FE	
251	FB	√⎺		255	FF	

ASCII CHART ORGANIZED BY TYPE

All ASCII codes are given in decimals notation

Arrows

24

27   26

25

Single horizontal, single vertical line boxes

196   194

218 ⌐   –   ⊤   ¬191

195 ⊢   197 ┼   ⊣180

179 | | |179

192 ∟   –   ⊥   ⌐217

196   193

Single horizontal, double vertical box

196   210

214 ╓   –   ╥   ╖183

199 ╟   215 ╫   ╢182

186 ‖   ╫   ‖186

211 ╙   –   ╨   ╜189

196   207

Double horizontal, single vertical box

          205   209

213 ╒   ═   ╤   ╕ 184

198 ╞   216 ╪   ╡ 181

179 │   ║   │ 179

212 ╘   ═   ╧   ╛ 190

          205   207

Double horizontal, double vertical box

          205   203

201 ╔   ═   ╦   ╗ 187

204 ╠   206 ╬   ╣ 185

186 ║   ║   ║ 186

200 ╚   ═   ╩   ╝ 188

          205   202

Foreign language characters

Ä   Å   â   ä   à   å   á   ª
142 143 131 132 133 134 160 166

Ç   ç
128 135

É   é   ê   ë
144 130 136 137

ï   î   ì   í
139 140 141 161

Ñ   ñ
165 164

Ö   ô   ö   ò   ó   º
153 147 148 149 162 167

Ü   ü   û   ù   ú
154 129 150 151 163

Foreign language characters

ÿ	Æ	æ	¿	i
152	146	145	168	173

¢	£	¥	₧	ƒ
155	156	157	158	159

Mathematical symbols

½	¼	∝	β	Γ	π	Σ
171	172	224	225	226	227	228

σ	ψ	τ	ϕ	θ	Ω	δ
229	230	231	232	233	234	235

∞	φ	∈	∩	≡	±	≥
236	237	238	239	240	241	242

≤	⌠	⌡	÷	≈	°	•
243	244	245	246	247	248	249

•	√	n	2
250	251	252	253

B
DOS Command Summary

Description	Interrupt	Service	Description	Interrupt	Service
Absolute Disk Read	25h		Check Input Status	21h	Bh
Absolute Disk Write	26h		Close File	21h	10h
			Close File	21h	3Eh
Append	2Fh	B7h	Commit File	21h	68h
Assign	2Fh	2	Create Directory	21h	39h
Critical Error Handler Address	24h		Create File	21 ı	16h
			Create File	21h	3Ch
Ctrl–Break Handler Address	23h		Create New PSP	21h	26h
			Delete Directory	21h	3Ah
Allocate Memory Block	21h	48h	Delete File	21h	13h
Auxiliary Input	21h	3	Delete File	21h	41h
Auxiliary Output	21h	4	Direct Console I/O	21h	6
Buffered Keyboard Input	21h	Ah	Disk Reset	21h	Dh
			Display String	21h	9
Cancel Device Redirection	21h	5Fh	Duplicate Handle	21h	45h
			Execute Program	21h	4Bh
Character Input without Echo	21h	8	Extended Open File	21h	6Ch
			Find First File	21h	11h
Character Input with Echo	21h	1	Find First File	21h	4Eh

Description	Interrupt	Service	Description	Interrupt	Service
Find Next File	21h	12h	Get Return Code	21h	4Dh
Find Next File	21h	4Fh	Get Time	21h	2Ch
Flush Input Buffer then Input	21h	Ch	Get Verify Flag	21h	54h
Get Current Disk	21h	19h	Get/Set Allocation Strategy	21h	58h
Get Current Directory	21h	47h	Get/Set Break Flag, Get Boot Drive	21h	33h
Get Date	21h	2Ah			
Get DBCS Lead Byte Table	21h	63h	Get/Set Code Page	21h	66h
Get Default Drive Data	21h	1Bh	Get/Set Country Information	21h	38h
Get DOS Disk Parameter Block	21h	32h	Get/Set File Date and Time	21h	57h
Get DOS Version Number	21h	30h	Get/Set File Attributes	21h	43h
Get Drive Allocation Information	21h	36h	Open File	21h	Fh
			Open File	21h	3Dh
Get Drive Data	21h	1Ch	Parse Filename	21h	29h
Get DTA Address	21h	1Ah	Printer Output	21h	5
Get Extended Error Information	21h	59h	Random Block Write	21h	28h
			Random Block Read	21h	27h
Get Extended Country Information	21h	65h	Random Read	21h	21h
			Random Write	21h	22h
Get File Size	21h	23h	Read File/Device	21h	3Fh
Get InDOS Flag Address	21h	34h	Redirect Device	21h	5Fh
			Redirect Handle	21h	46h
Get Interrupt Vector	21h	35h	Release Memory Block	21h	49h
			Rename File	21h	17h
Get Machine Name	21h	5Eh	Rename File	21h	56h
Get Printer Setup String	21h	5Eh	Resize Memory Block	21h	4Ah
Get PSP Address	21h	62h	Select Disk	21h	Eh
Get PSP Address	21h	62h	Sequential Write	21h	15h
Get Redirection List Entry	21h	5Fh	Sequential Read	21h	14h

Description	Interrupt	Service	Description	Interrupt	Service
IOCTL: Change Sharing Retry Count	21h	44h	Set Current Directory	21h	3Bh
			Set date	21h	2Bh
IOCTL: Check if Block Device is Remote	21h	44h	Set DTA Address	21h	1Ah
IOCTL: Check if Block Device is Removable	21h	44h	Set File Pointer	21h	42h
			Set Handle Count	21h	67h
IOCTL: Check if Handle is Remote	21h	44h	Set Interrupt Vector	21h	25h
IOCTL: Check Input Status	21h	44h	Set Printer Setup String	21h	5Eh
IOCTL: Check Output Status	21h	44h	Set PSP Address	21h	50h
IOCTL: Generic I/O Control for Character Devices	21h	44h	Set Relative Record Number	21h	24h
			Set Time	21h	2Dh
IOCTL: Generic I/O Control for Block Devices	21h	44h	Set Verify Flag	21h	2Eh
			Terminate-and-Stay-Resident	21h	31h
IOCTL: Get Device Information	21h	44h	Terminate Program	21h	
IOCTL: Get Logical Drive Map	21h	44h	Terminate Program	21h	0
IOCTL: Read Control Data from Block Device	21h	44h	Terminate Process with Return Code	21h	4Ch
			Unfiltered Character Input without Echo	21h	7
IOCTL: Read Control Data from Character Device	21h	44h	Write File/Device	21h	40h
IOCTL: Set Device Information	21h	44h	Disable Mouse Driver	33h	1Fh
IOCTL: Set Logical Drive Map	21h	44h	Enable Mouse Driver	33h	20h
IOCTL: Write Control Data to Block Device	21h	44h	Get Address of Alternate Mouse Event Handler	33h	19h
			Get Button Press Information	33h	5
IOCTL: Write Control Data to Character Device	21h	44h	Get Button Release Information	33h	6
			Get Language Number	33h	23h

Description	Interrupt	Service	Description	Interrupt	Service
Get Mouse Information	33h	24h	Set Mouse Sensitivity	33h	1Ah
Get Mouse Position and Button Status	33h	3	Set Text Pointer Type	33h	Ah
Get Mouse Sensitivity	33h	1Bh	Set User-Defined Mouse Event Handler	33h	Ch
Get Mouse Save State Buffer Size	33h	15h	Set Vertical Limits for Pointer	33h	8
Get Pointer	33h	1Eh	Show Mouse Pointer	33h	1
Hide Mouse Pointer	33h	2	Swap User-Defined Mouse Event Handlers	33h	14h
Read Mouse Motion Counters	33h	Bh			
Reset Mouse Driver	33h	21h	Turn Off Light-Pen Emulation	33h	Eh
Reset Mouse and Get Status	33h	0	Turn On Light-Pen Emulation	33h	Dh
Restore Mouse Driver State	33h	17h	Allocate Alternate Map Register Set	67h	5Bh
Save Mouse Driver State	33h	16h	Allocate DMA Register Set	67h	5Bh
Select Pointer	33h	1Dh	Allocate Handle and Raw Pages	67h	5Ah
Set Alternate Mouse Event Handler	33h	18h	Allocate Handle and Pages	67h	43h
Set Double Speed Threshold	33h	13h	Allocate Handle and Standard Pages	67h	5Ah
Set Graphics Pointer Shape	33h	9	Deallocate Alternate Map Register Set	67h	5Bh
Set Horizontal Limits for Pointer	33h	7	Deallocate DMA Register Set	67h	5Bh
Set Language for Mouse Driver Messages	33h	22h	Disable DMA on Alternate Map Register Set	67h	5Bh
Set Mickeys to Pixels Ratio	33h	Fh	Disable EMM Operating System Functions	67h	5Dh
Set Mouse Interrupt Rate	33h	1Ch			
Set Mouse Pointer Position	33h	4	Enable DMA on Alternate Map Register Set	67h	5Bh
Set Mouse Pointer Exclusion Area	33h	10h			

Description	Interrupt	Service	Description	Interrupt	Service
Enable EMM Operating System Functions	67h	5Dh	Get Status	67h	40h
			Get Total Handles	67h	54h
Exchange Memory Regions	67h	57h	Get Version	67h	46h
			Map Extended Memory	67h	44h
Get Addresses of Mappable Pages	67h	58h	Map Multiple Pages by Number	67h	50h
Get All Handle Names	67h	54h	Map Multiple Pages by Address	67h	50h
Get Alternate Map Registers	67h	5Bh	Map Page Numbers and Jump	67h	55h
Get Attribute Capability	67h	52h	Map Page Numbers and Call	67h	56h
Get Handle Pages	67h	4Ch	Map Page Segments and Jump	67h	55h
Get Handle Attribute	67h	52h	Move Memory Region	67h	57h
Get Handle Name	67h	53h	Prepare Extended Memory Manager for Warm Boot	67h	5Ch
Get Handle Count	67h	4Bh			
Get Handles for All Pages	67h	4Dh	Reallocate Page for Handle	67h	51h
Get Hardware Configuration	67h	59h	Release Access Key	67h	5Dh
Get Number of Mappable Pages	67h	58h	Release Handle and Extended Memory	67h	45h
Get Number of Page	67h	42h	Restore Page Map	67h	4Eh
Get Number of Raw Pages	67h	59h	Restore Partial Page Map	67h	4Fh
Get Page Frame Address	67h	41h	Save and Restore Page Map	67h	4Eh
Get Size of Alternate Map Register Save Area	67h	5Bh	Save Page Map	67h	4Eh
Get Size of Page Map Information	67h	4Eh	Save Page Map	67h	4Eh
Get Size of Partial Page Map Information	67h	4Fh	Save Partial Page Map	67h	4Fh
Get Stack Space for Map Page and Call	67h	56h	Search for Handle Name	67h	54h
			Set Alternate Map Registers	67h	5Bh

Description	Interrupt	Service	Description	Interrupt	Service
Set Handle Attribute	67h	52h	Standard Terminate and Stay Resident Handler	28h	
Set Handle Name	67h	53h	Terminate Address	22h	
Print Spooler	2Fh		Terminate and Stay Resident	27h	
Share	2Fh	10h			

C

DOS Shell Command Summary

DOS 4.0 consists of two parts: the DOS Shell and the File System. The DOS Shell lets you organize programs into groups. The File System lets you copy, delete, and rename files and directories.

DOS SHELL COMMANDS

Special keys:

F1	Displays help.
F3	Exits the DOS shell.
F10	Highlights the main menu bar.
Esc	Cancels previous command.
Shift – F9	Displays the traditional DOS prompt.
Ins	Toggles between insert and overtype mode.

MENU BAR COMMANDS

The DOS shell menu bar contains three menus: Program, Group, and Exit. Pressing F10 highlights the menu bar.

The Program Menu

The Program menu contains five commands for starting, adding, changing, deleting, or copying programs as they appear in the DOS shell.

Start Runs the program currently highlighted on the DOS shell. If no program is highlighted, this command appears dimmed on the menu.

Add   Adds a new program name to the DOS shell. You may add up to 16 programs or subgroups per group.

Change   Lets you modify the program entry.

Delete   Deletes a program name from the DOS shell.

Copy   Lets you copy a program entry to another group or subgroup.

The Group Menu

The Group menu contains three commands for adding, changing, or deleting groups and subgroups. The Reorder command lets you change the order of a subgroup or program.

Add   Adds a subgroup to a group. You cannot add a subgroup to an existing subgroup.

Change   Lets you modify the name or a subgroup.

Delete   Deletes a subgroup entry from the DOS shell.

Reorder   Rearranges the position of a subgroup or program within a group.

The Exit Menu

The Exit menu contains two commands: Exit and Resume Start Programs.

Exit   Exits from the DOS shell.

Resume Start Programs   Keeps the DOS shell displayed with the main menu bar highlighted.

START GROUP COMMANDS

Command Prompt   The Command prompt temporarily exits the DOS shell and displays the traditional DOS prompt C:>. To return to the DOS shell, you must type EXIT and press Enter. You can also choose this command by pressing Shift–F9.

File System   The File system displays the directory structure of a disk along with the files within each directory. See the section below on the File System for more information.

Change Colors   Change colors lets you choose from among four sets of colors.

DOS Utilities   Lists the most commonly used DOS commands: Set Date and Time, Disk Copy, Disk Compare, Backup Fixed Disk, Restore Fixed Disk, and Format. You can add or delete items if you want.

FILE SYSTEM MENU COMMANDS

The DOS 4.0 File System lets you manage files stored in directories. The File System menu displays four menu entries: File, Options, Arrange, and Exit.

The File Menu

The File menu contains 12 commands for manipulating selected files.

Open (start) Runs the selected file if the file is a .COM, .EXE, or .BAT file. If two or more files have been selected, this command will appear dimmed. As an alternative, you can highlight a file and press Enter.

Print Prints up to ten ASCII text files using the DOS print queue. If no files have been selected, this command appears dimmed.

Associate Lets you associate non-program files with the programs that created them. For example, you could associate all files with the .DBF file extension to a database program called DBASE.EXE. If you highlight a .DBF file and press Enter, DOS 4.0 will associate the .DBF file with the DBASE.EXE program, and run the DBASE.EXE program, loading the highlighted .DBF file.

Move Moves files between directories and subdirectories. If you only move one file, you can rename and move the file at the same time. If you move two or more files, you cannot rename the files as you move them.

Copy Copies a file to a different directory or to the same directory with a different name.

Delete Deletes one or more selected files or directories.

Rename Renames a file or directory.

Change attribute Changes a file's attribute. The three types of attributes are Read, Archive, and Hidden. If the Read attribute is on, you can only read but not change the file.

The Archive attribute indicates whether the file has been changed since it was last copied with the DOS BACKUP, RESTORE, or XCOPY commands. As soon as a file has been changed, the Archive attribute turns on.

The Hidden attribute "hides" a file from normal directory listings but will appear in the File System directory listing.

View Displays the contents of an ASCII text file. Will not work with non-ASCII text files.

Create directory Creates a new subdirectory to the currently marked directory.

Select all Selects all the files of the current directory.

Deselect all Unselects all the files previously marked with the Select all command.

The Options Menu

The Options menu contains three commands: Display options, File options, and Show information.

Display options   Gives you the option to display files alphabetically by name, by extension, by date, by size, or by disk order. The disk order refers to the physical location of each file on the disk.

The only time the disk order would affect anything would be if you manipulate multiple files. For example, if you want to copy multiple files, sorting them by disk order means the computer can perform this task faster.

File options   File options determine how the DOS shell works when you want to delete or replace a file. The default settings will display a confirmation box if you try to delete or replace a file.

Another option, Select across directories, is set off by default. When off, this option means that if you select a file and then change directories, the selected file is no longer selected. This is a safety feature to keep you from selecting a file, changing directories, and forgetting which files you previously selected. (Extremely important if you select a file, change directories, select more files, then choose the delete command, not realizing that this would delete your previously selected files as well.)

Show information   Displays the attribute, size, directory, and disk space available for a selected file.

The Arrange Menu

Defines how the File system displays directories and files on the screen. The choices are Single file list, Multiple file list, and System file list.

The Single file list displays the disk directory tree on the left side of the screen and the file contents of a selected directory on the right side of the screen.

The Multiple file list displays two directory trees on the left side of the screen, and the file contents of each directory tree on the right side of the screen. By choosing this option, you can view the directories and file contents of different disks simultaneously.

The System file list displays all the files on a disk, alphabetically, regardless of which directories they are in.

The Exit Menu

The Exit menu contains two commands: Exit File System and Resume File System. The Exit File System command exits to the DOS shell. You can also choose this command by pressing F3.

The Resume File System command keeps the File System displayed with the main menu bar highlighted.

D
One MByte Memory Map (Most DOS Based Operating Systems)

Address	Function
00000 - 0003F	Hardware/Software* Interrupt Vectors
00000 - 00003	Divide-by-Zero
00004 - 00007	Single Step
00008 - 0000B	Non-Maskable Interrupt (NMI)
0000C - 0000F	Breakpoint
00010 - 00013	Overflow
00014 - 00017	BOUND Exceeded, Print Screen* (Int 5)
00018 - 0001B	Invalid Opcode, Reserved* (Int 6)
0001C - 0001F	Processor Extension Not Available, Reserved* (Int 7)
00020 - 00023	Double Fault, IRQ0 Timer Tick* (Int 8)
00024 - 00027	Segment Overrun, IRQ1 Keyboard* (Int 9)
00028 - 0002B	Invalid Task-State Segment, IRQ2 Cascade from Slave 8259A PIC* (Int Ah)
0002C - 0002F	Segment Not Present, IRQ3 Serial Communications COM2* (Int Bh)
00030 - 00033	Stack Segment Overrun, IRQ4 Serial Communications COM1* (Int Ch)
00034 - 00037	General Protection Fault, IRQ5 Fixed Disk—PC or Parallel Printer LPT2—AT* (Int Dh)
00038 - 0003B	Page Fault, IRQ6 Floppy Disk* (Int Eh)
0003C - 0003F	Reserved, IRQ7 Parallel Printer LPT1 (Int Fh)
00040 - 0007F	BIOS Interrupt Vectors
00040 - 00043	Numeric Co-Processor Error, Video Services* (Int 10h)
00044 - 00047	Equipment Check* (Int 11h)
00044 - 0007F	Reserved
00048 - 0004B	Conventional Memory Size* (Int 12h)
0004C - 0004F	Disk Driver* (Int 13h)
00050 - 00053	Communications Driver* (Int 14h)
00054 - 00057	Cassette Driver—PC, I/O System Extensions—AT* (Int 15h)

Address	Function
00058 - 0005B	Keyboard Driver* (Int 16h)
0005C - 0005F	Printer Driver* (Int 17h)
00060 - 00063	BASIC* (Int 18h)
00064 - 00067	ROM BIOS Bootstrap* (Int 19h)
00068 - 0006B	Time of Day* (Int 1Ah)
0006C - 0006F	Ctrl–Break* (Int 1Bh)
00070 - 00073	ROM BIOS Timer Tick* (Int 1Ch)
00074 - 00077	Video Parameter Table* (Int 1Dh)
00078 - 0007B	Floppy Disk Parameters* (Int 1Eh)
0007C - 0007F	ROM BIOS Font—Characters 80h to FFh* (Int 1Fh)
00080 - 000FF	DOS Interrupt Vectors
00080 - 00083	Terminate Process* (Int 20h)
00084 - 00087	Function Dispatcher* (Int 21h)
00088 - 0008B	Terminate Address* (Int 22h)
0008C - 0008F	Ctrl–C Handler Address* (Int 23h)
00090 - 00093	Critical Error Handler Address* (Int 24h)
00094 - 00097	Absolute Disk Read* (Int 25h)
00098 - 0009B	Absolute Disk Write* (Int 26h)
0009C - 0009F	Terminate-and-Stay-Resident* (Int 27h)
00100 - 003FF	Assignable Interrupt Vectors
00100 - 00103	Idle Interrupt* (Int 28h)
00104 - 00107	Reserved (Int 29h)
00108 - 0010B	Network Redirector* (Int 2Ah)
0010C - 0011B	Reserved (Int 2Bh - 2Eh)
0011C - 0011F	Multiplex Interrupt* (Int 2Fh)
00120 - 0015F	Reserved (Int 30h - 3Fh)
00400 - 004FF	ROM BIOS Data Area
00400 - 00416	Hardware Parameters
00417 - 0043D	Keyboard Buffer/Status Bytes
0043E - 00448	Disk Status Bytes
00449 - 00466	Video Display Data
00467 - 00470	Option ROM and Timer Data
00471 - 00487	Additional Status Bytes
00488 - 004FF	Reserved
00500 - 005FF	DOS Data Area
A0000 - BFFFF	Video Display Area
A0000 - AFFFF	EGA 64KB
A0000 - BFFFF	VGA 256KB
A0000 - BFFFF	EGA 128KB
B0000 - B0FFF	Monochrome 4KB
B0000 - B7FFF	EGA Monochrome Emulation 32KB
B8000 - BBFFF	CGA 16KB
B8000 - BFFFF	EGA CGA Emulation 32KB
C0000 - F3FFF	BIOS Extensions
C0000 - C3FFF	EGA BIOS
C0000 - C5FFF	VGA BIOS

Address	Function
C6000 - C67FF	PGC BIOS
C6800 - C7FFF	Extended Mode EGA/VGA BIOS
C6800 - C7FFF	IBM 8514/A BIOS
C8000 - C9FFF	VESA 8514/A Primary BIOS
C8000 - CBFFF	XT Hard Disk BIOS
CA000 - CA7FF	IBM 8514/A BIOS
CC000 - CDFFF	RLL Drive
D0000 - D7FFF	Cluster Adapter BIOS
D0000 - DFFFF	PCjr Expansion Cartridges
D8000 - D9FFF	VESA 8514/A Alternate BIOS
D8000 - DFFFF	LIM/EMS Cards (Most Adapters Provide Alternate Address Capability)
E0000 - EFFFF	System ROM Extension
F4000 - FDFFF	System ROM/Stand-Alone BASIC
FE000 - FFFFF	ROM BIOS

* These addresses are assigned by software only. Because they are not hardwired into the machine, these addresses could change at any time.

Index

DS register, load (LDS), 94, 129
Dump command, CodeView, 37

E

80286 coprocessor
command additions, 175-185
instruction additions, 99
memory map for, 232
mnemonics to executable code
(A CodeView command), 34
sample program for, 176-177
80287 coprocessor
command additions, 185-186
control words, 185, 205
instruction set, 143-175
instructions, 97-99
registers, display contents (7
CodeView command), 30
status words, 185, 205
80386 coprocessor
command additions, 186-204
instruction additions, 100-101
memory map for, 232
mnemonics to executable code
(A CodeView command), 34
sample program for, 187-192
80387 coprocessor
command additions, 204-207
control words, 185, 205
instruction set, 97-99, 143-175
status words, 185, 205
8086 processor
Assembly Language sample
program, 102-111
flags, 112
instruction set, 94-97, 101-143
memory map for, 232
mnemonics to executable code
(A CodeView command), 34
8087 coprocessor
control words, 185, 205
instruction set, 97-99, 143-175
registers, display contents (7
CodeView command), 30
sample program listings,
144-162
status words, 185, 205
8088 processor
Assembly Language sample
program, 102-111
flags, 112
instruction set, 94-97, 101-143
memory map for, 232
mnemonics to executable code
(A CodeView command), 34
8253 programmable timer, 206-213
8254 programmable timer, 206-213

8255A programmable peripheral
interface (PPI), 216-224
8259 programmable interrupt
controller (PIC), 224-228
interrupt trapping, disable (/D
CodeView option), 29
interrupt trapping, enable (/I
CodeView option), 29
8514/A display adapter, 292-296,
350-366, 555
advanced function control
register, 359
application interface (AI)
commands, 350-353
background mix registers, 362
display control register, 357
display modes, 350
foreground mix register, 363-364
graphics processor
status/command register,
360-361
horizontal display, 355
horizontal sync registers, 355
memory control register, 365
pixel control register, 365
ROM page select, 359
short stroke vector (SSV) transfer,
362
standard registers, 353-354
subsystem status-control
registers, 357-359
sync status/horizontal total, 354
vertical sync registers, 356
vertical total/displayed, 356
EAX register, 208
load doubleword from string to
(LODSD), 195
store doubleword at string
(STOSD), 204
EDLIN, modify DOSSHELL.BAT,
11-13
effective address, load (LEA), 94,
129
enhanced commands, DOS 4.0,
3-10
Enhanced Graphics Adapter
(EGA), 267-281, 306-331, 555
alpha load, 435, 438
attribute controller register, 329
BIOS extensions, 267
bit mask register, 329
block specifier, set, 437
character map select register,
310
character set information, 444
character/attribute read, 421
character/attribute write, 422,
423

clocking mode register, 309
color compare register, 326
color don't care register, 329
color palette, set, 423
color plane enable register, 331
configuration of (MODE), 7
CRT controller overflow register,
318
CRTC register group index
values, 310
current video state, 425
cursor size/position, 415, 416
cursor start/end registers, 319
data rotate register, 327
display page, active, 417
display modes, 306
enable 43-line display mode (/43
CodeView option), 28
feature control register, 307
graphics registers, 325
horizontal blanking registers,
312-314
horizontal display enable, 312
horizontal PEL panning register,
331
horizontal retrace registers,
315-317
horizontal total register values,
311
input status registers, 308
intensify/blink toggle, 428
light pen position, 417
line compare register, 325
mask register, 309
maximum scan line register, 319
memory allocation information,
445
memory mode register, 310
miscellaneous register, 328
mode control register, 324, 330
mode register, 327
offset register, 322
output register, 307
overscan color register, 330, 427
palette register save and restore,
disable (/P CodeView option),
29
palette registers, set, 329, 425,
427
pixel dot, read/write, 424
preset row scan register, 318
print screen routine, alternate,
445
read map select register, 327
reset register, 308
ROM 8x14 character set, 442
ROM 8x16 character set, 443
ROM 8x8 character set, 443

restcur, 66
resume flag, 186
RET, 96, 136
RM.EXE, 89, 93
ROL, 95, 137
ROM BASIC, 516
ROM interrupts, 410-534
  global descriptor tables, 529-530
  hard disk drive/floppy diskette
    services, 463-482
  keyboard services, 482-491
  miscellaneous services, 491-521
  video services, 410-463
ROR, 95, 137
Rotate Left (ROL), 95, 137
Rotate Right (ROR), 95, 137
rounding to integer (FRNDINT), 172
RPL bits, compare and adjust
  (ARPL), 177

S

SAHF, 94, 138
SAL, 95, 138
sample rate, set, 510
SAR, 95, 138
savecur, 66
SBB, 95, 139
scale (FSCALE), 172
SCASB, 95, 139
SCASD, 101, 198
SCASW, 95, 139
screen swapping, enable (/S
  CodeView option), 29
scrolling, halt (Ctrl-S CodeView), 35
search and replace (see also
  matching)
  code (Alt-S CodeView
    command), 32
  find option (Ctrl-F CodeView), 35
  maximal matching, 64
  Microsoft Editor, 60-62
  minimal matching, 64
  regular expressions, Microsoft
    Editor, 62-66
  tagged expressions, 65
sectors (see hard disks, sectors)
segments
  addresses, 44
  limit, load (LSL), 181
  verify for read (VERR), 184
  verify for write (VERW), 185
SELECT, 3, 8
semaphores, event wait, 503
sequential mode debugging,
  enable (/T CodeView option), 29
sequential read/write, 568
serial ports, 228-230, 637-645

auxiliary input, 644-645
auxiliary output, 645
configuration of (MODE), 7
DOS service interrupts, 637-645
sample programs, 638-644
set byte instructions, 198-203
SETA, 100, 198
SETAE, 100, 199
SETB, 100, 199
SETBE, 100, 199
SETC, 100, 199
SETE, 100, 199
SETG, 100, 199
SETGE, 100, 199
SetKey(), 85, 87
SETL, 100, 200
SETLE, 100, 200
SETNA, 100, 200
SETNAE, 100, 200
SETNB, 100, 200
SETNBE, 100, 200
SETNC, 100, 201
SETNE, 100, 201
SETNG, 100, 201
SETNGE, 100, 201
SETNL, 100, 201
SETNLE, 100, 201
SETNO, 100, 201
SETNP, 100, 202
SETNS, 100, 202
SETNZ, 100, 202
SETO, 100, 202
SETP, 100, 202
SETPE, 101, 202
SETPO, 101, 203
SETS, 101, 203
SETZ, 101, 203
SGDT, 99, 183
SHARE.EXE, 546
shell program, DOS, 1, 10-24,
  845-848
  arrange menu, 848
  change colors, 11
  command prompt, 11
  create, File menu (Alt-F
    CodeView), 30
  DOS cmmand summary for,
    845-84
  DOS utilities, 11
  Exit Menu, temporary or
    permanent, 24, 846, 848
  File System menu, windows, 11, 847
  Group Menu, add, change,
    delete, reorder, 20-24, 846
  main menus of, 11-13, 845
  menu display, 13-15
  menu remove, 15

modify display/DOSSHELL.BAT,
  EDLIN for, 11-13
options menu, 848
Program Menu, add, edit, delete,
  copy, 15-20, 845
Start Programs menu, 10-11, 846
shift left (SHL), 95, 140
  double-precision (SHLD), 203
shift right (SHR), 95, 140
  double-precision (SHRD), 204
SHLD, 101, 203
SHR, 95, 140
SHRD, 101
SIDT, 99, 184
sign flag, 176, 186
signed numbers
  change sign (FCHS), 97, 164
  extended, move (MOVSX), 196
significand, extract (FXTRACT), 175
sine (FSIN; FSINCOS), 206
SLDT, 99, 184
SMSW, 99, 184
Software Interrupt (INT), 96
sound source, set, 520
source code file
  browse through (View CodeView
    command), 43
  search for expression
    (/ CodeView command), 42
  view (Alt-V, F3), 33, 39
spooler, print, 545
square root (FSQRT), 172
SS register, load (LSS), 196
stack frame, procedure parameters,
  make for (ENTER), 178
stacks
  place data on (PUSH), 94, 134
  place extended flags on
    (PUSHFD), 198
  place flags on (PUSHF), 94, 134
  remove data from (POP), 94, 134
  remove extended flags from
    (POPFD), 197
  remove flags from (POPF), 94,134
Start Programs shell menu, 10-11
states
  restore (FRSTOR), 172
  save with wait (FSAVE), 172
status words, 185, 205
  machine, load (LMSW), 181
  machine, store (SMSW), 184
  store (FNSTSW), 99, 171
  store with wait (FSTSW), 173
STC, 97, 141
STD, 97, 141
STI, 97, 141
STOSB, 95, 141

864   THE ULTIMATE DOS PROGRAMMER'S MANUAL

scroll up, 418
toggle cursor between dialog
box and (F6), 39
words
convert byte to (CBW), 95, 115
convert to doubleword (CWD),
117

doubleword extended conversion
(CWDE), 194

XCHG, 94, 142
XLAT, 94, 142

XOR, 95, 143

zero
extended, move (MOVZX), 196
flag, 176, 186
load value of (FLDZ), 98, 169

Other Bestsellers of Related Interest

**MS-DOS® BATCH FILE PROGRAMMING
—2nd Edition**—Ronny Richardson
Reviewer's praise of the first edition:
"By the end of this book, readers will be able to implement even the most difficult batch files, and will thoroughly understand the whole process." **—Computer Shopper**

Now, even the novice can take advantage of batch files—simple step-saving programs that can replace complicated DOS procedures. Includes DOS 4 and the latest in batch utilities. Comes with a disk containing all the batch files. 448 pages, 339 illustrations. Book No. 3537, $24.95 paperback, $36.95 hardcover

MS-DOS® Beyond 640K: Working with Extended and Expanded Memory
—James Forney

Find out how some relatively inexpensive hardware and software enhancements can give your 8088, 80286, or 80386-based computer the ability to run larger applications, create multiple simultaneous work environments, maintain larger files, and provide all the memory you need. This book provides a clear picture of all the alternatives and options available, even up-to-the-minute tips and techniques for using Lotus 1-2-3®, Release 3.0, in extended memory! 248 pages, Illustrated. Book No. 3239, $19.95 paperback, $29.95 hardcover

NORTON UTILITIES™ 4.5: An Illustrated Tutorial—Richard Evans

This completely revised edition of Richard Evans' bestselling guidebook demonstrates the vast capabilities of the Norton Utilities package, and features the exciting new additions to release 4.5. You'll find straightforward, step-by-step instruction on using every program in the Norton Utilities, for every version form 3.0 to the current 4.5. All the details of the command structure and common applications are presented. 224 pages, 98 illustrations. Book No. 3359, $16.95 paperback only

INVITATION TO DOS LIBRARY SERVICES: For Application Programmers
—Lana J. Chandler

Here's expert guidance in using support software to access and control DOS libraries and their directories. Using clear, easy-to-understand languages supported by numerous illustrations, Lana Chandler defines DOS libraries and shows you how simple it can be to access and control them once related software is mastered. Comparisons are made to core images, relocatable, source statement, and procedural libraries and their directories. 192 pages, Illustrated. Book No. 3261, $21.95 paperback only

LEARN DOS—GUARANTEED!
—Richard P. Cadway

Use DOS as the tool it was intended to be! This book tells you what you need to know to make MS/PC-DOS work for you, without making you try to digest an encyclopedia of specialized information and technical jargon. Cadway concentrates exclusively on technical jargon. Cadway concentrates exclusively on the most important DOS commands and most basic hardware installations—he explains what the major parts of DOS do, how the file system works, and just enough DOS to install and use your applications effectively. 192 pages, 28 illustrations. Book No. 3331, $14.95 paperback only

ADVANCED MS—DOS® BATCH FILE PROGRAMMING—Dan Gookin

Batch file programming is a way of communicating with your computer . . . a way of transforming DOS into a system that works the way you want it to. In this book, Dan Gookin explains unique methods of using batch files to create a work environment that will improve your efficiency, productivity, and overall relationship with your computer. All the necessary tools, batch file structures, commands, and helpful techniques can be found here. 400 pages, 733 illustrations. Book No. 3197, $24.95 paperback only

MS-DOS® UTILITY PROGRAMS: Add-On Software Resources—Ronny Richardson

Combining the most useful features of a product catalog and magazine reviews, this book is the most comprehensive guide available for finding the utility programs you need to optimize your DOS-based computer system. Richardson candidly describes the capabilities and operation of virtually even DOS utility on the market. He clearly explains what each package does, who might benefit from the package, and what specific problems it can solve. 672 pages, Illustrated. Book No. 3278, $24.95 paperback only

MASTERING PC TOOLS™ DELUXE—Paul Dlug

Master all the invaluable features of this program—including version 6.0 enhancements—from finding, previewing, and loading a file to using time- and effort-saving macros, and lots more! Each utility is explained in detail, with working examples and screen shots to illustrate specific features. Dlug covers data recovery, desktop tools, telecommunications, caching, DOS shells, hard disk backup. Arranged by utility, it makes a great reference, too! 272 pages, 279 illustrations. Book No. 3578, $16.95 paperback only

The Ultimate DOS Programmer's Manual

If you are intrigued with the possibilities of the programs included in *The Ultimate DOS Programmer's Manual* by John Mueller and Wallace Wang (TAB Book No. 3534), you should definitely consider having the ready-to-compile disk containing the software applications. This software is guaranteed free of manufacturer's defects. (If you have any problems, return the disk within 30 days, and we'll send you a new one.) Not only will you save the time and effort of typing the programs, but also the disk eliminates the possibility of errors that prevent the programs from functioning. Interested?

Available on either 5¹/₄″ or 3¹/₂″ disk requiring 512K at $29.95, plus $2.50 shipping and handling.